THE PAST IS A
FOREIGN COUNTRY

THE PAST IS A
FOREIGN
COUNTRY

DAVID LOWENTHAL

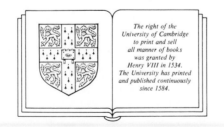

The right of the
University of Cambridge
to print and sell
all manner of books
was granted by
Henry VIII in 1534.
The University has printed
and published continuously
since 1584.

CAMBRIDGE UNIVERSITY PRESS

Cambridge
London   New York   New Rochelle
Melbourne   Sydney

Published by the Press Syndicate of the University of Cambridge
The Pitt Building, Trumpington Street, Cambridge CB2 1RP
32 East 57th Street, New York, NY 10022, USA
10 Stamford Road, Oakleigh, Melbourne 3166, Australia

© Cambridge University Press 1985

First published 1985

Printed in Great Britain at the University Press, Cambridge

British Library Cataloguing in Publication Data

Lowenthal, David
The past is a foreign country.
1. Past
I. Title
155.9'2   HM299

Library of Congress Cataloguing in Publication Data

Lowenthal, David.
The past is a foreign country.
Bibliography: p.
Includes index.
1. History – Philosophy.   2. History.   I. Title.
D16.8L52   1985   901   85-10990

ISBN 0 521 22415 2 hard covers
ISBN 0 521 29480 0 paperback

For Eleanor, past and present

CONTENTS

ILLUSTRATIONS

(Photographers' names in brackets; other photos by the author)

ACKNOWLEDGEMENTS

1, 8, 9, 10, 11, 12, 17, 18, 23, 24, 25, 29, 37–45, 47, 53, 54, 57, 58, 60, 64, 65, 66, 72, 75, 77, 82, 84, 85, 86, 89, 90, 91, 94, 96, 99–101: © David Lowenthal; 2, 61, 78, 104: National Trust (England and Wales); 3: York Archaeological Trust, Ltd; 4, 5: National Museum of Warsaw; 6: Groeningemuseum, Bruges; 7: Courtauld Institute of Art, University of London; 13, 79, 83: The British Architectural Library, RIBA, London; 14: National Gallery, London; 15, 16, 19: Warburg Institute, University of London; 20, 56, 73, 105: Victoria and Albert Museum, London; 21: Kunsthaus, Zürich; 22: Edwin Smith photo, Gordon Fraser Ltd; 26: David & Charles, Ltd, London; 27: Sir John Soane's Museum, London; 28, 67: Library of Congress, Washington, D.C.; 31: British Museum; 32, 49, 50: National Monuments Record, Royal Commission on Historical Monuments (England); 33: The Louvre, Paris; 35, 76, 80, 81, 88: © Wayne Andrews; 36: Chris Cromarty; 46: Walter H. Miller; 48: Richard Frear photo, U.S. National Park Service; 52: Herschel Levit; 55: Marquess of Zetland; 59: Museum of Lincolnshire Life; 62: English Life Publications Ltd; 63: Richard Dennis; 69: Amon Carter Museum, Fort Worth; 70: drawing by Kraus; © 1969 The New Yorker Magazine, Inc.; 71: drawing by Dana Fredon; © 1954, 1982, The New Yorker Magazine, Inc.; 74: Royal Commission on Ancient Monuments, Scotland; 87: Osbert Lancaster; 92: George Mott photo, © Thames & Hudson Ltd; 93: *Punch*; 97: Tate Gallery; 98: Imperial War Museum; 102: drawing by B. Tobey; © 1976 The New Yorker Magazine, Inc.; 103: © Alan Karchmer.

INTRODUCTION

The past is everywhere. All around us lie features which, like ourselves and our thoughts, have more or less recognizable antecedents. Relics, histories, memories suffuse human experience. Each particular trace of the past ultimately perishes, but collectively they are immortal. Whether it is celebrated or rejected, attended to or ignored, the past is omnipresent.

Nowadays the past is also pervasive in its abundance of deliberate, tangible evocations. To an American, the landscape of the 1980s seems saturated with 'creeping heritage' – mansarded and half-timbered shopping plazas, exposed brick and butcher-block decor in historic precincts, heritage villages, historic preservation; 'we have developed techniques of preservation that would have dumbfounded our forefathers', comments a fictional partisan of the past; 'we moderns have so devoted the resources of our science to taxidermy that there is now virtually nothing that is not considerably more lively after death than it was before'.[1] Once confined to a handful of museums and antique shops, the trappings of history now festoon the whole country. All memorabilia are cherished, from relics of the Revolution to artifacts from Auschwitz; antiques now embrace yesterday's ephemera; the zeal for genealogy ranges from Haley's *Roots* to the retrospective conversion of Mormon ancestors. Long uprooted and newly unsure of the future, Americans *en masse* find comfort in looking back; historic villages and districts become 'surrogate home towns that contain a familiar and reassuring landscape for people whose points of reference elsewhere have been altered beyond recognition'.[2]

An American transplanted to Britain espies similar trends even in a nation more secure in its older collective identity. While disdaining a Disneyfied history, British conservationists mount guard on everything from old churches to ancient countrysides, deplore the drain of heritage across the Atlantic, and solace present discontents with past glories. When the European Parliament recently suggested changing the name of Waterloo Station because it perpetuated unfortunate memories of the Napoleonic Wars, the British retorted, not wholly in jest, that it was 'salutary for the French to be constantly reminded

---

[1] Dennis, *Cards of Identity*, p. 165.   [2] Fortier, *Fortress of Louisbourg*, p. 19.

of Wellington's great victory', and expressed anxiety lest Britain be deprived of Nelson's Column, Trafalgar Square, and Blenheim Palace.[3]

Fashions for old films, old clothes, old music, old recipes are ubiquitous, and nostalgia markets every product. Traditions and revivals dominate architecture and the arts; schoolchildren delve into local history and grandparental recollections; historical romances and tales of olden days deluge all the media.

The past thus conjured up is, to be sure, largely an artifact of the present. However faithfully we preserve, however authentically we restore, however deeply we immerse ourselves in bygone times, life back then was based on ways of being and believing incommensurable with our own. The past's difference is, indeed, one of its charms: no one would yearn for it if it merely replicated the present. But we cannot help but view and celebrate it through present-day lenses.

'The past is a foreign country', begins L. P. Hartley's *The Go-Between*; 'they do things differently there.' That they did indeed do things differently is a perspective fundamental to this book. But it is a perspective of recent vintage. During most of history men scarcely differentiated past from present, referring even to remote events, if at all, as though they were then occurring. Up to the nineteenth century those who gave any thought to the historical past supposed it much like the present. To be sure, the drama of history recorded major changes of life and landscape, but human nature supposedly remained constant, events always actuated by the same passions and prejudices. Even when ennobled by nostalgia or depreciated by partisans of progress, the past seemed not a foreign country but part of their own. And chroniclers portrayed bygone times with an immediacy and intimacy that reflected the supposed likeness.

This outlook had two particular consequences. Past departures from present standards were praised as marks of virtue or condemned as tokens of depravity. And since past circumstances seemed comparable and hence relevant to present concerns, history served as a fount of useful exemplars. A past explained in terms similar to the present also suited views of *why* things happened as they had. Whether history unfolded in accordance with the Creator's grand design or with nature's laws, towards decline or towards progress, the pattern was irrevocable, immutable, and universal.

From time to time, prescient individuals like Erasmus realized that historical change made their present unlike any past circumstances. But awareness of anachronism ran counter to prevailing needs and perspectives. Only in the late eighteenth century did Europeans begin to conceive the past as a different realm, not just another country but a congeries of foreign lands endowed with unique histories and personalities. This new past gradually ceased to provide comparative lessons, but came to be cherished as a heritage that validated and exalted the present. And the new role heightened concern to save relics and restore monuments as emblems of communal identity, continuity, and aspiration.

For three centuries the archetypes of antiquity had dominated learning and law, informed the arts, and infused the whole of European culture. Antiquity was exemplary, beneficial, and beautiful. Yet its physical remains were in the main neglected or destroyed. Architects and sculptors were more apt to mine classical vestiges for their own works than to protect them against pillage and loss; patrons of the arts gave less thought to collecting

[3] 'British refighting Battle of Waterloo', *International Herald Tribune*, 29–30 Sept. 1984, p. 1.

antique fragments than to commissioning new works modelled on their virtues. Only in the nineteenth century did preservation evolve from an antiquarian, quirky, episodic pursuit into a set of national programmes, only in the twentieth has every country sought to secure its own heritage against despoliation and decay.

If recognizing the past's difference promoted its preservation, the act of preserving made that difference still more apparent. Venerated as a fount of communal identity, cherished as a precious and endangered resource, yesterday became less and less like today. Yet its relics and residues are increasingly stamped with today's lineaments. We may fancy an exotic past that contrasts with a humdrum or unhappy present, but we forge it with modern tools. The past is a foreign country whose features are shaped by today's predilections, its strangeness domesticated by our own preservation of its vestiges.

Preservation has deepened our knowledge of the past but dampened creative use of it. Specialists learn more than ever about our central biblical and classical traditions, but most people now lack an informed appreciation of them. Our precursors identified with a unitary antiquity whose fragmented vestiges became models for their own creations. Our own more numerous and exotic pasts, prized as vestiges, are divested of the iconographic meanings they once embodied. It is no longer the presence of the past that speaks to us, but its pastness. Now a foreign country with a booming tourist trade, the past has undergone the usual consequences of popularity. The more it is appreciated for its own sake, the less real or relevant it becomes. No longer revered or feared, the past is swallowed up by the ever-expanding present; we enlarge our sense of the contemporary at the expense of realizing its connection with the past. 'We are flooded with disposable memoranda from us to ourselves', as Boorstin puts it, but 'we are tragically inept at receiving messages from our ancestors'.[4]

Making this book has been a journey with specific points of departure, of concentration, and of conclusion. Like most historians, inclination commits me to an interest in the past. My particular concern with its impact stems from a study, begun in 1949, of the American polymath ecologist George Perkins Marsh. Comparing the consequences of deforestation in his native Vermont with the ancient denudation of Mediterranean lands and recent erosion by alpine torrents, Marsh gained unique insight into how human activities had reshaped – largely unintentionally, often disastrously – the habitable earth. Marsh's ability to read landscape history from the debris of nature and the relics of human occupance and his well-documented warnings of the need to restore a viable balance of vegetation and of river regimes made his *Man and Nature* (1864) the fountainhead of conservation consciousness.

Marsh urged the conservation of history as well as nature, but sought to preserve the artifacts of everyday life rather than the great monuments of antiquity. It was not the accoutrements of princes and prelates that would remind Americans of their antecedents, but the tools of field and workshop, the household implements and customary trappings of their own forebears. Closely linked with the Romantic nationalism that found roots in folklore and vernacular languages, Marsh's concern with common material vestiges came to fruition a generation later in Artur Hazelius's Skansen, and in the outdoor farm and

[4] 'Enlarged contemporary', p. 787.

industrial museums of our own day. Marsh's emphasis on the ordinary workaday past also prefigures today's populist bent in understanding, celebrating, and commemorating the heritage.

How we depict and reshape the world we inherit became my own next concern. The way people view their past seems to be a matter of universal concern, but the past plays very different roles in different cultures. For example, English attitudes toward locale seem permeated by antiquarianism – a settled bent in favour of the old or the traditional, even if less useful or beautiful than the new. To judge from sources Hugh Prince and I collected in the 1960s, all the arts and the whole built environment reflect this bias. Delight in continuity and cumulation is integral to English appreciation of *genius loci*, the enduring idiosyncrasies that lend places their precious identity.

The past seemed both less consequential and less intimate in American attitudes toward their surroundings. Far from venerating inherited vestiges, they had traditionally dero-gated them as reminders of decadence and dependency. The few admired relic features were either safely distant in Europe, sanitized by patriotic purpose as at Mount Vernon and Williamsburg, or debased by hucksters. Only a handful of wistful WASPs dwelt at length on their ancestries and their antiques; to most Americans the past was musty and irrelevant.

The early 1970s channelled my interests toward historic preservation and toward the past as a general concept. The impact of urban redevelopment on older city cores, nostalgic reactions to catastrophe and corruption and other failures of the brave new post-war world, the pillage of antiquities for sale to collectors increasingly enamoured of the past led me to wonder whether these trends might have common roots, and to speculate on the fate of a tangible heritage so intensively mined. Present needs seemed to reshape past remains in a fashion strikingly analogous to revisions of memory and history. Other linkages emerged, such as Freud's archaeological metaphors for excavating the psychological past. I began to realize that the pasts we alter or invent are as prevalent and consequential as those we try to preserve. Indeed, a heritage wholly saved or authentically reproduced is no less transformed than one deliberately manipulated. 'Re-created pasts ought to be based on the knowledge and values of the present', writes Kevin Lynch; they should 'change as present knowledge and values change, just as history is rewritten'.[5] Such change is in fact unavoidable.

The celebration of ethnic and national roots next caught my attention. American bicentennial memorabilia and modes of re-enactment revealed a Revolutionary past transformed to suit present needs. I looked at the effect of appreciation and protection on valued relics and relic landscapes, and at attitudes toward age and wear as distinct from historical antiquity. Experiences abroad led me to compare West Indian and Australian with North American orientations toward their pasts, as three New World realms where colonial and natural history had shaped distinctive ways of defining, vaunting, and rejecting various aspects of heritage.

In 1977 I began to devise the framework of this book and to fill gaps in my understand-ing. One was historic preservation, now a popular crusade. Visits with preservation spokesmen and educational programmes in Britain and the United States showed me how

[5] *What Time Is This Place?* p. 53.

much concern with the architectural heritage infused planning and development, yet left problems of gentrification, of public participation, even of motivation often unresolved. Why, after all, do people want to save things? To find out, Marcus Binney of SAVE Britain's Heritage and I organized a symposium, held in London in 1979 under the auspices of the International Council on Monuments and Sites, at which academics and practitioners discussed propensities for preserving everything from antiques to agricultural scenery, and resultant problems from authenticity to over-popularity.

Other byways beckoned, often to unlikely realms. The craze for time-travel fantasy led me to review imaginative journeys to the past in science fiction, folklore, and children's literature, as vivid instances of yearning for and coping with remote or remembered pasts.

The yearned-for past also inheres in its relics and records, to which nations attach increasing importance. Formerly subjugated peoples who have lost a major portion of a precious patrimony conjure up significant questions of rightful ownership, of safety, of conservation expertise, of appropriate locales for seeing the remains of the past. The issue of the Elgin Marbles offered a prime illustration of the political passions involved. While new and poor nations now seek the restitution of purloined relics and records, the continuing loss of heritage distresses all but the richest countries.

National and communal efforts to recall and refashion a praiseworthy if not a glorious past struck me as similar to the needs of individuals to construct a viable and believable life history. In reviewing alterations of the past, students of nationalism and psychoanalysis and literary criticism share an awareness that individuals, like states, must continually confront the competing pulls of dependence and autonomy, following and leading, tradition and creativity, infancy and maturity. It was striking to find the same metaphors for coping with a past, at once supportive and burdensome, employed across such a spectrum of disciplines and over European history from the Renaissance to the present. Such a convergence cannot be coincidental; our attitudes toward the past, and our reasons for preserving and altering its residues, reflect developments and predispositions common to history, to memory, and to relics.

This book comprises three broad themes. How the past alike enriches and impoverishes us, and the reasons we embrace or shun it, comprise Chapters 1 to 4. How our recollections and our surroundings make us aware of the past, and how we respond to such knowledge, occupies Chapter 5. Why and how we change what has come down to us, to what ends its vestiges, like our memories, are salvaged or contrived, and how these alterations affect our heritage and ourselves, are the themes of Chapters 6 and 7. Throughout I seek to show how the past, once virtually indistinguishable from the present, has become an ever more foreign realm, yet one increasingly suffused by the present.

Chapter 1 explores the age-old dream of recovering or returning to the past. Nostalgia transcends yearnings for lost childhoods and scenes of early life, embracing imagined pasts never experienced by their devotees or perhaps by anyone. Faith in reincarnation and past-life regressions seems unquenchable, fictional returns to previous times attract massive audiences, and scholarly surveys supply abundant evidence of desires to visit or relive some past period, whether recent and personal or historically remote.

To some people such imaginative returns promise immortality, to others a chance to undo errors or right wrongs, to still others an escape from the weight and woes of the present. The aims of would-be time travellers go beyond the customary needs for the past delineated in Chapter 2, but shed light on the goals we all seek in altering the lineaments or our images of bygone times. To conform the past with what it should have been; to safeguard its vestiges against unwonted and unwanted change: these conflicting urges dominate time-travel fantasy. They also underlie the universal desires, as shown in Chapters 2 and 3, both to profit from the past and to avoid its trammels.

Chapter 2 surveys the benefits the past actually supplies and the fears its influence arouses. The familiarity of recognition; the reaffirmation of belief and action; the guidance of example; the awareness of personal and communal identity; the diachronic enrichment of present experience; respites or escapes from the pace and pressure of the here and now are the most significant benefits. Culture and circumstance shape their relative worth and specific form. But they all stem from qualities felt to inhere uniquely in the past as distinct from the present or the future: traits linked with antiquity, such as precedence, primordiality, and ancientness; the sense of continuity and accretion engendered by relics and memories and chronicles; and termination – the fact that the past is over and hence can be summarized and summed up as the present cannot.

Against its benefits must be set the past's drawbacks. To endure present life we may want to forget or obliterate a malign or traumatic history. A glorious heritage may likewise overwhelm, its superiority extinguishing even the will to rival it. Traditional or inherited perspectives may seem pernicious to all but their few inheritors, and sometimes even to them.

Collective efforts to cope with a heritage at once revered and resented parallel individual needs both to follow and to reject parental precepts, an analogy perennially invoked in debates over imitation and innovation, ancients and moderns. Every inheritance is alike beneficial and baneful; every historically conscious society has had to reassess that balance for itself.

Chapter 3 considers conflicting views of the past's achievements and deficiencies in four epochs – the Renaissance, seventeenth- and eighteenth-century England and France, Victorian Britain, Revolutionary and post-Revolutionary America. Always passionately debated, the rival claims of past and present elicit arguments that reflect differing contexts in each epoch.

Far from precluding faith in modern genius, Renaissance reverence for classical antiquity fostered confidence that moderns might even surpass ancient greatness. Antiquity was distant; its scattered and dismembered vestiges could serve as exemplars only when resuscitated and made whole. Hence humanist reuse of antiquity had to be creative. Translating classical works into vernacular tongues, readapting pagan motifs to suit Christian iconography, redefining Greek and Roman architectural principles, the Renaissance drew sustenance from the past while avoiding servile indebtedness. Yet doubts about borrowing, about emulative rivalry, and about the merits of followers preoccupied humanists from Dante and Petrarch to Erasmus, Du Bellay, and Montaigne.

The seventeenth- and eighteenth-century quarrel between the Ancients and the Moderns polarized such tensions. The relative worth of modern and antique achievements hinged on several issues: the decline of men's powers presumed by the doctrine of universal decay; the concept that moderns were 'dwarfs on the shoulders of giants' who might see farther than more illustrious predecessors; distinctions drawn between science's cumulative achievements and art's isolated creations. By the Enlightenment the classical tradition had ceased to be the *ne plus ultra* in science but remained the fount of veneration, and of burdensome authority, in the arts – a weight now aggravated by the accomplishments of recent as well as remote precursors.

In Victorian Britain the past became a refuge from an all-too-new and disillusioning present. Changes set in train by the French and Industrial Revolutions radically sundered today from yesterday, and pride in material progress mingled with dismay at its brutal, ugly, and materialist consequences. Many ascribed to classical or medieval life all the virtues they thought modernity had destroyed. Increasing knowledge of antiquity and skill in delineating its forms encouraged a self-conscious and eclectic revivalism that precluded a self-respecting style of their own. A sentimentalizing regard for the past revived 'traditional' modes of life in the Arts and Crafts movement, vernacular building, the preservation and replication of the architectural heritage. Traditions seen to stem from time immemorial were sanctified as reflections of all that was ever best in Britain. But this obeisance to old times, old practices, old forms engendered and heightened demands to throw off a heritage seen as anachronistic and irrelevant – a conflict that exploded in *fin-de-siècle* despair and modernist iconoclasm.

The American colonial break with Britain generated explicit parental and filial metaphors for past–present confrontations. To support their political positions, both sides cited the bonds and reciprocal duties of parents and offspring. A revolution in child-rearing practices lent sanction to rebellions throughout the Americas and to a philosophy that condemned all past authority: the present generation must be sovereign. Taught to disdain inherited precepts, succeeding generations were then torn between antipathy toward authority and obligations to revere and defend the legacy of the Founding Fathers. To emulate them, they should throw off the shackles of the past; to safeguard their inheritance they must preserve, not create anew. These ideals were incompatible. And the tug of nostalgia many Americans felt for time-rooted Old World scenes offended the prevailing morality that smelled evil and autocracy in such vestiges. The Civil War ultimately resolved the dilemma over preserving or creating; tensions between progress and filial piety thereafter assumed other forms.

Each of these epochs thus confronted its inheritance with a double awareness of indebtedness and of resentment; each sought in different ways to compromise or to choose between reverence and rejection; each fostered images of past and present that reflected these painful dilemmas.

Chapter 4 explores responses to ageing, decay, and marks of use and wear as distinct from signs of an historical past. Because we tend to view artifacts and institutions as having life cycles like our own, such responses are customarily couched in analogies with human old age – a stage usually felt as unattractive if not repellent. Repugnance to old age and preference for youth are similarly manifest for the world and its parts, nations and states, and most artifacts; they are considered beautiful and virtuous when young, ugly and corrupt when aged and decrepit.

The prejudice is far from universal, however. Marks of age are felt to enhance the beauty and value of some types of artifact – notably buildings and paintings. But only since the sixteenth century has the look of age become widely appreciated, first as a means of confirming and authenticating historical antiquity, then as attractive in its own right. No longer largely noxious, monumental ruin and decay gained admiration as *memento mori* or for other symbolic associations and later as prototypes of a picturesque aesthetic. Appreciation of the look of age today extends from ancient Chinese bronzes and the neo-Romantic passion for fragmented sculpture to 'weathering-steel' buildings meant to rust and to intentionally evanescent works of art. But the public in general contemns the appearance of age, preferring even old things to look newly made. And continuing controversy over the cleaning of buildings and of paintings reveal impassioned differences of taste between embattled friends and foes of the patina of age.

Chapter 5 surveys the avenues along which we become aware of and informed about the past. The past itself is gone – all that survives are its material residues and the accounts of those who experienced it. No such evidence can tell us about the past with absolute certainty, for its survivals on the ground, in books, and in our heads are selectively pre-served from the start and further altered by the passage of time. These remnants conform too well with one another and with knowledge of the present to be denied all validity, yet residual doubts about the past's reality help to account for our eagerness to accept what may be dubious about it. There can be no certainty that the past ever existed, let alone in the form we now conceive it, but sanity and security require us to believe that it did.

As modes of access to the past, memory, history, and relics exhibit important resem-blances and differences. By its nature personal and hence largely unverifiable, memory extends back only to childhood, though we do accrete to our own recollections those told us by forebears. By contrast, history, whose shared data and conclusions must be open to public scrutiny, extends back to or beyond the earliest records of civilization. The death of each individual totally extinguishes countless memories, whereas history (at least in print) is potentially immortal. Yet all history depends on memory, and many recollections incorporate history. And they are alike distorted by selective perception, intervening circumstance, and hindsight.

The uses and misuses of memory suffuse much of modern literature (*Remembrance of Things Past* is the archetypal example) and literary criticism, which I review in conjunction with the history of memory training, psychoanalytical insights, developmental studies, and other psychological treatises. Among other facets touched on are how memory establishes personal identity; the links between personal and communal memory; how recollections are verified; the various types of memory that provide access to the past; the function of forgetting; how time alters old and invents new memories; and how new techniques from writing to film and tape progressively displace or transform the character of recollection.

Canons of historical inquiry and consensually shared data set historical knowledge on a seemingly firmer footing than what is known from memory alone. Yet historical know-ledge likewise is shaped by subjectivity, by hindsight, and by the insurmountable gulf between the actual past and any account of that past. Every account of the past is both more and less than that past – less because no account can incorporate an entire past, however exhaustive the records; more because narrators of past events have the advantage of knowing subsequent outcomes. Such epistemological problems are of small concern to practitioners for whom history is simply what historians do. But what they actually do depends on present views of what history ought to be about. If only to be understood, historians always rewrite the past from the standpoint of the present, in the process rearranging data and altering conclusions. And like historical rhetoric, chronology and narrative also shape accounts of the past. Finally, I review how history and fiction interrelate; and how understanding of the past differs from knowledge of the present.

Memory and history both derive and gain emphasis from physical remains. Tangible survivals provide a vivid immediacy that helps to assure us there really was a past. Physical remains have their limitations as informants, to be sure: they are themselves mute, requiring interpretation; their continual but differential erosion and demolition skews the record; and their substantial survival conjures up a past more static than could have been the case. But however depleted by time and use, relics remain essential bridges between then and now. They confirm or deny what we think of it, symbolize or memorialize communal links over time, and provide archaeological metaphors that illumine the processes of history and memory.

We respond to relics as objects of interest or beauty, as evidence of past events, and as talismans of continuity. These responses may mistake their original function, but do evince at least some concern with the past. All knowledge of the past requires caring about it – feeling pleasure or disgust, awe or disdain, hope or despair about some aspect of our legacy.

Chapter 6 examines how and why we change the past, and the effect of such changes on our environs and ourselves. The actual lineaments of surviving relics undergo ceaseless alteration, and simply to identify something as 'past' affects its ambience, for recognition entails marking, protecting, and enhancing relics to make them more accessible, secure, or attractive. Their appreciation if not survival may require moving them from original locales. Enshrined in historic precincts yet surrounded by the trappings of present-day management, vestiges of the past seem newly contrived. Thus present choices – whether to keep relics *in situ* or to remove them, to leave them in fragments or make them whole again – vitally affect how the past is experienced.

Imitations, fakes, and new works inspired by earlier prototypes extend and further alter the aura of antiquity. The scarcity of originals spurs the making of replicas that at least echo the old. Creations that hark back to or reflect some attribute of a bygone era have for five centuries dominated the cultural landscape of the Western world. Modern awareness of classical architecture derives from an amalgam of Hellenistic, Renaissance, Enlightenment, Romantic, and Victorian works in which extant Greek and Roman remains play only a minor role. It is not the original that seems 'authentic' but current views of what the past ought to have looked like. Much else that bespeaks the past, such as monuments to its memory, bears no resemblance whatever to its actual features.

We remould the past for reasons that mirror the benefits, outlined in Chapters 1 and 2, the past is felt to confer. Patriotic zeal or private pique persuade us to conform its remnants, like our recollections, to our needs and expectations. Most alterations accentuate past virtues to enhance our self-esteem or promote our interests. Thus we extend antiquity, contrive missing continuities, emphasize or invent ancestral prerogatives and achievements, minimize or forget defeat and ignominy.

Such changes have other, unintended consequences. Manipulation makes the past both more and less like the present – less because we set it apart, more because we put our own stamp on it. Even if we aim to preserve things just as they were or as we find them, protective and restorative devices mantle the past in the machinery of the present.

Alterations of the past likewise affect those who make them. They run counter to desires for a fixed and stable heritage and undermine our role as its continuators. Yet awareness of our propensity to alter what we inherit has compensations. Realizing that the past is not just what happened back then but is also a set of subsequent constructions, we discard the outgrown perspectives and anachronistic behaviour of an inflexible legacy, and learn that remaking that legacy is not only inevitable but salutary. 'There is nothing wrong with it', says an archaeologist of reinterpreting the past in present terms; the difficulty comes when we 'do not realize it and thereby are controlled by the process'.[6] Through construction and reconstruction each person achieves 'a useful and self-respecting past', writes a psychoanalyst, for 'a crucial aspect of the individual's sense of free will is a knowledge of his own history that does not dominate, overburden, or destroy him'.[7]

The much-heralded death of the past, and its supposed resurrection in the form of history, introduce Chapter 7. In the modernist view, industrial and post-industrial society no longer need the props and shibboleths of tradition; and the modern study of history emancipates us from the past's tyranny. But our rampant nostalgia, our obsessive search for roots, our endemic concern with preservation, the potent appeal of national heritage show how intensely the past is still felt. Yet new historical perspectives have outmoded once customary ways of feeling and using it. Wholehearted faith in tradition, the guidance of past examples, empathetic communion with great figures of antiquity, the solaces of a golden age, evocative ruminations over ruins and relics – these modes of engaging with bygone times have largely ceased to be credible. History has made them obsolete.

Along with once familiar modes of apprehension we have jettisoned part of the very fabric of the past. While the arena of historical scrutiny expands to embrace hitherto little-known peoples and realms of life, we have lost the ready familiarity with the classical and biblical heritage that long imprinted European culture and environment. This century's breach with that legacy leaves us surrounded by monuments and relics we can barely comprehend and scarcely feel are ours – an alienation especially evident in post-modernist efforts to overcome it.

The rage to preserve is in part a reaction to anxieties generated by modernist amnesia. We preserve because the pace of change and development has attenuated a legacy integral to our identity and well-being. But we also preserve, I suggest, because we are no longer intimate enough with that legacy to rework it creatively. We admire its relics, but they do not inspire our own acts and works. Precisely because preservation has become our principal mode of appreciating the past, it tends to preclude other uses, like

---

[6] Leone, 'Relationship between artifacts and the public in outdoor history museums', p. 309.
[7] Solnit, *Memory as Preparation*, p. 27.

Proust's Vinteuil who decides not to make use of a precious friendship, 'so as to have the wholly Platonic satisfaction of preserving it'.[8]

Relations with the past can neither be proscribed nor prescribed, for they are bound up with all our ideas and institutions. But heightened consciousness of how we now deal with the past, in the context of how others have done so, itself affects our attitudes and leads to change. Those who dispute this book's conclusions, no less than those who accept them, may thereby come to see the past in a different light.

Except in regretting the modernist breach with classical and biblical legacies, I hold no brief for any particular view of the past. The residues of bygone lives and locales affect, enrich, and inhibit our own in myriad ways. Awareness of things past comes less from information apprehended than from an appreciation of time's impact on all our words, all our deeds, all our relics. To know that we are simply the ephemeral lessees of age-old hopes and dreams that have animated generations of endeavour helps us to secure, if not to rejoice in, our place in the scheme of things.

Recognition of the past as a foreign country now colours our view of antiquity from primeval times down to yesterday. We have partly domesticated that past, where they do things differently, and brought it into the present as a marketable commodity. But in altering its remains we also assimilate them, ironing out their differences and their difficulties in the process. 'When "history" overtakes some new chunk of the recent past', a commentator reflects, 'it always comes as a relief – one thing that history does . . . is to fumigate experience, making it safe and sterile . . . Experience undergoes eternal gentrification; the past, all the parts of it that are dirty and exciting and dangerous and uncomfortable and real, turns gradually into the East Village.'[9]

Yet the past is not dead, as J. H. Plumb would have it; it is not even sleeping. A mass of memories and records, of relics and replicas, of monuments and memorabilia, lives at the core of our being. And as we remake it, the past remakes us. We kick over the traces of tradition to assert our autonomy and expunge our errors, but we cannot banish the past, for it is inherent in all we do and think. No one has not 'said things, or lived a life, the memory of which is so unpleasant to him that he would gladly expunge it. And yet' one achieves wisdom only by passing through 'all the fatuous or unwholesome incarnations . . . The picture of what we were at an earlier stage may not be recognisable and cannot, certainly, be pleasing to contemplate in later life. But we must not repudiate it, for it is a proof that we have really lived.'[10] We inherit a legacy no less precious for being often indecipherable or inconvenient. To be is to have been, and to project our messy, malleable past into our unknown future.

I have not conducted exhaustive research on most of the topics this book surveys. Instead I have tried to fashion a plausible synthesis out of quite heterogeneous materials. Necessarily trespassing beyond my own putative disciplines, I am bound often to have misinterpreted the art and architectural historians, the psychologists and psychoanalysts, the archaeologists and Renaissance scholars and others on whose research I have relied; for this I beg their pardon and my readers' forbearance. Apart from a few realms –

[8] *Remembrance of Things Past*, 1:163. [9] 'Notes and comment', *New Yorker*, 24 Sept. 1984, p. 39.
[10] Proust, *Remembrance of Things Past*, 1:923–4.

nineteenth-century American history, landscape perceptions, science fiction, historic preservation – original sources cited herein reflect no systematic sampling on my part, but selections whose representativeness is generally attested by modern authorities. My reversion to the originals mainly reflects needs to reconcile variant readings and to ensure that my citations are accurate and in context.

Though the past is a topic of almost universal concern, little research explicitly focuses on how people in general see, value, or understand it. I know of only half a dozen disparate surveys. Thomas Cottle's inquiry showed how much people said they would give, and why, to return for various lengths of time to personal and to historical pasts. Martin Taylor and Victor Konrad categorize past-related activities that appealed to residents of Toronto. Colin Morris analyses historical preferences revealed by responses to pictures of old and new buildings of various styles; Reid Bishop correlates perceived antiquity with attitudes toward old buildings in Guildford, Surrey. Barbara Szacka assesses 'antiquarian' and 'historicist' dispositions toward the past among Polish university graduates. Marquita Riel and I studied connections habitually made between American city scenes adjudged 'old' and other liked or disliked qualities. Given the wide range of subject-matter, the difficulties of definition, and the pitfalls of generalization, quantitative assessments can hardly be expected to shed steady light on attitudes toward any past. Even so, the virtual absence of large-scale inquiries into a topic of such consequence seems to me astounding.

That absence has forced me to rely mainly on the written record, and my syntheses reflect the collective wisdom of the various disciplines that have sampled that record. Such insights are heavily weighted toward literate elites who troubled to record their views and were probably more inclined than other folk to speculate about the past. My own conclusions necessarily depend mainly on generalizations that concern a small but influential minority of humanity, present and past. It is this minority to whom my use of 'we' and 'our' refers.

Present attitudes and those of our immediate forebears dominate this study, but exploring them often led me back to ancient times and even to prehistory. Standards of evidence, levels of confidence in sources, and our capacity to assimilate past ideas decline as the past recedes from us, but I have perforce had to move back and forth across the centuries with what some may judge casual disregard for such differences.

Spatially and culturally my conclusions are also parochial. Although I focus broadly on Western culture and rely on pan-European classical and subsequent scholarship, I pay only cursory attention to non-Anglophone literature and virtually none to cultures outside the European realm. Oriental and African views on the past and ideas of heritage are to me virtual *terrae incognitae*, for which equivalent studies might reach radically different conclusions.

A final caveat: I adduce such heterogeneous material as evidence – fiction, psychological treatises, interviews, autobiographies, advertisements for 'heritage' products, sources from the history of ideas, polemical diatribes on preservation and restoration – that readers may find the commingling wantonly eclectic or absurdly disparate. I do this not because I suppose all these sources are analogous nor because I accord them equal evidential value, but to make cogent what might otherwise go unnoted. Involving whatever I can recall or have culled over the years, whatever their antecedents, my sources resemble Henry James's grab-bag of memory more, I confess, than J. H. Hexter's coherence of history.

The range of materials this book includes makes my indebtedness manifold. For editorial assistance I thank Mary Alice Lamberty, and William Davies and Christine Lyall Grant at Cambridge University Press. Claudette John and subsequently Marian Plaskow superbly and cheerfully typed several drafts, and made word-processing a pleasure.

For access to materials I am grateful to the staff of the British Library, the Widener Library at Harvard, the Science Fiction Library at North East London Polytechnic, and the libraries of University College and the University of London, the Warburg Institute, and the Institute of Archaeology. Chris Cromarty skilfully made prints of most of the pictures, and Wayne Andrews generously supplied several of his own. My thanks to Philip Larkin and to Faber and Faber Ltd for permission to use part of his poem 'An Arundel Tomb' from *The Whitsun Weddings*, 1964.

Unpublished papers and reports were given me by Edwin Bearss, Richard Candee, John Fortier, Lucinda Irwin, Darwin Kelsey, Victor Konrad, Patrick McGreevy, David Nicholls, Graham Rowles, Gabrielle Spiegel, John Toews, and Ronald Witt. Help on a host of topics came from David Bomford, Nancy Burson, Gillian Clarke, Andrew Durham, James Marston Fitch, Richard Griffith, Max Hanna, Bunji Kobayashi, Bill Larrett, Roger Lonsdale, Robert Marten, Morris Pearl, Constantin Politis, Roy Schafer, Douglas Scovill, Marcella Sherfy, Sister Teresa of the Deaconess Community of St Andrew, Michael Steiner, and Garry Trompf.

Among the scores of people who gave up their time to be interviewed, I especially thank Ashley Barker, Edwin Bearss, David Bomford, Hugh Casson, Ralph Christian, Henry Cleere, John Cornforth, Martin Drury, Peter Fowler, St John Gore, Richard Haslam, Henry-Russell Hitchcock, Hermione Hobhouse, Donald Insall, Wayland Kennet, Alan Leavitt, Lois Lang-Sims, Michael Middleton, Eleanor Murray, Paul Perrot, John Popham, Peter Reynolds, John Shannon, John Summerson, Robert Utley, and Roy Worskett.

I am indebted for inspiration and guidance to the late Donald Appleyard, Jay Appleton, Daniel Boorstin, Kenneth Craik, Merle Curti, Thomas Greene, Fritz Gutheim, James Huhta, Chester Liebs, Richard Longstreth, the late Kevin Lynch, Robert Melnick, Murray Schafer, Sandra Semchuk, Albert Solnit, and Barbara Szacka.

Salutary responses to one or more chapters of earlier drafts came from Carolyn Adams, John Hale, Gad Heuman, Anne Lowenthal, Gerry McPherson, Kenneth Olwig, David Pearce, Valerie Pearl, P. M. Rattansi, Richard Rawles, Marion Shoard, Claudio Vita-Finzi, Jill Paton Walsh, and Peter Wason. Exhaustive, sometimes exasperated, but always constructive suggestions came from Ruth Elson, Michael Hunter, Antoinette Lee, and Betty Levin, who ploughed through entire typescripts, and from Edmunds Bunkše and Peter Quartermaine who endured the penultimate draft.

My most profound indebtedness is to Penelope Lively and Hugh Prince, who not only gave invaluable advice on the whole book but have inspired and encouraged me throughout many years of research and writing.

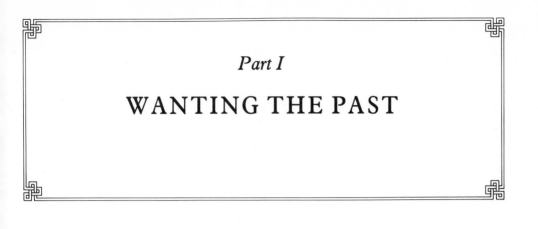

Part I

WANTING THE PAST

1

RELIVING THE PAST: DREAMS AND NIGHTMARES

Oh call back yesterday . . . bid time return.

Shakespeare, *Richard II*, 3.2

The miracle of life is cruelly circumscribed by birth and death; of the immensity of time before and after our own lives we experience nothing. Past and future are alike inaccessible. But, though beyond physical reach, they are integral to our imaginations. Reminiscence and expectation suffuse every present moment.

Past and future attract – and repel – in quite different ways. Most images of times ahead are hazy and uncertain. We cannot even know the consequences of our own acts, let alone foretell the larger future. In more confident times a generation ago, visionary planners saw the future as almost 'another country, which one might visit like Italy, or even try to re-create in replica', Reyner Banham recalls. 'Futurism was something suspiciously like a period style, a neo-gothic of the Machine Age.'[1] But today that future is just a nostalgic memory; what lies ahead, splendid, horrendous, or simply ordinary, is a scene that shifts with every viewer and moment. We are not privy to what will come. Wishes are notoriously unfulfilled, like the yearning for posthumous fame that led Beerbohm's Enoch Soames, a poet neglected in his own day, to compact with the devil so as to learn what posterity thinks of him. Returning a century later, Soames locates only one entry under his name in a literary history: 'an immajnari karrakter in a story by Max Beerbohm'.[2] We may affect the future's contingencies, but we can never control them. Borges's time-reversed Yahoos, who have foresight but lack hindsight, underscore the critical distinction between memory and divination.[3]

Unlike the vague lineaments of times ahead, the fixed past has been sketched by countless chroniclers. Its vestiges in landscape and memory reflect innumerable details of what we and our predecessors have done and felt. The richly elaborated past seems more familiar than the geographically remote, in some respects even more than our own nearby present; the here and now lacks the felt density and completeness of what time has filtered and ordered.[4]

[1] 'Come in 2001', *New Society*, 8 Jan. 1976, p. 63.
[2] *Seven Men and Two Others*, p. 36.
[3] 'Doctor Brodie's report'.   [4] Casey, 'Imagining and remembering'.

3

Moreover, we feel quite sure that the past really happened; its traces and memories reflect undeniable scenes and acts. The airy and insubstantial future may never arrive; man or nature may destroy humanity; time as we know it may end. By contrast, the past is tangible and secure; people think of it as fixed, unalterable, indelibly recorded.[5] 'How much nicer to go back', exclaims a fictional modern visitor to the world of 1820; 'the past was safe!'[6] It is on the whole unsurprising; its measure has been taken. We are at home in it because it *is* our home – the past is where we come from. And few have not wished on occasion to return to an earlier time. The revisited past may not always satisfy, but it seldom threatens so unpleasant a surprise as that which faced poor Enoch Soames.

Yet we can no more slip back to the past than leap forward to the future. Save in imaginative reconstruction, yesterday is forever barred to us; we have only attenuated memories and fragmentary chronicles of prior experience and can only dream of escaping the confines of the present. But in recent years such nostalgic dreams have become almost habitual, if not epidemic.

NOSTALGIA

When I was a lad, all this was open fields.

> Young cockney, in London's Charing Cross
> Underground tunnel, 1982[7]

Nostalgia is today the universal catchword for looking back. It fills the popular press, serves as advertising bait, merits sociological study; no term better expresses modern malaise. America's Nostalgia Book Club 'puts you years behind the times – by choice'. A Britain addicted to Mark Girouard's evocation of the Victorian cult of chivalry, to William Burges's neo-Gothic architecture, and to the film *Excalibur*, a reviewer surmised, would 'soon be appointing a Curator instead of a Prime Minister'.[8]

If the past is a foreign country, nostalgia has made it 'the foreign country with the healthiest tourist trade of all'. But like other tourists, those to the past imperil the object of their quest. 'An eco-nostalgic crisis [is] on the way', warned Sheridan Morley. 'Resources will have to be preserved, revivals ... strictly rationed.'[9] Nostalgia's profitability incites real estate agents 'to drum up interest by digging out every shred of history', whether the connection be with a king or a pop star; no echo of any past is too bizarre to appeal, not even the monument to the fraudulent Piltdown Man found at Barkham Manor, Sussex. Since 'people love nostalgia and firmly believe that' what is old 'is necessarily good', developers capitalize on proximity to historic dwellings; 'the old building adds credibility and status to the new building'.[10] Once unhappy with its nineteenth-century legacy, British Rail now finds steam engines and sepia scenes of bygone railway eras a source of pride and profit.

[5] 'The past ... is still an irrefutable and ubiquitous force: but the "future" is really nothing but a slightly normative fantasy' (Wyatt, 'In quest of change', p. 389).

[6] Aldiss, *Frankenstein Unbound*, p. 26.

[7] Quoted in Michael Dineen, 'The English village re-born', *Observer*, 19 Sept. 1982, p. 3.

[8] J. Mordaunt Crook, 'Honour and its enemies', *TLS*, 25 Sept. 1981, p. 1102.

[9] 'There's no business like old business', *Punch*, 29 Nov. 1972, p. 777.

[10] Caroline McGhie, 'Noel Coward played the piano here', *Sunday Times*, 17 July 1983, p. 39; Robert Troop, 'Making the most of moat and beam', *Sunday Times*, 27 March 1983, p. 27.

1 Rubbish into 'Antiques': Coventry, Vermont

2 Tudor nostalgia: Charles Wade's Snowshill Manor, Gloucestershire

Other peoples likewise pine for things past, especially things English: old oak beams from East Anglia (or glass-fibre copies of them) solace nostalgia in Helsinki and Osaka; *The Country Diary of an Edwardian Lady* and television's *Brideshead Revisited* tap world-wide markets. The remembrance of times past is a burgeoning business in almost every country, and any epoch will do. Russian nostalgia is most intense for images of pre-Revolutionary troikas, furs, and family samovars, but even the darkest Stalinist days now engender wistful memories of imagined idealism and heroic sacrifice.[11]

Formerly confined in time and place, nostalgia today engulfs the whole past. Antique dealers have jettisoned the former 100-year-old barrier, collectors treat 1930s art deco with reverence, critics admire 'canonically 1950s' juke-boxes. 'Memory men' revive Mary Quant, resurrect Bill Haley, keep Chuck Berry eternally youthful and Elvis Presley relentlessly alive. We increasingly focus on 'a past so recent that only an 11-year-old could possibly view it as past', in Russell Baker's phrase; 'the student anti-war demonstrations of the late 1960s ... are already being sentimentalized ... as some great turbulent but glorious phenomenon of a dead long-ago'; the city of Calgary is said to have had an architect search out its venerable buildings of the 1960s.[12] Obsolescence confers instant bygone status – no sooner is the fire truck out of sight than it becomes an emblem of a vanished past. By 1980, judged Bevis Hillier, 'history was being recycled as nostalgia almost as soon as it happened'. Indeed, Hillier portrayed the launching of his previous book on the subject as itself a nostalgic memory.[13]

Nostalgia has likewise expanded in space and theme. A Danish 'nostalgia index' embraces relics of every conceivable type.[14] *Henry VIII*, *Elizabeth I*, *Dad's Army*, *The Onedin Line*, *Upstairs Downstairs*, *The Forsyte Saga*, *The Pallisers*, *The World at War* celebrate a wide range of British pasts. 'The heartier facets of our heritage', from medieval thumbscrews to the Fire of London, cater for nostalgia at 'Merrie England' and the London Dungeon. *Good Old Days*, America's 'Magazine of Happy Memories', reminisces fondly about porches, cedar water buckets, hitching posts, woodsheds, showboats, Admiral Dewey, 'Casey at the Bat', Bonnie and Clyde; its readers collect Zane Grey books, Sears Roebuck catalogues, McGuffey readers, old sheet music.

The most trivial bygones have their devotees. 'Bring back Button B! Bring back proper kiosks', yearns Paul Jennings. 'Bring back trolley-buses ... Bring back cars with starting handles.'[15] The Smithsonian Institution's museum enshrines Washington's false teeth, trimmings from Lincoln's hearse, the tobacco plug Peary carried to the North Pole, the red-white-and-blue beard Gary Sandburg sported at the Bicentennial, black dentures exported to cater for nineteenth-century Polynesian taste; a Swiss collection of Sherlock

[11] Caroline Moorehead, 'The nostalgia that didn't get away', *The Times*, 15 Mar. 1980; Binyon, *Life in Russia*, pp. 140–2; Shipler, *Russia*, pp. 265, 300; Hedrick Smith, *Russians*, pp. 249–57; Philippa Lewis, 'Peasant nostalgia in contemporary Russian literature'.

[12] Baker, 'Shock of things past', *International Herald Tribune* (hereafter *IHT*), 2 May 1975, p. 14; Banham, 'Last boom-town'. Elvis Presley devotees throng Stanford University modern history courses when they reach the 1960s ('The great nostalgia kick', *U.S. News and World Report*, 22 Mar. 1983, p. 60).

[13] *Style of the Century*, p. 216, also pp. 206–15; *Austerity Binge*, pp. 187–9, 195.

[14] Newcomb, 'Nostalgia index of historical landscapes in Denmark', pp. 441–3; idem, *Planning the Past*, pp. 64, 214–15.

[15] *Sunday Telegraph*, 4 Feb. 1979, p. 16.

Holmes memorabilia includes a bottle of 'genuine London fog, certified by a lost passerby'.[16]

Intimate associations help sell the past. An advertisement for sepia-toned prints of Frith's late nineteenth-century photographs offers customers 'Your village, your town, your roots . . . your own personal piece of nostalgia.' The 'Imperial Tankard' commemorates for Britons 'the Empire they never knew, perhaps, but also the Empire they should not be allowed to forget'. And nostalgia attaches to times beyond our ken no less than to things we have experienced; few who flock to Bogart films, listen to Glenn Miller music, or throw 1960s parties are old enough to recall them.

What meanings emerge from this swarm of nostalgic invocations? Many seem less concerned to find a past than to yearn for it, eager not so much to relive a fancied long-ago as to collect its relics and celebrate its virtues. Yet to 'travel back forty years to a time when it was summer all year round and kids raided ice-wagons, . . . to take a Sunday walk the way we used to, with your silk parasol and your long dress whishing along, and sit on those wire-legged stools at the soda parlour', is more than one old man's obsessive dream.[17] 'Most old folks can remember a time when beer was cheaper . . . and people had more respect. Most of us remember odd patches of our lives with especial affection, sometimes patches that were not in themselves particularly pleasant.'[18] No matter if those days were in fact wretched: 'life was lovely back in the 1900s', elderly Irish folk raised in rural destitution recently assured an interviewer; the Courage beer campaign 'Fings are wot they used t'be' makes grubby associations of the 1930s endearing.[19] Even horrendous memories can evoke nostalgia. A Londoner a generation later recalled war-time bombing as 'pure, flawless happiness'; one suspects 'that many people experience this nostalgia and would dearly love to recreate the horrifying circumstances of their own childhood'.[20]

A past nostalgically enjoyed does not need to be taken seriously. Sightseers on London Transport's 1925 'Time Machine' bus imagine doing the Charleston or buying a house for under £1,000 in Pinner, and muse 'of times when every day seemed like high summer'; the attraction of a bus from 1940, when Britain stood alone against Hitler, is that 'you can dream as much as you like without the harsh realities of that almost forgotten world'.[21] A 'Vintage India' Maharaja-style trip around Rajasthan, each saloon's history enhanced by a period-costumed attendant, becomes an 'incredibly nostalgic package that brings back to life the vintage splendours'. One need not go abroad to taste the exotic; travellers on a Venice–Simplon train trip through comfortable Kent receive 'an Orient Express Certificate to remember your nostalgic journey into the opulent past'. Nostalgic excursions are often brief, circumscribed, inconsequential. The American 'Western' reflects 'a desire to get out of modernity without leaving it altogether; we want to relive those thrilling days of yesteryear, but only because we are absolutely assured that those days are out of reach'.[22]

[16] Tom Zito, 'Rummaging through America's attic', *IHT*, 11 Apr. 1980; Mavis Guinard, 'The case of the immortal detective', *IHT*, 17 Sept. 1982, p. 9.

[17] Ray Bradbury, 'Scent of sarsaparilla', pp. 193, 195.   [18] Michael Wood, 'Nostalgia or never', p. 343.

[19] Mary Kenny, 'When the going was bad', *Sunday Telegraph*, 19 Aug. 1979; Richard Milner, 'Courage cockneys tap taste for nostalgia', *Sunday Times*, 25 Apr. 1982, p. 49.

[20] Tom Harrisson, *Living through the Blitz*, p. 325; Maurice Lescoq, 'Leavetaking' (1961), in Moorcock, *English Assassin*, p. 1.

[21] Vintage Bus Service brochure, 'Take a ride in a time machine', *c.* 1980.

[22] Roger Rosenblatt, 'Look back in sentiment', *N.Y. Times*, 28 July 1973, p. 23.

Most of us know the past was not really like that. Life back then seems brighter not because things were better but because we lived more vividly when young; even the adult world of yesteryear reflects the perspective of childhood. Now unable to experience so intensely, we mourn a lost immediacy that makes the past unmatchable. Such nostalgia can also shore up self-esteem, reminding us that however sad our present lot we were once happy and worthwhile. Childhood thus recalled excludes the family quarrels, the outings dominated by waiting in queues for grubby loos; 'nostalgia is memory with the pain removed'. The pain is today. We shed tears for the landscape we find no longer what it was, what we thought it was, or what we hoped it would be.

Nostalgia is often for past thoughts rather than past things, 'a daydream in reverse, like thinking we loved the books of our youth, when all we love is the thought of ourselves young, reading them'.[23] People flock to historic sites to share recall of the familiar, communal recollection enhancing personal reminiscence. What pleases the nostalgist is not just the relic but his own recognition of it, not so much the past itself as its supposed aspirations, less the memory of what actually was than of what was once thought possible. Extolling the 1930s, when faith in reform, belief in political participation, and a sense of humour survived economic adversity, one sociologist expresses nostalgia for the Depression as a period when it was still possible to feel that life had a purpose.[24]

Nostalgic evocations long antedate our time. Virgil immortalized the heroic and the pastoral past; Petrarch sought refuge in antiquity from his own 'wretched' and 'worthless' age;[25] bitter-sweet regret for an Arcadian past suffused sixteenth- and seventeenth-century poetry and the canvases of Claude and Poussin. The late eighteenth century expressed nostalgia not only for antiquity but also for recent pasts and for previous stages of life: lost childhood was mourned along with lost childhood scenes. Wordsworth's evocations of Grasmere moved millions to nostalgic reflections of childhood as a time of peace and wholeness now unattainable, like Housman's

> . . . land of lost content,
> I see it shining plain,
> The happy highways where I went
> And cannot come again.[26]

Froude yearned 'but for one week of my old child's faith, to go back to calm and peace again, and then to die in hope'.[27]

The great changes of the times had made nostalgia pervasive. Revolutionary upheaval sundered past from present; after the guillotine and Napoleon the previous world seemed irretrievably remote – hence to many doubly dear. Industrialization and forced migration pushed millions into locales radically unlike those of their childhood. Romantics sheltered from devastating change in remembered or invented images of earlier times. From the

---

23 Cross, *Poetic Justice*, p. 140.
24 Robert Nisbet, 'The 1930s: America's major nostalgia' (1972), cited from Fred Davis, *Yearning for Yesterday*, p. 10.
25 To Livy, 22 Feb. 1349 (?), in *Petrarch's Letters to Classical Authors*, pp. 101–2; Peter Burke, *Renaissance Sense of the Past*, p. 22.
26 *Shropshire Lad* (1896), XL; Clausen, 'Tintern Abbey to Little Gidding', p. 417.
27 *Nemesis of Faith* (1849), p. 28.

so-called Ancients 'united in archaistic fervour' in Samuel Palmer's 'Arcadian' Shoreham, to 'medieval' knights jousting at Eglinton, to railway-age sufferers regretting the old stagecoach days, otherwise progressive Victorians made the past an object of nostalgic adoration,[28] and folk in other lands followed suit. City-dwellers expressed regret for idealized rural pasts. Reminiscences by 'An Old Inhabitant' and 'Glimpses from the Past' filled newspapers, vanished old inns were preferred to new public houses; in London's Kentish Town even 'the huddles of wooden shacks, the ancient "dwellings of the labouring poor"', Gillian Tindall remarks, 'were seen, once they had been swept away, with a sentimental eye'.[29]

By the turn of this century all Britain seemed bent on nostalgic quest. 'Let us live again in the past', urged P. H. Ditchfield, and 'surround ourselves with the treasures of past ages'.[30] The Poet Laureate sought out an 'old England', and 'the urbanity of the Past . . . with its washing days, home-made jams, lavender bags, recitation of Gray's *Elegy*'.[31] Kipling safeguarded 'Sussex medievalism' by banning the telephone and keeping up Saxon fence-gates at his Burwash home, and even D. H. Lawrence felt the tug of nostalgia: 'looking at the accomplished past' at Garsington Manor in 1915, he was tempted 'to lapse back into its peaceful beauty of bygone things, to live in pure recollection'.[32] The chivalric romance enabled even Americans 'to leave the present, so weighted with cumbersome enigmas and ineffectual activity, and go back . . . to other days, when men . . . moved forward unswervingly to the attainment of definite and obvious desires'.[33] 'A fair frame of mind' let Henry Adams travel back to the twelfth century and even 'see the children sporting on the shore'.[34]

Architects on both sides of the Atlantic made tangible this nostalgic myth by reviving an Old English vernacular. Mock-Tudor became the predominant domestic style of the 1920s and 1930s, 'quaint' and 'old-fashioned' became terms of praise; 'to be up-to-date now meant to look as old as possible'. Prime Minister Stanley Baldwin joined Poet Laureate John Masefield in shedding tears over the past. 'Our Bill', BBC's immensely popular 1930s programme, extolled the ancient traditions, the old churches, the wayside inns of the English countryside where one could 'step aside into some small pool of history, to be lapped awhile in the healing peace of a rich, still-living past'.[35] Actively reliving his Tudor nostalgia, Charles Wade at Snowshill worked with period tools, ate in an old-world kitchen, and slept in a cupboard bed.[36] Why not rejoice in so comforting a past? 'In England we may choose from any of a dozen different centuries to live in', said Kenneth Grahame; 'and who would select the twentieth?'[37]

[28] William Feaver, 'The intensity of Samuel Palmer's visions', *Observer*, 24 Dec. 1978, p. 18; Girouard, *Return to Camelot*.

[29] *The Fields Beneath*, pp. 174–5.

[30] *Story of Our English Towns*, p. 34; but Ditchfield adds, 'no wise man will wish to bring back that past'.

[31] Alfred Austin, *Haunts of Ancient Peace*, pp. 18–19; he took pride in uttering 'none but the very oldest and most out-of-fashion ideas'.

[32] Hopkins, *Rudyard Kipling's World*, p. 11; Lawrence to Cynthia Asquith, 3 Dec. 1915, in his *Letters*, p. 283. See Wiener, *English Culture and the Decline of the Industrial Spirit*, pp. 45, 57, 62, 76.

[33] Repplier, 'Old wine and new' (1896), p. 696.   [34] *Mont-Saint-Michel and Chartres* (1912), p. 2.

[35] Wiener, *English Culture*, pp. 66, 64, 74, 76. See Girouard, *Sweetness and Light: The 'Queen Anne' Movement*, pp. 5, 25–7, 60–2.

[36] H. D. Molesworth, 'A note on the collection', in *Snowshill Manor*, London: National Trust, 1978, pp. 30–1; Wade, *Haphazard Notes*, Cheltenham: National Trust, 1979.

[37] Grahame, *First Whisper of 'The Wind in the Willows'*, p. 26.

I have limned nineteenth- and early twentieth-century nostalgia mainly in an Anglo-American context. But the phenomenon was also Continental: equivalent yearning for lost pasts can be traced from Goethe and the Grimm brothers in Germany, from Victor Hugo and Viollet-le-Duc in France, and from much of the rest of Europe.

The original concept of nostalgic affliction, however, was quite different. Seventeenth-century nostalgia was a physical rather than a mental complaint, an illness with explicit symptoms and often lethal consequences. First medically diagnosed and coined (from the Greek *nosos* = return to native land, and *algos* = suffering or grief) in 1688 by Johannes Hofer, nostalgia was already common; once away from their native land, some people languished, wasted away, and even perished. Hofer saw the illness as a 'continuous vibration of animal spirits through those fibers of the middle brain in which the impressed traces of ideas of the Fatherland still cling'.[38] The neurologist Philippe Pinel later traced nostalgia's course: 'a sad, melancholy appearance, a bemused look, . . . an indifference toward everything; . . . the near impossibility of getting out of bed, an obstinate silence, the rejection of food and drink; emaciation, marasmus and death'. A physician found the lungs of nostalgia victims tightly adhered to the pleura of the thorax, the tissue of the lobe thickened and purulent.[39] They had in fact died of meningitis, gastroenteritis, tuberculosis; but everyone blamed nostalgia. To leave home for long was to risk death. 'I suffer homesickness', wrote Balzac from Milan, 'and if I remained this way for two weeks, I should die.'[40] One need not go far to become afflicted; Hofer found nostalgia symptoms in a young man who had left Berne to study 40 miles away in Basel.[41]

Swiss mercenaries throughout Europe were nostalgia's first victims. Simply to hear a familiar herder's tune made them deeply homesick for beloved alpine scenes.

> The intrepid Swiss, that guards a foreign shore,
> Condemn'd to climb his mountain-cliffs no more,
> If chance he hears the song so sweetly wild
> Which on those cliffs his infant hours beguil'd,
> Melts at the long-lost scenes that round him rise,
> And sinks a martyr to repentant sighs.[42]

No picture so vividly evoked the Alps as an alpine melody. Such music haunted the bearer with 'an image of the past which is at once definite and unattainable'. The memory 'of childhood reappears through a melody, . . . leaving us a prey to this "passion de souvenir"'.[43] The incessant clanging of cow bells in rarified alpine heights left the Swiss especially vulnerable to damage to ear drums and brain cells. To ward off nostalgia, Swiss soldiers were forbidden to play, sing, or even whistle alpine tunes.[44]

---

[38] Hofer, 'Medical dissertation on nostalgia' (1688), p. 384.

[39] Boisseau and Pinel, 'Nostalgie', and Leopold Auenbrugger, *Inventum novum* (1761), in Starobinski, 'Idea of nostalgia', pp. 97–8.

[40] Honoré de Balzac to Mme Hanska, 23 May 1838, quoted in ibid., p. 86n.

[41] 'Medical dissertation', p. 392.

[42] Rogers, *Pleasures of Memory* (1792), p. 26.   [43] Starobinski, 'Idea of nostalgia', p. 93.

[44] Charles A. A. Zwingmann, '"Heimweh" or "Nostalgic Reaction": A Conceptual Analysis and Interpretation of a Medico-Psychological Phenomenon' (1959), cited in Fred Davis, 'Nostalgia, identity and the current nostalgia wave', p. 415; Starobinski, 'Idea of nostalgia', p. 90. This prohibition was frequently reported by Rousseau and others in the nineteenth century but no documentary evidence for it has been found (Métraux, *Ranz des vaches*, pp. 53–7).

Medication included leeches, purges, emetics, and blood-letting; for nostalgia's later stages Hofer advised 'hypnotic emulsions', 'cephalic balsams', and opium. A Russian general in 1733 found terror efficacious: soldiers incapacitated by nostalgia were buried alive, and after two or three burials the outbreak of homesickness subsided. But malingering was seldom suspected; repatriation was considered the only effective cure. Even the beleaguered French army in 1793 gave recruits smitten with 'homesickness' convalescent home leave.[45]

Nostalgia long lingered on as an organic malady. A prize-winning medical treatise on the disease appeared in 1873.[46] As a 'contagious disorder' that might 'spread with the speed of an epidemic' through army induction centres, nostalgia figured on the U.S. Surgeon General's list of standard maladies during the Second World War, and as late as 1946 was termed a possibly fatal 'psycho-physiological' complaint by an eminent social scientist;[47] psychologists identified homesickness as a characteristic student affliction, and university health centres treated it along with flu and hepatitis.[48] But nostalgia's sociological connotations already overshadowed the physical malady. Today rarely associated with homesickness, nostalgia has become strictly a state of mind.

Once the menace or the solace of a small elite, nostalgia now attracts or afflicts most levels of society. Ancestor-hunters search archives for their roots; millions throng to historic houses; antiques engross the middle class; souvenirs flood consumer markets. In earlier times the challenge of new prospects assuaged the homesickness Americans often felt, but today 'the past looks like a keel to many people, so they're trying to get a hook into it, pull it alongside, and fix it in place'.[49] 'A growing rebellion against the *present*, and an increasing longing for the past', are said to exemplify the post-war mood. 'Never before in all my long life have I heard so many people wish that they lived "at the turn of the century", or "when life was simpler", or "worth living", or simply "in the good old days"', notes a science-fiction character. 'For the first time in man's history, man is desperate to escape the present.'[50]

Mistrust of the future also fuels today's nostalgia. We may not love the past as excessively as many did in the nineteenth century, but our misgivings about what may come are more grave. 'I can read your future', a palmist says, 'or, as so many seem to prefer these days, I can reminisce nostalgically about your past.'[51] Prospects of economic ruin, of resource depletion, of nuclear Armageddon make the past a crucial haven, and so extensive is our regression that one authority fears 'we are entering a future in which people may again die of nostalgia'.[52]

Beyond these nostalgic traits lurk truly pathological attachments to the past. Some entirely surround themselves with bygones. Others can dispose of nothing, like the old

[45] Hofer, 'Medical dissertation', p. 389; Starobinski, 'Idea of nostalgia', pp. 95–6.
[46] August Haspel, cited in Starobinski, 'Idea of nostalgia', pp. 99–100.
[47] Flicker and Weiss, 'Nostalgia and its military implications', pp. 386–7; Ruml, 'Some notes on nostalgia', p. 7.
[48] 'Homesickness is usual but it doesn't last long', *Parents Mag.*, 20 (Oct. 1945), 178; McCann, 'Nostalgia – a review of the literature' (1941); *idem*, 'Nostalgia: a descriptive and comparative study' (1943); Fodor, 'Varieties of nostalgia' (1950).
[49] Eric Sevareid, 'On times past', *Preservation News*, 14:10 (1974), 5.
[50] Finney, 'I'm scared' (1961), pp. 36–7.
[51] Ed Fisher, cartoon, *New Yorker*, 15 Mar. 1976, p. 39.
[52] Jay Anderson, quoted in *History News*, 38:12 (1983), p. 11.

woman's carefully saved 'Pieces of string too short to use', the man who hoarded thousands of jars of his own excrement, or the collector of bottles of dust recalling an old love affair, labelled 'Dust from dress of R. Dust by bed of R. Dust near door of R's room.'[53] Nostalgic obsession is the *raison d'être* of Nigel Dennis's pub for 'spiritual recapitulation', with its devotees of

medieval calligraphy, puzzling the postmen with their renascent addresses ... Some wore small, curved bowler hats and arrived ... in touring cars that had been built in the 1920s: they drank their beer out of old moustache-cups. Many were gardeners, and would grow only roses which had not been seen for some centuries ... [The pub] covered all periods from Thomist to Edwardian, and rejected nothing but the malaise of the present.

The onlooker at obsolescent ceremonies 'weeps drably to think that he is tied to the ever-miserable present'.[54]

'May we all be preserved from nostalgia', cries a critic, 'and still more from nostalgia for nostalgia.'[55] Too late: the seventeenth-century disease is now a drug that hooks us all. Until the 1970s nostalgia trips were 'fairly surreptitious and ambivalent', thinks Michael Wood, 'because we didn't want to relinquish our hold on the present, on whatever it meant to be modern'. Modernity has since lost its charm. 'Now that the present seems so full of woe, ... the profusion and frankness of our nostalgia ... suggest not merely a sense of loss and a time in trouble, but a general abdication, an actual desertion from the present.' The phrase 'they don't make them like that any more' has shed its former ironic edge and become a true lament.[56]

Nostalgia is now even planned for. Like Kierkegaard, we look back in the midst of enjoyment to recapture it for memory, and envisage nostalgia for future events: one young woman imagines herself as a grandmother recalling the infancy of her yet unborn daughters.[57] 'Just such a honeysuckle filtered, sunny conversational afternoon', a Margaret Drabble character subsequently remembers thinking, would later cause 'the most sad and exquisite nostalgia. She was sad in advance, yet at the same time all the happier ... for knowing that ... she was creating for herself a past.'[58] 'Remember nostalgia? Remember when you remembered the 1950s?' asks a satirist.

Remember remembering your first kiss? Remember remembering your first prom? Remember remembering your first name? ... Yes, those were the '70s – *innocent* days ... *simpler* days, when all you had to do for a good time was sit back and remember malt shops, doubledips, ponytails ... You cherish the memory of remembering these memories ... Yes, you remembered it all in the '70s, the Golden Age of Nostalgia, ... the most treasured memories you remember remembering ... And now here's your own grandmother to tell you how to order.[59]

Critics mock nostalgia's kitschy absurdities and deplore its enervation of present endeavour, its lack of faith in the future; it is put down as the 'most fashionable of palliatives for the spiritually deprived'.[60] As early as 1820 Peacock derided the nostalgic

[53] Pesetsky, 'Hobbyist', p. 42.   [54] Dennis, *Cards of Identity*, pp. 161–2, 171.
[55] Francis Hope, 'My grandfather's house', *New Statesman*, 1 June 1973, p. 807.
[56] Wood, 'Nostalgia or never', p. 346.
[57] Kierkegaard, *Either/Or*, 1:240–1; Davis, *Yearning for Yesterday*, p. 12.
[58] Drabble, *Jerusalem the Golden*, p. 93.
[59] George W. S. Trow, 'Bobby Bison's big memory offer', *New Yorker*, 30 Dec. 1974, p. 27.
[60] Barry Humphries, 'Up memory creek', *TLS*, 9 Apr. 1976, p. 418.

poet who 'lives in the days that are past, . . . with barbarous manners, obsolete customs and exploded superstitions'.[61] *Punch* poked fun at future views of 1944's hardships: 'I suppose in about thirty years' time', says a character in a shopping queue, 'people will insist on describing this as the good old days.'[62] To protect Williamsburg visitors from a deranged fondness for the past, the costumed guides should be toothless, and ready to admit that 'if we were really colonial people, most of us would be dead on account of the short life span'.[63]

Nostalgia is blamed for alienating people from the present. When not catastrophic or fearsome, today's world becomes 'undistinguished, unexciting, blank', charges a critic, 'a time that leaves nothing for our imaginations to do except plunge into the past'.[64] The enormous popularity of reconstructed 'landscapes that we never knew, but wish we had', suggests refusal to face up to the dilemmas of the present.[65]

If nostalgia is a symptom of malaise, it also has compensating virtues. Attachment to familiar places may buffer social upheaval, attachment to familiar faces may be necessary for enduring association.[66] Nostalgia reaffirms identities bruised by recent turmoil when 'fundamental, taken-for-granted convictions about man, woman, habits, manners, laws, society and God [were] challenged, disrupted and shaken' as never before, in one sociologist's view.[67] In reaction to the dislocations of the 1960s and early 1970s we became obsessed with bygone times, suggests an analyst, 'insisting that life was once liveable and, yes, yes, if we looked long and hard enough at some right thing in our past, it would be right again'.[68]

REPOSSESSING THE PAST

Is it not possible – I often wonder – that things we have felt with great intensity have an existence independent of our minds; are in fact still in existence? And if so, will it not be possible, in time, that some device will be invented by which we can tap them? . . . Instead of remembering here a scene and there a sound, I shall fit a plug into the wall; and listen in to the past . . . Strong emotion must leave its trace; and it is only a question of discovering how we can get ourselves again attached to it, so that we shall be able to live our lives through from the start.

Virginia Woolf, 'A sketch of the past'[69]

The pull of the past transcends nostalgic longing for a fancifully imagined or surrogate yesteryear. Some speculate at length about how to revisit the actual past. Such yearnings have long been a staple of imaginative literature. How common they are is hard to assess; a survey of 528 paramedical students in Michigan in 1974 revealed that fewer than one in three thought the historical past worth recovery at all. But two-thirds of the men and

---

[61] *Four Ages of Poetry*, p. 16.   [62] Mays, cartoon, *Punch*, 4 Oct. 1944, p. 299.
[63] Barry, 'Why I like old things', p. 50.
[64] Wood, 'Nostalgia or never', p. 344.
[65] Riley, 'Speculations on the new American landscapes', p. 6. On idealizations of rural pasts, see Raymond Williams, *The Country and the City*, pp. 44–5.
[66] Ruml, 'Some notes on nostalgia', p. 8.   [67] Davis, 'Nostalgia, identity', p. 421.
[68] Hasbany, '*Irene*: considering the nostalgic sentiment', p. 819. Loss of confidence in the present generated a spate of nostalgic themes, artwork, and typography in advertisements during the 1960s and 1970s (Moriarty and McGann, 'Nostalgia and consumer sentiment', pp. 82–5).
[69] 1939, in her *Moments of Being*, p. 74.

almost half the women would give substantial sums to relive a year of their personal lives, still more of them to retrieve a day or an hour.[70] Widespread belief in reincarnation and fascination with time regression likewise suggest absorption with retrieving the past.

A past beyond recovery seems to many unbearable. We know the future is inaccessible; but is the past irrevocably lost? Is there no way to recapture, re-experience, relive it? We crave evidence that the past endures in recoverable form. Some agency, some mechanism, some faith will enable us not just to know it, but to see and feel it. Sometime, somewhere, the daily life of our grandparents, the rural sounds of yesteryear, the conversations of Rousseau, the deeds of the Founding Fathers, the creations of Michelangelo, the glory that was Greece will be experienced afresh.

Many concur with Virginia Woolf that 'the past, like some immense, collective ghost, is here beyond all possibility of exorcism', quickening objects that receive its echoes, lying ready to enter minds attuned to it.[71] 'We live in . . . the past, because it is itself alive . . . Nothing ever dies.'[72] Hunting for sources, a fictional biographer cannot believe 'that the historic past was extinguished, gone; surely it must simply be somewhere else, shunted into another plane of existence, still peopled and active and available if only one could reach it'.[73] Certain careers and relics persuade onlookers that the past not only survives but resurfaces. Joseph Smith, who founded the Mormon church, persuaded thousands of followers he had lived long ago; from early youth he habitually described ancient peoples and folkways 'with as much ease . . . as if he had spent his whole life with them'.[74] Those who filmed Alceo Dossena creating 'classical' works of art were convinced he reincarnated the spirit of antiquity, and the forger Tom Keating claimed 'the spirits of the old masters came down and took over his work'.[75]

Retrieving the past has been a major preoccupation of science fiction ever since its late nineteenth-century origins. Such dwelling on previous times may surprise those who associate science fiction chiefly with future worlds, but a search reveals hundreds, if not thousands, of stories about returning to or recovering sight of the past, replaying historical experience through time travel.[76]

From H. G. Wells to *Doctor Who*, the immense popularity of time travel suggests that retrieving the past is of deep-seated interest to both writers and readers. I do not contend that science-fiction authors – any more than Mark Twain or Henry James, who also returned characters to the past – themselves believe in time travel. But their focus on what it would be like to see or live in bygone times, on how to get back there, on the consequences of such visits – underscores their own and presumably their readers'

---

[70] Cottle, *Perceiving Time*, Tables 8–12, pp. 222–4. The students, of whom four-fifths were male, were 17 to 21 years of age. According to a 1965 survey, 18 per cent of Polish university graduates would have preferred to live in the past, most of them long ago (Szacka, 'Two kinds of past-time orientation', p. 66).

[71] Matheson, *Somewhere in Time*, p. 37.   [72] Compton-Burnett, *A Father and His Fate*, p. 164.

[73] Lively, *According to Mark*, p. 110.

[74] Smith's mother, quoted in Silverberg, *Mound Builders*, p. 44.

[75] Hans Cürlis, *Alceo Dossena* film script, cited in Arnau, *Three Thousand Years of Deception in Art and Antiques*, pp. 223–5; Guy Rais, 'Old Masters' spirits took over, says Tom Keating', *Daily Telegraph*, 2 Feb. 1979.

[76] The Science Fiction Library, North East London Polytechnic, greatly helped my review. Peter Nicholls's *Encyclopedia of Science Fiction* includes articles (authors' names in brackets) on: 'Adam and Eve', 'Alternative worlds', 'Origin of man', 'Reincarnation' (Brian Stableford); 'Atlantis', 'Pastoral' (David Pringle); 'History in SF' (Tom Shippey); 'Mythology' (Peter Nicholls); 'Time paradoxes', 'Time travel' (Malcolm J. Edwards). See also Rose, *Alien Encounters*, pp. 96–138.

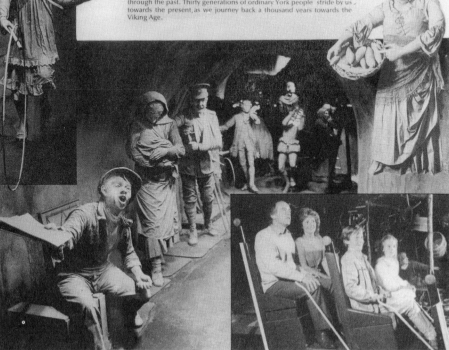

3 The lure of time travel: Jorvik Viking Centre 'Time Car', York

obsessions with the promises and perils of a visitable past. Science fiction is an invaluable clue to preoccupations about the past. Its fantasies yield insights into feelings no less valid for being impossible to consummate. Precisely because unbridled by common sense, they reveal passions and presuppositions that throw everyday concerns with the past into sharp relief. Indeed, the time-travel metaphor has spread beyond science fiction and now designates all manner of nostalgic entertainments. Visitors to York and Winchester take 'time trips' back through the centuries. 'My pupils were transported directly into Tudor times', a schoolmaster said of an historic-house theatrical. 'They bridged 400 years or so almost as though they were time travellers.'[77]

Modern science has given fresh impetus to an enduring tradition that promises the past's recovery. The belief itself is venerable. 'Every city and village and field will be restored, just as it was, over and over again', predicted the Stoics.[78] Faith in cyclical repetition has been a hallmark of many societies. But the retention and ultimate accessibility of an

---

[77] Quoted in Rich, 'Ten thousand children in need of a sponsor'.
[78] Bishop Nemesius of Emesa, *On the Nature of Man*, quoted in Whitrow, *Nature of Time*, p. 17.

historical past, in the mind or in the cosmos, became major preoccupations only in the eighteenth and nineteenth centuries.[79] Romantic poets and empirical scientists alike were persuaded that the past endured in the present as a reality which could be resurrected, although they knew not how. Echoing the Stoics, Thomas Hardy believed that 'once an event has happened, it not only can never be undone but enters a spacious realm containing all times where it goes on happening over and over again'.[80] 'Not a thing in the past', an H. G. Wells figure remarks, 'has not left its memories about us. Some day we may learn to gather in that forgotten gossamer, we may learn to weave its strands together again, until the whole past is restored to us.'[81] The wish was father to the thought for H. Rider Haggard's protagonist, whose imagination 'shot its swift shuttle back across the ages, weaving a picture on their blackness so real and vivid in its detail that I could almost for a moment think that I had triumphed o'er the Past, and that my spirit's eyes had pierced the mystery of Time'.[82]

Many saw memory itself as the receptacle. Because the past shaped everyone's present, no transient impression could be expunged from the mind; the storehouse of memory permanently preserved them all. The brain was 'a natural and mighty palimpsest', in De Quincey's view, that piled up 'everlasting layers of ideas, images, feelings. Each succession has seemed to bury all that went before. And yet, in reality, not one has been extinguished.'[83] To recall his childhood visits to the Montpelier Tea-gardens, Hazlitt had only to 'unlock the casket of memory, and draw back the warders of the brain; and there this scene of my infant wanderings still lives unfaded, or with fresher dyes'.[84]

Many believed that memory residues transcended present lifetimes. Shelley startled a mother by insisting that her few-weeks-old baby describe its pre-existence; surely so young a child had not already forgotten it![85] Swedenborg and other literati, including Coleridge and De Quincey, whose visions were opium-induced, retrieved vividly detailed pasts.[86] Fever likewise heightened such perceptions: in a delirium, George Gissing conjured up the thronged streets, processions, sepulchral marbles and great vases of ancient Croton two millennia before, reconstructing 'to the last perfection of intimacy, a world known to me only in ruined fragments'.[87]

The surrounding milieu often becomes the repository for memories, but one regains them only by revelation, not by will. Proust termed it 'a labour in vain to attempt to recapture' the past, hidden 'beyond the reach of intellect, in some material object . . . It depends on chance whether or not we come upon this object before we ourselves must die.' Such a trigger was the madeleine at Combray, whose smell and taste 'bear unflinchingly, in the tiny and almost impalpable drop of their essence, the vast structure of recollection'.[88]

Faith in memory retrieval animated Freudian psychology. Unconscious 'impressions are preserved, not only in the same form in which they were first received, but also in all the forms which they have adopted in their further developments', Freud maintained.

[79] Poulet, *Studies in Human Time*, pp. 185–200.
[80] J. H. Miller, 'History as repetition in Thomas Hardy's poetry', p. 247.
[81] *The Dream*, p. 236.   [82] *She* (1886), p. 199.   [83] *Suspira de Profundis* (1845–54), pp. 246–7.
[84] 'Why distant objects please' (1821), p. 257.
[85] Hogg, *Life of Percy Bysshe Shelley*, 1:239–40. See also Jenkyns, *Victorians and Ancient Greece*, pp. 233–4.
[86] Poulet, 'Timelessness and Romanticism'.   [87] Gissing, *By the Ionian Sea* (1901), pp. 82–4.
[88] *Remembrance of Things Past*, 1:47–8, 51.

'Theoretically every earlier state of mnemonic content could thus be restored to memory again.'[89] And although Freud's views on memory retention were not always consistent, he habitually termed them recoverable. 'Not only *some* but *all* of what is essential from childhood has been retained in these [screen] memories. It is simply a question of knowing how to extract it out of them [patients] by analysis.'[90] Psychoanalysis lent credence to turn-of-the-century faith that recollections were imperishable. 'My idea of integral conservation of the past', thought Bergson, 'has more and more found its empirical verification in the mass of experiments undertaken by the disciples of Freud.'[91] And with Proust, Joyce, and Mann, the storehouse of unconscious memory became a stock literary theme.

Further confirmation seemed to come from neuro-surgery in the 1930s. Using electrical stimulation, Wilder Penfield claimed to tap his patients' complete and authentic memory: 'There is a permanent record of the stream of consciousness within the brain. It is preserved in amazing detail. No man can, by voluntary effort, call this detail back to memory. But, hidden in the interpretative areas of the temporal lobes, there is a key to the mechanism that unlocks the past.'[92] Though little subsequent evidence supports Penfield's claim, his enduring fame largely explains why an overwhelming majority of psychologists still believe all memories potentially retrievable.[93]

Recapturing memories stored not only in individuals but in the species is a dream many scientists share. Since memory survives the loss of cerebral matter during life, the astronomer Gustaf Strömberg thought it might survive the dissolution of the brain cells after death, to 'become an eternal part of the cosmos'.[94] Genetic similarities might transfer memory from a past to a present mind, suggested J. B. S. Haldane[95] – an idea eagerly adopted by science fiction. 'The life experiences of our not-too-distant ancestors are inherited in certain cells of the brain, just as their physical characteristics are duplicated in our bodies', conjectures one writer; hypnotism might induce a man to relive ancestral episodes 'as if they were a part of his own experience'.[96] A fictional biophysicist surmises that some drug might 'enable us to see, hear, become cognoscent of things that happened in the past' by bringing to consciousness brain patterns inherited from primeval times.[97] Far from being limited to fiction, this notion animates the 'primal fantasies' Freud

[89] *Psychopathology of Everyday Life* (1901), p. 275.
[90] 'Remembering, repeating and working-through' (1914), 12:148.
[91] Bergson, *Pensée et le mouvant* (1934), p. 1316; see *idem, Matter and Memory* (1896); Lewin, *Selected Writings*, p. 405.
[92] 'Some mechanisms of consciousness discovered during electrical stimulation of the brain' (1958), quoted in O'Brien, 'Proust confirmed by neuro-surgery', pp. 295–7. See also Penfield, 'Permanent record of the stream of consciousness' (1955): 'The original record seems to be available . . . as long as a man may live and keep his wits' (p. 69); 'nothing is lost . . . the record of each man's experience is complete' (p. 67).
[93] That view is held by 84 per cent of psychologists and 69 per cent of the general public (Loftus and Loftus, 'On the permanence of stored information in the human brain' (1980), p. 410).
[94] *Soul of the Universe*, pp. 188–92: 'The memory of an individual is written in indelible script in time and space – it has become an eternal part of the cosmos in development' (p. 191). Kern (*Culture of Time and Space*, pp. 41–2) traces this belief from Henry Maudsley's *Organic Memory* (1867) and Samuel Butler's *Life and Habit* (1877) to Bergson and Freud; the view is immortalized, so to speak, in Bram Stoker's *Dracula* (1897).
[95] *Man with Two Memories*, pp. 137–9.   [96] Long, 'Reverse phylogeny', p. 33.
[97] Du Maurier, *House on the Strand*, p. 196.

attributed to phylogenetically-inherited experiences that were 'once real occurrences in primaeval times of the human family'.[98]

Many fancied retrievals are bolstered by reincarnation, a normative belief in many cultures that is still popular in our own. Although reincarnation need not entail familiarity with a pre-natal past, from Pythagoras and Empedocles on many have claimed to 'remember' previous lives. The Irish poet Æ 'recalled' his past personae sailing in galleys over the antique ocean, living in tents and palace chambers, lying tranced in Egyptian crypts; Salvador Dali vividly 'remembered' being St John of the Cross in his monastery.[99] As a child, the archaeologist Dorothy Eady 'recognized' a picture of the ancient Abydos temple as her 'home', and ultimately returned to live in Egypt as Om Seti, the nineteenth-dynasty temple waif she had once been; 'sometimes I wake up in the morning', she told a visitor, 'and can't remember whether it's B.C. or A.D.'[100] A graduate student of my own, convinced of a previous life as a seventeenth-century Romanian, made Bucharest his doctoral topic and married a Romanian girl to forge links with his past (alas, the dissertation remains unfinished and the marriage soon collapsed).

Cultists and converts feed public appetites for the past with intimate details: Joan Grant's 'far memory' of Egypt's First Dynasty, of the Nomarch of Oryx, of Rameses II; Arthur Guirdhan's Cathar 'recapture' of his lives in ancient Rome, Celtic Cumberland, Napoleon's navy; L. Ron Hubbard's 'rediscovery' of the locale of his life as a Carthaginian sailor – Hubbard's Scientologists do not 'recall' but literally 'relive' previous existences.[101]

Incarnations consciously recalled, however vivid to their possessors, are often unconvincing to others. But memories unlocked by hypnotic regression seem more persuasive because subjects remain unaware of the pastness of the events they recount; to them they are happening *now*. The 'previous life histories' elicited by hypnotist Helen Wambach, Virginia Tighe's *alter ego* Bridey Murphy, Jane Evans's York crypt that had sheltered a twelfth-century Jew, seem to yield authentic historical knowledge and behaviour unknown to their subjects when conscious.[102] But Ian Wilson has shown that all such accounts are riddled with anachronisms that betray their recent origins – origins disclosed when subjects are 'regressed' to the occasions they first read or heard about the remote past they have unwittingly absorbed. For example, Jane Evans's descriptions of ancient York embody long segments of Jean Plaidy's *Katharine, the Virgin Widow* (1961) and Louis de Wohl's *The Living Wood* (1959).[103] The memories divulged are also tainted by suggestions emanating from the hypnotists. Indeed, under hypnosis people are particularly prone to accept and imaginatively flesh out fragmentary memories, never realizing that they are

[98] Freud, *Totem and Taboo* (1913), pp. 155–9; Jacobson and Steele, 'From present to past', p. 358. See also Rupert Sheldrake's 'morphic-resonance' learning theory (*New Science of Life* (1981); and *New Scientist*, 18 June 1981, p. 766; 28 Apr. 1983, p. 218; 27 Oct. 1983, pp. 279–80).

[99] Æ, *Candle of Vision*, pp. 56–65, 143–7; Ben Martin, 'Dali greets the world' (1960), quoted in Head and Cranston, *Reincarnation*, p. 102.

[100] Christopher S. Wren, 'The double life of Om Seti', *IHT*, 26 Apr. 1979, p. 14; Lawrence Lancina, 'Watch on the Nile', letter, *IHT*, 5–6 May 1979, p. 4.

[101] Grant and Denys Kelsey, *Many Lifetimes* (1974); Guirdhan, *The Lake and the Castle* (1976); idem, *Cathars and Reincarnation* (1976); Peter Moss with Joe Keeton, *Encounters with the Past* (1981); Hubbard, *Have You Lived Before This Life?*; idem, *Mission into Time*, p. 33; idem, *Dianetics*, pp. 235–7.

[102] Wambach, *Reliving Past Lives* (1979); Morey Bernstein, *The Search for Bridey Murphy* (1956); Jeffry Iverson, *More Lives Than One?* (1977).

[103] Ian Wilson, *Reincarnation?* pp. 233–43.

erring and inventing. 'Hypnosis makes you more confident – and more inaccurate', psychologists conclude; verisimilar detail is no guide to accuracy, for those hypnotized describe the future with as much conviction as the past. Yet 'the folk belief that hypnosis taps memories indelibly recorded in the unconscious dies hard'.[104]

Others conceive of a past stored not in memory but in the material cosmos – though the notion of memory 'traces' implies their close affinity. Physical residues of all events may yield potentially unlimited access to the past. Many nineteenth-century scholars surmised that the whole historical record survived somewhere; given the right techniques, nothing would elude retrieval. The mathematician Charles Babbage saw every past event as a disturbance that reordered atomic matter and hence must have left 'an ineffaceable, imperishable record, possibly legible even to created intelligence',[105] just as tree rings reveal the climatic past: 'No motion impressed by natural causes, or by human agency, is ever obliterated . . . The air itself is one vast library, on whose pages are for ever written all that man has ever said or even whispered . . . and the more solid materials of the globe, bear equally enduring testimony of the acts we have committed.' Even unspoken thoughts must survive in the cosmic ether, where 'stand for ever recorded, vows unredeemed, promises unfulfilled'[106] – preservation in the service of Judgemental doom! Scientists long echoed this view. 'A shadow never falls upon a wall without leaving thereupon a permanent trace', thought John William Draper. 'Upon the walls of our most private apartment . . . there exist the vestiges of all our acts, silhouettes of whatever we have done.'[107]

The notion of a past permanently lodged in the remote reaches of the cosmos attracts adherents bemused by relativity theory as well as by science fiction. Since ancient terrestrial events are only now 'visible' in galaxies light-years away and will later be manifest still farther off, earth history could in theory be reviewed over and over again. 'Every detail of life – and all other events – remain recorded in the matrix of space-time', one writer suggests, 'capable of some sort of review.'[108] Spiritualists and story-tellers popularize such surmises. 'The faintest sound produces an eternal echo', Mme Blavatsky assured her followers; 'a disturbance is created on the invisible waves of the shoreless ocean of space, and the vibration is never wholly lost. Its energy . . . will live for ever.'[109] At the house in Derbyshire whence Mary Queen of Scots vainly tried an escape, Alison Uttley's heroine surmises that 'the vibrant ether had held the thoughts of the perilous ruinous adventure, so that the walls . . . were quickened by them, the place itself alive with the memory of things once seen and heard . . . The spoken words . . . had lain in some pocket of the ether and . . . pervaded my mind and became the most outstanding memory.'[110]

[104] Vines and Barnes, 'Hypnosis on trial', p. 16. See O'Connell, Shor, and Orne, 'Hypnotic age regression'; Dywan and Bowers, 'Use of hypnosis to enhance recall'; Orne, *et al.*, 'Hypnotically induced testimony', pp. 179–82, 192–4. Televised past-life regressions under hypnosis left one British viewer in five convinced of reincarnation (Brian Inglis, 'The controversial and the problematical', *The Times*, 20 Dec. 1980, p. 12).

[105] Marsh, 'Study of nature' (1860), p. 41, and *idem, Man and Nature* (1864), pp. 464–5n, paraphrase and extend Babbage's idea to human impact on the entire environment.

[106] Babbage, *Ninth Bridgewater Treatise* (1837), pp. 113–16.

[107] *History of the Conflict between Science & Religion* (1873), p. 111.

[108] Michael Kirsch, quoted in Peter Laurie, 'About mortality in amber', *New Scientist*, 3 Apr. 1975, p. 37.

[109] *Isis Unveiled* (1877), p. 114.

[110] *Traveller in Time*, p. 106. Mary was in fact held at nearby Wingfield Manor. 'That objects retain something of the eyes which have looked at them, that old buildings and pictures appear to us . . . beneath a perceptible veil

The recapture of past sounds is a recurrent imaginative theme. In the empty wastes of the Frozen Sea, Rabelais's Pantagruel is amazed to hear cannon booming, bullets whistling, the clangour of armour, the thud of battle axes, horses neighing, warriors shouting and groaning – battle sounds that had frozen in the air the previous winter and were now tumbling noisily down and melting into audibility.[111] A Munchausen tale describes a winter so cold that a postillion's tune froze in his horn, only later emerging as audible notes.[112] Mystic identification with past cultures enables Hermann Hesse's itinerant minstrels 'to perform the music of earlier epochs with perfect ancient purity'.[113] Old sounds linger on surfaces and in the air until vacuumed up by J. G. Ballard's 'Sound-Sweep', the walls and furniture throbbing for days with their resonating residues. To retrieve 'the mating-cries of mammoths, the recitations of Homer, first performances of the master-works of music' from ages past, one fabulist conjures up a light beam to overtake and reflect back sound that left the earth thousands of years before; another imagines recording Stone Age sonic history in reverse by slowly evaporating stalactites in once-inhabited limestone caves.[114] To recover valued past scenes a writer envisages 'delay-glass' of nearly infinite refractive index through which light may take years to pass; picture windows 'capture scenes of exceptional beauty which can be used . . . in place of more humdrum or ugly scenes of the here and now'.[115]

Science fiction deploys science not only to retrieve past sights and sounds but to return people bodily to previous times. 'We think the past is gone', says a fictional physicist, 'because the present is all we can see . . . We can't see the past, back in the bends and curves behind us. But it's there.' According to the unified field theory, 'a man ought somehow to be able to step out . . . and walk back to one of the bends behind us . . . If Albert Einstein is right . . . the summer of 1894 *still exists*. That silent empty apartment exists back in that summer precisely as it exists in the summer that is coming.' A time traveller could make his way 'out of that unchanged apartment and into that other summer'.[116]

Getting into the past is a feat imaginatively achieved in myriad ways – drugs, dreams, knocks on the head, pacts with the devil, lightning bolts, thunder claps, and, since H. G. Wells, time machines. Just as they do our memories, evocative relics of antiquity – votive axes, remnants of crosses, an heirloom fan – trigger many fictional transitions to the past. A fossilized sword arouses ancestral memories for a Francis Ashton hero who 'recognizes' it was long ago his own; a Celtic sword hilt found off the coast of Maine enables Betty Levin's twentieth-century children to travel back to Iron Age Ireland and early Christian Orkney as participants in ancient folk life; a painted shield puts Penelope Lively's 14-year-old in uncanny touch with the New Guinea tribe that had given it to her ethnologist great-grandfather.[117] In an old house battered by time and use a young visitor concludes that the past is real because things that have happened remain hidden in the

woven for them over the centuries by the love and contemplation of millions of admirers', Proust dismissed as scientific fantasy but adopted as psychological truth (*Remembrance of Things Past*, 3:920).

[111] *Five Books of Gargantua and Pantagruel*, Bk IV, Ch. 56, pp. 649–51.
[112] *Travels and Adventures of Baron Munchausen*, pp. 36–7.
[113] *Glass Bead Game*, p. 28.   [114] Ariadne, *New Scientist*, 25 Mar. 1975, p. 816; 26 Jan. 1978, p. 264.
[115] Bob Shaw, *Other Eyes, Other Days*, p. 48.
[116] Finney, *Time and Again*, pp. 52, 63.
[117] Ashton, *Breaking of the Seals*, p. 26; Levin, *Sword of Culann*; idem, *A Griffon's Nest*; Lively, *House in Norham Gardens*.

building; perhaps places, like clocks, can stop 'so that a moment goes on, as it were, forever', letting one see into other people's time.[118]

Reliving the past is usually felt to require wholehearted immersion. Empathetic association, detailed knowledge, profound familiarity with his chosen epoch are pre-requisites for the time traveller, who must avoid antagonizing – or perplexing – people he meets in the past. John Dickson Carr's historian is said to be the only man of the 1920s who knows the minutiae of seventeenth-century life well enough to carry off a return to it successfully.[119] Jack Finney's trainee time travellers live for months in simulated pasts that reproduce the sights and sounds and smells of their destinations, wearing the clothes, eating the food, speaking the dialect of the time to make sure they will feel completely at home.[120]

Such difficulties seldom deter those entranced by the promise of the past, and whose appetites for thoroughgoing returns are not assuaged by memory, history, or relics. Memories are partial and fleeting, history's evocations are often unimaginative, many physical remains are decayed or hard to reach or interpret; historical enclaves, whether actual backwaters or contrived reconstructions, seem tame or inauthentic. Thus addicts turn to imaginative voyages that will unlock gates to the past, let them see or roam there at will, and enjoy full-blooded experience of bygone times.

GOALS IN THE REVISITED PAST

If time came adrift . . . there's no reason why everyone shouldn't see things happen the way they want them to, . . . set free to live their lives to their deepest desires.

Peter Hunt, *The Maps of Time*[121]

Would-be time travellers long to experience an exotic antiquity, to live in times superior to today, to know what actually happened in history, to change the present or the past. The women Cottle interviewed would have liked simply to relive happy times, the men to excise past errors or to alter the course of their lives.[122] These goals highlight the hopes and dreams, the risks and nightmares often evoked by the past but generally cloaked or muted by its felt inaccessibility. A closer look at what time travellers seek offers insight into the sometimes extreme reactions to tradition and innovation the following chapters survey.

Strong feelings feature both the goals sought in the past and the sacrifices time travellers appear willing to make. Some find the urge to return overwhelming; like Faust or Beerbohm's Enoch Soames, they would traffick with the devil for the privilege of going back. 'The urge to see, to listen, to move amongst' the fourteenth-century folk he comes to care for was so intense that du Maurier's hero risks health and even life for his excursions back in time.[123] 'To know that just by turning a few dials you can see and watch anything, anybody, anywhere, that has ever happened' makes a time-viewer 'feel like a god'; to go back to the seventeenth century as his rich and well-born namesake at the court of Charles II, Carr's hero seems ready to sell his soul.[124]

---

[118] Lively, *Stitch in Time*, p. 104.   [119] *Devil in Velvet*, p. 9.   [120] *Time and Again*, pp. 48, 65.
[121] 1983, pp. 91, 123.
[122] Cottle, *Perceiving Time*, p. 55.   [123] *House on the Strand*, p. 241.
[124] Sherred, 'E for effort', p. 123; Carr, *Devil in Velvet*, pp. 13–14.

Not all such visits are so intense. Levels of fancied involvement range from glimpsing history from the safety of the present, to entry unseen by the past's inhabitants, to mutual contact, to active interference with past lives and events. Du Maurier's protagonist sees, hears, and smells as he walks through fourteenth-century Cornwall, but cannot be seen or interfere in any way; 'whatever happened I could do nothing to prevent it'.[125] An entrepreneur plans tours to 'daily life in ancient Rome, or Michelangelo sculpting the Pietà, or Napoleon leading the charge at Marengo'; venturesome travellers can visit Helen of Troy in her bath or sit in on 'Cleopatra's summit conference with Caesar'.[126] Time tourists envisage finding Attic poetry or fancy a Palaeozoic picnic. Brian Aldiss's travellers in the Devonian find the package-holiday past already overcrowded: 'We're making our way up to the Jurassic. Been there?' 'Sure, I hear it's getting more like a fair ground every year.'[127] Others seek trophies from the past: Sprague de Camp's safari hunters yearn to bring home tyrannosaurus heads as proof of their visit to the Cretaceous.[128] Still others envisage becoming famous characters in myth and history. Degrees of intervention vary with the intensity of these desires and with time travellers' motives for returning to the past.

Five reasons for going or looking back dominate time-travel literature: explaining the past, searching for a golden age, enjoying the exotic, reaping the rewards of temporal displacement and foreknowledge, and refashioning life by changing the past.

Explaining the past

To know how and why things happened is a compelling motive for witnessing past events. 'Most historians would give a great deal', writes one, 'to have had the chance of being actually present at some of the events they have described.'[129] To verify accounts of the Battle of Hastings, to hear Greek as actually spoken by Homer and Plato was what most appealed to H. G. Wells's protagonists.[130] Imagine how much trouble scholars would be spared 'if you could actually *see* what took place in the past, without having to infer it' from fragmentary records and traces![131] But what fictional historians mainly seek is new facts to solve old dilemmas. One envisages 'all the treasure houses of history waiting to be opened, explored, catalogued'; he wants 'to stand on the city wall of Ur and watch the Euphrates flood . . . to know how *that* story got into Genesis'.[132] To watch history revealing all its great secrets 'back to the dawn of time' stimulates Arthur C. Clarke's venturers.[133] Other curiosity is more explicit:

Think of the historical mysteries and questions you could clear up! You could talk to John Wilkes Booth and find out if Secretary of War Stanton was really behind the Lincoln assassination. You might ferret out the identity of Jack the Ripper . . . Interview Lucrezia Borgia and those who knew her and determine if she was the poisoning bitch most people think she was. Learn the identity of the assassins of the two little princes in the Tower.[134]

---

[125] *House on the Strand*, p. 40.   [126] Laumer, *Great Time Machine Hoax*, p. 35.
[127] Aldiss, *An Age*, p. 18.
[128] 'Gun for dinosaur'.   [129] Tillinghast, *Specious Past*, p. 171.   [130] *Time Machine*, p. 11.
[131] A. C. Clarke, 'Time's arrow', p. 139.
[132] Tucker, *Year of the Quiet Sun*, p. 107.   [133] 'Time's arrow', p. 143.
[134] Farmer, *To Your Scattered Bodies Go*, p. 44.

Establishing Mark Antony's exact birthdate, photographing Correggio's paintings in his studio, and recording 'the sonorous voice of Sophocles reading aloud from his own dramas' are one time traveller's ambitions.[135] Fred Hoyle's music historian seizes a chance to see classical Greece at first hand 'to settle all the controversy and arguments about ancient music'.[136] Like Isaac Asimov's 'chronoscope' inventor who yearns to disprove the slander that the Carthaginians immolated children as sacrificial victims,[137] historians eager to overturn the conventional wisdom may be especially anxious to see the actual past.

To revisit the past would do more than confirm or disprove historical facts; it would lend history a new dimension. If historians 'could go back in time and see what happened and talk to people who were living then', a Simak character conjectures, 'they would understand it better and could write better histories'.[138] An observer knowing how events turn out could 'write history as no one ever did before, for you'll be writing as a witness, yet with the perspective of a different period'. Ward Moore's fictional historian could 'write of the past with the detachment of the present and the accuracy of an eyewitness knowing specifically what to look for'.[139] In short, he combined immediacy with hindsight – an achievement to which historians have long aspired.

Origins obsess time-travelling as they do many actual historians. Darwin's *On the Origin of Species* engendered fictional visits to the dawn of mankind. Others sought the beginnings of fire, of agriculture, of Indo-European languages, of Alexander's conquests, of Columbus's voyages. A visitor to an immortal world seeks out its oldest inhabitants, for 'if the first of them are still alive then they might know their origin! They would know how it began!'[140] This obsession reflects the general cult of origins discussed in Chapter 2.

Curiosity about personal roots excites dreams of returning to some key episode or figure in one's own background. Simak's genealogists help clients to talk with or photograph ancient forebears; Scientology urges converts to recall their foetal experience, even their conception.[141] Incest may be one 'force behind the predisposition to look back': Moore's time traveller confesses 'a notion to court my grandmother and wind up as my own grandfather'.[142] As Chapter 3 will show, a seductive yet dreaded past often gives rise to such analogies.

Beyond the passion to know more about the past, such comments reflect science fiction's naïvety about how the past is known at all. Most would-be time travellers seem to assume that understanding derives only from observation made at the time things happen, that we lack any real insight into events that have already happened. They overlook the value of retrospection, minimize the importance of hindsight, and travel back to see the past as though it were the present, because for them things are explicable only in the present.

Searching for the golden age

Mirroring its readers' biases, most science fiction shows the world that was as a better place. Some admire all epochs; 'through the vistas of the years every age but our own seems

---

[135] Tucker, *Lincoln Hunters*, p. 112. [136] *October the First Is Too Late*, p. 96. [137] 'Dead past', p. 25.
[138] *Catface*, p. 54. [139] *Bring the Jubilee*, pp. 159–60, 169.
[140] Lafferty, 'Nine hundred grandmothers', p. 10.
[141] Simak, *Catface*, p. 163; Hubbard, *Dianetics*, pp. 266–8.
[142] Aldiss, *An Age*, p. 33; Moore, *Bring the Jubilee*, p. 164.

glamorous'; another finds any previous date 'vastly preferable to his own regimented day and age'.[143] Others fancy a lush, green, unpolluted world, teeming with plants and animals and but lightly tenanted by mankind, 'the time before the white men came, when there were only Indians', says a Simak character, or 'before there were any men at all'.[144] The prehistoric world of 15,000 B.C. seemed paradisaical to Philip José Farmer's expedition leader; 'damned few humans, and an abundance of wild life; ... this is the way a world should be'.[145] Virgin prehistory offers pioneers a whole new world: 'Give us the Miocene; we want another chance', cry Simak's ghetto-dwellers.[146]

Some opt for a more recent past, the familiar yet unspoiled era of their early childhood or youth. 'The quiet fifties [are] as early as I dare go without sacrificing the cultural comforts I desire. They are truly a magic moment', still idealistic yet also pregnant with the developing future.[147] Mary McCarthy's 1940s utopian community selects a locale 'arrested at the magical moment of [their] average birth-date ... forty years before, and ... at the stage of mechanization to which the colonists wished to return' – old carpet sweepers in place of vacuum cleaners, ice boxes instead of refrigerators. The 1910 buildings and furnishings 'took them back to the age of their innocence, to the dawn of memory'.[148]

Others, especially nostalgic ruralists, prefer a grand- or great-grandparental past. Drawing lines on old Ordnance Survey maps around bits of Britain that are now industrial or slummy – Dagenham, north Cardiff, much of Manchester – Hunt's young protagonist changes them back into countryside, rubbing away the 'filth and squalor' to remake things as they were in 1860: 'Pure. Clean.'[149] The late nineteenth century was by no means perfect, realizes Finney's hero, but 'the air was still clean. The rivers flowed fresh, as they had since time began. And the first of the terrible corrupting wars still lay decades ahead.'[150] In *Berkeley Square*, the quiet streets, gasolene-free air, and sedan chairs of 1784 make the taxis and efficient bustle of 1928 seem noisome and ugly.[151]

Whether recent or remote, the desired past exhibits strikingly similar traits: natural, simple, comfortable – yet also vivid and exciting. 'The old, gray, modern existence' had little to offer Robin Carson's hero compared with 'the new, colorful opulence' of Renaissance Venice.[152] A visitor who 'becomes' Cyrus in ancient Persia finds early warfare more enjoyable than modern foxholes.[153] The fourteenth-century world was 'cruel, hard, and very often bloody, and so were the people in it', learns du Maurier's protagonist, 'but, my God, it held a fascination for me which is lacking in my own world of today'.[154] It was old England's 'rough plenty' and 'sauntering life' along with 'its cool acceptance of

[143] Bester, 'Hobson's choice', pp. 147–8; Tucker, *Lincoln Hunters*, p. 43.   [144] *Catface*, p. 54.
[145] *Time's Last Gift*, pp. 79, 137. Many living-history buffs exhibit a comparable nostalgia. The thousand-odd American Mountain Men, who periodically (and arduously) 'relive' frontier conditions of 1800 to 1840, recruit only 'men who are willing to step back in time, ... to live life as man was meant to live it, a Free Individual, a true Son of the Wilderness' (AMM membership material, quoted in Jay Anderson, *Time Machines: The World of Living History*, pp. 160, 208).
[146] *Catface*, p. 241.   [147] Gerrold, *Man Who Folded Himself*, p. 122.   [148] *Oasis*, pp. 42–3.
[149] *Maps of Time*, pp. 58, 123. Kingsley Amis found rural nostalgia 'very rare' in British science fiction (*New Maps of Hell* (1961), p. 74), but it now seems as prevalent as across the Atlantic.
[150] *Time and Again*, p. 398.
[151] Balderston, *Berkeley Square*, pp. 37–8. But in Henry James's *Sense of the Past*, from which this play is adapted, the present (1910) is environmentally superior.
[152] *Pawn of Time*, p. 437.   [153] Poul Anderson, *Guardians of Time*, p. 68.
[154] *House on the Strand*, p. 267.

rudeness and violence' that William Morris anticipated experiencing were he landed in the fourteenth century.[155] Early Romans seldom lived long, admits a returning visitor, 'but while they lived, they *lived*'.[156] Today's faces seem 'much more alike and much less alive' to Finney's time traveller; 'there was also an *excitement* in the streets of New York in 1882 that is gone'. Back then people 'carried with them a sense of purpose ... They weren't *bored*, for God's sake! ... Those men moved through their lives in unquestioned certainty that there was a reason for being ... Faces don't have that look now.'[157]

The golden age that time travellers revisit bears little resemblance, of course, to any time that ever was; like other nostalgists, they create a past out of a childhood divested of responsibilities and an imagined landscape invested with all they find missing in the modern world.

Self-aggrandizement

Visitors to the past often fancy that advanced technology along with foreknowledge gives them an inestimable advantage; modern know-how will make them powerful, famous, or rich. In medieval England Twain's Hank expects to 'boss the whole country inside of three months; for I judged I would have the start of the best-educated man in the kingdom by a matter of thirteen hundred years'. Being in the sixth century immensely enhances his prospects:

I wouldn't have traded it for the twentieth. Look at the opportunities here for a man of knowledge, brains, pluck, and enterprise to sail in and grow up with the country. The grandest field that ever was; and all my own; not a competitor; not a man who wasn't a baby to me in acquirements and capacities; whereas, what could I amount to in the twentieth century? I should be foreman of a factory, that is about all.[158]

Another dreamer supposes that 'all the treasures of the past would fall to one man with a submachine gun. Cleopatra and Helen of Troy might share his bed, if bribed with a trunkful of modern cosmetics.'[159]

Foreknowledge is also alluring because it provides a past that is completed, even completed by ourselves. Unlike the insecure present, that past is safely mapped, its pleasures tried and tested, its perils already dealt with. To revisit the past is to be in a play whose plot we alone know. 'Watching old-timers' jaws drop in amazement while people who are 40 years ahead of them toy with them and give them the know-it-all treatment', Russell Baker comments, 'you are like a person playing poker with a stacked deck.'[160] Like visitors invited to 'have the time of *their* life' with Plimoth Plantation's simulated denizens of 1627, the time traveller becomes superior at the *expense* of the past's actual inhabitants.

In taking advantage of being modern, time travellers resemble historians, for whom hindsight is both inescapable and insightful. But whereas the historian eschews anach-

---

[155] 'Hopes of civilisation' (1885), p. 62.   [156] Merwin, *Three Faces of Time*, p. 33.
[157] *Time and Again*, pp. 218–19.
[158] *Connecticut Yankee in King Arthur's Court*, pp. 25, 63–4.
[159] Niven, 'Theory and practice of time travel', p. 123.
[160] 'Time-warped power', *IHT*, 30 Oct. 1981, p. 16.

ronistic judgements, the time traveller not only judges the past but uses foreknowledge to manipulate its outcomes.

Changing the past

The past as we know it is partly a product of the present; we continually reshape memory, rewrite history, refashion relics. The character of and reasons for such changes are discussed in Chapters 5 and 6. To revise what actually happened, as distinct from our ideas and its traces, is impossible, yet ardently desired. Three main motives impel would-be time travellers to tamper with history: to improve the past itself or the lot of those who live in it; to better present circumstances by changing what has led up to them; and to ensure the stability of the present by altering (or protecting) the past against interference by others.

Faith in progress is usually implicit in desires to improve the past. The ignorance and superstition, illiteracy and fecklessness of Arthurian England appal Twain's archetypal improver, who sets out to make life safer, happier, longer through scientific technology. Hank's civilizing mission envisions 'the destruction of the throne, nobility abolished, every member of it bound out to some useful trade, universal suffrage instituted, and the whole government placed in the hands of the men and women of the nation'. Within three years England is democratic and prosperous: 'Schools everywhere, and several colleges; a number of pretty good newspapers . . . Slavery was dead and gone; all men were equal before the law . . . The telegraph, the telephone, the phonograph, the typewriter, the sewing-machine, and all the thousand willing and handy servants of steam and electricity were working their way into favor.'[161]

Others seek analogous improvements. Rider Haggard's venturers into prehistory invent fire and save their tribe from starvation.[162] To avert the fall of the Roman Empire, William Golding's prescient envoy presents Caesar with a steamship, gunpowder, and the printing press, but all malfunction or presage disaster; the only modern appliance the gourmet emperor approves is a pressure cooker.[163] A Sprague de Camp reformer imports Arabic numbers, newspapers, telegraphy, distillation, double-entry book-keeping, and horsecollars into sixth-century Italy in an effort to save Europe from medieval retrogression; another introduces antiseptics and electricity into Lorenzo de Medici's Florence.[164]

Others improve the past by intervening in crucial events. Avoiding the 'mistakes' that destroyed Rome and corrupted the barbarians, one time traveller unites fifth-century Saxons and Romans under a form of Christianity 'which will educate and civilize men without shackling their minds'.[165] Preventing the ambush of Charlemagne's forces at Roncevalles in 778, R. A. Lafferty's characters forestall the breach with Spanish Islam and thus spare Christian Europe centuries of cultural isolation.[166] Aghast at the impending fate of Mary Queen of Scots, Uttley's heroine hopes to 'put back the clock of time and save her'.[167] Improving the past is seldom solely altruistic: in ameliorating historical conditions, time travellers also better their own lot. One advances Stone Age culture by

[161] *Connecticut Yankee*, pp. 79, 277, 359, 361.   [162] *Allan and the Ice-Gods*.   [163] 'Envoy extraordinary'.
[164] Sprague de Camp, *Lest Darkness Fall*; Wellman, *Twice in Time*. See Shippey, 'History in SF', p. 283.
[165] Anderson, *Guardians of Time*, p. 46.
[166] 'Thus we frustrate Charlemagne', pp. 172–3.   [167] *Traveller in Time*, p. 108.

teaching people 'fishing – so I could eat fish; raising beef, so I could eat steak – and, later on, painting pictures that I could look at and making music for me to hear'; an American nauseated by the slaughter of ancient Rome's gladiatorial games plans to replace them with less sanguinary football.[168]

The most compelling motive for altering the past is to change the present – to ward off global catastrophe, to secure national hegemony, to make one's own fame or fortune. Yearnings to repair an error, make good a loss, avert a tragedy, impel many fictional time travellers. One retrospectively rescues his fiancée from a bombing raid, another strives to save his seventeenth-century wife from being poisoned, a third eliminates a rival by sending him back as a prisoner of seventeenth-century buccaneers.[169] Others go back to prevent their present enemies from having been born or to make themselves millionaires by retrospectively investing money for their future.[170] Broader concerns for the future animate others to alter the past. The inventor of a time viewer seeks to alert the public to the evils of nationalist aggression, and hence to avert nuclear war, by filming the deceptions practised by wicked rulers throughout history.[171] To snuff out Soviet Communism at its inception, an American soldier during the Cold War is sent back to assassinate Lenin in 1917.[172]

To *ensure* the present that we now have is a third goal in changing the past. In a Poul Anderson story, Kublai Khan has discovered America in the thirteenth century and threatens to alter the whole course of history by conquering the hemisphere; 'our own world wouldn't exist, wouldn't ever have existed'. Destroying the expedition's horses and ships, Anderson's 'time patrol' ensures that the invaders will be absorbed without a trace into Eskimo and Indian populations, thus conserving the present as we know it.[173] Finding New York in 1960 full of 'kilted brachycephalic whites, mixed up with Indians and using steam-driven automobiles', another time patrol learns that prior interference in the Scipio–Hannibal conflict has changed all subsequent history, and goes back to refight that battle so that history will come out right.[174] Another preserver returns to the 1850s to forestall a fanatical Southern racist's deployment of modern weapons that would reverse the outcome of the Civil War.[175] A twentieth-century would-be witness of the Crucifixion takes on the Messiah's role, when he realizes the actual Jesus will not do so, because 'he wanted the events to be true. He wanted the New Testament to be right.'[176] *Catface*'s fundamentalists want to embargo travel to the time of Jesus, lest 'probing back . . . destroy the faith that has been built up through the ages'.[177] Such fears reflect a wider apprehension, as we shall see, that much of what lies undisclosed in the graveyard of the past had best remain buried there.

To change the past is none the less a compelling goal. It sharply contrasts the history we can have with the history we might want. We know and indeed depend on the fact that

---

[168] Laumer, *Great Time Machine Hoax*, p. 198; Merwin, *Three Faces of Time*, p. 140.
[169] Anderson, *Guardians of Time*, pp. 41–5; Carr, *Devil in Velvet*; Hubbard, *Typewriter in the Sky*.
[170] Reynolds, 'Compounded interest'; Henry Harrison, *Rebel in Time*. Like many SF ideas, this originated with Wells's *Time Machine* (p. 11).
[171] Sherred, 'E for effort'.
[172] Seabury, 'Histronaut'. He succeeds – but returns to 1968 to find Washington occupied by German forces.
[173] *Guardians of Time*, p. 102.   [174] Ibid., pp. 120–60.   [175] Harrison, *Rebel in Time*.
[176] Moorcock, *Behold the Man*, p. 37.
[177] Simak, p. 190.

what has occurred is fixed and irrevocable; but this does not prevent us from wishing that it might be otherwise.[178] The desire to alter what has happened is a common if futile response to a dilemma that confronts us all: past events have determined the world and ourselves as we are; yet we know that these events were not pre-ordained but simply contingent, that matters might have turned out otherwise. From that might-have-been we fantasize reaching back to make it so.

All these time-travel motives bear on concerns that characterize the more commonplace attachments to the past discussed in the next chapter. But just as time travellers' desires are intense, so are the attendant dangers grave, involving risks not only to themselves but to the cosmos. What are these consequences?

RISKS OF REVISITING THE PAST

Devotion to the past [is] one of the more disastrous forms of unrequited love.

Susan Sontag, 'Unguided tour'[179]

Suppose you *could* go back? What would the experience be like? What would be the consequences? Even those attracted by the rewards of time travel are dubious about its outcomes. The most optimistic venturers often find that the past's dangers or disappointments outweigh its supposed benefits. As will be seen, such reflections mirror widespread if seldom voiced feelings about risks inherent in the past.

Four potential drawbacks frequently alluded to are disappointment with the past, inability to cope with its circumstances, the danger of being marooned in it, and possible damage to the fabric of both past and present.

The past disappoints

History and memory so routinely glamorize the past that it should be no surprise to find the actuality disillusioning. 'I saw enough of the depression', says the embittered inventor of a time machine that will take him back only to the 1930s; 'I don't want to spend my old age watching people sell apples.'[180] Real life confirms how upsetting such returns can be. A recent nostalgic visit to New York's Lower East Side miserably disappointed former residents, some because they recognized too little, others too much; all wanted only to leave as soon as possible.[181] Even the very recent past can be a sorry eye-opener. Walking through the hippie encampment at Stonehenge's solstice rites in 1981 felt 'like stepping back in time', wrote a reporter. 'I have returned to the Sixties, . . . and it stinks.'[182]

That the past does literally stink is a lesson many time travellers would soon learn. A

---

[178] Anscombe, 'Reality of the past', pp. 47–8.   [179] 1977, p. 40.   [180] Gross, 'Good provider', p. 170.
[181] Richard F. Shepard, 'About New York: old neighborhoods visited mainly in memory', *N.Y. Times*, 18 Aug. 1977, p. B15. By contrast, a visit to Iowa's Living History Farm of 1900 made old people break down and cry from nostalgia (Jay Anderson, *Time Machines*, pp. 80–1).
[182] Stanley Reynolds, 'Stoned henge', *Sunday Times*, 28 June 1981, p. 35. Such a response, we will see in Chapter 6, would delight historic site curators seeking the authentic smell of the past. It is a mark of Plimoth Plantation's cramped, dung-splattered verisimilitude that 'after a day there, it has you yearning for the twentieth century' (Anderson, *Time Machines*, p. 52).

venturer disgusted by the late Roman Empire remarks that 'no restoration included all the dirt and disease, the insults and altercations' of the past.[183] Seeing the scuffed boots and worn coat of a Cromwellian soldier, the bedraggled look of a seventeenth-century village, Robert Westall's hero realizes he is in the actual, not a re-enacted, past: 'You can forget Merrie England . . . These houses straggled down a mud track, and they not only had no telly-aerials on the chimneys – most of them had no chimneys . . . The thatch looked old black and mouldy, the half timber was sagging and rotten, and the people . . . were all bloody midgets.'[184] Not even the supposed charms of yesteryear would commend themselves to its native inhabitants. 'If you told Mr. George Washington the reasons why you liked his time', an aspiring time traveller is cautioned, 'you'd probably be naming everything he hated about it.'[185]

Encounters with famous historical figures, their aura deflated by humdrum reality, likewise prove disillusioning. Lafferty's time viewers are revolted by Aristotle's 'barbarous north-coast Greek' and Tristan and Isolde's bear-grease pomade; they find Voltaire's wit a 'cackle' and Nell Gwynn 'a completely tasteless morsel'; listening to Sappho talk, they think the world fortunate 'that so few of her words have survived'.[186] Laumer depicts a paunchy, middle-aged William the Conqueror in ill-fitting breeches, a rust-speckled chain-mail shirt, and a moth-eaten fur cloak, yawning and belching at news of the Battle of Hastings.[187]

Moderns in the past miss the comforts of their own time. Fame and fortune in Renaissance Venice do not quench a time traveller's reverse nostalgia that 'came to him, ferocious and tugging, with a snatch of remembered music, with the desire for a cigarette, and in his memory of women of his era'.[188] An English girl in ancient Rome is chagrined to realize she may have to wait fifteen centuries for a cup of tea.[189] Henry James's Ralph Pendrel, at first in love with the past, ends by straining back to 'all the wonders and splendours' of his own modern world, 'of which he now sees only the ripeness, richness, attraction and civilisation, the virtual perfection without a flaw'.[190]

Inability to cope with the past

Modern knowledge might well prove a handicap rather than a royal road to success in the past. Lack of cultural preparedness, of processed materials, and of do-it-yourself skills would make much of current technology useless; and few moderns could quickly master the skills of an earlier era, even if they managed to escape cholera, smallpox, the gallows, and slavery. 'The Man Who Came Early' lacks the primitive know-how needed for survival in tenth-century Iceland; Richard Cowper's visitor to 1665 London dies of the plague before he can repair his damaged time machine; the Connecticut Yankee ends as a victim of his own scientific ingenuity.[191] Heretical innovations may prove fatal: Laumer's visitor

[183] Sprague de Camp, *Lest Darkness Fall*, pp. 13–14.   [184] Westall, *Devil on the Road*, p. 156.
[185] Bester, 'Hobson's choice', p. 146.
[186] 'Through other eyes', pp. 282–4.   [187] *Great Time Machine Hoax*, pp. 36–7.
[188] Carson, *Pawn of Time*, p. 57.
[189] Merwin, *Three Faces of Time*, p. 13.   [190] *Sense of the Past* , pp. 337–8.
[191] Anderson, 'Man who came early'; Cowper, 'Hertford Manuscript'.

to Llandudno in 1723 is not surprisingly burned as a witch for advocating birth control, evolution, and psychoanalysis.[192]

Innumerable, incommensurable differences from the present aggravate the risks of revisiting the past. 'How much can you learn in a totally strange environment', asks Anderson, 'when you can barely speak a word and are liable to be arrested on suspicion before you can swop for a suit of contemporary clothes?'[193] The most scrupulous schooling in past language and customs cannot make up for the absence of myriad shared recollections. Back in 1820, James's Ralph Pendrel is caught out again and again because he has no memory of intimate family and neighbourhood details. His knowledge, '*almost* as right as possible for the "period" ... and yet so intimately and secretly wrong', can never match that of persons then living, for his doubts and omissions appertain to his past, theirs to their future; anything he does or says, even opening his mouth to reveal well-cared-for teeth 'which that undentisted age can't have known the like of', is liable to betray him. It is 'one thing to "live in the Past" *with* the whole spirit, the whole candour of confidence and confidence of candour, that he would then have naturally had', concludes James, 'and a totally different thing to find himself living in it without those helps to possibility, those determinations of relation, those preponderant right instincts'.[194]

The mere act of moving back through time might have lethal consequences, were fantasy made real. Replaying the past as though it were their present, as recounted in Chapter 6, some historical re-enactors experience time-warp terror along with exultation. A young English woman, who believed herself in communion with a sixteenth-century man through a ouija board, became so obsessed with him that she killed herself, 'so that we can go back to live as we used to'.[195]

Problems of returning to the present

Among the past's other perils, some time travellers fear being forever exiled there. Terror at being unable to return, 'the horror ... of being *in* the past to stay, heart-breakingly to stay and never know his own precious Present again', corrodes Ralph Pendrel's pleasure in 1820 and vitiates the point of his visits there.[196] Hubbard's screen-writer fails to escape from buccaneers when he hears the diabolical clatter of the typewriter that keeps him trapped in the seventeenth century.[197] Changing the past may make return to the present impossible. A traveller back to the Battle of Gettysburg ensures the South will lose the Civil War but inadvertently kills the potential grandfather of the time machine's inventor, thereby marooning himself in the nineteenth century.[198]

Others return only to feel that sojourn in the past has unfitted them for the present or to

---

[192] *Dinosaur Beach*, p. 100. As Wells put it, 'Our ancestors had no great tolerance for anachronisms' (*Time Machine*, p. 11).
[193] *There Will Be Time*, p. 46.
[194] 'Notes for *The Sense of the Past*', pp. 295–6, 301. That candour and confidence the historian can acquire only in his own age (Wedgwood, 'Sense of the past', pp. 40–1).
[195] 'Mother killed by train "was obsessed"', *The Times*, 24 Apr. 1981, p. 4.
[196] James, 'Notes for *The Sense of the Past*', p. 294. The terror is vividly evoked in Marghanita Laski's *Victorian Chaise Longue*, whose tubercular modern protagonist finds herself back in 1864, unable to return to her own more medically enlightened time.
[197] *Typewriter in the Sky*, pp. 70, 75, 95.   [198] Moore, *Bring the Jubilee*.

find the modern world unliveable. The intensity of fourteenth-century experience alien-
ates du Maurier's protagonist from the drab present. Years spent in sixteenth-century
Venice incapacitate Carson's hero for twentieth-century America; coming back 'with a
skull full of maddening memories . . . I couldn't even qualify as an assistant professor of
Renaissance history'.[199] Disillusionment with the present might induce disastrous addic-
tion to a visitable past; dedicated to escaping from its own time, Aldiss's advanced but
nostalgic civilization is a paradigm of modern tourist experience.[200] Perennially dis-
satisfied 'time stiffs' in an Alfred Bester story who keep 'bumming through the centuries
. . . looking for the Golden Age' resemble American 'living-history' buffs who episodically
trade in old historical personae for new ones.[201] People who get time machines in Finney's
foredoomed twenty-first century simply stay in the past; ultimately most of the population
scatters back over the preceding two or three millennia, leaving a future world empty of all
but birds, insects, and rusting weapons.[202]

Endangering the temporal fabric

Interference involves risks to the past itself. Like historic restoration, time travel tends to
make the past thin and artificial, Fritz Leiber surmises, and may one day wear it out
altogether; the fabric of history can withstand only so much change. 'Every operation
leaves reality a bit cruder, a bit uglier, a bit more makeshift, and a whole lot less rich in
those details and feelings that are our heritage.'[203]

Indeed, the slightest alteration of the past – a grain of dust misplaced – may jeopardize
all that follows. 'The stomp of your foot, on one mouse, could start an earthquake, the
effects of which could shake our earth and destinies down through Time', Bradbury's
safari leader warns.[204] One might erase even oneself. Undoing some previous act courts
self-annihilation if one of our ancestors perishes in the process. 'If we once start doubling
back to tinker with our personal pasts, we'd soon get so tangled up that none of us would
exist.'[205] Time travellers adopt safeguards to minimize such risks: not interfering with the
course of events, not arousing suspicion that they come from a later epoch, not leaving
modern artifacts lying around. Others restrict travel to remote prehistory to allow enough
time for their modern artifacts to decompose. Sprague de Camp's machines visit only
epochs before 100,000 B.C.; Bradbury's Jurassic safari hunters kill only pre-selected
animals slated to die of natural causes within the next few minutes anyway; Simak's
resettlement colony for today's urban poor is remote enough in time to avoid collision with
subsequent humans.[206]

Some would-be travellers doubt that such impacts could significantly alter the past.
Time is a river into which billions of events are dropped; any individual can affect only a

---

[199] *Pawn of Time*, p. 433.　　[200] *An Age.*
[201] 'Hobson's choice', p. 146; Jay Anderson, *Time Machines*, p. 189: Those who change their 'impressions'
often sell their old costumes, and one battle re-enactment 'sutler has even gone into the business of recycling
authentic hand-made period clothing from worn-out personas'.
[202] 'Such interesting neighbours', pp. 16–18.
[203] *The Big Time*, p. 63. See also Laumer, *Dinosaur Beach*, pp. 19–20, 136.
[204] 'A sound of thunder', p. 77. See Finney, *Time and Again*, p. 73.
[205] Anderson, *Guardians of Time*, p. 52.
[206] Sprague de Camp, 'Gun for dinosaur'; Bradbury, 'Sound of thunder', p. 78; Simak, *Catface*, pp. 241–51.

few of these. 'You can't erase the conquests of Alexander by nudging a neolithic pebble', or 'extirpate America by pulling up a shoot of Sumerian grain'.[207] Similarly, 'if I went back to . . . the Middle Ages and shot one of FDR's Dutch forebears, he'd still be born in the late nineteenth century – because he and his genes resulted from the entire world of his ancestors'.[208] All his twentieth-century resources and detailed foreknowledge do not enable Carr's hero to change the past; he 'might alter a small and trifling detail here and there; [but] the ultimate result would be just the same'.[209] Finney's traveller quarrels with a man of the 1880s, but reassures himself that 'I hadn't really interfered with the past; something of the sort would sooner or later have happened anyway involving someone else, if I hadn't been here'.[210] In fact, you can't change anything, Larry Niven insists. 'You can't kill your grandfather because you *didn't*. You'll kill the wrong man if you try it; or your gun won't fire.'[211]

Others contend that the known present includes the effects of any temporal interventions. 'If time travel was going to make any changes, it had already done so', asserts a Farmer character. There was 'no question about his interference changing the course of events . . . Whatever he was to do had been done, and events and lives had been determined before he was born even if he had helped determine them.'[212]

The impossibility of changing the past frustrates a time traveller seeking retrospective revenge against his unfaithful wife. Going back to kill her grandparents, he returns to the present to discover her still in his rival's embrace. He then alters history more radically, murdering George Washington, Columbus, Mohammed – all to no avail. 'When a man changes the past, he only affects his own past – no one else's', he finally realizes. 'The past is like memory. When you erase a man's memory you wipe him out, but you don't wipe out anybody else's . . . We each travel into our own past, and no other person's.'[213]

To visit and alter the past ultimately leads to solipsistic isolation. Time flowing in both directions would deny sequential order; spontaneously generated events would lack both causes and effects; temporal episodes in the ocean of time would 'come drifting to us as randomly as dead animals on the waves'.[214] No aspect of the past could be depended upon. Can any of us 'be sure the memories we cherish were the same yesterday?' asks Moore. 'Do they *know* that a past cannot be expunged?'[215] The issue of the reality of the past goes far beyond time travel; I consider its wider context in Chapter 5. But any revisited past would be irreparably damaged. 'Lacking a past in the past, and having memories of the future', Ralph Pendrel thereby destroys the past he so intensely desires to belong to.[216] In seeking

---

[207] Leiber, 'Try and change the past', p. 94. See Finney, *Time and Again*, p. 140.

[208] Anderson, *Guardians of Time*, p. 130.

[209] *Devil in Velvet*, p. 15.   [210] *Time and Again*, p. 169.

[211] 'Theory and practice of time travel', p. 120.

[212] *Time's Last Gift*, pp. 12, 20.

[213] Bester, 'Men who murdered Mohammed', p. 129. The impossibility of changing the past is generally agreed by logicians. 'You cannot *change* the past: if a thing has happened, it has happened, and you cannot make it not to have happened' (Dummett, 'Bringing about the past', p. 341). Hence time travel too is impossible. 'Just to visit the Past would be to change the Past, and this cannot be', for 'were we able to visit the past we would bring with us our knowledge of the Future' (Danto, 'Narrative sentences', p. 160). Only a few suggest one might revisit the past without changing it (Horwich, 'On some alleged paradoxes of time travel') or that the paradoxes 'are oddities, not impossibilities' (David Lewis, 'Paradoxes of time travel', p. 145).

[214] Silverberg, 'In entropy's jaws', p. 188.   [215] *Bring the Jubilee*, p. 189.

[216] Bellringer, 'Henry James's *The Sense of the Past*', p. 210. Bellringer shows how in recapturing the past we deform or erase it: 'To relate back to historical figures is to alter them and to look back contactually at the past

to assimilate its details, he separates its own inhabitants from their moorings; his very concern reduces them to ghosts or zombies. 'You have been thinking of me in the past tense', says a horrified lady to the twentieth-century intruder into her world of 1784, 'talking about me as though I were already dead!'[217]

Those who ascribe power and purpose to the past feel that history will punish any interference with it, just as ancestor-worshippers fear their forebears' malicious reprisals if their memory is neglected or mistreated. More than others, fictional time travellers suffer the consequences of their obsession with the past, learning that escape from present reality is self-defeating. 'We shall never make the best of our present world', concludes Coulton after returning his protagonist from the Middle Ages, 'until we realize how false it is to hanker after the ideals of a dead past.' Having sought the splendour of medieval architecture, he was appalled by much else he found in those days, and returned 'strengthened to the common routine of life in our own soulless century'.[218] The past that time travellers seek is a mirage that reflects their own nostalgia.

People are normally aware that the actual past is irrecoverable. Yet memory and history, relic and replica leave impressions so vivid, so tantalizingly concrete, that we cannot help but feel deprived. Surely routes so enticing and well mapped should be open to us in reality! The hopes and fears that the past arouses are heightened by the conflict between our knowledge that its return is impossible and our desire, perhaps our instinct, that it must and can be reached.

The present alone is inadequate to our desires, not least because it is continuously depleted to further enlarge the past. Disenchantment with today impels us to try to recover yesterday. That discontent takes many forms: a devotion to relics, the treasuring of antiques and souvenirs, a tendency to value what is old simply because it is old, the rejection of change. These reactions lack the obsessive unreality of time travel but reflect the same yearning for times gone by.

It is easy to see what is amiss with that obsession. 'Through the vistas of the years every age but our own seems glamorous and golden', concludes Bester. 'We yearn for the yesterdays and tomorrows, never realizing . . . that today, bitter or sweet, anxious or calm, is the only day for us. The dream of time is the traitor, and we are all accomplices to the betrayal of ourselves.'[219] Yet the enduring dream of reliving the past also has some virtues. It brings history and memory vividly to mind, setting in sharp relief both the deficiencies and the virtues of the present; intense awareness of the past lends the present fullness and duration as well.

To live again in the past indeed implies that present life is but part of a long continuum. Coexisting in past and present convinces du Maurier's protagonist that 'there was no past, no present, no future. Everything living is part of the whole. We are all bound, one to the

---

is to attract its attention and alter its look' (p. 212). *The Sense of the Past* is 'a warning against historical infatuation' (p. 212) of which, as we shall see, James was frequently wary. See also Beams, 'Consciousness in James's "The Sense of the Past"'.
[217] Balderston, *Berkeley Square*, p. 80. Pendrel's 'very care for them [the past's inhabitants] had somehow annihilated them'; his uncanny understanding 'turned them to stone or wood or wax' (*Sense of the Past*, p. 213).
[218] Coulton, *Friar's Lantern* (1906), pp. 227, 34.　　[219] 'Hobson's choice', p. 148.

other, through time and eternity.' His vivid experience of fourteenth-century Cornwall 'proved that the past was living still, that we were all participants, all witnesses', hence more truly ourselves.[220]

Neither the dreams nor the nightmares of revisiting the past are less intense for their seeming unlikelihood. Moreover, they offer clues to what it is of the past we truly need and can accept or should avoid or reject. And they throw light on underlying perspectives toward both tradition and change. Intense devotion to the pursuit of the past is not so grievous an affliction as to lack feeling for the past altogether.

[220] *House on the Strand*, pp. 169–70.

2
BENEFITS AND BURDENS OF THE PAST

Only a good-for-nothing is not interested in his past.

Sigmund Freud[1]

The past is useless. That explains why it is past.

Wright Morris, *Cause for Wonder*[2]

Why do we need the past? What do we want it for? What burdens and risks does regard for it entail? How far do affections for the past reflect the extravagant yearnings and forebodings just explored? The consequences of our heritage are more momentous than those revealed in nostalgic dreams and time-travel fiction, for they concern real rather than make-believe worlds; yet the ensuing dilemmas have much in common.

The benefits the past supplies, the burdens it entails, and the competing claims of the old and the new are the subjects of the next two chapters. This chapter surveys attitudes toward the past in general and identifies those traits that make it seem desirable or reprehensible; Chapter 3 recounts how people in various epochs have dealt with the conflicting demands of past and present.

Reactions to the past are often ambiguous. Explicit avowals of admiration or disdain conceal their opposites; reverence for tradition underlies destructive iconoclasm; retrospective nostalgia coexists with impatient modernism. Revolutionaries exorcise recent evils by appealing to older exemplars, and end by resuscitating what they once rejected. Formerly avid to extirpate all traces of *anciens régimes*, Soviet and Chinese governments today turn a blind eye toward, and sometimes actively encourage, nostalgia for pre-Revolutionary customs and artifacts.[3] Expressions of feeling for and against the past moreover reflect vested interests. Antiquity may bolster the claims of some nations and individuals, innovation of others. To celebrate their patrons' regimes, Renaissance historians ran down the past in favour of the present, whereas antiquarians studying ruins

---

[1] Quoted in Bernfeld, 'Freud and archeology', p. 111.   [2] 1978, p. 53.
[3] Philippa Lewis, 'Peasant nostalgia in contemporary Russian literature', pp. 562–5; Binyon, *Life in Russia*, pp. 140–2; David Bonavia, 'China luxuriates in its pre-Mao past', *The Times*, 21 Apr. 1982, p. 7.

and relics magnified past achievements to the detriment of the present.[4] Modern sanitary engineers are professionally committed to replacing what is antiquated, museum curators to safeguarding obsolescent artifacts. But the antiquarian disposition – the enjoyment of antiques and historical sites, a preference for traditional form and design, an appreciation of the cultural creations of the past and a tendency to collect them – varies both socially and individually in ways that have been little examined.[5]

With these caveats, let us first review the past's advantages.

BENEFITS

The past for Poets; the Present for Pigs.

Samuel Palmer[6]

The legion of benefits the past provides clearly transcends nostalgia. 'The most Polite part of Mankind', wrote Vanbrugh almost three centuries ago, agree 'in the Value they have ever set upon the Remains of distant times.'[7] Today a large proportion of mankind share that view. A taste so widespread may be a necessity. But why is the past necessary? And what qualities make it so?

Reasons advanced for admiring the past are often vague or perfunctory; its desirability is simply taken for granted. 'The charm of the past is that it is the past', says Wilde's Henry Wotton,[8] as if to preclude further explanation. 'Generally, I love anything old, it's so proper', says a barrister of his clothes,[9] but he gives no clue as to what traits 'proper' embodies. Victorians prized the past less for any specific qualities than for its general ambience, and praise of the past today is so conventional that almost anything old may be thought desirable. So eclectic a past can embrace whatever is wanted, and even the newest artifacts feel 'immemorial' within a few years of their appearance.[10]

Equally ineffable is the concept of national heritage, normally evoked with sub-lyrical vagueness. 'I do not think in dictionary terms', writes the compiler of Britain's *Heritage in*

---

[4] Cochrane, *Historians and Historiography in the Italian Renaissance*, p. 441; Dobby, *Conservation and Planning*, p. 29. As the Florentine Alamanno Rinuccini flattered his patron in 1473, 'We need only look at you, my Lord Prince, and find the greatness of our age confirmed' (Dedicatory epistle, paraphrased in Gombrich, 'Renaissance conception of artistic progress and its consequences', p. 2).

[5] McKechnie ('Environmental Response Inventory in application', pp. 259, 273), distinguishes 'antiquarian' tendencies among various professions, S. M. Taylor and Konrad ('Scaling dispositions toward the past', pp. 290–3, 302–5), among various past-related activities. Barbara Szacka identifies two distinctive views of the past among Polish university graduates: an *historicist* orientation linking past with present and potential future achievements, and an *escapist* orientation seeing the past as better than and disconnnected from the present; the first is characteristic of the newly successful, the second of offspring of the older elite who have suffered a relative decline in status (Szacka, 'Two kinds of past-time orientation', pp. 67–72; *idem*, 'Historical consciousness', pp. 28–9). For Western parallels, see Fraisse, *Psychology of Time*, pp. 193–4; Cottle, *Perceiving Time*, p. 110.

[6] To Laura Richmond (1862), in Palmer, *Life and Letters*, p. 249. 'A preference for the present as a matter of taste is a pretty sure sign of mediocrity' (Palmer to F. G. Stephens, Sept. 1875, p. 250n).

[7] To the Duchess of Marlborough, 11 June 1709, in Vanbrugh, *Complete Works*, 4:29.

[8] Wilde, *Picture of Dorian Gray*, p. 153.

[9] John Hilton, quoted in Sally Brampton, 'Their strongest suits', *Observer Mag.*, 18 Apr. 1982. 'People who love wearing old clothes are romantics. They like the history that many of these clothes carry with them' (Donna Lawson, *Oldies but Goodies: How to Restyle Yesterday's Clothing and Castoffs into Exciting New Fashions for Today* (New York: Butterick, 1977), p. 12.

[10] The threshing machine was so seen within a few years of its appearance in England (Jefferies, *Life of the Fields*, 1884, p. 151).

Danger, 'but instead reflect on certain sights and sounds . . . a morning mist on the Tweed at Dryburgh where the magic of Turner and the romance of Scott both come fleetingly to life; . . . a celebration of the Eucharist in a quiet Norfolk church with the medieval glass filtering the colours.'[11] Those who drafted the National Heritage Act confess they 'could no more define the national heritage than we could define, say, beauty or art . . . So we decided to let the national heritage define itself.'[12] That heritage 'includes not only the Tower of London but agricultural vestiges visible only by the aid of aerial photography', writes the Secretary of the British Academy; 'not only the duke's castle and possessions but . . . the duke himself'.[13] No wonder heritage takes forms so diverse as to seem incommensurable. The British National Heritage Fund helped to preserve, among other things in 1981, Henry VIII's sunken flagship *Mary Rose*, the communion breadholder of Mary Queen of Scots, the State Bed of the Speaker of the House of Commons, Patrick Campbell's 'Bluebird', some Wordsworth manuscripts, the Astor Apostle spoons, trade union banners of the 1930s, a colony of Greater Horseshoe bats, and the elm-lined Cambridgeshire avenue whence Second World War bombers were guided home.[14]

Other links with the past are still more heterogeneous. Iron Age forts, Greek temples, Celtic jewellery, runic inscriptions, Georgian buildings, neo-Gothic whimsies, ridge-and-furrow plough marks, steam engines, windmills, Morris dancing, Macaulay's histories, art-deco cinemas, coronation mugs, 1930s juke-boxes, 1950s dress styles, 1960s movies, Golden Oldies, visits to Rome or Pompeii, the treasures of Tutankhamun and the horrors of Madame Tussaud's, childhood memories, chats with grandma, seaside souvenirs, family photographs, family trees, old trees, old money – all these connect with some treasured past. A typical Toronto resident, in Victor Konrad's portrayal, daily enjoys the past by lunching in a landmark restaurant, collecting Indian artifacts, and sifting through the remains of an old bottle dump.[15] The World Soundscape Project has recorded a vanishing sonic legacy that includes the ringing of old cash registers, scrubbing on washboards, butter-churning, razor-stropping, a hissing kerosene lamp, the squeak of leather saddle-bags, hand coffee-grinders, milk cans rattling on horse-drawn vehicles, heavy doors being clanked shut and bolted, school handbells, and rocking-chairs on wooden floors.[16]

What is appreciated about the past depends on a host of variables. For example, some live in patently ancient countries, others in lands whose lineaments are new or in constant flux. The latter may seek out the antiquities of the former: many Americans come to Europe to feel at home in time. Or they may focus on other aspects of their heritage, antiques or arrowheads or ancestral trees. 'Only in a country where newness and brevity of

[11] Cormack, *Heritage in Danger*, p. 14. The word 'heritage' now sounds either pompous or twee, 'redolent of Gifte Shoppes selling . . . crinoline-lady lavender bags and witch-balls in macrame slings' (Marghanita Laski, 'Lost for words', *The Times*, 2 Sept. 1983).

[12] Bommes and Wright, '"Charms of residence": the public and the past', p. 289; Charteris, 'Work of the National Heritage Memorial Fund', p. 327.

[13] J. P. Carswell, 'Lost for words on "the heritage"', letter, *The Times*, 8 Sept. 1983, p. 11.

[14] Charteris, 'National Heritage Memorial Fund', pp. 326, 328–31; National Heritage Memorial Fund, *Annual Reports*, 1980–3.

[15] Konrad, 'Orientations toward the Past in the Environment of the Present', p. 99; Konrad and Taylor, 'Retrospective orientations in metropolitan Toronto', p. 70.

[16] R. M. Schafer, 'Music of the environment', pp. 42–3; *idem*, *Tuning of the World*, p. 48.

tenure are the common substance of life', Henry James wrote of nineteenth-century New Englanders, would 'the fact of one's ancestors having lived for a hundred and seventy years in a single spot ... become an element of one's morality.'[17] In our time, massive migration and the loss of tangible relics have stimulated interest in genealogy. 'The more the ancient landmarks are destroyed, the more many of us hunger for a firm anchorage in time and place', asserts one authority. 'Through genealogy the transient flat-dweller of the cities can join himself to the peasant rooted in ancestral soil', and learn how his lineage derives from that older world. 'Cut off from his roots by profound changes in ways of living, by migration from home and by loss of contact with his kindred, modern man seeks more or less consciously to reconstruct human links.'[18] The growth of interest in roots is phenomenal. 'In the early 1960s there would be a *handful* of people looking through the census returns at the Public Record Office', recalls a herald at the College of Arms. 'Now they've got a special search room with 100 microfilm readers, and in the summer there's a big queue.' More than two Americans in three want to know more about their ancestors; interest in the family tree is second only to stamp and coin collecting as a hobby.[19]

Those who detach from themselves some part of their past commonly substitute another. Disavowing materialist values, many young Americans who forsook middle-class parental milieux for radical life-styles in the 1960s also flocked to prehistoric archaeological digs, finding an alternative heritage in remote antiquity. To compensate for their own lack of local roots, newcomers to old English villages may take keen interest in the local past; they often come to dominate historical and preservation societies, as militant defenders of old landmarks against bulldozers manned, likely as not, by unsentimental village old-timers.

Preservation is one popular use of the past, discussed at length in Chapter 7. Others, like revival architecture and reproduction furniture, adopt the forms and styles of yesteryear, or clothe new products in previous habiliments (see below, pp. 39–40, and Chapter 6). Still others ennoble ancient times by reanimating old myths, as the Victorians did with King Arthur.[20] Yet another is to find or create enclaves of the past where anachronistic remnants and traditions can be cherished (below, pp. 50–1).

All these actions imply general consensus about past-related benefits that are seldom articulated, however. I subsume them here within half a dozen categories: familiarity and recognition; reaffirmation and validation; individual and group identity; guidance; enrichment; and escape. No sharp boundaries delimit these benefits: a sense of identity is also a mode of enrichment; familiarity provides guidance. Yet some benefits conflict with others: using the past to enrich present-day life is at odds with wanting to escape from the present. But these categories are neither exhaustive nor logically coherent, they are simply heuristic, a means of surveying the whole spectrum of what the past can do for us.

---

[17] *Hawthorne* (1879), p. 14.   [18] Wagner, *English Genealogy*, p. 3; *idem*, *English Ancestry*, p. 6.

[19] Patric Dickinson, quoted in Martyn Harris, 'Mark the heralds', *New Society*, 9 Feb. 1984, p. 198; Harriett Van Horne, 'The great ancestor hunt', *Family Weekly*, 10 July 1977, p. 7. See Peter Hall, 'In pursuit of the past' *New Society*, 7 Apr. 1983, p. 21.

[20] Girouard, *Return to Camelot*, pp. 178–84; Merriman, 'Other Arthurians in Victorian England'.

Familiarity

The surviving past's most essential and pervasive benefit is to render the present familiar. Its traces on the ground and in our minds let us make sense of the present. Without habit and the memory of past experience, no sight or sound would mean anything; we can perceive only what we are accustomed to. Environmental features and patterns are recognized as features and patterns because we share a history with them. Every object, every grouping, every view is intelligible largely because previous encounters and tales heard, books read, pictures seen, have made them already familiar. Only habituation enables us to understand what lies around us. 'If you saw a slab of chocolate for the first time', suggests John Wyndham, 'you might think it was for mending shoes, lighting the fire, or building houses.'[21] The perceived identity of each scene and object stems from past acts and expectations, from a history of involvements. In Hannah Arendt's words, 'the reality and reliability of the human world rest primarily on the fact that we are surrounded by things more permanent than the activity by which they were produced'.[22]

The remembered past requires us all to behave, however unwittingly, as historians. Carl Becker's 'Mr. Everyman, when he awakens in the morning, reaches out into the country of the past and of distant places, . . . pulls together . . . things said and done in his yesterdays, and coordinates them with his present perceptions . . . Without this historical knowledge, this memory of things said and done, his to-day would be aimless and his tomorrow without significance.'[23]

Objects that lack any familiar elements or configurations remain incomprehensible. On C. S. Lewis's imaginary Malacandra a terrestrial visitor at first perceives 'nothing but colours – colours that refused to form themselves into things', because 'he knew nothing yet well enough to see it; you cannot see things till you know roughly what they are'.[24] But no terrestrial environment is totally novel to anyone: a life-long urbanite dropped unexpectedly into a tropical jungle would find day predictably alternating with night, rain with shine; would recognize trees, sky, earth, and water, and respond to up and down, back and forth much as on his own familiar streets. Every earthly locale has some connection with our experienced past.

Not only is the past recalled in what we see; it is incarnate in what we create. Familiarity makes surroundings comfortable; hence we keep memorabilia and add new things whose decor evokes the old. Electric fireplaces simulate Victorian coal or Tudor burning-log effects; plastic cabinets and vinyl-tile floors recall the 'natural' past with a wood-grain look; leaded lights painted on windows feign ancient cosiness; electric fixtures resemble candles or paraffin lamps.[25] Such embrace of the past is often unconscious. The designer may intend the anachronism of his concrete hearth logs or candle-drip light bulbs, but for most users they have ceased to evoke memories of the earlier prototypes that in fact lend them their familiar charm. Obsolete structures and artifacts similarly live on unobserved in contemporary language: newsmen make up pages 'on the stone' though that technology

---

[21] 'Pillar to post', p. 148.   [22] *Human Condition*, pp. 195–6. See Fraisse, *Psychology of Time*, p. 68.
[23] Becker, 'Everyman his own historian', p. 8.
[24] *Out of the Silent Planet*, p. 42. People born blind are similarly confused when given sight and faced with the unfamiliar visual world (von Senden, *Space and Sight*, pp. 158–69).
[25] Langer, *Feeling and Form*, p. 295.

has long been obsolete; children talk of 'pulling the chain' though handle-operated cisterns may be all they have seen; tarmac-flattening machines are still called 'steamrollers' and graphite sticks 'lead pencils'; my typescript was a 'manuscript'.

Surrogate and second-hand experiences further infuse present perception: we conceive of things not only as seen but also as heard and read about before. My image of London is a composite of personal experience, contemporary media, and historical images stemming from Hogarth and Turner, Pepys and Dickens. Despite the novelty and strangeness of the English scene, the American Charles Eliot Norton felt on arrival that an 'old world look' gave 'those old world things . . . a deeper familiarity than the very things that have lain before our eyes since we were born'.[26] Past impressions often so trenchantly embody the character of places they override our own immediate impressions. Constable's Suffolk has 'become the countryside . . . of all of us, even if we have a quite different landscape outside our windows', notes Nicholas Penny. 'We feel that we have grown up not only with jigsaws and illustrated biscuit tins showing that little boy on a pony beside the river with the mill in the distance, but with the reality represented . . . England was like that, we feel sure [and] we convince ourselves that his country is . . . still surviving today.'[27] Hardy's Wessex, Wordsworth's Lake District, Samuel Palmer's North Downs, all 'ghost features kept in existence by nostalgia', dominate our images of these landscapes, showing the power 'of a vanished past over a palpable present'; Monet so 'shaped our notion of the Ile de France . . . that we have trouble believing that his was not the complete, definitive and everlasting account of . . . Argenteuil, in particular'.[28] It is not just habituation that makes such impressions so enduring. Hindsight enables us to comprehend past scenes as we cannot those of the incoherent present; yesterday's more comprehensible remembered images dominate and obscure today's kaleidoscopic perceptions.

The past we depend on to make sense of the present is, however, mostly recent; it stems mainly from our own few years of experience. The further back in time, the fewer the traces that survive, the more they have altered, and the less they anchor us to contemporary reality.

Reaffirmation and validation

The past validates present attitudes and actions by affirming their resemblance to former ones. Previous usage seals with approval what is now done. Historical precedent legitimates what exists today; we justify current practice by referring to 'immutable' tradition. 'This is how it's always been done', we say, or 'Let's not set new precedents': precedence legitimates action on the assumption, explicit or implicit, that what has been should continue to be or be again.

The past validates the present in two distinct ways: by preserving and by restoring. Preservation invokes the continuance of practices that supposedly date from time immemorial; changes, if any, have been superficial, inconsequential. People in so-called traditional societies confidently assert that things are (and should be) the way they always

[26] To James Russell Lowell, 30 Aug. 1868, in Norton, *Letters*, 1:306.

[27] 'Constable: an English heritage abroad', *Sunday Times*, 11 Nov. 1984, p. 43.

[28] Prince, 'Reality stranger than fiction', p. 16; John Russell, 'In the mythical Ile de France', *IHT*, 15 July 1983, p. 9. See Tucker, *Monet at Argenteuil*, pp. 19–20, 176–86.

have been, for oral transmission accumulates actual alterations unconsciously, continually readjusting the past to fit the present. Literate societies less easily sustain such fiction, for written – and especially printed – records reveal a past unlike the present: the archives show traditions eroded by time and corrupted by novelty, by no means faithfully adhered to. Many literate societies none the less cling to supposedly timeless values and unbroken lineages that link them with antiquity, like Whig historians who viewed nineteenth-century England as the inheritor of legal and political forms fundamentally unchanged since medieval times.[29]

Restoring lost or subverted values and institutions is a second mode of validation. A remote past legitimates and fortifies the present order against subsequent mishap or corruption. Thus Renaissance humanists looked beyond the dark ages of evil and oblivion to the classical glories they aimed to reanimate. The most revolutionary innovators hark back to some legitimizing past: Luther invoked St Paul, the Girondists early Rome, nineteenth-century Pre-Raphaelites and ecclesiastical restorers 'pure' Gothic. Such harking back often happens in hard times; during the 1930s Americans viewed Founding Fathers with renewed respect, shoring up battered self-esteem by identifying with a successful past. Preservation and restoration are often commingled: Whig historians' affirmations of unbroken continuity alternated with abjurations to restore traditions interrupted by 'foreign' innovations.[30]

Those who feel they have transcended a sorry or infamous past may enjoy looking back to measure their progress, like *The Five Little Peppers* whose 'dear old things' at the beloved little brown house in Badgertown tangibly confirmed their rise from rags to riches.[31] We appreciate the bad old days partly as proof of our subsequent advance, as some commend preservation 'to reassure ourselves that life was really awful for our ancestors', hence a lot better for us.[32]

Various social modalities – family, peers, neighbourhood, ethnicity, state – validate various pasts, their custodial roles waxing or waning. As education becomes more centralized and parents increasingly reluctant or impotent consciously to impose beliefs on their offspring, the family has grown less and the state more significant as a transmitter of tradition.[33]

Identity

The past is integral to our sense of identity; 'the sureness of "I was" is a necessary component of the sureness of "I am"'.[34] Ability to recall and identify with our own past gives existence meaning, purpose, and value. The ancient Greeks equated individual existence with what was memorable, and post-Renaissance Europeans have increasingly seen the past as essential to personality. Rousseau's *Confessions* and Wordsworth's lyrics have taught us to view our identity in terms of our cumulated lives. Even traumatically

---

[29] Blaas, *Continuity and Anachronism*; Burrow, *Liberal Descent*; Butterfield, *Whig Interpretation of History*.
[30] A. H. Jones, 'Search for a usable past in the New Deal era', pp. 715, 720; Pocock, *Politics, Language and Time*, p. 248.
[31] Margaret Sidney, *Five Little Peppers Midway*, p. 148; Betty Levin, 'Peppers' progress', p. 170.
[32] Barry, 'Why I like old things', p. 49.
[33] Shils, *Tradition*, pp. 172–3.
[34] Wyatt, 'Reconstruction of the individual and of the collective past', p. 319.

painful memories remain essential emotional history; amnesiacs bereft of their past are also deprived of identity.[35] Identification with earlier stages of one's life is crucial both to integrity and to well being.

Many maintain touch with their past selves through attachment to natal or long-inhabited locales. 'A place in this sense cannot be bought; it must be shaped, usually over long periods of time, and then it must be preserved.'[36] Such places need not be magnificent to be memorable. Over and over again, in the most mundane surroundings, a chronicler of London's Kentish Town 'found exemplified the importance people attach to their roots and to their physical habitat actual or remembered'.[37] Helen Santmyer's childhood Ohio town was 'shabby, worn, and unpicturesque', yet it enabled her to cherish a full measure of stored impressions:

The unfastidious heart makes up its magpie hoard, heedless of the protesting intelligence. Valentines in a drugstore window, the smell of roasting coffee, sawdust on the butcher's floor ... – these are as good to have known and remembered, associated as they are with friendliness between man and man, between man and child, as fair streets and singing towers and classic arcades.[38]

Some need the tangible feel of native soil; mere traces of the past suffice to keep others in touch with their own development. The endurance even of unseen relics can sustain identity. 'Many symbolic and historic locations in a city are rarely visited by its inhabitants', writes Kevin Lynch, but 'the survival of these unvisited, hearsay settings conveys a sense of security and continuity.'[39]

Those who lack links with a place must forge an identity through other pasts. Immigrants cut off from their roots remain dislocated; discontinuity impels many who grow up in pioneer lands either to exaggerate attachments to romanticized homelands or stridently to assert an adoptive belonging. Wallace Stegner's history-starved boyhood on a frontier prairie was assuaged only by emotional ties with his ancestral but never-visited Norway.[40] 'Of all the bewildering things about a new country', in Willa Cather's words, 'the absence of human landmarks is one of the most depressing and disheartening.'[41]

Portable emblems of the past can lend continuity to new homes. Forced out of their ancient homeland, the East African Masai 'took with them the names of their hills, plains and rivers and gave them to the hills, plains and rivers in the new country, carrying their cut roots with them as a medicine'.[42] Those who sunder home ties often furnish new landscapes with replicas of scenes left behind. Azoreans reproduce in Toronto the flagstoned patios, wine cellars, and household saints of their island homelands; English suburb and High Street features embellish towns in Australia and Ontario, Hong Kong and Barbados; an Indian's homesickness in London is mitigated by familiar street furniture – the imperial British having previously imported it into India to add substance to their own remembrances.[43]

---

[35] Meerloo, *Two Faces of Man*, pp. 80–1; Pascal, *Design and Truth in Autobiography*, pp. 43–52. See Chapter 5, p. 197 below.

[36] August Heckscher, *The Individual and the Mass* (1965), quoted in Brett, *Parameters and Images*, p. 140.

[37] Tindall, *Fields Beneath*, p. 212.   [38] Santmyer, *Ohio Town*, pp. 307, 50.

[39] *What Time Is This Place?* p. 40.

[40] Stegner, *Wolf Willow*, p. 112. On pioneer nostalgia for the home country, see Blegen, 'Singing immigrants and pioneers', and my 'Pioneer landscape', p. 5.

[41] *O Pioneers!* p. 19.   [42] Dinesen, *Out of Africa*, p. 402.

[43] Holdsworth, 'Natives vs. newcomers'; Lynch, *What Time Is This Place?* p. 39.

Keepsakes also substitute for abandoned landscapes. Loading their jalopies for the trek to California, Steinbeck's uprooted Okies are told there is no room for such souvenirs as letters and old hats and china dogs, but knowing 'how the past would cry to them in the coming days . . . "How will we know it's us without our past?"' they refuse to leave them behind.[44] The elderly especially need mementoes and memories to redeem their loss of familiar places they can no longer even revisit. Many an old person, reduced in status and resources, 'makes frequent trips to the past' to validate himself in his own eyes, saying in effect: 'I was a strong, competent, beloved person once – therefore I am still a worthwhile person.'[45]

Photographs also serve as surrogates for roots. Abruptly severed from customary pasts, Americans and Japanese are notorious for embalming every passing moment in a snapshot, commemoration today in some measure compensating for dissociation from yesterday.[46] Most Britons, too, would be harder hit by the loss of family photographs than of jewellery or clothes or books; almost half those recently questioned treasured their photos above everything else.[47]

Possession of valued relics likewise enhances life. From Renaissance papal princes who amassed classical sculptures to modern treasure hunters avid for old coins, the passion for antiquities has been fuelled by the desire to own them. To have a piece of tangible history links one with its original maker and with intervening owners, augmenting one's own worth. An American in a John Cheever story gloats over his inherited antique lowboy 'as a kind of family crest, something that would vouch for the richness of his past and authenticate his descent from the most aristocratic of the seventeenth-century settlers'.[48] Many collectors expropriate without compunction relics quite unrelated to their own past. From the ruins of Palmyra Robert Wood 'carried off the marbles wherever it was possible', and had the hardihood to complain that 'the avarice or superstition of the inhabitants made that task difficult – sometimes impracticable'.[49] Carrying off fragments of Melrose Abbey for his own 'Gothic shrine', Walter Scott exulted in the 'treasures . . . hidden in that glorious old pile' as 'a famous place for antiquarian plunder. There are such rich bits of old-time sculpture for the architect, and old-time story for the poet. There is as rare picking in it as in a Stilton cheese, and in the same taste – the mouldier the better.'[50] Digging for antiquities at Saqqara in the 1870s, Amelia Edwards expressed remorse at participating in plunder, but

we soon became quite hardened to such sights, and learned to rummage among dusty sepulchres with no more compunction than would have befitted a gang of professional body-snatchers . . . So infectious is the universal callousness, and so overmastering is the passion for relic-hunting, that I do not doubt we should again do the same things under the same circumstances.[51]

---

[44] *Grapes of Wrath*, pp. 76, 79. See H. B. Green, 'Temporal stages in the development of self'.
[45] Kastenbaum, 'Time, death and ritual in old age', pp. 26–7. See Rowles, 'Place and personal identity in old age', p. 307. But Brennan and Steinberg doubt that reminiscence increases among the elderly, and claim that only a small proportion of such reminiscences express satisfaction with the past ('Is reminiscence adaptive?' p. 107).
[46] Sontag, *On Photography*, p. 10.   [47] Gallup survey, reported in *New Society*, 8 Sept. 1983, p. 358.
[48] 'The lowboy', p. 406.
[49] *Ruins of Palmyra* (1753), p. 2.   [50] Quoted in Irving, *Abbotsford and Newstead Abbey* (1835), p. 31.
[51] Edwards, *A Thousand Miles Up the Nile*, p. 51.

One French scholar termed the collector's desire for tangible relics 'a passion so violent that it is inferior to love or ambition only in the pettiness of its aims'.[52]

Historians not uncommonly covet – and sometimes acquire – the archives they research, though few exhibit the possessive greed of a Connecticut chronicler who culled what he wanted from his town's oldest newspapers and then burned them. 'The history of the Town of Bethel is my own personal business', he told other residents hunting data for the bicentenary. 'It's all mine now. Why should I tell you or anybody else? A man has a right to what is his.'[53]

To own a piece of the past can promote a fruitful connection with it. 'When I think of my own fierce joy on acquiring a Roman coin at the age of 15, and my frenzied researches into the dim, fourth-century emperor portrayed on it', Auberon Waugh recalls, 'there can be no doubt in my mind that it served a far more useful purpose than it would in the county museum.'[54] As honorary curator of one such museum, John Fowles defended public access to Dorset's fossiliferous cliffs, for 'what they pick up and take home and think about from time to time is a little bit of the poetry of evolution', a value overriding the protective tenets of 'vigilante fossil wardens'.[55]

To own the past today has become both a national crusade – the restitution of artifacts and archives felt integral to the cultural heritage (see Chapter 6), and a private goal – taking possession of our own personal history. A black youngster researching his past exemplifies the current zest for possession:

'I'm checkin' out my grandfather! I want to know everything there is to know about that ol' dude! Who he is, where he came from, what he used to eat for breakfast – the whole number, dig?'
'Why don't you just call him up and ask him?'
'Cause it's something I have to do on my *own*, man!'[56]

Awareness of history likewise enhances communal and national identity, legitimating a people in their own eyes. 'A collectivity has its roots in the past', in Simone Weil's phrase. 'We possess no other life, no other living sap, than the treasures stored up from the past and digested, assimilated, and created afresh by us.'[57] Groups lacking a sense of their own past are like individuals who know nothing of their parents. Parallels between personal and national identity, a powerful stimulus to early nineteenth-century European nationalism, culminated a century later in Max Dvorak's association of cherished family icons and heirlooms with the need to preserve national historic monuments.[58]

Identification with a national past often serves as an assurance of worth against subjugation or bolsters a new sovereignty. Peoples deprived by conquest of their proper past strive hard to retrieve its validating comforts. The loss of Welsh history 'hath eclipsed our Power, and corrupted our Language, and almost blotted us out of the Books of Records', lamented a late seventeenth-century chronicler; to mitigate these calamities,

---

[52] Quoted in Fagan, *Rape of the Nile*, p. 252.
[53] 'Chief has corner on town history', *N.Y. Times*, 18 July 1958, p. 4.
[54] 'A matter of judgment', *New Statesman*, 17 Aug. 1973, p. 220.
[55] 'Fowles defends fossil collectors', *The Times*, 10 Sept. 1982, p. 6.
[56] Garry B. Trudeau, 'Doonesbury', *IHT*, 10 Mar. 1977.   [57] Weil, *Need for Roots*, pp. 8, 51.
[58] Dvorak, *Katechismus der Denkmalpflege* (1916), cited in Rowntree and Conkey, 'Symbolism and the cultural landscape', pp. 470–1; Breitling, 'Origins and development of a conservation philosophy in Austria', pp. 54–5; Gutman, 'Whatever happened to history?' p. 554.

4 Securing a national symbol: Market Square, Old Town, Warsaw, after Nazi destruction, 1944 (J. Bułhak)

5 Securing a national symbol: Market Square, Old Town, Warsaw, after Polish reconstruction, 1970 (T. Hermanczyk)

scribes and antiquaries salvaged all they could of Welsh family lore and learning – lending credence to Vanbrugh's disparaging stereotype of Wales as 'a Country in the World's back-side, where every Man is born a Gentleman, and a Genealogist'.[59] Nineteenth-century Irish unearthed traditional forms to disprove English slurs that they were uncivilized savages; resurgent twentieth-century Turks conquered their past, as they had conquered their neighbours, so that it would appropriately reflect their title to present greatness.[60] Threatened states zealously guard the physical legacy felt to embody enduring communal identity. Rather than see their city destroyed, the Carthaginians beseeched their Roman conquerers to kill them all.[61] Saracen, Tudor, and Communard iconoclasts aimed to uproot the tangible emblems of enemy spirit. The Nazis sacked historic Warsaw to cripple the will of the Poles, who quickly rebuilt the medieval centre exactly as it had been; 'it was our duty to resuscitate it', explained the conservation chief. 'We did not want a new city ... We wanted the Warsaw of our day and that of the future to continue the ancient tradition.'[62] Many governments today nationalize their nations' past, outlawing pillage or excavation by foreign archaeologists and collectors and demanding the return of heritage previously taken as booty, sold, or simply stolen.

The past plays a paramount role in Icelandic national identity, where individual and communal roots intertwine to make history all-pervasive. Icelanders seem to feel that 'if they don't talk about their past they will have no future', a recent visitor remarked; 'their history is their identity'.[63]

Guidance

The past is most characteristically invoked for the lessons it teaches. The idea that the past can teach the present dates back to the dawn of written history and animates much of it. The Greeks thought history a useful guide because the rhythm of its changes implied the regular repetition of events. Study of the past might enable men to foretell, if not to forestall, the future. Thus Procopius wrote to warn 'future tyrants ... that retribution for their evil deeds will overtake them' and to console those who suffered injustice at their hands; they could at least learn from past example how to bear steadfastly the reverses of fortune.[64] During the Renaissance, historical episodes of virtue and vice likewise illustrated timeless truths, effective exhortations for right conduct and action. Scholars who sought classical sources had no doubt they would bear on present concerns; indeed, that was the main reason for seeking them. 'For about two centuries', concludes Myron Gilmore, the 'humanist tradition combine[d] a deeper historical knowledge of the classical past with an undiminished confidence in the relevance of lessons of that past.'[65]

---

[59] Thomas Jones, *The British Language in Its Lustre* (1688), quoted in Morgan, 'From a death to a view: the hunt for the Welsh past in the Romantic period', p. 45; Vanbrugh, *Aesop* (c. 1697), Pt I, Act 3, 2:33.

[60] Sheehy, *Rediscovery of Ireland's Past*; Alp, 'Reconstitution of Turkish history', p. 211.

[61] Appian, 'Punic Wars', in his *Roman History*, Bk 8, Pt I, Ch. 12, 1:545.

[62] Lorentz, 'Reconstruction of the old town centers of Poland', pp. 46–7. See also *idem*, 'Protection of monuments', p. 420.

[63] Stephen Klaidman, 'Iceland, where the past is prologue', *IHT*, 17 Feb. 1981, p. 4.

[64] Collingwood, *Idea of History*, pp. 24, 35–6; Fornara, *Nature of History in Ancient Greece and Rome*, pp. 106–15, quotation on p. 122. The Hittites used history in a similar admonitory fashion (Van Seters, *In Search of History*, pp. 114–17).

[65] *Humanists and Jurists*, p. 37.

Increasing scope and more rigorous techniques strengthened history's claims to teach useful lessons. Faith in the exemplary use of the past remained widespread through the eighteenth century, as Charles Duclos attested:

The usefulness of history . . . is a truth too generally receiv'd to stand in need of proof . . . The theatre of the world supplies only a limited number of scenes, which follow one another in perpetual succession. In seeing the same mistakes to be regularly follow'd by the same misfortunes, 'tis reasonable to imagine, that if the former had been known, the latter would have been avoided.[66]

Knowing the follies (if not the wisdom) of the past, men might not only foretell but partly determine the future. Those who treated history as exemplary understood the past much as they did the present. 'Mankind are so much the same, in all times and places, that history informs us of nothing new or strange in this particular', stated Hume. 'Its chief use is only to discover the constant and universal principles of human nature.'[67]

The high value of lessons based on such principles continued to suffuse European thought through the nineteenth century. 'Those who cannot remember the past are condemned to repeat it'[68] was one of scores of similar aphorisms. History taught morals, manners, prudence, patriotism, statecraft, virtue, religion, wisdom. 'Knowledge of history helped one to rise in the world, and knowledge of God's providence in history solaced', in F. S. Fussner's words.[69] Such guidance transcended the merely practical; it was also morally elevating. Like pilgrimages to the relics of antiquity, the study of history improved the character and inspired patriotism. Notwithstanding the manifest gulf between the industrial age and earlier times, supposed analogies with Romans, Greeks, and the Middle Ages stimulated classical and Gothic revivals in all the arts.

The kind of guidance the past provided, however, underwent a major shift. Men of the eighteenth century assumed the past to be so similar to the present that classical models exemplified eternal virtues: they saw antiquity's honour, patriotism, stoicism mirrored in their own times. In the nineteenth century, growing awareness of the past's diversity and dissimilarity from the present tempered its authority. But even when history ceased to provide explicit precedents or moral exemplars, parallels between past and present remained instructive.

Popular history today continues to apply past solutions to present difficulties. And even to professionals whom history no longer teaches lessons, it still teaches some things – that nothing lasts forever; that nothing is wholly predetermined; and that 'one of the more effective ways of inhabiting the present', in Edward Mendelson's phrase, 'is to learn how the past made it what it is'.[70] If it is no longer a model it remains a guide; if it cannot tell us what we should do it tells us what we might do; if it provides no specific precedents it still prefigures the present.

Enrichment

A well-loved past enriches the world around us. 'The present when backed by the past is a thousand times deeper than the present when it presses so close that you can feel nothing

---

[66] *History of Louis XI* (1745), 1:ii. I have slightly pruned Duclos's own translation.
[67] *Enquiry Concerning Human Understanding* (1748), sect. 8, Pt I, 4:68.
[68] Santayana, *Life of Reason* (1905), 1:284. [69] *Historical Revolution*, p. 59.
[70] 'Post-modern vanguard', *London Review of Books*, 3–16 Sept. 1981, p. 10.

else', writes Virginia Woolf.[71] Unlike America where 'the soil is not humanized enough to be interesting', in Oliver Wendell Holmes's comparison, 'in England so much of it has been trodden by English feet [and] has been itself a part of preceding generations of human beings, that it is in a kind of dumb sympathy with' its present occupants.[72] Even ghosts 'took their place by the family hearth', Hawthorne observed, 'making this life now passing more dense . . . by adding all the substance of their own to it'.[73] A day spent in a thirteenth-century house, his own tread hollowing the floors and his own touch polishing the oak, made Henry James feel that he had shared its six hundred years of life.[74]

The saturations of time made rooted old Ireland seem a far richer landscape than the English Pale, perched in its thin and isolated present. 'Those O'Connells, O'Connors, O'Callaghans, O'Donoghues – all the Gaels – were one . . . with the very landscape itself', writes their chronicler.

To run off the family names . . . was to call to vision certain districts – hills, rivers and plains; while contrariwise, to recollect the place-names in certain regions was to remember the ancient tribes and their memorable deeds. How different it was with the [English] Planters round about them. For them, all that Gaelic background of myth, literature and history had no existence . . . The landscape they looked upon was indeed but rocks and stones and trees.[75]

Norman peasants likewise infuse their locales with family history; every field and path recall some event, whereas immigrants without such memories inhabit only a meagre, monochrome present.[76]

The past lengthens life's reach by linking us with events and people prior to ourselves. Paradoxically, we are enriched by what underscores the brevity of our own span: living in an old house, communing with musuem relics, wandering in an ancient city imbues life with longevity. Rome's antiquity gives 'a perception of such weight and density in a by-gone life . . . that the present moment is pressed down or crowded out', Hawthorne observed. 'Side by side with the massiveness of the Roman Past, all matters, that we handle or dream of, now-a-days, look evanescent.'[77] We also enrich life by stretching present feelings backwards, like Benjamin Constant's lovers who strengthen their mutual devotion in asserting they have *always* loved each other.[78] To project present experience back magnifies it; to evoke the past makes it over as our own.

Sensory recall likewise enhances the present. Contemplating her treasured antiques, Henry James's Mrs Gereth feels that

everything was in the air – every history of every find, every circumstance of every struggle . . . old golds and brasses, old ivories and bronzes, the fresh old tapestries and deep old damasks threw out a radiance in which the poor woman saw in solution all her old loves and patiences, all her old tricks and triumphs.[79]

---

[71] *Moments of Being*, p. 98.   [72] *Our Hundred Days in Europe*, pp. 288–9.
[73] *Doctor Grimshawe's Secret*, p. 230.
[74] *English Hours*, pp. 145–6.   [75] Corkery, *Hidden Ireland*, pp. 64–6.
[76] L. Bernot and R. Blanchard, *Nouville, un village français* (1953), cited in Fraisse, *Psychology of Time*, pp. 169–70.
[77] *Marble Faun*, p. 6.
[78] Constant, *Adolphe* (1816), pp. 64–5. See Poulet, *Studies in Human Time*, pp. 205–22. We require apprehension of the 'antiquity' of each new love (Loewald, *Psychoanalysis and the History of the Individual*, pp. 29–51).
[79] *Spoils of Poynton*, p. 43.

Celebrating the pleasures of recollection, Proust's Marcel compares his present personality 'to an abandoned quarry ... from which memory, selecting here and there, can, like some Greek sculptor, extract innumerable different statues'.[80]

The treasures of the past can be literally as well as figuratively enriching. Supposedly therapeutic ingredients long made mummies merchandise; ancient Chinese bronzes, their potency a function of their age, protected owners against evil spirits. Today's collectors acquire antiques as investments, and anything old is turned to profit. 'People of the 18th and 19th centuries enrich our lives today', as the Early American Society advertises, partly because their residues have become modern riches.[81]

Escape

Besides enhancing an acceptable present, the past offers alternatives to an unacceptable present. In yesterday we find what we miss today. And yesterday is a time for which we have no responsibility and when no one can answer back.

Some prefer to live permanently in the past; others elect to visit it only occasionally. Even if today is rewarding and the past no golden age, historical immersion can alleviate contemporary stress. 'Come to Williamsburg ... Spend some time in gaol', urges an advertisement showing tourists grinning in the eighteenth-century stocks: 'it will set you free' – free from day-to-day cares in the workaday present. A desire to escape for a time from the tyranny of the modern lock-step world of digital watches and computers, to slacken the pace of life and regain a sense of rootedness, Jay Anderson finds, spurs weekend warriors and living-history re-enactors to engage in medieval revels or Civil War encampments.[82]

Arcadian dreams have ancient antecedents, but only after the eighteenth century did the past become a romantically attractive alternative to the present. As revolutionary change rapidly distanced all known pasts, yearning for what was felt to be lost suffused European imaginations. 'Drawn to history because he found in the past, in the study of huge folios and long dead chroniclers, much of the peace he could not get in contemplating the shifting scene of the present', Robert Southey typified early nineteenth-century feeling.[83] Re-created in verisimilar detail by novelists and painters, historians and architects, the past seemed a real and vivid alternative. Paintings of timeless rustic scenes offered respite from belching chimneys and huddled tenements.[84] In art or in actual landscape, many sought out relic islands of epochs encapsulated from modern progress.[85] Places that lagged behind the modern mainstream, half-forgotten enclaves of bygone worlds, retained the flavour of Thomas Hardy's 'street for a medievalist to revel in', where 'smells direct from the sixteenth century hung in the air in all their original integrity and without a modern taint'.[86] That taint was not easy to avoid even in Venice, Ruskin grumbled. 'Modern work has set its plague spot everywhere – the moment you begin to feel' that you have truly

[80] *Remembrance of Things Past*, 3:921.
[81] *Smithsonian*, 6:6 (1975), 110. See Michael Thompson, *Rubbish Theory*; Fagan, *Rape of the Nile*, pp. 44–7; David, *Chinese Connoisseurship*, p. 12.
[82] *Time Machines*, pp. 183–5.   [83] Peardon, *Transition in English Historical Writing*, p. 244.
[84] Gaunt, *Bandits in a Landscape*, p. 178.
[85] For example, Pater, *Marius the Epicurean* (1885), 1:109.   [86] *A Laodicean* (1881), 3:202.

escaped to the past, 'some gaspipe business forces itself upon the eye, and you are thrust into the 19th century; . . . your very gondola has become a steamer'.[87]

By the mid twentieth century, the sociologist Maurice Halbwachs termed such islands of the past desirable refuges from the pressures of modernizing change.[88] Provincial backwaters still offer such sanctuaries: club life in Hong Kong and Singapore attracts modern visitors as turn-of-the-century in dress and demeanour. Australians 'don't look like the British of today; more like the British looked two hundred years ago' or like the gnarled codgers in Victorian numbers of *Punch*. And when 'an English nanny-type' in Sydney brought the morning coffee on a silver salver, a journalist marvelled that 'these delightful dodos, extinct in England, [were] still extant in the former colonies'.[89]

The charm of these anachronistic places – and their fidelity to the past whose aura they convey – depends on unawareness. Their inhabitants are not moderns being quaint, but ordinary people leading normal lives. Once their datedness is widely enjoyed, such locales lose their authenticity and become period stage sets: 'primitive' places where one could formerly step back in time now purvey the past self-consciously. 'Fifteen years ago I could go into any muddy village in the Near East and step backward in time', remarked an art curator in 1970; 'today, in the tiniest Turkish town, you walk into the local merchant's and see tacked to the wall a list of Auction prices current issued by Sotheby's-Parke Bernet.'[90]

Even a contrived past, however, may alleviate rapid or dislocating change. Rest cures in historically frozen Amish villages or in the simulated past of Williamsburg and Mystic Seaport might be antidotes to the frenzy of modern life, where 'individuals who need or want a more relaxed, less stimulating existence should be able to find it', Alvin Toffler proposes. 'The communities must be consciously encapsulated, selectively cut off from the surrounding society . . . Men and women who want a slower life, might actually make a career out of "being" Shakespeare or Ben Franklin or Napoleon – not merely acting out their parts on stage, but living, eating, sleeping, as they did.'[91] Many Americans already visit historyland so habitually as to confirm Stephen Spender's charge of treating 'history as though it were geography, themselves as though they could step out of the present into the past of their choice'.[92]

Historical enclaves hold out further benefits. Just as we maintain genetic stocks of early plants and animals, so 'banks' of past ways of life might 'increase the chances that someone will be there to pick up the pieces in case of massive calamities'. Thus Robert Graves's fictional Scottish islanders and Catalans reproduce Bronze and early Iron Age conditions in a new 'ancient' community in Crete, sealed off for three generations from the rest of the world, so as ultimately to redeem modern civilization.[93]

Exotically remote ancient Greece and medieval Britain were the main loci of Victorian imaginative escape; our own escapist pasts are more often located in grandparental or great-grandparental times, 'far enough away to seem a strange country, yet close enough at

[87] Ruskin to his father, 14 Sept. 1845, in *Ruskin in Italy*, p. 201.   [88] *Collective Memory*, pp. 66–7, 135.
[89] Peregrine Worsthorne, 'Home thoughts from Down Under', *Sunday Telegraph*, 25 Feb. 1979, pp. 8–9. As 'refuges for those bewildered by the normal pace of change', certain 'backward regions' might be systematically retarded by delaying the transmission of innovations (Lynch, *What Time Is This Place?* pp. 77–8).
[90] Cornelius Clarkson Vermuele III, quoted in Karl Meyer, *Plundered Past*, p. 57.
[91] Toffler, *Future Shock*, pp. 353–4.
[92] *Love–Hate Relations*, p. 121.   [93] *Seven Days in New Crete*, pp. 41–2.

times to bring a tear to the eye'.[94] Many historical novels re-create eras of sixty to a hundred years ago, beyond the reach of our own memory but still intimately connected with people and places we hold dear. Reconstructed Stonefield, Wisconsin, remained always seventy-five years old, in a time 'which hasn't yet become dim, where the past can "merge into the present"'.[95]

One charm of a past of that vintage is that it barely antedates ourselves. 'The time just before our own entrance into the world is bound to be peculiarly fascinating to us; if we could understand it, we might be able to explain our parents, and hence come closer to persuading ourselves that we know why we are here.'[96] The nearer past often seems too close for comfort: it is too much bound up with our parents and our early childhood. (How attitudes toward parents bear on attitudes toward the historical past is explored at the end of this chapter.) Parents so impinge on our lives that their past may feel admonitory; grandparents are relatively impotent and their times less constraining. Out-of-date parents annoy and embarrass us, but grandparents are *supposed* to be *passé*: their world survives less in our minds than in their mementoes.[97] That is why it often seems quaintly anachronistic – a charming, touching, funny past beyond our view and yet under our own control.

James Laver's characterization of dress styles exemplifies preferences for the not-too-recent past. Clothes a year old are termed 'dowdy', those of ten and twenty years back 'hideous' or 'ridiculous', but fashions are 'amusing' at thirty, 'quaint' at fifty, 'charming' at seventy, 'romantic' at one hundred, and 'beautiful' one hundred and fifty years after their time. Before most old things can be properly appreciated, they must outlive a 'black patch of bad taste' often associated with parental times.[98] Nostalgia for the 1950s and 1960s notwithstanding, we display an uneasy ambivalence toward the recent past.

These various benefits frequently dovetail. For example, in contemporary American building design the past simultaneously justifies the present and suggests a refuge from it. Tradition sanctifies countless innovations in architectural decor: pedestrianized shopping enclaves, high-rise condominiums, 'heritage' villages, communal suburban fortresses supposedly derive from Puritan settlements, Southern plantations, Western missions, pioneer encampments. Yet their emblematic heritage also panders to dreams of escape from the shoddiness of modern building and the stress of modern milieux. And though 'the past way of life beckons to us with its harmony of scale, its variety of style, its closely built urban streets, its rich antiquity', few want to live in it wholly; instead they seek an up-to-date mix of past and present.[99]

The benefits the past confers vary with epoch, culture, individual, and stage of life. Different pasts – classical or medieval, national or ethnic – suit different purposes. Once morally instructive, the past has become a source of sensate pleasure. But most of the

---

[94] Oliver Jensen, *America's Yesterdays*, p. 11.

[95] Sivesind, 'Historic interiors in Wisconsin', p. 76. The purpose was to 'avoid the "discontinuity" which Lowenthal criticized' (in 'American way of history' (1966), pp. 31–2).

[96] Robert B. Shaw, 'The world in a very small space' (review of Cheever, *Stories*, q.v.), *The Nation*, 23 Dec. 1978, p. 706.

[97] Jervis Anderson, 'Sources', p. 112.   [98] Laver, *Taste and Fashion*, pp. 202, 208.

[99] Ziegler, *Historic Preservation in Inner City Areas*, p. 16.

benefits discussed above remain viable in some context. More than for any functional use, we treasure the old things in our homes for the pastness inherent in them; they reflect ancestral inheritance, recall former friends and occasions, and link past with future generations.[100]

VALUED ATTRIBUTES

Just wait until now becomes then. You'll see how happy we were.

Susan Sontag, 'Unguided tour'[101]

What traits of the past make it beneficial? What aspects of bygone times enable us to confirm and enhance identity, to acquire and sustain roots, to enrich life and environment, to validate or to escape from an otherwise overbearing present? Every part of a legacy benefits each inheritor in different ways. Enumerating the legatees and legacies of classical antiquity, George Steiner notes that the Greeks were

to Cicero and his successors, ... the incomparable begetters of philosophy, of the plastic arts, of the cultivation of poetic and speculative speech; ... to the Florentine Renaissance, ... the abiding model of spiritual, aesthetic, and even political excellence and experience; ... [to] the Enlightenment ... the architecture of Monticello and of the porticoes of our public edifices, ... the canonic source of beauty itself; ... [to] the modern imagination, ... the archaic, the Dionysian Hellas, with its ecstatic immediacy to the divine ... [and to Freud's] mapping of the unconscious.[102]

This list of particulars embraces a wide range of historical connotations. It is not, however, translatable into general traits – traits that would reckon not only with the perceived virtues of ancient Greece but also those of Rome, the Middle Ages, the Renaissance, and every epoch's more recent precursors, and with the bewildering diversity of individual as well as collective heritages.

No one to my knowledge has ever categorized the traits that make the past generally beneficial. Indeed, historical, cultural, and personal variables vitiate any such attempt. But the presumed benefits of the past discussed above none the less presuppose that such traits exist, even if barely articulated.

Four traits seem to me especially to distinguish the past from the present and the future, and to account for its principal advantages: I term them antiquity, continuity, termination, and sequence. As with the benefits the past confers, these ascribed traits comprise a heterogeneous array labelled here solely for heuristic and exploratory purposes.

Antiquity

'I just love history: it's ... it's so *old*.'[103] The American appreciating England's past typifies the gushing vagueness already shown to characterize tastes for antiquity. Antiquity's chief use is to root credentials in the past. Nations and individuals habitually trace

---

[100] Csikszentmihalyi and Rochberg-Halton, *Meaning of Things*, based on a 1977 survey of 82 families in northern Chicago.

[101] *New Yorker*, 31 Oct. 1977, p. 42.

[102] George Steiner, 'Where burning Sappho loved and sung', p. 115 (review of Jenkyns, *Victorians and Ancient Greece*), *New Yorker*, 9 Feb. 1981, p. 115.

[103] Quoted in Thompson, *Rubbish Theory*, p. 57.

back their ancestry, institutions, culture, ideals to validate claims to power, prestige, and property. Ancestral possession makes things ours; it is from forebears that we inherit.

Antiquity is, however, a more complex concept than any such listing can suggest. It involves at least four distinct qualities: precedence, remoteness, the primordial, and the primitive, each of which embodies particular antiquarian virtues.

Precedence evinces the concern to demonstrate a heritage, a lineage, a claim that antedates others: the competitive ducal pedigree, the Piltdown forgery, the ethnic French in Manitoba who claim linguistic rights because 'we were here as a nation before there was a Manitoba'.[104] Precedence makes many things precious: anything that was here before us gains status by virtue of its antecedence. 'These trees are older than I am and I can't help feeling that makes them wiser', writes a chronicler of England's New Forest.[105] That trees are 'natural' lends their antiquity further cachet.

Remoteness is another quality that commends antiquity, the 'so *old*' of the American tourist for whose countrymen, a British observer comments, 'it must be an embarrassment to possess a national history less than five centuries old'.[106] Sheer age lends romance to times gone by, and 'the more remote were these times', in Chateaubriand's words, 'the more magical they appeared'.[107] The older past has a status that later periods cannot match. It has proved hard to protect the *belle époque* architecture of Montreux, built with the opening of the Simplon tunnel, because elderly city fathers 'think that something from 1900 is no more valuable than something brand-new'.[108]

Sheer inaccessibility enhances the mystique of the very ancient past. Wordsworth's 'secrets older than the flood' and Shelley's 'thrilling secrets of the birth of time' express fascination with times hidden because so distant.[109] Remoteness also purifies, shifting the older past from the personal to the communal realm, like Japanese forebears who lose individuality some thirty-three years after death and merge indistinguishably with the whole ancestral community.[110] Distance purges the past of personal attachments and makes it an object of universal veneration, lending the remote a majesty and dignity absent from the homely, intimate good old days just gone.

How long ago 'remote' is depends on the context. Household artifacts that date back only a generation or two are often treasured for being ancient: 'It is very old', an American says proudly of her wicker armchair. 'It was given to me as a present by one of the oldest black families.' That such things have survived without damage is one reason for pride in their longevity, for it attests the owner's ability to protect things against the tooth of time. 'My grandmother brought [this cup] back from Newfoundland when she went back home

[104] Gilberte Proteau, quoted in Michael T. Kaufman, 'Ethnic French give Manitoba a language test', *IHT*, 3 Nov. 1982, p. 4.
[105] Peter Tate, *New Forest*, p. 14.
[106] Stephen Toulmin, 'The myth of the dinosaurs', *Punch*, 18 Aug. 1965, p. 224.
[107] *Genius of Christianity* (1802), Pt 3, Bk 1, Ch. 8, p. 385. See W. K. Ferguson, *Renaissance in Historical Thought*, p. 121.
[108] Jean-Pierre Dresco, cited in Calla Corner, 'Saving Montreux's belle époque heritage', *IHT*, 1 Nov. 1977, p. 14.
[109] Wordsworth, 'To enterprise' (1832), variant line 84, 2:283; Shelley, *Alastor* (1815), line 128, 2:48.
[110] Takeda, 'Recent trends in studies of ancestor worship in Japan', p. 136.

there on a trip 65–70 years ago. That's how long I've had it, and it's not even cracked. It's so old . . . I'm kind of proud that I've still got it.'[111]

From Vasari on, 'ancient' has been preferred to 'old' in the sense of preceding history, partaking of nature rather than culture.[112] 'New' countries like the United States and Australia compensate for relatively recent human histories by celebrating their prehistoric natural heritage and by inordinate attachment to dinosaurs and sequoias. Thoreau favoured the truly ancient over the merely old; the historical past seemed degenerate, primitive nature strong, pure, and free.[113] Many nineteenth-century Americans considered the primeval wilderness morally superior to historical scenes. They preferred a 'hoary oak' to a 'mouldering column' and contrasted Europe's 'temples which Roman robbers have reared' and 'towers in which feudal oppression has fortified itself' with their own 'deep forests which the eye of God has alone pervaded. What is the echo of roofs that a few centuries since rung with barbaric revels . . . to the silence which has reigned in these dim groves since the first Creation?'[114] Florida's sunset shores struck Henry James as older than the Nile, *previous* to any other scene, 'with the impression of History all yet to be made'.[115] Geological antiquity is still a source of American pride: witness the selection of Yellowstone National Park as a World Heritage site for its 'ancient volcanic remnants . . . with roots going back to Eocene time'.[116] All traces of seventeenth- and eighteenth-century cultivation were expunged from a new national park in the Virgin Islands so as to restore a 'wilderness' landscape.[117]

Australians with an even briefer recorded history are also solaced by natural antiquity, the unrecorded aeons of animals, plants, and rocks adding length to the meagre European past. Australian fiction, poetry, and painting emphasize this awesome antiquity.[118] Patrick White's novels convey the feeling of a primeval Australia larger because older than life; Rosemary Dobson's and Kenneth Slessor's poetic use of Greek legend lends Sydney a Mediterranean sense of history.[119] Analogies between Burke and Wills's Australian desert and early Christian landscapes, emphasized by 'Biblical' camels, imbue Sidney Nolan's Australian scene with Old World legend; the religious theme and landscapes suggestive of ancient walled cities antiquate the ill-fated Burke–Wills expedition by two millennia.[120]

Nolan's lengthening of Australian time resembles Wilson Harris's Guyanese jungle myths that create an antecedent historical framework for the Caribbean. Rejecting their colonial past as a dismal saga of slavery and exploitation, some West Indians seek a prior source of prideful identity in prehistory.[121] But West Indians look for their ancestral past among autochthonous Indian and African peoples more than in landscape, whereas Australians find roots in nature, not in aboriginal man. Indeed, nature's superior antiquity gives it a status that transcends any prehistoric artifacts. To see that living fossil, the

---

[111] Csikszentmihalyi and Rochberg-Halton, *Meaning of Things*, pp. 60, 82.
[112] Vasari, *Lives of the Artists*, 1:17.
[113] *Week on the Concord and Merrimack Rivers* (1849), pp. 55–6.
[114] Hoffman, *Winter in the West* (1835), 1:195–6.
[115] *American Scene* (1907), p. 462.   [116] 'World Heritage List established', p. 14.
[117] Olwig, 'National parks, tourism and the culture of imperialism', p. 246; *idem*, 'National parks, tourism, and local development', pp. 24, 28.
[118] Lowenthal, 'Australian images', p. 86.
[119] Kramer, 'Sense of the past in modern Australian poetry', pp. 24–6.
[120] Joppien, 'Iconography of the Burke and Wills expedition in Australian art', p. 59.
[121] Lowenthal, 'Caribbean region', pp. 62–5.

ginkgo, is to have an awed 'glimpse of Father Time as a boy'; the common horsetail is one of 'Nature's living ancient monuments, whose primeval patina ... is so much more exciting than the heap of stuff up on the Plain ... – Stonehenge ... – that somebody built yesterday.'[122]

The *primordial*, focused on origins rather than on ancientness, reflects a concern with roots, a search for beginnings typified in Alex Haley's quest for his African ancestor Kinte Kunte (see Chapter 5). Most of North America's initial (1979) World Heritage sites were mainly designated for their primordial quality: Canada's L'Anse aux Meadows as the site of the 'first' authenticated European structures in the new World, Mesa Verde as the 'earliest' Indian dwelling.[123] Nor is the cult of origins confined to artifacts: a tendency to seek complete explanations in beginnings and to account for everything in terms of the remotest past long dominated historical studies.[124] The supposed explanatory power of origins likewise led Freud and other analysts to seek the key to human development in so-called primal scenes and to consider original 'archaic' experience as the deepest and truest.[125]

The *primitive* promises a supposed innocence and purity unspoilt by later sophistication. Persuaded that modern technical skills cheapen and corrupt, late eighteenth-century *primitifs* abjured any architecture after the Doric, any literature later than Homer, any sculpture beyond Phidias as mannered, false, and ignoble.[126] The legendary origin of painting – the tracing of a departing lover's shadow on a wall – gave historical priority to the pure neo-classical outline; the linear simplicity of Greek vase painting inspired Flaxman's engravings and sculpture; the Pre-Raphaelites expunged subsequent artifice by reverting to the quattrocento's 'primitive' and 'natural honesty'.[127] Early twentieth-century neo-Romantics claimed kinship with archaic art, whose primary, elemental, unconscious character became a modernist touchstone.[128] An archaeological impulse again dominated the 1970s avant-garde; archaic nature and prehistory inspired many artists at odds with 1960s' formalism and high technology. The affinity of ancient artifacts with contemporary art is held to validate their archetypal appeal.[129]

Aesthetic attachment to prehistoric relics involves several facets of antiquarianism. Displaying ancient relics as works of art implies that they are beautiful *because* primitive.[130] Admiration of antiquity extends beyond the museum to the jewellery shop: stone

[122] Angela Milne, 'Ancient monuments', *Punch*, 8 Aug. 1962, p. 208.

[123] 'World Heritage List established'.

[124] Marc Bloch, *Historian's Craft*, pp. 29–35. 'When we come up to Oxford we never seem to get out of an infinite welter of "origins" and primitive forms of everything' (Frederic Harrison, *Meaning of History*, 1894, p. 134). See Butterfield, *Whig Interpretation of History*, pp. 43–63. A cult of origins still animates historians in quest of prefigurations and anticipations (Foucault, *Archaeology of Knowledge*, pp. 142–4), and curators of historic sites eager to maintain 'it all began here' (Horne, *Great Museum*, p. 113).

[125] Starobinski, 'The inside and the outside', pp. 333–4. [126] Gombrich, 'Dread of corruption', p. 242.

[127] Rosenblum, 'Origin of painting', pp. 283–5; Greenhalgh, *Classical Tradition in Art*, p. 214; Starobinski, *1789: Emblems of Reason*, pp. 142–4.

[128] Howard, 'Definitions and values of archaism and the archaic style'; Rosenblum, *Transformations in Late Eighteenth Century Art*, pp. 140–60; Rubin, 'Modernist primitivism'.

[129] Lippard, *Overlay*, pp. 4–8; Ehrenzweig, *Hidden Order of Art*, p. 77; Varnedoe, 'Contemporary explorations'.

[130] Wollheim, 'Preface' to Stokes, *Invitation in Art*, p. xxviii.

6 Lure of the primitive: Joseph-Benoit Suvée, *The Invention of Drawing*, 1791

7 Lure of the primitive: John Flaxman, 'Agamemnon and Cassandra', *Compositions from the Tragedies of Aeschylus*, 1795

arrowheads, blades, awls, and microliths from the Sahara, 'relics of man's remotest past' set in gold and diamond brooches and cufflinks, are advertised in a 1973 Garrard brochure as 'mute testimony of the dawn of man's striving to derive aesthetic pleasure from his own handiwork ... each painstakingly formed with a lost expertise'. Here all the virtues of antiquity converge: great age, uniqueness, scarcity, ancient skills, nonrecoverable techniques, and the assumptions that primitive man lived in harmony with nature, treated technology and art as one, and made everything for both use and beauty. By contrast, today's generally ugly utilitarian objects are seen as sharply differentiated from creations made solely for ornament or display.

Continuity

A Texan historical newsletter bears the title *The Endless Chain*. The phrase stands for continuity, the sense of enduring succession often manifest in historical annals and storied locales. Looking out from a Saxon boundary bank, W. G. Hoskins found it immensely satisfying

to know which of these farms is recorded in Domesday Book, and which came later in date in the great colonisation movement of the thirteenth century; to see on the opposite slopes, with its Georgian stucco shining in the afternoon sun, the house of some impoverished squire whose ancestors settled on that hillside in the time of King John and took their name from it; to know that behind one there lies an ancient estate of a long-vanished abbey where St Boniface had his earliest schooling, and that in front stretches the demesne farm of Anglo-Saxon and Norman kings; to be aware ... that one is part of an immense unbroken stream that has flowed over this scene for more than a thousand years.[131]

The unbroken stream is a peculiarly English virtue. A community of descent connects the earliest with the latest folk, the first with the last artifacts, and with surviving traces of intervening epochs. British Teutonic settlement 'becomes more of a living thing to one who finds', as E. A. Freeman did, 'that the boundary of the land which Ceawlin won from the Briton abides, after thirteen hundred years, the boundary of his own parish and his own fields'.[132] Hardly another country, claimed a celebrant of British royal tradition in 1937, 'has succeeded in so continually adapting its medieval institutions as to avoid their complete overthrow or their entire reconstruction'.[133]

English travellers likewise delight in palimpsests abroad. In Crete, Rose Macaulay enjoyed 'seeing the Achaean culture imposed on the last Minoan, the Dorian on the Achaean, the Roman on the Hellenic, the Byzantine on the Roman, then the Saracen, the Venetian, the Turkish, and the Cretan of to-day'. And at Morea, Arcadia, and Messenia the 'superimposition of medieval on ancient, modern on medieval, ... great Frankish castles thrust up on craggy heights from Byzantine or classical foundations' left a marvellous mosaic of 'the ghosts of dead ages sleeping together'.[134]

Continuity is most potent when subsequent artifacts reflect surviving relics. Six centuries of classical and Gothic adaptation and revival, consciously drawing on the forms

[131] Hoskins, *Provincial England*, p. 228.   [132] Freeman, *History of the Norman Conquest of England*, 5:ix–x.
[133] Schramm, *History of the English Coronation*, p. 105. See Cannadine, 'Context, performance and meaning of ritual: the British monarchy and the "invention of tradition"', *c.* 1820–1977', p. 146.
[134] Rose Macaulay, *Pleasure of Ruins*, pp. 113–27.

8 Charms of continuity: Bury St Edmunds, dwellings set into the medieval abbey front

9 Charms of continuity: Avebury, medieval tithe barn athwart prehistoric stone circle

10 Decor of diachrony: Roman wall and interwar house, near Southampton

and motifs of antiquity, give European landscapes a temporal density unmatched in other cultures where an ancient past uncomfortably jostles a modern present. Thus in Egypt 'stand pharaonic temples and concrete apartment houses, and nothing links them', observed Robin Fedden. 'What is missed and missing is the middle distance . . . Saladin is juxtaposed to cinemas, and To-day, having no ancestry, is uncertain of itself'.[135]

Traces of cumulative creation also engender a sense of accretion where each year, each generation, adds more to the scene. Accretion results from temporal asymmetry: the cumulations of time generally surpass its dissolutions, and yield sums greater than their parts. No single member of 'the obscure generations of my own obscure family . . . has left a token of himself behind him', muses Orlando in the ancestral house, 'yet all, working together with their spades and their needles, their love-making and their child-bearing, have left . . . this vast, yet ordered building'.[136] Residues of successive generations in ancient sites betoken partnership, harmony, and order. It is accretion, in particular, that generates the past's enrichment.

Accretions of enduring occupance captivate those from lands that lack them. Hawthorne's American visitor admired an English estate because 'the life of each successive dweller there was eked out with the lives of all who had hitherto lived there'; the past gave life 'length, fulness, body, substance'.[137] Henry James's American enjoys the 'items of duration and evidence, all smoothed with service and charged with accumulated mes-

[135] Fedden, 'Introduction: an anatomy of exile', pp. 9–10. See Tuan, 'Significance of the artifact', p. 470.
[136] Woolf, *Orlando*, p. 69.
[137] *Doctor Grimshawe's Secret*, p. 229.

sages', in his ancestral London house; the very air feels marvellously permeated with antiquity, 'and it seemed, wherever it rested, to have filtered through the bed of history'.[138]

Some benefits of cumulation need no great antiquity, however; a single lifetime may suffice. Coming back to her home town, Santmyer found it

immeasurably richer than when I was a child. It is the added years that make it so: . . . the town is richer by the life of a generation. Since I last stood here with a sled rope in my hand there has been that accretion: the roofs of the town have sheltered an added half-century . . . The humdrum daily life of the generations of mankind . . . has given to the scene that weight and density.[139]

Indeed, the mere contiguity of two distinct pasts may convey accretion, such as the medieval tithe barn athwart Avebury's prehistoric stone circle, the seventeenth-century dwellings hollowed into the west front of Bury St Edmunds's medieval abbey church.[140] A display of Trevelyiana at Wallington is commended for adding 'a distinct nineteenth-century chapter to a seventeenth-century house with an eighteenth-century interior'.[141] Roman and medieval walls in many English towns link on to twentieth-century terraces, merging traces of the past with one another and the present; continuity made diachronic.

Continuity expresses the conjunction of the whole or parts of the past, diachrony the endurance of the past in the present, enriching both: 'the life of the flitting moment, existing in the antique shell of an age gone by', as Hawthorne felt in Rome, 'has a fascination which we do not find in either the past or present, taken by themselves'.[142] And if we could 'join . . . our past and present selves with all their objects', as Adrian Stokes wrote, 'we would feel continually at home'.[143]

Intimate connections of past with present permeated William Maxwell's boyhood home:

When you walked in from outdoors, there were traces everywhere of human occupation: the remains of a teaparty on the wicker teacart in the moss-green and white living room, building blocks or lead soldiers in the middle of the library floor, a book lying face down on the window seat, an unfinished game of solitaire, a piece of cross-stitching with a threaded needle stuck in it, a paintbox and beside it a drinking glass full of cloudy water, flowers in cut-glass vases, fires in both fireplaces in the wintertime, lights left burning in empty rooms because somebody meant to come right back. Traces of being warm, being comfortable, being cozy together. Traces of us.[144]

The living room in Manderley bore similar 'witness to our presence. The little heap of library books marked ready to return, and the discarded copy of *The Times*. Ash-trays, with a stub of a cigarette; cushions, with the imprint of our heads upon them, lolling in the chairs; the charred embers of our log fires still smouldering against the morning.' We all need such a living history, rather than 'a desolate shell . . . with no whisper of the past about its staring walls'.[145] The devotion people lavish on inherited relics bespeaks their need for a living past. Through daily tending of her long-dead husband's shaving kit and

---

[138] *Sense of the Past*, pp. 64–5.   [139] Santmyer, *Ohio Town*, p. 309.
[140] Fedden, 'Problems of conservation', p. 377 (Avebury), and John Harvey, *Conservation of Buildings*, p. 193 (Bury), express opposing views on the propriety of these juxtapositions.
[141] John Cornforth, 'Some problems of decoration and display', *National Trust Newsletter*, No. 4 (Feb. 1969), 6.
[142] *Marble Faun*, p. 229.   [143] *Invitation in Art*, p. 61.   [144] Maxwell, *Ancestors*, p. 191.
[145] Du Maurier, *Rebecca*, p. 7.

watering her long-departed daughter's hanging plants, an elderly widow is able to re-create past relationships in the present.[146]

Even societies which deny that today differs from yesterday, or consider time but ceaseless replication, commingle past with present in commemorative rites. A talismanic shield confers symbolic immortality on a New Guinea tribesman: 'Accepting death, and yet denying it, he is not separated from his grandfather or his great-grandfather. They live on, protective and influential, represented by objects.'[147] Each stone or wooden *churinga* worked by the Aranda of central Australia 'represents the physical body of a definite ancestor and generation after generation, it is formally conferred on the living person believed to be this ancestor's reincarnation'. Lévi-Strauss comments that 'the churinga furnishes the tangible proof that the ancestor and his living descendant are of one flesh'. He likens churingas to archival papers whose loss would be 'an irreparable injury that strikes to the core of our being'. And he compares the initiation pilgrimages of Australian aborigines, escorted by their sages, with our conducted tours to the homes of famous men.[148]

Diachronic continuity enhances people, too; we see them not only as they are but also as they were, with layer under layer of previous life. 'We are none of us "the young", or the "middle-aged", or "the old"', comments a writer. 'We are all of these things.' Growing up, maturing, and ageing are guided by an awareness that the present develops from a past still inherent in it. 'Besides having a past, maturity means cultivating that past, integrating former experiences – previous ways of being – into the ongoing psychic activity.'[149] Household possessions and mementoes help maintain that temporal awareness past our own lifetimes. 'We have my great grandparents' bed which my daughter sleeps on', recounted one old woman. 'It's very small for a double bed and it amazes me that 3 sets of parents slept in it and conceived children in it!'[150] Linking oneself with ancestors and descendants lends continuity an intimation of immortality, much as the vitrification of the dead in the form of commemorative medallions was once proposed so as to derive permanence from transient lives and instil the virtues of ancestors in their descendants.[151]

The *ne plus ultra* in diachrony are Jeremy Bentham's clothed cadaver on display at University College London and his proposal for landscaping the dead: 'If a country gentleman had rows of trees leading to his dwelling, the Auto-Icons [embalmed bodies] of his family might alternate with the trees.'[152] A benefactor still extant more modestly stipulates that his cremated ashes go into an egg-timer, so he 'will be of some use again one day'.[153]

Celebrating continuity, as distinct from antiquity, is profoundly anti-escapist. The accretive past is appreciated less for its own sake than because it has led to the present; Napoleon and Louis Philippe both emphasized the continuity of their national lineage to

---

[146] Csikszentmihalyi and Rochberg-Halton, *Meaning of Things*, pp. 103–4.
[147] Lively, *House in Norham Gardens*, p. 51.
[148] Lévi-Strauss, *Savage Mind*, pp. 238–44. See Strehlow, *Aranda Traditions*, pp. 16–18, 55–6, 84–6, 132–7, 172.
[149] Lively, 'Children and memory', p. 404.
[150] Csikszentmihalyi and Rochberg-Halton, *Meaning of Things*, pp. 100, 215–16.
[151] Pierre Giraud, *Les Tombeaux, ou essai sur les sépultures* (1801), cited in Ariès, *Hour of Our Death*, pp. 513–16.
[152] Bentham, *Auto-Icon*, p. 3. See Marmoy, '"Auto-Icon" of Jeremy Bentham'.
[153] Tom Gribble, quoted in 'Old timer', *The Times*, 3 June 1983, p. 3.

show French history culminating with themselves.[154] Continuity implies a living past bound up with the present, not one exotically different or obsolete.

The virtues inherent in continuity often conflict with those prized in antiquity. Preservation and restoration principles reveal a similar opposition: those who hold antiquity supreme would excise subsequent additions and alterations to restore buildings to their 'original' condition; those devoted to continuity would preserve all the accretions of time, witnesses to their entire history.[155]

Termination

The past is appreciated because it is over; what happened in it has ended. Termination gives it a sense of completion, of stability, of permanence lacking in the ongoing present. Nothing more can happen to the past; it is safe from the unexpected and the untoward, from accident or betrayal. Because it is over, the past can be ordered and domesticated, given a coherence foreign to the chaotic and shifting present. Nothing in the past can now go wrong; as a Henry James character put it, 'the past is the one thing beyond all spoiling'.[156] And to some it seems cleansed of evil and peril because it is no longer active. Thus Carlyle regarded all the dead as holy, even those who had been 'base and wicked when alive'; and Communist states where religious worship is discouraged can yet take pride in their ancient churches: the past is forgiven the present's sins.[157]

Completion also makes the past comprehensible; we see things more clearly when their consequences have emerged. To be sure, the past has new consequences for each successive generation; we are forever reinterpreting it. But these interpretations all benefit from hindsight denied to perspectives on the present.

The relative simplicity of bygone things and processes also makes the past seem easier to understand: yesteryear's forms and functions were integral to life when we learned how things worked, whereas those of today often seem baffling because they stem from later, unfamiliar innovations. Hence the appeal of old tools and machinery: the steam engine is more comprehensible than the computer chip not only because its working parts are visible, but because it fits into an order of things familiar from childhood memory.[158]

A past too well ordered or understood loses some of its appeal, however; we prefer survivals to appear haphazard and organic, like Blunden Shadbolt's rambling, 'wibbly-wobbly' neo-Tudor dwellings.[159] To feel secure from present control or interference, the past must seem both completed *and* uncontrived.

---

[154] Haskell, 'Manufacture of the past in nineteenth-century painting', pp. 112, 118.

[155] See Chapter 6, pp. 278–80, and Chapter 7, p. 405 below.

[156] *Awkward Age*, p. 150.

[157] Carlyle, 'Biography' (1832), 2:256; Marvine Howe, 'Letter from Sofia: preserving the past', *IHT*, 26 Apr. 1982, p. 14; Binyon, *Life in Russia*, pp. 228–9; Shipler, *Russia*, pp. 334–5.

[158] The increasing mysteriousness of technology also fuels passions for vintage cars, steam locomotives, and old gramophones (Misha Black, 'The aesthetics of engineering', Presidential address, Section G, British Association for the Advancement of Science, Stirling, 1974).

[159] Campbell, 'Blunden Shadbolt'; Clive Aslet, 'Let's stop mocking the neo-Tudor', *The Times*, 11 June 1983, p. 8.

Sequence

The present is an indivisible instant, whatever duration we assign it; the past is a *length* of time. Length lets us order and segment the past and hence explain it. Time is linear and directional: the histories of all things begin in some past and go on in an unalterable sequence until they cease to exist or to be remembered. Sequential order gives everything that has happened a temporal place, assigns the past a shape, and sets our own lives in an historical context.

As commonly experienced, sequential order involves two distinct properties, one innate in the nature of time, the other a cultural construct. The first is simply that events precede and succeed each other; the past is a multitude of such events, each earlier than some and later than others. Their relation is one of potential cause and effect: what happens first may affect what happens later, but never vice versa. Sequence alone has inestimable value: to recognize that certain things happened before others enables us to shape memory, secure identity, and generate tradition. The second property, the segmentation of time into lengths of measurable duration, lets us divide the past according to generally accepted periods. Both properties apply prospectively to the future also, but the future's unpredictability severely curtails their use. It is mainly the past for which chronology counts. I explore relations between chronology, history, and narrative in Chapter 5.

An ordered chronology yields manifold rewards. We celebrate anniversaries, count up the days since important events, and base expectations on calendric regularities. We segment the past into equal or unequal intervals, marking off periods in our own lives along with those in other histories. Sequence clarifies, places things in context, underscores the uniqueness of past events, and forms them into the lineaments of a true landscape. But it remains a landscape we can now observe only from beyond, framed in an inalterably determined temporal grid.

The valued traits I have attributed to the past are seldom consciously identified. What people treasure about it arises out of needs and desires seldom analysed. None the less, each of these attributes – antiquity, continuity, termination, sequence – has a basis in actual experience. Together they give the past a character that shapes both its inestimable benefits and its inescapable burdens. To the latter I now turn.

THREATS AND EVILS

> Every past is worth condemning.
>
> Friedrich Nietzsche, *Use and Abuse of History*[160]

The past not only aids and delights; it also threatens and diminishes us. Most of its advantages involve drawbacks, most of its promises imply risks. This section reviews the evils felt to inhere in the past and the burdens it imposes, and discusses how such pasts are exorcized or neutralized.

[160] 1874, p. 21.

Traditionally, the past has been as much feared as revered. Most of its teachings have been threatening and doom-laden, dominated by ominous or tragic figures. As late as the nineteenth century, history was seen largely as a recapitulation of crimes and calamities, as in Browning's dying Paracelsus:

> I saw no use in the past: only a scene
> Of degradation, ugliness and tears
> The record of disgraces best forgotten
> A sullen page in human chronicles
> Fit to erase.[161]

Unlike Carlyle, many feel an evil past continues to endanger the present, its influence to be malign, its relics dangerous or corrupting. 'Where men have lived a long time', in J. B. Priestley's expression, 'the very stones are saturated in evil memories.'[162] The past as contagious malady is a recurrent metaphor, as seen with nostalgia. Walt Whitman warned Americans heading for the Old World that 'there were germs hovering above this corpse. Bend down to take a whiff of it, and you might catch the disease of historic nostalgia for Europe.'[163] The antique in Cheever's story mires its miserly inheritor in a miserable yesteryear; conjuring up the sordid unhappiness of the lowboy's previous possessors, he 'committed himself to the horrors of the past' and was 'driven back upon his wretched childhood'.[164] James Fenimore Cooper's *The Headsman* spells out the fearsome consequences of an inescapable heritage; the hereditary office of hangman in a Swiss canton, originally deemed a privilege, becomes an unendurable stigma to modern successors who 'can neither inherit or transmit aught but disgrace'.[165]

A past need not be evil or unhappy to have baneful effects on the present. Alceo Dossena's compulsion to fabricate anachronistic masterpieces exemplifies the burdens of 'Rome's great and overwhelming past, . . . at once a curse and a blessing', as Frank Arnau comments; 'no one can ever shake it off'.[166] The sheer persistence of a prosaic past may diminish the present. It saddens Hawthorne's Grimshawe 'to think how the generations had succeeded one another' in a venerable English village, 'lying down among their fathers' dust, and forthwith getting up again, and recommencing the same meaningless round, and really bringing nothing to pass . . . It seemed not worthwhile that more than one generation of them should have existed.'[167] History strikes Hardy's Tess as self-demeaning because repetitive: 'Finding out that there is set down in some old book somebody just like me, and to know that I shall only act her part' would deprive Tess of individuality and volition.[168]

The danger often lies in our tendency to overrate the past's importance or virtue by

---

[161] *Paracelsus* (1835), Pt 5, lines 814–16, 1:261–2. History, for the Comte de Portalis, was 'not merely a recapitulation of crimes, but a useful picture of the calamities which followed them' (Lovejoy, 'Herder and the Enlightenment philosophy of history', p. 180). See Plumb, *Death of the Past*, pp. 17, 21.

[162] *I Have Been Here Before*, Act 2, p. 41.   [163] Paraphrased in Spender, *Love–Hate Relations*, p. xi.

[164] 'Lowboy', pp. 401–11.

[165] 1833, 2:50. See Henderson, *Versions of the Past*, pp. 66–7.

[166] *Three Thousand Years of Deception*, p. 222.

[167] *Doctor Grimshawe's Secret*, p. 220.

[168] Hardy, *Tess of the d'Urbervilles*, p. 182. See Gordon, 'Origins, history, and the reconstitution of family: Tess' journey', p. 374.

comparison with the present. The American National Trust promotes historic preservation with the slogan 'They don't build them like they used to. And they never will again' – suggesting the inherent inferiority of today's architecture. The faces carved in a medieval cloister, more serious, grave, and experienced than modern faces, make Spender surmise that people in the past were 'more significantly alive'.[169]

A past too much esteemed or closely embraced saps present purposes, much as neurotic attachment to childish behaviour precludes mature involvement in the present. Many elderly people are so taken up with relics, heirlooms, and mementoes as to preclude concern for the living. Over-indulgence in memory likewise shuts out present experience. 'If the past makes such a bid for our attention, the present may escape us', Dickens felt. 'The past must be left buried in order that the living may experience life to the full.'[170] In Marx's phrase, 'the tradition of all past generations weighs like an alp upon the brain of the living'.[171] Reverence for the past is commonly seen to inhibit change, embargo progress, dampen optimism, stifle creativity. 'Your worst enemy', wrote Pavese, 'is your belief . . . in a happy prehistoric time, [and] that everything essential has already been said by the first thinkers.'[172]

The classic indictment remains Nietzsche's: over-attention to the past turns men into dilettante spectators, their creative instinct destroyed, their individuality weakened; seeing themselves as mere latecomers born old and grey, 'the latest withered shoots of a gladder and mightier stock', they succumb to passive retrospection; 'only in moments of forgetfulness . . . does the man who is sick of the historical fever ever act'.[173]

Nietzsche blames detrimental obeisance to the past on two retrogressive impulses. The practitioner of 'monumental history' invokes past authority to ensure present failure, as if to say, '"See, the great thing is already here!" . . . Hatred of present power and greatness masquerades as an extreme admiration of the past'; despising the present without loving the past, they really mean: '"Let the dead bury the living."' The practitioner of 'antiquarian history', a 'mad collector raking over all the dust heaps of the past', regards everything ancient as equally venerable. The indiscriminate antiquarian mummifies life with his 'insatiable curiosity for everything old'; able only to preserve, he 'hinders the mighty impulse to a new deed and paralyzes the doer'.[174]

Instances of antiquarian regression can be found throughout history. Widespread adulation of the past afflicted second-century Rome, when taste 'prostrated itself before Greek models, and educated Romans grew ecstatic over ruins', in Peter Gay's words. 'This indiscriminate antiquarianism was not so much a cause as a symptom – of exhaustion, of self contempt.'[175] Uncritical devotion to antiquity has been common since the fifteenth century; complaints about its stultifying effects have been no less rife. 'Transmitted with blind deference from one generation of disciples to another', in Gibbon's criticism, Greek authority 'precluded every generous attempt to exercise the powers,

---

169 *Love–Hate Relations*, p. 191.
170 Gent, '"To flinch from modern varnish": the appeal of the past to the Victorian imagination', p. 15.
171 Marx, *Eighteenth Brumaire of Louis Napoleon* (1852), p. 5. 'Former revolutions required historic reminiscences . . . The revolution of the nineteenth century must let the dead bury their dead' (p. 7). See Carne-Ross, 'Scenario for the new year: 3. the sense of the past', p. 247; Febvre, *New Kind of History*, pp. 40–1.
172 *This Business of Living*, diary entry 25 Aug. 1942, p. 132.   173 *Use and Abuse of History*, pp. 29, 48–51.
174 Ibid., pp. 17–20.   175 *Enlightenment*, 1:120.

or enlarge the limits, of the human mind'.[176] But the malign consequences of awesome antiquity were most keenly resented by early nineteenth-century Romantics and early twentieth-century Modernists, as discussed in Chapters 3 and 7. And today's intense absorption with the past is attributed to a no less dispiriting animus against the present. 'Beneath the visible attachment to "souvenirs", to photographs, memorabilia, old movies, old furniture, old styles in clothes, runs this sense that everything important is somewhere else, in another place or time.'[177]

Excessive devotion to the past precludes creative attention to the present if only because time, space, energy, and resources are finite. Were the 'enormous hosts of the dead . . . raised while the living slept', exclaims Dickens's 'Uncommercial Traveller', 'there would not be the space of a pin's point in all the streets and ways for the living to come out into, [and] the vast armies of the dead would overflow the hills and valleys far beyond the city'.[178]

Admiring the frieze of the Parthenon, the Elgin Marbles, Egyptian sarcophagi at the British Museum in 1856, Hawthorne none the less feared their incapacitating impact:

The present is burthened too much with the past. We have not time . . . to appreciate what is warm with life, and immediately around us; yet we heap up all these old shells, out of which human life has long emerged, casting them off forever. I do not see how future ages are to stagger under all this dead weight, with the additions that will continually be made to it.[179]

The additions made to museums in the century and a quarter since would have appalled him. And archival records likewise swamp our libraries and dismay historians; each successive American president's papers are said to outnumber those of his collective predecessors.[180] Even unwanted residues survive in quantities that daunt our powers of disposal. After God created all things, Katharine Whitehorn fancies, 'on the seventh day He saw all that He had made, and realised the way things would go. So on the eighth day He bestirred Himself again, and created moth and rust, His final stroke of mastery.'[181] But moth and rust cannot save us from the past's plastic or nuclear debris.

People often strive to forget or banish a baneful inheritance. Appalled by modern Jewish history, for example, some insist it 'be either forgotten or demolished'.[182] In this view, a past too painful to recall must be expunged from memory. Nietzsche urged that memory be curtailed or obliterated lest the past become the gravedigger of the present. 'No artist will paint his picture, no general win his victory, no nation gain its freedom' without forgetting the past.[183]

The need for exorcism is vividly expressed by V. S. Naipaul:

---

[176] Gibbon, *Decline and Fall of the Roman Empire*, 1:51–2.

[177] Brandt, 'Short natural history of nostalgia', p. 60.

[178] 'Night walks' (1860), p. 114.   [179] Hawthorne, *English Notebooks*, journal entry 26 Mar. 1856, p. 294.

[180] Lyndon B. Johnson's 31 million pages of papers exceed Library of Congress collections on all presidents combined up to this century (Boorstin, 'Enlarged contemporary', p. 778). And an ever-diminishing proportion of the mountain of surviving records is printed. 'So far from catching up with the past, we are actually losing ground' (Galbraith, 'Historical research and the preservation of the past', p. 314). See Chapter 5, p. 205 below.

[181] 'Dung-beetle urge', *Observer*, 2 Nov. 1980, p. 35.

[182] Yerushalmi, *Zakhor: Jewish History and Jewish Memory*, p. 97.

[183] *Use and Abuse of History*, p. 9.

We have to learn to trample on the past . . . There may be some parts of the world – dead countries, or secure and by-passed ones – where men can cherish the past and think of passing on furniture and china to their heirs . . . Some peasant department of France full of half-wits in châteaux; some crumbling Indian palace-city, or some dead colonial town in a hopeless South American country. Everywhere else men are in movement, the world is in movement, and the past can only cause pain.[184]

Wholesale destruction of a dreaded or oppressive past has marked iconoclastic excesses since time immemorial. Three times was the great Alexandria library sacked; twice was Carthage razed to the ground; during the English monastic dissolution soldiers were enjoined to destroy religious images 'so that no memory of them remain'.[185] Not only are public monuments effaced, but intellectual elites are slaughtered to make sure that the new order will forget the old.[186]

To exorcise bygone corruptions, even one's own treasured relics may have to be destroyed. 'Out they go – the Roman coins, the sea horse from Venice, and the Chinese fan', Cheever concludes. 'Down with the stuffed owl in the upstairs hall and the statue of Hermes on the newel post! ... Dismiss whatever molests us and challenges our purpose.'[187]

Some simply eradicate past vestiges, unconcerned with what will replace them. Naipaul's anti-colonial regime renames all the main streets, but 'no one used the new names, because no one particularly cared about them. The wish had only been to get rid of the old, to wipe out the memory of the intruder.'[188] Others eliminate the old so as to make way for the new. 'For something genuinely new to begin', many would echo Eliade, 'the vestiges and ruins of the old cycle must be completely destroyed.'[189] Medieval Cistercians, seventeenth-century New England Puritans, twentieth-century Futurists all felt that to create afresh they must remake the world in forms which owed nothing to historical traditions.[190]

Alternatively, one may destroy one's own ties with the past. When they find the weight of tradition unbearable, some Japanese break entirely with long-worshipped ancestors. Unfortunate inheritors, not only of ancestral identity but of particular forebears' woes and misfortunes, they escape the past's malign hold by joining a cult that shows them how to sever karmic bonds.[191] Similarly, because 'the character and fate of an ancestor is expected to be reproduced in his descendants', a Yoruba villager tries to erase the unfortunate history of an ancestor from collective memory by fudging his identity in a local printed text, lest the 'disgraceful anomaly ... affect his descendants' ambitions'.[192]

Others tame the past by giving its relics a new function. 'By displaying what had gone before and making an ornament of it', writes Lively, 'you destroyed its potency. Less sophisticated societies propitiate their ancestors; this one makes a display of them and renders them harmless.'[193] Agricultural implements hung on a wall can be admired by

---

[184] *Bend in the River*, pp. 152–3.
[185] Order in Council of 1547, quoted in M. S. Briggs, *Goths and Vandals*, pp. 34–5.
[186] Eiseley, *Invisible Pyramid*, pp. 100–1.   [187] Cheever, 'Lowboy', pp. 411–12.
[188] *Bend in the River*, p. 33.
[189] Eliade, *Myth and Reality*, p. 51.   [190] Kubler, *Shape of Time*, p. 124.
[191] Kerner, 'Malevolent ancestors'; Lebra, 'Ancestral influence on the suffering of descendants in a Japanese cult'.
[192] Peel, 'Making history: the past in the Ijesha present', p. 125.   [193] *Road to Lichfield*, p. 178.

11 The past neutralized as display: agricultural and other bygones, Woodstock, Vermont

those who neither know nor care what they were used for. We subdue an overbearing past by sequestering it. Once memorialized, it loses its power to harm the present – as with Nabokov's narrator who 'transformed everything we saw into monuments to our still nonexistent past ... so that subsequently when the past really existed for us, we would know how to cope with it, and not perish under its burden'.[194]

Satire is another mode of neutralizing the past. *Time Bandits* portrays Napoleon as obsessively touchy about his shortness and Robin Hood as a Mafia-type lout; thus made risible they cease to be figures of dread or even of consequence. Pretensions of ancient lineage are ridiculed by an American group, the 'Descendants of the Illegitimate Sons and Daughters of the Kings of Britain', one of whose prime aims is 'to emphasize that what a man makes himself is more important than who his parents may be'.[195] And a cartoon dialogue cuts the personal past down to size:

'I almost drowned yesterday, and my whole life flashed in front of me!'
'That must have been exciting!'
'Not really; I'd seen it before.'[196]

Other ways of neutralizing the past range from trying to understand it to selling it off. 'If the Past has been an obstacle and a burden', Lord Acton advised, 'knowledge of the Past is the safest and surest emancipation.'[197] Historians have reiterated Acton's message ever

194 'Admiralty spire', p. 313.
195 Alverson, pp. 28–32, 44–6; *Hereditary Register of the United States of America 1983*, pp. 241–3.
196 Hart, 'B.C.', *IHT*, 12 July 1979.   197 'Inaugural lecture on the study of history' (1895), p. 4.

since; history's emancipatory role is the main burden of J. H. Plumb's *Death of the Past* – a theme further explored in Chapter 7.

The evils attributed to the past are as manifold and complex as the benefits in whose wake they often follow. Malignant compulsions and coercive injunctions offset the past's attractions; excessive devotion to it thwarts action and diminishes individuality. To deny the past is less usual than to rejoice in it, but its demerits are none the less consequential. Explorers of the past usually find in it vices, as well as virtues, that contrast with or continue into our own day. And the newly found virtues may distress us no less than the vices. 'It is not just bad experiences we want to protect ourselves from but good experiences as well, and for some of the same reasons', notes an observer. 'It scares us to turn over a rock and find some worm of history we thought dead still crawling about; it scares us, too, though, to find the darkened present illuminated by some flickering light from the past.'[198]

TRADITION AND INNOVATION

In spite of all the direct precepts of tradition, the son advances in his own way. Aristotle was anxious to distinguish himself from Plato, Epicurus from Zeno ... The work of time proceeds to the good of the race by necessary opposition.

Johann Gottfried von Herder, *Reflections on the Philosophy of the History of Mankind*[199]

When I most want to be contemporary the Past keeps pushing in, and when I long for the Past ... the Present cannot be pushed away.

Robertson Davies, *The Rebel Angels*[200]

'Tradition shouldn't be the enemy of innovation.' That slogan appeared in 1982 in the windows of the Chemical Bank of New York. I asked my niece, who is the Chemical Bank's archivist, what it was supposed to mean. 'Oh, don't blame me', she said, 'it wasn't *my* idea. You see, the Chemical has all this history and tradition, and they're trying to persuade people that it doesn't really interfere with getting things done fast – you know, computing your statement in two seconds and giving you crisp new money and stopping holdups and stuff.'

But people realize that tradition *is* a brake on progress. They may acknowledge the virtues of yesteryear and the benefits of relics and roots, but they also know that the old has to give way, that youth must be served, that new ideas need room to develop – that the past does indeed constrain the present.

Stability and change are alike essential. We cannot function without familiar environments and links with a recognizable past, but we are paralyzed unless we transform or replace inherited relics; even our biological legacy undergoes continual revision. Yet to cope amidst change we also need considerable continuity with the past. The cultural legacy, too, is conservative *and* innovative: survival requires an inheritable culture, but it must be malleable as well as stable.[201]

---

[198] 'Notes and comment', *New Yorker*, 24 Sept. 1984, p. 39.   [199] 1784–91, Bk XV, Ch. 3, p. 104.
[200] 1983, p. 124.
[201] Mazzeo, *Varieties of Interpretation*, pp. 108–9. See Shils, *Tradition*; Maddock, 'Why industry must learn to forget'.

No nation or individual can ever be purely original: 'since each has received material transmitted by earlier generations', creative activity is never 'purely innovative but rather modifies the heritage', Wilhelm von Humboldt observed.[202] 'There is all this talk about originality, but what does it amount to?' asked Goethe. 'As soon as we are born the world begins to influence us, and this goes on till we die'.[203] Or in Emerson's admission, 'The originals are not original. There is imitation, model, and suggestion, to the very arch-angels, if we knew their history.'[204]

Yet the heritage is likewise doomed: the most faithful followers of tradition cannot avoid innovating, for time's erosions alter all original structures and outdate all previous meanings. Living in ever new configurations of nature and culture, we must think and act *de novo* even to survive; change is as inescapable as tradition.

Negative and positive responses to the past both imply their opposites. 'By perpetuating the past, by reproducing ritualistically its external features, we are actually exposing its pastness, pointing to its anachronism, putting it from us', writes Thomas Greene. 'By ostensibly ridiculing the past, by exposing its inconsequence and parodying its rhetoric, we may be revealing how we depend on it, how necessary it is to us, how little free of it we are, how we really stem from it.'[205] Although Nietzsche advocated ruthless forgetting, 'calling the past into court, putting it under indictment, and finally condemning it', he recognized this was futile, 'for as we are merely the resultant of previous generations, we are also the resultant of their errors, passions, and crimes; it is impossible to shake off this chain'.[206]

Every achievement in science or the arts 'either repeats or refutes *what someone else has done*', wrote Valéry, ' – refines or amplifies or simplifies it, or else rebuts, overturns, destroys, and denies it, but thereby assumes it and has invisibly used it'.[207] And the more we think we have escaped the past the greater our indebtedness; a forgotten precursor, as Harold Bloom put it, becomes a giant of the imagination who never ceases to haunt us.[208] Instancing Rousseau, Baudelaire, and Artaud, Paul de Man concludes that 'the more radical the rejection of anything that came before, the greater the dependence on the past'.[209] Every new movement is doomed to carry the past it rejects on its back, in Murray Krieger's phrase, so echoing its negated claims that 'the rejected predecessor comes also to be seen, somehow, as a precursor'.[210]

Coping with indebtedness to poetic precursors involves three sets of strategies identified by Bloom. One is to correct or complete the work of an exemplar who is presumed either not to have gone far enough or to have swerved off the true creative path. A second is to repress the memory of influence, either by detaching oneself from a supposed precursor or by disclaiming his uniqueness, thus denying the past's exclusive title to originality. The third is openly and actively to fight the venerated dead either by purging oneself and truncating the endowment, or by dispossessing them and making the past seem to model

[202] *Linguistic Variability & Intellectual Development* (1836), p. 28.
[203] To Eckermann, 5 Dec. 1825, in *Goethe: Conversational Encounters*, pp. 138–9.
[204] 'Quotation and originality' (1859), p. 286.   [205] Greene, *Light in Troy*, p. 195.
[206] *Use and Abuse of History*, p. 21.
[207] 'Letter about Mallarmé', 8:241.   [208] *Anxiety of Influence*, p. 107.
[209] *Blindness and Insight*, pp. 161–2.
[210] *Arts on the Level*, p. 37n.

itself after the present. Great poets late in life often employ this last strategy, Bloom suggests, in an effort to replace their precursors' immortality with their own. To such an extent has John Ashbery taken over his predecessor Wallace Stevens, for example, that 'when I read *Le Monocle de Mon Oncle* now . . . I am compelled to hear Ashbery's voice, for this mode has been captured by him, inescapably and perhaps forever'. So too did Browning, Dickinson, Yeats, Stevens 'achieve a style that captures and oddly retains priority over their precursors, so that the tyranny of time almost is overturned, and one can believe, for startled moments, that they are being *imitated by their ancestors*'.[211]

As with art, so with life. Those who seek to reject the authority of the past and those who avowedly wish for its return reflect two sides of the same coin, Wyatt and Lifton suggest of modern Japanese youth. At one extreme, conservatives who have internalized early prohibitions maintain rigid allegiance to the past, whose authority they vindicate by imbuing it with traditionalist symbols and institutions to be brought back in a redemptive future; but they feel secure in the restoration of their own past only if they can make others submit to it as well. At the other extreme, the modernist reformer vents his anger against the oppressive authority of his childhood, yet must avoid the secret pull of dependence on it; he fears the past, or he would not repudiate it with so much fervour.[212]

Viewing the past as wholly malign, the transformationist is nevertheless deeply nostalgic for a primordial state that blends childhood memory with the religious ritual of rebirth; and this imagined golden age shapes his vision of the future. Viewing the past as wholly ideal, the traditionalist seeks refuge in mystical connection with his great and ennobling heritage, but is partially absorbed in and subconsciously attracted to the new influences he affects to despise.[213]

Such ambivalence is an inescapable part of our being. Children grow up immersed in ideas and artifacts that antedate their birth; of necessity they copy, emulate, and venerate their elders. Yet to become adult they must throw off those models and make their own way, denying or transcending the parental heritage. Those who fail to do so remain fixated on and in the past and never achieve autonomy. Instead of recalling repressed memories as something belonging to the past, they repeat their childhood reactions as contemporary experience; the reanimated past appears to them as present reality.[214]

Ambivalence toward the past reflects or stems from problems of filial dependence. The self-realization of young people was inevitable and easily accepted when survival depended on physical strength; 'the old man must move over' was the saying among Austrian farmers, Bettelheim recounts. Generational succession was the natural order. But even before modern times the problem of succession was acute where physical strength was not the essential criterion: the old viewed the young with suspicion and fear and were unwilling to give way; the young, unsure when or even if they would gain dominance, had to fight for it. Young people kept economically and emotionally depend-

---

[211] Bloom, *Anxiety of Influence*, pp. 141–4.

[212] Lifton, 'Individual patterns in historical change', and Wyatt, 'In quest of change: comments on R. J. Lifton'.

[213] Wyatt, 'In quest of change', pp. 388–9.

[214] Freud, *Beyond the Pleasure Principle*, 18:18. The patient is 'obliged to *repeat* the repressed material as a contemporary experience instead of . . . *remembering* it as something belonging to the past'.

ent still suffer the consequences of these opposing imperatives.[215] Rebellion meets resistance not only from parents but from offspring who internalize their roles as devoted and obedient children. To disown father figures, as maturation requires, does violence to both generations. Some cling forever to their self-image as dutiful followers; others give it up only at great psychic cost; still others become ardent iconoclasts. For all of us, growing up is a ceaseless struggle between ingrained assumptions that parents deserve our homage and developing needs for autonomy that impel us to spurn their authority and example. Nor can autonomy be gained through amnesia. 'A father is a man's link with the past', in Tony Tanner's words. 'To be rid of all trace and knowledge of him is to be left "free and unencumbered" – but also without identity.'[216] 'To be an adult', writes a psychoanalyst, 'does not mean leaving the child in us behind.'[217] Indeed, to be adult means to be on good terms with the child within us, to know that we can still go home from time to time, that maturity does not preclude but embodies dependence.[218]

Since classical times the parent–child analogy has repeatedly been invoked to underscore the rival claims of past and present. To follow blindly the footsteps of past masters was to remain forever a child; one should aim to rival and finally to displace them. Inherited wisdom was a source of guidance and a fount of inspiration, but it should be assimilated and transformed, not simply revered and repeated. Only by manipulating the past to one's own purposes could one truly achieve autonomy. Admired precursors should never be slavishly copied: 'Even if there shall appear in you a likeness to him who, by reason of your admiration, has left a deep impress upon you', Seneca exhorted his followers, 'I would have you resemble him as a child resembles his father, and not as a picture resembles its original; for a picture is a lifeless thing.' The filial relationship, the family resemblance involved a healthy measure of *un*likeness: Seneca's son grows away from his father without ceasing to reveal the parental impress, but independence also enables him to acquire his own face.[219]

Nations and communities confront analogous dilemmas. They must draw sustenance from their past, yet to be fully themselves must also put it away from them. Societies, like individuals, imitate the ancients and pay homage to precursors, but also need to act for themselves, to innovate and create – hence to break with tradition and reject inherited patterns. Whether avowedly traditional or defiantly iconoclastic, every generation must reach a *modus vivendi* that simultaneously embraces and abandons precedent. And filial metaphors are employed to describe ambivalent relations with precursors in every aspect of life.

The tension between tradition and innovation has been recognized at least since Romans copied Greeks and fought off the implication that copying was uncreative, and Roman law coined the concept of *damnosa hereditas*.[220] The benefits and drawbacks of heritage have been perennially debated ever since. The conflict sharpened during the post-Renaissance

[215] Bettelheim, 'Problem of generations', pp. 70–6. Cultural and historical variations on this dilemma are of course myriad. For the American case, see Demos, 'Oedipus and America', and pp. 117–20 below.
[216] Tanner, *City of Words*, p. 245.   [217] Loewald, *Psychoanalysis and the History of the Individual*, p. 22.
[218] Albert J. Solnit, lecture, 30 Jan. 1984, University College London.
[219] Seneca, *Ad Lucilium epistulae morales*, 2:381. See Greene, *Light in Troy*, p. 75.
[220] Gaius, *Institutes*, 6.2.163; Nicholas, *Introduction to Roman Law*, pp. 236, 239–40. Through a mass of debts the heirs might find themselves with an inheritance 'more expense than it was worth' (J. A. Crook, *Law and Life of Rome*, p. 124).

quarrel between 'Ancients' and 'Moderns', the former insisting that antique excellence could never be matched, the latter that observation and experiment unfettered by tradition could generate insights transcending antiquity's. The arts of the past two centuries are especially full of injunctions, from those who found their legacy both rich and intimidating, to admire past examples but not to imitate them, to use their heritage without stultifying their own creative energies. Faced with the double burden of venerated precursors both remote and near, the 'Augustan' poets abandoned attempts to rival them. The classics of antiquity were hard enough to come to terms with; Elizabethan and Jacobean giants, notably Milton and Spenser, foreclosed their successors' autonomy.[221] Convinced they could never measure up to that past, later poets became all the more melancholy, for Romantic premises now demanded originality and self-expression. Our own growing subjectivity lengthens our precursors' shadows; Bloom terms us now 'more desperate' about our cultural heritage even than 'the Milton-haunted eighteenth century, or the Wordsworth-haunted nineteenth'.[222]

Intense historical awareness led to remarkable nineteenth-century insights into the past, but also left European society crippled by a despairing sense of being totally determined by it. Countering the past's determinative force, modernists rebelled against the entire heritage, and psychoanalysts sought to alleviate its burden through a better understanding of evolution, of primitive history, and of early life history. It was not to conserve the archaic past that Freud hoped to explain its consequences, but to render that past harmless.[223]

Education and example teach us to revere the great prototypes of the past and absorb their canonical virtues; but we are then forbidden to resemble these exemplars – a terrible double bind expressed in the Protestant tradition, notes Bloom, by divine injunctions to 'Be like Me', but 'Do not presume to be too like Me.'[224] W. J. Bate considers the conflict peculiar to the arts of the recent past, which enjoin us at the same time to admire and not to follow too closely what we admire.[225] But the dilemma is much more pervasive: the opposing demands of tradition and innovation, as we shall see in the next chapter, have deeply affected most aspects of life throughout much of the history of the Western world.

---

[221] Bate, *Burden of the Past and the English Poet.*   [222] *Anxiety of Influence*, p. 32.
[223] Erikson, *Life History and the Historical Moment*, p. 100; Mazzeo, *Varieties of Interpretation*, p. 57; Hughes, *Consciousness and Society*, pp. 33–9.
[224] *Anxiety of Influence*, p. 152.   [225] *Burden of the Past*, p. 133.

3

ANCIENTS VS. MODERNS

Speak of the Moderns without contempt, and of the Ancients without idolatry.

Lord Chesterfield, *Letters to His Son*[1]

How to enjoy the benefits of the past without being overwhelmed or corrupted by it is a dilemma that confronts us all. Each inheritance demands to be both revered and rejected. Whether or not people expressly articulate the conflict, rivalry between tradition and innovation engages every historically conscious society. Any effort to balance the past's benefits and burdens implies some awareness that we need to cherish the past and also need to get rid of it; either course of action embodies inherent contradictions. If we follow admired exemplars we can never hope to resemble them; if we deny our precursors' greatness we cannot match their accomplishments.

Cultures, like individuals, respond to this dilemma in quite different ways. Some look back with gratitude, others with regret, at the past that has made them what they are. Some can hardly imagine being parted from the past, however burdensome, or exhibit deep distress at its loss. Others are so daunted by it that they resign themselves to being inferior followers. Still others resolve to outdo past achievements or deny them any exemplary role.

This chapter illustrates with four case studies – the Renaissance; seventeenth- and eighteenth-century England and France; Victorian Britain; and pre- and post-Revolutionary America – how various epochs have endured and resolved the stresses of inheritance.

Several caveats are needed here. My aim is less to chronicle or to explain past–present conflicts in these epochs than to explore the rival stances adopted and to identify characteristic ambivalences toward things old and new. Disparities in the issues engaging attention, in the time spans and cultures involved, and in the evidence available preclude conformity of treatment among epochs or topics. For example, Renaissance confrontations with precursors came mainly in philosophy and the arts, articulated by a few score humanists who were not so much representative of the prevailing mentality as influential in reshaping it. By contrast, late eighteenth-century North American tensions over

[1] 22 Feb. 1748, 1:262.

74

patrimony had an explicitly political focus, and opposing views of the past as guardian and as tyrant engaged a substantial segment of the population. In Victorian Britain, the competing claims of tradition and innovation were voiced for a wide range of subjects – art and architecture, r ͏gion and morals, the material conditions of life, the nature of history itself – both by   onal advocates and by a large lay public. These diverse epochs and realms of di   manifold stresses between past and present, with concerns of every ki͏   n between tradition and change, imitation and innovation, pres͏

͏NAISSANCE AND THE CLASSICAL HERITAGE

  can ever swim well who does not dare to throw away the life preserver.

Erasmus, *Ciceronianus*[2]

  benefits and burdens of the past first came under sustained scrutiny in the Renais ͏ance. Previous epochs had not wholly ignored these issues – the promises and perils of imitating Greek forerunners were much debated in early imperial Rome[3] – but not until the mid fourteenth century, with Petrarch, did self-conscious concern about the rival merits of old and new become a dominant theme, first in Italy, then in France and England. Its importance followed directly from the Renaissance perspective that there was a past as such, a valued realm of antiquity admired by and distinct from the present.

How humanists reconciled their admiration for that past with their own creativity has had momentous consequences. They borrowed from Roman forerunners not only classical forms and precepts but Roman ways of dealing with their own indebtedness to the Greeks, elaborating imitative modes expounded by Cicero and Quintilian. Humanist insights and techniques remain vital down to our own time; most subsequent efforts to come to terms with precursors are variations on Renaissance themes.

Squaring devotion to antiquity with confidence in their own creative powers was an unremitting humanist preoccupation. Indeed, their reverence for antiquity reflected an overriding concern with the present. 'The ideal often lay in the past', Agnes Heller writes, 'but it was still the present which guided the individual's footsteps.'

However past-directed the thinking of Renaissance man may have been in some respects, in practice he lived entirely *in and for the present*. The past was the ideal, but keeping pace with the present was the true – and dynamic – motive of action. There have been few periods of history in which men gave themselves over so unconditionally to the present as they did during the Renaissance.[4]

Not all humanists always so highly esteemed their own epoch, but it was a general Renaissance view that present efforts could equal and perhaps surpass classical achievements.

Any assessment of opinions about ancients and moderns must take into account that the topic early became a rhetorical exercise. Statements about the relative merits of past and present may conceal views actually held, because many writers took up positions for

---

[2] 1528, quoted in Pigman, 'Versions of imitation in the Renaissance', p. 25.
[3] Wardman, *Rome's Debt to Greece*; Gordon Williams, *Change and Decline: Roman Literature in the Early Empire*.
[4] Heller, *Renaissance Man*, p. 194.

debating purposes. Authors who defended the moderns 'were not so much marching forward in the vanguard of a historical progression which would eventually lead to the overthrow of the authority of the ancients', Robert Black warns, 'as choosing the side of the argument' they felt their rhetorical task demanded.[5] Thus the Florentine chancellor Benedetto Accolti strove to show his virtuosity by upholding pro-modern positions many would deem incapable of defence. For example, he dismissed ancient rhetoric as rendered useless by the decline of Roman oratory; praised modern military innovations like the mercenary system, the arts of trickery and deceit, the invention of cannon and the use of armour; and defended the luxury of the modern Christian church and its paucity of martyrs on the ground that 'if there were more martyrs in antiquity, that was because there was more persecution'.[6] These arguments thinly disguise assertions of ancient superiority. Others likewise damned moderns with faint praise, suggesting for example that while Petrarch was superior to the ancients in poetry and prose together he was inferior to Cicero in prose and to Virgil in poetry.[7] Many seem to have felt genuine ambivalence. Almost every humanist on occasion compared his own epoch favourably with antiquity, yet at other times disparaged moderns as dwarfs compared with ancient giants, new work as mere dregs next to classical wine.

Changing viewpoints further obscure any supposed accordance of opinion. After the first flush of classical rediscovery, what R. F. Jones terms 'extravagant and servile worship' of the ancients crippled the initiative of Petrarch's immediate successors.[8] Petrarch himself held his own generation in contempt;[9] those who followed further disparaged the present and the recent past. Single-minded devotion to antiquity in the late fourteenth century precluded contemporary creativity, in Hans Baron's judgement. The humanist Niccolò Niccoli, who spent a fortune gathering ancient manuscripts and art relics, was so convinced it was futile to compete with the classics that he wrote practically nothing himself. Leonardo Bruni early in his career likewise despaired of modern efforts. So many regarded the ancients' attainments as now unmatchable, complained Domenico da Prato in 1420, as to paralyze creative energy.[10]

By then, however, the tide was already turning. If the classics left Petrarch's immediate successors too overwhelmed to achieve much of their own, a more enterprising spirit in the early fifteenth century viewed antiquity less as an irrecoverable golden age than as an exemplary parallel with the present, encouraging moderns to rival classical languages, literature, arts, and statecraft. Bruni exemplifies the transition: in 1408–9 he had termed his contemporaries hapless dwarfs; on his return from exile in 1418 he proclaimed Florence the equal of antiquity.[11] Alberti, who had previously derogated modern achievements in painting, came back to Florence in 1428 convinced that the

[5] 'Ancients and Moderns in the Renaissance', p. 28.
[6] Accolti, *Dialogue on the Preeminence of Men of His Own Time* (1462–3), paraphrased in Black, 'Ancients and Moderns', pp. 17–19, 25.
[7] Baron, *Crisis of the Early Italian Renaissance*, p. 259; Black, 'Ancients and Moderns', p. 15.
[8] Jones, *Ancients and Moderns*, p. 40.
[9] 'Epistle to Posterity' (1351), in *Letters from Petrarch*, p. 7.
[10] Baron, '*Querelle* of the Ancients and the Moderns', p. 17; Black, 'Ancients and Moderns', pp. 4–5; Baron, *Crisis*, p. 282.
[11] Baron, *Crisis*, pp. 282–3. See also Siegel, '"Civic humanism" or Ciceronian rhetoric?' pp. 9–28.

talents of Brunelleschi, Donatello, and Masaccio compared favourably with the ancient masters.[12] The painting of Fra Filippo Lippi, Fra Angelico, Luca della Robbia, the writing of Bruni, the sculpture of Ghiberti, the architecture of Alberti demonstrated that Italian talents of the present day rivalled ancient Greece.[13] Extravagant obeisance to antiquity excited opprobrium; the Florentine Alamanno Rinuccini reproached those who so praised ancient exploits and wisdom that they had to 'decry the manners of their own time, condemn its talents, belittle its men and deplore their misfortune which made them be born in this century'.[14]

Foreign invasion and occupation, along with literary formalism embodied in a rigidly imitative Ciceronian cult, again sapped Italian confidence in eclectic creativity during the early sixteenth century, and as the usable heritage narrowed to a few supreme figures, the past in general once more came to seem unmatchable.[15] Self-confidence *vis-à-vis* the past moved across the Alps and the English Channel. 'If our ancestors during the past hundred years due to an indolent veneration for antiquity had not dared to try anything new', we would not have most of our present great literature, claimed Guillaume Budé, assailing as 'absurd' the modern notion 'that the bare name of antiquity should be venerated as a deity'.[16] But such denials themselves suggest persisting veneration. The canonical virtues ascribed to ancient statues repressed creativity, as Gianfranceso Pico complained in 1512: 'any sculpture which is reported to be of recent make, even if it excels those made in ancient times, is considered inferior'. Statues supposed ancient were profusely praised, 'but as soon as it turns out that they are more recently made, . . . we get at once a thousand Aristarchuses [severe critics] and even a whistle of disapproval'.[17] That a reputed figure by Apelles cost twice one by Raphael or Tintoretto left no doubt that 'the age of an object renders it more valuable'.[18]

Three perspectives on the past were habitual in humanist consciousness. One was a sense of distance, a feeling that admired exemplars were remote in time, which allowed humanists considerable freedom in connecting with those precursors. A second was a theory of imitation, initiated in classical Rome but elaborated by the Renaissance sense of distance. A third was the notion of revival and rebirth – literally renaissance – associated with acts of unearthing and resurrecting, metaphors brought to mind by the past's remoteness and resultant fragmentation and burial; this too enlarged the purposes and practice of imitation. Distance, imitation, and revival were not perspectives exclusive to the Renaissance, but they then exerted a more prominent mediating role between past and present than ever before or since.

---

[12] Leon Battista Alberti, *Della pittura* (1436), cited in Gombrich, 'Renaissance conception of artistic progress and its consequences', p. 3.

[13] Matteo Palmieri, *Della vita civile* (1531–8); and Giannozzo Manetti, *De dignitate hominus*, cited in Baron, *Crisis*, pp. 282–3, 460–1, and in *idem*, 'Querelle', pp. 18–19.

[14] Dedicatory epistle (1473), quoted in Gombrich, 'Renaissance conception of artistic progress', pp. 1–2.

[15] Greene, *Light in Troy*, pp. 175–8.

[16] *De asse* (1532), quoted in Kinser, 'Ideas of temporal change and cultural process in France, 1470–1535', pp. 738–9.

[17] Pico, *De imitatione*, quoted in Gombrich, 'Perfection's progress', p. 3.

[18] Giovan Francesco Tinti, *La nobilta di Verona* (1592), quoted in Cochrane, *Historians and Historiography in the Italian Renaissance*, p. 441.

Distance

Nothing about the classical past was more critical for humanists than its sheer distance from their own times. Its very remoteness distinguished that past from the intervening dark ages – the more recent heritage the Renaissance sought to disown. Indeed, closeness to the original source of excellence, nature itself, helped to explain classical greatness. 'The first men were more perfect and endowed with more intelligence', wrote Vasari, for 'they had nature for their guide.'[19]

Yet remoteness also enabled humanists to engage more creatively with the venerated past than the Romans had with their Greek precursors, for example, or than later ages were able to do with the Renaissance itself. That over a thousand years separated humanists from antiquity actually stimulated self-confidence and creativity. The veil of historical distance and dark-age discontinuity that made antiquity so foreign also made it a more useful precursor, for the gulf between present and former circumstances required the past to be translated into modern idiom. Renaissance scholars needed to reshape the classics in order to use them at all, and translation into vernacular languages transformed them still more radically; having to reconstitute the past and make it their own they became creative in their own right. Had the classical past still been alive there would have been no need to revive it. Consciously distanced from their remote exemplars, Renaissance creations took on the character of rites of passage which modernized the past rather than merely recalling and preserving it.

Distance from antiquity also allowed humanists to feel superior to ancients who had in certain respects – notably religion – come too soon. Regretful that history had deprived the early Romans of Christianity, Petrarch feared lest his own classical zeal taint him with paganism, and his successors censured heroes of antiquity for their barbarous beliefs; classical mythology was a major fount of Renaissance art and literature, but its un-Christian tone and content gave cause for anxiety.[20] Christianity made other changes too seem inevitable and desirable. In discussing 'the mysteries of our religion', we should not 'use words as if [we] were writing in the times of Virgil and Ovid', noted Erasmus.[21] He went on to read the present back into the past by retrospectively Christianizing antiquity. 'He didn't speak like Cicero?' queries Erasmus's defender of strict imitation. 'No, he didn't', came the reply. 'Rather, he did because he spoke in the way in which Cicero probably would speak, if he were alive, about the same matters, that is, in a Christian manner about Christian matters.'[22]

Such historical awareness however raised problems for Renaissance improvers. Improving on antiquity implied that change was inherent in history, that the present could not really be like the past. Only Erasmus explicitly welcomed this insight. In criticizing sixteenth-century Ciceronians for slavish copying, he showed it was impossible to speak or write just like Cicero: since Cicero's time 'the religion, governmental power, magistracies,

---

[19] Vasari, *Lives of the Artists*, 1:5. On humanists' sense of distance from antiquity and denial of indebtedness to the Middle Ages, see Panofsky, *Renaissance and Renascences in Western Art*, pp. 36–8; idem, 'First page in Giorgio Vasari's "Libro"', pp. 189–90.

[20] Mazzocco, 'Antiquarianism of Francesco Petrarch', p. 223; idem, 'Case of Biondo Flavio', p. 192.

[21] Erasmus to John Maldonatus, 30 Mar. 1527, quoted in Pigman, 'Imitation and the Renaissance sense of the past', p. 160.

[22] *Ciceronianus*, quoted in Pigman, 'Imitation', p. 159.

commonwealth, laws, customs, pursuits, the very appearance of men – really just about everything – have changed radically.' And as 'the entire scene of human events has been turned upside down, who today can observe decorum [i.e., appropriateness] in his speech unless he differs greatly from Cicero?'[23]

Historical change thus validated present departures from past models. But Erasmus's insight was ignored or rejected by other humanists – and indeed by succeeding generations up to Vico and beyond – because it threatened to subvert two canonical uses of the past: imitation and history. The purpose of imitation was to assimilate the past for the benefit of the present; the purpose of history was to provide exemplary parallels. If Erasmus were right, if things had changed so fundamentally, then history would lose its relevance and imitation become pointless. Because an exemplary past was deemed essential to modern conduct, humanists repressed Erasmus's insight into the otherness of the past, or, like Vivès, wrestled it into triviality. To be sure, 'the whole way of living, dressing, lodging, waging war, and administering peoples and states has changed' since classical times and was 'being changed daily', but these changes were superficial, as Vivès put the normative Renaissance view. What really counted remained essentially unaltered:

Those things which are contained in human nature are never changed, that is to say, the causes of our mental emotions and their actions and effects ... Nothing from the ancients is so out of use and abolished that it cannot to a certain extent be adapted to our customs of living, because even if the form is now different, nevertheless the use remains the same.[24]

In short, as G. W. Pigman notes, 'when a historical awareness of the difference between present and past threatens to subvert the exemplarity of history, the past loses some of its difference, not its exemplarity'.[25]

But distance imperilled even those who refused to accept its implications. To bridge the gulf they had to engage antiquity in intimate dialogue, yet at the same time respect its alien quality, appreciating its outdated idioms and inflections while remaining men of their own time. Humanists who identified themselves with classical precursors risked submerging their own identities in a heritage all the more compelling because so remote.

Both confidence and anxiety *vis-à-vis* remote models of excellence increased as vernacular tongues began to replace Latin. Vernacular advocates like Bruni had earlier urged that moderns should act like the ancients rather than blindly follow them; since her own language had made Athens great, so should Dante's tongue exalt Florence.[26] Because the study of Greek and Latin took up time and effort that antiquity had been able to devote to creative work, Speroni considered moderns still inferior to ancients; they would rival them only when science and philosophy were composed in the vernacular.[27] Du Bellay likewise judged the French intellectually inferior to the ancients for wasting energy on dead languages: 'He who tries to write in the "famous" languages may be heard in more places', but his fame would be ephemeral.[28] Estranged from the classical spirit, imitators in Greek

---

[23] Ibid., p. 158.   [24] Vivès, *De disciplinis* (1531), quoted in Pigman, 'Imitation', p. 176.

[25] 'Imitation', p. 177. Gravelle ('Humanist attitudes to convention and innovation in the fifteenth century') takes issue with Pigman; she cites Salutati, Bruni, Guarino Veronese, and Lorenzo Valla as evidence of quattrocento recognition of historical change.

[26] *Oratio funebris* (1428), cited in Baron, *Crisis*, p. 452.

[27] *Dialogo delle lingue* (1547), cited in Baron, 'Querelle', pp. 20–1.

[28] *Deffence et illustration de la langue francoyse* (1549), paraphrased in M. W. Ferguson, 'Exile's defense: Du Bellay's *La Deffence*', p. 288 n. 30.

and Latin failed to revive the antique essence because the ancient languages were not their native tongues. The very absence of native classical antecedents gave the French an impetus to borrow and reject selectively; less 'defiled by the deposit of ages' than Italian humanists, they could restore with greater originality.[29]

The vernacular displacement of Latin and Greek helped humanists to see that change was essential, to accept the continual alteration of tradition, and in consequence to rate their own achievements more highly. Yet in eschewing classical languages they gained a freedom that was isolated and risky; by comparison with the great embalmed languages the vernaculars were unstable and localized. The discontinuity was especially dismaying in France and Britain, which lacked classicizing forerunners similar to Dante, Petrarch, and Boccaccio. 'Writers in both countries were likely to feel that they had to begin the task of revival at the begining', says Greene, 'thus perceiving an independence both daunting and liberating.'[30]

In sum, the felt distance of the past freed humanists from viewing classical antiquity as an unalterable, irreproachable forerunner. Regarding modern revisions as desirable and even necessary, they considered themselves potentially equal or superior to the ancients, but antiquity's remoteness at the same time aroused fears lest their own achievements alienate them from it, leaving them marooned between anachronistic worship of the past and a lonely modernity.

Imitation and emulation

Distance offered a new insight into the venerated past; imitation was the main mechanism for coming to terms with it. Renaissance imitation embraced a spectrum of meanings that our own narrow and pejorative usage of the term no longer suggests, meanings elaborated from Roman precursors expressly to cope with the glories and burdens of classical antiquity. The word *copy*, now also confined pejoratively to mere reproduction and repetition, then denoted eloquent abundance.[31]

Imitation taught Renaissance painters, sculptors, architects, and men of letters how to reanimate ancient models and yet also improve on them. The reuse of classical exemplars ranged from faithful copying to fundamental transformation, roughly paralleling what humanists termed *translatio*, *imitatio*, and *aemulatio*. Each mode of imitation expressed a different relationship with precursors, but most humanists employed not just one but several of these modes.

Translation meant to follow a model without deviation, reproducing an enshrined primary text or image with total fidelity. Exhorted to dig out relics of ancient times and hand them down unaltered as objects of veneration, Petrarch's disciples gathered phrases, passages, and figures from classical art and literature and transcribed them without revision. Poetic models become sacred exemplars whose greatness could never be too much praised – or too often reproduced. Paintings were copied to render originals more

---

[29] Budé, *De asse*, quoted in Kinser, 'Ideas of temporal change', p. 740. On French freedom from crippling precedent, see Huppert, 'Renaissance background of historicism', pp. 54–5.

[30] *Light in Troy*, p. 32.

[31] Gombrich, 'Style *all'antica*: imitation and assimilation'; Cave, *Cornucopian Text: Problems of Writing in the French Renaissance*, pp. 4–5, 9.

accessible, as with Rubens's faithful reproduction of Titian's *Rape of Europa*.[32] Shunning the style and vocabulary of his own time out of reverence for the great original, the purely reproductive painter or poet eschewed creative variation.

Eclectic exploitation of models was a second Renaissance imitative strategy. Using the classical past as a stockpile of traditions to draw upon at will, humanists heterogeneously excerpted phrases and allusions, so transfusing them that the new product seemed 'a birth of one's intellect, not something begged and borrowed from elsewhere'. Sources were concealed, originality was pretended: 'if we wish to imitate Cicero successfully, we must above all disguise our imitation of Cicero', as Erasmus put it.[33] The disguise was not meant to be total: 'imitation lies hidden ... It conceals rather than reveals itself and does not wish to be recognized except by a learned man.'[34] Eclectic imitation in painting synthesized diverse traditions, like Annibale Carracci combining Lombard–Venetian *colore* with Tuscan–Roman *disegno*, or like Rubens freely adapting from earlier painters.[35] Adding to and excerpting from Raphael's *Baldassare Castiglione* and Elsheimer's *Il Contento*, for example, Rubens infused the originals with his own more lifelike style.[36] But however far these departed from their models, they did not try to surpass them. Cicero's study of Zeuxis, whose painting of Helen of Troy combined the best features of five beautiful models, exemplifies these eclectic but limited refinements on past excellence.[37]

In a third more openly innovative mode of imitation the Renaissance painter or poet advertised his derivations from classical sources while consciously distancing himself from them, making the reader or viewer notice both his allusions to the past and his departures from it. Petrarch spelled out the rationale in a letter to Boccaccio:

> A proper imitator should take care that what he writes resembles the original without reproducing it. The resemblance should not be that of a portrait to the sitter – in that case the closer the likeness is the better – but it should be the resemblance of a son to his father ... With a basis of similarity there should be many dissimilarities ... Thus we may use another man's conceptions and the color of his style, but not use his words. In the first case the resemblance is hidden deep; in the second it is glaring. The first procedure makes poets, the second makes apes.[38]

Greene terms this awareness of vestiges 'sub-reading'. 'The resemblance of a poem to its model or series of models will never be fully articulated ... Rather, one sub-reads, patiently and intuitively, the dim, elusive presence of the model in the modern composition.' Innovative imitators 'produced buildings and statues and poems that have to be scrutinized for subterranean outlines or emergent presences or ghostly reverberations.' Through 'archaeological' analysis we penetrate the 'visual or verbal surface to make out the vestigial form below'. Knowing Virgil's *Aeneid*, Petrarch's reader was bound 'to perceive the Rome of the *Africa* as an archaeological construct ... He would superimpose

---

[32] J. M. Muller, 'Rubens's theory and practice of the imitation of art', p. 239.

[33] *Ciceronianus*, quoted in Pigman, 'Versions of imitation', p. 10.

[34] Johannes Sturm, *De imitatione oratoria* (1574), quoted in Pigman, 'Versions of imitation', p. 11.

[35] Agucchi, *Trattato* (1607–15) and G. P. Lomazzo, *Trattato dell'arte della pittura scoltura ed architettura* (1584), cited in Posner, *Annibale Carracci*, pp. 77–92.

[36] Muller, 'Rubens's theory and practice', p. 239.

[37] Cicero, *De inventione*, II, Ch. 1, para. 3, p. 169. Cicero applies these eclectic precepts to writing and rhetoric (p. 171). See Kidson, 'Figural arts', p. 415.

[38] 28 Oct. 1366, in *Letters from Petrarch*, pp. 198–9. Note the use of Seneca's father–son resemblance, Chapter 2 above.

present decay upon past glory and measure now the ironies of history.' As Greene notes, 'this habit of seeking out everywhere the latent vestiges of history is shared today by every tourist, but in Petrarch's century it was a momentous acquisition'.[39]

Such innovative imitation consciously married continuity with change: overcoming bondage to his precursors, the practitioner not only resuscitated but re-created. The confluence of ancient source with modern voice demanded awareness of the distinctive timbre of both the borrowed and the newly made. This mode of imitation, reshaping admired exemplars in accordance with modern perceptions and needs, materials and environments, moved beyond preservation to revival and renovation.

Most innovative was avowedly dialectical emulation: confronting sources expressly to improve on them. Past models, however inspiring, were outmoded; the emulative imitator gloried both in using and in departing from the ancients. Rubens explained his manipulations of certain originals in just such terms, eliminating the harsh rigidity and petrified effect of Mantegna's Hampton Court series and depicting famous Roman sculptures – the *Farnese Hercules, Laocoön, Apollo Belvedere, Venus de' Medici* – with an inner luminosity absent in the marbles themselves.[40] Rather than concealing indebtedness, emulation called attention to and challenged comparison with past masters. The urge to vie with exemplars combined a desire to surpass their achievements with a distaste for servile following. 'Better to do without a leader than to be forced to follow a leader through everything', in Petrarch's words.[41]

Contentious striving marked emulation of admired models. The emulator sought not just to equal antiquity but to best it. 'Imitation aims at similarity; emulation, at victory', wrote Erasmus,[42] whose emulative efforts were avowedly competitive. 'Aflame with a desire to compete with the ancients', Vida described his contemporaries, 'they delight in vanquishing them by snatching from their hand even material which has long been their peculiar possession ... and improving it.'[43] Unlike Longinus, who realized that Plato owed his greatness to struggling with Homer for pre-eminence but disapproved of that struggle's contentious violence, Renaissance emulators gloried in challenging the past. 'No brilliant minds can make substantial progress unless they have an antagonist', asserted Celio Calcagnini. Humanists must forgo reverent admiration for full-scale warfare against 'those who wrote in the past, ... otherwise we will always be speechless children [for] it is not only disgraceful but also dangerous ... to stick always to another's footsteps'.[44]

These strategies reveal the mixture of confidence and anxiety with which humanists approached their legacy, and the wide range of imitative modes underscores their ambivalence. But two features persistently recur. One was a commitment to individual creativity. Virtually every humanist, no matter how indebted to classical models, felt it crucial to form his own personal style. Even if that style were rude or unrefined, individuality was essential, as Petrarch remarked:

---

[39] Greene, *Light in Troy*, pp. 93, 90–1, citing *Aeneid* 8:347–8.
[40] Muller, 'Rubens's theory and practice', pp. 236, 240–2.
[41] To Boccaccio, quoted in Pigman, 'Versions of imitation', p. 21. Here Petrarch 'preserves Seneca's general idea, but much more determinedly rejects servile following' (p. 22).
[42] *Ciceronianus*, quoted in Pigman, 'Versions of imitation', p. 24.
[43] Vida, *De arte poetica*, Bk 3, lines 228–30, p. 101.
[44] Calcagnini to Giraldi, quoted in Pigman, 'Versions of imitation', pp. 17–18.

I much prefer that my style be my own, . . . made to the measure of my mind, like a well-cut gown, rather than to use someone else's style . . . Each of us has naturally something individual and his own in his utterance and language as in his face and gesture. It is better and more rewarding for us to develop and train this quality.[45]

Enforced conformity to any past model, added Pico a century later, violated this innate inclination – hence several exemplars were preferable to just one.[46] In painting, too, selective imitation helped to form an unmistakable personal style; Rubens absorbed the ancient sculptures so as to make his paintings the capstone of a living and changing tradition.[47]

A second persistent refrain was grave doubt about the rectitude of innovation. Simultaneously demanding subservience to the past and asserting independence from it, the doctrine of imitation seemed at once to proclaim and to deny the desirability of invention. Ritualistic repetition strengthened reverence for the classics; improvised emulation stimulated rebellion against them, implying sacrilege toward beloved ancients.

This peril was explicitly confronted in Du Bellay's *Deffence et illustration de la langue francoyse*. Advice to be original continually slips back into advice to imitate, Margaret Ferguson shows, because Du Bellay (like many Renaissance thinkers) cannot shed the belief that the first were necessarily the best. Though the modern poet's task is to cultivate a young plant (French culture) rather than to rescue one old and dying (classical Greek), the French plant can gain strength only by transfusion from those close to the source of invention; invention is by definition exclusive to those who came first.[48]

Du Bellay sought to minimize the present's indebtedness to classical precursors by pointing out that they too had borrowed – the Romans from the Greeks, the Greeks from India, Egypt, and the East. Since these masters themselves were not 'primary' inventors, modern imitators might hope to equal them.[49] Indeed, moderns might even dispense with ancient exemplars, for they stood between the artist and his true source of inspiration, nature itself. 'Nobody should ever imitate another's manner', advised Leonardo da Vinci, 'because as far as art is concerned he will be called a grandson and not a son of Nature.'[50]

Yet the classical past remained problematic. Implicit in Du Bellay's claim that imitation had so enriched their language that the French *almost* equalled the Greeks (they had not yet produced an epic) was an assumption that the Greek heritage impeded modern poetic powers. Imitation fell short of resolving the past–present dilemma because its polarized modes of action – reverential copying and iconoclastic transformation – were irreconcilable. The faithful follower sought to merge with his model, regarding his own additions as mere surface beneath which the essential spirit of the relic remained intact; but translators lacked the language and the ability of their exemplars. The emulative contender sought to alter the essence of the original, changing rather than merging with the past; but he corrupted, devoured, or effaced the relic on which he based his own work. Du Bellay shunned both polarities – the reverent form of imitation that neither captured the spirit of

---

[45] To Boccaccio, 1359, in *Letters from Petrarch*, p. 183.

[46] Cited in Pigman, 'Imitation', p. 164. The argument for eclectic borrowing derives from Quintilian's *Institutio oratorio*.

[47] Muller, 'Rubens's theory and practice', pp. 235, 243–4.   [48] Ferguson, 'Exile's defense', p. 280.

[49] Ibid., pp. 280–1, 289.

[50] *On Painting* [1508–15], p. 32.

the past nor rivalled its excellence and the critical form that profaned, transformed, and even abolished the past. Even where he most acrimoniously contended against antiquity Du Bellay's figures of speech reflect an underlying devotion to it.[51] His ambivalence echoes in Montaigne, who warned that exclusive reliance on the past could stifle present efforts and sought to rescue contemporary experience from thraldom to memory, yet also venerated antiquity, termed moderns fallible, and upheld tradition as essential to stability.[52]

Rubens expressed a similar tension between creativity and adherence to tradition. Pointing out how knowledge of ancient sculpture could integrate artistic personality, he stressed that such knowledge be used with great caution, lest imitation go 'to the point of the extermination of their art'.[53] The practice of imitation left humanists precariously balanced between submergence in the past and self-assertion against it.

Revival as creation

Conscious enactment of revival further shaped Renaissance relations with antiquity – the idea of the past reborn, the dead resurrected, the very notion of renaissance. So remote was the classical heritage that its use required strenuous recovery and reanimation. Distance led to doubts whether re-creations could ever be truly authentic or worthy of the great originals.[54] But if the humanistic mission was fraught with anxiety, it was also intensely fulfilling.

Humanists conceived the revival of antiquity as creative obeisance; retrieving ancient learning was not an inferior chore but a proof of their own high talents. This was a just appraisal, for until printing became widespread the rescue of lost texts from oblivion was the main path to scholarly progress. 'An "inventor" was ... a person who found something which had been lost', as Keith Thomas puts it, 'not one who devised a new solution unknown to previous generations.'[55] The retrieval of classical texts promised much that was still novel; of his description of ancient Roman coinage, Budé boasted that 'I am the first to have undertaken to restore this aspect of antiquity.'[56] Early-modern scientists spoke of their own creative contributions as restorations of ancient wisdom because innovation and renovation were for them one and the same.[57] Indeed, to bring figures from the past to life again was to deploy power the ancients themselves never had. 'To restore great things is sometimes not only a harder but a nobler task than to have introduced them', asserted Erasmus.[58]

From the time of Petrarch, retrieving antiquity took on necromantic overtones of rebirth, resuscitation, reincarnation, even of resurrection. Petrarch described lost and fragmented literary remains as 'ruins'; his canzone 'Spirto gentil' makes the Scipios, Brutus, and Fabricius rejoice at the imminent prospect of release from their Roman

---

[51] Ferguson, 'Exile's defense', pp. 283–6.   [52] Quinones, *Renaissance Discovery of Time*, pp. 234–7.

[53] Rubens, *De imitatione statuarum* (c. 1608), quoted in Muller, 'Rubens's theory and practice', p. 229.

[54] Renaissance writers feared that being second-hand might make them second-rate (Giamatti, 'Hippolytus among the exiles', p. 14).

[55] *Religion and the Decline of Magic*, p. 511.

[56] *De asse*, quoted in Kinser, 'Ideas of temporal change', p. 740.

[57] Eisenstein, *Printing Press as an Agent of Change*, pp. 292–3.

[58] To Leo X, 1 Feb. 1516, letter 384, *Correspondence*, 3:221–2.

tombs; he himself was lauded for 'exhuming' the Latin language.[59] The recovery of ancient texts was conceived in explicitly archaeological terms. Just as antiquarians pieced together pictures of long-vanished imperial Rome from surviving vestiges of temples and statuary, scholars who collated remnants of classical authors were 'unearthing fragments'. To bring together such fragments was seen as a laudable act of healing. Poggio announced his rediscovery in 1446 of Quintilian's complete works, previously available only in 'a mangled and mutilated state', as restoring him 'to his original dress and dignity, to his former appearance, and to a condition of sound health'.[60] Echoing both the reintegration of Virgil's fragmented *Aeneid* and the return of Aeneas, Poggio likened himself to Aesculapius, who had remade Hippolytus and brought home from exile a dispersed people. And like Lycurgus, who had brought back whole to Greece the scattered work of Homer, humanists came to see themselves as physicians who restored lacerated heroes – the ancient exiled texts – to a safe and honourable home.[61]

Digging up crumbled remains to recover lost or buried antiquities thus implied a further act of healing: the exhumed and lacerated relics – of a building, a text, or an ethos – had to be reconstructed. Resurrected relics became nutriment for new metamorphoses. Metaphors of digestion, appropriation, arrogation, making things one's own opened up the past for present and future use. The restored work of illustrious ancients would now enrich the humanists themselves. Again like Hippolytus, the healing humanist reassembled himself too, reconstituting out of the fragments of his own past an identity that combined a consciousness at once old and new.[62] As a block of stone ceased to belong to nature when it became the sculptor's, so creative reuse consumed textual relics in order to shape them anew.[63] Petrarch 'digested' the works of Virgil, Horace, Livy, and Cicero not only to fix them in memory but to absorb them into his very marrow, refashioning ancient literature in the honey of his own creations:

Take care that the honey does not remain in you in the same state as when you gathered it; bees would have no credit unless they transformed it into something different and better. Thus if you hit upon something worthy while reading or reflecting, change it into honey by means of your style.[64]

Such resurrection demanded not simply the rebirth but the replacement of the past. 'The reader must devour his models, destroying their alien substance so that they may be regenerated in his living utterance as a product of his own essential nature', notes Terence Cave. 'The dead must be devoured and digested before new life can ensue.'[65] Humanist creativity required both the pre-existence of exemplars and their subsequent destruction. What merely degenerated could not be regenerated; as in Eliade's cycle of replacement, the old world had to be destroyed before it could be re-created.[66]

Resurrection and appropriation of the past left many humanists profoundly uneasy, however. Were they not robbers dishonouring a heritage they could never rival, of whose

[59] Greene, *Light in Troy*, p. 92. Unlike 'resurrection', however, the terms rebirth, renewal, revival, and restoration all refer to a *new* cycle of time (Frye, *The Great Code*, p. 72).
[60] Poggio Bracciolini to Guarino of Verona, in *Petrarch's Letters to Classical Authors*, p. 93.
[61] Giamatti, 'Hippolytus among the exiles', pp. 24, 26.
[62] Greene, *Light in Troy*, pp. 96–9; Giamatti, 'Hippolytus among the exiles', pp. 23–5.
[63] Sturm, *De imitatione*, cited in Greene, *Light in Troy*, p. 187.
[64] Petrarch, quoted in Greene, *Light in Troy*, p. 99.
[65] Cave, *Cornucopian Text*, paraphrasing Erasmus and Du Bellay.
[66] *Myth and Reality*, p. 52.

very ruins they were unworthy? The poet grouping for Latin quotations was as much a pillager as the contractor picking up shards from an ancient slag heap. Du Bellay likened the pillage of Roman antiquities to his own imitative verse. 'The contemporary mason, collecting broken statuary for the foundations of a modern palazzo', in Greene's gloss, is the poet too, Renaissance man writ large; but whether he gleaned ancient stones or ancient words he would 'sow no new seed, make no new design; . . . true creation is denied him'.[67]

Renaissance attitudes toward the past remained complex and ambivalent. No summary statement will suffice for the thought of a period so multifariously involved with its heritage, deeply divided in its own mind, and increasingly fragmented by national identity.

A few general points can none the less be made. The Renaissance was uniquely defined by humanists' relationship with the past. To be sure, the term 'renaissance' is ours, not theirs, but the awareness was theirs too; they saw themselves as shaped by the ways they recognized, revived, and came to terms with precursors. Aware of their need both to admire and to transcend the classical past, they did not simply oscillate between devotion and rejection, worship and sacrilege, preservation and transformation, but kept these contrarieties in balance. If humanists could seldom resolve those tensions to their own satisfaction, no one since has been able to do so either.

Renaissance admiration of antiquity presupposed execration of the medieval past. Identification with Greece and Rome went along with sustained efforts to disown more recent precursors, blackening medieval reputations while crediting classical times with every achievement but Christianity. The humanists were not the first or the last to prefer remote to proximate ancestors – imperial Rome and Revolutionary France are familiar examples – but the Renaissance preference was neither a self-pitying nostalgia nor a rationale for revolution; it was the core of their self-awareness. Reviving a distant past for its own uses, the Renaissance was the first epoch to see itself as 'modern', as distinct from both the immediate past it discredited and the remote past it idolized.

The awareness of distance, the embrace of imitation, the implications of revival left humanists uncertain about their ability or even their right to overcome the burdens of a past at first shouldered with crusading zeal. Such action ultimately risked dismembering or annihilating the heritage that was the touchstone of their identity. But if these doubts clouded they did not erase general confidence that, wonderful as past accomplishments had been, moderns could rival and should aim to surpass them. The great works of their contemporaries buttressed humanist confidence. 'I sometimes like to glory in the fact that I was born in this age, which produced countless numbers of men who so excelled in several arts and pursuits that they may well bear comparison with the ancients', thought Rinuccini.[68] 'Since we see in our age letters restored to life', wrote Budé, 'what prevents us from expecting to see among us new Demosthenes, Platos, Thucydides, Ciceros?'[69] Moderns would surpass ancients, claimed Vivès, for they had come to realize that progress was the essence of human thought.[70]

[67] *Light in Troy*, pp. 240–1. See Du Bellay, *Antiquitez de Rome* (1558), sonnets 19, 27, 32, pp. 27–43.
[68] 1473, quoted in Gombrich, 'Renaissance conception', p. 2.
[69] Quoted in Kelley, *Foundations of Modern Historical Scholarship*, p. 78.
[70] *De disciplinis* (1531), cited in Baron, '*Querelle*', p. 13.

Growing faith in material advances; dawning pride in nationality; the felt superiority of Christianity to paganism; the replacement of Latin by vernacular tongues; a conception of history that saw in antiquity exemplary parallels yet also standards for universal aspiration; the perfecting of vigorous and self-conscious emulation; the assumption that the recovery of antiquity, the resurrection of a long-buried past, was a novel and creative act – these were the principal traits that enabled Renaissance spokesmen to turn the past to advantage, to absorb its manifest benefits without being swamped by its manifold burdens.

FROM THE 'QUERELLE' TO THE ENLIGHTENMENT

> In *Words*, as *Fashions*, the same Rule will hold;
> Alike Fantastick, if *too New*, or *Old*;
> Be not the *first* by whom the *New* are try'd,
> Nor yet the *last* to lay the *Old* aside.
>
> Alexander Pope, *An Essay on Criticism*[71]

The vices and virtues of the past became most sharply polarized during the aftermath of the Renaissance. The seventeenth-century *'querelle'* of the Ancients and the Moderns set those who insisted on the enduring superiority of classical antiquity against those who believed they could or already had surpassed the ancients and who deplored subservience to them. Few subscribed wholly to the past or wished wholly to discard it, but embattled advocates generated passions that emphasized extreme views.

What accounts for the virulence of the quarrel, and how was it finally dissipated, if not decided? Three interrelated trends generated its content and polemical rhetoric: the presumed decay of everything in nature; the impact of printing on attitudes toward the past; and antagonism between guardians of classical traditions and a new breed of scientists who found their own experience and observations more reliable guides.

Decay of nature

Widespread belief in universal decay predisposed many in the late sixteenth and early seventeenth centuries to suppose everything in the past superior to anything in the present. The origins and implications of the decay hypothesis are explored in Chapter 4; here it is enough to note that the Renaissance rediscovery of antiquity's greatness seemed to confirm that human intellect shared the general degeneration. An inundation of classical learning made the present seem a 'stony' or an 'iron' age compared with the 'golden' past; the evident superiority of the ancients reinforced plaints of present decline.[72]

The belief that nature had run its course and was tottering to final dissolution blinded many to the virtues of their own times. They rated the present retrograde because they held modern immorality responsible for continuing decline. The conviction that former times were better times amounted to what Gordon Davies terms 'a group inferiority

---

[71] 1711, lines 333–6, 1:276.
[72] Victor Harris, *All Coherence Gone*, pp. 135–6; Williamson, 'Mutability, decay, and seventeenth-century melancholy', p. 135.

complex on a gigantic scale',[73] made endurable only by faith in ultimate redemption. Decay became a stock theme, especially of English Protestant thought from Francis Shakelton's *A Blazing Starre* (1580) through George Goodman's *Fall of Man* (1616) to Thomas Burnet's *Sacred Theory of the Earth* (1684), but the notion of general decline was not confined to England. 'What can we degenerates do in this wayward age?' asked Rubens; it seemed to be God's will that human talents should decay along with the ageing world.[74] Closer to nature's original perfection, unscathed by senescent corruption, mankind during antiquity had been stronger and wiser – the heroic giants depicted in ancient sculpture and Renaissance painting.

Against the doctrine of decay, others argued that nature's plenitude, constancy, and stability proved progress possible, perhaps inevitable. Since the cosmos had not changed since antiquity, reasoned Louis Le Roy, neither had men's abilities; indeed, the fullness of nature guaranteed that moderns would surpass ancients.[75] Mankind showed no signs of decline, asserted George Hakewill, whether in strength and stature, wit and inventions, or manners and conditions.[76] Indeed, advances in religion, history, mathematics, painting, and the sciences were legion. The misperceptions of decay and antique superiority were attributed to elderly men who 'wish againe for the pleasures of youth', being 'so affectionate to antiquitie, that they are ignorant of the Countrie, and time wherein they live'.[77] The *'morosity* and crooked disposition of old men, alwais complaining of the hardnesse of the present times' and given to 'excessive admiration of *Antiquitie*', was a consequence of their own ageing; 'men thinke the world is changed, whereas in truth the change is in themselves'.[78]

By the latter part of the century the corruption of nature seemed no longer justified either by theology or by empirical evidence, and ceased to be a significant argument for the superiority of the past. Subsequent debates over decay were restricted to decline in the arts. In other spheres of nature and material life ideas of progress came to hold sway.

Effects of printing

From the late sixteenth century, the diffusion of printed materials engendered confidence that men would transcend their predecessors' achievements. This optimism stemmed from several causes. Reproduction in print ensured the survival of precious texts without laborious transcription; energies released from tasks of retrieval and preservation could focus on other creative activities, thereby detaching inspiration from the bondage of imitation.

Printing likewise made obsolete the scribal assumption that, because hand-copied texts blurred and blotted ancient learning more than they improved it, and errors increased with time, the most ancient were the most right. Widespread dissemination in print also made it

[73] *Earth in Decay*, p. 6.
[74] *De imitatione statuarum* (*c.* 1608), quoted in Muller, 'Rubens's theory and practice', p. 231.
[75] *De la vicissitude, ou variété des choses en l'univers* (1575), cited in Kelley, *Foundations of Modern Historical Scholarship*, p. 83.
[76] Hakewill, *An Apologie or Declaration of the Power and Providence of God*, 1635, Bks 3 and 4.
[77] Le Roy, *De la vicissitude*, quoted, and Jean Bodin, *Methodus ad facilem historiarum cognitionem* (1566), cited in Harris, *All Coherence Gone*, pp. 100–1, 104. See also Le Roy, 'Excellence of this age', pp. 91–101.
[78] Hakewill, *Apologie*, Bk I, Ch. 3, sect. 5, 1:25. See Tuveson, *Millennium and Utopia*, p. 58.

easy to compare classical texts, and comparison was often fatal to their credibility. Since sources frequently proved at odds, variant texts clearly contained errors, and no traditional authority could be implicitly trusted. Thus the very ability of print to preserve the past led men to question its authority, concludes Eisenstein; 'veneration for the wisdom of the ages' declined as great ancients formerly thought infallible came to be seen as 'individual authors – prone to human error . . . and plagiarism'.[79] The exposure of myriad forgeries and transcription errors deepened mistrust of the past accomplishments touted by scribal texts. Ancient historians were denigrated as careless and biased, their works as self-serving, their times as undeserving of later esteem.[80]

Printing not only preserved the glories and exposed the errors of the past, it also made new additions to mankind's stock of knowledge cumulative, secure against obliteration and alteration. Since each present could now build on all preceding pasts, their accumulated inheritance made moderns *ipso facto* superior, even if individually inferior. 'We are like dwarfs standing on the shoulders of giants', Peter of Blois anticipated the idea in the twelfth century; 'thanks to them, we see farther than they.'[81] The advent of print made the metaphor of moderns on the shoulders (or heads) of ancient giants a commonplace for transcending the past. Even if individually dwarfed, moderns grasped secrets the ancients lacked because they came after them. Later scholars not only built on the past's accumulated knowledge but benefited from its errors. 'We are under obligations to the ancients', asserted Fontenelle, 'for having exhausted almost all the false theories that could be formed.'[82] Fontenelle underestimated mankind's perennial capacity for fallacious invention, but the point was valid: past trial and error spared the present many wrong turnings.

Indeed, the passage of time was felt to make moderns the real ancients. 'Ancient times [were] the youth of the world; these times are the ancient times' was a Baconian dictum often reiterated.[83] Time's cumulations seemed to Pascal to make progress inevitable:

The whole succession of human beings throughout the course of the ages must be regarded as a single man, continually living and learning; and this shows how unwarranted is the deference we yield to the philosophers of antiquity . . . Old age in the universal man must be sought, not in the times nearest his birth, but in the times most distant from it. Those whom we call the ancients really lived in the youth of the world, and the infancy of mankind; and as we have added to their knowledge the experience of the succeeding centuries, it is in ourselves that is to be found the antiquity we venerate in them.[84]

Inverting antiquity and modernity long remained a popular trope for demoting the past. 'I honour antiquity, but that which is commonly called old time is young time', thought Hobbes.[85] 'By the longevity of their labours', wrote Edward Young, moderns who eschewed subservience to the past 'might, one day became antients themselves'.[86]

[79] Eisenstein, *Printing Press*, pp. 289–90, 112–25; quotation on p. 122.
[80] Hazard, *European Mind*, pp. 35–7; Momigliano, 'Ancient history and the antiquarian', pp. 10–18.
[81] *Epistolae* (1180), quoted in Merton, *On the Shoulders of Giants*, p. 216.
[82] *Digression sur les anciens et les modernes* (1688), p. 165.
[83] *Novum Organum*, I, lxxxiv, p. 82; *Advancement of Learning*, Bk I, p. 78. See also Leyden, 'Antiquity and authority'.
[84] Blaise Pascal, 'Fragment d'un traité du vide' (*c.* 1651), in his *Pensées*, 2:271.
[85] 'Answer of Mr. Hobbes to Sir William Davenant's preface before Gondibert' (1650), 4:456.
[86] *Conjectures on Original Composition* (1759), pp. 31–2.

Freeing men from excessive reliance on past authority, the preservative powers of print in other ways made the past more oppressive. Bygone models of excellence became permanent exemplars and each generation's legacy more burdensome to the next: the sheer accumulation of data inhibited efforts to rival precursors. 'The acquisition of knowledge occupies time that might be bestowed on invention', in Adam Ferguson's view; prior occupation of 'every path of ingenuity' militated against new efforts; 'we become students and admirers, instead of rivals; and substitute the knowledge of books, instead of the inquisitive or animated spirit in which they were written'.[87] Thus the past's now all-too-immortal riches at length discouraged the very confidence initially quickened by the printed word. Faced with their predecessors' cumulative achievements, moderns had either to confess their own inferiority or deny the past entirely. As we shall see, this dilemma became a crucial concern for post-Enlightenment poets and philosophers.

The new science

What most sharply polarized the ancients–moderns conflict was the advent of a scientific spirit in seventeenth-century Britain and France. The revelations of immediate sensory experience convinced many scholars that contemporary observations and experiments must supplement, correct, and even supplant past knowledge. William Gilbert dedicated his *De magnete* (1600) to men 'who look for knowledge not in books but in things themselves';[88] as one such man asked, half a century later, why 'subject ourselves to the authority of the Ancients, when our own experience can inform us better?'[89] Current advances made it apparent that much remained to be learned; Columbus's voyages showed how ignorant of fundamental geography antiquity had been, and Magellan's circumnavigation of the globe surpassed ancient discoveries.

Scientists held undue admiration of antiquity a serious impediment. Modern discoveries were discredited, William Watts complained, because ancient dictates preoccupied opinion and discouraged new inventions.[90] 'Too great Reverence borne to *Antiquity* is an error extreamly prejudicial to the advancement of Science', wrote Noah Biggs, 'as if our Ancestours resting places, were to be like the *Hercules* pillars, inscrib'd with a *Ne Plus Ultra*.'[91]

The most influential though one of the least polemical critics of the past was Francis Bacon. Conceding the ancients remarkable powers of abstract meditation, Bacon charged them with generalizing too readily from a few instances; 'new discoveries must be sought from the light of nature, not fetched back out of the darkness of antiquity'.[92] Although Bacon's followers often waxed more vehement, none advocated wholesale repudiation of the past. They knew well what they owed their predecessors, for they depended as much

[87] *Essay on the History of Civil Society* (1767), Pt V, sect. 3, p. 217.
[88] Quoted in Armstrong, 'Introduction' to Bacon, *Advancement of Learning*, p. 9. But Eisenstein notes that Gilbert probably gleaned as much from books as from his own observation and experiments (*Printing Press*, p. 520); see also Zilsel, 'Origins of William Gilbert's scientific method'.
[89] Jeremy Shakerly, *Anatomy of Urania Practica* (1649), quoted in R. F. Jones, *Ancients and Moderns*, p. 123.
[90] 1633, cited in Jones, *Ancients and Moderns*, pp. 72–4.
[91] *Mataeotechnia medicinae praxeos* (1651), quoted in Jones, *Ancients and Moderns*, p. 132.
[92] *Novum Organum*, I, cxxii, p. 109; also I, cxxv, p. 111.

on the printed dissemination of manifold past observations as on the new instruments that magnified their own ability to observe nature. To praise exclusively either the old or the new was foolish and self-defeating. 'Antiquity envieth there should be new additions, and novelty cannot be content to add but it must deface', warned Bacon against both extremes; innovation progressed best along paths marked out by accumulated experience.[93]

Not until the late seventeenth century did traditionalist attacks impel some scientists to exaggerate their claims and to advocate explicit rejection of certain classical traditions.[94] Accused of forsaking time-hallowed traditions for self-serving novelties, Royal Society members retorted that they found in nature an authority previous to the ancients and were simply discarding corrupt copies for originals.[95] Nature's primordial antiquity became a stock defence against accusations of sacrilege. When theologians condemned findings of a change in the shores of the Baltic as contrary to Genesis, scientists replied that 'God had made both the Baltic and Genesis, and ... if there was any contradiction between the two works, the error must lie in the copies that we have of the book rather than in the Baltic Sea, of which we have the original'.[96]

Scientists were not alone in complaining that obeisance to classical learning hampered present-day needs; vernacular literacy made Greek and Latin increasingly irrelevant. Immensely exciting when first rediscovered, the classics were by now so familiar that their majesty had become commonplace. Classical learning was enervating where veneration was compulsory, as in English universities: an Oxford statute extant in 1583 made 'Bachelors and Masters who did not follow Aristotle faithfully ... liable to a fine of five shillings for every point of divergence'.[97] Critics inveighed against the universities' 'stupendous bulk of blinde learning' and 'shreds of *Latine*' for propagating old errors and suppressing new truths.[98] 'A looking back, and prescribing Rules to ourselves from Antiquity, retards and lessens even our Appetite to that which we might easily attain', wrote Clarendon. 'There is not ... a greater Obstruction to the Investigation of Truth, or the Improvement of Knowledge, than ... to admire too much those who have gone before, and like Sheep to tread in their Steps.'[99]

Classicists retaliated in kind: they upheld the ancients as begetters of time-tested truths and accused arrogant scientists of leaving 'the old beaten and known path, to find out wayes unknown, crooked and unpassable'.[100] The old learning seemed to them also an indispensable moral safeguard; they feared lest scientific contempt for antiquity foresha-

---

[93] *Advancement of Learning* (1605), Bk I, p. 77. Bacon in fact wrote a treatise on the wisdom of the ancients (*De sapientia veterum*, 1609).

[94] Jones, *Ancients and Moderns*, pp. 184–201, 237–40.

[95] Sprat, *History of the Royal Society* (1667), p. 371. 'Moderns' of Protestant persuasion professed to rediscover 'Adamic' wisdom whose recovery heralded the end of the Christian terrestrial drama (Rattansi, review of Jones, *Ancients and Moderns*, p. 254).

[96] Charles Ducros, *Les Encyclopédistes* (1900), quoted in Arthur Wilson, *Diderot*, p. 143.

[97] Quoted in McIntyre, *Giordano Bruno*, p. 21. See Highet, *Classical Tradition*, p. 276.

[98] Biggs, *Mateotechnia*, and Francis Osborne, *Miscellany of Sundry Essayes . . .* (1659), quoted in Jones, *Ancients and Moderns*, pp. 100, 146.

[99] Clarendon, *Of the Reverence Due to Antiquity* (1670), pp. 218, 239.

[100] Alexander Ross, *Arcana microcosmi* (1652), quoted in Jones, *Ancients and Moderns*, p. 122. These polemics probably exaggerate the importance of the ancients–moderns antithesis. Entirely absent from many significant works of natural philosophy, the dispute was often conducted in terms not of ancients against moderns, but of Aristotle against other ancients (Rattansi, review of Jones, *Ancients and Moderns*, p. 254).

dow a materialism that would destroy religion, corrupt education, and brutalize society. To deny homage to the ancients was both seditious and atheistical.[101]

The ultimate accolades to ancient learning were William Temple's *Essay on Ancient and Modern Learning* (1690) and Jonathan Swift's 'Battle of the Books'. In Temple's view the ancients excelled the moderns in every particular. Swift assailed exclusive reliance on modern genius as selfish, unproductive folly. Enlarging on Aesop, he likened the modern to a spider skilled in architecture and mathematics but which scorned to admit any obligation and consequently spun a poisonous cobweb out of its entrails. By contrast, the bees (ancients), owning nothing but their wings and voices, garnered riches from every good source; their honey and wax thus furnished mankind with 'Sweetness and Light'.[102] But unlike the bees of Renaissance emulative practice, Swift's bees did not transform and digest what they took in. That omission epitomizes the sterility of the ancients' position by the end of the seventeenth century.

Sciences vs. arts

Few avowed partisans remained, by then, on either side of the *querelle*; most struck a balance between the triumphs and shortcomings of past and present. 'Men are subject to errors', wrote Algernon Sidney, 'and it is the work of the best and wisest to discover and amend such as their ancestors may have committed, or to add perfection to those things which by them have been well invented.'[103] Clarendon kept 'a just Reverence' for the ancient Church Fathers 'as great Lights which appeared in very dark Times; we admire their Learning and their Piety, and wonder how they arrived to either in Times of so much Barbarity and Ignorance'. But 'the best way to preserve the Reverence that is due to Age' was 'hoping and believing that the next Age may know more, and be better'.[104]

The end of the seventeenth century left ancients and moderns embattled in principle but in practice dividing the honours. The *querelle* increasingly led men to distinguish arts and sciences as different realms. Scientific knowledge was clearly cumulative, a grand collective enterprise ever adding to the stock of knowledge. But artistic talent showed no such cumulative benefits, and superiority depended on individual effort; for the modern poet or painter, architect or composer, past achievements were less a boon than a burden, monuments to greatness which he could seldom if ever rival.[105] It seemed in the nature of science that the moderns should win the day, and in the nature of the arts that they should lose.

The distinction itself was seen as detrimental to artistic endeavour. Proclaiming the progressive genius of modern science, William Wotton conceded that the past might continue to outshine the present in the arts and philosophy, where achievement had to be judged solely on non-cumulative merits.[106] William Collins termed the arts exceptions to present-day improvements:

[101] Especially Meric Casaubon and Henry Stubbe, cited in Jones, *Ancients and Moderns*, pp. 241–62.
[102] 'Battle of the books' (1698), p. 151.
[103] *Discourses Concerning Government* (1698), Ch. 3, sect. 25, p. 364.
[104] *Of the Reverence Due to Antiquity*, pp. 237, 224, 220.
[105] Kristeller, 'Modern system of the arts', pp. 525–6; Scheffer, 'Idea of decline in literature and the fine arts in eighteenth-century England'.
[106] *Reflections upon Ancient and Modern Learning* (1694), pp. 5, 9.

Each rising art by just gradation moves,
Toil builds on toil, and age on age improves:
The Muse alone unequal dealt her rage,
And graced with noblest pomp her earliest stage.[107]

Joseph Priestley drew an analogous distinction: since science knew no bounds, Newton's discoveries had not discouraged other philosophers but inspired them to new discoveries; but because there were perceptible limits to artistic advance, previous achievements closed off new prospects.[108]

Not everyone considered all modern arts inferior. Boileau admitted that contemporary epic, oratory, elegy, and satire did not match the classical Augustans, but believed his own the greatest age for tragedy, philosophy, and lyric poetry.[109] But literary champions of the modern cause, notes Paul de Man, were themselves by and large inferior in talent to advocates of the ancients.[110]

Thus whereas the sciences increasingly shook off dependence on antiquity, the arts became more oppressed by the past's now redoubled burden. Eighteenth-century poets had to cope not only with classical precursors but with the closer eminence of Montaigne and Rabelais, Spenser and Milton. 'The virtues of their immediate predecessors' made it harder for princes to govern, remarked Samuel Johnson, and 'he that succeeds a celebrated writer has the same difficulties to encounter'.[111] The remote past might seem admirable, but the recent past 'extinguishes emulation, and sinks the ardour of the generous youth', in Hume's phrase; a man confronted by many models of native eloquence 'naturally compares his own juvenile exercises with these; and being sensible of the great disproportion, is discouraged from any farther attempts, and never aims at a rivalship with those authors, whom he so much admires'. Yet only rivalry could overcome undue reverence for the past; 'a noble emulation is the source of every excellence. Admiration and modesty naturally extinguish this emulation.'[112] No one felt the dilemma more keenly than Goethe, one of the few to transcend it: the demons themselves, he believed, 'set up isolated figures who are so alluring' – a Raphael, a Mozart, a Shakespeare – 'that everyone emulates them and yet so great that no one can equal them'.[113] So pernicious was this allure, thought Vico, that no talented artist could afford to keep past exemplars around him; men 'endowed with surpassing genius, should put the masterpieces of their art out of their sight'.[114]

The very recognition of previous excellence thus condemned eighteenth-century

---

[107] 'Epistle addressed to Sir Thomas Hanmer' (1744), p. 391.

[108] *Lectures on History, and General Policy* (1788), p. 382. John Stuart Mill later drew the same contrast in terms of the learned and the masses: 'The wisest men in every age generally surpass in wisdom the wisest of any preceding age, because . . . [they] possess and profit by the constantly increasing accumulation of the ideas of all ages; but the multitude . . . have the ideas of their own age, and no other' ('Spirit of the age', 1831, p. 36).

[109] To Charles Perrault, cited in Highet, *Classical Tradition*, p. 281.   [110] *Blindness and Insight*, pp. 153–4.

[111] *The Rambler*, No. 86, 12 Jan. 1751, in Johnson, *Works*, 2:87.

[112] Hume, 'Of the rise and progress of the arts and sciences' (1742), 3:196. Hume's own precursor was Velleius (*Historiae Romanae*, c. A.D. 30; see Scheffer, 'Idea of decline', pp. 157–60). Hume also blamed foreign importations: 'So many models of ITALIAN painting brought into ENGLAND, instead of exciting our artists, is the cause of their small progress'.

[113] To Eckermann, 6 Dec. 1829, in *Goethe: Conversational Encounters*, p. 208.

[114] Vico, *On the Study Methods of Our Time* (1709), p. 72: 'Our possession of the Farnese Hercules and of other masterpieces of ancient sculpture . . . has prevented our sculpture from reaching its consummate fruition' (p. 71). See Bloom, *Poetry and Repression*, p. 4.

painters and poets to inferiority; the sanctified past left the modern spirit no role beyond imitation of matchless precursors. 'Impossible', was the constant refrain. 'Nature being still the same', concluded Richard Steele, 'it is impossible for any modern writer to paint her otherwise than the ancients have done';[115] originality was inconceivable. 'It is impossible for us, who live in the latter Ages of the World', wrote Addison, 'to make Observations . . . which have not been touched on by others.'[116] Great precursors *'engross* our attention, and so prevent a due inspection of ourselves; they *prejudice* our judgment in favour of their abilities, and so lessen the sense of our own; and they *intimidate* us with the splendor of their renown, and thus under diffidence bury our strength'.[117]

French Enlightenment *philosophes* likewise excluded the arts from the general march of progress. Voltaire believed routine imitation the only alternative to 'senseless eccentric-ity'; Condillac thought imaginative decline evident and artistic exhaustion inevitable.[118] Sprawled at the foot of a classical colossus, Henry Fuseli's painter (Illus. 21, p. 155 below) epitomized the modern artist at once inspired and abased by the grandeur of the past.[119]

Their precursors' felt superiority led eighteenth-century poets, painters, and critics to judge artistic decline pervasive. But their pessimism stemmed from assumptions quite unlike the now discredited 'decay of nature'; moral and artistic decline seemed a consequence of general *advance* in knowledge and civilization, an impoverished imagin-ation the ultimate price of scientific progress.[120] Material improvement was held to deprive modern poets and painters of passion, the corrosion of criticism to discourage fluency, and mass audiences to subvert aesthetic standards. Fear of originality magnified these drawbacks; the creative impulse felt to be lacking was at the same time deprecated as *outré* and unseemly. Consciousness of past excellence, thought James Marriott, incited excessive novelty, causing the arts to degenerate. Moderns ambitious to rival past perfection 'are tempted to turn aside into unbeaten tracks of nicety and affectation', corrupting what Voltaire termed their predecessors' 'beautiful simplicity of nature'.[121] Since the modest despair of attaining fame 'and the opulent may think it too precarious to pursue', in Goldsmith's view, the defence of modern talents 'may at last devolve on indigence and effrontery', for only the conceited or the desperate would aim to improve on the past.[122] Modern tastes for complexity and novelty were partly to blame for decline, thought Lord Kames – though he also felt that past achievements had been so superior 'as to extinguish emulation' even in science, where 'the great Newton, who, having surpassed all the ancients, has not left to his countrymen even the faintest hope of rivalling him'.[123]

Previous perfection similarly inhibited modern sculpture, 'necessarily destroy[ing] that

---

[115] *The Guardian*, quoted in Bate, *Burden of the Past*, p. 40.

[116] *Spectator*, No. 253, 20 Dec. 1711, 2:483–4: 'We fall short at present of the Ancients in Poetry, Oratory, History, Architecture, and all the noble Arts and Sciences which depend more upon Genius than Experience, but exceed them . . . in Doggerel, . . . Burlesque, and all the trivial Arts of Ridicule' (ibid., No. 249, 15 Dec. 1711, 2:467).

[117] Young, *Conjectures on Original Composition* (1759), p. 9.   [118] Bate, *Burden of the Past*, p. 46.

[119] *The Artist Moved by the Grandeur of Ancient Ruins* (1778–9), cited in Honour, *Neo-classicism*, p. 53.

[120] Manuel, *Shapes of Philosophical History*, pp. 67–8.

[121] Marriott, 1755, cited, and Voltaire, 'An essay on taste' (1757), quoted in Scheffer, 'Idea of decline', pp. 162, 164.

[122] *Enquiry into the Present State of Polite Learning in Europe* (1759), p. 260.

[123] Kames, *Sketches of the History of Man* (1788), 1:296–7; see also pp. 281–2. In Italy 'Michael Angelo, Raphael, Titian &c. are lofty oaks that keep down young plants in their neighbourhood, and intercept from them the sunshine of emulation' (p. 300).

noble emulation which alone can stimulate to excellence', in Robert Cullen's words. 'Conscious of being unable to surpass the great models which he sees, the artist is discouraged from making attempts. The posts of honour are already occupied; superior praise and glory are not to be reached; and the ardour of the artist is checked by perceiving that he cannot exceed' or perhaps even equal his predecessors.[124]

How did the *querelle* shift allegiances between past and present, old and new? As with the Renaissance, no single conclusion can suffice. Some see the idea of progress as ever more triumphant. Even before the Enlightenment, European scholars 'suddenly dropped the cult of antiquity', in Paul Hazard's view; regarding four millennia of history as 'nothing to be proud of but, on the contrary, an intolerable burden', they 'turned their backs on the past [as] something evanescent, Protean, something impossible to grasp and retain, something inherently and inveterately deceptive' and untrustworthy. By the end of the seventeenth century 'the past, with all its mighty dead, was set at nought'.[125] Eighteenth-century *philosophes* expressed gratitude that mankind had left behind the infamous past, on whose horrors they continually harped.[126] Only those ignorant of history could regret the good old days, asserted Chastellux; no past had been so happy as the present. 'What educated man', asked the Abbé Morellet, 'would really wish he had lived in the barbarous and poetical time which Homer paints?'[127] In Volney's view, the opulent splendours of ancient empires had made their inhabitants neither wise nor happy.[128] Antiquity was derogated to emphasize the progress made by moderns – and, as these examples show, to dispel lingering traces of nostalgia.

'The Past abandoned; the Present enthroned in its place!'[129] is not, however, an accurate assessment of the temper of the time. New confidence in progress did not banish older doubts, and many remained variously attached to the past. As we have seen, even so confident a modern as Bacon continued to revere antiquity. A century later John Locke termed the *querelle* a conflict between unreasonable prejudices; it was 'fantastical' to attribute 'all knowledge to the ancients alone, or to the moderns'; one should 'get what helps he can from either'.[130]

The legacy of the *querelle* was an amalgam of confidence about the march of progress, apathy in the face of overshadowing precursors, and ambivalence about the proper role of the past in the present. Contentious early issues – the idea of decay, the urge to unshackle science from classical precedents, the role of vernacular languages – were resolved or outdated; but the *querelle*'s very vehemence generated new issues, and set past against present as implacable rivals.

Cumulative progress eventually became the hallmark of scientific knowledge, but in culture and the arts great precursors were felt to inhibit modern prowess, and novelty meant not advance but decline. Both realms acknowledged the power of the past for either

---

[124] *Lounger*, No. 73 (1786), quoted in Scheffer, 'Idea of decline', p. 173.
[125] Hazard, *European Mind*, pp. 29–30.
[126] Becker, *Heavenly City of the Eighteenth-Century Philosophers*, p. 118.
[127] Chastellux, *Essay on Public Happiness* (1772); Morellet, quoted in Bury, *Idea of Progress*, pp. 192–3.
[128] Volney, *Ruins; or, A Survey of the Revolutions of Empire* (1789), Ch. 11, pp. 49–61.
[129] Hazard, *European Mind*, p. 30.
[130] *Conduct of the Understanding* (1706), sect. 24, 'Partiality', pp. 47–8.

good or evil, but in science and material civilization men felt they had absorbed and overcome the past, whereas in the declining arts the glories of antiquity inspired but also haunted moderns who felt themselves belated inferiors. To follow precursors had been a creative option in the Renaissance but was now simply a mark of subservience; imitation had become incompatible with innovation. Thenceforth, revolutionary and Romantic iconoclasm became major challenges to the weight and authority of the past.

VICTORIAN BRITAIN

> The new things are based and supported on sturdy old things, and derive a massive strength from their deep and immemorial foundations, though with such limitations and impediments as only an Englishman could endure. But he likes to feel the weight of all the past upon his back; and, moreover, the antiquity that overburdens him has taken root in his being, and has grown to be rather a hump than a pack, so that there is no getting rid of it without tearing his whole structure to pieces . . . As he appears to be sufficiently comfortable under the mouldy accretion, he had better stumble on with it as long as he can.
>
> Nathaniel Hawthorne, 'About Warwick'[131]

Unprecedented change radically sundered the present from even the recent past in nineteenth-century Europe and North America. Consciousness of that change magnified both the virtues and vices of a heritage better known but less retrievable than ever before. And revolutionary upheaval at both ends of the century unleashed iconoclastic impulses that aimed to render the past impotent if not wholly to efface it, but at the same time triggered reactionary nostalgia for ways of life felt to be forever lost.

Ambivalence towards a past transcended and discarded, yet also passionately embraced or yearned for, was most manifest in Victorian Britain. No people since the Renaissance combined such confidence in their own powers with so much antiquarian retrospection. But nineteenth-century Britain was not fifteenth-century Italy; although echoes of the earlier ambivalence still resonated, fundamental changes in material life, in modes of government, and in conceptions of man and nature, time and change – not least that the Victorians conceived the Renaissance as part of their own past – made for tensions of a wholly different order.

British life after 1815 (the end of the Napoleonic Wars marks a more significant divide than the accession of Victoria) left the past behind in many things social and material, but clung to its vestiges in many things aesthetic and spiritual, largely as a consequence of three great upheavals. First, society was profoundly shaken by the French Revolution, after which it seemed that nothing would ever again be the same. Whether seen as the deserved downfall of a corrupt and frivolous ruling class or as a demonic blood-bath under mob rule, the Revolution replaced the fall of the Roman Empire as history's sternest and most dramatic moral lesson, in J. W. Burrow's apt comparison.[132] The destruction of tradition reverberated in other Continental uprisings – 1830, 1848, 1871 – and the Hyde Park riots of 1866 seemed a harbinger of anarchy at home. Social and political flux endangered all institutions based on past authority.[133]

---

[131] 1862, p. 70.   [132] 'Sense of the past', p. 124.
[133] Arnold, *Culture & Anarchy* (1869), pp. 50–7, 171–4, 214–18; Houghton, *Victorian Frame of Mind*, pp. 54–8.

Second, British reform movements of the 1820s and 1830s emphasized discontents analogous to those across the Channel. The Utilitarians and political economists condemned tradition, precedent, prescriptive right, ancient privilege. And anti-traditional doctrine provoked a fervent defence of heritage in the medievalist reactions of the 1830s and 1840s.

Third, British manufacturing spurted ahead so rapidly after Waterloo that the face of the country and the lives of most of its inhabitants seemed transformed beyond recognition and, for many, beyond redemption. Revulsion against this transformation was overwhelming, notwithstanding or even on account of the immense wealth it created. Romantics and reactionaries blamed the brutal 'machinery' of change (alike of the French and the Industrial Revolutions) for a mean and rootless modernity.[134] Reacting against the present, early and mid Victorians propped up and reinstated anachronistic features of pre-industrial pasts. Denunciations of the soulless, ugly, degrading present continued well into the twentieth century, for the widening franchise, the railways, steamships, telegraph, and trams made the two generations after 1840 as dramatically disorientating as the two generations before. So much did preferences for the past dominate British life and landscape that turn-of-the-century guides on Manchester and Birmingham stressed their origins in remote antiquity to the virtual exclusion of their modern growth, while archaic anachronisms such as royal rituals and London's Lord Mayor's show were served up as popular spectacles.[135]

No other society had so rapidly embraced innovation and invention or seen its everyday landscapes so thoroughly altered. Yet no other society viewed its past with such self-congratulatory gravity or sought so earnestly to reanimate its features. Scott's historical novels, Gothic Revival architecture, neo-chivalric fashions of dress and conduct, classical standards of beauty, successive passions for all things Roman, Greek, Egyptian, Chinese, early English – all this betokened a people besotted with the past. John Stuart Mill thought his fellow countrymen all 'carry their eyes in the back of their heads'.[136]

As an antidote to the dreadful present, the exotic past supplied missing virtues – especially medieval England with its shared and ordered life, so poignant a contrast to modern tawdriness, secularism, and lack of community.[137] Precisely because medieval art belonged to 'a world that is now no more', Victorians found it 'salutary and refreshing to be taken back to men and times with whom we have so little in common'.[138] Many began to wish for, and consequently to find, more in common with them. 'We *are* medievalists and rejoice in the name', wrote the architect G. E. Street, 'wishing to do our work in the same simple but strong spirit which made the man of the thirteenth century so noble a creature.'[139] 'The Middle Ages are to me the only ages', declared Ruskin. 'That miracle-believing faith produced good fruit – the best yet in the world'; modern science and philosophy had yielded only abortions.[140] Thirteenth-century builders' freehand

---

[134] Burrow, 'Sense of the past', p. 125.
[135] Cannadine, 'Context, performance and meaning of ritual', pp. 122, 138; Asa Briggs, *Victorian Cities*, pp. 391–2. See Tuveson, *Millennium and Utopia*, p. 218.
[136] 'Spirit of the age' (1831), p. 29.   [137] Girouard, *Return to Camelot*.
[138] J. Beavington Atkinson in *Art-Journal* (1859), quoted in Haskell, *Rediscoveries in Art*, p. 106.
[139] In *Ecclesiologist* (1858), quoted in J. M. Crook, *William Burges*, p. 55.
[140] To Charles Eliot Norton, 8 Jan. 1876, in Ruskin, *Collected Works*, 37:189.

drawings were crude, their perspective poor, their knowledge of mechanics and geometry nil, conceded William Burges – but they left us Amiens, Westminster, Cologne, and Beauvais cathedrals. By contrast, the ugly scientific etching and shading of modern architects had produced nothing of merit. And so Burges based his own drawings on what he thought was medieval practice.[141]

An exchange in a novel by Robert Kerr, whose architect protagonist Georgius Old-housen stands for Burges, imparts the quintessential tone:

> 'We're getting on, you know. We're standing in the ancient ways a great deal more than we used to . . . Of all things in the world I hate things that are modern.'
> 'Just so . . . And do you really think the sixteenth century is ancient enough?'
> 'No', says Georgius, 'I don't . . . Don't I wish I had been born in the thirteenth century!'[142]

So narcotic was medievalist infatuation that some late Victorians 'belonged' to the past in a fashion more quixotic than Petrarch's love-affair with the ancients. 'A pity 'tis I was not born in the Middle Ages', exclaimed Burne-Jones in 1897. 'People then would have known how to use me – now they don't know what on earth to do with me.'[143] Others created the past they hoped posterity would accord them: Hardy set himself up as the Aeschylus of Wessex; Arnold's *Sohrab and Rustum* echoed Homer to impress future commentators; Tennyson marked where *Idylls of the King* imitated Homer and Pindar; and Robert Leighton's self-portrait shows an ancient Greek in Victorian London, in Richard Jenkyns's phrase, confirming the persona already assigned him by the Henry James narrator who always had 'an odd sense of our speaking of the dead . . . His reputation was a kind of gilded obelisk, as if he had been buried beneath it; the body of legend and reminiscence of which he was to be the subject had crystallised in advance.'[144] These living time-capsules remind one of the ghostly classical reverberations of Petrarch's texts. But nothing was less like Renaissance imitative strategies – concealing or openly contending against exemplars for creative ends – than Victorian harking back to past models whose fame alone justified their successors' puny efforts.

Not all Victorians were so deluded about the past. George Eliot regretted the loss of bygone folkways, but believed herself 'better off for possessing Athenian life solely as an inodorous fragment of antiquity', and was happy not to have lived 'when there were fewer reforms and plenty of highwaymen, fewer discoveries and more faces pitted with small-pox'.[145] Proud of his own progressive age, Dickens often condemned the past, mocked its partisans, and hated to hear 'those infernal and damnably good old times extolled'.[146] Archaeology and history revealed much to deprecate as well as to laud: a classical world less noble and pure than previously supposed; medieval superstition, vice,

---

[141] Crook, *William Burges*, pp. 62–5.

[142] Kerr, *His Excellency the Ambassador Extraordinary* (1879), 1:330–1, 2:101.

[143] *Memorials of Edward Burne-Jones*, 2:318. See Buckley, 'Pre-Raphaelite past and present: the poetry of the Rossettis', p. 137.

[144] Jenkyns, *Victorians and Ancient Greece*, pp. 34–8, 309–10; James, 'Private life' (1893), 17:226.

[145] Eliot, 'Looking backward!' in her *Impressions of Theophrastus Such* (1879), pp. 24, 27.

[146] To Douglas Jerrold, 3 May 1843, in Dickens, *Letters*, 3:481. Dickens named his shelf of dummy books 'The Wisdom of our Ancestors' and subtitled them 'Ignorance. Superstition. The Block. The Stake. The Rack. Dirt. Disease' (Burrow, 'Sense of the past', p. 125). See Sanders, *Victorian Historical Novel*, pp. 70–1; Houghton, *Victorian Frame of Mind*, pp. 45–53.

and cruelty. Such imperfections required lovers of the past to wear selective blinkers.[147] Walter Scott, the past's supreme delineator, himself preferred to live in the present; for all its historical trappings, his Abbotsford was also Scotland's first gas-lit house.[148]

The sorry consequences of besottedness with the past were the subject of ceaseless self-criticism. Writers bemoaned the burden of the past, their own inability to produce epics, their sense of belonging to a lesser age. 'We are lost in wonder at what has been done', wrote Hazlitt, 'and dare not think of emulating it.'[149] Shelley termed the surviving fragments of Greek perfection 'the despair of modern art'; the weight of past greatness crushed the life out of modern poets who felt that everything worth saying had already been said.[150] In Florence, George Eliot was 'thrown into a state of humiliating passivity by the sight of the great things done in the far past' and felt 'so completely dwarfed by comparison that I should never have courage for more creation of my own.[151]

The rich architectural legacy was likewise intimidating. The sheer accumulation of drawings and pictures of antique buildings terrified modern taste and frightened 'original talent . . . into servile imitation'.[152] The heritage was a grave psychological burden: 'All that is excellent in art has been transmitted to us from past ages', an observer summed up current views, and 'all the productions of modern skill are mere imitations of the ancient.' Many felt that human imagination had run its course; 'the maturer age of the world' was not conducive to fresh creation, and could only apply for models to 'legacies from the superior intelligence of former ages'. Progress was not to be hoped for; 'unable to improve upon the splendid individualities of the past, we are left to reclassify and re-employ them'. Another critic almost wished 'that the temples of Greece had long ago perished if the study of them is to supersede all invention on our part'.[153]

To profess devotion to progress in general while mistrusting artistic innovation struck Ruskin as absurdly inconsistent. 'While we . . . act in accordance with the dullest modern principles of economy and utility, we look fondly back to the manners of the ages of chivalry, and delight in . . . the fashions we pretend to despise, and the splendors we think it wise to abandon.' It was deplorable that 'the furniture and personages of our romance are sought . . . in the centuries which we profess to have surpassed in everything', while 'the art which takes us into the present times is considered as both daring and degraded . . . In this we are wholly different from all the races that preceded us . . . The Greeks and mediaevals honored, but did not imitate, their forefathers; we imitate, but do not honor.'[154] But then Ruskin held the material and social 'improvements' of his time responsible for its moral and aesthetic retrogression.

What undermined self-confidence, many complained, was less the actual superiority of

[147] Honour, *Romanticism*, pp. 211–13.   [148] Daiches, 'Sir Walter Scott and history', p. 464.
[149] 'Schlegel on the drama' (1816), p. 66.
[150] Shelley, *Hellas* (1822), Preface, p. ix; Byron, cited in Jenkyns, *Victorians and Ancient Greece*, p. 23.
[151] To John Blackwood, 18 May 1860, in Eliot, *Letters*, 3:294. As shown above, she subsequently recovered her creative self-confidence.
[152] 'Public buildings of Edinburgh' (1820), p. 370.
[153] E. Trotman, 'On the alleged degeneracy of modern architecture' (1834); *Athenaeum* (1829); George Wightwick in *Loudon's* (1835); *Foreign Quarterly Review* (1830); all quoted in Kindler, 'Periodical criticism 1815–40: originality in architecture', p. 25.
[154] *Modern Painters*, III, Pt IV, Ch. 16, sect. 15, pp. 255–6.

the past than excessive attention to it; the past weighed heavily because it was a burden voluntarily shouldered. 'The idea of comparing one's own age with former ages . . . had occurred to philosophers' previously, observed Mill, 'but it never before was itself the dominant idea of any age.'[155] And Hazlitt noted that 'a constant reference to the best models of art necessarily tends to enervate the mind . . . and to distract the attention by a variety of unattainable excellence'.[156] Close study of the ancient masters deprived moderns of original genius; Constable chided artists 'intent only on the study of departed excellence'.[157]

Above all, Victorians feared lest obeisance to the past cheat their era of its own identity. 'A house may be adorned with towers and battlements, or pinnacles and flying buttresses', wrote Richard Payne Knight early in the century, 'but it should still maintain the character of the age and country in which it is erected; and not pretend to be a fortress or monastery of a remote period or distant country.'[158] Greater knowledge of the past and skill in reproducing its forms threatened to deprive Victorians of any distinctive style of their own.

Even those who doted on the past expressed strictures against its toils. The champion of the Gothic Revival, George Gilbert Scott, feared that the 'effect of working with this vivid *panorama* of the past placed constantly in our view, is to induce a capricious eclecticism – building now in this style, now in that – content to pluck the flowers of history without cultivating any of our own'.[159]

Made abject by their borrowings, Victorians sought an identity to gain self-respect. But many saw such an effort was doomed by its very self-consciousness. No age had ever formed a style of its own by deliberately seeking it, added Scott; creativity had flourished among the Greeks and in the Renaissance, he assumed, because 'no one thought much of the past – each devoted his energies wholly to the present. Their efforts were consequently *concentrated*.'[160] Only by likewise forgetting its predecessors could his epoch achieve a distinctive individuality.

The Victorians exemplified Nietzsche's complaint that 'we moderns have nothing of our own'; young minds were stuffed with 'an enormous mass of ideas, taken second hand from past times and peoples, not from immediate contact with life'.[161] The past burdened them because they remembered it so well, while vainly hoping that it might be possible to forget it again.

Self-conscious sophistication was felt to forfeit other virtues, too. Aesthetic revivals gleaned only the husk of past exemplars when passionate involvement had given way to academic authentication. Cathedrals like Amiens could no longer be built, asserted Heine, because 'the men of old times had convictions, we moderns have only opinions'.[162] The Gothic Revival was 'a vain endeavour to reanimate deceased Art', thought Constable, which could only 'reproduce a body without a soul'.[163] That devoted Gothicist Burges

---

[155] Mill, 'Spirit of the age', p. 28.   [156] 'Fine arts' (1814), 18:41.
[157] 'Various subjects of landscape characteristic of English scenery' (1833), p. 10.
[158] *Analytical Inquiry into the Principles of Taste* (1806), Pt II, Ch. 2, p. 99.
[159] 'Remarks on architectural character' (1846), quoted in Pevsner, *Some Architectural Writers of the Nineteenth Century*, p. 177.
[160] Ibid. See Lang, 'Richard Payne Knight', p. 96.   [161] *Use and Abuse of History*, pp. 24, 67.
[162] 'Ueber die französische Bühne' (1837), p. 279.
[163] 'Lecture on landscape' (1834–5), p. 70.

concluded in 1868 that he and his contemporaries had 'not been very successful, either in our copies or in our own efforts . . . [They] want spirit. They are dead bodies; they don't live.'[164]

The spirit of the age, thought the architect T. L. Donaldson, 'trying by an amalgamation of certain features in this or that style of each and every period . . . to form a homogeneous whole with some distinctive character of its own', simply led to 'injudicious thraldom'.[165] Responding to calls for 'an architecture of our period, a distinct, individual, palpable style of the nineteenth century', architects laboriously borrowed from a multitude of sources.[166] But this aroused criticism as withering as that directed against single-minded devotion to Greek or Gothic. 'We have all the centuries but our own', Alfred de Musset had complained of eclecticism; 'unlike any other epoch, we take all that we find, this for its beauty, that for its commodity, the other for its antiquity, this other even for its ugliness; consequently we live only among debris, as though the end of the world were at hand.'[167] Fifty years later, William Morris deplored all nineteenth-century revivals, from 'pure' Gothic ('London has not yet begun to look like a fifteenth-century city') to Queen Anne, for bequeathing an 'avowedly imitative' vulgar and unimaginative architecture.[168]

Querying not only the efficacy but the morality of borrowing, Victorian artists and architects faced anew the old problem of originality. They had inherited conflicting traditions: one stemming from the classics that stressed faithful following, the other from the Romantics (and in part the Enlightenment) that stressed innovation and individuality. But for the Victorians, as for their humanist precursors, to innovate still meant to reuse the past; they asserted individuality through reconstruction. The past was the creative architect's touchstone; 'the more richly he stores his mind with the ideas of others', wrote a critic, 'the more likely will he be to bring forth new ideas of his own'.[169] Invention for its own sake was abhorrent; 'the continual attempt at *novelty*' had been the 'ruin' of modern Italian architecture.[170] But critics also scored architects who pilfered and tacked together Palladian fragments in unthinking imitation. A balance of stylistic stability and change was wanted, a compromise between 'copyism' and 'originality',[171] a difference from the past without rejecting the past – 'that which is new and more or less unexpected', in Bray's words, but 'at the same time an organic development of that which is already well known and familiar'.[172] In short, Victorians sought to swim while keeping on Erasmus's life-preserver.

That life-preserver was also needed by Whig historians who remade the past into a cosy or uplifting simulacrum of the present. Unlike nostalgic medievalists, they merged their chosen period with modern times, emphasizing points of presumed resemblance rather than differences and relishing the enduring continuities. 'The more one revered the

---

[164] 'Art and religion' (1868), quoted in Crook, *William Burges*, p. 127.

[165] *Preliminary Discourse . . . Lectures on Architecture*, 1842, p. 30.

[166] T. L. Donaldson (1847), quoted in Pevsner, *Some Architectural Writers*, p. 82.

[167] *Confession d'un enfant du siècle* (1836), p. 89. Because the nineteenth century lacked its own 'decisive color', echoed the Austrian architect Ludwig von Förster, it borrowed visual idioms from every past (Schorske, '*Fin-de-Siècle*' Vienna, p. 36).

[168] 'Revival of architecture' (1888), p. 326. See Summerson, 'Evaluation of Victorian architecture', pp. 38–9.

[169] 'The Conductor', *Loudon's* (1834), quoted in Kindler, 'Periodical criticism', p. 26.

[170] 'Restoration of the Parthenon in the National Monument' (1819), p. 143.

[171] Pevsner, *Some Architectural Writers*, Ch. 22, 'The battling *Builder*: copyism v. originality', pp. 222–37.

[172] *History of English Critical Terms* (1898), pp. 211–12.

ancients, the more exciting it was to find that one had something in common with them', as Jenkyns puts it.[173] Rather than praising the past at the expense of the present, they respected but were not confined by their heritage, cherished the past while denying it any binding force; they married belief in continuity with faith in progress.[174] Compromise between tradition and change was their leitmotiv: change occurring within the confines of tradition, and hence controllable; tradition made malleable by change, and hence progressive. The assumed continuity of English institutions allowed the seemly incorporation even of the most extensive transformations.

It was loss of faith in those continuities that eventually cost late Victorians much of the security they had found in the past. Far too much was now known by historians, anthropologists, classicists and other specialists to sustain the old view that past and present were similar, that history was exemplary. The unlikeness of the past, the awareness of historical change that Erasmus's contemporaries had ignored or explained away, Vico's unbridgeable diversity of epochs and cultures each with its own, not our own, way of looking at life – these insights could no longer be denied; the past evidently *was* a foreign country. Its contrasts might amuse, shock, or even instruct the present but could no longer sustain faith in its exemplary role.[175] The past's intellectual bankruptcy as much as its suffocating weight spawned the turn-of-the-century modernist crusade (see Chapter 7) against past precepts, past artifacts, past modes of thought.

Nineteenth-century Britain consummated the ancients–moderns distinction between the forward-looking sciences and the backward-looking arts. In science, engineering, and manufacturing, Britain became the prototype of innovative self-confidence. In the arts, education, religion, and politics, troubling ambivalence left the past sometimes a refuge, sometimes a burden. The manifold consequences of industrialization hardened the *revanchiste* mentality aroused by the French Revolution. To secure themselves against the evils of rampant change and the dangers posed by the new industrial order, Victorians took refuge in one or another past, pasts not so much preserved as extravagantly re-created in architecture, art, and literature. But as the century wore on, increasing knowledge and new historical insights made re-creation and revival alike more demanding and confining. 'How had the burden of precedent increased!' exclaimed Marius of what Pater supposed a similarly beholden era. 'It was all around me – that smoothly built world of old classical taste, and accomplished fact, with an overwhelming authority on every point of the conduct of one's own work ... There might seem to be no place left for novelty or originality.'[176] Demands for a style that would incorporate the genius of the entire past fed an eclecticism that scarcely satisfied the earlier Romantic urge toward creative individuality, let alone the later modernist urge to dispense with the past altogether.

By the turn of this century the past had lost its exemplary and pedagogical justification but continued to supply intimate connections with pre-industrial ways of life. In apparent defiance of technological growth, the trappings of chivalry proliferated within and beyond

---

[173] *Victorians and Ancient Greece*, p. 81. See Burrow, 'Sense of the past', pp. 127–8.
[174] Views exemplified in William Stubbs's *Constitutional History of England* (1874–8); see Burrow, *Liberal Descent*, pp. 102–7.
[175] Blaas, *Continuity and Anachronism*.   [176] *Marius the Epicurean* (1885), 1:107.

12 The look of antiquity: seventeenth-century manor house, Sibford Gower, Oxfordshire, remodelled 1915

13 The look of antiquity: Ernest Newton, design for Fouracre, West Green, Hampshire, *c.* 1902

the newly expanded knighthood and the ceremonially revived monarchy. The concurrent birth of the Ancient Monuments Act, *Country Life* magazine, the Society for the Protection of Ancient Buildings, the National Trust, and the Arts and Crafts movement attest the pervasiveness of the pre-industrial cult; architects designed new 'Old English' and 'Queen Anne' cottages that felt as old as, if not older than, actual relics of those times.[177]

England's new schools and colleges illustrate how innovation accommodated and was then engulfed by tradition. Designed for sons of rising industrial magnates and of a growing middle class, these establishments at first made change palatable by cloaking innovative aims in traditionalist garb – Gothic buildings, pastoral landscapes, classical fixtures and features, ceremonies and curricula. But as new entrepreneurs were domesticated into landed gentry, academe became preoccupied with the past in its own right, a past morally, socially, and environmentally superior to the present and now endangered by material progress.[178]

That past was no longer really alive, however. Indeed, the very fact that it was dead made its revival possible, now that it posed no threat to the present. 'Concern with the past did not conflict directly with the progress of modernization', concludes Charles Dellheim. A Bradford businessman was no less dedicated an entrepreneur for his interest in collecting Roman coins; business in Bradford's neo-Gothic Wool Exchange was thoroughly modern. Indeed, Dellheim suggests that middle-class devotion to historical paraphernalia diminished the past's prescriptive force by reinterpreting its meaning in the light of modern aspirations. Relegated to the realms of art, leisure, and ceremonial ritual, anti-modern forces had a negligible impact on the practical world of technology.[179]

Nor did the worship of ancient architecture require any commitment to its institutions or ideals, as had earlier been the case; late Victorians could safely preserve medieval remnants because the medieval past was gone for good. Conflicts between saving the past and building the future were minimized by preserving specified monuments and – notwithstanding manifestos defending the entire heritage – quietly forsaking the rest.[180] But it is wrong to suppose that cultural attachments to the past had no influence on other British institutions. Martin Wiener has shown how the nostalgic attachments of the older elite became emblems of acceptance for the rising rich, and suggests that finding solace in obsolete modes of living and working still preoccupies Britain to the continuing detriment of industrial innovation.[181]

Whether British attachment to things past was – and is – wholly pervasive, as Wiener argues, or largely decorative, as Dellheim thinks, its significance for British letters and landscape is beyond question. The past was a burden willingly assumed by an elite who

---

[177] Girouard, *Sweetness and Light*; Wiener, *English Culture*, pp. 44–70; Jan Marsh, *Back to the Land: The Pastoral Impulse in Victorian England*.

[178] Wiener, *English Culture*, pp. 11–24. American architecture, education, and *belles-lettres* exhibited similar reactionary tendencies (Lears, *No Place of Grace: Antimodernism and the Transformation of American Culture 1880–1920*, pp. 5, 60–1, 159–66, 188–9; Conn, *Divided Self*, Chs. 2, 7, 8).

[179] Dellheim, *Face of the Past*, pp. 179–81.   [180] Ibid., p. 180.

[181] Wiener, *English Culture*, pp. 158–66. Dellheim himself notes that rapidly expanding Leeds, Manchester, and Middlesbrough emphasized their pre-industrial antiquity to mitigate newness and rootlessness (*Face of the Past*, pp. 65–6).

identified with it and who felt genuine alarm lest massive change subvert national character and environment. A recent expression of such a feeling is James Lees-Milne's reflection on the loss of a benevolent aristocracy. 'This evening the whole tragedy of England impressed itself upon me', he wrote in 1947 while negotiating the National Trust's acquisition of Brockhampton, Herefordshire. 'This small, not very important seat in the heart of our secluded country is now deprived of its last squire [John Talbot Lutley]. A whole social system has broken down. What will replace it beyond government by the masses, uncultivated, rancorous, savage, philistine, the enemies of all things beautiful?'[182]

AMERICAN FOUNDING FATHERS AND SONS

Whatever is old is corrupt, and the past turns to snakes. The reverence for the deeds of our ancestors is a treacherous sentiment.

Ralph Waldo Emerson, 'Works and days'[183]

American attitudes toward the past, perhaps more sharply polarized than any other, are most vividly expressed in the metaphors of filial conflict noted in Chapter 2. On the one hand, freedom from the encumbering past was a virtual dogma of the Revolution and the new republic; on the other, Americans deplored their historically meagre landscapes and reverently protected the Founding Fathers' achievements. They could square neither their nostalgia nor their filio-piety with the national mission to sweep away past precept and tradition.[184]

The binding force of the past had troubled Puritan New Englanders even in the seventeenth century. Frontier circumstances made it increasingly hard for children and grandchildren of the original settlers to follow the patriarchal precepts of their elders. The Puritan ideal of the community as a large family – hierarchical, disciplinarian, earnestly dedicated to religious purpose – came to seem reactionary and unenforceable. But their predecessors' moral superiority posed a painful choice: 'They could continue to idealize, and seek to perpetuate, the temper of the Founding Fathers; or they could try to adapt themselves to drastic change in political, economic, and intellectual conditions', in Peter Gay's words. 'Rigid, they would turn themselves into anachronisms; flexible, they would betray their Puritanism.'[185]

More burdensome than outgrown colonial beginnings, as time wore on, became the imperial heritage: Britain, British political institutions, British modes of thought. In severing imperial bonds, Americans discarded not only the mother country but many of its traditions. Three interrelated ideas helped justify dismissal of the past: a belief that autonomy was the birthright of each successive generation; an organic analogy that assigned America a place of youth in history; and a faith that the new nation was divinely exempt from decay and decline.

[182] Lees-Milne, *Caves of Ice*, diary entry 16 June 1947, p. 172.   [183] 1870, 7:177.
[184] Lowenthal, 'Place of the past in the American landscape'.
[185] *Loss of Mastery: Puritan Historians in Colonial America*, p. 110. See also J. P. Walsh, 'Holy time and sacred space in Puritan New England', p. 94.

Autonomy and generational freedom

The parent–child analogy was persistently invoked by British and American antagonists in the late eighteenth century. Tories used filial metaphors to chastise unruly colonists for disobedience to the mother country, Patriots to castigate Britain as an unnatural and tyrannical parent. Such metaphors were already common coin: analogies between family and state authority pervaded seventeenth-century English debates over 'natural' freedom and 'social contract'. Principles and practices of child-rearing were in flux, the traditional authoritarian household gradually giving way, with the rise of a market economy, to a more open and egalitarian structure.[186]

Earlier views, epitomized in Robert Filmer's *Patriarcha* (1680), emphasized two related precepts: a father held absolute lifelong power over his offspring; subjects owed their sovereign the same unquestioning obedience. It was to rebut these propositions that John Locke wrote *Two Treatises of Government*. Against Filmer's patriarchal family, Locke argued that a man 'cannot by any compact whatsoever bind his children or posterity'; sons when grown were by nature as free as their fathers. And against Filmer's divine-right precept, Locke argued that governmental trust required the consent of the governed; absolutism flouted natural rights and forfeited citizens' obedience. Along with Locke's arguments, growing faith in progress eventually disallowed genetic or familial justifications of political authority.[187]

Punitive family norms that had kept children dependent well into adulthood increasingly gave way to Locke's precepts to instil obedience through example and tender guidance, lest 'children, when grown up, weary of you; and secretly ... say within themselves, "When will you die, father?"'[188] Education should enable offspring released from the paternal yoke to seek the divine, a step essential to their salvation.[189] Rousseau reached a similar conclusion: 'Children remain bound to their father only so long as they need him for their own self-preservation. The moment this need ceases, the natural bond is dissolved.'[190] Some felt reform had gone too far: 'the last age taught mankind to believe that they were mere children and treated them as such till they were near thirty years old', wrote a theologian, but he equally deplored that 'the present gives them leave to fancy themselves complete men and women at twelve or fifteen'.[191]

Changes in child-rearing were especially rapid across the Atlantic. Seventeenth-century colonial parents had kept adult sons dependent by curtailing access to land and the transmission of wealth; the breakdown of these controls enabled eighteenth-century sons to establish independence, leave home, and reach maturity far earlier, often assuming adult responsibilities by the age of 13. One reason the Revolutionary epoch produced so

---

[186] Schochet, *Patriarchalism in Political Thought*; Trumbach, *Rise of the Egalitarian Family*; Fliegelman, *Prodigals and Pilgrims: The American Revolution against Patriarchal Authority*; Rogin, *Fathers and Children*.

[187] Locke, *Two Treatises of Government* (1690), II, Ch. 8, para. 116, p. 180, and Chs. 6, 7, 15, 18; Schochet, *Patriarchalism*, pp. 273–6. Locke himself did not apply this analogical reasoning, let alone use it to defend revolution (Burrows and Wallace, 'American Revolution', pp. 188–9).

[188] Locke, *Some Thoughts Concerning Education* (1693), para. 4, p. 34.

[189] 'The first moment one is loosed from the paternal yoke becomes identified with the first moment one may *choose* to seek the divine yoke ... To impede that passage was virtually to interfere with a necessary stage of the salvational process' (Fliegelman, *Prodigals and Pilgrims*, p. 285).

[190] Rousseau, *Social Contract* (1762), Bk 1, Ch. 2, p. 4.

[191] Isaac Watts, *Improvement of the Mind* (1747), quoted in Fliegelman, *Prodigals and Pilgrims*, p. 19.

many outstanding leaders, some historians suggest, is that fathers actively encouraged sons to take on such responsibilities.[192] Britain had treated colonials as infants dependent on their elders and subject to their whims; pent-up resentment against the subordination exploded with the Revolution. Colonies would wean themselves when they came of age, James Harrington had predicted in *The Commonwealth of Oceana* (1656); John Adams observed in 1774 that 'the colonies are now nearer manhood than ever Harrington foresaw they would arrive' in so short a time. 'You have been children long enough', lectured Noah Webster, 'subject to the control and subservient to the interest of a haughty parent.'[193] In this perspective, Britain had blocked the colonial rite of passage by refusing to prepare Americans for maturity, and George Washington became the indulgent parent – the Father of his Country – who, in one eulogist's words, freed the 'infant country from a state of childhood and weakness to that of manhood and strength'.[194]

'Enlightenment is man's emergence from his self-imposed nonage', Kant had put it, 'from the inability to use one's own understanding without another's guidance ... Laziness and cowardice are the reasons why such a large proportion of men ... gladly remain immature for life.'[195] Even worse was to have adulthood denied by despotic parents. In Paine's words, 'To know whether it be the interest of the continent to be independent, we need only ask this easy, simple question: Is it the interest of a man to be a boy all his life?'[196]

Revolutionary allegiances accorded with modes of upbringing. Kenneth Lynn shows that every important Loyalist was either raised by uncompromising patriarchs who brooked no opposition and demanded prolonged filial fealty or so lacked parental guidance that he never outgrew the need for authoritarian figures; neither type could afford to sever bonds with Britain, the supreme parental surrogate. Most prominent Patriots, by contrast, were reared on Lockean principles, their individuality respected, their autonomy nurtured, their spirit of liberty praised. Those who led the break from Britain were prepared by their upbringing to face separation and independence with resourceful confidence.[197]

South American revolts against Spain evinced similar resentment against an imposed permanent childhood. The young colonials who became Chilean Revolutionary leaders felt themselves held back by ageing imperial tyrants. As Bolívar declared in 1815, Latin Americans owed no loyalty to Spanish rule that 'kept us in a state of permanent childhood'.[198]

---

[192] Handlin and Handlin, *Facing Life: Youth and Family in American History*, pp. 12–18; Lynn, *A Divided People*, pp. 68–9, 98–9. The speed and ease with which young American boys achieved adulthood long continued to impress foreign observers (Tocqueville, *Democracy in America* (1840), 2:202–3). Well into the twentieth century, American sons were brought up to be independent and resourceful, and distanced themselves from rivalled fathers on whom they modelled themselves but to whom they owed nothing (Demos, 'Oedipus and America', pp. 35–6).

[193] Adams, *Novanglus*, 4:104; Webster, 'On the education of youth in America' (1787–8), p. 77.

[194] Josiah Dunham, *A Funeral Oration* (1800), quoted in Fliegelman, *Prodigals and Pilgrims*, p. 203, and p. 185; see Burrows and Wallace, 'American Revolution', pp. 188–9.

[195] Kant, 'An answer to the question: "What is enlightenment?"' (1784), p. 54.

[196] 'The American crisis', III (1777), p. 203.

[197] Lynn, *A Divided People*.

[198] Felstiner, 'Family metaphors and the language of an independence revolution', quoting Simon Bolívar, 'Jamaican letter' (1815), p. 167.

The notion of continuing freedom of choice legitimized American rebellion. Proud of their own rupture with the past, Americans assumed their descendants would continue to slough off ancestral things and thoughts. Filial autonomy underlay Paine's and Jefferson's doctrine of the sovereignty of every maturing generation: each generation was a 'distinct nation' that should erase inherited institutions and choose its own. 'The dead have no rights', as Jefferson put it. 'Our Creator made the world for the use of the living and not of the dead ... One generation of men cannot foreclose or burden its use to another.'[199] Against the English common-law rationale which rooted judicial precedent in the immemorial past, many Americans held that the legal code ought to expire every nineteen years or so – an adult generation's average duration.[200] They disowned the dead, reiterating the doctrine that no generation should bind its successors.

The youth of America

In the organic analogy then current, nations like individuals invariably moved from infancy and youth to maturity and old age.[201] The virtues of youth had long been associated with America; contrasting the pristine purity of American life with Britain's degeneracy at the time of the South Sea Bubble, Bishop George Berkeley celebrated New World virtues:

> Not such as Europe breeds in her decay
> Such as she bred when fresh and young
>   ★ ★ ★
> Westward the course of Empire takes its way
> The first four acts already past,
> A fifth shall close the drama with the day
> The world's great effort is the last.[202]

America's early stage in the life cycle also justified her inhabitants' disregard of the past. 'It belongs to the character of youthful and vigorous nations to concern themselves with the present and the future rather than with the past', wrote George Perkins Marsh; 'not until the sun of their greatness ... is beginning to decline [is] a spirit of antiquarian research' aroused.[203] The very lack of a long and glorious past augured a long and glorious future. 'It is for other nations to boast of what they have been; ... the history of their youthful exploits ... only renders decrepitude more conspicuous', asserted a chauvinist.

[199] Paine, 'Dissertation on the first principles of government' (1795), p. 576; Jefferson to John W. Eppes, 24 June 1813, to Samuel Kercheval, 12 July 1816, to Thomas Earle, 24 Sept. 1823, in his *Writings*, 12:260–1, 15:42–3, 15:470. Commager, *Empire of Reason*, pp. 202–4, suggests Jefferson's disavowal of the dead dates from at least 1785. See Woodward, 'Future of the past', pp. 721–2; Alexander Laing, 'Jefferson's usufruct principle', *The Nation*, 3 July 1976, pp. 7–16. Animus against the tyranny of the past did not prevent Jefferson from admiring and following many of its precepts (Colbourn, *Lamp of Experience*, pp. 158–84; Somkin, *Unquiet Eagle*, p. 69).

[200] Boorstin, *Lost World of Thomas Jefferson*, pp. 206–10; Pound, *Formative Period of American Law*, pp. 7–8, 144–5. Jeremy Bentham urged Americans to shut their ports 'against the Common Law, as we would against the plague' (quoted in Boorstin, *The Americans: The National Experience*, p. 36).

[201] See Chapter 4, pp. 127–8, 140–2 below.

[202] 'America, or the Muse's refuge', in letter from Berkeley to John Percival, 2 Oct. 1726, *Works*, 8:153.

[203] Marsh, *Goths in New-England* (1843), p. 7. Marsh feared, however, that lack of reverence for antiquity would cost Americans dear; see my *George Perkins Marsh*, pp. 59, 101.

'Ours is the more animating sentiment of hope, looking forward with prophetic eye.'[204] A New York City mayor attributed Europe's decrepitude to its glut of relics: 'Did we live amidst ruins' and evidence of 'present decay, . . . we might be as little inclined as others, to look forward. But we delight in the promised sunshine of the future, and leave to those who are conscious that they have passed their grand climacteric to console themselves with the splendors of the past.'[205]

A-historical uniqueness

A period of youth that kept the corrupt old past temporarily at bay was not enough: many Americans conceived their country as exempt from decay because *eternally* youthful. Newly created by rational and blameless men, America lay outside the historical process; Providence had specifically spared it from history. Building on seventeenth-century Protestant millennialism, Colonial theologians had viewed Americans as a chosen people destined to complete the Reformation and to restore a prelapsarian state of grace. The Puritan errand was simply the ripening of this millennial seed; the promised millennium would preserve America from otherwise universal corruption.[206] America need never suffer the fate of Europe, long mature and now 'nearly rotten',[207] for the Deity had exempted it from the final period of ageing, even from death itself. 'If such is the youth of the Republic, what will be its old age?' asked a French statesman, and Senator Lewis Cass answered: 'Sir, it will have no old age.'[208] The American nation resembled Mackinac Islanders who lived to a great age; 'if people want to die, they can't die here – they're obliged to go elsewhere'.[209]

Eternally vigorous and youthful, Americans continued to depict their destiny in a-historical terms. One of America's most influential nineteenth-century historians, George Bancroft, ascribed his country's development to the realization of God's unchanging truth; his successors, though eschewing Bancroft's romanticism and religiosity, still identified America with an immutable covenant, unswerving principles, and immunity from time's corrosion.[210] Not until the end of the nineteenth century was confidence in dispensation from history seriously challenged, and well into the twentieth century – whether as isolationists withdrawing from contamination by the decadent outside world, or as messianic activists bent on its reform – Americans conceived themselves as uniquely exempt from secular historical processes.[211]

[204] Paulding, 'The American naval chronicle' (1815), quoted in J. M. George, 'James Kirke Paulding', p. 96.
[205] Colden, *Memoir, at the Celebration of the Completion of the New York Canals* (1825), pp. 77–8.
[206] Tuveson, *Redeemer Nation*, pp. 103–6, 110–11; Dorothy Ross, 'Historical consciousness in nineteenth-century America', p. 912; Pocock, *Machiavellian Moment*, Ch. 15.
[207] Bory St. Vincent to Constantine Rafinesque, in *Western Minerva*, 1 (1821), 70 (facs. reprint, Gloucester, Mass., 1949).
[208] *Congressional Globe*, 29:2 (1846–7), p. 1192, quoted in Merle Curti, *Roots of American Loyalty*, p. 64.
[209] Marryat, *Diary of America* (1839), p. 122. See Somkin, *Unquiet Eagle*, pp. 72–83.
[210] Ross, 'Historical consciousness', pp. 916, 921, 924. Not all were so confident America was immune from the life cycle. 'There is never a rising without a setting sun', warned John Quincy Adams. 'Let us remember that we shall fall . . . into the decline and infirmities of old age' ('The former, present, and future prospects of America', 1787), quoted in Van Tassell, *Recording America's Past*, p. 45). See Persons, 'Progress and the organic cycle in eighteenth-century America'; *idem*, *American Minds*, pp. 123–6; Perry Miller, 'Romantic dilemma of American nationalism and the concept of nature'.
[211] Ross, 'Historical consciousness', p. 928; Tuveson, *Redeemer Nation*, pp. 158–60, 213–14.

The useless and crippling past

As a new creation rather than an organic outgrowth, America held aloof from history in general. 'We have no interest in the scenes of antiquity', declared an exponent of American manifest destiny, 'only as lessons of avoidance of nearly all their examples.'[212] For Americans history was truly just a catalogue of errors. Like the scientists who defended their Baltic Sea findings against charges of impiety, Paine thought it pointless 'to roam for information into the field of antiquity; the real volume, not of history but of facts, is directly before us, unmutilated by the errors of tradition'.[213] Truth was the observable present, falsehood the hearsay past; Americans were pleased they lacked a past and felt sorry for Europeans lumbered with one. 'A nation is much to be pitied, that is weighed down by the past', says a James Fenimore Cooper character; 'its industry and enterprise are constantly impeded by obstacles that grow out of its recollections.'[214]

The sheer novelty of America made historical analogies irrelevant. 'With the Past we have literally nothing to do. Its lessons are lost and its tongue is silent', asserted a future Missouri governor. 'Precedents have lost their virtue and all their authority is gone.'[215] Envious Europeans echoed these presentist accolades. In Goethe's lines:

> America, you are more fortunate
> Than our old continent
> You have no ruined castles
> And no primordial stones
> Your soul, your inner life
> Remain untroubled by
> Useless memory . . .[216]

Americans who linked institutional decay with old age also viewed Europe's ivy-clad monuments and ancient ruins as marks of evil reflecting Old World senility. 'It is said that *our* country has no past, no history, no monuments!' exclaims an American in an Emma Southworth best-seller, on seeing the decayed dungeons of an ancient British castle. 'I am glad of it! Better her past should be a blank page than be written over with such bloody hieroglyphics as these! When I consider these records and reflect upon the deeds of this crime-stained old land, I look upon our own young nation as an innocent child!'[217]

As the nation shook off the historical past, so its citizens divested themselves of family heritage. The ideal American became 'an individual emancipated from history, happily bereft of ancestry, untouched and undefiled by the usual inheritances of family and race; an individual standing alone, self-reliant and self-propelling', in R. W. B. Lewis's words. Time and memory had corrupted Europeans; Americans were like Adam before the Fall. 'The national and hence the individual conscience was clear just because it was unsullied by the past – America . . . had no past, but only a present and a future.'[218]

To renounce the past meant especially to reject parental influence. 'I have lived some

---

[212] O'Sullivan, 'Great nations of futurity' (1839), p. 427.   [213] *Rights of Man* (1791–2), p. 376.

[214] *Home as Found* (1849), p. 23.

[215] Benjamin Gràtz Brown (1850), quoted in Walter Agard, 'Classics on the Midwest frontier', p. 166.

[216] 'Vereinigten Staaten' (1812), p. 405–6. I am grateful to Gillian Clarke for help in translating this poem.

[217] *Self-raised; or, From the Depths* (1864), pp. 433–4.

[218] Lewis, *American Adam*, pp. 5, 7. For the Emersonian dismissal of memory, custom, and filiation, see Quentin Anderson, *Imperial Self*, especially Ch. 1, 'The failure of the fathers'.

thirty years', Thoreau declared, 'and I have yet to hear the first syllable of valuable or even earnest advice from my seniors.'[219] Democracy made men forget their ancestors and 'imagine that their whole destiny is in their own hands', observed Tocqueville: in America 'the tie that united one generation to another is relaxed or broken; every man there loses all traces of the ideas of his forefathers or takes no heed of them'.[220]

Americans excised history from their surroundings as well as from their minds: the 'sovereignty of the present generation' applied no less to law than to landscape. Inherited property epitomized the tyranny of forebears, the burden of the past. Old houses were 'heaps of bricks and stones' that a man builds 'for himself to die in, and for his posterity to be miserable in';[221] the glory of America, thought George Wharton, was that everything was periodically pulled down.[222]

Art mirrored life in espousing material evanescence. The reformer Holgrave in Hawthorne's *House of the Seven Gables* envisaged the day 'when no man shall build his house for posterity' and extolled the ephemeral:

Our public edifices – our capitols, state-houses, court-houses, city-halls and churches – ought [not] to be built of such permanent materials as stone or brick. It were better that they should crumble to ruin, once in twenty years, or thereabouts, as a hint to the people to examine into and reform the institutions which they symbolize.[223]

Thoreau would destroy all relics of the past: America must disown the habits of England, 'an old gentleman who is travelling with a great deal of baggage, trumpery which has accumulated from long housekeeping which he has not the courage to burn'. His *Walden* proposes a programme of 'purifying destruction'.[224] The Old World idea 'that houses, like wines, improve with age' was termed simply 'absurd'.[225]

Dislike of old dwellings extended to historical revivals. 'Since they cannot live in real old houses, our lovers of antiquity ... imitate old barbarisms in their new structures', charged a critic. 'Building new houses to resemble old ones, is quite as ridiculous as it would be for a young man to affect the gait of his grandfather.'[226] It might be 'quite pardonable in Horace Walpole and Sir Walter Scott to build gingerbread houses in imitation of robber barons and Bluebeard chieftains, ... but there can be nothing more grotesque, more absurd, or more affected' than for an ordinary American 'who knows no more of the middle ages than they do of him, to erect for his family residence a gimcrack of a Gothic castle'.[227] 'Gothicized' churches and 'imitation mediaeval cathedrals' were likewise condemned: 'the gray moss of centuries, the clothing ivy, the irregular antique street, the humble hovel, the cloister pale, the stately palace, the dignity of age' were alien to the American landscape and the American mind.[228]

Oblivion was praised as foresight. 'Instead of moralising over magnificence in a process of decay', the European traveller in America would 'watch resources in a process of

---

[219] *Walden* (1854), p. 8.   [220] *Democracy in America* (1840), 2:104–6.
[221] Hawthorne, *House of the Seven Gables* (1852), p. 263.
[222] Cited in Perry Miller, *Life of the Mind in America*, p. 303. See also Anderson, *Imperial Self*, p. 33.
[223] Pp. 183–4. See also Hawthorne, 'Earth's holocaust' (1844), 10:381–95.
[224] Pp. 60–1. See Woodward, 'Future of the past', pp. 722–3.   [225] 'Our new homes' (1847), p. 392.
[226] Ibid., pp. 392–3.
[227] *New York Mirror* review of William H. Ranlett, *The American Architect* (1846), quoted in Hamlin, *Greek Revival Architecture in America*, p. 325.
[228] 'Church architecture in New-York' (1847), p. 140.

development'.[229] Crèvecoeur found it 'better to occupy one's thinking with bright futures and new speculations . . . than to wander through the uncertain and questionable paths of antiquity, only to contemplate tottering ruins, demolished buildings, or the effects of devastating revolutions'.[230] The *tabula rasa* spurred Americans on:

> Though we boast no ancient towers,
> Where ivied streamers twine;
> The laurel lives upon our shores;
> The laurel, boy, is thine.[231]

Faith that they had banished the past and owed nothing to forebears, to tradition, to example, animated Americans up to the Civil War. The new American Adam, unencumbered by inherited ideas and habits, was the Transcendental ideal. Countless essays and tales approvingly portrayed Americans heedless of heritage and sloughing off everything old.

Even the classical past, at first exempt from this animus, ultimately fell into disfavour. Like most who have thrown off an evil or crippling proximate heritage, disaffected colonials identified with remoter epochs whose virtues they thought mirrored their own. They likened themselves to Plutarch and Livy, Cicero and Sallust, who had similarly mourned the loss of innocence, deplored moral disintegration, and 'contrasted the present with a better past'.[232] During the Revolution, Americans continually harked back to ancient Roman virtues. Washington's fancied resemblance to Cincinnatus was one of a hundred parallels that helped to validate the new republic, and citations from Polybius, Cato, and other ancient authors lent classical authority to American constitution-makers.[233]

Like Romans who claimed to surpass Greece, however, Americans claimed superiority to the ancient republics. And veneration of the classical past was soon tempered and later largely relinquished. Pioneer settlers continued to lend the frontier culture and prestige with antique place-names and Greek Revival buildings, but by the mid nineteenth century the classical experience became 'a matter of *curiosity*, rather than of instruction'.[234] Pompey and Caesar were names for slaves; Greek and Roman literature was more to be avoided than imitated. The New World was beyond the farthest ken of classical authors; what could progressive Americans learn from them? Those who sought ancestral advice or worshipped heroes replaced Cato and Cicero with Washington and Jefferson. Democracy, anti-intellectualism, materialism, and faith in progress made the classical past useless and

---

[229] Oliphant, *Minnesota and the Far West* (1855), p. 1.
[230] *Journey into Northern Pennsylvania and the State of New York* (1801), p. 456.
[231] Joseph Bartlett Burleigh, *The Thinker, a Moral Reader . . .* (1855), quoted in Elson, *Guardians of Tradition: American Schoolbooks of the Nineteenth Century*, p. 36.
[232] Bailyn, *Ideological Origins of the American Revolution*, pp. 25–6. See Mullett, 'Classical influences on the American Revolution'; Gummere, *American Colonial Mind and the Classical Tradition*, pp. 97–119. For the role of the classics in American schooling, see Middlekauff, *Ancients and Axioms: Secondary Education in Eighteenth-Century New England*, pp. 75–91, 120–3.
[233] Wills, *Cincinnatus: George Washington and the Enlightenment*; Chinard, 'Polybius and the American Constitution'; Gummere, *American Colonial Mind*, pp. 173–90. Washington was also spoken of as Fabius, Lycurgus, and Solon (Matthews, 'Some sobriquets applied to Washington').
[234] Thomas S. Grimké, *Address on the Expediency and Duty of Adopting the Bible as a Class Book* (1830), quoted in Miles, 'The young American nation and the classical world', p. 259. See Hamlin, *Greek Revival Architecture*; Gowans, *Images of American Living*, pp. 276–7; Buchanan, 'Owego architecture: Greek Revival in a pioneer town'; Zelinsky, 'Classical town names in the United States'.

derisory.[235] Persuading William Henry Harrison to delete some obscure classical references from his 1840 inaugural address, Daniel Webster bragged that he had 'killed seventeen Roman proconsuls as dead as smelts'.[236]

Ambivalence

But if Americans had shed the incubus of the past, why did they need to detest it so excessively? What made their disavowals of tradition so shrill and persistent? Why bother to castigate a now impotent rival? Why did Thoreau demand 'purifying destruction' of a heritage already forsworn? Clearly, the past somehow remained fearsome to the American spirit. Verbal assaults against tradition, against antiquity, against heirlooms, against inherited houses, as exemplified in the *The House of the Seven Gables*, show that the past many nineteenth-century Americans claimed to have left behind was still a baneful living presence. Hawthorne himself showed endless ambivalence toward the past. 'Let us thank God for having given us such ancestors', he wrote of the original Puritan forefathers; 'and let each successive generation thank him, not less fervently, for being one step further from them in the march of ages.' What alarmed Hawthorne about his revered forebears was not merely that 'the discipline which their gloomy energy of character had established' had dispirited their immediate successors, but that not yet had 'we even thrown off all the unfavorable influences' they had bequeathed.[237]

Emerson was equally ambivalent. The premier apostle of the new certainly doubted his fellow countrymen's willingness to put the past behind them. 'Our age is retrospective', he complained at Harvard in 1836. 'It builds the sepulchres of the fathers.' Like some anxious English Victorian, Emerson accused his own times of excessive devotion to antiquity: 'The foregoing generations beheld God and nature face to face; we, through their eyes; . . . why should not we also have a poetry and philosophy of insight and not of tradition?'[238] In *Self Reliance* he again inveighed against 'this worship of the past' and the American who dared not say, '"I think, I am," but quotes some saint or sage'.[239] But what made Emerson himself, fifteen years after taking Americans to task for imitating the Founding Fathers rather than relying on themselves, turn around to blame them for not fully resembling the Fathers? Hanging a portrait of Washington in his dining-room, Emerson commented that 'I cannot keep my eyes off of it'.[240] Why did the past he had exhorted others to abandon so mesmerize the Sage of Concord?

After Paine and Jefferson had so firmly established the sovereignty of the present generation, why should any American need to encourage children to 'think "that they may be great themselves"', instead of always subservient to dead men'?[241] How could any mid-century writer contend that their upbringing made Americans 'worshippers of the past' or term their obeisance to tradition an 'almost insurmountable obstacle . . . against real advancement'?[242] How do laments over this 'retrospective age', this 'worship of the

[235] Miles, 'Young American nation', pp. 263–74; Agard, 'Classics on the Midwest frontier'.
[236] Quoted in Peter Harvey, *Reminiscences and Anecdotes of Daniel Webster*, p. 163.
[237] 'Main-street' (1849), 11:68.   [238] 'Nature' (1836), 1:3.   [239] 2:66–7.
[240] *Journals and Miscellaneous Notebooks*, 6 July 1852, 13:63. See Bloom, *Poetry and Repression*, pp. 242–54.
[241] 'The East and the West' (1848), p. 408.
[242] 'Daniel Webster: his political philosophy in 1820' (1848), p. 130.

past', this 'subservience to dead men', accord with a half century's self-congratulatory dismissals of the past? American conquest of the past sounds strangely incomplete.

In fact, few Americans wholly rejected the past, and some embraced much of it. Opposing the 'party of Hope', as Emerson called those who looked forward, a 'party of Memory' yearned for a storied past.[243] Many adopted both perspectives, simultaneously embracing and rejecting history. Those who felt the pull of the past had the more strongly to resist it; the New World could not afford to be corrupted by nostalgia, but Americans were nostalgic all the same.

Nostalgia for Old World antiquity

One cause of ambivalence toward the past was the paucity of its tangible remains in America. Injunctions to throw off allegiance to antiquity alternated with complaints about its absence – the lack of hoary relics, romantic crumbling ruins, vestiges of continuity with centuries of forebears. 'I had never in my life seen an *old* building', Henry Ward Beecher explained when he wept at Kenilworth Castle; 'I had never seen a ruin.'[244] European ruins especially attracted Americans: Piranesi's Roman scenes were widely popular; Longfellow termed the ruined Alhambra 'wonderful in its fallen greatness'; the Colosseum enraptured Mrs Hawthorne because it looked 'hoary with the years that have passed'.[245]

If Europe's ruins spelled depravity by contrast with the purity of American nature, the same ruins helped make American nature familiarly endearing. The landforms of the American West became ruin metaphors. 'The same processes that sheared fragments from the Pantheon fractured the canyon walls', Paul Shepard sums up explorers' responses to Yellowstone's 'architectural' look.[246] Western Nebraska's escarpments and bluffs compelled comparison with the remnants of ancient castles; Chimney Rock seemed 'the ruins of some vast city erected by a race of giants, contemporaries of the Megatherii and Ichthyosaurii'.[247]

Raw, unfinished America dismayed sensitive souls who shared Mme de Staël's view that 'the most beautiful landscapes in the world, if they evoke no memory, if they bear no trace of any notable event, are uninteresting compared to historic landscapes'.[248] Historical associations were prime attractions in painting and poetry, delineation of the past a

---

[243] 'Historic notes of life and letters in New England' (1883), p. 514.   [244] *Star Papers* (1855), p. 14.

[245] H. M. Jones, *O Strange New World*, p. 236; Longfellow, *Outre-Mer* (1835), p. 227; Sophia Hawthorne, *Notes on England and Italy* (1870), pp. 407–8. American attraction to ruins was anachronistic; the taste for the picturesque in Europe had long passed its heyday (Novak, *Nature and Culture: American Landscape Painting 1825–1875*, pp. 214–15).

[246] *Man in the Landscape*, p. 253. 'The very idea of the Gothic style of architecture', mused the geologist Ferdinand V. Hayden at Yellowstone, might well have 'been caught from such carvings of Nature' (quoted in W. C. Bryant, *Picturesque America*, 1:300). See also Nathaniel Pitt Langford, *The Discovery of Yellowstone Park* (1905), University of Nebraska Press, 1972; Roderick Nash, *Wilderness and the American Mind*, pp. 208–16.

[247] Samuel Parker, *Journal of an Exploring Tour Beyond the Rocky Mountains* (1838), pp. 60–1; Edwin Bryant, *What I Saw in California* (1847), quotation on p. 102. British rocks too were seen as ruins; the products of erosion in Nidderdale were thought carved by ancient Druids (Rooke, 'Some accounts of the Brimham Rocks in Yorkshire', 1787). See Dymond, *Archaeology and History*, p. 25.

[248] *Corinne* (1807), 1:222.

major focus of the arts. 'What are the most esteemed paintings?' asked an American schoolbook of 1806. The answer: 'Those representing historical events.'[249]

The absence of a 'pictured, illuminated Past', felt Motley, gave America 'a naked and impoverished appearance'.[250] This was a typical moan that what was new was empty; lacking 'the associations of tradition which are the soul and interest of scenery', America had 'the beauty of a face without an expression'.[251] 'History, as yet, has left in the United States but so thin and impalpable a deposit that we very soon touch the hard substratum of nature', wrote Henry James, 'and nature herself ... has the peculiarity of seeming rather crude and immature. The very air looks new and young ... the vegetation has the appearance of not having reached its majority. A large juvenility is stamped upon the face of things.'[252]

Europe's historical depth fulfilled needs the American juvenility could not. The foremost celebrants of the new confessed the pull of the old. Thomas Cole's paintings romanticized the American wilderness, yet he also yearned for the past; antique temples and towers festoon several of his landscapes, re-creating the storied Rhine along the Hudson's wild shores.[253] 'He who stands on the mounds of the West, the most venerable remains of American antiquity, *may* experience ... the sublimity of a shoreless ocean un-islanded by the recorded deeds of man', Cole explained, whereas 'he who stands on Mont Albano and looks down on ancient Rome, has his mind peopled with the gigantic associations of the storied past'.[254] Cooper scorned European ruins and celebrated wilderness virtues, but royalties from *Leatherstocking Tales* let him gothicize and castellate his family home and play at being an Old World country squire.[255] When not inveighing against the accumulated rubbish of antiquity, Thoreau found it 'much more agreeable to sit in the midst of old furniture [which has] come down from other generations, than in that which was just brought from the cabinet-maker's and smells of varnish, like a coffin!'[256] Hawthorne wished 'the whole past might be swept away' and the burdensome Parthenon marbles 'burnt into lime', but found it hard to write about places devoid of antiquity: 'romance and poetry, like ivy, lichens, and wallflowers need ruin to make them grow'.[257]

Ambivalence exaggerated both the charms of the past and its evils. As American consul at Liverpool, Hawthorne disparaged visiting fellow countrymen who sought ancestral links, yet sympathized with 'this diseased American appetite for English soil': he himself confessed wishing 'to find a gravestone in one of those old churchyards, with my own name upon it'.[258] But his protagonist in *Doctor Grimshawe's Secret* eventually renounces the rich

[249] Charles Peirce, *The Arts and Sciences Abridged* ... (1806), quoted in Elson, *Guardians of Tradition*, p. 233.
[250] Motley, 'Polity of the Puritans' (1849), p. 493–4. See Strout, *American Image of the Old World*, pp. 74–83; David Levin, *History as Romantic Art*, pp. 7–9.
[251] W. C. Bryant, 'On poetry in its relation to our age and country', quoted in W. C. Bryant II, 'Poetry and painting: a love affair of long ago', p. 875.
[252] James, *Hawthorne* (1879), pp. 12–13.
[253] E. S. Vesell, 'Introduction' to Noble, *Thomas Cole*, p. xxiii; Nash, *Wilderness and the American Mind*, pp. 78–82.
[254] 'Essay on American scenery' (1835), p. 577.
[255] Van Wyck Brooks, *World of Washington Irving*, pp. 421–5.
[256] *Journals*, 3 Oct. 1857, 10:59.
[257] *English Notebooks*, 29 Sept. 1855, and 27 Mar. 1856, pp. 243, 294; *Marble Faun*, p. 3.
[258] 'Consular experiences', p. 20; Hawthorne letter in J. T. Fields, *Yesterdays with Authors*, p. 74.

English past for America's 'poor tents of a day, inns of a night'.[259] For Longfellow too, Old
World history at length gave way to New World duty; foreshadowing the science-fiction
angst explored in Chapter 1, a character in *Hyperion* likens his preposterous nostalgia to
'falling in love with one's own grandmother'.[260]

Fending off nostalgia, Americans condemned historic European scenes as immoral,
decadent, unpatriotic – symbolic of the oppression and tyranny cast off by the Founding
Fathers. Nineteenth-century worthies repeatedly advised young men to shun European
corruptions and seductions. 'Please don't get expatriated', Longfellow entreated a friend;
'life is not all cathedrals or ruined castles, and other theatrical properties of the Old
World.'[261] Repelled by Italy's 'vast museum of magnificence and misery', Mark Twain
rebuked tourists for gawking at ruins and castles.[262] Henry Greenough likened Italy to
'the skeleton of some mighty mastodon, among whose bones jackals, mice, and other
vermin were prowling about'; American schoolbooks termed all of Italy a horrid ruin.[263]
Rome's unearthly beauty struck Hawthorne as also sinister. By contrast with Kenyon's
New World (in the *Marble Faun*) where 'each generation has only its own sins and sorrows
to bear, here, it seems as if all the weary and dreary Past were piled upon the back of the
Present'. For an American to immortalize himself with a marble bust, 'leaving our features
to be a dusty-white ghost among strangers of another generation', seemed to Hawthorne
dreadful and self-defeating, for the brevity of American families meant that few would
know their great-grandfathers; hence one should 'leave no more definite memorial than
the grass'. The world 'will be fresher and better', says Hawthorne's Miriam, 'when it flings
off this great burthen of stony memories' piled up by the pious ages on the back of the
present.[264]

Even green and living English landscapes seemed too full of the past. Hawthorne's
mistrust of old houses, old institutions, long lines of descent made him 'an American of
Americans', in Henry James's judgement, if not 'more American than many [who] have
often a lurking esteem for things that show the marks of having lasted'.[265] Hawthorne
found the old Warwickshire village of Whitnash tedious and moribund.

Rather than the monotony of sluggish ages, loitering on a village-green, toiling in hereditary fields,
listening to the parson's drone lengthened through centuries in the gray Norman church, let us
welcome whatever change may come – change of place, social customs, political institutions, modes
of worship – trusting that . . . they will but make room for better systems, and for a higher type of
man to clothe his life in them, and to fling them off in turn.[266]

To be sure, there was 'something beautiful and touching in the associations' of England's
'old manor houses and country halls . . . where, age after age, the descendants of one family
have lived, and loved, and suffered, and died . . . sheltered by the same trees and guarded
by the same walls', confessed the landscape architect A. J. Downing. But for Americans
such a heritage would not do: 'It is only an idyll, or only a delusion to us. It belongs to the

[259] P. 230.   [260] 1839, p. 137.
[261] To Louise Chandler Moulton, in Wagenknecht, *Henry Wadsworth Longfellow*, p. 195; for Longfellow on
    Europe, see pp. 188–92.
[262] *Innocents Abroad* (1869), pp. 182–5.
[263] Greenough, *Ernest Carroll, or Artist-Life in Italy* (1858), quoted in Novak, *Nature and Culture*, p. 217; Elson,
    Guardians of Tradition, p. 150.
[264] *Marble Faun*, pp. 301–2, 119.   [265] James, *Hawthorne*, p. 130.
[266] Hawthorne, 'Leamington Spa', 5:60.

past ... It could only be reanimated at the sacrifice of the happiness of millions of free citizens.'[267]

No American felt the pull of the past more acutely than Henry James. London and Paris filled him with 'nostalgic poison' and a keen regret for the paucity of history in America.[268] As we saw in Chapter 1, James's *Sense of the Past* highlights the perils of historical charm for a protagonist who finds the American past 'deplorably lacking intensity'. Ralph Pendrel's old house in London comes alive as 'a conscious past, recognising no less than recognised', but also one of evil. Mesmerized by family portraits, Pendrel finds himself back in the previous century as the lover of a long-dead collateral forebear – the Longfellow grandmother syndrome. A past too vividly evoked becomes an abode of nightmare, from which Pendrel barely extricates himself to return to his fiancée 'Aurora' in present-day America.[269] The Old World past comes at a fatal cost.

The debt to the Founding Fathers

A second cause of post-Revolutionary ambivalence toward the past was the conflict of two moral imperatives. Enjoined to throw off allegiance to tradition and rely solely on their own efforts, Americans were at the same time exhorted to revere the Founding Fathers and protect their achievements. They ardently admired their immediate forebears, yet also asserted total independence from the past. The Revolutionary generation had 'bequeathed to us almost all we have that is worth having', a precious legacy that must be zealously safeguarded; 'we inherited it from our fathers, and it is our duty to preserve it for those who come after us'.[270] In short, while the past in general was to be sloughed off, the immediate past was to be venerated and preserved.

As during the break from 'mother' England, family metaphors dominated the 'infancy' of the republic. George Forgie shows that the Founding Fathers offered ideal, indeed inescapable, paternal models.[271] 'So deeply rooted is the principle of imitation in our nature and so ceaseless is our reverence for those who have gone before us', wrote a journalist, 'that the habits and opinions of the people are almost moulded after those of their fathers and especially the first founders.'[272] The rising generation must revere them as fathers: 'as soon as he opens his lips ... every American child should rehearse the history of his own country', bade Noah Webster; 'he should lisp the praise of those illustrious heroes and statesmen who have wrought a revolution in [liberty's] favor'.[273] Senator Rufus Choate agreed that national polity required paternal history to 'be central to the emotional life of the child from the start'.[274] So deeply ingrained were such filial adjurations that in 1864, when a Connecticut state senator opposed repeal of the Fugitive

---

[267] Downing, *Architecture of Country Houses* (1850), pp. 268–9. [268] James, *Reverberator* (1888), 13:195.
[269] *Sense of the Past*, quotations on pp. 33, 65.
[270] 'Reminiscences of a walker round Boston' (1838), p. 80; 'The Missouri Compromise line', *Utica Daily Observer*, 7 Jan. 1861, in Perkins, *Northern Editorials on Secession*, 1:298.
[271] *Patricide in the House Divided*; see also Rogin, *Fathers and Children*, pp. 36–54.
[272] 'Machiavel's political discourses upon the first decade of Livy', *Southern Literary Messenger* (1839), quoted in Forgie, *Patricide*, p. 18n.
[273] 'On the education of youth in America' (1787–8), pp. 64–5.
[274] 'Oration before the Young Men's Democratic Club, in Tremont Temple' (1858), quoted in Forgie, *Patricide*, pp. 19–20.

Slave Law of 1793 on the ground that 'our fathers' would disapprove, a well-known editor doubted that 'worship of ancestors has ever been carried much further than this even in China'.[275]

Such injunctions posed the sons a terrible dilemma. They could not resemble the Founding Fathers without endangering their legacy, or preserve it without acknowledging their subordination. Simply to save the legacy relegated them to everlasting inferiority as sons unable to act on their own. The father's achievements ironically made their example inimitable; 'a hero cannot be a hero', in Hawthorne's words, 'unless in a heroic world', and that world was now gone; as early as 1822 Emerson judged that his country had moved from 'strength, to honour, ... & at last to ennui'.[276] A generation later American life seemed 'no longer a contest of great minds for great ends, but a pot-house squabble'.[277] The present was condemned to a lesser role; 'it is for us to *preserve*, and not to create', concluded Charles Francis Adams.[278] 'We can win no laurels in a war for independence', asserted Daniel Webster. 'Earlier and worthier hands have gathered them all. Nor are there places for us by the side of Solon, and Alfred, and other founders of states. Our fathers have filled them.' Instead, Webster's contemporaries were bequeathed the dubious consolation of having to 'praise what we cannot equal, and celebrate actions which we were not born to perform'.[279] Amidst encomiums to present progress and forecasts of their manifest destiny, Americans also incessantly harked back to the 'earlier and better days of the Republic', terming their present prosaic prosperity 'the forcing-house of mediocrity' and themselves the second-rate progeny of heroic forebears.[280]

Sons with a sacred duty to preserve the inheritance could never match their fathers and thus never reap like rewards. The fathers would forever be remembered for what they had done; who would remember the sons, who did nothing but protect what they had inherited? The founders were justly famed; the preservers would be forgotten.

Several circumstances exacerbated this dilemma while inhibiting awareness of it. One was the prolonged survival of the actual fathers, living memorials to their own splendid deeds for half a century beyond the Revolution. The first five presidents had all played major roles as Founding Fathers. For Americans growing up in the 1820s, the continuing presence of Adams and Jefferson symbolized Revolutionary immortality, and President Monroe made special appearances in his old army uniform 'as if to ward off not the British, but time itself'.[281] Panegyrists could easily treat history as domestic and timeless while 'the heroes ... were still walking among the people'.[282] Their longevity buttressed the view that Americans were exempt from the running of time; 'the presence of these few

[275] E. L. Godkin, 'The Constitution, and its defects', p. 126.

[276] Hawthorne, *American Notebooks*, 7 May 1850, p. 501; Emerson to John Boynton Hill, 3 July 1822, in his *Letters*, 1:120.

[277] 'American despotisms', *Putnam's Monthly* (1854), quoted in Forgie, *Patricide*, p. 67.

[278] 'Hutchinson's third volume' (1834), p. 157.

[279] Webster, 'Bunker Hill Monument' (1825), pp. 153–4, and 'Completion of the Bunker Hill Monument' (1843), p. 262. See Forgie, *Patricide*, pp. 67–8; Schwartz, 'Social context of commemoration', p. 386.

[280] Lowell, 'Self-possession *vs.* prepossession' (1861), p. 763; Forgie, *Patricide*, pp. 73, 173–4.

[281] Forgie, *Patricide*, p. 49. Monroe's appearance was 'a living reminder of some past sufficiently distant for everyone to be proud of it' (Dangerfield, *Awakening of American Nationalism*, p. 22).

[282] 'Henry Clay as orator', *Putnam's Monthly* (1854), quoted in Forgie, *Patricide*, p. 10; also pp. 35–49. Mason Locke Weems's *The Life and Memorable Actions of George Washington* (1800) became the fount of mythology about the Father of his Country.

Revolutionary patriots and heroes among us seems to give a peculiar character to this generation', noted Edward Everett, binding it to the momentous beginnings.[283] Practically all Americans enjoyed such Revolutionary links; 'a *living history was* to be found in every family', Lincoln later recalled, 'bearing the indubitable testimony of its own authenticity, in the limbs mangled, in the scars of wounds received, in the midst of the very scenes related'.[284]

So long did the heroes linger that emancipation from them was difficult even after they had gone; Americans continued to refer to them as immortals. But if the fathers never died, the sons could never assume power or patrimony. Some feared less that their cords with the Founding Fathers would snap than that the dead would use them to strangle the living. Thus filial devotion was edged with resentment against perdurable fathers; because 'the sire would live forever', a Hawthorne character observes, 'the heir [would] never come to his inheritance, and so he would at once hate his own father, from the perception that he would never be out of his way'.[285] Pervasive if unacknowledged hostility suggests why many monuments commemorating Founding Fathers were often opposed, their completion long delayed.[286]

The sons also exaggerated the fathers' antipathy to the past the better to validate their own. Needing to view the new nation as an orphan devoid of parental impress, they obscured the Revolutionaries' dependence on earlier precedent and portrayed them as thorough-going modernists.[287]

The beckoning frontier buoyed up faith in an Adamic destiny untrammelled by any ancestral past; it also postponed a showdown between the duty to preserve and the urge to transcend the inheritance. The ever-renewable West sustained the illusion that the past has been left behind, obviating any need to rebel against it. 'Each frontier did indeed furnish a new field of opportunity', in Frederick Jackson Turner's words, 'a gate of escape from the bondage of the past'; hence 'scorn of older society, impatience of its restraints and its ideas, and indifference to its lessons' marked the frontier mentality.[288] Some who revered the fathers none the less believed they had broken all ties with the past. Others repressed their antipathy to the past like Hawthorne's Holgrave, who ungratefully accepted the inheritance he had inveighed against. 'Claiming simultaneously to be good sons of the fathers and to be adults unburdened by the past', writes Forgie, they 'took their booty and moved into their fathers' house.'[289]

A few realized how ominous was the stress between veneration and aspiration, how dangerous any attempt to emulate the Founding Fathers. A man who now acted like

---

[283] 'Circular' of the Bunker Hill Monument Association (1824), p. 112.

[284] 'Address before the Young Men's Lyceum of Springfield, Illinois' (1838), 1:115. The virtues of this intimate heroic legacy impressed a Prussian historian who visited the United States in 1845. Unlike Europeans who 'go back in sentiment through the twilight of ages', Americans' 'great, undoubted historical past lies near them; their *fathers* did great things, not their *great-great-grandfathers!*' (von Raumer, *America and the American People*, p. 300). But Lincoln saw this living memory as 'now all but gone' and the republic consequently at risk. See Goodrich, *Recollections of a Lifetime* (1857), 1:22–3.

[285] 'Septimius Felton', 13:127.   [286] Forgie, *Patricide*, pp. 92–3.

[287] Ibid., pp. 100–1. Revolutionary leaders had contended they sought only to restore traditional liberties, embedded in Anglo-Saxon forms of government, but radically abrogated by the mother country (Colbourn, *Lamp of Experience*, pp. 190, 199; Hatch, *Sacred Cause of Liberty*, pp. 81–7).

[288] Turner, 'Significance of the frontier in American history' (1893), p. 38; Forgie, *Patricide*, pp. 103–10.

[289] *Patricide*, p. 122.

Washington would no longer be a patriot but a tyrant, warned Judge Beverly Tucker;[290] revolutionary behaviour today would not preserve the republic but subvert it. Lincoln early expressed alarm lest frustrated ambition turn patricidal. Since 'towering genius [that] *scorns* to tread in the footsteps of *any* predecessor' however illustrious would scarcely rest content with memorializing the fame of the fathers, Lincoln feared that adventurers with nothing left to build up would 'set boldly to the task of pulling down'.[291] Those who followed an heroic age might even foment war so as to demonstrate their own heroism.[292]

These anxieties mounted with sectional strife; invective against blind obedience to the past and 'the mouldering tombs of the eighteenth century'[293] alternated with impassioned appeals to restore original principles now subverted. 'It is the cant of the day to repudiate the past', one reviewer complained; it became the counter-cant to lament that repudiation, notes Forgie.[294] Disregard of the past was deemed a besetting and perhaps fatal flaw in the national character; judging that no other generation 'made so little use of the past as ours', critics found Americans too disposed 'to reject the experience and authority of others', and deplored 'our careless indifference to the associations and memory of the past'.[295] The parlous state of Washington's homestead epitomized the decline. Edward Everett urged Mount Vernon's rescue from threatened despoliation as a token of national salvation. 'The Father of his country cries aloud to us ... to be faithful to the dear-bought inheritance which he did so much to secure to us'; pilgrimages to Washington's home and tomb, once restored, might help to heal sectional animus.[296]

Significantly, such appeals no longer aimed at holding on to the past but at *returning* to it. The proclaimed mission of the Republicans was not to preserve but to rescue, to 'restore the government to the policy of the fathers', in Lincoln's words.[297] Their opponents merely remembered the Revolution; the Republicans re-enacted and brought it back into the present. 'The dogmas of the quiet past', which Lincoln had once thought unalterable, were not 'adequate to the stormy present; as our case is new, so we must think anew, and act anew. We must disenthrall ourselves, and then we shall save our country.'[298] Forgie suggests that Lincoln saw himself as the republic's protector against those evil sons whose parricide he had prophesied; 'if the evil figure did appear, and if Lincoln fought and defeated him, and saved the fathers' work, then he too would become immortal'.[299]

The Civil War released Americans from merely preservative filio-piety: as crusaders restoring the founders' edifice, they like them earned descendants' gratitude and deserved undying fame. The previous generation could only revere the founders; the Unionists in

---

[290] 'A discourse on the genius of the federative system of the United States' (1839), cited in Forgie, *Patricide*, p. 235.

[291] 'Address' (1838), 1:114. 'This field of glory is harvested, and the crop is already appropriated. But new reapers will arise, and *they*, too, will seek a field.' Can the gratification of their ruling passion be found 'in supporting and maintaining an edifice that has been erected by others? Most certainly it cannot' (pp. 113–14).

[292] 'Great men, a misfortune', *Southern Literary Messenger* (1860), cited in Forgie, *Patricide*, pp. 279–80.

[293] News correspondent, 1853, quoted in Forgie, *Patricide*, pp. 97–8.

[294] Tuckerman, 'American society' (1855), p. 30; Forgie, *Patricide*, p. 175.

[295] Peabody, 'Arnold *and* Merivale: the History of Rome' (1851), p. 443; 'Civilization: American and European', *American Whig Review* (1846); Boston *Daily Advertiser* (1858); all quoted in Forgie, *Patricide*, p. 175.

[296] Everett (1858), quoted in Forgie, *Patricide*, p. 171; on Mount Vernon, see Hosmer, *Presence of the Past*, pp. 41–62.

[297] 'Speech at Edwardsville' (1858), 3:93.   [298] Lincoln, 'Annual Message to Congress', 1862, 5:537.

[299] *Patricide*, p. 86.

the Civil War, who matched paternal deeds and valour, could also criticize them. Achieving inheritance by their own sacrifices, they won freedom from burdensome father-worship. They themselves noted the end of that thraldom. 'The nation in its childhood needed a paternal Washington', declared a popular novelist; 'but now it has arrived at manhood', and that need was past.[300]

Centennial comforts of the Colonial past

The Civil War may have freed Americans from the burden of filial piety, but in its wake came a wave of nostalgia for other periods or aspects of the American past. Increasing dissatisfaction with the present led Americans to yearn for the fantasized ideals and artifacts of the Colonial or Revolutionary golden age.

Several circumstances inspired affection for these supposedly happier times. Photograph albums memorializing the Civil War dead and depicting the fields of carnage brought nostalgically to mind the more congenial, less sanguinary Revolutionary struggle. Glorious early America à la Currier & Ives outshone both today's tawdriness and yesterday's desolation.[301]

Although few historical themes marked the 1876 Philadelphia Centennial Exhibition, the occasion moved many to retrospection, and historians adjudged the century's earlier decades more fruitful, harmonious, and admirable than the later ones. In the beginning all had been progress: trans-Allegheny settlement, the clearing of the wilderness, the acquisition of the West, the growth of culture and prosperity. But from the mid century events had taken a more sombre turn. Territorial conquests excited foreign jealousies, slavery exacerbated sectional discord, industrial growth engendered class conflict. Initially virtuous and high-minded, America had become corrupt, acquisitive, imperialistic; many mourned the loss of supposed past felicities.[302]

Massive industrialization and mass immigration likewise led disillusioned Americans to seek refuge in the past. Noisome and odious industrial cities seemed more and more remote from the old agrarian ideal, and late nineteenth-century immigration accentuated urban evils. The millions of newcomers from southern and eastern Europe, manifestly alien in religion, language, family patterns, and temperament, seemed unassimilable and dangerously un-American.[303]

Many older Americans retreated defensively into history. An exclusive WASP heritage, the Colonial past offered a perfect escape. The British heritage was no longer disparaged; early America became an offshoot of Old England, decently Protestant and charmingly

[300] Trowbridge, 'We are a nation' (1864), p. 773. But the rhetoric lingered on. The 1936 edition of David Savile Muzzey's *American History*, long the most popular school text, exhorted readers to keep up the 'beautiful country estate' they had inherited. 'You would be ungrateful heirs indeed if you did not care to know who had bequeathed the estate to you, who had planned and built the house [and defended] it from marauders and burglars' (quoted in Fitzgerald, *America Revised*, p. 62).

[301] Van Tassell, *Recording America's Past*, pp. 95–110; Curti, *Roots of American Loyalty*, p. 191; Gowans, *Images of American Living*, p. 352; Lynes, *Tastemakers*, pp. 67–70.

[302] J. B. Jackson, *American Space: The Centennial Years, 1865–1876*, pp. 104–5; Elson, *Guardians of Tradition*, pp. 27–8.

[303] Strout, *American Image of the Old World*, pp. 135–8; Hays, *Response to Industrialism*, pp. 24–5, 40–3; Higham, *Strangers on the Land*. The Chicago Haymarket riot of 1886 and labour strife generally encouraged escapism (Wallace, 'Visiting the past', pp. 65–8).

quaint, the Revolution a temporary disruption of close fraternal bonds. The 1880s and 1890s saw the birth of scores of Sons, Daughters, Dames, and other commemorative genealogical societies, with Anglo-Saxon origins a *sine qua non* of membership.[304]

Native-born Americans also surrounded themselves with fancied ancestral landscapes, homes, and furnishings. Household decor copied Colonial models. The passion for antiques soon outran the resources of the past, but patriots' homes and relics were refurbished, new monuments erected, old folkways reanimated. There was no instant volte-face from faith in progress to a passion for the past, to be sure. Earlier generations had their devotees of olde times; some at the century's end still spurned antiques and antiquities. But the balance had shifted. Up to the centennial, most Americans were avowed modernists: they felt fortunate to have left the outmoded past behind. The 1880s and 1890s heard a new note: the past had been *better* than the present. The party of Memory for the first time began to outvote the party of Hope.

Unlike the sons of the Founding Fathers, the great-grandsons who looked back with nostalgia were untroubled by any sense of inferiority. The ugliness of urban life, the savagery of industrial disputes, the subversive evils of immigration and other signs of decline were not *their* fault. Far from feeling burdened by the heritage they admired, they saw in the past a haven for traditional values that might, in time, restore their idealized America, and would, in the mean time, safeguard them from the sordid present. And they treasured Colonial relics partly to show that even if they had lost the present the past was theirs; the possession of antiques vouched for having been around long enough to hand them down.[305]

The poignancy of Americans' earlier dilemma inhered in having to protect the fruits of a Revolution whose main tenet was to disregard the past. It is a most burdensome past that insists on obedience while denying its own legitimacy. Acutely aware that they owed everything to their immediate forebears, post-Revolutionary Americans sought desperately to escape the implications of that debt – implications that threatened their innermost being. To that end they denigrated the past more intensely, it seems to me, than any culture before or since.

With the niceties of imitation and emulation that engaged Renaissance and Enlightenment and Victorian minds Americans had little concern; they recognized the seeming contradictions between following and resembling admired exemplars, but scarcely bothered to distinguish one form of imitation from another. Nor did the old *querelle*'s distinction between cumulatively progressive sciences and already perfected arts speak to Americans with any pertinence, for they believed whatever they did improved on the past. While they took particular pride in mechanical innovation and dismissed the European artistic legacy as of small account, Americans were not seriously inhibited by the achievements of distant precursors. Only the superiority of their own immediate forebears consigned them to inferiority, and not until after the Civil War could that judgement about past and present be reassessed.

[304] See my 'Place of the past in the American landscape', p. 108.
[305] Stillinger, *Antiquers*, pp. xiii. Boston Brahmins especially like 'to greet each new dawn with the word "old": old families, old names, old money. This, by entail, becomes the right schools and occupations, "antique"

Turn-of-the-century writers still reiterated the virtue of returning to 'what the republic used to be', and Woodrow Wilson couched his Progressivism in terms of 'rebirth' and 'reconstruction' that 'harks back' to the great age of American democratic origins.[306] But residues of this dilemma today survive less in traditionalistic indebtedness to forefathers than in American ambivalence toward ancient European continuities. Inhabiting an empty and recent land, bereft of history not only by historical chance but by deliberate choice, American heirs of Hawthorne and Henry James retain a half-guilty fascination with the longer, fuller Old World heritage that both enriches the present and threatens its autonomy.

Increasingly enamoured of their own history, Americans now long to see it everywhere, adding historical flavour to the most modern aspects of life. Every landscape and townscape advertises its unique heritage, every product boasts time-honoured virtues, every politician trumpets his devotion to the Founding Fathers' principles. The 'great awakening' to their own heritage makes it no longer 'necessary to travel abroad to see Europe's sultry castles and dusty cathedrals', in the words of a recent local guidebook.[307] But nobody is fooled; Americans keep on going back to Europe for the past they lack at home.

The periods reviewed above reveal an extraordinary range of attitudes toward the past. There have been times of archaistic zeal which vilified the present in favour of a lost or revived past; times of reluctant acceptance of a dominating heritage; times of self-confident improvement on valued precursors; times of iconoclastic frenzy which scuttled the past to aggrandize the present; and times of hapless ambivalence. Most epochs exhibit instances of all these inclinations, and many individuals fluctuate from one to another depending on the topic at hand, the mood of the moment, and their own stage in life.

To draw creative strength from the past without being overwhelmed by it is not a rare circumstance; most art of lasting merit exhibits respect for tradition combined with self-respect. But such achievement requires a delicate balance between what was once disparaged as 'novelty' and what is now disparaged as 'imitation'. Each epoch has had to come to terms with a past seemingly better placed. The classical models Renaissance humanists admired (and contended against) seemed superior because antecedence put them closer to that primordial original, nature. Victorians despaired of rivalling the Greeks, whose achievements they linked with an historical unselfconsciousness no longer open to themselves. Post-Revolutionary Americans believed that their own pedestrian and less demanding times condemned them to unheroic secondary roles. Like many sons of famous fathers, societies overshadowed by illustrious precursors are prone to consign themselves to the rubbish heap of history.

Such despair is much more likely when the venerated past is near rather than remote, parental rather than ancestral. Great distance from the Renaissance made antiquity a tolerable precursor, for the gulf required the past to be translated into modern idiom. But

---

woods in the parlors, Canton china, and so on' (Elizabeth Hardwick, 'Cheever, or the ambiguities', *N.Y. Review of Books*, 20 Dec. 1984, p. 3).

[306] David Graham Phillips, *The Plum Tree* (1905), quoted in Conn, *Divided Mind*, pp. 60, 70; Croly, *Progressive Democracy* (1914), p. 19.

[307] Hans G. Egli, *Guide/History of Jim Thorpe* (formerly Mauch Chunk), n.d.

whereas Renaissance scholars became creative in their own right through that necessary reconstitution of the classical past, eighteenth-century arts were felt to stagnate because more recent exemplars were still wholly accessible in unaltered form; these precursors were formidably enervating precisely because they were *not* dead and lost but still loomed over successors as active constituents of the present. The resurrection and assimilation of a remote past thus distinguishes Renaissance humanism from efforts to come to terms with nearer precursors in Enlightenment Europe and post-Revolutionary America.

   Conflict between the competing demands of past and present has sharpened further since the turn of this century. Many anxious to shed inherited burdens deny past example any merit whatsoever. Modernists no longer vie with admired exemplars; concerned only with present deeds, they have no interest in comparing themselves with precursors they refuse to acknowledge. Leaders in most of the arts in the early 1900s considered the past so intolerable that they sought to scrap every vestige of it, to rid themselves of any obeisance to tradition, to begin completely afresh. Modern technological and social change demanded entirely new ideas, structures, artifacts, institutions; a strong and relevant present needed to reject the past, to liquidate history, to eliminate memory, as Pierre Boulez puts it.[308] Well into the mid century, authority and tradition were denounced as *ipso facto* evil.

The consequences of modernist iconoclasm – notably the collective amnesia it imposed – are discussed in my last chapter. Here it is enough to note that dismissing the past as irrelevant has not succeeded in exorcizing it. The past remains an integral component in all of us and all of our works, no matter how burdensome it may also be. Attempts to make moderns wholly autonomous deprived them of recognized forerunners but left them with powerful ancestors. To be a modern one must grant the ancients their place, for without ancients there can be no moderns.

[308] *Conversations with Célestin Deliège*, pp. 31–3.

4

THE LOOK OF AGE

How does the look of age come? . . . Does it come of itself, unobserved, unrecorded, unmeasured? or do you woo it and set baits and traps for it, and watch it like the dawning brownness of a meerschaum pipe, and make it fast, when it appears, . . . and give thanks to it daily? Or do you forbid it and fight it and resist it, and yet feel it settling and deepening about you, as irresistible as fate?

Henry James, *A Passionate Pilgrim*[1]

The awareness of things past derives from two distinct but often conjoined traits: antiquity and decay. Antiquity involves cognizance of historical change, decay of biological or material change. The benefits and burdens of the past discussed above mainly concerned age in its historical sense, though often couched in metaphors of youth and old age. This chapter explores attitudes toward age in its biological sense and how they affect feelings about the past in general.

The manifestations of old age are quite distinct from the marks of antiquity, such as anachronistic styles or historical associations. Things seem biologically aged owing to erosion or accretion. Ageing is a worn chair, a wrinkled face, a corroded tin, an ivy-covered or mildewed wall; it is a house with sagging eaves, flaking paint, furnishings faded by time and use. Whatever their historical connections, objects that are weathered, decayed, or bear the marks of long-continued use *look* aged and thus seem to stem from the past.

The ageing of wear and tear takes myriad forms: cracked varnish, scuffed shoes, gnarled tree trunks, rubble-strewn demolition sites, even river meanders and eroded peneplains. Sounds that seem worn or flawed strike the ear as products of decay: a scratchy record, a muffled church bell, a wheezy car engine suggest prolonged use. A quavering voice conveys a sense of age because we assume it comes from someone old.

Such signs of decay also betoken imminent extinction. No product of man or nature endures forever.

---

[1] 1871, 13:392.

> Since brass, nor stone, nor boundless sea,
> But sad mortality o'ersways their power
>   *   *   *
> ... rocks impregnable are not so stout,
> Nor gates of steel so strong, but Time decays.[2]

Only the gods are immune from age and death, Oedipus reminds Theseus; 'All other things almighty Time disquiets. Earth wastes away; the body wastes away.'[3] Even art is mortal; 'the Bust outlasts the throne, the Coin Tiberius', in Gautier's phrase,[4] but the remnants of bust and coin finally commingle with the dust of those they commemorate. Conservators acknowledge the ultimate mortality of the artifacts they strive to save. 'No canvas is impervious to the ravages of time. Modern restoration techniques, advanced as they are, cannot preserve a painting for eternity.'[5] In Etienne Gilson's words, 'there are two ways for a painting to perish: the one is for it to be restored; the other is for it not to be restored'.[6] Like most works of art, monuments are made to last; longevity is their *raison d'être*. But as Ausonius noted, death comes even to the names inscribed on monumental stones.[7]

Some things endure for millennia, others for moments; each species and kind of object ages at its own tempo. A cat may look old at seven years, a man at seventy, a cathedral at a thousand, a mountain in a hundred million; a car may seem worn in a decade, a pair of shoes in a year, a sand-castle in ten minutes. Comparing life spans of aardvarks and apples, vaccines and vehicles, Kendig and Hutton also note those of waste products: paper boxes disintegrate within weeks, plastic bottles endure half a century or more, the half-life of some nuclear wastes is tens of thousands of years.[8] Attrition is often irregular: some things age most rapidly at the outset, others towards the end, and environmental circumstances may retard or accelerate decay.

Durability also varies among component parts of organisms and artifacts – blood, nerves, eyes, and skin age at differing rates – and the apparent age of any being or environment depends on how these components interact.[9] Other variables also affect impressions of artifact age. 'Everything in Liverpool is old', commented a mid nineteenth-century American visitor, 'yet nothing is worn out.' By contrast, New York impressed Fanny Kemble as 'an irregular collection of temporary buildings ... not meant to endure for any length of time'.[10] Yet a modern English visitor terms New York 'a very old city, indeed one of the oldest I have ever seen', because of the speed with which its abandoned components aged. 'That pot-hole became old as I watched it. The broken-down, burnt and charred remains of piers on the Hudson waterfront look as old as Roman remains.' The juxtaposition of old and new heightens one's awareness of age: Americans do not bother to repair something old, 'they would rather give it a new face, even if that means leaving a lot of old faces around pending replacement. So for every glistening new

---

[2] Shakespeare, Sonnet 65.   [3] Sophocles, *Oedipus at Colonus*, lines 609–10, p. 107.
[4] Gautier, 'L'Art' (1857), p. 129; I have used Austin Dobson's free translation.
[5] Francis Kelly, *Art Restoration*, p. 120.   [6] *Painting and Reality*, p. 99.
[7] Ausonius, *Epitaphs*, Bk vi, no. 32, 1:159.
[8] *Life-Spans or How Long Things Last.*   [9] Kubler, *Shape of Time*, p. 99; Gombrich, 'Style', p. 357.
[10] W. W. Brown, *American Fugitive in Europe* (1855), p. 41; Kemble, *Journal of a Residence in America* (1835), p. 97.

Pepsodent-fresh landmark in New York, there are at least a couple of rotting black teeth.'[11]

Little is known of reactions to attrition. Aside from the cult of ruins, most discussions of relics indiscriminately lump biological with historical age. Visitor response to wear and tear in museum displays is seldom noted, and public preferences are more surmised than surveyed. Yet 'whether a particular thing ought to appear old or new affects everything we look at', attests one museum curator; even though 'on the whole we never think about it', the look of age or youth arouses intense feelings and 'irrational conflicts'.[12]

The balance of evidence, however, shows general dislike of age and decay. We prefer youth, not only in living creatures but in our surroundings, including our own creations. A large-scale assessment of four American cities showed that scenes regarded as 'new' were regularly adjudged beautiful, clean, rich, and likeable, while those felt to be 'old' were concomitantly ugly, dirty, poor, and disliked; semantic tests confirmed these and other negative associations with age.[13] Distaste for the marks of age is far from universal; attachments to some things that look old, affection for certain patinas of age, are well attested. But such admiration is the exception: few old or long-used features exhibit what anyone considers 'pleasing decay', and wear and tear usually portend loss of function, senescence, imminent demise – grievous or repellent states. We generally treasure relics more for being old-fashioned than for being old, and favour the look of youth even in things whose historical antiquity we prize.

This chapter explores responses to ageing in man, in nature, and in artifacts. I begin by examining the organic analogy – parallels commonly drawn between our own lives and the careers of natural features, social institutions, and relics – and show how antipathy toward decaying objects and institutions reflects abhorrence of old age in humans. I then deal with the contrary view, ascribing beauty and value to the marks of age and wear. Finally I discuss what taste and distaste for age imply for other apprehensions of the past.

DISTASTE FOR AGE

That doesn't mean they're old, dear. Prunes are *supposed* to be wrinkled.

'Dennis the Menace'[14]

The organic analogy

Most attitudes toward ageing suppose a similitude between human beings and things of natural and human make. The human body has habitually served as an image for everything around us; two such instances – the decay of nature and the life cycle of states – were touched on in Chapter 3. Organic analogies often go beyond metaphor. Cosmos,

---

[11] Miles Kington, 'Moreover . . .', *The Times*, 2 Nov. 1982, p. 12.

[12] Roy Strong, 'Making things as good as new', *The Times*, 16 Feb. 1985, p. 8.

[13] Lowenthal and Riel, *Structures of Environmental Associations*, pp. 5, 7, 23; *idem, Milieu and Observer Differences in Environmental Associations*, pp. 31–2; *idem, Environmental Structures: Semantic and Experiential Components*, pp. 6–7. Carried out between 1966 and 1968, these studies involved 292 observers of various locales in New York, Boston, Cambridge, Mass., and Columbus, Ohio, and 97 respondents to a semantic questionnaire, both groups including a wide range of ages, occupations, and educational and residential backgrounds. All the statistical correlations mentioned were overwhelming.

[14] Ketcham, cartoon, *IHT*, 10 Oct. 1984.

church, and state were long believed to be creatures animated with life. Diverse strands of thought – Hellenic ideals of unity and proportion; the Pauline doctrine of the mystical body of Christ; the humanist image of man as the measure of all things; late Renaissance notions about the body politic – fostered anthropomorphic perceptions. Artifacts, institutions, and aspects of nature were described in explicitly human terms – for example, rocks as bones, soil as flesh, grass as hair, tides as the pulse, the sun and the moon as eyes.[15]

Natural features and artifacts seen as organisms also exhibit stages of birth and growth, decay and death. After seasonal and diurnal rhythms, the life cycle is our most familiar temporal experience, furnishing metaphors for virtually everything in existence; indeed, we would hardly know how to describe temporal change without referring to stages in our own lives. 'Infancy', 'youth', 'maturity', and 'old age' are terms continually applied to nations and neighbourhoods, arts and sciences, rocks and relics.

Organic metaphors confirm, and perhaps help to generate, preferences for earlier and aversion to later stages of existence. Repugnance to human old age is well-nigh universal; likening 'old' artifacts and institutions and natural features to old people induces or exaggerates a similar antipathy, and with few exceptions we consequently disparage their 'old age'. To be sure, we do not prefer the pristine to the antiquated solely because we connect the one with youth and the other with senescence; but organic terminology strengthens such biases, and indeed is often used to put the new and fresh in the best possible light, the old and stale in the worst.

So influential is repugnance to old age that some devotees of the organic analogy shun its logical conclusion. Both Patristic philosophers and Renaissance humanists hesitated to project cosmos or state beyond maturity to degeneration or death. Gregory the Great's three ages of the Church were boyhood, youth, and maturity; St Augustine's City of God was incompatible with old age.[16] Nor did decay necessarily portend death; 'all that totters does not fall', noted Montaigne: certain ancient buildings endured despite decrepitude, their very hoariness a source of strength.[17] Some liken features, institutions, and artifacts not to mortal individuals but to immortal species.

Literal belief in the world as an organism and society as a body politic faded out in the seventeenth and eighteenth centuries, but the rhetoric endured and even intensified, as I have shown, in conflicts between imperial and colonial 'fathers' and 'sons'. Following Herder, historians compared institutions and nations at supposedly similar points of organic growth or decline, and evolutionary biology revived organic political analogies, notably stimulated by Herbert Spencer's *Principles of Sociology* (1876–96). Today nature and culture are less often analysed as organisms, but still commonly seen and sometimes deliberately conceived in life-cycle terms.[18]

How well we like cultural and natural features bears closely on their place in a supposed life cycle. Beauty and goodness are almost universally linked with youth, ugliness and evil with old age. The 'new-born' is innocent and lovely, the old is decrepit and foul, alike in

---

[15] Raleigh, *History of the World* (1614), Bk I, Ch. 2, sect. 5, p. 30; G. L. Davies, *Earth in Decay*, p. 19.

[16] Trompf, *Idea of Historical Recurrence in Western Thought*, pp. 214, 282; Panofsky, 'First page of Giorgio Vasari's "Libro"', pp. 216–20.

[17] Montaigne, 'Of vanitie', 3:202.

[18] D. G. Hale, *Body Politic: A Political Metaphor in Renaissance English Literature*, pp. 135–7; Coker, *Organismic Theories of the State*; Schlanger, *Métaphores de l'organisme*.

nations, artifacts, and the world as a whole. This bias arises from – and is starkly exhibited in – attitudes toward ourselves.

The remainder of this section traces aversion to old age in humans and shows how similar distastes apply to the earth and its features, to states and institutions, and to artifacts. Discussion of preferences for old age is reserved for the following section.

Aversion to age in humans

Heightened concern with ageing masks repugnance toward old age. But, contrary to popular myth, our own epoch is not uniquely averse to the elderly; it is their growing numbers and increasing longevity that explain the surge of geriatric concern. Preference for youth and antipathy toward old age are immemorial and almost universal sentiments.

From classical times to the present, ageing has been held a misfortune, if not a condign punishment. Senile immortality was the dreadful fate of Swift's Struldbrugs who by the age of 90 lacked teeth, eyesight, and memory; 'every Man desires to live long', Swift concludes, 'but no Man would be old'.[19] A Grimm fairy-tale relates that God originally set the life span for all creatures at 30 years; finding so long a life wearisome, the ass, the dog, and the monkey had theirs reduced by 18, 12, and 10 years respectively. Only man wished a longer life, and added to his previous span what the other creatures relinquished. He paid dearly for longevity; at 48 his condition became that of the ass, carrying countless burdens; at 60 like the dog's, growling toothlessly and dragging himself from corner to corner; and at 70 like the monkey's, a derisory, witless creature. 'Thou shalt not grow old', the Eleventh Commandment of present-day Californians, is an ancient adage common to most searches for fountains of youth.[20]

Save for Roger Bacon and his alchemist followers and Luigi Cornaro and the hygienists, Europeans have seldom sought longevity as such. Some Protestant creeds encouraged the elderly to accept their biblically sanctioned role by maintaining health and social useful-ness to the end, ticking on like an old grandfather clock up to the age of 90 (an American popular song conveying this message sold 800,000 copies on publication in 1876). But this encouraging perspective succumbed to secularism and to medical views linking old age with unavoidable, irreversible, often pathological decline. In this century, senescence became senility.[21]

Degradation of the aged is no doubt more usual in some societies and eras than in others. Early American Puritans, David Hackett Fischer contends, respected and deferred to their elders; 'The hoary head is a crown of glory' was a Puritan commonplace. Old age was a sign of God's special favour, longevity betokening salvation. Not only had the Puritans' God a face older than time; even their Christ, taken from the Book of Revelation, had hair white as wool or snow.[22] The god-like elderly gave valued advice:

---

[19] *Gulliver's Travels* (1726), Pt III, Ch. 10, pp. 257–60; Swift, 'Thoughts on various subjects' (1727), 4:246.
[20] 'Span of life', *Grimm's Fairy Tales* (1812–15); W. I. Thompson, *At the Edge of History*, p. 15.
[21] Gruman, 'History of ideas about the prolongation of life', pp. 49–71; Thomas R. Cole, 'Aging, meaning, and well-being', pp. 331–2; Haber, 'From senescence to senility', p. 43. The Taoist, who aims to live to a great age as a bent and diminutive figure like the dwarfed plants in Japanese gardens, is characteristic of Oriental, not of European, culture (Tuan, *Dominance and Affection*, p. 62; Gruman, 'Prolongation of life', pp. 28–49).
[22] Fischer, *Growing Old in America*, pp. 26–76. For contrary views see Stone, 'Walking over grandma'; 'Growing old: an exchange'; Demos, 'Old age in early New England'. Perukes made of grey hair were

> His hoary hairs, and grave aspect made way,
> And all gave ear, to what he had to say,

in Anne Bradstreet's lines.[23] Yet Puritans honoured the old more in theory than in practice. It may have been ungodly 'to treat Aged Persons with disrespectful and disdainful language only because of their age', but people none the less commonly spoke with contempt of *'Old Such An One'*.[24] That 'respect and reverence for old age formed a conspicuous feature ... of the ancient commonwealths' was 'well known', asserted John Stuart Mill,[25] but then, as now, the benefits the elderly were previously thought to have enjoyed came from a reading of precepts, not from a knowledge of practice; ritualistic deference toward old age was everywhere mistaken for authentic respect.[26]

Some elderly folk were perhaps better off when there were fewer of them. The rare octogenarian in seventeenth-century France was a legendary sage, 'widely regarded with the superstitious awe commonly accorded to champions'. But while a rich old man might be venerated as a wise patriarch, the aged poor were scorned and cast out.[27] Up to the Second World War, 'old age would appear in its most mocking, most terrifying guise' among English country folk, notes Ronald Blythe; 'the fate of the common labourer and his wife in old age was to be punished by society for daring to grow old', so off they went to the workhouse to 'scrub and peel and chop their paths to the grave'.[28]

Increasing numbers have begun to win the elderly political influence and a measure of economic security; America's Gray Panthers form a formidable lobby. But growth likewise makes old people more burdensome to their juniors, as the mounting cost of old-age pensions attests. And the speed of technological change devalues the experience of old people whose accumulated knowledge is now simply obsolete and whose counsel is unsought. The British Company of Veteran Motorists has renamed itself the Guild of Experienced Motorists for fear of being thought a bunch of dodderers; to the young, 'veteran' no longer means 'experienced' but simply 'old'.[29]

Old age increasingly implies uselessness and senility, and signs of approaching extinction are also more apt to stigmatize the elderly. Most labouring people in the past aged early, as bent and withered at forty as some folk of eighty today; few lived long enough to exhibit the geriatric infirmities that now afflict so many. The rare survivors to advanced old age often kept fit until the end. Elderly ministers, teachers, statesmen seldom retired; patriarchs clung to power and office, Hawthorne's 'Gray Champions' to the last. In the past, old people deprived of social roles soon perished; today's elderly often survive

considered the best and cost the most in mid eighteenth-century England (Brummell, *Male and Female Costume*, p. 100), but little other evidence supports Fischer's claim that insignia of age were actually preferred.

[23] 'Of the four ages of man' (1678), lines 49–50, p. 52. Old age is less attractively limned elsewhere in the poem: 'My memory is bad, my brain is dry: / ... / My grinders are few, my sight doth fail / My skin is wrinkled, and my cheeks are pale' (lines 416–20, p. 63).

[24] Increase Mather, *The Dignity and Duty of Aged Servants of the Lord* (1716), quoted in Fischer, *Growing Old in America*, pp. 59–60.

[25] Mill, 'Spirit of the age' (1831), p. 64.

[26] Kastenbaum and Ross, 'Historical perspectives on care', p. 432; Hendricks and Davis, 'Age old question of old age'.

[27] Goubert, *Louis XIV and Twenty Million Frenchmen*, p. 21.

[28] *The View in Winter: Reflections on Old Age*, p. 52.

[29] 'Times diary', *The Times*, 28 May 1983, p. 8.

twenty or thirty years beyond their ability to contribute – or society's willingness to let them.

Old age today is more closely linked with death because – war and violence aside – it is now mainly the old who die. Death formerly struck with little warning at all ages, most frequently in infancy; the elderly were felt to be no nearer death's door than other folk. In countries where medical science nowadays saves all but a few of the young, only the elderly seem mortal. 'Old age is dreaded because it has become the only *normal* death-age', writes Blythe.[30] The old are avoided not only as helpless nuisances but as harbingers of mortality.

The look of age seldom wins admiration even where white hair commands respect. Age-linked changes in stature, facial appearance, and voice almost always connote weakness.[31] In many languages 'young' and 'beautiful' are synonyms, implicitly disparaging the old.[32] Classical writers and orators decried old age as dismal and repugnant: Mimnermus hoped to die before he became an old man 'repulsive to young women'; Juvenal deplored 'doddering voices and limbs, bald heads, running noses'; Ovid warned a young woman that 'her fair face will be marred by the long years, and wrinkles of age will' ruin her beauty.[33]

Scriptural annals likewise doted on the appearance of youth. Icons celebrated the young Virgin, and Jesus as a child and young man; St Irenaeus alone among the Church Fathers suggested that He might have lived to be old so as to sanctify 'each stage of life by a likeness to himself ... Therefore he passed through every stage, ... sanctifying the older men, and becoming an example to them also.'[34] But, in the usual view, it was almost 'necessary for Christ to die in the prime of his beauty and vigour'.[35] In God's years 'there is no climacter', thought Thomas Browne, lest 'long life be but a prolongation of death'.[36] During the Renaissance the young Son gained pictorial supremacy while the white-bearded Father was decreasingly depicted; old men no longer appear as great warriors and wise rulers but as drowsy, senile, unappetizing invalids in the 'Ages of Man'.[37] To charges that Michelangelo's painting of the Virgin made her look too young, Vasari replied that 'spotless virgins keep their youth for a long time' – just as saints' bodies were exempt from earthly decay, so beauteous youth signified sanctity.[38]

Father Time came to symbolize decay and dissolution, his scythe, hour-glass, and crutches linking old age with poverty and decrepitude. Often a one-legged cripple or skeletal demon, Time was a procurer of death who lurked among barren trees and ruinous buildings, waiting to devour his own children.[39]

Adoration of human beauty made old age seem all the more odious; aged women were reviled and old men mocked for their looks. The transience of beauty and the inevitability of ugly old age obsessed Elizabethans.

[30] *View in Winter*, p. 96.   [31] G. D. Jensen and Oakley, 'Aged appearance and behavior'.
[32] Thus in rural Cyprus 'antika' means 'ugliness' (Herzfeld, *Ours Once More*, p. 20).
[33] Mimnermus, 'Censure of age', in *Greek Lyric Poetry*, pp. 102–3; Juvenal, *Satires*, No. 10, lines 191–5, p. 128; Ovid, *Tristia*, Bk III, Ch. 7, lines 33–7, p. 129. See Kastenbaum and Ross, 'Historical perspectives on care', pp. 428–30.
[34] Irenaeus, *Adversus Haereses* (c. 180), II.xxii. 4, p. 110.   [35] Whistler, *Initials in the Heart*, p. 204.
[36] Browne, *Religio Medici* (1635), p. 57.
[37] De Beauvoir, *Old Age*, pp. 159–60; Ariès, *Hour of Our Death*, p. 299.
[38] Vasari, *Lives*, 4:115; Huizinga, *Waning of the Middle Ages*, p. 128.
[39] Panofsky, 'Father Time'.

14 The evils of age: Pompeo Batoni, *Time orders Old Age to destroy Beauty*, 1746

When I have seen by Time's fell hand defac'd
The rich-proud cost of outworn buried age;
* * *
Ruin hath taught me thus to ruminate –
That Time will come and take my love away.

'Time's injurious hand' and 'confounding age's cruel knife' destroyed beauty along with youth.[40]

Old age seemed ridiculous when not ugly. Seeking youthful pleasures, Falstaff is reminded that he has a moist eye, a dry hand, a yellow cheek, a white beard, and an increasing belly. 'Is not your voice broken, your wind short, your chin double, your wit single, and every part about you blasted with antiquity?'[41] Dryden's Florimell 'resolved to grow fat and look young till forty, and slip out of the world with the first wrinckle, and the reputation of five and twenty'.[42]

Beauty is still confined to youth. 'They are old, *they are old*', a boy of 17 describes the elderly; 'they are ill and ugly and their life is over.'[43] The elderly are at best ludicrous, like Philip Larkin's character whose 'eccentric appearance' would harmonize 'with the caricaturing onset of age'.[44] Billy Wilder hopes that 'maybe some day somebody will see beauty in gray hair and some sort of wisdom in experience, not just dirty old men and crazy old ladies in tennis shoes'.[45] It is a forlorn hope. 'What would happen to the face-lift trade', a critic wonders, 'if our culture accepted the beauty of Rembrandt's mother as he painted her?'[46] In fact, the elderly are not much admired in paintings, either. Though fascinated by the features of old age, Rembrandt habitually portrayed older faces – including his own – as less attractive than younger ones.[47] An 'Age Machine' which produces pictures forecasting what people may look like twenty or thirty years ahead, based on characteristic atrophying in facial skin and muscles, seems less likely to bring people to terms with ageing, as the machine's inventor suggests,[48] than to arouse dismay.

Old people themselves shun the look of age. 'I really must not meet my image in a mirror', wrote the ageing Gide – 'these bags under the eyes, these hollow cheeks, those drawn features.'[49] Yet age-segregation more and more condemns the elderly to locales where decrepitude is pervasive. 'You know what bugs me?' one Florida oldster in a cartoon says to another. 'Everybody I know is wizened.'[50]

Sexual pulchritude especially requires unblemished youth; a few wrinkles and a slight

---

[40] Shakespeare, Sonnets 64, 63.   [41] Shakespeare, *Henry IV, Part 2*, I.ii, lines 206–10.

[42] *Secret Love, or, the Maiden Queen* (1668), III.i, 9:160.

[43] Blythe, *View in Winter*, p. 120. A study of 180 American children aged from 3 to 11 confirms the stereotype of the elderly as 'sick, sad, tired, dirty and ugly' (Jantz *et al.*, *Children's Attitudes toward the Elderly*). Many studies confirm these negative images (J. L. Burke, 'Young children's attitudes and perceptions of older adults'; S. M. Miller *et al.*, 'Children and the aged'). These negative attitudes are by no means confined to Britain and America; children in Paraguay, Australia, and the Aleutian Islands exhibit them in like measure (Seefeldt, 'Children's attitudes toward the elderly: a cross-cultural comparison', p. 326).

[44] *Girl in Winter*, pp. 192–3.

[45] Mary Blume, 'Billy Wilder tackles the only taboo left', *IHT*, 3–4 Sept. 1977.

[46] Penelope Gilliatt, 'Study of a man under the axe', *New Yorker*, 13 Sept. 1976, p. 127.

[47] Kaufmann, *Time Is an Artist*, p. 59.

[48] The inventor is Nancy Burson, whom I thank for information. See Hank Herman, 'What will *you* look like in 25 years?' *Family Health*, Feb. 1979. p. 12.

[49] *So Be It*, p. 67; I have conflated Justin O'Brien's translation of *Ansi soit-il* with Simone de Beauvoir's, *Old Age*, p. 333.

[50] Stan Coren, *New Yorker*, 2 Dec. 1974, p. 56.

sag in the buttocks put Hugh Hefner's bunnies on the shelf at 28. A seventeenth-century traveller likened the ruins of Rome to fair ladies in old age, 'yet so comely, that they ravish still the beholders eye with their Beauties',[51] but they were clearly *more* beautiful when young. Benjamin Franklin recommended knowledgeable, grateful, and prudent older mistresses, but in adding that 'when women cease to be handsome, they study to be good', he implicitly conceded his preference for physical youth.[52]

The ageing of formerly seductive women excites extreme revulsion. When Rider Haggard's Ayesha starts to look her two thousand years, her lover sees on her withered and shapeless face a 'stamp of unutterable age . . . too hideous for words'.[53] Orwell's George Bowling can scarcely credit the ravages that have transformed his long-lost girl friend, then a comely wench of 22, into an old hag of 47.[54] Finding his former lover now a 'foul and rotted ancient woman', a Carlos Fuentes protagonist sees this devastation as 'something worse than time', the work of disease and of immeasurable evil.[55]

The archetype of age abhorrence, however, is a male: Oscar Wilde's Dorian Gray dreads the 'day when his face would be wrinkled and wizen, his eyes dim and colourless, the grace of his figure broken and deformed . . . He would become dreadful, hideous, and uncouth.' The portrait's conflation of age with evil, wickedness with decay, foretold a dreadful future:

It might escape the hideousness of sin, but the hideousness of age was in store for it. The cheeks would become hollow or flaccid. Yellow crow's feet would creep round the fading eyes and make them horrible. The hair would lose its brightness, the mouth would gape or droop, would be foolish or gross, as the mouths of old men are. There would be the wrinkled throat, the cold, blue-veined hands, the twisted body.[56]

Dorian Gray hides his picture because he cannot bear its signs of age. Concealing our own ravages of time is a common pursuit. Fortunes are spent on face-lifts, to dye greying hair, to smooth wrinkles, to firm flabby flesh. 'INVEST IN FEAR', runs a beautician's advertisement; 'we're all afraid of growing older'. Today's message is to '*remain young and youthful looking*', for the look of age connotes misery and misfortune.[57] 'Golden Oldies' are records; applied to people, the term is derisive. Other words cut worse: one teenager explained that her father's generation were 'oldies', folk in their sixties 'wrinklies', her great-grandmother 'the crumblie';[58] French teenagers refer to parents as 'les ruines'. The white locks, grizzled cheeks, and shuffling gait of a lone elderly outcast in the film *Logan's Run* make him in youthful eyes not only weird but obscene.[59]

Repugnance to old age extends to its accessories. 'Serviced with dentures, lenses, tiny loudspeakers, sticks, and hip-pins', writes Blythe, 'the flesh has become absurd and can no longer be taken seriously.'[60] Russell Baker expresses dismay at such gifts as a rocking-

---

[51] Lassels, *Italian-Voyage*, 2:74. The image of Rome as a still comely old lady dates back at least to Petrarch (Mortier, *Poétique des ruines en France*, p. 28).
[52] 'Old mistresses apologue'.   [53] *She*, p. 299.   [54] *Coming Up for Air*, p. 205.
[55] *Terra Nostra*, pp. 536–7.
[56] *Dorian Gray*, pp. 91, 171.   [57] Judith Sans franchise, *Wall Street Journal*, 10 Aug. 1978, p. 23.
[58] 'Times dairy', *The Times*, 31 Aug. 1976, p. 10. We already age more rapidly. '"Oldies" today start at 25; "wrinklies" follow at 35'; at 45 one 'becomes a "crumblie"' (Charles Wolfe Keene, 'Brave face on it', letter, *The Times*, 11 Feb. 1985, p. 15).
[59] William F. Nolan and George C. Johnson's text only hints at this.   [60] *View in Winter*, p. 200.

chair, treated paper for cleaning bifocals, hair pomade guaranteed to conceal the grey, a stair-rail lift, and – the ultimate put-down – a copy of *How to Avoid Probate*.[61]

Age in animals and plants is also usually derogated. The old creature – spent, bedraggled, often lame – is less attractive than the playful cub or the virile adult; we love the faithful old dog despite his look (and smell) of age. The long-lived tortoise is a curiosity, not a beauty. And withered flowers have small allure. Only old gnarled trees are partly exempt from such opprobrium. 'While animal decay is ugly', asserted Bosanquet, 'vegetable decay is beautiful or tolerable'; he offers no examples, but trees are frequent symbols of communal unity and patrimonial continuity.[62] Trees are often most appealing in old age: England's gnarled oak, the enduring American redwood, the shade of the old apple tree, the old familiar oak that George Pope Morris sought to save from the woodman's axe, for 'In youth it sheltered me, / And I'll protect it now.'[63] Wordsworth bemoaned the loss of 'a brotherhood of venerable Trees' which, like Felicia Hemans's 'stately Homes of England' beautiful 'amidst their tall ancestral trees', attested long continuity of land and homestead.[64] Picturesque ruins, as we shall see later in this chapter, attract similar terms of approbation.

Even aged trees are odious, however, when numerous and moribund. Old age is offensive when it is the only age in view: the very notion of life cycle requires a varied panoply, a spectrum ranging from infancy to senescence. Thus the massed remains of England's deciduous groves, some time-worn relics of Parliamentary enclosures, others victims of Dutch elm disease, arouse sorrow, even disgust. 'A certain amount of death and decay' is essential, Mary Powell points out, but 'an excessive number of dying trees is a disagreeable symptom of a landscape out of balance, offensive to the taste for vitality'.[65]

Widespread arboreal decay has other disturbing implications. Whereas the occasional dying tree in a mature grove connotes continuity, wholesale extinction – like the 'ghastly gray . . . dilapidated black and lifeless' skeletons among the furnaces of the Black Country that James Nasmyth termed 'vegetable death in its saddest aspect'[66] – signals ruthless agricultural or industrial change. While a few 'ancient trees still in splendid condition . . . can stimulate a kind of nostalgia for a glorious past', too many degenerating specimens become unpleasant reminders of the passing of beloved familiar landscapes.[67]

This repugnance toward the look of old age in living beings colours attitudes toward the world's natural features, toward nations and institutions, and toward man-made objects – in short, toward most things under the sun.

The decay of the world and its features

Long after Galileo, most Europeans took the earth to be an animate being. Alive, it had a life history: classical, Christian, and humanist literature detail the world's birth, maturing, ageing, and prospective death. The Renaissance concept of man as the microcosm of

---

[61] 'Christmas orange', *IHT*, 21 Dec. 1979, p. 18.
[62] *History of Aesthetic*, p. 436; Schlanger, *Métaphores de l'organisme*, pp. 199–204.
[63] 'The Oak', in Morris, *Deserted Bride*, p. 19.
[64] Wordsworth, 'Degenerate Douglas', in his *Memorials of a Tour in Scotland*, Sonnet XII, line 6, 3:83; Hemans, 'Homes of England' [1827], *Poems*, p. 412. [65] 'Variations on a theme of dying trees', p. 26.
[66] *Engineer: An Autobiography*, p. 163. [67] Powell, 'Dying trees', p. 26.

nature, the world as the macrocosm of man, reinforced the organic analogy; the terrestrial life cycle mirrored the human. And as astronomy revealed change even in the heavens previously thought immutable, the idea of organism spread to the sun and the stars.[68] 'All things have their *birth*, their *growth*, their *flourishing*, their *failing*, their *fading*', in George Hakewill's words.[69] 'That which we see in every particular body, the same we perceive to be in the whole frame and course of the world', wrote Pierre de la Primaudaye. 'For the world hath had his infancie, next his youth, then his mans estate, & now he is in his old-age.'[70]

The organic cosmos was long considered in the last stages of decay. A twelfth-century chronicler saw the City of Earth (as opposed to the City of God) 'already failing and . . . drawing the last breath of extremest old age'[71] Medieval Christians believed the world had passed through six stages of life into a final decrepit seventh; 'an ende by putrefaction' was conventionally assumed.[72]

Belief in cosmic decline became still more pervasive after humanists portrayed the human body as the image of the world. The world's decay now echoed man's own sins. According to Luther, Adam had initiated not only the fall of man but the decay of nature, and as man's sins multiplied, nature further deteriorated.[73] The six thousand allotted years were now almost spent; signs of cumulative corruption foreshadowed an imminent end. In England, where sombre scenes of monastic ruin reinforced awareness of decay, both Anglicans and Puritans held mankind responsible.

> Heaven's just displeasure & our unjust ways
> Change Natures course, bring plagues dearth and decays.
> This turns our lands to Dust, the skies to Brass,
> Makes old kind blessings into curses pass.
>   ⋆   ⋆   ⋆
> The dregs and puddle of all ages now
> Like Rivers near their fall, on us do flow.[74]

Man 'drew the Curse upon the world', added Henry Vaughan, 'and Crackt / The whole frame with his fall.'[75]

Since nature shared complicity in man's fall from grace, the penalty of mortality extended from Adam to the whole world. Heaven, earth, cities, and men were 'Nature's nest of Boxes' in which Donne saw 'decay and age in the whole frame of the world and every piece thereof'.[76]

Once predicted, decay and death could be found in every falling leaf. Science seemed to confirm religion; deterioration infected the entire cosmos. In Giordano Bruno's words, 'the earth seems to grow grey with years, and . . . all the great animals of the universe perish

---

[68] Victor Harris, *All Coherence Gone*; Davies, *Earth in Decay*; Barkan, *Nature's Work of Art: The Human Body as Image of the World*.
[69] *Apologie or Declaration of the Power and Providence of God* (1635), Bk III, Ch. 6, sect. 2, 1:259.
[70] *L'Académie française* (1577–94), quoted in Harris, *All Coherence Gone*, p. 197.
[71] Otto of Freising, *Two Cities*, p. 323. See Trompf, *Idea of Historical Recurrence*, pp. 226–8.
[72] Polydore Vergil, *De rerum inventiborus* (1499), quoted in Harris, *All Coherence Gone*, p. 87.
[73] *Luther on the Creation* and *Luther on Sin and the Flood*, cited from Nicolson, *Mountain Gloom and Mountain Glory*, pp. 100–4.
[74] Vaughan, 'Daphnis' (1666), lines 143–50, p. 679.   [75] 'Corruption', lines 15–16, p. 440.
[76] 'Devotions upon emergent occasions' (1624), p. 523.

like the small'.[77] 'On crutches yesterday', Thomas Dekker's world was now 'bed-rid', declining into its dotage.[78] The spotted and blemished sun 'now waxeth weary' and 'shineth more dimly'; the moon grew paler, the stars 'weake & suspicious'.[79] Men themselves were smaller and weaker; giants, once common, were now seldom seen. 'As all things under the Sunne have . . . a youth and beautie, and then age and deformitie', wrote Raleigh, 'so Time itselfe . . . hath wasted and worne out that lively vertue of Nature in Man, and Beasts, and Plants.'[80] Wheat mildewed, wood rotted, iron rusted more than ever before.[81]

Mountains, the 'bones of the world', notably suggested organic change. Mountain erosion seemed prime evidence of terrestrial decay, and to Bishop Burnet their very existence spelt dissolution. Again and again he likened them to architectural ruins: 'what can have more the figure and mien of a ruine, than Crags and Rocks and Cliffs?'[82] The rude and ragged earth, 'lying in its rubbish', was 'the Image or Picture of a great Ruin'. Today's mountains were the 'ruines of a broken World', God's originally smooth and endless plain shattered by the Deluge into wild and undigested heaps.[83]

The assumption of terrestrial decay was challenged, as we have seen, by Bodin and Le Roy in France and Hakewill in England. It was impious to suppose that the Creator would make a corruptible earth, argued Hakewill against the doctrine of decadence; the world changed but did not degenerate. He saw no loss of strength in living things: trees were as great, herbs as potent, as ever; the sun and moon seemed more spotted only because the telescope enabled men to see them better. Scripture foretold that 'the heavens shall wax old like a garment', yet this 'doth not necessarily imply a *decay*', but perhaps 'a *farther step and accesse to a finall period*'. Nature would end when God willed it; meanwhile His power and providence were manifest not in the world's decline but in its conservation.[84]

Scholarship and liturgy increasingly stripped the concept of decay both of emotional force and of intellectual conviction – exempting parts of the cosmos, regarding the process of decay as complete, or no longer blaming it on man's continuing sins. Yet the notion remained popular even at the end of the seventeenth century. That all things diminish and decay was 'the received Opinion, not only of the Vulgar, but even of Philosophers themselves from Antiquity down to our times', according to John Ray.[85] It reverberated well into the eighteenth century. The sparsely-peopled earth struck Montesquieu as evidence that nature had 'lost the wonderful fruitfulness of the first ages. Can it be that she is already old and fallen into decay?'[86] Decay was evident in the humbler scale of housekeeping, higher prices, scarcer coinage – even jaded palates: 'In the Infant Age of the World', wrote a *Compleat Housewife*, 'Mankind stood in no need of additional Sauces, Ragoos, Etc.', required to stimulate appetites in the present elderly epoch.[87]

[77] *Infinito* (1584), quoted in McIntyre, *Giordano Bruno*, p. 221.
[78] *Old Fortunatus* (1600), quoted in Harris, *All Coherence Gone*, p. 121n.
[79] John Dove, *Confutation of Atheism* (1605), quoted in Harris, *All Coherence Gone*, p. 117.
[80] *History of the World*, Bk I, Ch. 5, sect. 5, pp. 76–7.
[81] La Primaudaye, *L'Académie française*, cited in Harris, *All Coherence Gone*, p. 98.
[82] *Sacred Theory of the Earth* (1684), p. 41.
[83] Ibid., pp. 91, 115.   [84] Hakewill, *Apologie*, Bk II, Ch. 1, sect. 4, 1:84; also Bk V, 2:141.
[85] *Miscellaneous Discourses concerning the Dissolution and Changes of the World* (1692), p. 41.
[86] *Persian Letters*, No. 113 (1718), p. 250.   [87] Mrs Smith (1736), quoted in Bate, *Burden of the Past*, p. 68.

Those who believed the world decrepit also thought its 'crooked old age' ugly and vile.[88] 'As a garment the older it waxeth, the lesse comely it is, the lesse able to warm him that weares it: so the materiall heavens by continuance of yeares decreas in beauty and vertue.'[89] Spenser lamented that 'the world is runne quite out of square ... And being once amisse, growes daily wourse and wourse' – more and more deformed and senescent.[90] Such plaints were an early seventeenth-century commonplace. The earth's last age also seemed its very dregs.

Cosmologists drew comparisons with human senescence, depicting a worn, corrupted earth decaying into an 'odious mass, weake through age and drunk with bloud', or a limping, feeble, and childish world.[91] Although Milton refused to envisage the earth in 'loathsome old age', stricken with 'the years' insatiable hunger, and filth, and rust', and doubted that the face of nature would 'really wither away and be furrowed all over with wrinkles',[92] his words reflect the disgust that ageing elicited. Terrestrial old age repelled both those who accepted and those who rejected the doctrine of decay.

Irregularities of land and sea recalled loathsome diseases, as in Charles Cotton's tirade against Chatsworth:

> Like Warts and Wens, Hills on the one side dwell
> To all but Natives Inaccessible;
> Th' other a blue scrofulus Scum defiles
> Flowing from th' Earth's imposthumated Boyles.[93]

Or as others satirized the analogy:

> Swell'd with a dropsy, sickly Nature lies
> And melting in a diabetes, dies.[94]

Burnet's dismay at the marks of terrestrial decay focused on mountain forms. Before the Deluge the earth had been 'smooth, regular, and uniform; without Mountains, and without a Sea; ... it had the beauty of Youth and blooming Nature, fresh and fruitful, and not a wrinkle, scar or fracture in all its body'. But now in old age it was all rocks and mountains, than which 'nothing in Nature [is] more shapeless and ill-figur'd'.[95] As Donne had put it, mountains were 'warts, and pock-holes on the face of th' earth'.[96] Esteem for man's own relics was no reason to admire nature's; old things might be instructive, but were not therefore attractive. 'We are pleas'd in looking upon the Ruins of a Roman Amphitheatre, or a Triumphal Arch, tho' Time may have defaced its Beauty', argued Burnet, but while 'a man may be pleas'd in looking upon a Monster, will you conclude therefore that he takes it for a Beauty?'[97]

[88] Lambert Daneau, *Physica Christiana* (1576), quoted in Harris, *All Coherence Gone*, p. 95.
[89] Samuel Rowlands, *Heavens Glory* (1628), quoted in ibid., p. 144.
[90] *Faerie Queene* (1590), Bk V, Prologue, stanza 1, 2:159.
[91] William Alexander, *Doomes-Day* (1614); Barnabe Rich, *The Honestie of the Age* (1614), quoted and cited in Harris, *All Coherence Gone*, pp. 123, 135.
[92] 'Naturam non pati senium' (c. 1627), lines 11–14, p. 61.
[93] 'Wonders of the peak' (1681), quoted in Nicolson, *Mountain Gloom*, p. 66.
[94] John Gay, Pope, and Arbuthnot, *Three Hours after Marriage* (1717), p. 142.
[95] Burnet, *Sacred Theory of the Earth*, pp. 53, 64, 112.
[96] 'Anatomy of the world: the first anniversary' (1611), lines 300–1, p. 205.
[97] *Answer to the Exceptions* (1690), quoted in Nicolson, *Mountain Gloom*, p. 269.

Terrestrial ugliness, like decline, seemed a consequence of man's continuing misdeeds. 'Our landlord has left us a fair house, and we suffer it quickly to runne to ruin', wrote Thomas Adams.[98] 'The gross irregularities of earth's surface, with its warts and pock-holes, were abiding evidence of the sin of man', Marjorie Nicolson summarizes reactions, and 'with each of man's major sins, the earth has grown increasingly ugly'.[99]

The allegory of mountain decay held the popular imagination long after theology outdated Burnet. Mountain scenery especially conjured up 'the Revolutions of past Ages, the fleeting forms of Things, and the Decay even of this our Globe', wrote Shaftesbury. 'The wasted Mountains shew [men] the World itself only as a noble Ruin, and make them think of its approaching Period.'[100] Even at the gentler 'friendly hills' near Bath:

> The shattered rocks and strata seem to say,
> Nature is old, and tends to her decay.[101]

And as late as 1810, Scott unlovingly termed

> Crags, knolls, and mounds, confusedly hurl'd
> The fragments of an earlier world.[102]

Well into the nineteenth century, Ruskin divided earth history into periods of youth (crystallization), strength (sculpturing), and, in his own day, decrepitude, when 'all mountain forms are suffering a deliquescent and corroding change'.[103]

Life-cycle analogies also attracted students of temporal change in landforms and rivers. An eighteenth-century hydraulic engineer likened fluvial to human stages of development:

A river, from its source to the sea, depicts the different ages of man . . . Its INFANCY is frolicsome and capricious; it turns mills and eddies playfully beneath the flowers. Its YOUTH is impetuous and hasty; it buffets, uproots and overturns. Its MIDDLE COURSE is serious and wise; it makes detours and yields to circumstances. In OLD AGE its step is measured, peaceful, majestic and silent; its tranquil waters roll softly and soon lose themselves in the immense ocean.[104]

Of the Mississippi a geologist wrote that 'the young river made an indenture in the sweep of the shores; the mature river filled it in'.[105] ('Ol' man river' had long been its folk designation.) Indices of 'youth' and 'topographic old age' were terms common in American geomorphology. 'The degradation of the driftless region [of Wisconsin] has passed beyond the time of youth', wrote Chamberlin and Salisbury. 'The ultimate result . . . is old age declining again to the level of childhood.'[106]

The most memorable use of life cycles in geomorphology was William Morris Davis's land-mass 'life history'. Davis termed the smoothness and shallow lakes of an uneroded surface 'truly infantile features'; during 'adolescence' rivers establish narrow and well-

---

[98] *The Spirituall Navigator* (1615), quoted in Harris, *All Coherence Gone*, p. 137.

[99] *Breaking of the Circle*, p. 114.

[100] Shaftesbury, *Moralist* (1709), Pt 3, sect. 1, p. 201.

[101] Mary Chandler, 'A description of Bath' (1743), quoted in Nicolson, *Mountain Gloom*, p. 228.

[102] *Lady of the Lake* (1810), Canto I, sect. xiv, p. 211.

[103] *Deucalion* (1875), Ch. 2, 'The three aeras', 26: 117, 123. See Buckley, *Triumph of Time*, pp. 66–9.

[104] L.-G. du Buat, *Principes d'hydraulique* (1779), quoted in Chorley, Dunn, and Beckinsale, *History of the Study of Landforms*, 1:88.

[105] Greenwood, *Rain and Rivers* (1857), p. 185. On Greenwood, see Davies, *Earth in Decay*, pp. 231–4.

[106] 'Driftless area of the Upper Mississippi Valley' (1884–5), quoted in Chorley, Beckinsale, and Dunn, *History of the Study of Landforms*, 2:133–4.

marked courses; 'maturity' exhibits maximum topographic differentiation; finally relief diminishes, slopes become gentler, and the terrain is 'almost as low, flat and featureless . . . as it was at birth . . . This is simple old age, a second childhood in which infantile features are imitated.'[107] Davisonian rivers passed from infancy and adolescence to maturity and senescence, when 'the flood-plains of maturity are carried down to the sea, and at last the river settles down to an old age of well-earned rest'. With age came deterioration. Elderly rivers exhibited a 'general fading away of strength and variety', Davis concluded. 'Extreme old age or second childhood is, like the first childhood, characterized by imperfect work.'[108] Thus 'old age' remained a metaphor for terrestrial degradation more than two centuries after ideas of decay had ceased to buttress the organic analogy.

Natural features were, to be sure, adjudged beautiful or ugly for qualities other than their presumed youth or age. Medieval men shunned mountains before they thought of them as 'old', but the life-cycle analogy reinforced the negative response. Uniformity, regularity, symmetry, and smoothness epitomized beauty long before Burnet linked them with the earth's innocent infancy, but this linkage strengthened existing bias against agedness. Only in the late eighteenth century, when roughness, irregularity, and assymetry became 'sublime' or 'picturesque', did mountain forms, like ruins, gain favour.[109] But those who then admired mountains saw in them not terrestrial senescence, but God's original work. Just as ruined buildings symbolized the triumph of nature over the transience of artifice, so wild and rugged nature no longer signified the elderly but the primeval.

The superiority of youthful nations

Human institutions seem no less subject to the ravages of time than natural features. The perpetual demise of old states and the genesis of new ones has struck countless observers as an organic process. In the second century before Christ, Polybius likened human institutions to living creatures: 'Every body or state or action has its natural stage of growth, then of prime, and finally of decay.' And like human beings and terrestrial features, nations were vaunted in youth and belittled in old age. 'Everything is best at its zenith' and worst in decay.[110] Ever since, national old age has betokened corruption, decay, impotence; and denizens of ageing lands are tainted, like Dorian Gray, by cruelty and debauchery.

The Romans made the analogy explicitly human, denoting historical epochs of birth, infancy, childhood, youth, maturity, and senescence. Seneca connected Rome's infancy with Romulus, its adolescence and 'manly strength' from the banishment of Tarquinius to

[107] Davis, 'Geographic classification' (1885) and 'The rivers and valleys of Pennsylvania' (1889), quoted in Chorley, Beckinsale, and Dunn, *History of the Study of Landforms*, 2:165–6, 190.
[108] 'Physical geography as a university study' (1894), p. 177.
[109] Nicolson, *Mountain Gloom*, pp. 269–323. Nicolson terms Burnet an unconscious precursor of Romantic taste: 'Theologically Burnet condemned mountains; actually he was obsessed by them . . . In the midst of a condemnation of the uncouth holes and hollows of a broken world' (p. 213), Burnet praises them for inspiring 'a kind of superstitious timidity and veneration' (*Sacred Theory*, p. 94) and finds 'something august and stately' in mountains 'that inspires the mind with great thoughts and passions; they fill and over-bear the mind with their Excess, and cast it into a pleasing kind of stupor and admiration' (pp. 109–10).
[110] Trompf, *Historical Recurrence*, pp. 4–115; quotations from Polybius on p. 24. See Barkan, *Nature's Work of Art*.

the end of the Punic Wars, its old age, hastened by over-expansion, leading to second childhood under Augustus. In the second century Florus credited Trajan with averting old age and postponing senescence; in the fourth century Ammianus Marcellinus limned the complexity of the Eternal City's 'degeneration': old Rome was slack and declining, yet also venerable, peaceful, and stable.[111]

Though some Patristic and medieval historians felt uneasy about the organic analogy for its implied lack of faith in Divine Creation, life-cycle terminology borrowed from classical history suffused Christianity's Great Week of world history. St Augustine termed the antediluvian 'day' mankind's infancy, the 'day' from the Flood its childhood, that from Abraham its adolescence, that from David its prime of life; a 'weakened and broken' old age stretched from the Exile to the Incarnation.[112]

Like many classical modes of thought, the institutional life cycle gained new currency in the Renaissance. Fifteenth- and sixteenth-century historians reiterated the Polybian framework, invoking biological explanations for the growth, decay, and ruin of states. All were ultimately devoured by disease, though few sixteenth-century states averted calamity long enough to expire of 'inward sicknesse'.[113] So too with elements of culture. Like human beings, wrote Vasari, the arts of painting and sculpture 'have their birth, growth, age and death'; like empires, added William Drummond, 'arts and sciences have not only their eclipses but their wanings and deaths'.[114] Reintroduced by Winckelmann, the organic analogy gained currency in nineteenth-century views of art – Peacock termed poetry 'the mental rattle that awakened the attention of intellect in the infancy of civil society'; Dyce saw art's 'infancy', 'adolescence', and 'manhood' in various epochs of Venetian painting. Extending the life-span analogy to whole cultures, Herder saw their decay as an inescapable consequence of their flowering.[115]

Political like geological metaphors of decay long remained prevalent. 'The affairs of all nations proceed in their rise, progress, mature state, decline and fall', thought Vico, who envisaged a terminal decay into senile impotence.[116] The life-cycle fate of nations was a recurrent eighteenth-century worry. 'The best constituted governments, like the best constituted animal bodies', wrote Bolingbroke, 'though they grow and improve for a time, they will soon tend visibly to their dissolution.'[117] In Fielding's *Amelia* every great kingdom is said to decline from youth to old age, when 'it is enervated at home – becomes contemptible abroad; and such indeed is its Misery and Wretchedness, that it resembles a Man in the last decrepit Stage of life, who looks with Unconcern at his approaching Dissolution'.[118]

---

[111] Trompf, *Historical Recurrence*, pp. 188–91; Momigliano, 'Time in ancient historiography', pp. 189–90.

[112] *De Genesi contra Manichaeos*, cited in Trompf, *Historical Recurrence*, pp. 212–14.

[113] Trompf, pp. 276–82, 301–2; Manuel, *Shapes of Philosophical History*, pp. 52, 59, quoting Bodin.

[114] Vasari, *Lives*, Preface, 1:18; Drummond, *Cypresse Grove* (1623), p. 245.

[115] Peacock, *Four Ages of Poetry* (1820), p. 18; William Dyce, *The National Gallery – its formation and management considered* ... (1853), quoted in Haskell, *Rediscoveries in Art*, p. 104; Manuel, *Shapes of Philosophical History*, p. 77.

[116] Vico, *New Science* (1744), Bk I, para. 349, p. 93; see also Bk V, para. 1096, p. 372; Conclusion, para. 1106, p. 381; Berlin, *Vico and Herder*, pp. 63–4.

[117] *Idea of a Patriot King* (c. 1740), Ch. 8, p. 65. See Kramnick, *Bolingbroke and His Circle*, pp. 35, 166–8.

[118] 1751, Bk XI, Ch. 2, p. 461. 'The state follows the man ... infirm and corrupt in his old age ... sinking with decrepitude into despotism' (Chateaubriand, *Genius of Christianity*, Bk III, Ch. 2, p. 420). See Spacks, *Imagining a Self*, pp. 274–5.

Only the rebel offshoot of Fielding's great kingdom across the Atlantic used the analogy with unconcern because, as shown in Chapter 3, Americans fancied themselves in infancy or vigorous (and permanent) youth, Europeans in their dotage. 'Nations are oft compared to individuals and to vegetables, in their progress from their origin to maturity and decay', stated Noah Webster, and 'the resemblance is just and fair.'[119] National youth was preferable 'to complete manhood and old age, when we every day become less active, and less pleased' – and, others added, more impious, debauched, and vicious. Nations already mature had nothing to look forward to but 'decline and mortification'.[120] Loyalists lamely refuted these implications of English seniority; when Alexander Hamilton termed England 'an old, wrinkled, withered, worn-out hag', Samuel Seabury rejoined that England, though indeed ancient, was a 'vigorous matron, just approaching a green old age'.[121]

National decay was still a leitmotiv of Western thought a century later. States past maturity should welcome quiet dissolution, in Herder's view, 'lest the graves of ancient institutions ... rob the living of light, and narrow their habitations'. Hegel, Schelling, Gobineau, and Marx variously expressed contempt for civilizations that prolonged an uncreative torpor amidst the ash-heap of history.[122] Spengler allotted cultures life spans of a thousand years; China and India had long lingered as 'wornout giants of the primeval forest thrust[ing] their decaying branches towards the sky', and the 'metaphysically exhausted soil of the West' betokened a similarly protracted end; he attributed the decline of the West to institutional senescence.[123] J. A. Symonds, echoed by Pater and Lytton and later by Louis MacNeice, likened the final senility of Greek literature to late-Victorian decadence. Futurist assaults against tradition invoked the organic analogy to denounce the 'smelly gangrene' of the decaying past.[124]

Institutional and cultural decline is now mainly seen as historically contingent, not organically determined. None the less the organic analogy remains persuasive. Images of flowering, maturing, and fading lead many to speak of 'the birth of an art', the 'life of a style', the 'death of a school', even when they are well aware that styles do not behave like people or plants. Historians continue to refer to the Ottoman Empire as the 'sick man of Europe' and to the 'death agony of Byzantium'.[125] Newly sovereign states contrast their youthful energies with the corrupt old West; hardly a day passes without public comment on the 'hardening of Britain's industrial arteries' or 'the English disease'. Such references are almost always pejorative, implying distaste for 'old age'.

[119] Webster, *An American Selection of Lessons in Reading and Speaking* (1787), quoted in Van Tassell, *Recording America's Past*, p. 45.

[120] Thomas Barnard (1794) and others, quoted in Persons, *American Minds*, pp. 122–5.

[121] Hamilton; and Seabury, *A View of the Controversy* (1774), quoted in Bailyn, *Ideological Origins of the American Revolution*, p. 137.

[122] Herder, *Reflections on the Philosophy of the History of Mankind*, p. 79; Manuel, *Shapes of Philosophical History*, pp. 59, 122–7; Schlanger, *Métaphores de l'organisme*, pp. 186–9.

[123] *Decline of the West* (1918), pp. 106–7; Dray, *Perspectives on History*, pp. 107, 113.

[124] Jenkyns, *Victorians and Ancient Greece*, pp. 73, 293–6; Marinetti, 'Founding and manifesto of Futurism' (1909); see Chapter 7, p. 380 below.

[125] Kidson, 'Figural arts', pp. 403–5; Kubler, *Shape of Time*, p. 5; Peter Burke, 'Tradition and experience: the idea of decline from Bruni to Gibbon', p. 144.

Rejection of age and wear in artifacts

We endow artifacts even more than nations and nature with life cycles like our own; indeed, most metaphors for ageing refer to artifactual decay. Such decay is by and large obnoxious; we normally prefer the new to the old, the fresh to the worn. (The opposite view, ascribing value to a patina of age or decay on certain artifacts, is discussed later.) A furniture conserver worries about 'what happens when like us in our old age, things start to fall off or wear out'.[126] But ageing artifacts are mostly jettisoned without compunction when they have served their use. A half century ago, Le Corbusier noted that we piously preserve the Colosseum, merely endure the Roman aqueduct, and let the locomotive rust on the scrap-heap.[127] Aqueducts and even locomotives now join the Colosseum in the heritage, but the scrap-heap is as full as ever.

Artifacts age in varying ways, reflecting different substances and kinds of use and wear. Biodegradable objects moulder and erode; plastic materials discolour or shatter. Yet we apply the same life-cycle language to them all. 'Men's Workes have an age like themselves', as Thomas Browne observed, 'and though they out-live their Authors, yet they have a stint and period to their duration.'[128] Decay is described in metaphors of human frailty or illness – the fatigue of metals, the ageing of glass. Like any patient, ailing art objects are said to require first aid, diagnosis, and treatment.[129] Technical terms such as 'tin pest' and 'bronze disease' make metal corrosion seem an organic malady. As Webster's Antonio remarks,

> . . . all things have their end,
> Churches and Cities (which have diseases like to men)
> Must have like death that we have.[130]

However venerated a relic, its decay is seldom admired. 'Antiquitie I unfainedly honour', in Hakewill's words, 'but why should I bee bound to reverence the rust and refuse, the drosse and dregs, the warts and wenns thereof?'[131] The search for constitutional precedents among 'rotten parchments under dripping and perishing Walls' struck Edmund Burke as an unseemly contrast with the living tradition of those precedents; he treasured the fact of antiquity but despised the look of age.[132] Burke's revulsion was customary. Shakespeare's list of time's corrosions –

> To ruinate proud buildings with thy hours,
> And smear with dust their glittering golden towers;
> To fill with worm-holes stately monuments,
> To feed Oblivion with the decay of things
> To spoil antiquities of hammered steel,
> And turn the giddy round of fortune's wheel[133]

---

[126] Anne Jordan, 'Lamb dressed as mutton', *Interior Design*, 17 (1977), 464–5.

[127] *City of To-morrow* (1925), p. 51. [128] Browne, *Religio Medici* (1635), Pt I, sect. 23, 1:35.

[129] Zwart, *About Time: A Philosophical Inquiry into the Origin and Nature of Time*, p. 46; W. G. Constable, 'Curators and conservation', p. 99.

[130] *Duchess of Malfi*, V.iii, p. 124. [131] Hakewill, *Apologie*, Bk V, 2:133.

[132] To the Duke of Richmond, post- 15 Nov. 1772, in Burke, *Correspondence*, 2:377.

[133] *Rape of Lucrece*, lines 944–7, 951–2.

– is not just an admission of decay's inevitability but a catalogue of its horrors, as the words 'ruinate', 'spoil', 'smear', and 'worm-holes' attest. The mutilated English monasteries were long abhorred, their 'rotten Foundations, ruinous Arches and Pillars, mouldering and tottering Walls' arousing general revulsion.[134] Not until the eighteenth century did travellers begin to find them picturesque.

The picturesque apart, the texture of age has rarely been a tenet of antiquarian taste. Renaissance and Enlightenment neo-classicists reprobated the look of age that accompanied time's erosions. Classical art as revived or emulated was bright, clean, new. Jacques-Louis David, Benjamin West, and others commonly depicted antique structures as newly built or in perfect repair. Not even their ruins are crumbling: chipped or exfoliated stones exhibit clean breaks and are devoid of moss and ivy, the romantic insignia of age and wear. Neo-classicists decried 'crooked-bodies, old and rent, full of Knots and Hollownesses', in Gerard de Lairesse's phrase, and the 'rough or ruined Buildings with their Parts lying up and down in Confusion'[135] that later attracted lovers of the picturesque.

Romantic taste apart, decay continued to arouse general revulsion. Simply because their softening tones enhanced some old buildings did not mean that age and decay were good in themselves.[136] Only the eccentric cultivated dust and filth; as Le Corbusier put it, people who washed their clothes and cleaned their houses disdained the patina of age.[137]

Devotees of wear and tear confess their own predilection aberrant, embarrassing, even perverse. Arthur Marshall terms 'idiotic' his 'increasing fondness for material objects that have grown old along with one'.[138] A young historian in Lively's *Treasures of Time* is hard put to justify English taste for decay to Japanese tourists. 'Is all broken down. What a pity', they respond to his own partiality for Minster Lovell. 'Well, yes', he answers, 'but it's rather nice, all the same.' And he adds lamely that the English are fond of ruins 'partly because we've got so many, we've had to make the best of them'.[139]

In some artifacts any signs of decay repel. A rusting car, a corroded washing machine, a verminous mattress, peeling wallpaper excite general disgust. And an absence of decay enhances the value of many old things. The used-car dealer expunges signs of wear. Old clothes are cleaned, fabrics renewed not just to conserve them but to prevent them from looking scruffy. Buildings undergo periodic repainting and repointing for looks as well as maintenance; an old house may be charming, but no one wants a tattered wreck. Holes in sleeves, cracks in walls, mould on the ceiling, grass thrust up between paving stones, tumble-down houses are distressing because they betoken failure to forestall decay.

Decay and wear usually detract from the appeal of antiquity. 'We love old buildings . . . for what they stand for rather than for what they look like', as John Piper characterized English taste. 'Even *pleasing* decay is not allowed by the officials who look after a ruined building, because if they allowed it *people would think they were not looking after the building*

---

[134] George Starkey, 'Epistolar discourse' (1665), quoted in R. F. Jones, *Ancients and Moderns*, p. 214. Starkey used metaphors borrowed from reactions to monastic ruination to attack traditional medicine (Aston, 'English ruins and history: the Dissolution and the sense of the past', pp. 242–3).

[135] *Art of Painting* (1738), quoted in Monk, *The Sublime*, p. 91.

[136] William White, 'Restoration vs. conservation' (1878), cited in Tschudi-Madsen, *Restoration and Anti-Restoration*, p. 62.

[137] *When the Cathedrals Were White*, p. 46.   [138] 'As time goes by', *New Statesman*, 19 May 1978, p. 671.

[139] P. 160.

at all.'[140] Most National Trust visitors prefer historic houses fresh and sparkling; they laud spotless and immaculate Clandon, disdain 'tatty' Knole and 'shabby' Chiddingstone village.[141] Tourists in York prefer old buildings well kept up to those that seem 'seedy'.[142] Justifying cleaning on the ground 'that originally all must have been new and bright and complete, our restorers share with the Victorians ... a disregard for the real and noble signs of age often amounting to hatred', thinks John Schofield, deploring their 'insidious compulsion' to supplant worn medieval sculptures, scour and redecorate Elizabethan tomb figures, and 'tinker with every square inch of ancient surface'.[143]

For valued antiquities to look new is standard practice in the United States. The restored and replica buildings in Colonial Williamsburg, 'as neat and well painted as the houses in a new suburb', historian Daniel Boorstin comments, 'will never have the shabbiness that many of them must have shown in the colonial era'.[144] Shabbiness seldom brings history to life; the only way the past can seem real is if its relics are in their prime.

A worn and tattered authentic artifact 'generally contradicts any feeling that it could possibly have been used by someone really alive'. Thus the objects that train Jack Finney's time traveller to feel at home in 1882 are not actual survivals but freshly minted reconstructions. An 1880s' dress from a museum, now faded and shrivelled, is rejected, for 'the women of the eighties ... were *living women*, and they would never have worn that rag!' Instead of mildewed books 'whose faded pages ... only a ghost could ever have read', bright new 'titles fresh-stamped in shining gold leaf, their pages pure white, the fresh black print still smelling of ink', bring the old days to life.[145] The plaster cast replicas at the Victoria and Albert Museum strike a critic as more attractive than the worn, dispersed originals; and some television viewers complained that recent programmes on Henry VIII and Elizabeth I showed dark old oak furniture rather than the brand-new pieces that the sixteenth century would have had.[146] Most who return to the past in imagination like to see it as 'new' as it seemed to those who lived in it. (Advocates of decay, as we shall see, turn these tastes on their head.)

Marks of wear and tear were deliberately expunged from artifacts in the Smithsonian Institution's 1976 Bicentennial exhibition, a reproduction of the Philadelphia Centennial. As the 1876 exhibitors had shown their finest, newest wares, 'most of the objects displayed *had* no history'; to be faithful to the spirit of modernity, century-old objects in the 1976 show had to look new. Original artifacts too worn or damaged to be rejuvenated were replaced by unused substitutes or new replicas.[147] Indeed, Americans seem reluctant to allow anything to decay: old things are acceptable only as long as they remain visibly and functionally fit.

The most venerable antiquities are imperilled by instinctive desires to renovate and rid them of patina. Measures to arrest decay of the Sphinx's ancient stonework came to a halt in 1980 when over-zealous masons were found dismantling its left front paw. The

---

[140] 'Pleasing decay' (1947), pp. 90, 96.   [141] Martin Drury, National Trust, interview 12 Sept. 1978.
[142] John Shannon, York Civic Trust, interview 20 Sept. 1978.
[143] 'Repair not restoration', p. 154.   [144] *America and the Image of Europe*, pp. 93–4.
[145] Finney, *Time and Again*, pp. 77–9.
[146] Jules Lubbock, 'Victorian vistas: the Cast Courts, V & A', *New Statesman*, 7 May 1982, p. 27; Binns, 'Importance of patina on old English furniture', p. 58.
[147] Post, *1876: A Centennial Exhibition*, p. 25. See Schlereth, *Artifacts and the American Past*, pp. 130–42.

16 Age improves art: William Hogarth,
Time Smoking a Picture, 1762

15 The perils of age: François Perrier,
Time the Destroyer, 1638

workmen 'had all these nice, new limestone blocks', an Egyptologist explains, 'and they thought they would look better than the old, dirty ones'.[148]

Decay also symbolizes failure. In Elizabeth Hardwick's desolating iconography of backwoods Maine squalor, worn-out household goods imply the decay of hope and spirit.

Everywhere a crowd, a multitude of rust, breakage, iron, steel, and tin. Here, almost blocking the door, is the rusting wheel of an automobile ... A slide upside down, the ladder broken; a huge tin garbage pail, dented everywhere, as if from a thousand blows, its bottom a sieve. A battered baby stroller, clumps of wood, old chair legs, bed springs, a tarpaulin in which an old puddle of water nests. A sled, a barrel, rubber tires. All crowned by the object just to the left, the car itself, leprously scarred ... What is an old appliance except a tomb of sorrow, a slab of disappointment, a fraud not really acknowledged but kept around mournfully, a reminder of life's puzzling lack of accommodation?[149]

Some offended by the look of decay do not tolerate anything old around them. 'Continually threatened by the presence in the house of piles of dying commodities', they permit possessions only the beginnings of lives. 'No sooner have Christmas presents been unpacked from their wrappings than there is talk of "coping with the junk" ... There is always the fear that something or other may be on "its last legs"'. Some go so far as rigorously to exclude all dying things, odds and ends and junk; everything they have must be 'alive and purposeful and well'.[150]

Decay is most dreadful when it seems our fault. Like seventeenth-century theologians who blamed nature's decay on mankind's sins, some writers suggest that desecration may cause relics to wither away. Brian Moore posits the mysterious appearance of a mass of priceless Victorian relics brought to life again in perfect condition in a California motel parking lot. But these historic artifacts rapidly decay, 'like invalids suffering some wasting disease', under the glare of publicity, the philistine gaze of tourist throngs, and the schemes of greedy entrepreneurs:

Machinery either warps or breaks down, the canvas cracks, the dolls' eyes no longer move, the damask and linen have brown stains, ... the statuary has developed cracks, even in the cast-iron pieces. The musical instruments all give out false notes, there are mysterious bare patches on the collection of sables and ermines, the Ross telescope lens is misted.

Everything becomes mouldy, mildewed, moth-eaten. Still worse, artifacts lose their authenticity. 'The original materials now seem false; ... hallmarks have faded completely, so that I can't tell any more whether it's silver, or silver plate'; blocks of glass look like lucite; obvious imitations and blatant shams spoil the ambience of the remaining originals, which finally waste away entirely.[151]

Taste for the appearance of youth is ubiquitous, and almost every life-cycle analogy deprecates old age. When the earth and its features are 'aged' they are also considered ugly; when nations and institutions seem 'senescent' they are thought impotent and corrupt. Features as various as ruins and 'elderly' rivers suffer decay. Buildings, utensils, clothing, even antiquities are best appreciated when just fashioned. We constantly make fresh

---

[148] 'Near faux pas for the Great Sphinx', *IHT*, 6 Feb. 1980, p. 1.
[149] Elizabeth Hardwick, 'In Maine', *N.Y. Review of Books*, pp. 4, 6.
[150] Laurie Taylor, 'Living with things'.
[151] Moore, *Great Victorian Collection*, pp. 149, 203; see also pp. 173–5.

starts, new brooms sweep clean, youth is served, age comes before – and thus contrasts with – beauty.

Yet some marks of age at times provide comfort or pleasure or beauty. When and how did ruin and decay come to be appreciated, and how does this taste affect apprehension and treatment of the past in general?

APPRECIATING THE LOOK OF AGE

Time truly works wonders. It sublimates wine; it sublimates fame; enriches and enlightens the mind; ripens cherries and young lips; festoons old ruins, and ivies old heads; . . . smooths, levels, glosses, softens, melts, and meliorates all things . . . All [is] the better for its antiquity, and the more to be revered . . . Time hoared the old mountains, and balded their old summits, and spread the old prairies, and built the old forests, and molded the old vales. It is Time that has worn glorious old channels for the glorious old rivers . . .

Herman Melville, *Mardi*[152]

'I mean to go in for letting the workmen have the use of all the rooms, with liberty to smudge them as much as they like, and so at the end we shall have a sort of antique effect.'
'They will be dirty.'
'You may call it dirt; I call it Art.'

Robert Kerr, *Ambassador Extraordinary*[153]

When fourteenth- and fifteenth-century humanists opened their eyes to the glories of Greece and Rome, what they saw, beyond much-copied classical texts, were the worn and mutilated remnants of antique architecture and sculpture. They admired these eroded fragments, but not their state of decay or ruin; the classical past came to life more vividly in their own fresh re-creations of it than in the time-worn survivals.

Yet these tattered remnants none the less helped to reinspire passion for the forms and ideas of antiquity. The ruins of Rome enchanted Petrarch; Francesco Colonna rhapsodized over lovers walking among fallen columns, broken sculptures, dilapidated temples, overgrown pillars, and funerary vaults; Du Bellay was typical of visitors overwhelmed by the magnitude and meaning of half-buried Rome.[154]

Exemplifying the transience of great men and deeds, the consequence of depravity, or the triumph of justice over tyranny, ruins inspired reflections on what had once been proud and strong and new but was now decrepit, corrupt, degraded. And as reminders of the evanescence of life and the futility of effort, ruins became a staple of eighteenth- and nineteenth-century response to the past.

First valued as residues of a splendid past and tokens of true antiquity, ruins later attracted interest for their own sake. The patina of age became an adjunct to worthy sentiments and then a canon of taste, a prime ingredient of Romantic scenery. Time was felt to 'ripen' artifacts, the marks of age to enhance art and architecture. Picturesque taste

---

[152] 1849, pp. 270–1.   [153] 1879, 3:168.
[154] Petrarch, *Roma instaurata* (1443) and *Roma triumphans* (1459), cited in Mazzocco, 'Antiquarianism of Francesco Petrarch'; Colonna, *Hypnerotomachia poliphili* (1499), cited in Mortier, *Poétique des ruines*, pp. 33–5; Du Bellay, *Antiquitez de Rome* (1558); Weiss, *Renaissance Discovery of Classical Antiquity*, p. 123.

enshrined ruins as consummate exemplars of the irregular, the accidental, and the natural; for the sake of pleasing decay houses were deliberately made ruinous and new ruins manufactured.[155] In the nineteenth century even antique sculptural fragments came to seem beautiful, and mutilated torsos and heads were preferred to intact originals.

The popularity of ruined castles, the price of patinated bronzes, the market for 'distressed' furniture attest the continuing appeal of marks of age. Corrosion not only enhances the sense of antiquity but is sometimes esteemed in itself. Artists celebrate evanescence with works intended to decay and perish. The worn and tattered state of treasured mementoes – battered jugs, old cigarette packets, dog-eared theatre programmes – is integral to their companionable value.

I shall discuss fondness for the look of age in terms of four themes: the idea that old things should look old; faith in decay as a guarantor of antiquity; aesthetic delight in wear and tear; and the reflections conjured up by ruins and fragments.

Old things should look old

The Renaissance rediscovery of classical masterpieces made the marks of age crucial adjuncts to historical antiquity. A patina of age commended paintings to seventeenth-century Venetians, who felt that no modern work could measure up to their sixteenth-century predecessors; old pictures that looked their age lent prestige to their owners. The cult of the 'old master' – 'a painting which was not merely venerable as old in time', in Denis Mahon's words, but 'was a respected testimony from the past' – spread throughout Europe.[156] Even when the 'length [and] injuries of time' damaged old masters, collectors preferred them to look their age. 'By giving testimony to their antiquity', Francesco Algarotti observed, the patina of time 'renders them proportionably beautiful in the superstitious eyes of the learned.'[157]

Learned appreciation of patina now extends to myriad historical artifacts. Many museum specimens should not be cleaned, testifies a Smithsonian Institution conservator; their 'handsome patina ... should be left intact, both to show their age and for aesthetic reasons'.[158] Bruises and hard knocks commend antiques to connoisseurs, explains an eminent restorer, for 'normal daily use imparts, merely by the touch of the human hand, the brush of a sleeve, and the stubbing with a leather-clad toe, the natural, not-too-perfect appearance that period furniture really should present'.[159] Antiquity justifies rough imperfections that would not pass muster in new work: rough-hewn floors and blackened timbers are valued not for beauty but for their impression of great age. Because 'worn' sounds powerfully evoke a sought-after sense of the past, recording studios preserve scratches in old recordings,[160] and the Retrospect Collectors Society distributes records with 'characteristic surface effects retained in the interests of authen-

---

[155] As early as the sixteenth century, Girolamo Genga built a house resembling a ruin for the Duke of Urbino at Pesaro (Vasari, *Lives*, 3:263–4).

[156] 'Miscellanea for the cleaning controversy', p. 464.   [157] *An Essay on Painting* (1764), p. 56.

[158] Bethune M. Gibson, quoted in Greif, 'Cleaning up the treasures of history', p. 298.

[159] Philp, 'Restoring furniture and clocks', p. 59.

[160] John Cornwell, 'Secrets of the recording studios', *Observer Mag.*, 19 Oct. 1975, pp. 20–30, reference on p. 26.

17 The noble patina of soot: Robert Smirke, St Philip's, Salford, Manchester, 1825

18 Renewing the old: Canterbury Cathedral cloisters, 1978

ticity'. Cleopatra's Needle was left unprotected in London during the Second World War partly in the faith that a few scars might add to its historic ambience.[161]

Treasured wear and tear need not require great antiquity. It was a look of seamy conformability that James Agee admired in the clothing of rural Southerners, prolonged use giving each man's garment 'the shape and beauty of his induplicable body'; sun, sweat, laundering, and age rendering the colour and texture of cloth 'ancient, veteran, composed, and patient'; buttons 'blind as cataracts' slipping into holes still older; overall legs as minutely wrinkled as the skin of aged faces; softened and faded substances sleeping 'against all salients of the body in complete peace'.[162] Used agricultural implements in a farm museum seem 'natural' and 'convincing' because 'they looked as if they had seen some hard work'; another museum seeks a late nineteenth-century calendar which 'should be well thumb-marked and bearing all the signs of constant use'.[163]

Marks of age and use especially suit structures whose natural place is out of doors, subject to continual weathering. The taste for building decay is intimately linked with late nineteenth-century restoration philosophy. One reason not to renovate ancient buildings was that restoration takes away 'the appearance of antiquity . . . from such old parts of the fabric as are left', argued William Morris.[164] 'To us every item which is spick and span and new . . . is something which requires an apology', asserted a leading architect.[165] In France, Delacroix preferred 'the smallest village church as time has left it, to Saint-Ouen de Rouen restored'.[166] G. E. Street decried the 'irreverent hands' that threatened at Reims and Laon cathedrals to 'scrape off every weather stain, repair every damaged feature and leave the whole as clean and new looking as it was when first built'.[167] In the United States, Henry James deplored the self-conscious air of 'desperate clean freshness' that marked Salem's old colonial houses; a sense of true antiquity needed 'musty secrets in the eaves'.[168]

That old buildings should look old is a not uncommon view. Unlike people, 'buildings are expected to gain by the process of growing old', and 'it is part of the quality we admire in them that they have their history written on their faces'. Some value any marks of age, even encrustations of dirt. The velvety patina conferred by soot 'allows a building to proclaim its age', argued the *Architectural Review* against cleaning St Paul's Cathedral. It provides 'that subtle combination of architecture and history that gives old buildings their value, . . . the visible evidence that the monument – like the nation – has weathered centuries of storm and crisis and come through battered but unbowed'.[169] Other soot-encrusted façades are variously defended as reminders of 'London's foggy past', as 'a monument to the age of smoke', and 'as noble and meaningful as any other texture of history'.[170]

[161] Ball, *Cleopatra's Needle*, p. 29.   [162] *Let Us Now Praise Famous Men*, pp. 267–9.
[163] Rhodes, Smith, and Shishtawi, 'Manor Farm, Cogges', p. 16; John Norwood, Worthing Museum, photo caption in Eric Joyce, *Observer Suppl.*, 17 Feb. 1980.
[164] 'Restoration' (1877).   [165] Sidney Colvin, at SPAB, 1878, quoted in Wiener, *English Culture*, p. 70.
[166] *Journal*, 29 Aug. 1857, 3:122.
[167] 'Destructive restoration on the Continent' (1857), quoted in Tschudi-Madsen, *Restoration and Anti-Restoration*, pp. 82–3.
[168] *American Scene*, p. 268.   [169] 'St Paul's: black or white?' (1964).
[170] Feliks Topolski, 'In praise of London grime', letter, *The Times*, 9 Nov. 1977; other examples in Lowenthal and Prince, 'English landscape tastes', pp. 218–19.

Even American preservationists sometimes deplore 'revivals' that eliminate marks of age. 'We must be wary of becoming our own worst enemies', warns the National Trust for Historic Preservation about a recently rediscovered old neighbourhood. 'A restoration could ruin the community's character, removing the patina of the years.'[171] That some flavour of the past survives in Boston's restored Quincy Market is due not merely to the nineteenth-century lettering on the shopkeepers' signboards but also to their lovingly preserved flaking paintwork and decayed wood.

Decay demonstrates and secures antiquity

Wear and tear confirms as well as adorns antiquity. The antique patina of early bronzes attested alike to their age and their genuineness. Many collectors assume that 'the more crude and gnarled and battered a piece of furniture looks, the earlier it must be', and would not believe a piece in perfect condition was genuine.[172] The owners of the Hôtel Crillon in Paris wanted its façade left unwashed when the Place de la Concorde's other historic palaces were cleaned in the 1960s, because the dirt served as a guarantee to visiting Americans that the Crillon was genuinely historic.[173] The marks of age – peeling paint, cracked putty, corroded metal – on Kew Gardens' Palm House are held to confirm its authenticity and yield a sense of the past which a stainless steel, plastic-coated replacement could never convey.[174] Other marks of wear are prized as personal links with the past, like the arms of an old rocking-chair whose lacquer and staining had succumbed to long and constant rubbing; preferring to keep this reminder of her mother's former presence, the owner refused to have them revarnished.[175]

Reliance on the aura of age as an historical bona fide tempts forgers to simulate weathering or abrasion. Roman fondness for Greek art led to the production of 'weathered' copies. But faking along with liking the marks of time first became widespread in the Renaissance. Fifteenth- and sixteenth-century Italian bronzes were artificially darkened to make them look older; Lorenzo de' Medici persuaded Michelangelo to pass off his statue of Cupid as an antique by burying it for a time in acidic soil.[176]

Ageing techniques are manifold. After darkening a painting with smoke, Terenzio da Urbino added variegated layers of varnish and dressed a decrepit frame with shabby gilt 'so that his work eventually looked as though it were really old and of some value'.[177] Another seventeenth-century painter antiquated pictures by tempering their colours with chimney soot and then rolling them up to cause minute fissures.[178] A German goldsmith 'aged' coins by shaking them in a mixture of fatty broth and iron filings on carriage journeys.[179]

---

[171] 'The enemy within', *Preservation News*, 16:10 (1976), 4.
[172] Binns, 'Restored and unrestored pieces of early oak furniture', p. 186.
[173] Janet Flanner ('Genet'), 'Letter from Paris', *New Yorker*, 3 Feb. 1962, p. 84.
[174] Rhona Hall, 'Restoration of the Palm House, Royal Botanic Gardens, Kew', course paper, Dept. of Geography, University College London, 1984.
[175] Rowles, 'Place and personal identity in old age', p. 306.
[176] Vasari, *Lives*, 4:113–14. Earlier, Michelangelo had 'antiqued' a sculptured faun's head by knocking out one of its teeth (4:111). See Arnau, *Deception in Art and Antiques*, pp. 28, 100; Kelly, *Art Restoration*, p. 193; Karl Meyer, *Plundered Past*, p. 109.
[177] Giovanni Baglione, *La Vite de pittori* . . . (1642), quoted in Arnau, *Deception*, p. 43.
[178] Sanderson, *Graphice* (1658), p. 17.
[179] Rieth, *Archaeological Fakes*, pp. 24–5.

Van Meegeren passed off his forged Vermeers by endowing paint with a solidity which resembled centuries of natural drying.[180]

Freshly carved ivory simulates the fine cracks on genuine old ivory; a few hours of mechanical smoke gives meerschaum pipes the warm honey colour of years of leisurely smoking.[181] Elaborate techniques fabricate ancient worm-holes and scratches in reproduction furniture, the scuff and fading of old jeans. One firm sells a do-it-yourself staining kit for 'that "200-year-old" look'; another markets 'wine dust' to make bottles seem old.[182] A Yale University architect gave his neo-Gothic building historical verisimilitude by grinding down its steps to suggest the passage of centuries of plodding students; an artful use of old tiles and vegetation gives new resorts like Port Grimaud on the Riviera a settled immemorial air, similar to Blunden Shadbolt's 1930s neo-Tudor structures that seemed to have been settling for centuries.[183]

Those who treasure decay as proof of antiquity are often satirized as well as duped. Salvator Rosa mocked the seventeenth-century practice of artificially ageing paintings; Hogarth's *Time Smoking a Picture* (1762) pokes fun at naïve lovers of the antique.[184] In Mark Twain's 'Capitoline Venus', an unappreciated modern sculpture acquires value by being mutilated, buried, and dug up as an antiquity.[185] In Stephen Leacock's 'Old Junk and New Money', a clock artfully broken by an Italian expert in destruction is praised as 'hardly to be distinguished from a genuine *fractura*' found in clocks actually flung from windows in the thirteenth century. But the best old things 'rust and rot in a way you simply cannot imitate'; Leacock's collectors wax ecstatic over a ninth-century drinking horn 'all coated inside with the most beautiful green slime, absolutely impossible to reproduce'.[186]

Besides authenticating or fabricating antiquity, erosion augments interest in its study and concern for its preservation. To see and touch palpably aged documents heightens the appeal of the past. History students were thrilled to handle nineteenth-century diaries and travel logs with 'some crinkle of antiquity about them . . . The idea, however illusory, that some major discovery might be lurking in those yellowed pages added a further luster to the assignment.'[187]

Decay yields valuable information about the past. A ceramics specialist welcomes 'old, clear abrasion' on archaeological specimens and cherishes 'eloquent scratches' indicative of use.[188] Some decay even helps to preserve: like blueing steel and anodizing aluminium, a patina in stable equilibrium with its environment may protect against further erosion. This effect was early appreciated. 'Nothing contributes so much to the conservation of brass or copper coins', wrote an expert in 1808, 'as that fine rust, appearing like varnish,

[180] Arnau, *Deception*, pp. 255–8.   [181] Ibid., pp. 101–2.

[182] *Cohasset Colonials*, Hagerty catalog, 1967, p. 22 ('Our specially compounded colors faithfully reproduce the mellow tones of centuries old milk paints', p. 23); Gordon Bennett & Associates, Palo Alto, cited in 'How to dust off the latest wine', *IHT*, 28 Apr. 1979, p. 12.

[183] Ryan, 'Architecture of James Gamble Rogers at Yale University'; Kidney, *Architecture of Choice: Eclecticism in America 1880–1930*, p. 61; Philippa Toomey, 'Coming up roses on the Riviera', *The Times*, 12 Sept. 1981, p. 15; Campbell, 'Blunden Shadbolt'. For a similarly 'aged' resort in Corfu, see Binney, 'Oppression to obsession', p. 207.

[184] Rosa, *La Pittura* (1640s), cited in Mahon, 'Cleaning controversy', p. 465 n. 32; M. D. George, 'Hogarth to Cruikshank', pp. 27–8.

[185] Twain's story was inspired by the Cardiff Giant hoax (Chapter 6, p. 330 below).

[186] Quotation on pp. 274–5.   [187] McKenna, 'Original historical manuscripts and the undergraduate', p. 6.

[188] Chernela, 'In praise of the scratch', pp. 174, 177.

19 The grandeur of ruins: Giovanni Paolo Panini, *Capriccio with Belisarius*, 1730–5

20 The grandeur of ruins: John Constable, *Stonehenge*, 1835

21 Henry Fuseli, *The Artist Moved by the Grandeur of Ancient Ruins*, 1778–9

which their lying in a particular soil occasions.'[189] Other decay is less beneficial. Bronzes rich in tin and buried in loam or dry earth acquire protective patinas, but patinas on bronzes high in zinc or buried in sandy soil induce deterioration, and oxidation further corrodes cast bronze sculpture. Metal corrosion can, however, help to preserve adjacent organic materials, notably artifacts of wood, leather, and wool.[190]

The beauty of patina

A patina of age that authenticates or preserves antiquity is apt to be thought aesthetic. Venetians for whom paintings gained esteem over time also felt that time improved their colours. Post-Renaissance painters welcomed the effects of patina, sculptors the dark encrustations on their bronzes, and architects the mellowness of weathered stone.[191] 'One

189 John Pinkerton, *Essay on Metals*, quoted in Nielson, 'Corrosion product characterization', p. 17. See C. S. Smith, 'Some constructive corrodings'.
190 R. T. Foley, 'Measures for preventing corrosion of metals'; John Musty, *The Ancient Monuments Laboratory* (London: H.M.S.O., 1977), p. 14.
191 P. D. Weil, 'Review of the history and practice of patination', pp. 83–6.

of the greatest charms of old furniture', remarks a restorer, 'is the change in colour and surface condition brought about by . . . hundreds of years' exposure to light and heat, dust and dirt, smoke from wood and coal fires, the application of beeswax and turpentine and the abrasion of countless polishing cloths.'[192]

Aesthetic pleasure in the patina of age is first recorded from China. Ninth-century collectors delighted in the colours given ancient Shang and Chou bronze urns by a thousand years or more of burial in the ground or under water, or by simply being passed down from generation to generation. Once unearthed and cleaned, ancient bronzes were smoothed and massaged by hand over many years to produce the admired brownish yellow or lustrous 'tea-dust' green. Although artificial patinating was practised during the Sung dynasty (960–1279), connoisseurs agreed that only great age gave bronzes the desired mellowness.[193]

In Europe, few marks of age were considered attractive until the mid eighteenth century. A pioneer of taste for decay praised Rome's ruined aqueducts both for engineering expertise and for their visual conformity with emerging tenets of Romantic taste.[194] Irregularity of form, a tension between previous unity and subsequent corrosion, and the prospect of variation through further decay made ruins ideal exemplars of the picturesque. Earlier depictions of decay – the stark, unsentimental realism of sixteenth-century artists like Hieronymus Cock, Hendrik van Cleve, and Maerten van Heemskerk – gave way to ruined structures as scenic background that harmonized with Poussin's and Claude's Arcadian themes; and in the eighteenth century crumbling and overgrown structures half-reverting to nature became foci of attraction. Next to Piranesi's powerful sketches of Roman antiquities, the ruins themselves seemed small and pallid to such observers as Goethe and Flaxman.[195]

Late eighteenth-century taste gauged artifacts and landscapes by the 'pictorial' criteria embodied in ruins. Time and weather made old trees and buildings picturesquely rough, explained Uvedale Price, while moss, lichen, and other encrustations added tonal richness. Irregular dead branches partly revealed the landscape behind them, and decaying Gothic turrets and pinnacles pierced skylines.[196] William Gilpin, the chief exponent of the picturesque, approvingly observed that at Tintern Abbey 'time has worn off all traces of the chissel: it has blunted the sharp edges of rule and compass, and broken the regularity of opposing parts', though 'a mallet judiciously used . . . might be of service in fracturing some' of the too regular remaining gable ends.[197] Extreme decay features J. T. Smith's etching of a neglected Surrey cottage whose 'patched plaster, of various tints and discolorations, . . . weather-beaten thatch, bunchy and varied with moss – the mutilated chimney top – the fissures and crevices of the inclining wall – the roof of various angles and inclinations – . . . and the unrepaired accidents of wind and rain' allured

[192] Binns, 'Importance of patina', p. 59.

[193] David, *Chinese Connoisseurship*, p. 9; van Heusden, *Ancient Chinese Bronzes of the Shang and Chou Dynasties*, pp. 60–1.

[194] Charles de Brosses, *Lettres familières écrites d'Italie en 1739 et 1740*, cited in Daemmrich, 'Ruins motif as artistic device in French literature', p. 454.

[195] Daemmrich, 'Ruins motif', pp. 455–7; Mortier, *Poétique des ruines en France*; Hartmann, *Ruine im Landschaftsgarten*; Honour, *Neo-classicism*, p. 53.

[196] Price, *Dialogue on the Distinct Characters of the Picturesque and the Beautiful* (1801), 3:200–3; *On the Picturesque, &c.*, 1:51–6. [197] *Observations on the River Wye . . . 1770*, pp. 47–8.

the artist's eye.[198] In the mouldering landscapes of Piranesi and Panini, lilliputian figures meander among classical remnants softened by soggy atmosphere, porous stone, and rampant underbrush.[199]

Picturesque devotees visited locales like John Dyer's *Grongar Hill*, where amid 'huge heaps of hoary mouldered walls . . . the pois'nous adder breeds / Concealed in ruins, moss and weeds',[200] and David Mallet's

> . . . Place of Tombs
> Waste, desolate, where *Ruin* dreary dwells,
> Brooding o'er sightless Sculls and crumbling Bones
> . . . the Column grey with Moss, the falling Bust
> The Time-shook Arch, the monumental Stone,
> Impair'd, effac'd, and hastening into Dust.[201]

These bizarre extremes are ridiculed in Jane Austen's suggestion that Henry VIII had abolished the monasteries and left them to 'the ruinous depredations of Time' mainly to improve the English landscape – unaware that Gilpin had seriously praised Cromwell for having 'laid his iron hand' upon Raglan Castle and 'shattered it into ruin'.[202]

But nature, not man, was the prime author of 'pleasing decay'. Ivy, mosses, lichens, maiden-hair, penny-leaf were to Gilpin 'ornaments of time that gave those full blown tints, which add the richest finishing to a ruin'.[203] These effects made Fountains Abbey 'a sacred thing. Rooted for ages in the soil, assimilated to it, and become, as it were, a part of it; we consider it as a work of nature, rather than of art.'[204] At villas near Rome, 'the more broken, weather-stained, and decayed the stone and brickwork, the more the plants and creepers seem to have fastened and rooted in between their joints, the more picturesque' Uvedale Price found them.[205] 'The rents, or fractures, or stains, or vegetation', concluded Ruskin, 'assimilate the architecture with the work of Nature, and bestow upon it those circumstances of color and form which are universally beloved by the eye of man.'[206] To be sure, architects added their own efforts: the Temple of 1780 in Ermonenville Park re-created 'in real leaf and stone . . . the sad spectacle of the works of man slowly being absorbed by the organic forces of nature', in Robert Rosenblum's words.[207] But no craftsman could truly achieve picturesque decay. 'It is hardly possible to put stones together with that air of wild and magnificent disorder which they are sure to acquire by falling of their own accord', wrote Cowper apropos ruins artfully rebuilt by Lord Holland.[208] Lack of contrivance was essential both to the look and to the very concept of ruins, Gilpin explained:

To give the stone its mouldering appearance – to make the widening chink run naturally through all the joints – to mutilate the ornaments – to peel the facing from the internal structure . . . – and to scatter heaps of ruin around with negligence and ease . . . you must put your ruin at last into the

[198] *Remarks on Rural Scenery . . . relative to the Pictoresque* (1797), p. 9.
[199] Rosenblum, *Transformations in Late Eighteenth Century Art*, pp. 113–15.
[200] 1761, lines 80–3, pp. 90–1.   [201] *Excursion* (1728), p. 23.
[202] Austen, *Love and Freindship* [1790], p. 89; Gilpin, *River Wye*, p. 89.
[203] *River Wye*, p. 48.
[204] Gilpin, *Observations . . . made in the Year 1772, on . . . the Mountains, and Lakes of Cumberland, and Westmoreland*, 1:188.
[205] *Essay on Artificial Water* (1794), p. 114.   [206] *Seven Lamps of Architecture* (1849), p. 183.
[207] *Transformations*, p. 116.   [208] To William Unwin, July 1779, in Cowper, *Correspondence*, 1:155.

22 Pleasing decay: nature's work. Lichen at Montacute, Somerset (Edwin Smith)

23 Pleasing decay: man's work. William Chambers, ruined arch, Kew Gardens, 1759–60

hands of nature to adorn, and perfect it ... It is time alone, which meliorates the ruin; which gives it perfect beauty; and brings it ... to a state of nature.[209]

Nor could any artist adequately depict decay. George Crabbe's hapless painter of a ruined tower fails to match the effect of time:

> ... see how Nature's Work is done,
> How slowly true she lays her colours on;
>
>   ★   ★   ★
>
> ... till in unnotic'd Years
> The stony Tower as grey with age appears;
>
>   ★   ★   ★
>
> And wouldst thou, Artist! with thy Tints and Brush,
> Form Shades like these? Pretender, where thy Blush?
> In three short Hours shall thy presuming Hand
> Th' effect of three slow centuries command?[210]

As Trollope observed, 'no colourist that ever yet worked from a palette had been able to come up to this rich colouring of years crowding themselves on years'; ivy and creepers on Ullathorne's walls produced 'that delicious tawny hue which no stone can give, unless it has on it the vegetable richness of centuries'.[211]

Romantic musings heightened appreciation of picturesque decay. The antique aspect of Oxford's colleges enraptured Hawthorne: 'So gnawed by time as they are, so crumbly, so blackened ... The effect of this decay is very picturesque, ... greatly enriching the Grecian columns, which look so cold when the outlines are hard and distinct.[212] Ageing also beautified sculpture: the Elgin Marbles for Keats mingled 'Grecian grandeur with the rude Wasting of Old Time'; the cracks and old weather stains of Venetian stone conveyed to Ruskin the rich hue of ten centuries; the *Venus de Milo* was enhanced for Walter Pater by time rubbing away its original precision of outline.[213]

Patina's most celebrated effects relate to paintings. That ageing adds beauty, with colours becoming more perfect as time goes on, was the common view of connoisseurs by the seventeenth century. The Italian word '*patena*', originally a dark varnish applied to shoes, denoted the flattering tones time induced on varnished paintings.[214] Dryden's verses to the royal portraitist Kneller epitomize confidence in patina:

> For Time shall with his ready Pencil stand;
> Retouch your Figures, with his ripening hand
> Mellow your Colours, and imbrown the Teint;
> Add every Grace, which Time alone can grant:
> To future Ages, shall your Fame convey;
> And give more Beauties, than he takes away.[215]

---

[209] *Observations on ... Cumberland, and Westmoreland*, 1:67–8.

[210] *The Borough* (1810), Letter 2, pp. 16–17.

[211] *Barchester Towers* (1857), p. 203. Ullathorne was modelled on Montacute House, Somerset.

[212] *English Notebooks*, 5 Sept. 1856, p. 412.

[213] Keats, 'On seeing the Elgin Marbles' (1817), lines 12–13, *Poetical Works*, p. 478; Clegg, *Ruskin and Venice*, pp. 53–6; Pater, cited in Jenkyns, *Victorians and Ancient Greece*, p. 58.

[214] Mario Boschini, *La carta del navegar pitoresco* (1660), cited in Kurz, 'Varnishes, tinted varnishes, and patina', pp. 56–9; Weil, 'History and practice of patination', pp. 201–2.

[215] 'To Sir George Kneller' (1694), lines 176–81, 4:466.

Eighteenth-century painters assured clients that a few decades would mellow their raw new colours; as with new-killed meat and newly gathered fruit, time softened and sweetened pigments that were at first too sharp and strong.[216] Patina bestowed 'an extraordinary degree of harmony upon the colours of a picture', thought Algarotti; many painters simulated the time-darkened tones of their predecessors.[217] Addison depicts Time as an ancient craftsman who 'wore off insensibly every little disagreeable Gloss', adding 'a beautiful Brown . . . and Mellowness that . . . made every Picture appear more perfect than when it came fresh from the Master's Pencil'.[218]

The mellow patina of age became especially important in nineteenth-century England, where the treatment of paintings in the National Gallery, founded and initially furnished by Sir George Beaumont, profoundly affected popular taste. Beaumont adored brown varnish; for him an old picture's subdued tints were more 'picturesque' and hence more desirable than any new one could be.[219] The 'subtle tonal unity' of old master paintings was in fact induced more by dirt and London fog than by the patina of centuries, but widespread admiration of the 'golden glow' of age led restorers to heap varnish on early masterpieces.[220] Considered too 'fresh' for an old master, the blue skies of some Luca Giordano paintings were retouched with age-like green.[221]

Much as fig leaves made classical sculpture respectable, so did time domesticate gaudy Mediterranean scenes. Many Victorians 'felt that several coats of dirt and dulled varnish made brightly coloured paintings, especially of the Italian and Spanish schools, seem more English, less foreign, less Catholic', in Kenneth Hudson's words. 'They felt uneasy when the original picture was revealed, almost as if it had had its clothes taken off.'[222] And since patina obscured much detail, viewers found in old paintings whatever their imaginations sought. 'The romantic amateur loves the rust and haze of the varnish', commented a critic, 'for it has become a veil behind which he can see whatever he desires.'[223]

Unlike their predecessors, some present-day restorers remove varnish and overpainting along with dirt. Decrying 'old master' patina as sentimental nostalgia, they aim to return paintings to their original freshness.[224] Many eminent connoisseurs and art historians, however, continue to value the marks of age. In their view, varnish was intended to harmonize colours that time would alter – a harmony irreversibly deranged by radical cleaning.[225] For example, time has eclipsed Vermeer's greens with blue, and made the

[216] Charles Perrault, *Paralelle des anciens et des modernes* (1688), quoted in Wotton, *Reflections upon Ancient and Modern Learning*, p. 76.

[217] *Essay on Painting*, pp. 56–7.

[218] *Spectator*, No. 83, 5 June 1711, 1:356. Ageing did not beautify all pictures: whereas patina slowly reduced Guido Reni's colours to 'a true and satisfactory semblance of nature', he claimed that time blackened and flattened the colours of other artists (Carlo Cesare Malvasia, *Felsina pittrice* (1678), cited in Mahon, 'Cleaning controversy', p. 466; see Kurz, 'Varnishes', p. 58). L.-J.-F. Lagrenée's allegorical *Le Temps colore les bons tableaux et détruit les mauvais* (c. 1798–1804) exemplified these selective effects (Kurz, 'Time the painter', p. 97). See Walden, *Ravished Image*, p. 52.

[219] Hussey, *Picturesque*, pp. 262–3; Walden, *Ravished Image*, p. 134.

[220] Ruhemann, *Cleaning of Paintings*, pp. 228–9; Brommelle, 'Material for a history of conservation: the 1850 and 1853 reports on the National Gallery', pp. 179–81.

[221] Mahon, 'Cleaning controversy', p. 469.   [222] *Social History of Museums*, p. 82.

[223] Horsin Déon, *De la conservation* (1851), quoted in Ruhemann, *Cleaning of Paintings*, p. 85.

[224] Brandi, 'Cleaning of pictures, in relation to patina, varnish and glazes'. The public, too, 'no longer wants to see the "old master glow"', wrote Theodore Rousseau of the Metropolitan Museum of Art ('Cleaning of pictures: introduction', *Museum*, 3 (1950), 110).

[225] W. G. Constable, 'Curators and conservation', p. 100; Walden, *Ravished Image*, p. 32.

blues of Poussin and Claude aggressively glaring, standing out from other colours and upsetting the original balance. A 'light patina masks the harshness of colour discords and restores the balance among the values', argued René Huyghe when director of the Louvre, 'covering up the injuries [of time] and so making them less obvious to the eye'.[226]

The battle was joined in the National Gallery 'cleaning controversy', provoked by post-war displays of newly restored pictures whose bright colours and flat tones shocked British viewers accustomed to dark old varnish. Passions aroused by patina engendered a rancorous exchange that ranged from the correspondence columns of *The Times* to the *Burlington Magazine*.[227] Art historians contended that painters had customarily exaggerated colours that time would tone down; they and their patrons had welcomed the ageing effects of varnish. Restorers who sought to confute this view were accused of ignorance and of warping historical facts. When 'literary evidence regarding the technique of the old masters [did] not tally with the views held at the National Gallery', Otto Kurz charged, restorers made 'a concerted effort . . . to discredit the principal witnesses'. Thus advocates of radical cleaning were said to discount evidence from the painter Boschini because he was a '"picture dealer" with a vested interest in the sale of old masters', from the writer P. J. B. Nougaret as an 'assiduous collector of gossip', and from Joseph Vernet because his assertion that 'my works improve with time which imparts to them vigour, colour, and harmony' happened to be addressed to a diplomat; Kurz thought even a diplomat 'might occasionally be told the truth'. One restorer had proposed 'that historians should submit their findings to the authorities of the National Gallery for "sifting"', but 'when the arguments advanced turn out to be speculations about the possible attitude of Titian's patrons, when documents are interpreted against the elementary rules of grammar, or when we are told that a sixteenth-century author was dependent on a book published in 1929, any form of collaboration becomes impossible'.[228]

More fundamental matters are at issue than these polemics reveal, however. Even the most radical restorers consider themselves faithful to the 'true' look of age. Time does alter pigments on a canvas: oils harden and dry out and a network of fine cracks (*craquelure*) covers the surface; some tones darken, others become transparent, revealing what was painted under them (*pentimenti*). These marks of age are as integral to a painting's historical 'truth' as its style and content.[229] Each epoch selects its own aesthetic and historical truths, however. The patina (*craquelure* and *pentimenti*) that modern restorers accept was distasteful to and concealed by nineteenth-century connoisseurs, who instead enjoyed the 'golden tone' of antiquity now considered disfiguring and spurious.

Irreversible change in pigments makes it impossible to return any old painting to its initial condition. But assumptions about original intentions in any case reflect restorers' own biases. 'The "restored" Cathedrals of England, France, and Germany are sufficient reminders of what can happen when renowned experts claim to know the intentions of bygone ages', warned Gombrich. No matter how knowledgeable the restorer or worthy his aims, he is bound to be 'influenced by his scale of values, his unconscious bias, and his

---

[226] 'Louvre Museum and the problem of the cleaning of old pictures', p. 191.
[227] See *Museum*, 3 (1950); *Burlington Magazine*, 91 (1949), 183–8; 92 (1950), 189–92; 104 (1962), 51–62, 452–77; 105 (1963), 90–7; *British Journal of Aesthetics*, 1 (1961), 231–7; 2 (1962), 170–9.
[228] Kurz, 'Time the painter', pp. 94–5. See Gombrich, 'Controversial methods and methods of controversy'.
[229] Kelly, *Art Restoration*, pp. 108–20; Adams, *Lost Museum*, pp. 225–6.

24 Ruin enlivens a landscape: Folly, Hodnet Hall, Shropshire, *c.* 1970

25 Unpleasing decay: former cement works, near Snelling, California

conscious convictions'.[230] Today, these favour bright colours and strong contrasts: the restorer is apt to boast he 'has cleaned a Rembrandt so successfully that its colours remind one now of Monet', and the restored paintings of various epochs in New York's Frick Collection strike a recent observer 'as though they had been painted by the same artist, probably an Impressionist'.[231] Radical restorers 'achieve more nearly the firm tones to which the modern eye is accustomed', writes Huyghe, so that 'the state in which old pictures finally emerge is almost akin to that of modern pictures ... Our generation then marvels at an altogether artificial youth, which is not in fact that of the picture but of its assimilation to our own conceptions.'[232] To know what an old master looked like when first made we need to see not restored old paintings but recent ones, Gilson suggests, for 'any youth resembles any other youth more than he resembles the old man he will someday have to be'.[233] Meanwhile, however, the cult of youth continues to dominate modern sensibilities in art as in life.

Varieties of aesthetic decay

Appreciation of wear and tear varies with the composition and use of artifacts. Whether decay ornaments or blemishes often depends on whether it affects something made for utility or for ornament. We expect most functional artifacts to become less attractive as they age, but hope that most art objects will remain perennially fresh.

But the distinction between art and use breaks down in practice. Patina improves buildings more than paintings, even though buildings are 'useful' and paintings are not. Homely relics gain authenticity by exposure to time and use: dog-eared books, frayed curtains, pitted and earth-stained spades and mattocks lend reality to the past. Yet renovated workshops of olden times – forge and smithy, grain mill, printing press, bakery – must yield goods that are fresh, not rusty, stale, or mildewed.

Some substances age less well than others. Concrete becomes more ugly every passing year, looking greasy if smooth, squalid if rough; glass-fibre decays more disagreeably than stonework, as the Brighton Pavilion's minaret replacements have shown. The aesthetics of metal decay reflects a host of chemical and cultural variables. Much corrosion – rust on iron, tarnish on silver, white crusts on lead and tin – is normally odious; only to copper and bronze does a time-induced oxidized surface add the lustre of a 'noble' patina. And even copper and bronze, as noted above, can suffer unsightly decay.[234]

Some bias against metal corrosion has been overcome by Cor-Ten or 'weathering steel'. First used in the 1930s by Eero Saarinen at the John Deere plant in Moline, Illinois, Cor-Ten has promoted a taste for rust. Its adherent oxide coating acquires 'an attractive natural colour', advertises the British Steel Corporation, 'particularly pleasing in rural surroundings'. Once past an unattractive stage of salt contamination and run-off staining, it weathers into beauty. 'After one cleared one's mind of the nasty word *rust*, the amazing

[230] Gombrich, 'Dark varnishes', p. 55; *idem*, 'Controversial methods and methods of controversy', p. 93.
[231] Kurz, 'Varnishes', p. 59; Richard Boston, 'The lady varnishes', *Guardian*, 25 Sept. 1984, p. 11.
[232] 'Louvre Museum', p. 198. See Walden, *Ravished Image*, pp. 6, 13, 92.   [233] *Painting and Reality*, p. 103.
[234] Blomfield, *Modernismus*, p. 77; Plenderleith and Organ, 'Decay and conservation of museum objects of tin'; Organ, 'Current status of the treatment of corroded metal artifacts'; Gettens, 'Patina: noble and vile'.

conclusion was that it was a beautiful material such as only nature can produce.'[235] With steel as with ruins, 'nature' validates the aesthetics of ageing.

The patina of age is most appreciated on stonework. Finding 'actual beauty' in the marks of age,[236] Ruskin felt that ageing ennobled all sculptural ornament:

The effect of time is such, that if the design be poor, it will enrich it; if overcharged, simplify it; if harsh and violent, soften it; if smooth and obscure, exhibit it; whatever faults it may have are rapidly disguised, whatever virtue it has still shines and steals out in the mellow light.

No fine building 'is not improved up to a certain period by all its signs of age', nor was 'any building so ugly but that it may be made an agreeable object' by marks of antiquity. The façade of The Queen's College, Oxford, seemed to Ruskin otherwise reprehensible, but few 'could have looked with total indifference on the mouldering and peeled surface' of the unrestored limestone.[237] William Morris's dictum that 'the natural weathering of the surface of a building is beautiful, and its loss disastrous'[238] became a canon of taste throughout Europe.

Materials and climate also affect virtues of stone corrosion, however; even that champion of pleasing decay, John Piper, agrees that 'not all decay in buildings is pleasing'.[239] Structures that weather beautifully in unpolluted or arid locales become unsightly in sulphur-laden or humid air. Time's patina may dignify some sculpture, but runnels of soot make the giant statue of Atlas at Rockefeller Center in New York seem neither wrinkled with age nor lined with wisdom, but merely dirty.[240] And while stone façades can become attractive ruins, painted or plastered walls exposed to the elements look dilapidated and forlorn. Lack of shelter quickly destroys stucco work and frescoes. The art of ancient Pompeii would soon vanish, archaeologists warn, were its care left to 'the romantic visitor, who would prefer a discoloured wall overgrown with weeds to a painted wall protected by a roof and a curtain'.[241]

Awareness of an old building as a still functioning organism immuring a lengthy past ennobles its decay with 'some mysterious suggestion of what it had been, and of what it had lost'.[242] Ruskin eulogized an ancient church tower at Calais as

useful still, going through its own daily work [though with] the record of its years written so visibly, ... its slates and tiles all shaken and rent, and yet not falling; its desert of brickwork full of bolts, and holes, and ugly fissures, and yet strong, like a bare brown rock – as some old fisherman beaten grey by storm, yet drawing his daily nets ... It completely expresses that agedness in the midst of active life which binds the old and the new into harmony.[243]

What made the tower charming to Ruskin was, in fact, just those features that enfeebled it.

[235] British Steel Corporation, *Cor-Ten Steel* brochure (1973), p. 4; John Dinkeloo, quoted in Denney and O'Brien, 'Introduction to weathering steels', pp. 962, 966. The American sculptor Ellsworth Kelly specializes in Cor-Ten weathered slabs whose raised or incised textured surfaces rust to gray-brown or green (Hayward Gallery, London, exhibition, Apr. 1980).

[236] *Seven Lamps of Architecture*, pp. 178, 183.

[237] *Modern Painters*, I, Pt 2, sect. 1, Ch. 7, para. 26, p. 104. On the refacing of Queen's College, see Arkell, *Oxford Stone*, pp. 152, 168.

[238] 'Beauty of life' (1880), 22:69.   [239] 'Pleasing decay', p. 93.

[240] Bovey, 'Boats against the current', p. 577.

[241] Maiuri, 'Recent excavations at Pompeii' (1950), p. 102. See Pane, 'Some considerations on the meeting of experts ... 1949', p. 74.

[242] Ruskin, *Seven Lamps of Architecture*, Ch. 6, sect. 18, p. 185.

[243] *Modern Painters*, IV, Pt 5, Ch. 1, paras. 2–3, pp. 2–3.

26 Picturesque misery: Gustave Doré, 'Houndsditch', London, 1872

In short, Ruskin admired decrepitude. By picturesque tenets, 'a broken stone has necessarily more various forms in it than a whole one; a bent roof has more various curves in it than a straight one; every excrescence or cleft involves some additional complexity of light and shade, and every stain of moss on eaves or wall adds to the delightfulness of color'. Erosion lent beauty a temporal dimension, for 'set in the deeper places of the heart [is] such affection for the signs of age that the eye is delighted even by injuries which are the work of time'.[244]

Many share Ruskin's view that the organic nature of buildings ennobles their wear and tear. John Soane sketched his buildings as they would look not only when new but after centuries of use. 'Men should make buildings, as God made men, to be beautiful in age as well as in youth', comments Piper; a building's architect should bear in mind that 'some people will see it as an aged warrior or matron, not just as a brave baby'.[245]

Pleasure in diminished strength and function did seem perverse to some, however, especially when picturesque tenets called for old-timers as well as old ruins. The similarly 'irregular' features of a hypothetical parson's house and of his daughter provoked Uvedale Price to contemplate a future with the daughter grown even more picturesque, 'when her

[244] Ibid., para. 8, p. 6; I, Pt 2, sect. 1, Ch. 7, para. 26, p. 104.   [245] 'Pleasing decay', p. 89.

27 Imagined decay: Joseph Michael Gandy, *Architectural Ruins:
A Vision. The Bank of England . . .* 1832

cheeks were a little furrowed and weather-stained, and her teeth had got a slight incrustation'. But as consistency required 'the same happy mixture of the irregular and picturesque . . . throughout her limbs', responded Richard Payne Knight, 'consequently she must have hobbled as well as squinted; and had hips and shoulders as irregular as her teeth, cheeks, and eyebrows'. 'You will hardly find any man fond enough of the picturesque', Price had to admit, to marry a girl so thoroughly deformed.[246]

Ruskin himself deplored the heartless 'lower picturesque' delight in 'the look that an old laborer has, not knowing that there is anything pathetic in his grey hair, and withered arms, and sunburnt breast'. The slum-dwellers of Amiens in 1845 seemed to him 'all exquisitely picturesque, and no less miserable . . . Seeing the unhealthy face and melancholy mien, . . . I could not help feeling how many suffering persons must pay for my picturesque subject and happy walk.'[247] In America, Melville reproved those who hung 'povertiresque' pictures in their drawing-rooms while denying the existence of misery.[248] Taste for 'the plaster falling in blotches from the ancient brick-work' and other picturesque stains of time in Italian houses made Hawthorne 'suspect that a people are waning to decay and ruin, the moment that their life becomes fascinating either in the poet's imagination or in the painter's eye'.[249]

[246] Price, *Dialogue on the Distinct Characters of the Picturesque and the Beautiful* (1801), 3:292–3; Knight, *Analytical Inquiry into the Principles of Taste* (1805), quoted in Hussey, *Picturesque*, p. 75; also pp. 73–4.
[247] Ruskin, *Modern Painters*, IV, Pt 5, Ch. 1, paras. 7 and 12n, pp. 5, 10n. The description of Amiens comes from Ruskin's diary, 11 May 1854. Ruskin felt that the 'noble picturesque' of Turner and Prout, by contrast, exhibited sympathy with suffering, poverty, and decay 'nobly endured' (Hewison, *John Ruskin: The Argument of the Eye*, pp. 48–60).
[248] *Pierre* (1852), Bk 20, pp. 276–7. See Litman, 'Cottage and the temple: Melville's symbolic use of architecture', p. 634.   [249] *Marble Faun*, p. 296.

28 Abandoned decay: Vicksburg, Mississippi, 1933 (Walker Evans)

29 Arrested decay: Calico Ghost Town, moved to Knott's Berry Farm, Buena Park, California

The equivalence between painting and reality posited by Melville and Ruskin has long been disregarded, however, if indeed it was ever accepted. Real squalor repelled, but its pictorial representation in the past might be enjoyed. The ancient abbey and the anti-quated cottage deserved preservation for their pictorial qualities, Humphry Repton argued, but no one would suggest that a modern English gentleman should actually *live* in one.[250] As painters' canvases served no utilitarian purpose, viewers could appreciate the artifacts and people they depicted as departures from ideal types.[251] Rotten and withered trees were 'capital sources of picturesque beauty', in Gilpin's view; hollow trunks made invaluable foregrounds, withered tops lent scenic diversity, and when 'ideas of wildness and desolation are required, what more suitable accompaniment can be imagined, than the blasted oak, ragged, scathed, and leafless?'[252] Fantasizing decay afforded romantic artists welcome relief from the humdrum present. Hubert Robert's ruinous *Louvre*, Joseph Gandy's decrepit *Bank of England* were pleasing partly because the imputation of decay abolished their workaday functions.[253] Pictures even of human decay can seem attractive if remote enough in time to make their realism quaint. Hence the appeal of Doré's grim sketches of the London poor and of nineteenth-century photographs of slums and child labourers.[254]

The keenest admirers of decay admit that beyond a point it no longer beautifies. Views differ as to when that point has arrived: British colleagues chided me for junking a frayed old briefcase which I found both unsightly and unserviceable; my newer one is made acceptable in their eyes by the old rope that replaces its broken leather handle. But even Ruskin agreed that after a 'certain period' decay negated the pleasing effects of weathering on the finest of buildings, which 'like all other human works ... necessarily declines'.[255]

Ruins present further problems. A building may be more beautiful as a ruin than in its prime,[256] but ruination in its later stages loses evocative power. Ruins should seem on the verge of dissolution, suggests Summerson. 'A building which has simply had its roof burnt and windows broken is usually perfectly uninteresting as a ruin; it demands to be re-roofed. A building which has become a chaotic and meaningless heap of masonry is like-wise valueless; it demands to be removed.' Aesthetics require a balance between architec-ture and nature, but the balance must seem uncontrived: any suggestion that the ruin is an artifice or that its decay has been deliberately arrested lessens our appreciation of it. 'We

---

250 Repton, *Sketches and Hints on Landscape Gardening* (1795), Ch. 7: 'How void of taste must be that man who could desire a chimney or roof to his country-house when we are told that Poussin and Paul Veronese built whole cities without a single chimney and with only one or two slanting roofs' (p. 238 n. 33).
251 'The most *beautiful* pictures may be produced by the most ugly and disgusting objects' (Price, *Dialogue*, 3:303). See Hussey, *Picturesque*, pp. 70–1, 169; Gaunt, *Bandits in a Landscape*, pp. 99–100.
252 *Remarks on Forest Scenery and Other Woodland Views* ... (1794), 1:8–14.
253 Mortier, *Poétique des ruines*, p. 92; Hussey, *Picturesque*, pp. 202–3; Macaulay, *Pleasure of Ruins*, p. 38; Carlson, *Hubert Robert*; Lukacher, 'Gandy's dream revisited'.
254 'The nineteenth-century photographs of child laborers or urban slum apartments are so beautiful that they transcend their subject. To look at them, or at the Victor Gatto painting of the Triangle shirtwaist factory fire, is to see not misery or ugliness but an art object' (Fitzgerald, *America Revised*, p. 15).
255 *Modern Painters*, I, Pt 2, sect. 1, Ch. 7, para. 26, p. 105.
256 Stendhal, *Roman Journal*, p. 16; Price, *Dialogue*, 3:332–3.

30 Fragments: paintings and ruins

need to have the reassurance of accidental creation', Summerson adds. If it is a sham 'we begin to criticize it as a work of art, . . . if it is known to be preserved the ruination seems no longer the work of pure accident'.[257]

But decay is inexorable, and no ruin can long survive without interference. The conserved ghost towns of the American West, whose brief, colourful lives ended with the mining booms which built them, exemplify the problem. To maintain sagging roofs and broken windows in a state of arrested decay and stabilize the fragile patina of age is not only technically taxing but aesthetically unreasonable,[258] for 'decay is not a stationary condition but a growing and continuing process', as Piper writes. 'A building in which decay has been arrested smells, however faintly, of the museum; and in a few years it has the "dated" look of somebody or something that has outlived its time.'[259]

Whether decay enhances or detracts from a work of art depends on the artistic medium. Whereas patina alters one of a painting's essential elements, its colour, 'patina on a sculpture or a building adds something to them without substantially interfering with the main thing, their form', writes a restorer.[260] The distinction is said to depend on how erosion is perceived: most pictures represent a three-dimensional reality on a flat surface;

---

[257] Summerson, 'The past in the future', p. 237. See Kenneth Clark, *Gothic Revival*, p. 57.
[258] *Ghost Towns and Mining Camps*: Nelson, 'Bodie: a ghost town stabilized', pp. 5–10, discusses some technical problems; Hart, 'Interpretive case study: Custer, Idaho', pp. 25–8, questions the propriety of preserving decay.
[259] 'Pleasing decay', pp. 89, 91.   [260] Ruhemann, *Cleaning of Paintings*, p. 218.

31 Fragments: the Elgin Marbles. Dione and Aphrodite (?), east pediment

to sustain this illusion, injury and decay that interrupt the composition must be concealed or minimized. But sculpture, pottery, silver, ivory, buildings do not represent objects, they *are* objects; the observer's imagination corrects defects engendered by erosion or accident. We admire a sculpted headless figure but view askance a decapitated portrait.[261]

History clouds this distinction, however, as shifting fashions in antique statuary show. Fragmented relics and damaged specimens of archaic art outraged Renaissance sensibilities. Mutilated and disfigured antique pieces, like ancient texts, were restored to the lovely wholeness of youth. Humanists aimed to reassemble the mangled body of classical learning – Thomas Traherne's 'worthless shreds and Parcels' of fragmented relics 'lost and buried in Ruines' – into an 'Intire piece',[262] as we saw in Chapter 3. Collectors reconstituted scattered classical fragments; pieces that did not fit were forced into place, their edges bevelled off and joint marks hidden. Restorers followed the sculptor Lorenzetto and Cardinal Andrea della Valle in replacing parts of statues, and sculptors made or forged facsimiles of anything missing, down to such details as ear-lobes.[263] 'Antiquities thus restored certainly possess much more grace than those

[261] David Bomford, 'Theoretical and practical considerations in the restoration of damaged paintings', lecture at Art Historians' conference, London, 26 Mar. 1983; Walden, *Ravished Image*, p. 153.
[262] *Centuries of Meditation*, 'Fourth Century', No. 54, 1:196.
[263] Weil, 'Contribution toward a history of sculpture techniques: I', p. 83; Arnau, *Deception*, p. 82; Haskell and Penny, *Taste and the Antique*, pp. 26–7.

mutilated trunks, members without hands, or figures defective and incomplete', noted Vasari; through the eighteenth century restored statues invariably fetched higher prices than mutilated ones.[264] The Danish sculptor Thorvaldsen added new heads and limbs to antique torsos so skilfully that he himself later could not tell his own work from the original.[265] Wholeness was still *de rigueur* in the 1850s at the Louvre, where restorers filled in missing pieces, concealed broken edges, and repainted old Etruscan vases where glaze had flaked off.[266]

Decay and mutilation gained favour in the late eighteenth century owing to picturesque taste and the increasing cachet of authenticity. The emotional power of a mutilated marble was held to more than compensate for its lost formal perfection. Just as they enjoyed ruined buildings, connoisseurs of the 'aesthetic of rupture' took delight in armless and legless torsos and scorned 'modern reparations' that 'degraded' antique fragments.[264]

The Elgin Marbles illustrate the revolution in taste. When negotiating for the Acropolis sculptures, Lord Elgin took it for granted that they would be sent to Rome for restoration, but Canova refused the task; time and barbarism had sadly injured the statues, but they remained the unretouched 'work of the ablest artists the world had ever seen [and] "it would be sacrilege in him or any man, to presume to touch them with a chisel"'. Flaxman likewise declined, fearing 'it would be a source of dispute among Artists, whether the restored attitudes were correct, or otherwise', and sharing Canova's view that 'the execution must be far inferior to the original parts. [Few] would set a higher value on a work of Phidias . . . with a modern head and modern arms than they would in their present state.' After 1814 Elgin was persuaded to leave the statues unrestored.[265] Repair was no longer required for antiquities to be appreciated; fragmentation was becoming a positive virtue.

The taste for fragments spread from sculptural remains to other works of art, old and new. Literary creations like Goethe's *Faust* were advertised as 'Fragments'; poets' lives themselves often seemed curtailed and truncated, much as the present now seemed sundered from the past.[269] 'Many works of the ancients become fragments', wrote Friedrich Schlegel; 'many works of the moderns are so at their genesis.'[270] Viewing the

---

[264] Vasari, *Vite de' pui eccelenti pittori* . . ., Pt III, in his *Opere*, 4:579–80 (abridged in the English edition); St. Clair, *Lord Elgin and the Marbles*, p. 151.

[265] Arnau, *Deception*, p. 301. Prints customarily filled in missing or damaged parts of the objects they depicted (Ivins, *Prints and Visual Communication*, p. 142).

[266] Bousquet and Devambez, 'New methods in restoring ancient vases in the Louvre'.

[267] Mortier, *Poétique des ruines*, pp. 97–103; E. D. Clarke, *Greek Marbles Brought from the Shores of the Euxine, Archipelago, and Mediterranean*, . . . (1809), p. iii.

[268] Canova in *Memorandum on the Subject of the Earl of Elgin's Pursuits in Greece* (1815), Flaxman in William Richard Hamilton to Elgin, 23 June 1807, and 8 Aug. 1802, quoted in A. H. Smith, 'Lord Elgin and his collection', pp. 255, 297–8, 227; St. Clair, *Lord Elgin and the Marbles*, pp. 151–3.

[269] McFarland, *Romanticism and the Forms of Ruins*, pp. 22–5; Kaufmann, *Time Is an Artist*, pp. 61–3. 'When the fragments of Sappho's poetry became known in the nineteenth century, their fragmentary condition was thought to improve them, and French and English poets began to invent fragments of their own' (Peter Levi, 'Wondrous pleasures' (review of Hugh Lloyd-Jones and Peter Parsons, *Supplementum Hellenisticum*), *The Times*, 5 Jan. 1984, p. 9).

[270] Quoted in McFarland, *Romanticism and the Forms of Ruin*, p. 24.

Elgin Marbles recently deposited in the British Museum, Benjamin Haydon overheard this exchange:

'How broken down they are, a'ant they?'
'Yes, but how *like life*.'[271]

Mutilated and incomplete fragments evoked imaginative reconstruction that made them intensely alive; intact works of antiquity lacked the dynamism of relics worn by time and accident. 'It is not that we prefer time-worn bas-reliefs, or rusted statuettes as such', explains Malraux, 'but the sense of life they impart, from the evidence of their struggle with Time.'[272] Classical fragments even inspired new art whose truncation was deliberate. William Rimmer left his *Dying Centaur* armless in the manner of an unrestored Greek statue; Gaston Lachaise and Arthur Lee did likewise.[273] Painters fragmented their own canvases: Wilhelm Leibl cut up, signed, and sold off separate pieces of his paintings.[274]

Some modern artists disdain durability and purposely create things to decay and perish.[275] Picasso relished the erosions of time as proof that his paintings had a volition of their own, and enjoyed giving tiresome admirers graphic *dédicaces* in the knowledge that they would soon fade and ultimately vanish.[276] Auto-destructive art visibly disintegrates, fragments being ejected, carbonized, or pulverized, peeling or sliding off, liquifying, imploding, or shattering on impact. 'The aesthetic of revulsion' is often didactic rather than decorative: 'corrosion is regarded as an enemy of our civilization', expounds Gustav Metzger. 'Society is deteriorating. So is the sculpture ... Auto-destructive art sets up a kind of mirror image of reality.'[277] *Memento mori* was the message of Leopoldo Maler's self-sculpture in ice, H_2OMBRE, taken out of a freezer to melt over a day or so in a New York gallery. 'Tomorrow it is not there anymore', said Maler, sipping tea made from H_2OMBRE melt-water, 'maybe like me.'[278]

Much so-called earth art is intentionally evanescent. Will Ashford's giant 'Mona Lisa', outlined by the selective spreading of fertilizer near Alamo, California, in 1979, highlighted the role of natural change. The picture 'grew' with the grass, matured with rain and sun, and at last yellowed and wilted into invisibility.[279] Whether fugitive art gradually

[271] Haydon, *Diary*, 28 May 1817, 2:120.
[272] *Voices of Silence*, p. 635. See Meiss, 'Discussion', 'Aesthetic and historical aspects of the presentation of damaged pictures', p. 166; Fuller, *Art and Psychoanalysis*, pp. 128–9; Fisher, 'The future's past', p. 597.
[273] Naeve, *Classical Presence in American Art*, p. 27.
[274] Langer, *Wilhelm Leibl*, pp. 65–6, and plates of *Nelkenmädchen* (1880) fragments; Schug, 'Dismembered works of art – German painting', p. 141. The taste for fragmentation has largely waned; 'See the glories of the past as a whole, rather than as a collection of fragments', advertised Swan's Hellenic Cruises in 1983.
[275] Althöfer, 'Fragmente und Ruine'. The intent is often deliberately paradoxical. Man Ray's *Object to Be Destroyed* lasted thirty-five years until German art students smashed it; his facsimile reproduction is entitled *Indestructible Object* (Adams, *Lost Museum*, p. 228).
[276] John Richardson, 'Crimes against the Cubists', p. 33.
[277] *Auto-Destructive Art*, pp. 16, 18–19.
[278] 'Artist delights in work's limited life', *N.Y. Times*, 10 May 1982.
[279] Georg Gerster, 'Grow your own Mona Lisa', *Sunday Times Mag.*, 17 Feb. 1980, pp. 26–8.

decays or speedily disintegrates, ageing is crucial to its appreciation, as exemplified in the butterfat-and-chocolate work of Dieter Roth.[280]

Ideas evoked by decay

The attractions of decay are seldom solely aesthetic. Indeed, it was the sad, sinister, or violated look of ruins that appealed to Romantics.[281] Dismay as well as delight at the look of age give rise to manifold reflections. 'No one of the least sentiment or imagination can look upon an old or ruined edifice without feeling sublime emotions', declared a late eighteenth-century essayist; 'a thousand ideas croud upon his mind, and fill him with awful astonishment'.[282] We have heard the aesthetic overtones of these 'sublime emotions'; what were the sentiments evoked?

The 'thousand ideas' decaying and moribund artifacts elicit once bore on every realm of life. The veneer of age on paintings and *objets d'art* symbolized long-standing social continuities; the ruinous decay of sombre mansions embodied some dreadful hidden crime; the crumbling stones of ancient ruins conveyed a haunting sense of temporal remoteness.[283] Retrospective wonder was a common Renaissance response – admiration not for existing remains but for the greatness of the original structures they recalled. And in England monastic ruins 'sett the thoughts a-worke to make out their magnificence, as they were when in perfection'.[284] Contrasts of present decay with former grandeur inspired poets and painters well into the nineteenth century.

Decay also served as an exemplary warning against sin and depravity; Archbishop Hildebert in 1116 urged that ancient Rome's remains be left unrestored as witnesses of heavenly chastisement.[285] Ruins made manifest the melancholy lesson that all men's works moulder to insignificance. 'I could hardly keep back my tears faced with such mutations of time', wrote a sixteenth-century German visitor to the Colosseum.[286] The scars left by monastic mutilation were likewise cautionary. The 'extreme povertie, nakedness, and decay' of sixteenth-century Canterbury struck William Lambarde as divine retribution, and the remains of Romanism 'record [ed] for posterity the exemplary abuses of the religious past'.[287] Ruins attested human retribution too; those who wreaked havoc against enemies 'found emotional joy in the contemplation of the ruinous results.'[288]

---

[280] *Paint & Painting* (London: Tate Gallery, 1982), pp. 50–1; Althöfer, 'Fragmente und Ruine', pp. 81, 162. Roth directed that his *Self Portrait at a Table* (1973–6), bought by the Tate Gallery, should be allowed to deteriorate without intervention (interview, 25 Oct. 1977). It was still in good condition, despite the changed appearance of the chocolate, in October 1984 (Andrew Durham, Tate Gallery Conservation Dept.).

[281] Hugo, 'Temps et les cités' (1817); Mortier, *Poétique des ruines*, pp. 218–22.

[282] 'On the pleasure arising from the sight of ruins or ancient structures', *European Magazine* (1795), quoted in Monk, *Sublime*, p. 141.

[283] Slive and Hoetink, *Jacob van Ruisdael*, pp. 66–8; Kander, *Deutsche Ruinenpoesie*; Kaufmann, *Time Is an Artist*, p. 74.

[284] John Aubrey, *Wiltshire . . . A.D. 1659–70*, quoted in Aston, 'Dissolution and the sense of the past', pp. 251–2; Michael Hunter, *John Aubrey and the Realm of Learning*, pp. 178–9, 234–5, from the Bodleian Mss.

[285] *De Roma*, cited in Macaulay, *Pleasure of Ruins*, p. 12. See Daemmrich, 'Ruins motif', p. 451.

[286] A. von Buchell, *Iter Italicum* (1587), quoted in Mortier, *Poétique des ruines*, p. 43.

[287] *Perambulation of Kent* (1576), quoted in Aston, 'Dissolution and the sense of the past', p. 247; Aston, ibid.

[288] Macaulay, *Pleasure of Ruins*, p. 1.

32 Skeletal death menaces its victim: Louis-François Roubiliac, Tomb of Lady Elizabeth Nightingale, Westminster Abbey, 1761

As emblems of tyranny overcome, ruins bespoke fearsome rulers gone to just deserts, once-sumptuous mansions decaying into humble abodes. 'The ruin of the palace enables it to acquire the virtues of the cottage', wrote Diderot.[289] Volney's *Ruins* was much cited by Americans to whom the Old World's mouldering castles stood for oppression.[290] The English too came to see ruins as evidence of tyranny's downfall, 'a symbol of time's destruction of ancient autocratic power', in Stuart Piggott's phrase, 'standing for freedom from the corrupt oppression by monks or barons'.[291] Uvedale Price admired crumbling castles and abbeys not just as picturesque objects but as witnesses that Britain's former 'abodes of tyranny and superstition are in ruin'.[292]

Decay heightened temporal awareness generally, inducing nostalgic and other reflections on time's changes. The imagination is 'more taken with prospects of the ruinous kind', wrote Gilpin of England's ragged monastic remnants, 'than with most smiling Views of Plenty and Prosperity in their greatest perfection'.[293] Admiring the 'ruins of a noble tree', Gilpin felt that 'these splendid remnants of decaying grandeur speak to the imagination in a stile of eloquence, which the stripling cannot reach: they record the history of some storm, some blast of lightening, or other great event, which transfers its grand ideas to the landscape'.[294] Wear and tear suggested not only the past but the passage of time, as with the Yale University steps noted above, and the patina accruing from passers-by who stroked the San Francisco Hyatt's bas-relief fountain to impart a sense of history to that hotel.[295]

The dominant association with decay is our own transience. Marks of dissolution figure as *memento mori*, compelling reminders of death's imminence. 'As I am, so you shall be' is one of a thousand epitaphs warning the reader that he too must die. The ruin of England's monasteries 'puts us in minde of our mortalitie', wrote John Weever, 'and consequently brings us to unfained repentence'. Many like Weever sought out 'mournfull remains' to reflect on their own impending demise.[296]

Images of mortal decay had obsessed medieval Europeans beset by plague and famine; in the wake of the Black Death, depictions of skeletal death menacing his victims served as common admonitions. Sculptured figures of the dead in splendid regalia with *transi* of their decomposing corpses beneath them set everlasting life against earthly decay.[297] Such images, like the self-humiliation of flagellants, evinced the deceased's contrition, lest eternal damnation punish him for worldly pride and greed. In an epoch of intense anxiety over extremes of debauchery and piety, *transi* denigrated the flesh, contrasting hideous death with youthful beauty; 'after man, worms, and after worms, stench and horror', as inscribed on the *transi* of Cardinal Jean de Lagrange (d. 1402).

Transi representations might be shrouded, emaciated, shrivelled, or putrescent. In a fresco at Campo Santo, Pisa (*c.* 1350), three hunters find their own corpses in various

---

[289] Diderot, *Salons* (1767), 3:246; see Weinshenker, 'Diderot's use of the ruin-image', pp. 324–5.
[290] Davidson, 'Whither the course of Empire?' p. 60.
[291] *Ruins in a Landscape*, p. 120.   [292] *Essay on Architecture and Buildings* (1794), p. 264.
[293] *Dialogue upon the Gardens . . . at Stow in Buckinghamshire* (1748), p. 5.
[294] *Remarks on Forest Scenery*, 1:9.
[295] Fleming, 'Lovable objects challenge the Modern Movement', p. 92.
[296] *Ancient Funerall Monuments . . .* (1631), quoted in Aston, 'Dissolution and the sense of the past', p. 247.
[297] Kathleen Cohen, *Metamorphosis of a Death Symbol: the Transi Tomb*, pp. 4–7, 21–8, 47–8.

33 Decay and resurrection: Girolamo
della Robbia, rejected *transi* of Catherine
de Medici, 1566

stages of decomposition. A memorial in a chapel in the canton of Vaud shows François de
la Sarra (d. 1363) as he might have looked after several years of putrefaction, with worms
slithering in and out of the cadaver and toads covering the eyes and genitals. A mouse, a
serpent, a worm, a frog, and a beetle devour the likeness of John Wakeman's *transi*
(*c.* 1529) at Tewkesbury Abbey. Each creature conveyed a specific message: snakes
emerged from spinal marrow, frogs and toads symbolized sins, worms signified repen-
tance or the pangs of conscience. But by the sixteenth century, Kathleen Cohen maintains,
most *transi* no longer expressed a fearful abasement but a confident faith. It was well
known that, aside from saints, bodies must decay before they could become immortal;
corruption was a necessary prelude to resurrection. Thus the cadaverous likeness of René
de Châlons (killed in battle in 1544) after three years' envisaged decay, with a heaven-
pointing hand holding a heart, displays a decomposing body not as passive food for worms
but as an active affirmation of eternal life.[298]

[298] Ibid., pp. 103, 114–19, 171, 177–81; Panofsky, *Tomb Sculpture*, pp. 56–64, 80. Boase, *Death in the Middle
Ages*, p. 102; Baltrušaitis, *Moyen Age fantastique*, pp. 238–40. But Ralph Giese (review of Cohen, *Speculum*,
52 (1977), 637–41) doubts that *transi* ever came to symbolize resurrection.

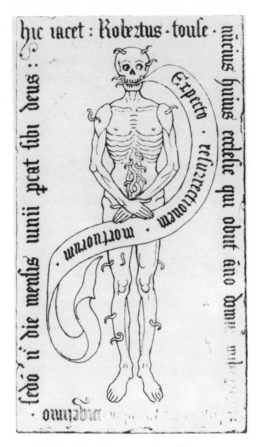

34 Death and resurrection: 'Expecto
resurrectionem mortuorum': inscription
on slab tomb of Robert Touse, d. 1422

Delight in the look of mortality revived in the nineteenth century, as in the maudlin
Methodist hymn:

> Ah lovely appearance of death
> What sight upon earth is so fair!
> Not all the gay pageants that breathe
> Can with a dead body compare.[299]

The evident frailty of ruins made manifest their kinship with mortal beings. Contemplating some architectural fragments, a character in an Ann Radcliffe romance finds

the comparison between himself and the gradation of decay, which these columns exhibited, . . . but too obvious and affecting. 'A few years,' said he, 'and I shall become like the mortals on whose relics I now gaze, and like them too, I may be the subject of meditation to a succeeding generation, which shall totter but a little while over the object they contemplate, ere they also sink into dust.'[300]

---

[299] Jill Paton Walsh, *Unleaving* (New York: Avon, 1977), p. 21. On 'beautiful death' in the nineteenth century, see Ariès, *Hour of Our Death*, pp. 610–13.
[300] *Romance of the Forest* (1791), pp. 21–2.

Other writers emphasized transience ('all passes but God'), the futility of vanity ('A little rule, a little sway, / A sunbeam in a winter's day, / Is all the proud and mighty have / Between the cradle and the grave')[301] or the brevity of men's lives compared with their works ('what is my existence in comparison with this crumbling stone?'). On finishing his *Decline and Fall of the Roman Empire*, Gibbon found solace in knowing that man's 'monuments, like himself, are perishable and frail; and in the boundless annals of time his life and labours must equally be measured as a fleeting moment'.[302] Ruins taught Diderot that 'everything is annihilated, everything perishes, only time endures'.[303]

For painters too ruins and decay suggested the transience of man's life and works. Guardi's moist landscapes and mouldering buildings echo the decline of eighteenth-century Venice;[304] Piranesi and Hubert Robert depicted time and nature devouring the relics of antiquity. Rousseau's classicizing tomb, designed to be glimpsed 'as if it were a fragment of antique marble just visible within a landscape by Hubert Robert', stirred ruminations on splendours long past.[305] Gazing on Italy's ruins, Thomas Cole conceived his final *Course of Empire* painting as a scene of desolation where 'ruined temples, broken bridges, fountains, sarcophagi [toll] the funeral knell of departed greatness'.[306] Such associations varied with age, with agency of decay, and with style: Gothic ruins were felt to exhibit 'the triumph of time over strength', a melancholy but not unpleasant thought, 'a Grecian ruin ... the triumph of barbarism over taste, a gloomy and discouraging thought'.[307]

Decay shed some of its aura of gloom in the nineteenth century. English water-colourists depicted ruined abbeys and castles in prosaic, even cheerful terms. Home-made memorial embroideries festooned American parlour and bedroom walls with maidens contemplating classical tombstones in landscapes of willows (for sadness) and withering oaks (transitory life), often embellished with ships (departure) on the sea (tears); but this iconography reflected no sad or recent bereavements; the pictures instead commemorated remote and long-dead relatives, national heroes like George Washington, or figures from Romantic literature, notably Goethe's Werther.[308] Signs of transience in Constable's time-eroded beings and artifacts – the sense of imminent destruction in *Hadleigh Castle*, the ancient decay of *Stonehenge*, the gnarled stump set off by tender leaves in *Leaping Horse* – are not *memento mori* but celebrations of life in all its stages.[309]

The taste for *memento mori* also persisted, however. Ivy creeping over a broken window tracery, the sky glimpsed through a fallen banqueting hall roof 'moved to melancholy pleasure minds which dwelt gladly on the impermanence of human life and effort', in Michael Sadleir's words; a childhood spent amid crumbling overgrown buildings left James Stevens Curl 'intensely aware of the nearness of death and of the dead'.[310]

Recognition that individual decay was biologically essential, already evident in the

[301] Dyer, *Grongar Hill* (1761), lines 90–3, p. 91.   [302] 1787, 3:863.   [303] *Salons* (1767), 3:228.
[304] Gaunt, *Bandits in a Landscape*, p. 65.
[305] Rosenblum, *Transformations*, p. 177. Hubert Robert had helped design Rousseau's tomb.
[306] Cole to Luman Reed, 18 Sept. 1833, in Noble, *Life and Works of Thomas Cole*, p. 310. See Craven, 'Thomas Cole and Italy'.
[307] Kames, *Elements of Criticism* (1762), 3:313. See Charlton, *New Images of the Natural in France*, pp. 98–9.
[308] Muto, 'A feminist art – the American memorial picture'.
[309] Kroeber, *Romantic Landscape Vision: Constable and Wordsworth*, pp. 55, 113–15.
[310] Sadleir, '"All horrid?": Jane Austen and the Gothic romance', p. 176; Curl, *Celebration of Death*, p. xxiv.

Enlightenment, became a nineteenth-century commonplace. Baudelaire celebrated ageing and death as concomitants of growth, putrefaction as a consequence of generation; Ruskin and Morris insisted that buildings be left to age into ancient beauty and then allowed to perish. Precious marks of decrepitude, far more than historical associations or artistic worth, explained and validated the rising cult of historical monuments, stated Alois Riegl in 1903; their evanescence was the best testimony to the whole cycle of organic existence. Viewing every human creation as a natural organism, Riegl applauded their transience. In portending the inevitable end, the ageing of artifacts reconciled the observer to his own impending fate; hence no artifice should be used to lengthen their life or dim awareness of inescapable decline.[311]

Decay implies not just evanescence but the accretion of experience. As wear and tear reveals furniture's long life and faded fabric makes historic buildings feel lived in, so Russell Baker takes 'comfort from an authentic life-hewn face, looking like a man who had made the usual excursions into life and been affected by them much the way most of us are'.[312] Lineaments of age link past and present, reassuring us life goes on even if death is around the corner.

A full sense of being requires awareness of ageing and decay, for all that lives is partly nascent, partly penultimate. 'A life spent without any contemplation of death', in Curl's words, is 'a denial of life, since death is the logical and inevitable end for us all.' One can have too many such reminders, to be sure; the young may find ruins beautiful, remarked the elderly Chateaubriand, but the old have quite enough of their own debris.[313]

Imminent dissolution renders many things more precious, and reminders of life's transience can enhance what remains of it; miniature jointed skeletons passed around at Roman banquets purportedly heightened diners' enjoyment.[314] Anticipation of Venice's approaching demise intensified that city's beauty for Ruskin.[315] 'Because we know their transience', concludes Gregory Sohns, 'the delight and beauty of the world are invested with a special poignancy, and we value them the more.'[316] The ephemeral can be deeply affecting: 'old toys, made for brief use, seemingly so fragile, associated with a passing and vulnerable phase of life, are much more emotive symbols than are permanent, serious memorials', writes Kevin Lynch.[317] We love things partly because we know they will perish:

> All beauteous things for which we live
> By laws of time and space decay.
> But oh, the very reason why
> I clasp them, is because they die.[318]

In portending its end, the marks of age add substance to life. Some argue that our own great creations ought also to age and perish rather than to endure an arid immortality. 'Trying to preserve a century by keeping its relics up to date is like keeping a dying man

[311] Charlton, *New Images of the Natural in France*, pp. 101–3; Riegl, *Moderne Denkmalkultus*; Rasch, 'Literary decadence: artistic representation of decay', pp. 205–15.

[312] 'Ageless idols', *IHT*, 21 Apr. 1978, p. 16.

[313] Curl, *Celebration of Death*, p. 1; Chateaubriand to John Fraser Frisell, 20 Dec. 1828, quoted in Mortier, *Poétique des ruines*, p. 191.

[314] Curl, *Celebration of Death*, p. 2.   [315] Clegg, *Ruskin and Venice*, p. 53.

[316] Gregory Sohns, letter, *N.Y. Times*, 28 July 1978.

[317] *What Time Is This Place?* p. 44.   [318] Cory, 'Mimnermus in church', *Ionica*, p. 6.

35 Romanesque monumentality for America: H. H. Richardson, Cheney Building, Hartford, Connecticut, 1875 (Wayne Andrews)

alive by stimulants', protests F. Scott Fitzgerald's Gloria at Robert E. Lee's too-restored home. 'There's no beauty without poignancy and there's no poignancy without the feeling that it's going, men, names, books, houses – bound for dust – mortal.'[319] The scars of time are the signs of life. It is 'all the infinite scratches, bumps, scars, and declivities, some the tricks of art, some the wear of fortune, which give such noble vitality' to the horses of San Marco, Jan Morris feels; putting them away in a museum to forestall corrosion denies them 'the slow dignified decline into age and dust which is the privilege of all living things'.[320]

[319] *The Beautiful and the Damned*, p. 140.
[320] 'Horses of San Marco', *Sunday Telegraph*, 2 Sept. 1979, pp. 76–83; quotation on p. 83.

The effects of time on man's and nature's works can presage immortality as well as death. Byron saw ivy as 'The garland of eternity, where wave / The green leaves over all by time o'erthrown.'[321] H. H. Richardson's heavy Romanesque buildings gave late nineteenth-century American cities a needed solidity, stability, security; they appeared 'to rise from roots sunk deep in the subsoil', their ponderous forms seeming 'to stand for and from eternity'.[322]

Beyond an individual perspective, ageing and death intimate collective immortality. 'We are but the most recent lessees of similar bodies preceding ours and of similar ones to come after', writes Stephen Spender, 'the momentary organs of sensibility of what is redeemable of the whole of human existence.'[323] Briefer life spans make ours seem well-nigh infinite. 'Isn't it good to see the autumn come?' asks an insect in a fable. 'My reaction is different', replies another; 'my species is annual.' In human terms all 'these innumerable little lives quickly pass while ours endure . . . The autumnal spectacle of the cessation of life on the earth, nature's yearly tragedy', in W. H. Hudson's phrase, 'multiplies our years and makes them so many that it is a practical immortality.'[324]

Decay also signifies companionability with our surroundings. 'The joy of familiarity requires intimacy, wear, usage, and the accumulation of memories', as Hough writes; 'the companionship of a house is nourished by mellowing and shabbiness.'[325] Marks of age consecrate the longevity of our linkages with familiar things.

Fondness for the look of decay followed appreciation of its manifold evocations. Bereft of these, decay's attractions are meagre and the picturesque lacks appeal. The look of age still has devotees, but those who prefer a new or remade past consider attachment to patina and 'pleasing decay' morbid. Decay arouses repugnance not simply because ageing makes things less useful, but because it suggests our own old age. This aversion reflects fears of decrepitude and mortality, from which we shrink not as reminders of the past but as harbingers of the future. But ageing and death are natural, indeed inevitable, processes. All things around us, both natural and man-made, are more or less worn by time and subject to incessant decay. To find some virtue in the marks of age, not in unblemished youth alone, enhances all the rest of life.

What kind of relics make the past most vivid? Those that are bright and clean, some insist, full of the sparkle of youth they had when new. For others the marks of use and time are crucial to living continuity. A past freshly made or revived and a past convincingly scored by time and use answer different needs and inspire different consequences.

The contrast between neo-classical and Romantic evocations of antiquity in the late eighteenth century exemplifies this distinction. The relics of classical antiquity, Rosenblum points out, on the one hand stimulated attempts to reconstruct remote glories in the service of modern progress and on the other a retrospective nostalgia for a lost, irretrievable past. The virtue of antiquity for neo-classicists was its suggestive vitality and

---

[321] *Childe Harold's Pilgrimage*, Canto IV. 99, lines 888–9, p. 240.
[322] Gowans, *Images of American Living*, p. 352. See Hitchcock, *Architecture of H. H. Richardson*, pp. 164–6, for the Cheney building.
[323] *Love-Hate Relations*, p. 192.   [324] *Nature in Downland*, p. 180. See *idem, Afoot in England*, p. 76.
[325] *Soundings at Sea Level*, p. 98.

innocence, giving rise to virile new architectural and social forms; the virtue of antiquity for Romantics lay in the hypnotic power of its remains, evoking reflections on transience and decline.

Eschewing decay and ruin led activists to appropriate antiquity for new programmes; emphasizing decay and ruin led to melancholy meditations on achievements that could be neither retrieved nor emulated. Those who enjoyed a bright new past assumed they could reanimate it in their own epoch; those who enjoyed a decayed and ruined past assumed it was unrepeatable. Whereas mouldering relics suggested a past beyond reach, new creations inspired by antiquity brought ancient ideals and forms once more to life.[326]

These viewpoints shape conflicting but often coexisting perspectives on the look of age. The past can be seen as a prototype of our own epoch or alternatively as an era made distinctive by the erosions and accretions of its own remains. The choice of perspective affects not only what we decide to recall and preserve, but how we distinguish past from present. That distinction is the subject of the next chapter.

[326] Rosenblum, *Transformations*, Ch. 3, 'Aspects of neoclassic architecture'.

Part II

KNOWING THE PAST

5

HOW WE KNOW THE PAST

The poetry of history lies in the quasi-miraculous fact that once, on this earth, on this familiar spot of ground, walked other men and women, as actual as we are today, thinking their own thoughts, swayed by their own passions, but now all gone, one generation vanishing after another, gone as utterly as we ourselves shall shortly be gone like ghosts at cock-crow.

G. M. Trevelyan, 'Autobiography of an historian'[1]

In talking about the past we lie with every breath we draw.

William Maxwell, *So Long, See You Tomorrow*[2]

Awareness of the past is in myriad ways essential to our well-being. Previous chapters discussed the range of these needs; this one surveys the routes by which we become apprised of the past as a precondition of meeting those needs.

How do we come to know about the past? How do we acquire this essential background? The simple answer is that we remember things, read or hear stories and chronicles, and live among relics from previous times. The past surrounds and saturates us; every scene, every statement, every action retains residual content from earlier times. All present awareness is grounded on past perceptions and acts; we recognize a person, a tree, a breakfast, an errand because we have seen or done it before. And pastness is also integral to our own being: 'We are at any moment the sum of all our moments, the product of all our experiences', as A. A. Mendilow put it.[3] Centuries of tradition underlie every instant of perception and creation, pervading not only artifacts and culture but the very cells of our bodies.[4]

Of most such residues we remain unconscious, assigning them simply to the ongoing present; to *recognize* that they stem from the past demands conscious effort. 'I must be modern: I live now', muses a Robertson Davies character. 'But like everybody else . . . I live in a muddle of eras, and some of my ideas belong to today, and some to an ancient past, and some to periods of time that seem more relevant to my parents than to me.'[5] The

---

[1] 1949, p. 13. [2] 1980, p. 29. [3] *Time and the Novel*, p. 223; see also p. 230.
[4] Bergson, *Creative Evolution*, p. 20; Shils, *Tradition*, pp. 34–8, 169–70.
[5] *Rebel Angels*, p. 124.

185

temporal *mélange* generally goes unnoticed, taken for granted as the normal nature of the present. The facets of the past that live on in our gestures and words, rules and artifacts, appear to us as 'past' only when we know them as such.[6]

Recognition of the past as a temporal realm distinct from the present, some scholars suggest, is a distinguishing feature of Western thought.[7] But some awareness of the past is common to all humans save infants, the senile, and the brain-damaged. At the very least, we remember what we repeat, recall that there was a yesterday, and sense the organic processes of growth and ageing, flowering and decay, discussed in Chapter 4. Fuller awareness of the past involves familiarity with processes conceived and completed, recollections of things said and done, stories about people and events – the common stuff of memory and history.

'The past is never dead', in Gilbert Highet's phrase; 'it exists continuously in the minds of thinkers and men of imagination.'[8] Indeed, it exists in the minds of all of us. We are continually made aware not only of our own previous thoughts and actions, but of other people's, whether directly witnessed or learned about at second hand. Even the imprints of exceedingly remote experience can come into consciousness. Herbert Butterfield expresses how this takes place:

> The mind of every one of us holds a jumble of pictures and stories . . . that constitute what we have built up for ourselves of the Past, . . . called into play by a glimpse of some old ruin . . . or by a hint of the romantic . . . A cathedral bell, or the mention of Agincourt, or the very spelling of the word 'ycleped' may be enough to set the mind wandering into its own picture galleries of history.[9]

The past Butterfield refers to is both historical and memorial: its scenes and experiences antedate our own lives, but what we have read and heard and reiterated makes them part of our memories too.

We are in fact aware of the past as a realm both coexistent with and distinct from the present. What joins them is our largely unconscious apprehension of organic life; what sets them apart is our self-consciousness – thinking about our memories, about history, about the age of things around us. Deliberation often distinguishes the here and now – tasks being done, ideas being formed, steps being taken – from bygone things, thoughts, and events. But conflation and segregation are in continual tension; the past has to be felt both part of and separate from the present. 'We do call the past, *as such*, into being by recollecting and by thinking historically', wrote R. G. Collingwood; 'but we do this by disentangling it out of the present in which it actually exists.'[10]

What the conscious past contains, why it is dwelt upon, how much and in what ways it is felt to be a realm apart – these matters vary from culture to culture, from person to person, and from day to day. Some are so enlivened (or oppressed) by remembered or imagined pasts that all present experience resonates with memories of them; to others the past has little to say, the present and future pre-empting their conscious attention. But whether meagre or copious, dead or alive, a realm apart or one meshed with the present, the past comes to conscious apprehension along the same routes.

---

[6] Heller, *Theory of History*, p. 201.   [7] Kelley, *Foundations of Modern Historical Scholarship*, p. 3.
[8] *Classical Tradition*, p. 447.
[9] *Historical Novel*, p. 1.   [10] 'Some perplexities about time', p. 150.

Three sources of past knowledge are considered in this chapter: memory, history, and relics. Memory and history are processes of insight; each involves components of the other, and their boundaries are shadowy. Yet memory and history are normally and justifiably distinguished: memory is inescapable and prima-facie indubitable; history is contingent and empirically testable. Unlike memory and history, relics are not processes but residues of processes. Man-made relics are called artifacts; those that are natural lack a distinctive name. Both attest to the past biologically, through ageing and weathering, and historically, through anachronistic forms and structures.

Each route to the past – memory, history, relics – is a domain claimed by specialist disciplines, explicitly by psychology, history, and archaeology. But knowing the past embraces wider perspectives than these disciplines normally treat. Hence my exploration will depart from and sometimes transcend these realms of professional expertise.

Before considering how memory, history, and relics bear on the past, I shall try to show how it is generally experienced and believed. The fact that the past is no longer present clouds knowledge of it with uncertainty. Assigned varying durations, insecurely linked with the present, its very existence unproven, the past often seems disconcertingly tenuous. Because these doubts colour most of what we think we know of the past, they deserve extended examination.

THE PAST AS EXPERIENCED AND BELIEVED

All past events are more remote from our senses than the stars of the remotest galaxies, whose own light at least still reaches the telescopes.

George Kubler, *The Shape of Time*[11]

Already a fictitious past occupies in our memories the place of another, a past of which we know nothing with certainty – not even that it is false.

Jorge Luis Borges, 'Tlön, Uqbar, Orbis Tertius'[12]

Memory, history, and relics continually furbish our awareness of the past. But how can we be sure that they reflect what has happened? The past is gone; its parity with things now seen, recalled, or read about can never be proved. No statement about the past can be confirmed by examining the supposed facts. Because knowing occurs only in the epistemological present, as C. I. Lewis puts it, '*no* theoretically sufficient verification of any past fact can ever be hoped for'.[13] We cannot verify it through observation or experiment. Unlike geographically remote places we could visit if we made the effort, the past is beyond reach. Present facts known only indirectly could in principle be verified; past facts by their very nature cannot.

To name or to think of things past seems to imply their existence, but they do not exist; we have only present evidence for past circumstances. 'The past simply as past is wholly unknowable', concludes Collingwood; 'it is the past as residually preserved in the present that is alone knowable.' A past that continued to exist would be a 'limbo, where events which have finished happening still go on'; it would imply 'a world where Galileo's weight

[11] 1962, p. 79.   [12] 1961, pp. 42–3.   [13] *Analysis of Knowledge and Valuation*, p. 200.

is still falling, where the smoke of Nero's Rome still fills the intelligible air, and where interglacial man is still laboriously learning to chip flints'.[14]

From the past's absence two doubts ensue: that anything like the generally accepted past ever did exist; and if it did, that what it was can ever be truly known. I shall treat these doubts in turn.

Did events we believe took place in fact happen? Perhaps a fictitious past occupies our memories, as Borges speculates. For all we can tell, we may be like Ron Hubbard's simulacra who were convinced they lived in a real world and 'thought they remembered long pasts and ancestors'.[15] Historical records and memories may delude us into supposing that there was a past at all. The planet could have been created five minutes ago, Bertrand Russell surmised, with a population that 'remembered' an illusory past.[16] A writer embellishing Russell's scenario imagines a newspaper found in the fossilized jaws of a 70-million-year-old tyrannosaurus in Cretaceous strata, proving that 'the universe was in fact created at about five past nine this morning and whoever did it slipped up by leaving this copy of *The Times* lying around'.[17]

These hypothetical new-made worlds differ only in their recency and brevity from received biblical doctrine. Previously assigned diverse dates, the Creation was at length calculated to general satisfaction at 4004 B.C. by Archbishop James Ussher. The six millennia allotted to the past then sufficed all known events; without modern geochronology, seventeenth-century scholars felt no deficiency of time behind them. Even nineteenth-century Scripturalists could fit the then known *human* past into six millennia. Rock and fossil evidence of earlier existence was discounted as spurious and impious: seemingly antediluvian erosions and successions were part of the single act of Creation. But geology and palaeontology made the orthodox view increasingly hard to sustain; everywhere were marks of a terrestrial past far more ancient than biblical Creation seemed to allow.[18]

P. H. Gosse's *Omphalos*, which sought to explain why the newly created earth had to contain marks of apparent pre-existence, is nowadays dismissed as risible. But it raised fundamental questions that prefigure Russell's scepticism. Gosse knew the historical past existed, for men who wrote about events they themselves saw left direct witness of it.[19] But prehistory left no such accounts; no one was there to see and record it. And evidence of such a past from fossils, geological strata, and living tissues lacked the reliability of eyewitnesses.

No one . . . declares he actually saw the living *Pterodactyle* flying about, or heard the winds sighing in the tops of the Lepidodondra. You will say, 'It is the same thing; we have seen the skeleton of the one, and the crushed trunk of the other, and therefore we are as sure of their past existence as if we had been there at the time.' No, it is . . . not quite the same thing [for] only by a process of reasoning [do] you infer they lived at all.[20]

[14] Collingwood, 'Limits of historical knowledge', pp. 220–1.   [15] *Typewriter in the Sky*, p. 60.

[16] *Analysis of Mind*, p. 159. See Fain, *Between Philosophy and History*, pp. 114–26.

[17] Karl Sabbagh, *New Statesman* competition, 11 Aug. 1967, p. 183.

[18] G. L. Davies, *Earth in Decay*, pp. 13–16; R. J. Butler, 'Other dates', pp. 23–4; Rupke, *Great Chain of History*, pp. 51–7.

[19] *Omphalos* (1857), p. 337.   [20] Ibid., p. 104.

Were such inference extended, 'the sequence of cause and effect . . . would inevitably lead us to the eternity of all existing organic life'. And that would be nonsense. Everything including fossils, 'ancient' rock strata, and the apparent progenitors of all living things must at *some* point have been created.[21]

Every living thing evinced pre-existence – the rings of trees, man's navel – which at the moment of Creation were 'false'. 'The "cuttle-bone" is an autographic record, indubitably genuine, of the Cuttlefish's history. Yes, it is certainly genuine; it is as certainly autographic: but it is *not true*. That Cuttle has been this day created.'[22] A deity who gave newly made creatures a factitious appearance of prior existence might be considered perverse – 'God hid the fossils in the rocks in order to tempt geologists into infidelity' was the memorable gibe[23] – but it was not so, Gosse countered: 'Were the concentric timber-rings of a created tree formed merely to deceive? . . . Was the navel of the created Man intended to deceive him into the persuasion that he had had a parent?' No, they were so made because the Creator decided to call the globe into existence 'exactly as it would have appeared at that moment of its history, if all the preceding eras of its history had been real'.[24]

Notwithstanding Gosse's faith in eyewitness accounts, similar scepticism seems to imperil the reality even of the historical past. Had God chosen to create the world not in 4004 B.C. but in A.D. 1857 (Gosse's present), it would none the less appear just as it now was, full of 'evidence' of a past:

houses half-built; castles fallen into ruins; pictures on artists' easels just sketched in; wardrobes filled with half-worn garments; ships sailing over the sea; marks of birds' footsteps on the mud; skeletons whitening the desert sands; human bodies in every stage of decay in the burial grounds. These and millions of other traces of the past would be found, *because they are found in the world now*; . . . not to puzzle the philosopher, but because they are inseparable from the condition of the world at the selected moment of irruption into its history; . . . they make it what it is.[25]

In short, the historical past may be as illusory as the prehistoric.

To doubt the historical past, however, raises additional problems. A world created during historical times would falsify not just some but *all* accounts of previous history, with dire implications for human credibility. To disavow every account of the past, to doubt the veracity or the sanity of all those who massively documented what had not happened would call into doubt our own sanity and veracity as well. And Russell's extension of Gosse's hypothesis to a Creation just five minutes old posits the falsity not merely of all physical and historical evidence of the past, but also of our own memories; if the past began five minutes ago, all our recollections would be delusory.[26]

Would it make any difference had there been no past? Would we not behave just as we

---

[21] Ibid., p. 338.　　[22] Ibid., p. 239.　　[23] Edmund Gosse, *Father and Son* (1907), p. 67.
[24] *Omphalos*, pp. 347–8, 351. Half a century before, Chateaubriand had explained the apparent antiquity of the fresh Creation in aesthetic terms: 'God might have created, and doubtless did create, the world with all the marks of antiquity and completeness which it now exhibits. If the world had not been at the same time young and old, the grand, the serious, the moral would have been banished from the face of nature; for these are ideas essentially inherent in antique objects . . . Without this original antiquity, there would have been neither beauty nor magnificence in the works of the Almighty' (*Genius of Christianity* (1802), Bk IV, Ch. 5, pp. 135–7). See also Borges, 'The Creation and P. H. Gosse', pp. 22–5.
[25] *Omphalos*, pp. 352–3.
[26] Murphey, *Our Knowledge of the Historical Past*, pp. 9–10; Danto, *Analytical Philosophy of History*, pp. 66–84.

do anyway? 'What matters . . . is not what my past actually was, or even whether I had one', argues H. H. Price; 'it is only the *memories* I have now which matter, be they false or true.'[27] But in fact nothing would be the same. Tradition would be farcical. Few would heed the consequences of their actions. No one would apprehend wrong-doers if there was no past when their crimes could have taken place. Effects could not be traced back to causes, nor behaviour to motives. Nothing could be proved, for 'to doubt our sense of past experience as founded in actuality, would be to lose any criterion by which either the doubt itself or what is doubted could be corroborated; and to erase altogether the distinction between empirical fact and fantasy', C. I. Lewis reasons.[28] Scepticism carried to this extreme puts all reality in doubt and ends in utter solipsism.

Few are so dubious. None the less, the past's empirical absence leaves a grain of doubt which philosophical analysis cannot wholly allay. 'We have had to take on faith the unproven events of unproven years', writes Ray Bradbury. 'The reality, even of the immediate past, is irretrievable . . . For all the reality of ruins and scrolls and tablets, we fear that much of what we read has been made up.'[29]

Why one might seek to expunge the actual past and replace it with a false past is explored in two cautionary tales that convey the ensuing sense of helpless unreality. Big Brother in Orwell's *Nineteen Eighty-Four* controls the present by controlling the past. Since 'past events . . . have no objective existence, but survive only in written records and in human memories', it follows that 'the past is whatever the records and the memories agree upon', and therefore 'whatever the Party chooses to make it . . . Recreated in whatever shape is needed at the moment, . . . this new version *is* the past, and no different past can ever have existed.' To secure the Party's infallibility, 'the past, starting from yesterday, has been actually abolished . . . Nothing exists except an endless present.'[30] The inquisitor uses Gosse's argument to undermine Winston's faith in an ancient past:

'The earth is as old as we are, no older. How could it be older? Nothing exists except through human consciousness.'
'But the rocks are full of the bones of extinct animals – mammoths and mastodons and enormous reptiles which lived here long before man was ever heard of.'
'Have you ever seen those bones, Winston? Of course not. Nineteenth-century biologists invented them. Before man there was nothing.'[31]

Scepticism engendered by efforts to replicate a lost past is the theme of David Ely's 'Time Out'. To ensure that no one will know about the nuclear accident that wiped out Britain some decades earlier, an American–Soviet task force is re-creating 'every stick and stone, . . . every blade of grass, every hedge and bush, every mansion, palace, hut and hovel. *Everything*', along with archival and reliquary evidence of Britain's entire past – even of the events that would have occurred had there been no holocaust.[32] Dragooned into creating this new past, an American historian, Gull, complains that people are bound to find out:

---

[27] *Thinking and Experience*, p. 84. See also Butler, 'Other dates', pp. 16–19.
[28] *Analysis of Knowledge and Valuation*, p. 358. See Danto, *Analytical Philosophy of History*, pp. 68–70, 77–8; Murphey, *Our Knowledge of the Historical Past*, pp. 10–12; Earle, 'Memory', p. 10.
[29] 'Machine-tooled happyland – Disneyland', p. 102.   [30] Pp. 170, 126–7.   [31] Ibid., p. 213.
[32] Pp. 95, 90.

'What are they supposed to think when they see the construction squads putting up Blenheim Palace . . . ?'

'They'll think like true-born Englishmen, Gull, because they'll have been reared that way. If the history books and the teachers tell them that Blenheim was completed in 1722, that is the date they will accept, regardless of the evidence of their eyes.'

'Brainwashing.'

'Possibly. But that's the way the young always have been brought up. You and I too, Gull. Why do we accept 1722 for Blenheim?'

'Because it's true . . . or was true.'

'Because we've been trained to accept it.'[33]

The painstaking re-creation finally leads Gull to wonder whether 'perhaps it had all happened before. Suppose this were the second time . . . or the tenth? The England they were so diligently copying now, that might have been bogus too.'[34] Historical forgeries are known to abound; could not the entire past be a contrivance?

For all our progress toward recovering and understanding the past, the doubts of Orwell's and Ely's protagonists still haunt us. 'Knowing the past', as Kubler says, 'is as astonishing a performance as knowing the stars';[35] and it remains no less elusive for being well documented.

The ultimate uncertainty of the past makes us all the more anxious to validate that things were as reputed. To gain assurance that yesterday was as substantial as today we saturate ourselves with bygone reliquary details, reaffirming memory and history in tangible form. We like to imagine that those who lived back then wanted us to know how real it was. Displaying nineteenth-century pioneers' diaries and letters, the Colorado Heritage Center commented in 1978: 'They took time to record their observations and feelings, leaving us records of their most intimate thoughts', as if a concern that *we* should know their past had led them to chronicle their lives.

Yet we are all the while aware that the past can never be known like the present. The past *is* L. P. Hartley's foreign country, where they do things differently. What is now known as 'the past' was not what anyone ever experienced as 'the present'.[36] In some respects we know it better than those who lived it; we sense 'the past in a way and to an extent which the past's awareness of itself cannot show', T. S. Eliot remarks.[37] We interpret the ongoing present while living through it, whereas we stand outside the past and view its finished operation, including its now known consequences for whatever was then the future. Old fen drainings become one phase in a series of successive reclamations; retrospective exhibitions show a painter's early work prefiguring his later; subsequent impacts on offspring, political heirs, scientific successors throw new light on careers long since ended. The implications of hindsight for what we make of the past are discussed later in this chapter.

Our capacity to understand the past is in many other ways deficient. The surviving residues of past thoughts and things represent a tiny fraction of previous generations'

---

[33] Ibid., p. 104.   [34] Ibid., pp. 130–1.   [35] *Shape of Time*, p. 19.
[36] Piaget and Inhelder, *Memory and Intelligence*, pp. 398–9.
[37] 'Tradition and the individual talent', p. 16.

contemporary fabric. 'Even when we are conscious of participating in a great historical event . . . we feel clearly that this event, as it will be inscribed in history, will be only a part of what it has been for us in the present', argues Eugène Minkowski. 'We know perfectly well that what is "historic" in it is only a part, only an aspect of what we do and of what we live.'[38]

Memory feels no less residual than history. However voluminous our recollections, we know they are mere glimpses of what was once a whole living realm. No matter how vividly recalled or reproduced, the past progressively becomes more shadowy, bereft of sensation, effaced by oblivion. 'Recognition does not always give us back the warmth of the past', writes Simone de Beauvoir; 'we lived it in the present; . . . and all that is left is a skeleton.' A long-ago scene recalled is 'like a butterfly pinned in a glass case: the characters no longer move in any direction. Their relationships are numbed, paralysed.' Her decaying 'past is not a peaceful landscape lying there behind me, a country in which I can stroll wherever I please, and which will gradually show me all its secret hills and dales. As I was moving forward, so it was crumbling.' Time's erosion grievously afflicts what memories remain: 'Most of the wreckage that can still be seen is colourless, distorted, frozen; its meaning escapes me.'[39]

The very certainty of today makes yesterday tenuous. 'The main reason why the past is so weak is the extraordinary strength of the present', Carne-Ross suggests.

To try now to achieve a real 'sense of the past' is like looking out of a brilliantly lit room at dusk. There seems to be something out there in the garden, the uncertain forms of trees stirring in the breeze, the hint of a path, perhaps the glimmer of water. Or is there merely a picture painted on the window, like the Furies in Eliot's play? Is there nothing out there at all and is the lit room the only reality?[40]

The past also lacks temporal consensus. Depending on content and context, it passes into the present anywhere from an instant to an aeon ago. The Holocene or 'recent' era ends the geological past about 10,000 years ago; the edaphic and floristic past extends within a few centuries of today; the so-called specious present lets us refer to 'this century' as though 1901 were 'now'. The human past sometimes ends with our own birth, occasionally coincides with the calendar year, often impinges on the present moment. Some pasts remain a constant interval behind us; others keep falling back or catching up. The 'Old West' survives in American folk memory as a period that has always ended about forty years ago; fifty years from now, an historian predicts, people will maintain that the defunct Old West was still flourishing back in the 1980s.[41]

Dubious owing to its very absence, inaccessible yet intimately known, the character of the past depends on how – and how much – it is consciously apprehended. How such apprehension takes place, and how it shapes our understanding, is the main subject of this chapter.

[38] *Lived Time*, p. 167.   [39] *Old Age*, pp. 407–8.
[40] 'Scenario for a new year: 3. the sense of the past', p. 241.
[41] L. B. Meyer, *Music and Arts and Ideas*, p. 169; Josephy, 'Awesome space: . . . interpretations of the Old West'.

MEMORY

> The past is what you remember, imagine you remember, convince yourself you remember, or pretend to remember.
>
> Harold Pinter[42]

All awareness of the past is founded on memory. Through recollection we recover consciousness of former events, distinguish yesterday from today, and confirm that we have experienced a past.

The range of meanings commonly attached to memory, however, transcends and sometimes obscures these relations with the past. Mnemonic systems attract much attention, and a lot of memory effort – recalling people to be seen, things to be done, routes to be followed – focuses on the future.[43] Such aspects of memory bear only tangentially on our knowledge of the past. But while the everyday use of memory goes beyond knowledge of the past, much psychological research neglects such knowledge. Short-term memory of the very recent past and the recall of contrived material have pre-empted psychologists' attention, for these topics best lend themselves to replicable, value-free, quantitative laboratory analysis; 'memories' that last less than a minute are a major focus of contemporary texts on the subject. So abstruse are psychologists' concerns that one of them, Ulric Neisser, charges that 'if X is an interesting or socially significant aspect of memory, then psychologists have hardly ever studied X'. When asked what interests them about memory, people are apt to mention their inability to recall early childhood, difficulties in remembering names or appointments, an aunt who could endlessly recite poetry by heart, how much or how little changed the old home seemed after thirty years' absence, discrepancies between their own memory and other peoples', the pleasure or sorrow of recollection; on most such topics psychological research has virtually nothing to say.[44] If scientific study of natural and everyday memory is more active than it used to be, as one reviewer of Neisser claims,[45] the results have not yet diffused beyond the specialist journals. Insight into the uses of memory come less from psychologists than from novelists, historians, and psychoanalysts; it is on such sources that Neisser's *Remembering in Natural Contexts* most heavily draws.

Suffering from a dearth of scholarly enquiry, ordinary memory is also lumbered with a misleading mythology. One enduring myth is that memory consists of physical inputs permanently stored in the brain, which some mechanism can restore to present consciousness; 'they can take away fifty feet of your intestines', as an old man in a hospital said, 'but they can't take away fifty seconds of your memory'.[46] The implications of this belief for hypnotic and other recall were explored in Chapter 1. Another widely held myth holds that the nature and potential power of memory are the same in us all and incapable of fundamental modification. A mass of evidence shows that on the contrary, both inherited dispositions and experiences throughout life affect memory capacity.[47]

---

[42] Quoted in Adler, 'Pinter's *Night*: a stroll down memory lane', p. 462.

[43] Meacher and Leiman, 'Remembering to perform future actions'.

[44] Neisser, 'Memory: what are the important questions?' pp. 4–5.

[45] Alan Baddeley, 'Keeping things in mind', *New Scientist*, 2 Sept. 1982, p. 636.

[46] Marcus Nathaniel Simpson, quoted in Cottle and Klineberg, *Present of Things Future*, p. 49.

[47] Neisser, 'Memorists'; Gruneberg, Morris, and Sykes, *Practical Aspects of Memory*, 'Individual differences', pp. 337–65; Belmont, 'Individual differences in memory'.

A third myth holds that because people in oral ('primitive') societies do not store or transmit thoughts in writing, they have better developed memories and a greater repertoire of detailed recall than people in literate societies – a belief controverted by much evidence.[48] A fourth prevalent view is that the more you can remember the better off you are. In fact, to generalize and act effectively requires not an encyclopaedic but a highly selective memory and the ability to forget what no longer matters.

My main concern in these pages is the nature and value of memorial knowledge, rather than the process of memory itself. I first review the personal and collective character of memory; go on to show how recollection bears on our sense of identity; and then discuss how far the 'truth' of memories can be confirmed. Various types of recall, willed and unbidden, learned and innate, reveal diverse aspects of things past, combining to reflect our past as a whole. The need to use and reuse memorial knowledge, and to forget as well as to recall, force us to select, distil, distort, and transform the past, accommodating things remembered to the needs of the present.

Memory pervades life. We devote much of the present to getting or keeping in touch with some aspect of the past. Few waking hours are devoid of recall or recollection; only intense concentration on some immediate pursuit can prevent the past from coming unbidden to mind. But the memories that permeate the present are subsumed within a hierarchy of habit, recall, and memento.

Habit embraces all mental residues of past acts and thoughts, whether or not consciously remembered. Recall, more limited than habitual memory but still pervasive, involves awareness of past occurrences or states of being. Mementoes are cherished recollections purposely salvaged from the greater mass of things recalled. This hierarchy resembles relics: everything familiar has some connection with the past and can be used to evoke recollection; out of a vast array of potential mnemonic aids we keep a few souvenirs to remind us of our own and of the wider past. Like a collection of antiquities, our store of precious memories is in continual flux, new keepsakes all the time being added, old ones discarded, some rising to the surface of present awareness, others sinking beneath conscious note.[49]

Memories in all these senses tend to accumulate with age. Although some are always being lost and others altered, the total stock of things recallable and recalled grows as life lengthens and as experiences multiply.

Personal and collective

The remembered past is both individual and collective. But as a form of awareness, memory is wholly and intensely personal; it is always felt as 'some particular event [that] happened to *me*'.[50] We recall only our own experiences at first hand, and the past we remember is innately our own. 'Nothing is so uniquely personal to a man as his memories',

---

[48] Neisser, 'Literacy and memory'; Vansina, *Oral Tradition*, p. 40. Oral narrative seldom involves verbatim memory, as Milman Parry and Walter B. Lord have shown (Scholes and Kellogg, *Nature of Narrative*, pp. 21–3); only ancient Israel reverenced the *ipsissima verba* (Gerhardsson, *Memory and Manuscript: Oral Tradition and Written Transmission in Rabbinic Judaism and Early Christianity*, pp. 130–1). See below, p. 200.
[49] Fred Davis, *Yearning for Yesterday*, p. 48; Piaget and Inhelder, *Memory and Intelligence*, pp. 387–8.
[50] Earle, 'Memory', p. 13.

notes B. S. Benjamin, 'and in guarding their privacy we seem almost to be protecting the very basis of our personality.' But memory is by its nature inviolable; most of our remembering is done in private, and 'we do not have to learn how to keep our recollections private'; they remain so unless we decide to make them public. Even then they can never be fully shared; for someone else to know *about* my memory is not at all the same as *having* it. 'Though we speak of sharing our memories with others, we could no more share a memory than we could share a pain.'[51]

The content of what we remember likewise makes it uniquely personal: it includes minute and intimate details of past events, relationships, and feelings. The secret language I invented, my fear of the man next door who disliked my dog, the discomfort of a bee-sting, the trauma of a broken arm are memories of my 12-year-old self that no one else can have. The essential privateness of Austin Wright's boyhood favourites – a chosen baseball star, opera singer, steamboat, ice-cream soda – is the leitmotiv of his *Morley Mythology*, in which a sinister caller reminds Morley of things that Morley knows he alone could remember.[52]

Memory also converts public events into idiosyncratic personal experiences. As part and parcel of facts about the New Deal, for example, I remember my parents' partiality to Roosevelt, my grandparents' animus against labour unions; political history has become an annexe to family history. Things we are bidden to recall often give way to more frivolous private recollections. 'The sight of an old textbook', notes Frances Fitzgerald, 'is much less likely to bring back the sequence of Presidents or the significance of the Smoot-Hawley Tariff Act than it is to evoke the scene of an eighth-grade classroom.'[53]

Private memories also feel like private property. 'In memory we recognize *immediately* that our own past experiences belong to us', notes a philosopher. 'Once I have experienced putting my daughter to bed, that experience remains *mine*.'[54] Indeed, some prize their personal past as they would a valuable antique. They congratulate themselves on having had the experience they recall, treasuring memories that enhance their self-regard.[55]

Since they are inherently personal, many memories are extinguished at every death. 'The love of Helen died with the death of some one man', writes Borges, in whose 'Tlön' tangible continuance depends on memory: 'all things tend to become effaced and lose their details when they are forgotten. A classic example is the doorway which survived so long as it was visited by a beggar and disappeared at his death.'[56] Among the Swahili, the deceased who remain alive in the memory of others are called the 'living-dead'; they become completely dead only when the last to have known them are gone.[57] Unable to pass on her inherited store of memories, the lone elderly survivor of an ancient lineage bears the heavy burden of being 'the Last Leaf'. 'Generations remain alive only in the flickering memory of

---

[51] Benjamin, 'Remembering', p. 171.
[52] The nostalgic musings elicited by Fred Davis, however, revealed 'secret' pasts that were more alike than unique (*Yearning for Yesterday*, p. 43).
[53] *America Revised*, p. 17.   [54] R. G. Burton, 'Human awareness of time', p. 307.
[55] Schachtel, *Metamorphosis*, p. 311.
[56] 'The witness'; idem, 'Tlön, Uqbar, Orbis Tertius', p. 39.
[57] Uchendu, 'Ancestorcide! are African ancestors dead?' p. 287. 'While the departed person is remembered by name, he is not really "dead": he is alive . . . in the memory of those who knew him in his life as well as being alive in the world of the spirits', and this may continue for four or five generations (Mbiti, *African Religions & Philosophy*, p. 25).

a person whose own days are drawing to a close', in a gerontologist's description. 'Her mind is the final common pathway, the last preserve of all that has gone on before in one branch of human existence.' The Last Leaf 'is all that the past still has to rely upon – and she knows it'.[58] Not all regret that loss, to be sure. With so much feeling bound up in her past, Anna Freud in old age could not bring herself to share her recollections 'with the reading public, . . . so I allow myself the privilege of taking it all with me'.[59]

The uniquely personal nature of memory not only condemns it to ultimate extinction but flaws its communication of the past. Doubts assail us about a memory that is only private. 'Because it is not shared, the memory seems fictitious', felt Wallace Stegner when he returned to his boyhood prairie home and found 'not a name that I went to school with, not a single person who would have shared as a contemporary my own experience' of his childhood. 'I have used those memories for years as if they really happened, I have made stories and novels of them. Now they seem uncorroborated and delusive . . . How little evidence I have that I myself have lived what I remember . . . I half suspect that I am remembering not what happened but something I have written.'[60]

The origins like the reliability of recollections lie shrouded in doubt. We can seldom distinguish primary from secondary memories, remembering things from remembering remembering them, Wordsworth's 'naked recollection' from 'after-meditation'.[61] Recalling childhood days in St Ives, Virginia Woolf seemed 'to be watching things happen as if I were there . . . My memory supplies what I had forgotten, so that it seems as if it were happening independently, though I am really making it happen.'[62] These doubts implicate other people; many events we think we recall from our own experience were in fact told to us and then became an indistinguishable part of our memory. 'Very often . . . when I recall an event of my own past, I "see myself", which I obviously didn't do in the past', writes Paul Brockelman; for example, 'I "see myself" getting out of bed' – a scene probably recounted by his mother.[63] Other people's recollections of past events occlude and often masquerade as our own.

In fact, we need other people's memories both to confirm our own and to give them endurance. Unlike dreams, which are wholly private, memories are continually supplemented by those of others. Sharing and validating memories sharpens them and promotes their recall; events we alone know about are less certainly, less easily evoked. In the process of knitting our own discontinuous recollections into narratives, we revise personal components to fit the collectively remembered past, and gradually cease to distinguish between them.[64]

The late development of memory in infancy, and our continuing connection with older kin and a prior world, likewise make this collective overlay inescapable. 'No one ever is, or can be, the first to know who he or she is'; without the odds and ends of parental and

---

[58] Kastenbaum, 'Memories of tomorrow', p. 204.

[59] 1977; quoted in Muriel Gardiner, 'Freud's brave daughter', *Observer*, 10 Oct. 1982, p. 31.

[60] Stegner, *Wolf Willow*, pp. 14–17.

[61] Anscombe, 'Experience and causation', pp. 27–8; Fraisse, *Psychology of Time*, p. 162; Wordsworth, *The Prelude*, Bk III, lines 614–16, p. 107. See also Mendilow, *Time and the Novel*, p. 219.

[62] *Moments of Being*, p. 67.

[63] 'Of memory and things past', p. 319. See also Martin and Deutscher, 'Remembering'.

[64] Halbwachs, *Collective Memory*, pp. 23–5, 47–61, 75–8.

grandparental memory we would have to invent a greater portion of ourselves.[65] Elder siblings too supply memories that partly preclude our own, as Anne Tyler notes: 'Like most youngest children, he had trouble remembering his own past. The older ones did it so well for him, why should he bother? They had built him a second-hand memory that included the years before he existed, even.'[66] He might perhaps bother out of need for some past that belonged solely to him, Cottle suggests; to shape that time he must either leave home or wait until his elders die and his siblings depart.[67] But in any event, what we remember from childhood is immersed in a sea of both general and family history and thus bears their stamp. 'Running parallel to public matters', in Lively's words, 'your own doings [are] interwoven with the coarser and more indestructible fabric of history.'[68]

We treasure these connections with the wider past. Gratified that our memories are our own, we also seek to link our personal past with collective memory and public history. People vividly recall their own thoughts and actions at moments of public crisis because they jump at the chance to connect themselves with a meaningful cosmos. A high proportion of those old enough to recall Lincoln's and Kennedy's assassinations many years later also vividly remembered their own circumstances at the time: where they were, who told them, what they were doing, how they reacted, what they did next.[69] But these recollections are often as erroneous as they are vivid. Indeed, the gross inaccuracies emphasize the point: people are so eager to be part of 'history' that they falsely 'remember' their responses to, or even having been present at, some momentous event.[70]

Memory and identity

Remembering the past is crucial for our sense of identity: as noted in Chapter 2, to know what we were confirms that we are. Self-continuity depends wholly on memory; recalling past experiences links us with our earlier selves, however different we may since have become. 'As memory alone acquaints us with the ... succession of perceptions', Hume reasoned, ''tis to be consider'd ... as the source of personal identity. Had we no memory, we never shou'd have any notion ... of that chain of causes and effects, which constitute our self or person.'[71] The Greeks identified the forgotten past with death; save for a privileged few, the dead had no memories.[72] Amnesiacs suffer a similar loss. 'I felt nothing', said a man whose memory had been lost for several years; 'when you have no memory, you have no feelings.'[73] Loss of memory destroys one's personality and deprives life of meaning. As Gabriel García Márquez envisages an amnesiac's plight, 'the recollec-

---

[65] Jervis Anderson, 'Sources', p. 112. Erasmus (*Copia*, sect. 172, pp. 539–40) distinguishes memories of one's own lifetime (*nostra aetate*) from memories of things seen by and heard from the older generation (*nostra memoria*) and memories transmitted from great-grandparents and remote forefathers (*patrum memoria*).

[66] *Clock Winder*, p. 293.   [67] *Time's Children*, p. 63.   [68] Lively, *According to Mark*, p. 27.

[69] Colegrove, 'Day they heard about Lincoln'; Roger Brown and Kulik, 'Flashbulb memories'; Linton, 'Memory for real-world events', pp. 386–7.

[70] Buckhout, 'Eyewitness testimony', p. 119; Neisser, 'Snapshots or benchmarks?' The twentieth anniversary of Kennedy's assassination was marked by articles featuring recollections of where people had been and what they were doing when they heard the news.

[71] *Treatise of Human Nature*, Bk I, Pt 4, sect. 6, 1:542. See Biro, 'Hume on self-identity and memory', p. 29.

[72] Eliade, *Myth and Reality*, p. 121; S. C. Humphries, 'Death and time', pp. 274–5.

[73] Theo Goossens, quoted in Marjorie Wallace, 'The drug that gave this man his memory back', *Sunday Times*, 24 Apr. 1983, p. 13. The classic amnesiac is Luria's *Man with a Shattered World*, especially pp. 87–108; for a recent parallel, see Oliver Sacks, 'The lost mariner', *N.Y. Review of Books*, 16 Feb. 1984, pp. 14–19.

tion of his childhood began to be erased from his memory, then the name and notion of things, and finally the identity of people, and even the awareness of his own being, . . . until he sank into a kind of idiocy that had no past.'[74]

We synthesize identity not simply by calling up a sequence of reminiscences, but by being enveloped, like Virginia Woolf's Orlando, in a unifying web of retrospection.[75] Groups too mobilize collective memories to sustain enduring corporate identities, much as legal instruments endow firms and estates with potential immortality.[76]

No personal synthesis can be complete: we do not remember being born, we forget much and become alienated from more of our past. And some 'live more momentary, disjointed, fragmented lives than others', leaving much 'of the concrete detail of their lives' behind them, not relating meaningfully to past experiences and feelings. By contrast, remarks a philosopher, 'those who bring more of their past into their present' thereby both confirm their own identity and enrich the present with the past's amplified residues.[77] As Mr. Sammler put it, 'Everybody needs his memories. They keep the wolf of insignificance from the door.'[78]

Awareness that memory forms identity is relatively recent. To be sure, memory helped to ward off the horror of oblivion both for the ancient Greeks and for medieval and Renaissance Europeans, but the memories thus preserved were usually posthumous.[79] Lives were conceived not as diachronic continuities but as instances of constant, universal principles. Individual identity was fixed, consistent, and vested wholly in the present. Well into the eighteenth century even reflective men took life to be 'a discontinuous succession of sensory enjoyments' interspersed with abstract reflections, in Starobinski's phrase, with 'chance events and momentary excesses' featuring successive unrelated episodes. 'Such lives had no distant goal, no finality beyond the limits of the imminent moment of time.'[80] The identities revealed in eighteenth-century autobiographies and novels stay the same over time; events do not affect a malleable consciousness, but simply figure as fortuitous moments in careers unmarked by introspective connections with previous stages in life.[81]

Even after men began to make such life-history connections, they remained unsure of their validity. 'The same objects are before us – those inanimate things which we have gazed on in wayward infancy and impetuous youth, in anxious and scheming manhood – they are permanent and the same', as Walter Scott's Jonathan Oldbuck said; 'but when we look upon them in cold, unfeeling old age, can we, changed in our temper, our pursuits, our feelings – changed in our form, our limbs, and our strength – can we be ourselves called the same? or do we not rather look back with a sort of wonder upon our former selves, as beings separate and distinct from what we now are?'[82]

[74] *One Hundred Years of Solitude*, p. 46.   [75] Shore, 'Virginia Woolf, Proust, and *Orlando*', p. 242.
[76] Halbwachs, *Collective Memory*, p. 143.
[77] Ehman, 'Temporal self-identity', p. 339.   [78] Bellow, *Mr. Sammler's Planet*, p. 190.
[79] Vernant, 'Death with two faces'; Quinones, *Renaissance Discovery of Time*, pp. 84–5, 232–3; S. C. Humphries, 'Death and time', p. 270.
[80] Starobinski, *Invention of Liberty 1700–1789*, p. 207. See also Poulet, *Studies in Human Time*, pp. 13–23.
[81] Spacks, *Imagining a Self: Autobiography and Novel in Eighteenth-Century England*, pp. 8–11, 284–5. See also More, 'Criticism', pp. 241–2; Ellis, 'Development of T. S. Eliot's historical sense', pp. 293–5.
[82] *The Antiquary* (1816), p. 91.

Awareness of memory as the key to self-development, securing and magnifying identity through life, was a late eighteenth-century revelation whose only harbinger had been biblical narrative.[83] Identity sanctioned by memory now came to incorporate change. 'We are ourselves, always ourselves, and not for one minute the same', in Diderot's words.[84] And identity over a lifetime secured the reality of the past: since the self had persisted despite change, the past must also have been real.

Followers of Rousseau and Wordsworth began to see their childhood selves forming their adult identity, and hence to view life as an interconnected narrative; within a few decades the relation of the sense of the past to personal memory became part of the mental equipment and expectations at least of the educated.[85] Reiterated impressions reinforced present with recollected experience. Awareness of memory stimulated degrees of self-consciousness previously unknown, often narcissistic and autobiographical, usually suffused with Romanticist sensibility. 'Today when our literature and whole conduct of life is unthinkable without a sense of time and of the past', writes Christopher Salvesen, 'when practically no emotion can be felt without some reference of it to earlier experience or to childhood', it is hard to realize that this sense of personal continuity was rare before the nineteenth century.[86] At the century's end, self-conscious concern with the past became a cardinal feature of psychoanalysis: in Morse Peckham's terms, just as Wordsworth's *The Prelude* had historicized the personality, so Freud aimed to make Wordsworths out of his patients.[87]

But we have since become far less confident about looking back over our past. The signals we now recall often seem confused, even self-contradictory; the memories that define us are apt to be tacit rather than explicit, somatic rather than self-conscious, involuntary rather than deliberate. Modern habits of self-analysis render dubious the integrity of our own remembered past. And the frequency with which we update and reinterpret our memory weakens coherent temporal identity. 'What used to be taboo becomes *de rigueur*, what used to be obvious becomes laughable' almost overnight, concludes Peter Berger. 'We go through life refashioning our calendar of holy days, raising up and tearing down again the signposts that mark our progress through time toward ever newly defined fulfilments.'[88]

These incessantly readjusted memories are rarely integrated into any consistent self-definition. 'Rather we stumble like drunkards over the sprawling canvas of our self-conception, throwing a little paint here, erasing some lines there, never really stopping to obtain a view of the likeness we have produced.'[89] The pace and scope of alteration

---

[83] Scholes and Kellogg, *Nature of Narrative*, pp. 123–68; Walter Kaufmann, *Time Is an Artist*, pp. 36–40.

[84] *Refutation suivie de l'ouvrage d'Helvétius intitulé L'Homme* (1773–4), 2:373.

[85] Salvesen, *Landscape of Memory: A Study of Wordsworth's Poetry*, pp. 42–4; Weintraub, 'Autobiography and historical consciousness', pp. 835, 843–4; *idem, Value of the Individual.*

[86] *Landscape of Memory*, p. 172. LeVine's assumption that 'all normal persons in all societies view themselves as continuous entities ... from their earliest memories to the present, ... think about themselves in a chronological context', and aim at 'long-range goals representing cumulative performance in a culturally defined career pathway' ('Adulthood and aging in cross-cultural perspective', p. 2) is confuted by all the historical evidence.

[87] 'Afterword: reflections on historical modes in the nineteenth century', p. 279. 'Psychology became history; personality became history; the manifestation of the self became history' (Peckham, *Triumph of Romanticism*, p. 46).

[88] Berger, *Invitation to Sociology*, pp. 72–3.   [89] Ibid., p. 75.

preclude a consistent self-view anchored in memory. Yet few can afford to become aware of this deficiency; it is too painful to recognize the discrepancies between one's present and past views. 'No one lives comfortably with the knowledge that he or she cannot recall a continuous past if one wants to', in Jan Vansina's words, for 'belief about the continuity or discontinuity of [one's] opinions in the past is a core part of every personality.'[90]

Confirmability

The subjective nature of memory makes it both a sure and a dubious guide to the past. We know when we have a memory, and whether true or false that memory bears in some way on the past. Even an error of memory involves the recall of something, however distorted; no memory is totally delusive. Indeed, a false recollection firmly believed becomes a fact in its own right.[91]

Memories inspire faith because we believe they were recorded at the time; they have eye-witness status. And memories in general are prima-facie credible because they are consistent. Particular memories often do turn out to be wrong or even invented, but we remain confident about most of them because they are congruent; they hang together too well to be dismissed as illusions. And we cannot impeach all our memories, as noted above, or present experience would make no sense.

No such faith attests the truth of any particular memory, however. To remember a thing is at best to credit it as probable; although their present or future consequences may confirm some memories, they can be checked only against other recollections of the past, never against the past itself.[92]

The personal character of memories magnifies the difficulty of confirming them. No one else can wholly validate our own unique experience of the past. Memories proved wrong or inaccurate are not thereby dispelled; a false recollection can be as durable and potent as a true one, especially if it sustains a self-image. '"I did that", says my memory. "I could not have done that", says my pride and remains inexorable', as Nietzsche wrote: 'Eventually the memory yields.'[93]

Memory not only yields; it also alters, often imperceptibly. The unreliability of recall is a matter of common experience. Plagued by erroneous alterations of the Torah, Jewish law-makers insisted that even copyists legendary for their mnemonic feats should not transcribe a single letter without the text before their eyes.[94] Such caution is exceptional: on the whole, we place unjustified confidence in our own memories, seldom questioning their reliability. But we realize that *other* people generally remember less than they think,

---

[90] 'Memory and oral tradition', pp. 266, 269. It was in the late nineteenth century that the sense of coherence gave way to one of discontinuity, thinks Jackson Lears (*No Place of Grace*, pp. 36–8); Foucault places the change a century earlier (*Order of Things*, pp. 367–70).

[91] Burton, 'Human awareness of time', pp. 308; Roy Schafer, *A New Language for Psychoanalysis*, pp. 29–50; idem, *Psychoanalytic Life History*.

[92] Lewis, *Analysis of Knowledge and Valuation*, pp. 334–8, 353–62.

[93] *Beyond Good and Evil*, p. 86; quoted approvingly by Freud in a note added in 1910 to *Psychopathology of Everyday Life*, p. 147n.

[94] Gerhardsson, *Memory and Manuscript*, pp. 29, 46; Stratton, 'Mnemonic feat of the "Shass Pollak"'.

imagine part of what they believe they remember, and reshape the past to accord with present self-images.[95]

The reception of John Dean's testimony at the U.S. Senate Watergate hearings exemplifies faith in the supposed infallibility of a detailed memory. Dean was able to expose President Nixon's cover-up because the specificity of his recollected conversations with Nixon, Ehrlichman, and Haldeman persuaded senators of their accuracy. Dean's memory did confirm what emerged as the general truth about Watergate. But comparison with tapes of the actual White House conversations reveals striking disparities between what Dean said and heard and what he thought and claimed to have said and heard. Although Dean conveyed the gist of the discussions, only where he had frequently rehearsed his own words did he give anything approaching a verbatim account; elsewhere, hardly a single detail conformed with the facts.[96]

Types of memory

Memories are as multiform as Brockelman's evocative listing suggests:

I remember where – as a child – I used to swing, and I remember the feel of the air rushing by my face. I remember who beat Napoleon at Waterloo, and I remember that 8×9 is 72. I haven't forgotten how to swing a bat; and I remember – no, I feel it again in the weakness in my legs and wrists and in the nausea in my stomach – the terror I felt when the captain made me a 'volunteer' on the first search and destroy mission in the Ashau Valley. I remember the party we had when I got married – the music, the friends, the food, the wine; but (oh God!) I can't remember any more the face of my dearest friend who died a year ago . . . There are all sorts of memory, and they pervade and define me.[97]

Not all these kinds of recall provide perspectives on the past – we walk, write, brush our teeth, swing a bat without recalling how or when we learned to do so. Memorized semantic learning – the multiplication table, lines of verse, the structure of amino acids, the capitals of nations, our accumulated store of words, facts, and meanings – sheds no light on the past in which it was acquired. Being able to recite a poem does not enable me to tell when or where or how I learned it or to recall other times I have recited it; I recognize a friend in the street but am not conscious of the former meetings that make that recognition possible.[98]

To be sure, some memorized facts are themselves historical – the sovereigns of Britain, the presidents of the United States, any chronological series. Memorizing helps us to know *about* the past by locating such events in time, but unless they are related to other aspects of history the dates of Washington's presidency convey no *sense* of the past.

To be in touch with the past requires recall that is usually conscious, often self-conscious. Unlike semantic and sensory-motor memory, so-called episodic memory bears on specific events in our life.[99] We remember the past as a congeries of distinctive

---

[95] Spacks, *Imagining a Self*, p. 19, for eighteenth-century trust in memory; Berger, *Introduction to Sociology*, p. 71, for our own time.

[96] Neisser, 'John Dean's memory'.   [97] 'Of memory and things past', p. 309.

[98] Russell, *Analysis of Mind*, pp. 166–7; Waters, 'The past and the historical past', p. 254.

[99] Tulving, *Elements of Episodic Memory*, pp. 17–120; see also 'event' and 'factual' memory in Perry, 'Personal identity, memory, and the problem of circularity', p. 144. Repeated recall can transform episodic into semantic memory, like John Dean's rehearsed recollections becoming stable, unchanging, and divorced from sense of self. See Flavell, *Cognitive Development*, pp. 184–9.

occasions, recognizably different from yet not altogether unlike the present: different enough to know it as another time, similar enough to make us aware of our continuity with it.

The intensity of episodic recall varies with its purpose. Least evocative is instrumental everyday memory – remembering a friend's name, where we had dinner on holiday, when we paid the rent. Such recall resurrects facts, not feelings: 'In what year was I an intern in Lariboisière Hospital? Let's see, it was two years after my sister died; that would be 1911' – reactions to being in hospital or to the sister's death do not intrude.[100] Instrumental memory abstracts from former events without evoking the sensations that accompanied them.

The instrumentally remembered past is a conventionalized and barren landscape. In the shapeless plain of time, bleak calendric pinnacles, the sole survivors of former rich environments, pre-empt our attention. Scenes and events are not recalled, but only their order and location. Such 'memory reflects life as a road with occasional signposts and milestones', writes the psychoanalyst Ernest Schachtel, 'rather than as the landscape through which this road had led'. We identify the outstanding events to which the signposts point but remember little of the events themselves; 'not the concrete abundance of life [but] only the fact that such an event took place'.[101]

Adult social conventions make instrumental memory prevalent. Children see and hear what is there; adults see and hear what they are expected to and mainly remember what they think they ought to remember. That we recall little of our earliest years stems less from repression than from the loss of sensate recollections that adults can no longer even imagine experiencing. Adult memory schemata have no room for the smells, tastes, and other vivid sensations, or for the pre-logical and magical thinking of early childhood; deeply felt experience fails to register or is forgotten if it is socially inappropriate.[102] Instrumental recall is a purposeful set of markers and grids that resembles a road map, a guide book, a calendar. Many memories suffer similar attrition: the subjects of Bartlett's famous experiments reduced the complex stories they were asked to recall to blandly conventional tales so as to render them 'acceptable, understandable, comfortable, straightforward'.[103]

Unlike instrumental recall, reverie includes and even highlights remembered feelings. Reverie yields explicit but manifestly incomplete images of the past, particular aspects of bygone scenes that leave us conscious more *could* be recalled. To recover a lost impression, to see and feel again what we have experienced before, often requires a deliberate effort at the outset, after which states of reverie become self-generating.

Affective memory of greatest intensity reveals a past so rich and vivid we all but relive it – like the reviewer who did not 'remember' the film *Kagemusha* when he closed his eyes,

[100] E. Pichon, 'Essai d'étude convergente des problèmes du temps' (1931), quoted in Minkowski, *Lived Time*, p. 152.

[101] Schachtel, *Metamorphosis*, p. 287.

[102] Ibid., pp. 279–322; Piaget and Inhelder, *Memory and Intelligence*, pp. 378–401; Albert J. Solnit, lecture at University College London, 6 Mar. 1984.

[103] Bartlett, *Remembering* (1932), p. 89. Critics suggest that Bartlett's subjects made such extensive changes because they were pressed to reproduce coherent and finished memories (Gauld and Stephenson, 'Some experiments relating to Bartlett's theory of remembering').

but 'saw it again'.[104] Recalling his stay in Venice, Brockelman can 'see the buildings, I hear the talk, I feel the texture of the chair I sat on; . . . I smell the breeze from the bay, hear the cloud of pigeons at my feet; I feel the frustration I felt, and my heart constricts as I "re-await" the arrival of my lover . . . I can sit here in recall and almost lose myself, almost slip into the past.'[105]

It is not introspection that yields these heightened recollections, but the chance reactivation of forgotten sensations, commonly a touch or smell or taste or sound. Like nostalgia's alpine melody, the village bell was Cowper's triggering mechanism:

> Clear and sonorous, as the gale comes on!
> With easy force it opens all the cells
> Where mem'ry slept. Wherever I have heard
> A kindred melody, the scene recurs,
> And with it all its pleasures and its pains.[106]

An overwhelmingly 'ancient, unbearable recognition' of the past came for Stegner 'partly from the children and the footbridge and the river's quiet curve, but much more from the smell. For here, pungent and pervasive, is the smell that has always meant my childhood', compounded of river water, mud, damp bench boards, the burlap-tipped diving-board, that for a moment conjured memory into reality.[107] Such recall seems visceral; in Proust's phrase, 'our arms and legs are full of torpid memories'.[108]

These intense recollections are uniquely involuntary, and the more vivid the sensation the less accessible it is to deliberate retrieval. But although they come unbidden, such apparitions come only if we truly want them. Recall so intense is often anguishing; even an agreeable memory can painfully re-evoke an ancient conflict. As in analytic therapy, such remembered events lose their coercive hold and fade into the neutral past only when that conflict has been resolved.[109]

Certain heightened recollections seem to bring the past not only to life, but into simultaneous existence with the present, making it appear 'closer than the present, which it both haunts and hypnotizes'.[110] De Quincey describes an old woman whose paramnesia combined total recall with temporal concurrence: 'In a moment, in the twinkling of an eye, every act, every design of her past life, lived again, arraying themselves not as a succession, but as parts of a coexistence.'[111] Like *déjà vu* – the sensation that we have seen before what we know we are now seeing for the first time – paramnesia coalesces a still distinguishable past and present. Poulet traces this obsessive, often opium-induced, experience from Rousseau to Coleridge, Byron, Blake, and Swedenborg through De Quincey, Baudelaire, and Proust.[112] 'I sometimes seemed to have lived for 70 or 100 years in one night', reported De Quincey, who amplified experienced time to gain an illusion of eternity, swelling life's

---

[104] Robert Hatch, 'Films', *The Nation*, 15 Nov. 1980, p. 522.   [105] 'Of memory and things past', p. 321.
[106] *The Task* (1785), Bk VI, lines 10–14, p. 220.   [107] *Wolf Willow*, p. 18.
[108] *Remembrance of Things Past*, 3:716.
[109] 'Actually relived in all its intensity', the past 'seems, even in the case of an agreeable memory, to be an agonizing pain' (Pichon, 'Essai . . . des problèmes du temps', quoted in Minkowski, *Lived Time*, p. 152; see also pp. 159–61). See Poulet, *Studies in Human Time*, p. 298.
[110] Shattuck, *Proust's Binoculars: A Study of Memory, Time, and Recognition in 'A la recherche du temps perdu'*, pp. 48–9; see Shore, 'Virginia Woolf, Proust, and *Orlando*', pp. 237–41.
[111] *Suspira de Profundis* (1845), p. 245.
[112] 'Timelessness and Romanticism'. 'It was no mere analogous sensation nor even a mere echo or replica of a past sensation . . . it was that past sensation itself' (Proust, *Remembrance of Things Past*, 3:907).

narrow span with as many memories as possible.[113] Proust's *Recherche du temps perdu* was 'an infinite quest to bring back the past into the present, the past not as past, not as a series of points in time, but as a simultaneous whole possessed in its entirety'.[114] But par-amnesiac convergence leaves addicts unable to distinguish past from present – perhaps even life from death. Walking in a town in 1928, Borges conjectures his childhood existence there, and then 'the facile thought *I am in eighteen hundred and* . . . ceased being a set of approximate words and deepened into a reality. I felt dead, I felt myself an abstract perceiver of the world', unable to separate 'one moment belonging to its apparent past from another belonging to its apparent present'.[115]

Each type of recall subtends its own perspective on the past. Instrumental memory lacks involvement; its schematized past simply points toward the more important present. Reverie recalls particular feelings and encourages us to compare past with present states of being. Total recall immerses us willy-nilly in the past; the present is hag-ridden by previous events so consequential or traumatic they are relived almost as though they were still occurring. Minkowski's wartime recollections exemplify these distinctions: 'Completely different attitudes toward the past are involved when we recount what we did during the war, when we try to relive what we experienced during that torment, and finally, when we feel it still present in the very fibers of our being, when we feel it thus become a part of our present even more than the *actual* present.'[116]

Normally, however, memory juxtaposes these types of recollection, the emphasis continually shifting from one to another. The whole continuum from functional recall through reverie to virtual immersion in a bygone time together fashion our awareness of the remembered past. Stemming from such disparate levels of apprehension, that past can feel bewilderingly multiform. Yet memory, however protean, seems to be a distinct category of experience. Remembering the feel of sand between the toes at the seashore is quite unlike recalling where we left the house keys, but we are none the less conscious that both involve awareness of the past. Nor are these levels of memory segregated; we experience them as an ensemble. Instrumental recall mingles with unbidden recollection; we simultaneously day-dream about last summer's holiday while trying to remember where we put those keys. Different modes of memory afford differing perspectives into the past, but the process of recall merges all of them together.

And they do after all have something in common. All memory transmutes experience, distils the past rather than simply reflecting it. We recall only a small fraction of what has impinged on us, let alone of all the environment displays. Thus memory sifts again what perception had already sifted, leaving us only fragments of the fragments of what was initially on view.

Forgetting

For memory to have meaning we must forget most of what we have seen, lest we become like 'Funes, the Memorious':

---

[113] *Confessions of an English Opium-Eater* (1822), p. 115. [114] Poulet, 'Timelessness and Romanticism', p. 22.
[115] 'A new refutation of time', p. 55. Compare this despair with James's protagonist in *Sense of the Past.*
[116] *Lived Time*, p. 153.

He remembered the shapes of the clouds in the south at dawn on the 30th of April of 1882, and he could compare them in his recollection with the marbled grain in the design of a leather-bound book which he had seen only once, and with the lines in the spray which an oar raised in the Río Negro on the eve of the battle of the Quebracho ... Funes not only remembered every leaf on every tree of every wood, but even every one of the times he had perceived or imagined it ... *'My memory, sir, is like a garbage disposal.'*

The weight of these disjoined and unselective recollections in the end proves unbearable. 'To think is to forget a difference, to generalize, to abstract. In the overly replete world of Funes there were nothing but details.'[117]

Memories must continually be discarded and conflated; only forgetting enables us to classify and bring chaos into order. 'An important condition of remembering', as Whitrow put it, 'is that we should be able to forget.'[118] Like Henry James we must deliberately circumscribe our recollections: 'The ragbag of memory hung on its nail in my closet, though I learnt with time to control the habit of bringing it forth.'[119] Memory too frequently resorted to no longer vivifies but inundates the present. Indeed, to remember more than a small fraction of our past would be enormously time-consuming. As with Tristram Shandy, who took a year to recount just the first day of his life, 'it would take a life-time to record a life-time', notes Charles Rycroft, 'and anyone who attempted to write a blow-by-blow account of his life would get caught in an infinite regress, having to spend time and words describing his autobiographizing'.[120]

The most vividly remembered scenes and events are often those which were for a time forgotten. 'If an image or a sensation out of the past is to be truly recognized, ... it must be summoned back ... after a period of absence', Roger Shattuck interprets Proust. 'The original experience or image must have been forgotten, completely forgotten ... True memory or recognition surges into being out of its opposite: *oubli*.'[121] In Proust's own words:

As Habit weakens everything, what best reminds us of a person is precisely what we had forgotten. It is thanks to this oblivion alone that we can from time to time recover the person that we were, place ourselves in relation to things as he was placed ... Owing to the work of oblivion, the returning memory ... causes us to breathe a new air, an air which is new precisely because we have breathed it in the past, ... since the true paradises are the paradises that we have lost.[122]

Indeed, the convoluted length of *Remembrance of Things Past* makes the reader forget what he had read at the start, to recall it at the end with a shock of recognition.[123]

Much forgetting is not just desirable; it is unavoidable. Repetitive events merge in recall: since any time I go to buy bread is practically like the time before, only the first and last experiences are apt to be remembered.[124] Contrary to common belief, we forget most

---

[117] Borges, pp. 40, 42–3. For an actual instance of such eidetic memory, see Oliver Sacks, 'The twins', *N.Y. Review of Books*, 28 Feb. 1985, p. 16.

[118] Whitrow, *Natural Philosophy of Time*, p. 85, elaborating on Théodule Armand Ribot's *Diseases of Memory* (1885). See also Aristides, 'Disremembrance of things present', p. 164.

[119] James, *A Small Boy and Others*, p. 41.

[120] Sterne, *Tristram Shandy*, Bk IV, Ch. 13, 2:49; Rycroft, 'Analysis and the autobiographer'. Vansina estimates a 40-year-old might require six months to recall all he potentially could ('Memory and oral tradition', p. 265). On the Shandy paradox, see Mendilow, *Time and the Novel*, p. 184.

[121] *Proust's Binoculars*, p. 63. See Joseph Frank, 'Spatial form in modern literature', pp. 238–9.

[122] *Remembrance of Things Past*, 1:692, 3:903.

[123] Shattuck, *Proust's Binoculars*, pp. 100, 105.   [124] Vansina, 'Memory and oral tradition', p. 264.

of our experiences; the greater part of what happens to us is soon irretrievably lost. 'I expect memories to be long-lasting because, like everyone else, I can assess a large number of very old memories, some of them from two or three decades past', but Marigold Linton found her expectation delusive: we remain unaware of the many things we have forgotten, precisely because we have forgotten them. Linton's periodic reviews of her diary, in which she had noted the outstanding events of her each day in 1972, revealed that memory grossly altered events recorded two years back; after three or four years many items failed to trigger any recollection at all. Originally significant details of her life became fragments of nonsense, whole phrases utterly unintelligible, and her ability to recall items dwindled as time distanced them until after six years one-third of her recorded events had entirely vanished from memory.[125]

These losses leave the remembered past as 'islands in a confused and layered landscape, like the random protrusions after a heavy snowfall, the telegraph pole and hump of farm machinery and buried wall', in Lively's words.[126] 'We relive our past years not in their continuous sequence, day by day', wrote Proust, 'but in a memory focused upon the coolness or sunshine of some morning or afternoon'; between these isolated scenes lie 'vast stretches of oblivion'.[127] Oblivion is the fate of many events of utmost consequence when they happened. Comparing wartime experiences with memories of them thirty-five years later, Tom Harrisson found that most people had forgotten things they could not imagine losing track of. For example, the writer Richard Fitter failed to remember having been to Coventry and 'could hardly believe his eyes when shown his hand-written accounts of a long visit to the place, including important conversations with leading high-ups'.[128]

Revising

Memories are also altered by revision. Contrary to the stereotype of the remembered past as immutably fixed, recollections are malleable and flexible; what seems to have happened undergoes continual change. Heightening certain events in recall, we then reinterpret them in the light of subsequent experience and present need.

Intelligibility is one such need: things initially ambiguous or inconsistent become coherent, clear, straightforward. 'Memory is the great organizer of consciousness', Susanne Langer writes. 'Actual experience is a welter of sights, sounds, feelings, physical strains, expectations', perceptions that memory simplifies and composes. Above all, memory transforms the experienced past into what we later think it should have been, eliminating undesired scenes and making favoured ones suitable.[129]

Subsequent recollections reshaped recorded wartime experiences to conform with canons of approved behaviour and feeling. Playing the piano on a September day in 1939, a young girl in Stepney missed Neville Chamberlain's announcement and the first siren alert; her mother then burst in shouting at her, her father began issuing peremptory commands and useless advice. Memory transformed it all: 'We were gathered in our little

---

[125] Linton, 'Transformations of memory in everyday life', p. 86. See *idem*, 'Real-world memory after six years'.
[126] Lively, *Going Back*, p. 11.   [127] *Remembrance of Things Past*, 2:412–13.
[128] Harrisson, *Living through the Blitz*, p. 327.
[129] *Feeling and Form*, p. 263. 'The past rises before us . . . by having gained sufficient unity to be remembered as such' (Casey, 'Imagining and remembering', p. 203).

living room . . . all together for once', she recalled, listening to the wireless and 'shaken to the roots' by the siren she in fact never heard. For years she told this story, which appears nowhere in her candid original document, as a true account of her early war days. And Harrisson adds that 'those who kept no records would normally distort even more'.[130]

Equally faulty are memories of Orwell elicited from associates who 'witnessed' incidents Orwell had in fact invented or who 'remembered' holding views about him they could have formed only from subsequent reading. For example, Orwell's sister detested the little she knew of his work while he was alive; her familiarity with and admiration for it came only with his posthumous fame; a BBC interview soon after Orwell's death shows how 'the sea-change also contaminated her memories of the past', now laced with retrospective approval of her brother's work. 'The past is filtered through what one subsequently learns', concludes Bernard Crick:

Cherokee chiefs read books on anthropology before being interviewed by anthropologists, and distinguished men of letters reread their early essays on Orwell just before being interviewed and then recounted them with commendable accuracy . . . Memories of a famous man in his days of obscurity can become badly confused by reading and recalling subsequent writings on him . . . It is simply very difficult to get through to genuine remembrances or re-remembrances.[131]

These caveats apply just as much to our own past. Like 'the confessing husband who reinterprets the love affairs of his past to bring them into a line of ascent culminating in his marriage', notes Berger, 'we keep reinterpreting our biography very much as the Stalinists kept rewriting the Great Soviet Encyclopedia'.[132] Such revisions may seem culpable, but they are normal and even necessary; like other historians we incessantly rewrite our own personal histories because at the time events occur we can seldom predict what or how much they will later signify.[133] Conversion can dramatically transform our whole remembered past: Augustine's *Confessions* and Newman's *Apologia pro vita sua* reveal newly periodized and reinterpreted previous lives; our own kin emerge from the conceptual cauldron of psychonanalytic revelation 'as metamorphosed figures of the Freudian pantheon'; everything in the past only *now* makes sense.[134] An autobiography is thus 'a record by oneself of what all its preceding selves have chosen to remember of their predecessors', the outcome of a dialectic 'between present "I" and past "me", at the end of which both have changed'; the psychoanalyst sees himself 'as an assistant autobiographer' who can 'point out biases in the direction of, typically, self-denigration or self-justification, and to discriminate between [the analysand's] own true voice and his learned imitations of other, typically, ancestral voices'.[135]

Revision is often as unintentional as forgetting, however. John Dean's much-touted memory unconsciously transformed what actually happened into what he himself had felt and wanted to happen; his memories like everyone's were constructed, staged, and self-centred.[136]

Unlike the schematized landscape of functional memory, events passionately recalled

[130] *Living through the Blitz*, pp. 325–6.   [131] 'Orwell and biography'.
[132] *Invitation to Sociology*, pp. 75, 71.
[133] Linton, 'Transformations of memory', p. 88.
[134] Berger, *Invitation to Sociology*, pp. 76–7. See Hankiss, 'Ontologies of the self: on the mythological re-arranging of one's life-history'; Gagnon, 'On the analysis of life accounts'.
[135] Rycroft, 'Analysis and the autobiographer', p. 541.   [136] Neisser, 'John Dean's memory', p. 157.

are often more emphatic than when originally experienced. Just as we forget or elide scenes that initially failed to strike us, we exaggerate those that did. A place may be wrongly remembered as uniformly icy and windswept if a blizzard was our most memorable experience there; the memory of Cape Town's rare 1926 snowfall, photo-enshrined in its parlours, gives a completely false impression of that city's customary climate. We mask diversity and collapse countless earlier images into a few dominant memories, accentuating any impressive characteristic and exaggerating its splendour or fragility.[137] Such emphases underpinned the classical art of memorization. 'When we see in every day life things that are petty, ordinary, and banal, we generally fail to remember them, because the mind is not being stirred by anything novel or marvellous', according to an ancient text. 'But if we see or hear something exceptionally base, dishonourable, unusual, great, unbelievable, or ridiculous, that we are likely to remember for a long time.'[138] Memory training thus concentrated on striking, vivid, even grotesque images.

Remembered places tend to converge unless highly distinctive: a score of successive scenes may conflate to one or two recalled with the generic features of them all. The visitor's memory syncretizes Oxbridge colleges, transposes Exmoor to Dartmoor, conceives the South Downs and the North Downs as one. Memory also reorders events in time, shuffling the sequence of cities visited, presenting episodes in the order they should have occurred. When calendrical precision is not essential, remembered dates are often vague or kaleidoscopic; 'long ago' or 'the other day' suffices. The recollected past is not a consecutive temporal chain but a set of discontinuous moments lifted out of the stream of time. 'We may vividly recall certain events of our past without being able to date them', Siegfried Kracauer suggests, and the more readily we recollect them the more apt we are to 'misjudge their temporal distances from the present or play havoc with their chronological order'.[139] Most people

date things by events, they don't date them by years. They don't say 'that happened in 1930' or 'that happened in 1925' or things like that. They say 'that happened the year after the old mill burned down' or 'that happened after the lightning struck the big oak and killed Farmer James' or 'that was the year we had the polio epidemic'. So naturally, of course, the things they do remember don't go in any particular sequence ... There are just bits poking up here and there.[140]

Memory retrieval is seldom sequential; we locate recalled events by association rather than by working methodically forward or backward through time, and treat the past as 'an archaeological museum of fragments ... haphazardly juxtaposed'.[141]

Whether ordered or haphazard the recollected past substantially diverges from the original experience. We can no longer accept Bergson's view that memory's function is to conserve the entire past, or Penfield's that every apprehended event can be precisely reconstituted. On the contrary, the passage of time induces qualitative memory change as well as loss. New experiences continually alter the mental schemata that shape what we have previously remembered. 'Throughout our life, we reorganize our memories and ideas of the past', write Piaget and Inhelder, 'conserving more or less the same material, but

[137] Ian Hunter, *Memory*, p. 279.
[138] *Ad Herennium* (c. 86–82 B.C.), quoted in Yates, *Art of Memory*, p. 25; also pp. 17–41.
[139] 'Time and history', p. 69. See Fraisse, *Psychology of Time*, p. 161.
[140] Christie, *By the Pricking of My Thumbs*, p. 174.
[141] Donato, 'Ruins of memory: archeological fragments and textual artifacts', p. 595.

adding other elements' that change its meaning and significance.[142] As Freud realized, 'our childhood memories show us our earliest years not as they were but as they appeared to us at the later periods when the memories were aroused'.[143] Indeed, each occasion of remembering alters memories again. Recitation likewise changes them, for 'the very act of talking about the past tends to crystallize it in specific but somewhat arbitrary language', notes Donald Spence; once related as a story, the original memory can never again be experienced as a vague Wordsworthian reverie.[144] To communicate a coherent narrative, we must not only reshape the old but create a new past. 'Far from being a time machine by which one may travel back to see what one has been made of', in Roy Schafer's phrase, the analyst (or any auditor, for that matter) puts his own stamp on our past by eliciting, and frequently retelling in his own words, a narrative shaped by his interaction with us.[145]

Other changes are inherent in maturing, ageing, and generational displacement. When we are children our parents seem wholly unlike our grandparents; as we grow up and our parents age they come increasingly to resemble them. After Proust's grandmother died, his mother appeared to take on many of her traits, partly as a function of her own old age, partly as a repository for memories once linked with the grandmother; 'the dead annex the living who become their replicas and successors'.[146] Remembered images of earlier periods, themselves previously altered, antiquate the more recent past.

The balance between our own and other people's memories also shifts with age. A world dominated by seniors endowed with memories longer and earlier than ours gives way, as we grow older, to one of juniors who share only our recent experiences. Childhood memories of the young are continually amplified by the recollections of seemingly omniscient elders, whereas the elderly, now the sole eyewitnesses of their own earlier years, enjoy incontestable memories of them. But their interpretations of recent events diverge from those of the young who share that past with them.[147] Evolving connections with various segments of time, now uniquely custodial, now contested by those with longer or briefer memories, thus alter both the content and the veracity of the past.

Since current mental processes continually reorganize memory, how can apprehension of the past be shown to differ from apprehension of the present? Piaget's answer is that experience and memory excite different temporal expectations. Action incessantly infuses present perception, altering things at will or by chance. But the past has already been enacted; no matter how skewed or modified the recall, things remain what they were and can never be revoked.[148] A sense of completedness stemming from hindsight is inescapable in memory as in history. As Walter Benjamin put it, a man who dies at the age of thirty-five is remembered 'at every point of his life [as] a man who dies at the age of thirty-five';[149] we cannot divest knowledge of his subsequent demise from our memories of his earlier years.

Prior knowledge explains why memory often disappoints. 'The images of the past that

---

[142] *Memory and Intelligence*, p. 381.
[143] 'Screen memories' (1899), 3:322. See Kris, 'Recovery of childhood memories', p. 56.
[144] *Narrative Truth and Historical Truth*, pp. 92, 173, 175.
[145] 'Narration in the psychoanalytic dialogue', p. 33.
[146] *Remembrance of Things Past*, 2:796–7. See Halbwachs, *Collective Memory*, p. 67.
[147] Kastenbaum, 'Time, death and ritual in old age', pp. 24–5; Halbwachs, *Collective Memory*, pp. 68–9.
[148] *Memory and Intelligence*, pp. 399–404.   [149] 'The storyteller', p. 100.

we recover are dated', feels de Beauvoir. 'Our life escapes us – it was freshness, novelty and bloom. And now that freshness is out of date.'[150] Retrieval falls short of initial experience. Revisiting Tintern Abbey after five years, Wordsworth regretted his failure to recapture the immediacy of his first visit there: 'An appetite; a feeling and a love, / That had no need of a remoter charm, / By thought supplied.'[151] But it was the reflections animated by the second visit that gave rise to the poem itself. Memory diminishes original experiences only when we expect them to be duplicated; its transformations can enhance them.[152] It is by relating past to present that memories become important to Proust, and to us all. 'The remembered image is combined with a moment in the present affording a view of the same object', Shattuck explains. 'Like our eyes, our memories must see double; those two images then converge in our minds into a single heightened reality.'[153]

The prime function of memory, then, is not to preserve the past but to adapt it so as to enrich and manipulate the present.[154] Far from simply holding on to previous experiences, memory helps us to understand them. Memories are not ready-made reflections of the past, but eclectic, selective reconstructions based on subsequent actions and perceptions and on ever-changing codes by which we delineate, symbolize, and classify the world around us. And recollections remote from present frameworks of thought, such as early childhood's vivid sensory experiences, or of no current consequence, such as obsolete school lessons, are truly lost beyond recall.

None the less we remember far more than we need simply to cope with ongoing life. Memory, which steals 'fire / From the fountains of the past, / To glorify the present',[155] enables us not merely to follow but to build on previous efforts, not just to survive in today's world but to elaborate our moments and days with a densely woven skein of time that makes the mortal mind seem all but imperishable.

HISTORY

> The historian does simply not come in to replenish the gaps of memory. He constantly challenges even those memories that have survived intact.
>
> Yosef Hayim Yerushalmi, *Zakhor: Jewish History and Jewish Memory*[156]

> The study of memory teaches us that all historical sources are suffused by subjectivity right from the start.
>
> Jan Vansina, 'Memory and oral tradition'[157]

History extends and elaborates memory by interpreting relics and synthesizing reports from past eyewitnesses. In its broadest sense, historical awareness concerns not only the annals of civilization but the aeons of prehistory that lack written records. Their absence

---

[150] *Old Age*, p. 407.   [151] 'Lines composed a few miles above Tintern Abbey' (1798), lines 80–2, 2:261.
[152] Donato, 'Ruins of memory', p. 580.   [153] *Proust's Binoculars*, p. 47.
[154] Hunter, *Memory*, pp. 202–3. 'Not only does the present experience rest on the past, but the present supplies the incentive for the viewing of the past' (Kris, 'Recovery of childhood memories', p. 55). See Spence, *Narrative Truth and Historical Truth*, p. 98.
[155] Tennyson, 'Ode to memory' (1830), lines 12–13, p. 211. See J. D. Hunt, 'Poetry of distance', p. 94; Kissane, 'Tennyson: passion of the past and the curse of time'.
[156] 1982, p. 94.   [157] 1980, p. 276.

does not prevent our realizing that preliterates had a history nor preclude insight into that history. Oral narratives, films, fictional tales, works of art – pictures and sculpture that represent or reflect ideas about the past – convey historical understanding of both prehistory and later times. Even in literate societies, most if not all information about the past is orally transmitted.

Voiceless nature has also had an historical career. 'Stones, trees, animals have a knowable past, but no history', thought Vico, because no conscious purposes animated that past;[158] yet historical understanding subsumes the past of non-human entities. Historical zoology, botany, geology, and astronomy lack the motivating agencies of human history, but the past they disclose is none the less 'historical'.

The substantive scope of historical apprehension also transcends conventional history, encompassing a broader perspective, a wider range of sources, and a more inclusive notion of 'truth'.[159] Our sense of the historical past comes less from history books than from the everyday things we see and do from childhood on.

> History isn't handed down,
> It's handed up ...
> History is in the bounce of a ball,
> In the flick of a skipping-rope.[160]

Beyond and around events he has personally experienced, Carl Becker's Everyman embroiders 'a more dimly seen pattern ... of things reputed to have been said and done in past times which he has not known ... Out of the most diverse threads of information, picked up in the most casual way, from the most unrelated sources ... he somehow manages, undeliberately for the most part, to fashion a history.'[161] And Everyman's history is far more pervasive than the professonals'. For all the expertise of historians and archaeologists, history remains, in Rosemary Harris's phrase, 'something of an odd, semi-fictional subject, part fact, part myth, and guesswork'.[162]

Understanding of the past embraces all modes of exploration. Just as various levels of memory merge to yield composite knowledge, so these heterogeneous historical materials – things previous to memory, beyond the range of our personal experience, or dependent on accounts by others – likewise converge in Everyman's efforts.

Perspectives on historical understanding are as diverse as its components. They include what is sometimes derogated as mythological. 'In the history of history a myth is a once valid but now discarded version of the human story', notes Becker, 'as our now valid versions will in due course be relegated to the category of discarded myths.'[163] In perceptions of India's past, there are 'no criteria for differentiating between myth and

---

[158] Berlin, *Vico and Herder*, p. 29.

[159] Pocock, 'Origins of the study of the past', p. 215. Jacques Le Goff envisages 'a total history' that 'will embrace all the studies concerned with man and time' (*Nouvelle histoire*, p. 11).

[160] W. R. Rodgers, quoted in Vicky Payne, 'Taking Ireland's history off the streets', *Observer Mag.*, 2 Dec. 1979, pp. 75–7.

[161] Becker, 'Everyman his own historian', pp. 14–15.

[162] 'How to enjoy the first lessons in developing a sense of the past', *The Times*, 31 Jan. 1973, p. 10. Historical consciousness is enlarged also by surmises about unrecorded events and those for which records are lost or destroyed; by speculations about a past which might some day happen, or one which could never have happened, like an encounter between Tamerlane and Joan of Arc; and by counter-factual ruminations generally (Keller, 'Time out: the discontinuity of historical consciousness', pp. 288–90).

[163] Becker, 'Everyman his own historian', p. 16.

history ... What the Westerner considers as history in the West, he would regard as myth in India; ... what he calls history in his own world is experienced by Indians as myth.'[164] Soothsayers and priests, storytellers and minstrels are historians too. Advocating a 'metaphorical' history, Nietzsche disparaged 'factual' explanation in favour of mythic insight from drama and fable.[165] And written history may acquire the poetic, universalizing character of myth as time outdates its specific factual content; we no longer read Gibbon as Roman history but as an eloquent meditation on human decline and fall, exemplified by Caesar's Rome.[166]

Our sense of history goes beyond knowledge to empathetic involvement. In constructing his own history, Everyman 'works with something of the freedom of a creative artist; the history which he imaginatively re-creates ... will inevitably be an engaging blend of fact and fancy', dominated by data 'that seem best suited to his interests or promise most in the way of emotional satisfaction'.[167] Professionals' insights come in much the same way, through 'a sudden perception which gradually makes sense of a whole large area of the past'. And R. W. Southern deems it 'more important that the initial perception should be sharp and vivid than that it should be true. Truth comes from error more easily than from confusion. It is only by having a vivid perception that an energetic search can begin.'[168]

History is thus both more and less than what historians study, but the discrepancies are not so great as those between memory and professional psychology. Psychologists study much besides memory, to which few of them solely devote themselves; historians' central task is the study of history, their discipline wholly defined (as is archaeology) in terms of knowledge of the past. Psychologists generally confine themselves to aspects of memory testable or replicable in the laboratory; historians study the past by scrutinizing accounts of what has happened in the real world. Most psychologists deal with a 'memory' remote from ordinary awareness; most historians deal with the past as it is normally apprehended. None the less, the divergences between history as a discipline and historical knowledge as discussed here are manifold and significant.

History and memory

Comparing these two routes to the past distresses some historians 'because they know history to be hard work while recollection seems passive, noninferential, and unverified'.[169] History differs from memory not only in how knowledge of the past is acquired and validated but also in how it is transmitted, preserved, and altered.

We accept memory as a premise of knowledge; we infer history from evidence that includes other people's memories. Unlike memory, history is not given but contingent: it

---

[164] Panikkar, 'Time and history in the tradition of India', p. 76. A more mordant view is that the 'golden Indian past is not to be possessed by inquiry; it is only to be ecstatically contemplated. The past is a religious idea, clouding intellect and painful perception, numbing the stress in bad times' (Naipaul, 'India: paradise lost', p. 15).

[165] *Use and Abuse of History*, pp. 39–42. The historian's task is not merely to render the strange familiar but to render the familiar strange, reconstituting past lives 'in all their strangeness and mystery ... to remind men of the irreducible variety of human life' (Hayden White, 'Foucault decoded', p. 50).

[166] Frye, *Great Code*, pp. 46–7.   [167] Becker, 'Everyman his own historian', p. 15.

[168] Southern, 'The historical experience', p. 771.

[169] Mink, 'Everyman his or her own annalist', p. 234.

is based on empirical sources which we can decide to reject for other versions of the past. Unless I implicitly trust my memory I must surrender any claim to knowing the past; but in the absence of validating evidence historical data can reasonably be doubted.

Ambiguity and overlap confound this distinction, however. As we have seen, 'memory' includes second-hand accounts of the past – that is, history; 'history' relies on eyewitness and other recollections – that is, memory. We treat other people's memories like history, as empirically testable, as we sometimes do our own autobiographical accounts.[170] Even if initially derived from the autobiographer's memory, external events – when things happened, who met whom, what consequences ensued – can be verified or falsified by public records; the wise autobiographer checks his memory against historical sources. But he can rely only on his memory for his past feelings about those events, for he alone is privy to such knowledge. All he can check those memories against are his own previous accounts.[171]

To discriminate the historical and memorial components of our recollections is extremely difficult. If I am unaware that part of what I remember is a bit of history cribbed from someone else, I treat it as prima-facie true, just like the rest of my memory. And even when external sources are distinguishable from primary memories, I may be disclined to treat them historically. In everyday life we accept what spouses and neighbours and colleagues tell us happened much as we accept our own memories; only when conflicting evidence or innate improbability arouse serious doubts do we subject their memorial knowledge to historical criticism.

History and memory are distinguishable less as types of knowledge than in attitudes toward that knowledge. Not only original memories but all the history they include is normally taken as given and true; not only historical but memorial sources are on occasion scrutinized for their accuracy and empirical validity.

History's collective nature sets it apart from memory, however. Whereas the past that I remember is partly shared with others, much of it is uniquely my own. But historical knowledge is by its very nature collectively produced and shared; historical awareness implies group activity. 'An isolated individual could remember no past other than his personal recollections', writes J. G. A. Pocock, whereas 'the word "past" as historians use it connotes a state of affairs of some social complexity existing over a period long enough to make it intelligible'. To remember and communicate such a past requires complex and enduring institutions. Hence 'history must be studied as a social activity'.[172]

Just as memory validates personal identity, history perpetuates collective self-awareness. To understand 'what they are or what they might become', notes Gordon Leff, groups 'define themselves through history as an individual does through memory'.[173] Indeed, the enterprise of history is crucial to social preservation. 'Since all societies are organised . . . to ensure their own continuity', collective statements about the past help to conserve existing arrangements, and the diffusion of all manner of history,

---

[170] Murphey, *Our Knowledge of the Historical Past*, pp. 10–12.
[171] Collingwood, *Idea of History*, pp. 295–6. By comparing retrospective reports with those given at the time, one might partly discount autobiographical bias (Kohli, 'Biography: account, text, method', p. 71).
[172] 'Origins of the study of the past', p. 211.   [173] *History and Social Theory*, p. 115.

whether fact or fable, fosters the feeling of belonging to coherent, stable, and durable institutions.[174]

Endurance also distinguishes historical knowledge. Whereas most memories perish with their possessors, history is potentially immortal. Indeed, preserving knowledge of the past is one of history's prime *raisons d'être*: both oral accounts and archival records have long been kept against the lapse of memory and devouring time. History is also less open to alteration than memory: memories continually change to conform with present needs, but the historical record to some extent resists deformation. To be sure, history is continually revised to take account of subsequent events and to be comprehensible to new generations, but printing preserves source materials virtually as they were.[175]

The stability of history is largely due to its dissemination in print, but much knowledge of the past survives scribal and even oral transmission more or less intact. Despite the prevalence of forgeries and copying errors, many manuscripts remain reasonably veracious accounts. Orally transmitted history cannot be checked against previous records, but residual anachronisms show that some knowledge persists largely unchanged from narrator to narrator.[176] And those who recount and receive histories – oral, scribal, and printed – rely on their being stable and faithful records, whereas we expect memory often to mislead us.

Historical knowledge also differs from memory in telling us things about the past not known to those who lived at the time. To be sure, time-transformed recollections likewise invent and discover new facts; like histories, memories review the past with present hindsight. But whereas memory is seldom consciously revised, historians deliberately reinterpret the past through the lenses of subsequent events and ideas. Both history and memory engender new knowledge, but only history intentionally sets out to do so.

History is less than the past

Historical knowledge is by its nature consensual. Because it is seen or heard in much the same form by many people, it can often be verified or falsified as memories seldom can be. Countless historical impostures have been foisted on a credulous world, but the weight of evidence ultimately corrects many errors and exposes mendacities. Its public character makes historical knowledge even of quite remote events more reliable than many eyewitness recollections of the recent past.

Yet it is impossible to recover or recount more than a tiny fraction of what has taken place, and no historical account ever corresponds precisely with any actual past. Three things limit what can be known: the immensity of the past itself, the distinction between past events and accounts of those events, and the inevitability of bias – especially presentist bias. I shall discuss each in turn.

First, no historical account can recover the totality of any past events, because their

---

[174] Pocock, 'Origins of the study of the past', p. 211. See Shils, *Tradition*, pp. 162ff; Peel, 'Making history', pp. 112–13.

[175] Kelley, *Foundations of Modern Historical Scholarship*, pp. 215–33; Eisenstein, *Printing Press as an Agent of Historical Change*, pp. 112–15; Goody and Watt, 'Consequences of literacy', pp. 57–67.

[176] J. C. Miller, 'Introduction: listening for the African past', pp. 37–49; Goody and Watt, 'Consequences of literacy', pp. 28–31; Vansina, *Oral Tradition*, p. 46.

content is virtually infinite. The most detailed historical narrative incorporates only a minute fraction of even the relevant past; the sheer pastness of the past precludes its total reconstruction. Most information about the past was never recorded at all, and most of the rest was evanescent. The historian must accept Herbert Butterfield's 'tremendous truth – the impossibility of history':

> The ploughman whom Gray saw, plodding his weary way, the rank and file of Monmouth's rebel crowd – every man of them a world in himself, a mystery of personality . . . – these have left no memorial and all that we know about them is just enough to set us guessing and wondering. Things by which we remember an old friend – his peculiar laugh, his way of drawing his hand through his hair, his whistle in the street, his humour – we cannot hope to recapture in history [just as we] cannot hope to read the hearts of half-forgotten kings. The Memory of the world is not a bright, shining crystal, but a heap of broken fragments, a few fine flashes of light that break through the darkness.[177]

Second, no account can recover the past as it was, because the past was not an account; it was a set of events and situations. As the past no longer exists, no account can ever be checked against it, but only against other accounts of that past; we judge its veracity by its correspondence with other reports, not with the events themselves. Historical narrative is not a portrait of what happened but a story about what happened. The historian does not even select from the totality of what has happened (*res gestae*), but from other accounts of what happened (*historia rerum gestarum*); in this respect, so-called primary sources come no closer to the reality of the past than derivative chronicles do. No process of verification can totally satisfy us that we know the truth about the past, for we accept or reject any account solely on the basis of its internal plausibility and its conformity with other known and trusted accounts. In short, we cannot refute Munz's sceptical view that 'any particular event . . . can be said to have occurred only because somebody thought it did', of Lévi-Strauss's assertion that 'historical fact has no objective reality; it only exists as . . . retrospective reconstruction'.[178]

This is not to deny that historical consensus and collective memory are anchored in reality and provide real knowledge of the past. Indeed, it is only our sense of cumulative temporal experience that gives present judgements any meaning; 'without it, there could be no answer to any question, nor any question to be answered, because there could be no such thing as fact and no intelligible discourse', C. I. Lewis concludes. 'Without genuinely knowable past experience [and] its relevance to the future, we could have no such sense of empirical reality.'[179] But just as recollection never strictly corresponds with original events, no historical account strictly corresponds with them; *historia rerum gestarum* is not *res gestae*.

Historians have been reluctant to face this epistemological limitation partly because of their need to see themselves as robustly commonsensical. Even J. H. Hexter, usually critical of his fellow historians' scientific self-ascription, takes refuge in an imagined dialogue that trivializes the issue:

---

[177] Butterfield, *Historical Novel*, pp. 14–15.
[178] Munz, *Shapes of Time*, pp. 184–5, 204–13, quotation on p. 209; Claude Lévi-Strauss (1965), quoted in ibid., p. 186. See von Leyden, 'Categories of historical understanding', pp. 55–9.
[179] *Analysis of Knowledge and Valuation*, pp. 361–2. See McCullagh, *Justifying Historical Descriptions*, pp. 26–7.

PHILOSOPHER (*loud and clear*): Men cannot really know the past.

HISTORIAN (*stupidly*): What did you say?

PHILOSOPHER (*irritably*): I said, 'Men cannot really know the past', and you know damn well that's what I said,

assuming 'a kind of knowing about the past' that makes communication possible and is 'good enough' for historians, who should 'mind their own business' and not worry about philosophy[180] – a comment that admits and then shrugs off the problem.

Third, historical knowledge however communal and verifiable is also invariably subjective, biased both by its narrator and by its audience. Unlike memory or relics, history usually depends on someone else's eyes and voice: we see it through an interpreter who stands between past events and our apprehension of them. To be sure, written history circumscribes the narrator's tyranny by allowing his audience access to original sources: since distant predecessors can communicate to us in their own words we are not entirely dependent, as are folk in oral societies, on the views of tradition transmitted by immediate precursors. 'Not one but a hundred generations', in W. Lloyd Warner's words, 'are now sending their own delayed interpretations of what both they and we are.'[181] Whether narrators are single and recent or multiple and spread over time, however, we cannot escape the framework they impose on the past.

Nor can we escape our own. The narrator's perspective and predilections shape his choice and use of historical materials; our own determine what we make of them. The past we know or experience is always contingent on our own views, our own perspective, above all our own present. Just as we are products of the past, so is the known past an artifact of ours. No perceiver, however immersed in the past, can divest himself of his own knowledge and assumptions, or 'recall past events without in some subtle fashion relating them to what he needs or desires to do'.[182] Our hopes and fears, expertise and intentions continually shape the historical past as they do our memories. To 'explain' the past to themselves and their audience, historians go beyond the actual record to frame hypotheses in present-day modes of thought. Editing data from his chosen era, synthesizing commentaries, the historian reaches an understanding distinctively of his own time. Such biases have creative as well as limiting implications, to be sure, implications shortly to be examined; the point here is that bias is inescapable.

Above all, the passage of time that has outdated the past limits our understanding of it, for everything we see is filtered through present-day mental lenses. Different presuppositions and modes of discourse constrain both the historian's understanding and his ability to communicate to those of another age. 'We are moderns and our words and thoughts can not but be modern', noted Maitland, 'it is too late for us to be early English'; hence we cannot see the past with their eyes.[183] 'No recipe exists from which to concoct the

---

[180] *History Primer*, pp. 338–9.   [181] *The Living and the Dead*, p. 217.

[182] Becker, 'Everyman his own historian', p. 12. 'There can be no history without a point of view, even if it is only that the historian should have no point of view' (Leff, *History and Social Theory*, p. 91). Quentin Skinner shows how the unconscious application of paradigms inapplicable to the past unavoidably contaminates historical studies ('Meaning and understanding in the history of ideas', pp. 4–28). Indeed, McCullagh holds that historians justify their conclusions less by their coherence with other accepted beliefs than by present observable evidence; they have much greater confidence in what they perceive than in the truth of written history (*Justifying Historical Descriptions*, pp. 91–2).

[183] *Township and Borough* (1898), p. 22.

thoughts, values, and emotions of people who lived in the past', cautions another historian. 'Even having steeped ourselves in the literature of the period, worn its clothes, and slept on its beds, we never shed [today's] perspectives and values.'[184] And today's perspective makes us more likely to misinterpret the past as remoteness multiplies its anachronisms.

The language of historical accounts also restructures images of the past. The historian translates his impressions into words; to absorb these impressions, the reader or auditor reconverts the words into images – but the images differ from the historian's originals. Any distance – in time, in space, in culture, in point of view – widens the gulf between narrator and audience. And every language imposes its own conventions on users' sense of the past, conventions that reshape their understanding or the original record.[185]

Dilemmas over the recent revision of the Bible highlight the errors that can result from anachronism. Thanks to its rhetorical virtues and to liturgical traditionalism, the King James version has survived almost four centuries. But time has made much of its language archaic and obsolete; few modern readers have the historical skill to understand it, and even they find the text anachronistic because scholarship has revealed so many mistakes and errors of translation or omission. King Solomon sounds splendid with peacocks, but once one knows the 1611 translators got it wrong, the peacocks must be replaced by monkeys (they should actually be baboons).[186] Anachronistic unintelligibility is the fate not only of fixed written texts but also of faithful oral accounts, incomprehensible even to their narrators when their language is obsolete or refers to customs now extinct.[187]

Lastly, hindsight paradoxically limits our ability to understand the past by giving us greater knowledge than people of the time could have had. 'Can we really be fair to men of the past', asked A. F. Pollard, 'knowing what they could not know? Can we, indeed, understand them at all ... with our minds prepossessed by a knowledge of the result?'[188] The question raises an issue that transcends the limits to historical understanding, for it implies that bias does not merely reduce the historical past but also enlarges it. To these additions I now turn.

History is more than the past

Hindsight as well as anachronism shapes historical interpretations. To explain the past to the present means coping not only with shifting perceptions, values, and languages, but also with developments after the period under review. We are bound to see the Second World War differently in 1985 than in 1950, not merely because masses of new evidence have come to light, but also because the years have unfolded further consequences – the Cold War, the United Nations, the revival of the German and Japanese economies.

In translating knowledge into modern terms and in using knowledge previously

---

[184] Sherfy, 'The craft of history', p. 5. 'We cannot arrive at a full understanding of the past because the past is something outside our experience, something that is other ... The men who lived then were different from us' (Vansina, *Oral Tradition*, pp. 185–6). See also Richard Ronsheim, 'Is the past dead?' *Museum News*, 53:36 (1974), 62.

[185] Scholes and Kellogg, *Nature of Narrative*, p. 83.

[186] Henry Mitchell, 'Monkeying with the King James Bible', *IHT*, 25 Aug. 1982, p. 5.

[187] Vansina, *Oral Tradition*, pp. 44–5.

[188] 'Historical criticism' (1920), p. 29. See also Blaas, *Continuity and Anachronism*, p. 281.

unavailable, the historian discovers both what has been forgotten about the past or improperly pieced together and things that no one ever knew before.[189] Concepts like 'the Renaissance' or 'classical antiquity' were 'not perceived to exist, at the beginning of the process, and . . . could only be fully recognized and articulated at the end of it', notes R. S. Humphreys. 'People and societies are caught up in processes which can be perceived and described only in hindsight [and] documents are ripped out of their original context of purpose and function . . . to illustrate a pattern which might well not have been meaningful to any of their authors.'[190]

Knowing the future of the past forces the historian to shape his account to come out as things have done. The tempo, contractions, and time scale of his narrative reflect his retrospective knowledge, for he 'must not only know something of the outcomes of the events that concern him; he must use what he knows in telling his story'. Citing the 1951 National League baseball pennant race, when the Giants pulled up from last place at mid-season to a first-place tie on the final day, Hexter shows that 'unless the writer has the outcome in mind as he writes the story, he will not know how to adapt the proportions of his story to the actual historical tempo'.[191]

The very process of communication demands creative change to make the past convincing and intelligible. Like memory, history conflates, compresses, exaggerates; unique moments of the past stand out, uniformities and minutiae fade away. 'Time is foreshortened, details selected and highlighted, action concentrated, relations simplified, not to alter or distort the actors and events but to bring them to life and to give them meaning . . . amid the uncompassable multiplicity of the past.'[192]

The contingent and discontinuous facts of the past become intelligible only when woven together as stories. Even the most empirical chroniclers invent narrative structures to give a shape to time. 'Res gestae may well be one damned thing after another', Munz argues, 'but it cannot possibly appear as such', for all meaning would then be extruded from it.[193] And because intelligible stories emphasize explanatory linkages and play down the role of accidents, history as known to us appears more predictable than we have reason to believe the past was.[194]

Unless history displays conviction, interest, and involvement, it will not be understood or attended to. That is why subjective interpretation, while limiting knowledge, is also essential to its communication. Indeed, the better a narrative exemplifies an historian's point of view the more credible his account. History is persuasive because it is organized by and filtered through individual minds, not in spite of that fact; subjective interpretation gives it life and meaning. 'Rhetoric is ordinarily deemed icing on the cake of history', but

---

[189] Modern interpretations of past events are both more intelligible to moderns and psychologically 'truer': 'charisma' better explains the rise of a dynasty than the relics it possessed, although people at the time believed in relics and would have found charisma incomprehensible. To understand what happened, we have to add thoughts of our own which did not exist back then (Munz, *Shapes of Time*, pp. 80, 93).

[190] 'The historian, his documents, and the elementary modes of historical thought', p. 12. The historian discovers not only what has been completely forgotten but also 'what, until he discovered it, no one ever knew to have happened at all' (Collingwood, *Idea of History*, p. 238). See Danto, *Analytical Philosophy of History*, pp. 115, 132; von Leyden, 'Categories of historical understanding', pp. 68–70.

[191] 'Rhetoric of history', p. 378. This invalidates Spence's distinction in *Narrative Truth and Historical Truth*. History is no less subject to deformation than any other narrative.

[192] Arragon, 'History's changing image', p. 230.   [193] *Shapes of Time*, p. 239.

[194] Mink, 'Narrative form as a cognitive instrument', p. 147.

in fact 'it is mixed right into the batter. It affects not merely the outward appearance of history, ... but its inward character, its essential function – its capacity to convey knowledge of the past as it actually was.' Historical knowledge depends on emotive language, for if the historian fails to communicate what he believes it will not become publicly available or testable by other historians, but remain disjointed, arbitrary, unintelligible.[195]

Hexter shows how footnotes, quotations, and lists of names serve such rhetorical needs. Quotations confront the reader with a veritable slice of the past, to make him not simply respond 'Yes', but exclaim 'Yes, indeed!' Omitting attributions makes a list of names convincingly allusive:

The Christian Revival, that intensification of religious sentiment and concern, . . . in its full span had room for Cardinal Ximenes and Girolamo Savonarola, Martin Luther and Ignatius Loyola, the Reformed churches and the Jesuits, John of Leiden and Paul IV, Thomas Cranmer and Edmund Campion and Michael Servetus.

We are deliberately *not* told who they are, but by implication, to 'draw on the reservoir of your knowledge of the times in which these men lived to give meaning to this list'. What matters is not just the names but their order, whose meaning could have been emphasized by listing identifying characteristics *instead* of names:

The pre-Reformation cardinal who reformed the church in Spain, and the pre-Reformation monk who was burned at the stake for his reforming efforts in Florence; the first great figure of Reformation and the first great figure of the Counter Reformation, . . .

or the list might have included names *and* explications:

Cardinal Ximenes, the pre-Reformation cardinal who reformed the church in Spain, and Girolamo Savonarola, the pre-Reformation monk who was burned at the stake for his reforming efforts in Florence; Luther, the first great figure of the Reformation and Loyola, the first . . .

Each list is correct and apposite. But instead of alerting the reader to give them meaning himself, the more overtly informative lists would have signalled: 'Stop drawing on the reservoir of your knowledge. I have already told you how I want you to think about these men', thus damming up his imagination rather than letting it flow freely. The historian may have erred in supposing readers would know enough to make sense of the names, in gambling that the connotative list would communicate better than the exhaustive one. But the point is that all historians constantly have to judge how much their audience already knows, when to be allusive rather than precise, or sacrifice fact for evocative force.[196] To do so effectively 're-creates the past in the present, and gives us, not the familiar remembered things, but the glittering intensity of the summoned-up hallucination'.[197]

Chronology and narrative

It is so customary to think of the historical past in terms of narratives, sequences, dates, and chronologies that we are apt to suppose these things attributes of the past itself. But they are not; we ourselves put them there, as shown in Chapter 2. The ability and propensity to order events in datable sequences is a relatively recent cultural achievement.

[195] Hexter, 'Rhetoric of history', pp. 390, 380–1.   [196] Ibid., pp. 386–9.   [197] Frye, *Great Code*, p. 227.

Historical facts are timeless and discontinuous until woven together in stories. We do not experience a flow of time, only a succession of situations and events. Much historical apprehension remains almost as temporally vague as memory, lacking dates or even sequences.[198] In oral narrative calendric specificity is rare: with little opportunity to reflect or compare, narrators and auditors overlook or alter temporal distances. Without dates or permanent records to refer back to, one can neither assess the duration of past events nor verify their order; oral narratives telescope, expand, and rearrange segments of the past in line with the significance attributed to them.[199] Perceived changes tend to cluster within discrete periods separated by long intervals of stasis, with important events relegated either to a mythic time of origin or to the very recent and hence recollectable past. Thus dynastic founders get credit both for their own deeds and for their successors', whose own times are passed over without comment. The repetitive regularity of most of the orally transmitted past is consistent with the belief that 'nothing happened' between the beginnings and recent times. By contrast, many modern literate historians focus on middle periods whose incremental changes shed light on ongoing historical processes.[200]

The temporal traits of oral communication persisted well into the scribal age, when chronicles were still mainly read aloud. Medieval audiences shuffled Caesar, Charlemagne, Alexander, David, and other ancients like cards in a pack; it took two centuries of printing to habituate Europeans to the mental process of reaching back through an orderly sequence of chapters in history.[201] Even in modern book-learning societies, the past for most people is largely chaotic and episodic, a hodgepodge of chronologically unknown or mistakenly connected figures and events. In this heaving and formless sea stand a few islands of stratified narrative, on which we huddle for calendric security.

Time is, to be sure, linear and directional. The histories of all things begin in a more or less remote past and extend in an unalterable sequence until they cease to exist or to be remembered. Sequential order potentially gives everything a temporal place, lends history shape and form, enables us to set our own lives in the context of external events. But even when writing made dating easier, equally spaced segmentation of the past was long limited mainly to tax collecting, census-taking, and the periodic selection of office-holders.[202]

It was the need for a firmly based sacred calendar, most manifest in efforts to calculate the occurrence of Easter, that made chronology of major consequence. Although the Christian calendar was not fully accepted for more than a millennium after its construction in the sixth century, it enabled medieval and later chroniclers to overcome the deficiencies of oral narrative. Annalistic accounts replaced event-dominated chronicles; year-by-year frameworks became more important than the episodes they framed. Specific happenings – a plague, a coronation, an invention, a royal birth – were assigned to particular years in these annuaries, and when no event seemed significant enough, enumerated years were simply left blank; what mattered was the enumeration itself. Representing the years of our

---

[198] Mink, 'History and fiction as modes of comprehension', pp. 545–6; Goody, *Domestication of the Savage Mind*, pp. 91–2; Kracauer, 'Time and history'.

[199] Henige, *Chronology of Oral Tradition*, pp. 2–9.

[200] J. C. Miller, 'Listening for the African past', pp. 16, 37. Oral societies perceive the past in quite different ways, however; see Maurice Bloch, 'The past and the present in the present'; Peel, 'Making history'.

[201] Eisenstein, 'Clio and Chronos: an essay on the making and breaking of history-book time', p. 52; Peter Gay, *Enlightenment*, 1:344–5; Hay, *Annalists and Historians*, p. 91.

[202] Goody, *Domestication of the Savage Mind*, pp. 91–2.

Lord unfolding from a known beginning toward a predetermined end, the chronology possessed a God-given fullness and continuity in its own right.[203]

Such chronology dominated historical texts through the eighteenth century. When things happened, who succeeded whom, how long epochs lasted – questions like these gave rise to countless tables of dates based on dynasties and Olympiads, consulates and tribunates, the lineal descendants of Romulus and Remus, Adam or Abraham, Noah or Aeneas. But growing conflicts between Christian and scientific history made the calendric commingling of the mythical with the verifiable, of cosmic and sacred with secular events, seem increasingly futile and absurd.[204]

A mystique about the start and end of millennia, centuries, and decades still permeates thought. From millennial forebodings preceding the year 1000, a kind of decimal determinism came to ascribe reality to epochs neatly demarcated by century, with profound *fin-de-siècle* malaise around 1800 and 1900.[205] Recently, even decades have become clothes-horses for calendric fashions. We attribute to the 'Gay' nineties, the 'Depression' thirties, the 'Swinging' sixties distinctive modes of life, particular personalities that give way abruptly at the decade's end to another unique set of features. What began as an identifying shorthand – fifth-century Athens, seventeenth-century England – has become a retrospectively defining framework. Like other synthetic constructs, such as 'the Middle Ages' or 'the Renaissance', calendric stereotypy hardens and reifies thought about the past, the nineteenth century or the 1930s becoming a 'thing' like a battle or a birthplace, and the cause of causes.[206]

These excesses aside, we are apt to forget how much we owe the chronologists: the clock, the calendar, and the numbered page have so accustomed us to chronological sequence that we nowadays take its value almost for granted. But only the printing press and the spread of literacy secured the acceptance and fixity of temporal order. And it took centuries of painstaking correlation from primary sources to provide the ready-made sequences on which we now depend.[207]

Chronology or 'history-book time' until recently encouraged the educated to view the past as an all-inclusive narrative. Each of us early learned to use it 'to sort out and arrange almost any portion of the past he encounters, to find his ancestors or to "find himself"', notes an historian.[208] A sequence of readily identifiable monarchs makes Britain the fortunate possessor, in Richard Cobb's view, of 'a national time scale immediately understandable to any English child'.[209] Another writer recalls that her 1950s Oxford course 'began at the beginning of English history' and went 'on in a nice straight line without any gaps', providing 'an orderly, chronological image, ... a nice, linear,

---

[203] Hay, *Annalists and Historians*, pp. 22–7, 38–42; Mink, 'Everyman his or her own annalist', pp. 233–4. But even after the Middle Ages, deeds and charters were dated by regnal years rather than *anno Domini* because the king's coronation was a more recent and publicly remembered date (Clanchy, *From Memory to Written Record*, p. 240).

[204] Eisenstein, 'Clio and Chronos', p. 43; J. W. Johnson, 'Chronological writing', pp. 137, 145. For confusions over Scriptural time, see Hazard, *European Mind*, pp. 43–7.

[205] Kermode, *Sense of an Ending*, pp. 96–8. Fischer, *Historians' Fallacies*, p. 145. An early instance of ordering by centuries was Alexandre Lenoir's post-Revolutionary disposition of French historical treasures in his Musée des Monuments (Bann, *Clothing of Clio*, p. 83). On the *fin-de-siècle*, see Chapter 7, p. 379 below.

[206] Butterfield, *Man on His Past*, p. 136.

[207] Johnson, 'Chronological writing', p. 145; Grafton, 'Joseph Scaliger and historical chronology'.

[208] Eisenstein, 'Clio and Chronos', p. 59.   [209] 'Becoming a historian', pp. 21–2.

uninterrupted memory'.[210] My own school-boy perspective framed Western civilization from the Egyptians and Babylonians up to the twentieth century. Many epochs in this continuum were scarcely known to me, but the sequence made them seem readily retrievable. Charts aligning pharoahs and kings and presidents in one chronological column with discoveries and inventions or poets and painters in another bolstered faith that all history was knowable because datable.

Reliance on chronology was sometimes rigid or simplistic, to be sure. Certain American history school-books, for example, evaluated each president at a point in the text corresponding to the year of his death, regardless of when he had served in office or what was currently going on.[211] But chronology was the keystone that enabled most students to see history as an interlinked, continuous process. This faith was epitomized in the so-called 'Western Civilization' course that set before undergraduates the sum total of Euro-American history – as one historian put it, 'a panorama ... true to ... the whole scheme of things entire as we know them'.[212]

Dates and chronology are now out of fashion. Especially since the Second World War, human history has been seen to follow not one line but those of many different cultures, impossible or pointless to lump within a common sequence. The Western Civilization course declined along with the ethnocentrism which viewed that civilization as canonically pre-eminent; historians discovered not only the Third World but the West's previously neglected 'minorities' – women, children, Jews, peasants, blacks.[213] New emphases on economic, social, and intellectual history further vitiated the relevance of chronology: cultures and ideologies were less datable than kings and conquests. Increasingly accessible and germane, these new-found aspects of the past 'impinge on the modern consciousness from so many directions', concludes Eisenstein, 'that they tax the capacity of the human intelligence to order them coherently'.[214]

One response to this dilemma is to scrap narrative history entirely, as Lively's plausible headmaster urges a history teacher:

'Children under fifteen just aren't ready for a chronological approach to history. And yet here we are teaching them history as narrative, one thing after another.'
'That's what it is. One thing does happen after another.'
'Yes, but that's a very sophisticated concept . . . – children can't grasp it. So you . . . give it to them in nice digestible chunks, as themes or projects. You teach them about revolutions, or civil wars, or whatever.'[215]

The dating of events, not long ago the *sine qua non* of historical knowledge, has been so

---

[210] Lively, 'Children and the art of money', p. 200.

[211] Fitzgerald, *America Revised*, p. 50.

[212] Preserved Smith, 'The unity of knowledge and the curriculum' (1913), quoted in Allardyce, 'Rise and fall of the Western Civilization course', pp. 697–8.

[213] Allardyce, 'Rise and fall of the Western Civilization course', p. 719; Rossabi, 'Comment' [on Allardyce]. The textbook market for world history is still only 20 to 25 per cent that for 'Western Civilization', however (Karen J. Winkler, 'Textbooks: the rise and decline of Western Civilization' *American Historical Association Perspectives*, 21:3 (1983), 11–13); a community college history teacher in the South notes that 'Western Civ continues to thrive out in the boondocks' (Evelyn Edson, 'Reflections on the history of Western Civilization', ibid., 22:2 (1984), p. 16).

[214] 'Clio and Chronos', p. 63.

[215] *Road to Lichfield*, pp. 87, 188. I have conflated the teacher's discussion with the headmaster and her subsequent retelling of it.

far abandoned that most French schoolchildren are said to know neither that the French Revolution began in 1789 nor to what century that year belongs.[216] More than one person in three interviewed recently in Guildford, England, had little sense of a datable past, and virtually none of any time before their grandparents' day. 'My grandfather went to school with' a past owner, one respondent remarked of a seventeenth-century structure, so 'the building must go back a very long time, perhaps to about 1880'. Some linked still more ancient buildings with their parents and grandparents. 'I'm not surprised that it is 400 years old instead of 100', said one when told of his underestimate. 'Old is old, it doesn't matter how old.'[217]

Narrative's linear nature does constrain historical understanding. The auditor or reader has to follow a single track from start to finish. But *awareness* of the past involves more than linear movement; social, cultural, and myriad other circumstances are superimposed on the narrative, together with histories of other peoples, other institutions, other ideas. While historical narration is one-dimensional, the past is multiform, much more complex than any sequential story line.[218]

Yet historical and other stories have moved well beyond the straightforward, unilinear, annalistic framework inherited from chronologists. Historical intelligibility requires not merely past events occurring at particular times, but a coherent story in which many events are skipped, others are coalesced, and temporal sequence is often subordinated to explanation and interpretation.[219] Just as we think back and cast ahead in recapitulating the remembered past, so do historical narratives back-track to clarify causal connections. Such 'polychronicity', in Dale Porter's term, matches our intuition that the sequential structure alone cannot capture complex historical reality.[220] Narrative history holds great appeal, James Henretta suggests, 'because its mode of cognition approximates the reality of everyday life; most readers view the past in the same manner as they comprehend their own existence – and ... in terms of a series of overlapping in interwoven life-stories'.[221]

Historians weary of cliometrics, of deterministic models, and of psycho-history have recently rediscovered the virtues of narrative. But they mainly eschew the once-popular broad sweep over entire cultures or nations, now condemned as egregiously simplistic, to scrutinize particular institutions and arenas circumscribed in time and space – Montaillou's handful of Pyrenean peasants over two decades in the fourteenth century is the classic example. Concerned with the lives and loves of the poor and obscure, armed with new kinds of source materials and insights derived from fiction and symbolism and psychoanalysis, the new narrative historians seek to shed light on the inner realities of past societies. But the focus is sometimes so narrow that 'case studies' seem eccentric

---

[216] Thomas Kamm, 'French debate teaching of history', *IHT*, 11 Apr. 1980, p. 6. 'They ask me a question, 16-year-olds', says a French history teacher – 'the Hundred Years' War, was that in 1914–18?' (in Brian Moynahan, 'Teaching: it's trendy to be trad', *Sunday Times*, 10 Feb. 1985, p. 15).

[217] Reid Bishop, 'Perception and Importance of Time in Architecture', pp. 149, 190.

[218] Frank Kermode, 'Time and narrative', lectures at Architectural Association, London, 8 and 15 Mar. 1982.

[219] Munz, *Shapes of Time*, pp. 28–43. See also Strout, *Veracious Image*, pp. 9–10.

[220] *Emergence of the Past: A Theory of Historical Explanation*, pp. 113–14. See also Goodman, 'Twisted tales; or, story, study and symphony'.

[221] 'Social history as lived and written', pp. 1318–19.

rather than characteristic; failing to relate the lives and events they treat to larger trends, they further fragment knowledge of the past.[222]

Yet in forgoing dates and narrative much is lost; events are jumbled into a grab-bag of epochs and empires, significant figures and social movements cut adrift from any particular period.[223] So-called thematic history – for example, Revolutions that lump together the Puritan, the French, the American, the Russian, the Cuban – traces illuminating parallels but plays down the fact that people at *each* of these times lived lives, acted from motives, and fashioned milieux that were distinctively different. Understanding the past demands some awareness of the temporal location of people and things; a chronological framework clarifies, places things in context, underscores the essential uniqueness of past events. The way history is now taught, with 'glittering pearls of Romans, cavemen, the battles of the First World War, medieval monks, and Stonehenge, suspended in temporal, non-causative isolation, hardly enhance[s] appreciation of the necklace of time'.[224] The pearls of history take their value not merely from being many and lustrous, but from being arranged in a causal narrative sequence; the narrative lends the necklace meaning as well as beauty.

History, fiction, and faction

The most pellucid pearls of historical narrative are often found in fiction, long a major component of historical understanding. More people apprehend the past through historical novels, from Walter Scott to Jean Plaidy, than through any formal history.[225] Some novels use history as a backdrop for imaginary characters; others fictionalize the lives of actual figures, inserting invented episodes among real events; still others distort, add, and omit. As in science fiction, some fictional pasts are paradigms of the present, other exotically different; both invent pasts for readers' delectation. Yet historical novelists also declare intentions similar to historians', striving for verisimilitude to help readers feel and know the past.

Many historians consider analogies with fiction even more invidious than comparisons with memory. Their distaste is the greater because, as we have seen, they cannot avoid 'fictional' rhetoric in their own narratives. Resembling novelists as story-tellers, historians seek to distance themselves as scholars, emphasizing that history is scrupulous to the facts of the past and open to the scrutiny of other observers, whereas fiction is heedless of both constraints.[226]

Both the distinction and the distaste are recent, however. In former times, history and fiction often coalesced or conveyed mutually supportive insights. Oral rhapsodists transmit history in much the same fashion as chroniclers, and with equal credibility.[227] Aristotle

---

[222] Stone, 'Revival of narrative' (1979). See also Jerry White, 'History Workshop 3: beyond autobiography', and Chapter 7, p. 367 below.

[223] 'In the minds of modern illiterates ... who know how to read and write and even teach in schools and at universities, history is present but blurred, in a state of strange confusion. Molière becomes a contemporary of Napoleon, Voltaire a contemporary of Lenin' (Milosz, 'Nobel Lecture, 1980', p. 12; see Chapter 6, below, p. 349).

[224] P. J. Fowler, 'Archaeology, the public and the sense of the past', p. 67.

[225] 'Scott and Dumas will always have a larger history class than any two regular historians you care to name' (Ernest Baker, *Guide to Historical Fiction* (1968), p. viii). See Leah Leneman, 'History as fiction', *History Today*, 30:1 (1980), 52–5.

[226] Hexter, 'Rhetoric of history', p. 381.   [227] Vansina, *Oral Tradition*, pp. 32–6.

termed fiction, showing what might and explaining how it might have happened, superior to history, which more prosaically showed what had happened. Instancing Homer's *Iliad*, Erasmus commended pagan historians for devising 'appropriate' fictional dialogue, 'for everyone accepts that they are allowed to put speeches into the mouths of their characters' (Erasmus allowed Christian historians less scope for invention).[228] Style and language mattered more than fidelity to historical facts; through the eighteenth century, history was read less for what it said about the past than for how it was said.[229]

The segregation of historical from fictional narrative was a by-product of late-Renaissance concern about the validity and accuracy of historical sources. Previously fused in classical and medieval epic, the two genres were increasingly segregated into 'history' (actual events open to scrutiny from other sources) and 'poetry' or 'romance' (which eschewed any pretence to historical fidelity). The aristocracy in late medieval France recorded its ideology in prose, the preferred language of factuality.[230] Others preferred fiction, for 'the poet may say or sing things, not as they were but as they ought to have been', as *Don Quixote*'s Samson remarks, while 'the historian must write things, not as they ought to be, but as they have been, without adding or taking aught from the truth'.[231] Constrained to seem faithful to known facts, historians surrendered the authorial omniscience that epic bards had had. And as history retreated to the arid confines of empirical rigour, novelists took over the richer if more fanciful aspects of the past that historians relinquished.[232] 'To make the past present, to bring the distant near, . . . to invest with the reality of human flesh and blood, . . . to call up our ancestors before us with all their peculiarities of language, manners, and garb, to show us over their houses, to seat us at their tables, to rummage their old-fashioned wardrobes', as Macaulay put it, 'these parts of the duty which properly belongs to the historian, have been appropriated by the historical novelist.'[233]

As history's handmaid fiction gained general acclaim in the nineteenth century. Scott's imaginative empathy with the past made history itself enormously popular; he taught that 'bygone ages . . . were actually filled by living men, . . . with colour in their cheeks, with passions in their stomach', as Carlyle attested, 'not by protocols, state-papers, controversies and abstractions'.[234]

The historical novel not only made history vivid; it was held a more trustworthy guide to the past. 'Out of the fictitious book I get the expression of the life of the time – the old times live again', Thackeray asserted. 'Can the heaviest historian do more for me?'[235] Fiction dealt with common everyday things as well as with the momentous episodes to which history was mostly confined. 'I would have History familiar rather than heroic', echoed his Henry Esmond.[236] No wonder the Marxist critic Georg Lukács commended Scott. The poetic awakening of ordinary people caught up in great historical events mattered more

[228] Fornara, *Nature of History in Ancient Greece and Rome*, pp. 94–5, 135, 163–5; Erasmus, *Copia*, Bk II, 24:649. See Gilmore, *Humanists and Jurists*, pp. 95–6; Bolgar, 'Greek legacy', p. 460.
[229] Cochrane, *Historians and Historiography in the Italian Renaissance*, pp. 488–90.
[230] Spiegel, 'Forging the past: the language of historical truth in the Middle Ages', pp. 271, 277.
[231] Cervantes (1615), II, Ch. 3, 2:21.   [232] Scholes and Kellogg, *Nature of Narrative*, pp. 265–6; also p. 252.
[233] 'Hallam' (1828), 1:115. See Sanders, *Victorian Historical Novel*, pp. 4–5.
[234] Carlyle, 'Sir Walter Scott' (1838), 3:214. See Honour, *Romanticism*, pp. 192–3; Peardon, *Transition in English Historical Writing*, p. 215.
[235] *English Humourists of the Eighteenth Century* (1853), p. 78.   [236] *Henry Esmond* (1852), Bk I, Ch. 1, p. 46.

than the events themselves; through the humble annals of the poor, readers could re-experience what led men of the past to think, feel, and act as they did.[237] To bring out 'the nature and power of a people's genius', academic history should give way to historical fiction.[238]

Scholars turned novelist the better to convey the past to their readers. Newman, Wiseman, and Kingsley wrote historical fiction to get across their religious messages – the holiness of the medieval church, the need to restore it in contemporary creeds – to the widest public in the most convincing way.[239] In their means if not their ends the Oxford Tractarians saw eye to eye with Hegel, who praised novels for making the past accessible to those with little learning.[240]

That the novelist deliberately invented was held a virtue; his past was more vital than the historian's *because* it was partly self-created. So profoundly did the popular demand for imaginative views of the past permeate nineteenth-century fiction that many identified it wholly with the past; a realistic contemporary novel, the Goncourts said, was simply an historical novel about the present.[241]

Historical fiction found its staunchest advocate, however, in a twentieth-century historian. 'The past as it exists for all of us is history synthesised by the imagination, and fixed into a picture by something that amounts to fiction', wrote Butterfield. The historical novel fulfilled two needs. First, it let readers *feel* the past as formal history could not:

The life that fills the street with bustle, that makes every corner of a slum a place of wonder and interest, the life that is a sad and gay, weary and thrilling thing in every hillside cottage, is a dim blurred picture in a history. Because of this, history cannot come so near to human hearts and human passions as a good novel can; its very fidelity to facts makes it ... farther away from the heart of things ... To make a bygone age live again, history must not merely be eked out by fiction; ... it must be turned into a novel.[242]

Second, fiction put readers in the past like people of the time, who could not know what was coming next. Encumbered with hindsight, the historian was not content to let the past tell its own tale but hauled it 'into relationships with the whole of subsequent development'; thus 'the reader does not lose himself in the past; he stands aside to compare it with the present', and seeing from a distance a world finished and ended he is forcibly reminded that he is not in the past.[243]

It is not enough to know that Napoleon won a certain battle; if history is to come back to us as a human thing we must see him on the eve of battle eagerly looking to see which way the dice will fall ... The victory that is achieved on one day must not be regarded as being inevitable the night before ... To the men of 1807 the year 1808 was a mystery and an unexplored tract; ... to study the year 1807 remembering all the time what happened in 1808 ... is to miss the adventure and the great uncertainties and the element of gamble in their lives; where we cannot help seeing the certainty of a desired issue, the men of the time were all suspense ... History does not always give us [these] irrecoverable personal things; but we know they existed.

---

[237] Lukács, *Historical Novel*, especially p. 44.
[238] *Bentley's Miscellany* (1859), quoted in Sanders, *Victorian Historical Novel*, p. 15.
[239] Sanders, *Victorian Historical Novel*, pp. 120–47, referring to Kingsley's *Hypatia* (1852–3), Wiseman's *Fabiola* (1854), and Newman's *Callista* (1855).
[240] Cited in Lukács, *Historical Novel*, p. 58.   [241] Peckham, *Triumph of Romanticism*, p. 141.
[242] *Historical Novel* (1924), pp. 22, 18, 23.   [243] Ibid., pp. 22, 26.

These things 'are the very touches that are needed to turn history into a story'. Unlike history, Butterfield believed, fictional narrative could forget or transcend hindsight.[244]

The distinctions between history and fiction Butterfield elaborated left each with a clearly defined role: 'To the historian the past is the whole process of development that leads up to the present; to the novelist it is a strange world to tell tales about.'[245] That is no longer the case. Each genre has encroached on the domain once exclusive to the other; history has grown more like fiction, fiction more like history.

Both the structure and the content of contemporary fiction substantially rearrange the past. Gone is the linear time of nineteenth-century fiction; flashbacks, streams of consciousness, duplicitous narrators, and multiple endings now decompose temporality.[246] Although – or perhaps because – *The French Lieutenant's Woman* is saturated with history, John Fowles suggests that the reader make up his own ending.[247] Best-selling books confound the two categories; the 1982 Booker prize for fiction went to Thomas Keneally's *Schindler's Ark*, which the author terms a true history, but then, as the prize chairman temporized, 'history is always a kind of fiction'. Many novelists share this view. 'There's no more fiction or nonfiction now, there's only narrative', asserts E. R. Doctorow, who calls his novel *Ragtime* 'a false document'; novelists are said to transcend 'the inconsequential distinctions we constantly make between fact and fiction'.[248]

This presumed convergence tempts some novelists to exaggerate fictional understanding of the past. 'Historical fiction is more truthful than history itself', say compilers of the former genre, arguing that history often pretends to be true but is false, whereas historical fiction claims only that much of its content is 'true to life and much fictional', leaving the reader to decide which is which.[249] Some novelists relegate historians to the 'outside' of the past while arrogating to themselves the 'inner' undocumentable truths. 'An historian can tell you just what happened at Borodino, but only Tolstoy, often dispensing with facts, can tell you what it really was to be a soldier at Borodino', writes William Styron, enlarging on Butterfield; the novelist's 'imaginative truth . . . transcends . . . what the historian can give you'. Styron degrades history into a barren chronicle, while elevating the novelist into a superior historian who tells it like it really was.[250] Other contemporary novelists present fact as fiction because they consider fiction 'the higher reality, not limiting and arbitrary

---

[244] Ibid., pp. 23–4. It had been Plutarch's aim to infuse the dizzying and upsetting emotions of the actual participants into his narrative (Fornara, *Nature of History in Ancient Greece and Rome*, p. 129); an aim exemplified in Michelet's *Histoire de France* (Bann, *Clothing of Clio*, pp. 49–50).

[245] Ibid., p. 113. 'Scientific' historians of the late nineteenth-century charged 'literary' historians with eschewing fact for fable; initially inspired to explore the past by Scott's novels, von Ranke later renounced historical romance because Scott's portrayals of Charles the Bold and Louis XI in *Quentin Durward* so offended his standards of historical evidence (Wedgwood, 'Sense of the past', p. 27; *idem*, 'Literature and the historians', p. 71). See Anne Green, *Flaubert and the Historical Novel*, p. 1.

[246] Hayden White, 'Burden of history', p. 126; Strout, *Veracious Imagination*, p. 10.

[247] Strout, *Veracious Imagination*, p. 18.

[248] Doctorow, quoted in Foley, 'From *U.S.A.* to *Ragtime*', pp. 102, 99; Larzer Ziff, quoted in Edwin McDowell, 'Fiction: often more real than fact', *N.Y. Times*, 16 July 1981, p. C21. See Walcott, 'Muse of history', p. 2.

[249] McGarry and White, *World Historical Fiction Guide*, p. xx.

[250] Styron, and C. Vann Woodward, 'The uses of history in fiction: a discussion' (1969), quoted in Strout, *Veracious Imagination*, pp. 167, 164. Historians – and blacks – criticized Styron's portrait of Nat Turner as a fiction that misled by excluding salient facts (John Henrik Clarke (ed.), *William Styron's Nat Turner; Ten Black Writers Respond* (1968); John White, 'Novelist as historian: William Styron and American Negro slavery', *Journal of American Studies*, 4 (1971), 233–45); James M. Mellard, 'This *unquiet* dust: the problem of history in Styron's *The Confessions of Nat Turner*', *Bucknell Review* 36 (1983), 523–43.

like historical truth'.[251] As a Vidal narrator says, 'there is no history, only fictions of varying degrees of plausibility. What we think to be history is nothing but fiction.'[252]

But few of these comminglings effectively convey the spirit of the past. Modern sensibilities in John Barth's picaresque seventeenth-century world blur the line between facts and fictionalized versions of facts, suggesting that Barth 'does not believe in such a thing as history even while his narrative pretends to evoke it'.[253] In 'modernizing' well-known historical figures, *Ragtime*'s racial confrontation subverts the specific realities of both the 1960s and the Edwardian era.

Fiction criticizes history while cannibalizing it; history derogates fiction's claims while adopting fictional insights and techniques. New materials and recording devices enable contemporary historians to do what Victorians thought only fiction could do – chronicle the everyday past. The resurgence of narrative has brought back the past in the form of stories. And historians are increasingly aware of the need for the fictive rhetoric championed by Hexter.[254]

Some go still further, like David Ely's protagonist avowing errors and omissions as integral to historical validity. Alex Haley thus defended *Roots* when much of his eighteenth-century data was shown to be invented or transformed. The actual facts could never be known, Haley retorted, and in any case mattered less than his fictionalized symbolic past with which millions of black Americans identified. He acknowledged that the Juffure he described was a Juffure that never existed, but justified it as a composite likeness of Gambian villages of the time. Haley's Juffure was in fact much more than that – it amalgamated West Africa with Avalon, Eden, and idealized small-town America in a Club Méditerranée type of Platonic city-state.[255] Indeed, only such anachronisms enabled black Americans to identify *their* past with this remote and unlikely place; had Haley depicted Juffure as it actually was, his picture would have been not just disbelieved but ignored. In short, factual faithfulness was jettisoned for a symbolically serviceable past. And that past has triumphed, for tourist fame has since begun to transform Juffure into a facsimile of Haley's eighteenth-century idealization.[256]

The historical novelist similarly heightens illusion at the expense of accuracy. Because he must 'give his readers as complete an illusion as possible of having lived in the past', according to Hervey Allen, 'he is *under obligation* to alter facts, circumstances, people, and even dates'.[257]

The novelist most critically affects the past by modernizing it. 'To all situations one brings a modern spirit', in Goethe's words, 'for only in this way can we understand them and, indeed, bear to see them.'[258] As Scott explained, 'it is necessary, for exciting interest of any kind, that the subject [be] translated into the manners, as well as the language, of the

---

[251] Larzer Ziff (see n. 248 above).   [252] *1876*, pp. 196–7, 194.

[253] Tanner, *City of Words: American Fiction 1950–1970*, p. 245, referring to Barth's *Sot-Weed Factor*.

[254] But most historians still employ the narrative form of the late nineteenth-century novel, leading to 'the progressive antiquation of the "art" of historiography itself' (Hayden White, 'Burden of the past', p. 127).

[255] Mark Ottaway, 'Tangled roots', *Sunday Times*, 10 Apr. 1977, pp. 17, 21; Israel Shenker, 'Few U.S. historians upset by charges', *IHT*, 11 Apr. 1977, p. 5.

[256] To others Juffure still seems an ordinary West African village (Brian Whitaker, 'The shade of the mango', *Sunday Times*, 2 Oct. 1983, p. 26; Robin Laurance, 'Back to the roots in a peanut republic', *The Times*, 10–16 Sept. 1983, p. 2).

[257] Quoted in Werrell, 'History and fiction', p. 6.   [258] 'Teilnahme Goethes aus Manzoni' (1827), 14:838.

age we live in'.[259] Scott's Anglo-Saxon and Norman characters not only spoke more or less modern English, they expressed historical relationships far more clearly than men and women of the time could have done.[260] In short, fictional anachronism is both desirable and essential. Butterfield to the contrary, historical fiction shares with history the burdens of hindsight, not just to make the past intelligible but to account for processes of change not originally apparent.

All accounts of the past tell stories about it, and hence are partly invented; as we have seen, story-telling also imposes its exigencies on history. At the same time, all fiction is partly 'true' to the past; a really fictitious story cannot be imagined, for no one could understand it. The truth in history is not the only truth about the past; every story is true in countless ways, ways that are more specific in history and more general in fiction.[261]

Thus historians who assert their unique fidelity to the past and writers of fiction who claim total exemption from such fidelity both delude themselves and their readers. The history–fiction difference is more one of purpose than of content. Whatever rhetorical devices the historian deploys, the tenets of his craft forbid him knowingly to invent or to exclude things that affect his conclusions; in terming himself an historian and his work a history, he chooses to have it judged for accuracy, internal consistency, and congruence with the surviving record. And he dares not fabricate a character, ascribe unknown traits or incidents to real ones, or ignore incompatible traits so as to make his tale more intelligible, because he could neither hide such inventions from others with access to the public record nor justify them when found out.[262]

By contrast, the historical novelist is bound to invent characters and events, or imaginary thoughts and actions for real people of the past. The constraints the historian gladly embraces are intolerable to the writer of fiction, as John Updike found when gathering materials for a life of President Buchanan. Suffocated by the determinable facts of history, Updike could not leap the divide from fiction to fact. 'Researched details failed to act like remembered ones, they had no palpable medium of the half-remembered in which to swim; my imagination was frozen by the theoretical discoverability of *everything*. An actual man, Buchanan, had done this and this, exactly so, once; and no other way. There was no air.'[263]

To deny that history and fiction are either mutually exclusive or utterly indistinguishable routes to the past, however, is not to condone a compromise that claims the virtues of both while accepting the limitations of neither. What is called 'faction' imitates much new fiction and some new history in smudging the distinction between them, but displays a pretentious omniscience that traduces both approaches.

Glossing over the past's alien nature, faction resembles certain Victorian novels which made the past popularly accessible by enlivening it in present-day terms. Now obvious, the anachronisms of such fiction then went largely undetected. Few realized that while humanizing everyday life in the past it also glamorized it, even while 'claiming to do the opposite', writes Jenkyns; 'lending a bogus sense of intimacy with Pompeii' by flattering

---

[259] 'Dedicatory epistle to the Rev. Doctor Dryasdust, F.A.S.', *Ivanhoe* (1820), p. 15. See Scott, *Prefaces to the Waverley Novels*, p. 34; David Brown, *Walter Scott and the Historical Imagination*, pp. 173–86.
[260] Lukács, *Historical Novel*, p. 69.
[261] Munz, *Shapes of Time*, pp. 214, 338 n.10. See also Mink, 'Everyman his or her own annalist', pp. 238–9.
[262] Hexter, *History Primer*, pp. 289–90.   [263] *Buchanan Dying: A Play*, 'Afterword', p. 259.

the masses they had 'a special knowledge denied to pedants and professors'; bringing people into intimate relation with the past but at the same time diluting its passions through the sieve of distance.[264] Sheer verisimilitude made the late-Victorian novel seem historically valid, but it perverted public understanding of the past by denying, taming, or explaining away its utter strangeness; in such fiction, as in Whig histories, the past was present, the present past, anachronism became decoration, and residues too dreadful to digest were hidden or bowdlerized. Apropos all such re-creations, Henry James objected that Sarah Orne Jewett's *Tory Lover* sought to do the impossible – to represent 'the old *consciousness*, the soul, the sense, the horizon, the vision of individuals in whose minds half the things that make ... the modern world, were non-existent, ... [people] whose own thinking was intensely otherwise conditioned'.[265]

Reluctance to face up to that impossibility makes factional portrayals shoddy and disingenuous. While 'firmly anchored to the facts', as one producer says, television documentaries like historical novels must in the end 'make a stab at the personality'[266] – in other words, abandon fact for fiction, letting go of the anchor while pretending still to be grasping it. The adaptation of history to television exacerbates tendencies to accept versions of the past as gospel. Even when producers confess that shows commingle fact and fiction, viewers mistake them for literal accounts of what actually happened and what life was really like, assuming that what costs so much and is seen by so many must be true.

'This is how it was' heralds faction shows, rather than 'It may have happened something like this'; the tone of all-knowing certitude, cloaked in authoritative anonymity, lends such sagas a stamp of revealed truth.[267] In written histories, the author's voice usually alerts us at the outset to his own perspective; in television sagas, presentation eliminates authorial specificity and responsibility. Faction 'includes so much known to be true, and shown with such patient expertise, that the rest of it is swallowed in ... easy credulity'. And visual images are more convincing than written accounts. 'In the good old days, people believed things they read', says a critic. 'This sweet faith in the invariable veracity of books and newspapers' has given way to the belief 'that the television camera never lies ... You can actually see it, so it must be true.'[268] Even film-makers formerly shared this faith. Those who made *The Birth of a Nation* (1914), along with 'most of the people who saw it, regarded it as exact history; "You will see what actually has happened"', said director D. W. Griffiths, '"there will be no opinions expressed, you will merely be present at the making of history ... The film could not be anything but the truth."'[269]

Gone are the breezily cynical days of Moviola, when few knew and none cared where fact ended and palpable fiction began, like Nicholas Bentley's Cecil B. de Mille, who:

> Rather against his will
> Was persuaded to leave Moses
> Out of the *Wars of the Roses*.

[264] *Victorians and Ancient Greece*, pp. 83–6.

[265] To Jewett, 5 Oct. 1901, in James, *Selected Letters*, pp. 234–5: 'You may multiply the little facts that can be got from pictures and documents, relics and prints as much as you like – the *real* thing is almost impossible to do.'

[266] Ralling, 'What is television doing to history?' p. 43.   [267] Ibid., p. 42.

[268] Patrick Brogan, 'America's history being rewritten on TV by confusing fact–fiction serials', *The Times*, 11 Oct. 1977. See Fledelius, *History and the Audio-Visual Media 1*.

[269] Sorlin, *Film in History: Restaging the Past*, pp. viii–ix.

In place of ignorance or philistinism we are now so besotted by the past that anything goes as long as it is 'authentic'. In what purports to be history, such as Haley's *Roots*, 'authenticity' means fidelity to feeling that swamps facts in anachronistic invention, a search for roots so *engagé* as to include very little of the actual past.[270]

In what purports to be fiction, the passion for authenticity perverts the tale by larding it with painstakingly genuine detail. Viewers may spot Trollopian or Dickensian costume dramas as palpable fables, but what can they conclude from *Brideshead Revisited*, whose producers went to the trouble of securing Waugh's actual rooms at Oxford, of speckling pullets' eggs to simulate the novel's breakfast plovers' eggs, and of adding simulated marble columns and Felix Kelly's murals (echoing Vanbrugh and Hawksmoor) to Castle Howard? Was all this actually done, as claimed, to make it 'real for the actors'?[271] Seeing Oxford, Castle Howard, and Venice on the screen degrades the novel's fantasy world by making it seem a slice of the actual past, with real rather than fictional events. Nineteenth-century tourists went to Kenilworth 'not to see a place where the acts of history had really happened long ago but to see a place where the deeds of fancy were fictionally recurring forever', writes Christopher Mulvey;[272] today a *National Geographic* type of geography is enlisted to contrive an historically authentic framework, turning past fiction into present fact.

Past and present

Memory, I have suggested, is innately and immediately distinguishable from present experience. The distinction between the historical past and the present is not innate but acquired, and often uncertain or absent. Where knowledge of the past is orally trans-mitted, for example, or where no records exist, the past is perceived entirely in terms of present accounts. Whatever changes may have occurred, continually reshaped narratives seek to make it appear that tradition has survived unaltered all along; no line divides the historical past from the present. In such societies 'remembered truth was flexible and up to date, because no ancient custom could be proved older than the memory of the oldest living wise man; hence there was no conflict between past and present practice'.[273] Some oral societies view the present as a mere manifestation of an all-encompassing past; others are so present-orientated that the past is never a topic of discourse; both deny firm distinctions between past and present.[274] The past in oral cultures 'is not felt as an itemized terrain, peppered with verifiable ... "facts" or bits of information', concludes Walter Ong. 'It is the domain of the ancestors, a resonant source for renewing awareness of

---

[270] Arragon, 'History's changing image', pp. 231–2; John J. O'Connor, '"Docu-ramas" – authenticity is still the key', *N.Y. Times*, 10 Aug. 1980, p. D29.

[271] Derek Granger, quoted in Geoffrey Wansell, 'The battle of the megaseries', *The Times*, preview, 9–15 Oct. 1981. Castle Howard's owner, George Howard (BBC chairman when the ITV Granada *Brideshead* series was shown), lauded Kelly's murals for 'their heart-searching nostalgia [and] Never-never Land appeal' (Felix Kelly: The Castle Howard Murals, Partridge Gallery, London, 1982, and Geraldine Norman review, *The Times*, 27 Oct. 1982). See Steven Rattner, 'A visit to the real "Brideshead"', *IHT*, 9 Feb. 1982.

[272] *Anglo-American Landscapes*, p. 18.

[273] Clanchy, *From Memory to Written Record*, p. 233. See Goody and Watt, 'Consequences of literacy', pp. 32–4; Henige, 'Disease of writing', pp. 255–6.

[274] Maurice Bloch, 'The past and the present in the present', p. 288.

present existence, which itself is not an itemized terrain either.'[275] According to Goody and Watt, 'the pastness of the past depends upon a historical sensibility that can hardly begin to operate without permanent written records'.[276] Only the preservation and dissemination of historical knowledge through writing, and especially through print, sets the past firmly apart from the present.

While permanent records reveal and ultimately enforce that distinction, its recognition was long resolutely resisted. In the Middle Ages history was a unified Christian drama with no scope for or interest in differences between present and past. 'The men of those ages had no past', concludes E. A. Freeman; 'unconscious, unreflecting, uncritical, they wrote their own history in their own works rather than spelled out that of their forefathers in the relics they had left.'[277] As Raymond de l'Aire of Tignac put it in the early fourteenth-century, 'There is no other age than ours.'[278] Only with Petrarch did awareness of antiquity as another time begin to figure in men's minds. But Renaissance fascination with classical sources was predicated on their relevance to present concerns; the past might be another country, but it could not safely be a foreign one. Relevance required history to illustrate repetitive patterns of eternal virtues and vices. We saw in Chapter 3 how most humanists denied or ignored Erasmus's perception of historical change; but the clearer the image of antiquity became, the less it seemed to resemble the modern world. Historical consciousness enabled some Enlightenment *philosophes* to rediscover the classical world only to realize how far away it had become, how unattainable the model of antique harmony; they were traits of a past now truly irrecoverable.[279]

Seeing the past as a different realm was no historical revolution, as it is sometimes termed, but a plant of slow growth nurtured by secularism, increasing scrutiny of evidence, and awareness of anachronism.[280] As late as the nineteenth century, history remained for many a seamless whole scarcely distinguishable from the present, human nature the same in all epochs.[281] Whig historians stressed the familiarity and continuity of pasts they found exemplary. The immemorial open-air gatherings of the democratic Swiss cantons vividly conjoined past and present for Freeman; Macaulay witnessed the passage of the Reform Act in his own time as 'like seeing Caesar stabbed in the Senate House, or seeing Oliver Cromwell taking the mace from the table'; late-Victorian classicists found Homer's world a mirror image of their own and ascribed to Aristotle and Plato their own

---

[275] *Orality and Literacy*, p. 98. But like Bloch, Ong over-simplifies; see Peel, 'Making history', pp. 128–9.

[276] 'Consequences of literacy', p. 34. Some fundamentalists continue to deny that pastness. Adhering 'to the letter of their authentic founding documents' and relying solely upon the words of their prophets and sages, Karaite Jews and Muslim and Protestant extremists live 'in a religious present rather than religious past'. But once 'a tradition has ceased to be the exclusive compendium of its adherents' interests', its apologists seek historical confirmation of its authority, and externalize the past (Schwartzbach, 'Antidocumentalist apologetics', p. 374).

[277] *Preservation and Restoration of Ancient Monuments* (1852), pp. 16–17.

[278] Le Roy Ladurie, *Montaillou*, p. 282. Apart from a rare interest in lineage or genealogy, villagers took no interest in earlier decades and 'lived in a kind of "island in time"', even more cut off from the past than from the future' (pp. 281–2).

[279] Gilmore, *Humanists and Jurists*, pp. 14, 95–6, 101, 109; Starobinski, *1789: The Emblems of Reason*, p. 272.

[280] Preston, 'Was there an historical revolution?' p. 362.

[281] Lyons, *Invention of Self*, p. 5; W. H. Walsh, 'Constancy of human nature'; Gossman, *Medievalism and the Ideologies of the Enlightenment*, p. 250. Gibbon knew himself less credulous than Livy, but believed they spoke 'the same language' and that he could 'have taught Livy to be as sceptical as an educated eighteenth-century Englishman' because their minds were essentially alike (Munz, *Shapes of Time*, pp. 188–9).

thoughts.[282] Evolutionary paradigms reinforced these perspectives: the seeds of the present seemed immanent in the past, the consequences of the past everywhere evident. And the modern cult of roots, seeing ancestors foreshadowing descendants, family and ethnic traits enduring through time, reflects similar genetic prepossessions.[283]

Alongside these continuing predilections, however, other perspectives emphasized the diversity of historical experience. Herder and his successors taught that every historical period, as well as each culture, had its own unique and incomparable character; uniformity was a myth, differences between the present and any past incommensurable. The late eighteenth-century Romantic imagination delighted in the unique spirit of times past; many such epochs served the nineteenth century as nostalgic refuges.[284] But the past's alien character came to be widely recognized and accepted only near the turn of this century, when a 'Chinese wall between past and present' was definitively erected.[285] The past really was dead, noted Froude, a precursor of such awareness; remoteness, not intimacy, made the Middle Ages poignant:

In the alteration of our own character, we have lost the key which would interpret the characters of our fathers, and the great men even of our own English history before the Reformation seem to us almost like the fossil skeletons of another order of beings ... Now it is all gone; ... and between us and the old English there lies a gulf of mystery which the prose of the historian will never adequately bridge. They cannot come to us, and our imagination can but feebly penetrate to them.[286]

Recognizing the past as a foreign country cost historians dear. Distanced and differentiated, it ceased to be a source of useful lessons and became a heap of quaint anachronisms. Historians were left at a loss to explain the causal relations of past and present. 'To live in any period of the past', as V. H. Galbraith thought an historian bound to try to do, 'is to be so overwhelmed with the sense of difference as to confess oneself unable to conceive how the present has become what it is.'[287]

Against the irrelevance of so alien a past, certain benefits also emerged. With the loss of its exemplary role, the past ceased to exert so crippling an influence over the present. To bring about the 'death of the past' and thus relieve the present of its burdens became an avowed function of historical study.[288] Maitland saw 'the office of historical research as that of explaining, and therefore lightening, the pressure that the past must exercise upon the present ... Today we study the day before yesterday, in order that yesterday may not paralyze today, and today may not paralyze tomorrow.'[289] And for Croce 'the writing of history liberates us from history, ... from slavery to events and to the past'.[290]

---

[282] Freeman (1864), *Growth of the English Constitution* (1874), pp. 1–7; Macaulay to Thomas Flower Ellis, 30 Mar. 1831, in his *Letters*, 2:9; Frank Turner, *Greek Heritage in Victorian Britain*, pp. 175–86, 418–27. See also Burrow, *Liberal Descent*, pp. 70, 169–70.

[283] Dorothy Ross, 'Historical consciousness in nineteenth-century America', pp.923–4; Buckley, *Triumph of Time*, pp. 15–16; Hijia, 'Roots: family and ethnicity in the 1970s', pp. 553–4.

[284] Berlin, *Vico and Herder*, p. 145; Honour, *Romanticism*, pp. 175–84, 197ff; Girouard, *Return of Camelot*; Harbison, *Deliberate Regression*, pp. 139–40.

[285] For Raphael Samuel, that wall is 'one of the chief legacies of the von Rankean revolution in historiography' ('History Workshop I: truth is partisan', p. 250).

[286] Froude, *History of England* (1856), 1:3, 62.

[287] 'Historical research and the preservation of the past' (1938), p. 312. See Blaas, *Continuity and Anachronism*, p. xiv.

[288] Plumb, *Death of the Past*; see Chapter 7, pp. 364–5 below.   [289] 'A survey of the century' (1901), 3:439.

[290] Croce, *History as the Story of Liberty*, p. 44.

If recognizing the past's foreignness relaxed its tyranny over the present, it also enhanced the virtues of hindsight. History depicts a past more definitive and magisterial than the present, for hindsight clarifies yesterday as it cannot clarify today: historical consequences are at least partly worked out and understood, whereas the results of present acts are yet to be seen. By contrast with contemporary experience, 'the examples which history presents to us, both of men and of events, are generally complete: the whole example is before us', as Bolingbroke wrote. 'We see [men] at their whole length in history, ... through a medium less partial at least than that of experience.'[291]

History is never wholly sealed off, to be sure; however keen our present retrospective insights, new consequences of past events will ever continue to emerge. But any degree of hindsight makes knowledge of the past more conclusive than that of the present, as Elizabeth Gaskell ironically observed:

> In looking back to the last century, it appears curious to see how little our ancestors had the power of putting two things together, and perceiving either the discord or the harmony thus produced. Is it because we are farther off from those times, and have, consequently, a greater range of vision? Will our descendants have a wonder about us, such as we have about the inconsistency of our forefathers, or a surprise about our blindness? ... Such discrepancies ran through good men's lives in those days. It is well for us that we live at the present time, when everybody is logical and consistent.[292]

In short, historical explanation surpasses any understanding available while events are still occurring. The past we reconstruct is more coherent than the past was when it happened. 'What we recognize as the Roman Empire was a series of disconnected experiences for the generations who made it up', says Gordon Leff. 'It is we who give them coherence.'[293] Even more than memory, history clarifies, tidies, and elucidates. This is the point of Namier's conundrum that historians 'imagine the past and remember the future':[294] they explain what has happened by bearing subsequent events in mind.

Narrative exigencies magnify these differences. To make history intelligible, the historian must reveal a retrospectively immanent structure in past events, creating an illusion that things happened as they did because they had to. As we have seen, he not only knows the outcome of the past but uses that knowledge to shape his account into a story, with a sense of fullness and completion. But the present is never described in this way. Hence the strikingly definitive tone of many historical chronicles: following a line of proven virtues, old diaries and journals now reveal an ordered clarity in marked contrast with the chaos of the authors' actual lives, not to mention the imprecision of our own unfinished lives.[295]

As this implies, however, historical understanding merges past with present as well as differentiating them; we cannot avoid mixing up what goes on now with what went on then. To understand what happened, as distinct from what people in the past thought or

---

[291] *Letters on the Study and Use of History* (1752), 1:37. 'Experience is doubly defective; we are born too late to see the beginning, and we die too soon to see the end of many things. History supplies both these defects' (1:42). See also Lovejoy, 'Herder and the Enlightenment philosophy of history', and Heller, *Theory of History*, p. 17. Ghostly figures in Thomas Hardy's poems transcend the distinction, viewing 'the present as something which has already happened and which has already been followed by its inevitable consequences' (J. H. Miller, 'History as repetition in Thomas Hardy's poetry', p. 231).
[292] *Sylvia's Lovers* (1863), pp. 58–9.   [293] *History and Social Theory*, p. 105.
[294] *Conflicts: Studies in Contemporary History*, p. 70.
[295] Vendler, 'All too real', p. 32.

wanted others to think was happening, we must introduce our own thoughts.[296] And just as present thoughts shape the known past, awareness of the past suffuses the present. A literary historian must write 'not merely with his own generation in his bones', in T. S. Eliot's phrase, 'but with a feeling that the whole of the literature of Europe from Homer ... has a simultaneous existence and composes a simultaneous order'.[297]

To span the mental gulf between past and present, to communicate convincingly, and to invest historical accounts with interpretive coherence requires their continual reshaping. No absolute historical truth lies waiting to be found; however assiduous and fair-minded the historian, he can no more relate the past 'as it really was' than can our memories. But history is not thereby invalidated; faith endures that historical knowledge casts *some* light on the past, that elements of truth persist in it. Even if future insights show up present errors and undermine present conclusions, evidence now available proves that some things almost certainly did happen and others did not. The curtain of doubt does not cordon off historians from the past; they look through the fabric and beyond, secure in the knowledge they approximate to the truth.[298]

Absolute 'truth' is a recent and uncommon criterion for evaluating accounts of the past. In most oral societies, the status of historical accounts depends more on the reputation of their narrators than on their faithfulness to known facts or their explanatory validity. For the Kuba, the true past is what the majority think worthy of belief; for the Trobriands, it is whatever the ancestors have declared to be true, even events everyone knows did not happen. Seldom querying the logical feasibility of what they hear, oral audiences may comfortably embrace contradictory testimonies about the past, even conflicting accounts by the same informant.[299]

In our own culture, historical accounts have traditionally served many functions other than 'truth', and sometimes at cross-purposes with it – to secure the pedigrees of existing rulers, for example, or to promote patriotic zeal, or to sanction religious or revolutionary causes. Expressly concerned to keep records 'lest age or oblivion destroy the memory of modern events',[300] twelfth- and thirteenth-century chroniclers none the less aimed to convey 'a deliberately created and rigorously selected version of events', M. T. Clanchy notes. The 'historical truth' of monastic annals was 'what really should have happened, . . . a providential truth . . . Documents were created and carefully conserved so that posterity might know about the past, but they were not necessarily allowed to accumulate by natural accretion over time nor to speak for themselves, because the truth was far too important to leave to chance.'[301] Only within the past century or two has describing the past as it actually was become some historians' major commitment. Purged of their predecessors' biases, successive generations have erroneously fancied themselves free of bias. Montesquieu thought himself unprejudiced; exposing Montesquieu's unconscious prejudices,

---

[296] Munz, *Shapes of Time*, p. 110. [297] 'Tradition and the individual talent', p. 14.
[298] Murphey, *Our Knowledge of the Historical Past*, pp. 15–16. 'There is ... a knowable past ... I am sure we can make statements about the past which are either true or false' (Steinberg, '"Real authentick history" or what philosophers of history can teach us', pp. 471–2).
[299] Vansina, *Oral Tradition*, pp. 102–3; d'Azevedo, 'Tribal history in Liberia', pp. 266–7.
[300] Matthew Paris, *Chronica majora* (1250), quoted in Clanchy, *From Memory to Written Record*, p. 118.
[301] Clanchy, *From Memory to Written Record*, p. 118–20, 147.

Marat believed he himself had none.[302] It was the rare scholar who recognized the fallibility of his own age. 'Our ancestors, ... I doubt not, thought themselves as little under the influence of prejudice and idle fancy, as we may deem ourselves', wrote an astute late eighteenth-century chronicler.[303] Alert to bias in others, nineteenth-century historians likewise fancied themselves rational and impartial.

Those who assert their objectivity also tend to minimize the difficulties that prevent its realization. Hence the misconception endures that history can achieve a wholly faithful and final account of the past. Many historians who implicitly accept the limitations on knowledge discussed above are unwilling to admit them to themselves, Hexter suggests, because they assent to or feel oppressed by a view that accords cognitive value only to precise and univocal scientific language.[304] But even those who explicitly acknowledge these limitations often shun their implications, as a recent exchange illustrates. On the one hand, historians are told that the facts of the past are embedded in structures they themselves frame, 'that historical explanations are crafted forms', and that

the most illuminating works of history are those governed by the most imaginative and capacious regulative fictions. The blurring of lines between history and fiction ought to humble historians, reminding them how fragmentary and oblique their view of the past must always be; it ought also to alert them to new possibilities. Giving up a positivist epistemology, they might ... reveal a broader range of historical truths. They might even acknowledge the truth-telling power of literary fictions.

For example, García Márquez's *One Hundred Years of Solitude* 'devastates positivist assumptions about linear causality and historical truth', Jackson Lears argues, 'but also tells some profound historical truths about the 'modernization' of a colonial society'.[305]

On the other hand, only a faith that the past really exists gives historians the confidence to collect and order evidence and 'bring[s] us closer to knowing the truth about that past "as it really was", even if the full and complete truth about the past will always remain beyond their grasp'. Old-fashioned this epistemology may be, concedes Gordon Wood, but only such faith 'makes history writing possible. Historians who cut loose from this faith do so at the peril of their discipline.'[306]

Viewing historical knowing in its broadest context, as I have tried to do here, leaves me dubious about prescriptions that tie historians to standards of exactitude they cannot help but infringe, while remaining reluctant to explore what professional history has in common with Becker's Everyman. Michael Oakeshott distinguishes the completely disinterested historian concerned with the past entirely for its own sake from 'non-histori-

---

[302] Gossman, *Medievalism and Ideologies of the Enlightenment*, pp. 350–1.

[303] Joseph Berington, *History of the Lives of Abeillard and Eloisa* (1793), 1:li–liii. 'The time will arrive, when this age may also be denominated, dark: and who knows, but they may say, we were *credulous*?' (1:li).

[304] Hexter, 'Rhetoric of history', p. 381. Other critics are more severe. 'Historians alone among all scientists still believe that the only reason why truth eludes them is that they show too much bias, or that their sources do, or that there are missing "facts"' (Munz, *Shapes of Time*, p. 221). 'Since the middle of the nineteenth century, most historians have affected a kind of willful methodological naivete ... This suspicion of sytem ... has led to a resistance throughout the entire profession ... to almost any kind of critical self-analysis' (Hayden White, 'Burden of history' (1978), pp. 111–13). Michael Kammen suggests that a revolution in methodological awareness since the 1970s outdates these critiques ('Introduction: the historian's vocation and the state of the discipline in the United States' (1980)), but in Britain there are few signs of any such revolution. See Steinberg, '"Real authentick history"', pp. 455, 463.

[305] 'Writing history: an exchange', p. 58.   [306] Ibid., p. 59.

cal', 'practical' people who use the past to understand, sustain, or reform the present.[307] But the distinction is unreal: the practical man's past is seldom exclusively operational; the historian too is unavoidably present-minded. Oakeshott's types are both 'historical' in the same sense.

The historian's vocation, declares Michael Kammen, is to provide society with a discriminating memory.[308] Indeed, to communicate effectively he must discriminate. Only by selectively shaping available sources can any historian, whether a professional academic or a creator of romance, coherently convey knowledge of the past. Many do provide society with this discriminating memory, but little use is made of it: the gulf between sophisticated chroniclers and the public at large seems to widen all the time. More about the past is known than ever before, and is ever less shared. The 'Progressive' synthesis that marked American history writing up to twenty years ago, for example, has given way to a congeries of fragments slanted toward different ethnic, age-graded, and class-based audiences.[309] The growth of historical romance and of nostalgic cults contrasts starkly with the drop of enrolments in academic history and the decline of historical knowledge among university students, of whom 'the majority cannot identify Socrates, confuse the Enlightenment with the name of a rock band, and draw a blank when McCarthy, Kennedy, or Vietnam are mentioned'.[310]

Why has professional erudition failed to dispel public ignorance? Some blame historians for increasingly narrow specialisms, for forbidding technical paraphernalia, and for turning their backs even on educated readers in order to satisfy their academic peers. 'We may choose to ignore it', one historian warns, 'but the devilish truth is that both fragmentation and overspecialization have stultified the intellect of much of the profession.'[311] But there is little evidence that historians today are narrower or more scientistic; most continue to eschew jargon for ordinary language, and their work is more accessible than that of most other scholars.

I attribute the gulf rather to the enormous expansion of historical knowledge. Widespread literacy and the preservative powers of print allow everything known about the past to accumulate, and formal history has broadened to include the past of non-European cultures and of a host of new phenomena. As a result, no one person can take in more than a tiny fraction of it.[312] We are all specialists now, the football fanatic who knows the past scores of every team no less than the expert on the lives of saints or the history of majolica.

[307] 'Activity of being an historian'; *idem, On History*, pp. 35–9, 43.

[308] 'Vanitas and the historian's vocation', pp. 19–20.

[309] Gutman, 'Whatever happened to history?' p. 554.

[310] Burns, 'Teaching history: a changing clientele and an affirmation of goals', pp. 20–1. See John Lukacs, 'Obsolete historians'.

[311] Burns, 'Teaching history', p. 20. 'Historians are more and more specialized, experts on single decades or single subjects, and still they cannot keep up with the profusion of monographs. Most now make no pretense of writing for the educated public. They write for each other, and with all their scientific paraphernalia . . . they can sometimes count their readers on their hands' (Gordon Wood, 'Star-spangled history', p. 4). See also Yardley, 'Narrowing world of the historian'.

[312] 'The mere size of the literate repertoire means that the proportion of the whole which any one individual knows must be infinitesimal in comparison with what obtains in oral culture. Literate society, merely by having no system of elimination, . . . prevents the individual from participating fully in the total cultural tradition to anything like the extent possible in non-literate society' (Goody and Watt, 'Consequences of literacy', p. 57).

Professional historians themselves perforce remain ignorant of most aspects of the past studied by their own colleagues.

The cumulation of historical knowledge has also widened the gap betwen literate and non-literate, between what is apprehended from reading and from hearing about the past. How the highly literate imbibe history sets them more and more apart from the rest of the world. The gap also divorces adult knowledge of the past from that of unschooled youngsters. Indeed, it estranges adults from their own childhood pasts, for the habits of literacy, like the conventions of maturity, preclude grown men and women from making sense of the perceptions they had before they could read.[313]

Consensual knowledge of the past thus seems inversely proportional to how much is known *in toto*. In oral societies historical chronicles are meagre and sometimes hoarded as secret, yet most knowledge of the past is in fact shared. In literate societies printed historical texts are widely disseminated, but most knowledge of the past is fragmented into segments exclusive to small clusters of specialists, and the consensually shared past shrinks to a thin media-dominated veneer.[314]

RELICS

> Most of the marks that man has left on the face of the earth during his two-million year career as a litterbugging, meddlesome and occasionally artistic animal have one aspect in common: they are things, they are not deeds, ideas or words.
>
> Glynn Isaac, 'Whither archaeology?'[315]

Tangible relics survive in the form of natural features and human artifacts. Awareness of such relics enhances knowledge gained through memory and history. But no physical object or trace is an autonomous guide to bygone times; they light up the past only when we already know they belong to it. Memory and history pin-point only certain things as relics; the rest of what lies around us seems simply present, suggesting nothing past. And daily familiarity divests of their pastness many artifacts formerly identified as relics.[316]

The tangible past is none the less immeasurably voluminous. Few artifacts are entirely new-made, and even these usually have recognizable antecedents. Links with prototypes are ubiquitous, comprising not just ruins and reconstructions but everything marked by age, use, or memorial purpose.

Such remains form an assemblage incomparably greater than what is only of the present day. 'Above and under the earth', in Rose Macaulay's words, are 'far more ruined than unruined buildings.'[317] Any observer of the living landscape, at least in England, constantly comes 'up against the dead and the dying – prehistoric earthworks, Roman villas, Norman *mottes*, dead and decaying towns, deserted villages, nineteenth-century disused railways'.[318] Archaeology inherits the earth; most places contain the debris and cradle the memory of innumerable past events.

Relic features that mark the land and impress the mind include not only human artifacts

---

[313] Eisenstein, *Printing Press*, pp. 432–3.   [314] Miller, 'Listening for the African past', p. 11.
[315] 1971, p. 123.
[316] Tuan, 'Significance of the artifact', p. 469.   [317] *Pleasure of Ruins*, p. xvii.
[318] Glyn Daniel, *Idea of Prehistory*, p. 140.

but products of nature. The image of the earth as a geological and archaeological treasury inspired Thomas Browne:

The treasures of time lie high, in Urnes, Coynes, and Monuments, scarce below the roots of some vegetables. Time hath endlesse rarities, and shows of all varieties; which reveals old things in heaven, makes new discoveries in earth, and even earth it self a discovery. That great Antiquity *America* lay buried for thousands of years; and a large part of the earth is still in the Urne unto us.[319]

Much of the past is yet to become visible. But what is potentially visible is omnipresent.

Ubiquitous as they are, relics suffer greater attrition than do memories or histories. Whereas history in print and memories recorded on tape can be disseminated without limit and are thus potentially immortal, physical relics are continually worn away. However many vestiges remain to be found, resurrected, and deciphered, the tangible past is ultimately a finite and non-renewable resource, except as time engenders new relics. Earlier structures inexorably give way to subsequent ones if only because two things cannot occupy the same space at the same time. Were artifacts like memories, everything ever built might be brought to light again, Freud suggests; for example, Rome would be a city 'in which nothing once constructed had perished, and all the earlier stages of development had survived alongside the latest',[320] like van Poelenburgh's and Weenix's Roman landscapes juxtaposing lost and surviving relics with present features.[321] Remote and recent memories often survive along with present impressions of the same scene, but for artifacts the new must displace the old; material things emerge by discarding previous integuments. Otherwise past and present would blur into unintelligibility, like the palimpsest of the Roman Campagna 'crowded so full with memorable events that one obliterates another', in Hawthorne's words, 'as if Time had crossed and re-crossed his own records'.[322]

Artifacts are ceaselessly effaced, whether suddenly destroyed by earthquake or flood, war or iconoclasm, or slowly perishing by erosion. Less of last week survives than of yesterday, less of last year than of last month. 'You can see yesterday; most of it is still left', Jack Finney's fictional inventor reflects. 'And there's plenty of 1965, '62, '58. There's even a good deal left of nineteen hundred. And ... there are fragments of still earlier days. Single buildings. Sometimes several together: ... still-surviving fragments of a clear April morning of 1871, a gray winter afternoon of 1840, a rainy dawn of 1783.'[323] But most of the remote past is wholly gone or unrecognizably transformed. 'Could the England of 1685 be, by some magical process, set before our eyes, we should not know one landscape in a hundred or one building in ten thousand. The country gentleman would not recognise his own fields. The inhabitant of the town would not recognise his own street. Everything has been changed, but the great features of nature, and a few massive and durable works of human art.'[324] How much more true now, more than a century since T. B. Macaulay penned those words.

[319] *Hydriotaphia, Urne-Burial* (1658), p. 135.
[320] Freud, *Civilization and Its Discontents* (1930), p. 17. See his *Psychopathology of Everyday Life*, p. 275n; Bernfeld, 'Freud and archeology', p. 120. The novelist Régine Robin uses the composite temporality of history to enable 'multiple generations to rediscover themselves in the image of Freud's Rome' ('Toward fiction as oblique discourse', p. 242; see also Robin, *Cheval blanc de Lénine ou l'histoire autre*, pp. 138–50).
[321] Eunice Williams, 'Introduction', *Gods & Heroes*, p. 24. See p. 287, below.   [322] *Marble Faun*, p. 101.
[323] *Time and Again*, p. 56.
[324] T. B. Macaulay, *History of England* (1848), 1:281.

Relics succumb to attrition of meaning as well as substance. Our own past landscapes will lose consequence for our descendants as our present and imminent future become constituents of *their* past. 'All our yesterdays diminish and grow dim', in Becker's phrase: 'in the lengthening perspective of the centuries, even the most striking events . . . must inevitably, for posterity, fade away into pale replicas of the original picture, for each succeeding generation losing, as they recede into a more distant past, some significance that once was noted in them, some quality of enchantment that once was theirs'.[325]

Perceiving the tangible past

How much we apprehend the past in its surviving relics varies with several circumstances. One is the apparent antiquity of things around us. Certain locales, cities, houses, furnishings markedly reflect the past – landscapes saturated with ruined cities, prehistoric earthworks, memorials to the dead; rooms full of antiques, mementoes, souvenirs, old family photographs. Other locales, new, fresh, or provisional, suggest much less depth in time. Recently settled landscapes conspicuously lack the monuments and ancient buildings, the attics and trunks and museums, that invest older ones with a palpable human past.[326]

The felt past is a function of atmosphere as well as locale. 'Very much depends on the time of day at which one visits', cautions a guide to Britain's antiquities. 'A Neolithic barrow seen at high noon in summer-time, surrounded by a spiked Ministry of Works fence, dustbins and warning notices, that seems drained of all mystery, will have an entirely different aspect at sunset when the other visitors have departed.'[327] Weather can augment – or dispel – an illusion of history. In the Thames valley, autumn fog 'may blot out the far hills completely, and the ancient forests of the valley, leaving only the sights and sounds of the harsh industrial jungle', notes Paul Johnson. But at other times rain over the airport may make 'the jets invisible and unaudible, while . . . Windsor Castle emerges from the mists, . . . the sun glittering on the stone battlements and the royal standard straining from the citadel. For a few moments, the landscape becomes in all essentials what the people . . . must have glimpsed when Chaucer was still writing.'[328]

Like memories, relics once abandoned or forgotten may become more treasured than those in continued use; the discontinuity in their history focuses attention on them, particularly if scarcity or fragility threatens their imminent extinction. Artifacts of initially transient and diminishing value that fall into the limbo of rubbish are often later resurrected as highly valued relics.[329]

Our propensity and ability to detect antecedents, linking what now exists with earlier times, also determines how far we sense things as relics. Some gaze on ancient stones wholly unaware of their history; others invest even the new and the barren with bygone associations. Overlooking palpable differences, many traditional societies draw no distinc-

---

[325] 'Everyman his own historian', pp. 22–3.   [326] Stegner, *Wolf Willow*, p. 29.

[327] Newby and Petry, *Wonders of Britain*, p. xv.

[328] Paul Johnson, 'London diary', *New Statesman*, 13 Sept. 1968, p. 314. In fact, the scene Johnson describes is largely the nineteenth-century work of Jeffry Wyatville, and Windsor's 'pretensions to genuineness would hardly deceive a four-year-old' (Lancaster, 'Future of the past: some thoughts on preservation', p. 127).

[329] Michael Thompson, *Rubbish Theory*.

tion between contemporary artifacts and those ancestrally made or long used. Awareness of relic forms thus requires not only actual differences between survivals and present-day materials, but the capacity and willingness to recognize those differences. Rapid obsolescence and frequent replacement encourage us to identify things as 'antique'; we easily spot anachronisms that were, so to speak, born only yesterday.[330]

Whether we see the past in things also depends on when and how frequently we have seen them or their like before. To recognize features as relics we must recall circumstances unlike those of the present, yet not too dissimilar. Scenes viewed every day change so imperceptibly that past merges with present; those revisited after a prolonged absence may seem altered beyond recall.

How far back memory extends also affects judgements about how much remains of the past – and what should be done with it. Demolition and rebuilding in Bloomsbury have left Georgian remnants so pathetic that those who remember the squares of a generation ago see little point in saving them from the wrecker. By contrast, younger or more recent inhabitants and visitors who cannot recall the good old days zealously cherish the few remaining treasures.[331] As sad reminders of an entire past the eighteenth-century relics are worth little; to newcomers who remember nothing else they are precious specimens of antiquity.

Alterations in ourselves – growth from childhood, decline into old age, or simply the weight of added experience – may imbue unchanged scenes with an aura of time. 'I failed at first to recognise her', Proust's Marcel says on seeing ageless Odette after a lapse of many years, 'not because she had but because she had not changed.'[332] Old movies seen again after many years seem different not because they have altered but because we have. Our betrayed memories – resentment perhaps that they have become faded or jaded or disillusioning – reflect mainly the alteration in ourselves made by the passage of time and social change.[333]

Every relic thus exists simultaneously in the past and in the present. What leads us to identify things as antiquated or ancient varies with environment and history, with individual and culture, with historical awareness and inclination.

Three distinct processes alert us that things stem from or link with the past: ageing, embellishment, and anachronism. The first, decay and wear attributed to ageing, was the subject of Chapter 4. The second, embellishments that memorialize or otherwise call attention to some aspect of the past, is discussed in Chapter 6. The third, historical distance, makes relics feel like emanations of a previous age. 'Old-fashioned' things – open-field traces, moustache cups, vintage cars, classical pediments – exhibit or echo outdated forms or styles. Some such survivals are usable, others obsolete; some are in the scrap-heap, others in the museum. What they have in common is seeming to derive from an earlier epoch: they are anachronistic. To be conscious that things are anachronistic entails historical insight.

We believe artifacts stem from the historical past if they seem old-fashioned. They may

[330] J. G. Mann, 'Instances of antiquarian feeling in medieval and Renaissance art', p. 255.
[331] Ashley Barker, Greater London Council, Historic Buildings Division, interview 4 May 1978.
[332] *Remembrance of Things Past*, 3:990.
[333] David Robinson, 'The film immutable against life's changes', *The Times*, 7 Dec. 1983, p. 11.

or may not retain their original functions – watermills sometimes do, oast-houses do not, but neither are built nowadays except in imitation of the traditional genre. Thatched roofs are still useful, and their popularity has spawned fireproof glass-fibre copies; but new and even simulated thatch has an aura of antiquity because it *looks* old-fashioned.

Plant and animal species of hoary antiquity or at an evolutionary dead end seem similarly outdated. Remnant exemplars of the coelacanth, the tuatara, the Joshua tree are anachronisms more at home in previous than present environments. Fossil traces conjure up the histories of now extinct species, also antiquating the strata that embody them. And the very absence of fossils imparts antiquity to Pre-Cambrian rocks: devoid of any trace of subsequent life, the ancient Canadian Shield conveys a haunting sense of the primordial.

Sounds like substances can appear out of date. Musical themes, tones, and styles seem 'old' when identified as early or archaic, and listeners familiar with the history of music can chronologically locate a work even if they have never heard it before. Even a particular key may evoke the musical past: some *cognoscenti* 'cannot hear B minor without our subconscious being stirred by memories of the Kyrie of Bach's Mass, the first movement of the Unfinished Symphony, and Tchaikovsky's *Pathétique*'.[334]

The timbre of music can suggest the historical past, as Chapter 4 showed. Certain instruments produce tones that sound archaic whatever their actual age. We conceive early music as characteristically thin, reedy, quavering, or nasal; it also lacked a well-tempered pitch and featured acoustical traits – the castrato voice, for example – rare in our own epoch. Hearing such sounds today, we feel in the presence of the past.

The presumption of antiquity may be mistaken: few musical relics match the pedigreed authenticity of the Ukrainian mammoth bones Cro-Magnon man used as percussion instruments 20,000 years ago, which even now yield 'hard, resonant, and musically expressive' sounds.[335] Many 'early' instruments are in fact recent copies; some modern music is meant to sound acoustically antique or, like Stravinsky's *Lyke-Wake* cantata, is set to antiquated verse. But it is the assumption of antiquity that concerns us here, not its veracity. A deliberately archaic style lends music historical depth even when we know the semblance of age is contrived. We associated archaisms with previous epochs; when we hear such sounds they therefore seem ancient.

Little historical expertise is needed to identify most things as anachronistic. The veriest tyro in architectural history, unable to tell classical from neo-classical, Queen Anne from Georgian, Tudor from mock Tudor, rightly sees that all these styles have some connection with the past. Countless clues certify furniture, silverware, clothing, paintings as 'antique'. The very prevalence of fakes substantiates the point: deceptions are only convincing if they incorporate the insignia of antiquity. So too with avowed emulations and imitations, period architecture, self-consciously nostalgic fashions: some complain

---

[334] Abraham, *Tradition of Western Music*, pp. 34–5. Popular music ages rapidly: 'The record was old-fashioned, and had a tinny quality only partly due to the needle ... Little empty tricks of syncopation ... recalled the outmoded dresses of the girls that had danced to it. It was strange to think it had once sounded modern. Now it was like an awning propped in the sun, nearly white, that years ago had been striped bright red and yellow' (Larkin, *Girl in Winter*, pp. 118–19).

[335] Bibikov, 'A Stone Age orchestra' (1975), quotation on p. 30. Melodiya, the Soviet gramophone concern, has issued a 'hypnotic' recording of music played on these bones (Michael Binyon, 'Paleolithic record of prehistoric rhythm', *The Times*, 22 Nov. 1980, p. 5).

they debase the true coin, but the objection admits the resemblance and, as Chapter 6 will show, affirms the link with the past.

Defects and virtues of reliquary knowledge

The tangible heritage has both advantages and drawbacks as a source of awareness. One limitation is the restricted scope of the past it discloses. As a Naipaul character testifies, '"The past is here." He touched his heart. "It isn't here." And he pointed at the dusty road.'[336] Attitudes and beliefs can only be conjectured from relics; to demonstrate past reactions and motives, artifacts must be amplified by accounts or reminiscences. This is a severe handicap, for 'thoughts, feelings, actions … are the stuff of history, not sticks, stones and bombasine'.[337] Unlike history and memory, whose sheer existence betoken the past, the tangible past cannot stand on its own. Relics are mute; they require interpretation to voice their reliquary role.

Relics are also static. Whereas the recorded and remembered past can convey the sense of a sweep through time, most tangible survivals yield only arrested moments. The high visibility of relics, especially of old buildings, leads many to over-estimate – and over-value – the stability of the past. The aura of antiquity in a much-preserved locale does not really connote historical vitality but a dearth of later innovative energy. 'Although people walked the pavements, there was a feeling of desertion as though this were a place from which, a long time ago, everyone had gone', as Lively describes the Cotswold town of Burford. 'Every building was old, many were beautiful: they seemed to be there together in sad abandonment like textbook illustrations of the past.'[338] All the relics felt dead.

A living, diachronic sense of the past demands a 'dynamic tension between what you see and what you know to have existed once and still to exist in some fragmented or symbolic form', suggests Gillian Tindall – a dynamism rare in heavily preserved localities. She contrasts the ongoing continuities of Kentish Town with the precious and static air of well-known London show-pieces:

So-called 'historic' areas – including many Conservation Areas – are precisely those in which time has stopped, that have to some extent died and been pickled at some point in the past. Townscapes which have managed to retain such a homogeneous aspect … are, by definition, areas which have not suffered the complex social upheavals and physical dislocations that make their history worth studying … Paradoxically, those places in which local 'concern for the past' is often so marked among successive generations of moneyed and leisured inhabitants, actually tell one less about the past as a whole … than do more ordinary, battered places.[339]

---

[336] *Bend in the River*, p. 123.
[337] Hale, 'Museums and the teaching of history', p. 68. 'When the raw material does not contain traces of thought, the doors to the past remain closed'; hence the archaeologists' picture of the past is not only poor but bizarre, as though 'beaker-folk' or 'Hallstadt Culture' 'were genuine societies' (Munz, *Shapes of the Past*, pp. 179–80). For an opposing view of the explanatory power of relics, even for cognitive processes, see Renfrew, *Towards an Archaeology of Mind*, pp. 16–23.
[338] *House in Norham Gardens*, p. 121. Ian Jack describes Cotswold villages as 'lovely shells, periwinkles inhabited by hermit crabs' ('The new gentry in a fine and private place', *Sunday Times*, 8 Mar. 1982, pp. 16–25, quotation on p. 20).
[339] *The Fields Beneath*, p. 116.

Places now pickled in aspic may, to be sure, have enjoyed a prolonged equilibrium. But when much survives from any particular epoch, not much can have happened since; otherwise most of those old things would have been replaced. Early Pompeii endured in complete detail only because there was no later Pompeii. In West Wycombe 'we get vivid glimpses of how life must have been', the proprietor maintains, precisely because there 'time appears to have stood still'.[340] But time does not stand still, and to see it so misconceives the past.

The artifactual route to the past also has special virtues, however. One is a relative lack of intentional bias. From the Renaissance on, scholars aware of textual forgeries and corruptions turned to relics as more reliable past witnesses.[341] Although it is now evident that artifacts are as easily altered as chronicles, public faith in their veracity endures; a tangible relic seems *ipso facto* real. Relics are also felt to counter the traditional predilection of historians for the extraordinary, the grand, or the precious. Tangible vestiges are seen as more characteristic of everyday life. To be sure, decay itself discriminates against the commonplace: the most imposing and costly artifacts best withstand attrition, attract protection, and encourage imitation. But intentional preservation accounts for only a small fraction of what survives. In resurrecting the way of life of the millions who have left no archival trace, artifacts partly redress the bias of written sources, and hence make historical knowledge more populist, pluralistic, and public.[342]

This function of relics, consonant with the homely virtues of the historical novel, was first stressed in the nineteenth century. 'We do not understand the ancients', wrote Niebuhr, 'unless we form distinct notions of such objects of their everyday life, as we have in common with them, under the forms their eyes were accustomed to.'[343] Because the tombs of Thebes depicted familiar scenes of everyday life, George Perkins Marsh thought them 'fraught with richer lore than ever flowed from the pen of Herodotus', just as he felt 'an hour of buried Pompeii is worth more than a lifetime devoted to the pages of Livy'. Marsh urged that everyday domestic and industrial artifacts – agricultural and mechanical tools, furniture, utensils – be preserved to reveal the lineaments of past ordinary lives – a practice only now become common.[344] Some preferences for artifacts may stem from philistine as well as populist bias. Thus Henry Ford, ridiculed for asserting that 'history is more or less bunk', determined 'to build a museum that's going to show industrial history, and it won't be bunk ... That's the only history that is worth observing ... By looking at things people used and that show the way they lived, a better impression can be gained than could be had in a month of reading.'[345]

[340] Francis Dashwood, West Wycombe brochure (1977), p. 1.

[341] Cochrane, *Historians and Historiography*, pp. 432–6; Hay, *Annalists and Historians*, pp. 127–8; Momigliano, 'Ancient history and the antiquarian', pp. 11–16.

[342] Schlereth, 'Pioneers of material culture'; I. N. Hume, 'Material culture with the dirt on it', pp. 37–8; L. S. Levstik, 'Living history – isn't'; Lynch, *What Time Is This Place?* p. 31; Schlereth (ed.), *Material Culture Studies in America*, especially Kouwenhoven, 'American studies: words or things?' (1964), pp. 79–92; Wilcomb E. Washburn, 'Manuscripts and manufacts' (1964), pp. 101–5; John T. Schlebecker, 'Use of objects in historical research', pp. 103–16, and Robert Ascher, 'Tin*can archaeology', pp. 325–37.

[343] Niebuhr, *History of Rome* (1811), 1:xxiii.

[344] *American Historical School* (1847), p. 11; Lowenthal, *George Perkins Marsh*, pp. 101–3.

[345] Ernest G. Liebold, Reminiscences, quoted in Roger Butterfield, 'Henry Ford, the Wayside Inn, and the problem of "History is bunk"', p. 57, and slightly varied, in Hosmer, *Preservation Comes of Age*, p. 80; Alexander, *Museums in Motion*, p. 92.

Accessibility is another advantage of tangible remains. Relics open to public inspection and potentially visible to any passerby provide unmediated impressions of the past. Seeing history on the ground is a less self-conscious process than reading about it: texts require deliberate engagement, whereas relics can come to us without conscious aim or effort. 'More open than the written record', in Lewis Mumford's words, 'buildings and monuments and public ways . . . leave an imprint upon the minds even of the ignorant or the indifferent.'[346] History and memory usually come in the guise of stories which the mind must purposefully filter; physical relics remain directly available to our senses.

This existential concreteness explains their evocative appeal. Noting 'the content a man has to see and handle the very same individual things which were in use so many ages ago', a seventeenth-century antiquary termed coins the real proof of the past. 'Would you see a pattern of the . . . funeral pile, burnt at the canonization of the Roman emperors? would you see how the Augur's hat and *lituus* [wand] were made? Would you see true and undoubted models of their temples . . .? Repair to old coins, and . . . there shall you find them excellently and lively represented.'[347] Protestants who spurned reputed fragments of the Cross and Judas's pieces of silver as idolatrous frauds themselves idolized classical relics; fascinated by a nail of Corinthian brass from the ruins of Nero's Golden House, John Evelyn felt the thrill of immediate touch with ancient civilization.[348] 'Examination at first hand of surviving monuments is a direct door into the human past', Vico judged, 'and casts a steadier light both on what men were and did, and on their reasons and motives for it, than the stories of later chroniclers and historians.'[349] Gibbon's visit to Rome, seeing 'each memorable spot where Romulus *stood*, or Tully spoke, or Caesar fell', provided his crucial inspiration: 'On the 15th of October, 1764, as I sat musing amidst the ruins of the Capitol, while the barefooted friars were singing vespers in the Temple of Jupiter, . . . the idea of writing the decline and fall of the city first started to my mind.'[350] The effigies of the French kings in the Musée des Monuments vivified national history for the young Michelet; 'the sword of a great warrior, the insignia of a celebrated sovereign', argued the historian Prosper de Barante in urging a subsequent government to buy the Musée de Cluny collection, were 'relics which people like to see', more impressive than 'the dead letter' of the history book.[351]

Romantic evocations of tangible monuments, epitomized in Shelley's 'Ozymandias', heightened appreciation of relics as witnesses. Historical training should begin not in library archives, thought J. R. Green, but in the quaint old streets of Bury St Edmunds, to 'work out the history of the men who lived and died there'.[352] The taste, feel, and sight

[346] *Culture of Cities*, p. 4. Linguistic characteristics and ceremonial traits, 'realities just as much as the flint hewn in the stone age', are likewise apprehended at first hand, notes Marc Bloch (*Historian's Craft*, pp. 54–5). But unlike physical objects, these residues have to be translated from symbolic into physical representations. On the immediacy of material relics, see Daniel, *Idea of Prehistory*, pp. 160–3; Bronner, '"Visible proofs": material culture study in America'.

[347] Peacham, *Complete Gentleman* (1622), Ch. 12, 'Of Antiquities', pp. 126–7.

[348] *Diary*, 13 and 27 Feb. 1645, pp. 185, 195.

[349] *New Science*, paraphrased in Berlin, *Vico and Herder*, p. 57. See Luck, 'Scriptor classicus', p. 154.

[350] *Autobiography* (1796), pp. 84–5. This was actually a much-altered recollection. In the original, Gibbon was not in the Capitol but in the Church of the Franciscan friars; in fact, by 1764 the ruins of the Capitol had long been effaced (Randolph Bufano, 'Young Edward Gibbon', letter, *TLS*, 10 Sept. 1982, p. 973). The discrepancies are instructive but do not detract from the event's significance.

[351] Michelet, *Ma jeunesse* (1884), pp. 44–6; Barante, 'L'Acquisition du Musée du Sommerard' (1843), 2:421.

[352] *Stray Studies from England and Italy* (1876), p. 218; Burrow, 'Sense of the past', p. 122.

that etch relics into memory can also vividly conjure up their milieux. 'Picking up for one's self an arrow-head that was dropt centuries ago, and has never been handled since', Hawthorne fancied he had received it 'directly from the hand of the red hunter', thereby envisaging 'the Indian village, amid its encircling forest', and recalling 'to life the painted chiefs and warriors, the squaws at their household toil, and the children sporting among the wigwams; while the little wind-rocked papoose swings from the branch of a tree'.[353]

Relics lent immediacy to exotic as well as domestic history; archaeological discoveries in the Holy Land and in Greece brought biblical and classical worlds alive. Millions thrilled to Amelia Edwards's eyewitness accounts of Egyptian temples. Every dawn at Abu Simbel 'I saw those awful brethren pass from death to life, from life to sculptured stone', almost believing 'that there must sooner or later come some one sunrise when the ancient charm would snap asunder, and the giants must arise and speak'. At Karnak's Great Hall 'every breath that wanders down the painted aisles . . . seems to echo back the sighs of those who perished in the quarry, at the oar, and under the chariot-wheels of the conquerer'.[354]

Today the relics of antiquity arouse less extravagant responses, but the feeling of immediacy endures. London's historical flavour overwhelms Helene Hanff: 'I went through a door Shakespeare once went through, and into a pub he knew. We sat at a table . . . and I leaned my head back, against a wall Shakespeare's head once touched, and it was indescribable.'[355] The shiver of contact with ancient sites brings to life their lingering barbarity or sanctity, and merely touching original documents vivifies the thoughts and events they described.[356]

The historian who sees for himself the locale of his work heightens its impact for his audience. George Bancroft trod the ground which Wolfe had walked and 'marked as near as I could the spot where Jacques Cartier may have landed'.[357] Margery Perham's biography of Lord Lugard gains verisimilitude from her own Nigerian tour of duty; Bruce Catton knew the Civil War battlefields he describes; Samuel Eliot Morison made a point of tracking Columbus's voyages by sail.[358]

Tangible familiarity enhances the effect of historical fiction, too. Virgil sought out places visited by Aeneas, Scott reconnoitred the locales his tales describe. 'Does not our sense of that classic struggle between Holmes and Moriarty quicken if we have seen the Reichenbach Falls, above the Englischer Hof?'[359] Even re-created locales can convey historical immediacy: Poussin painstakingly built models of the Greek and Roman scenes

---

[353] Hawthorne, 'The old manse' (1846), 10:11.

[354] *A Thousand Miles up the Nile* (1877), pp. 285, 152. See Hudson, *Social History of Archaeology*, pp. 73–83.

[355] *Duchess of Bloomsbury Street*, p. 30.

[356] Fairley, *History Teaching through Museums*, pp. 2–3; Galbraith, 'Historical research and the preservation of the past', p. 305; Drabble, *A Writer's Britain*, p. 17. 'Nothing seems to bridge the gap of the years so much as the unfolding and reading of ancient letters; sometimes minute particles of sand which had long adhered in some thick down stroke where the ink had been wet, detach themselves after three hundred years to blow away and join with yesterday's dust' (Wedgwood, 'Sense of the past', p. 25). It is awesome to handle an object that is real in the present, yet unreal because from a different past (K. C. P. Smith and Apter, 'Collecting antiques – a psychological interpretation'). Modern technology and institutions that attenuate face-to-face transactions may have increased our need to touch the past (Hindle, 'How much is a piece of the True Cross worth?' pp. 5, 10).

[357] To his sister, 8 Aug. 1837, quoted in David Levin, *History as Romantic Art*, p. 17.

[358] Morison, *Admiral of the Ocean Sea*, 1:xvi–xviii. On the more 'authentic' and nearly disastrous voyage of the *Niña II*, see Jay Anderson, *Time Machines*, pp. 115–16.

[359] A. P. Middleton and Adair, 'Case of the men who weren't there', p. 173.

that inspired his Arcadian pictures so as to see the past with his own eyes and feel it with his own hands.[360] For Robert Wood the sense of place magnified the sense of the past; steeping himself in Greek landscapes, he felt the closeness as well as the remoteness of the Greek literature he read there: 'the Iliad has new beauties on the banks of the Scamander'.[361]

A past lacking tangible relics seems too tenuous to be credible. Ruskin grumbled that because England had only 'a past, of which there are no vestiges; . . . the dead are dead to purpose. One cannot believe they ever were alive, or anything else than what they are now – names in school-books.' By contrast, 'at Verona we look out of Can Grande's window to his tomb', and feel 'that he might have been beside us last night'.[362] To be certain there was a past, we must see at least some of its traces. 'Like very old, once famous people whom everyone has thought dead for half a century but who turn out to be living in a furnished room somewhere, with half a dozen cats', places redolent of age prove 'that the past really existed once, that it wasn't made up by experts on the basis of archives'.[363] His tangibly old chair, table, and tavern in Chester reassured Frederick Law Olmsted that 'his experience of the past was [not] a fabrication and that at any minute a bell would ring and scene-shifters' dismantle the ancient town before his eyes.[364] Preserving the ruins of Oradour is essential, French survivors feel, to convey conviction of the horrendous Nazi massacre; as with old houses which 'have stood and watched the processes of change, . . . you must keep the shells inside which such things happen, in case you forget about the things themselves'.[365]

Coexistence with the present is another vital quality of the tangible past: something old or fabricated to seem old can bring the past to us, palpable and potent. 'To see the emperors, consuls, generals, orators, philosophers, poets, and other great men . . . standing as it were in their own persons before us', John Northall reacted to the antique statues at Rome in 1752, 'gives a man a cast of almost 2000 years backwards, and mixes the past ages with the present.'[366] The past was similarly present for Amelia Edwards at Philae. 'One forgets for the moment that anything is changed. If a sound of antique chanting were to be borne along the quiet air – if a procession of white-robed priests . . . were to come sweeping round between the palms and the pylons – we should not think it strange.'[367] Crusading a century ago to save Boston's Old South Meeting House, Wendell Phillips assured his audience that the Revolutionary heroes 'Adams and Warren and Otis are to-day bending over us, asking that the scene of their immortal labors shall not be desecrated or blotted from the sight of men'.[368] Disneyland's moving, speaking model of Abraham Lincoln helps us believe in our past by bringing it into the present, 'not be

---

[360] Praz, *On Neoclassicism*, pp. 28–9.

[361] *Ruins of Palmyra* (1753), p. 2: 'Classical ground not only makes us always relish the poet, or historian more, but sometimes helps us to understand them better.'

[362] *Modern Painters*, IV, Pt 5, Ch. 1, sect. 5, pp. 4–5.   [363] Zweig, 'Paris and Brighton Beach', p. 512.

[364] Olmsted, *Walks and Talks of an American Farmer in England*, pp. 88–90; quotation from Mulvey, *Anglo-American Landscapes*, p. 51.

[365] Lively, *House in Norham Gardens*, p. 12. See Andrew Spurrier, 'Oradour: the town that came back to life after a massacre', *IHT*, 4 June 1980, p. 7; Diana Geddes, 'Oradour: the agony that cries out for vengeance', *The Times*, 4 June 1983, p. 8. Compare the horrified response of a Lidice survivor who returns 'to find nothing there, not even ruins' (Cox, 'Restoration of a sense of place', p. 422).

[366] *Travels through Italy*, p. 362.   [367] *A Thousand Miles up the Nile*, p. 207.

[368] Speech of 1876, quoted in Hosmer, *Presence of the Past*, p. 104.

history *was* but history *is*'.[369] Finding an 1864 volume on Henry Clay in the British Library, its pages still uncut, instantly made John Updike intimate with that past: 'I was the prince whose kiss this book had been awaiting, asleep, for over a century.'[370]

Because artifacts are at once past and present, their historical and modern roles interact. A flavour of antiquity permeates a row of houses famed for architects and residents of various epochs, their different longevities adding character to the present-day ensemble. Landscapes commingling old with new reinforce feelings of temporal coexistence: the mass of ancient artifacts on Dorset's hills, all 'seen at once, as from the perspective of eternity', gave Thomas Hardy the sense of history in layered proximity.[371]

Yesterday's relics thus enlarge today's landscapes. The endurance of buildings carries habits and values 'over beyond the living group', in Mumford's words, 'streaking with different strata of time the character of any single generation'.[372] Old relics hand down their stored-up past: rubbing an Elizabethan silk bobbin-boy against her cheeks 'to get the essence of the ancient thing', Alison Uttley's modern heroine felt it 'smooth as ivory, as if generations of people had held it to their faces, and I suddenly felt a kinship with them, a communion through the small carved toy'.[373] For an old man in Bradbury's story, keepsakes in an attic harbour and enliven the past.

It was indeed a great machine of Time, this attic, . . . if you touched prisms here, doorknobs there, plucked tassels, chimed crystals, swirled dust, punched trunk hasps and gusted the vox humana of the old hearth-bellows until it puffed the soot of a thousand ancient fires into your eyes . . . Each of the bureau drawers, slid forth, might contain aunts and cousins and grandmamas, ermined in dust.[374]

Pictures and images of things past likewise help to convey moderns back through time. The medieval costumes in C. A. Stothard's *Monumental Effigies* were meticulously authenticated so as to 'arrest the fleeting steps of Time' and enable readers to 'live in other ages than our own'.[375] Historical reconstructions likewise persuade visitors either that they are in the past or that the past is alive in the present. U.S. Park Service managers of prehistoric Indian ruins are exhorted 'to convey the notion to the visitor that the ancients who lived there might come back this very night and renew . . . the grinding of corn, the cries of children, and the making of love and feasting' – though this last dictum 'must not be taken too literally'.[376]

Things thus differ from thoughts and words in their temporal nature. Written history demarcates past from present; verbal tense clearly distinguishes now from then. But artifacts are simultaneously past and present; their historical connotations coincide with their modern roles, commingling and sometimes confusing them, as in a recent National Trust notice: 'CHEDWORTH ROMAN VILLA ... COMPLETION DUE AUTUMN 1978'. The tangible past is in continual flux, altering, ageing, renewing, and always interacting with the present.

As enduring emblems of history and memory, tangible relics also symbolize national

---

[369] Bradbury, 'Machine-tooled happyland', p. 104.   [370] *Buchanan Dying*, 'Afterword', p. 256.
[371] J. H. Miller, 'History as repetition in Hardy's poetry', pp. 227–8.
[372] *Culture of Cities*, p. 4.   [373] *Traveller in Time*, pp. 49–50.   [374] 'Scent of sarsaparilla', pp. 196–7.
[375] 'Prefatory essay', *Monumental Effigies of Great Britain* (1832), p. ix.
[376] Tilden, *Interpreting Our Heritage*, p. 69.

identity. Places answer this purpose much better than books, as protectors of Washington's headquarters at Newburgh argued in 1850:

If our love of country is excited when we read the biography of our revolutionary heroes, . . . how much more will the flame of patriotism burn in our bosoms when we tread the ground where was shed the blood of our fathers, or when we move among the scenes where were conceived and consummated their noble achievements.[377]

Such patristic links have played a major role in the crusade for historic preservation, to be discussed in Chapter 7.

For most people, relics render the past more important but not better known. Laymen glean little historical information from, say, a table that has been in the family for generations; 'one does not know its history in the way an art historian knows the pedigree of a picture. It brings . . . rather a "sense of the past".'[378] But that tangible sense persuades us that the past we recall and chronicle is a living part of the present.

INTERCONNECTIONS

We live in a world where . . . the music that drifts down from the medieval walls into the garden where we sit is an old recording of Vivienne Segal singing 'Bewitched, Bothered and Bewildered'.

John Cheever, 'The Duchess'[379]

Memory, history, and relics offer routes to the past best traversed in combination. Each route requires the others for the journey to be significant and credible. Relics trigger recollection, which history affirms and extends backward in time. History in isolation is barren and lifeless; relics mean only what history and memory convey. Indeed, many artifacts originated as memorial or historical witnesses. Significant apprehension of the past demands engagement with previous experience, one's own and others', along all three routes.

Which route we follow at any given moment is not always clear. Uncertain where memory ends and history begins, we often attribute to one what comes from the other, jumbling early memories together with stories later heard and read, much as oral narrative conflates recent recollections with tales immemorially told. The 'living memory' of Kentish Town residents included events long before their birth, Tindall found. People 'remembered' farms which had ceased to exist in their grandparents' prime:

I was again and again told 'Cows were grazed at Gospel Oak when I was a girl', or 'It used to be all fields around here, dear; I remember before such-and-such a street was built.' Reference to a map of the period shows . . . [that] every street in central Kentish Town was there before the birth of the oldest person now living . . . Regularly reproduced by gullible local newspaper editors, . . . these 'reminiscences' [reflect] the fact that people of all ages *wish* to believe . . . that these fields still exist in the safety of memory.[380]

The need for substantiation often directs us from memory to history; relics and re-enactments vitalize history by retranslating it into memory. Handed down from generation to generation, Peruvian *quipus* (carved sticks) and Benin bronze plaques

[377] Richard Caldwell, *A True History of the Acquisition of Washington's Headquarters at Newburgh by the State of New York* (1887), quoted in Hosmer, *Presence of the Past*, p. 36.
[378] Carne-Ross, 'Scenario for a new year', p. 239.　　[379] 1978, p. 347.　　[380] *The Fields Beneath*, p. 129.

preserve socially important memories;[381] knocking an English youngster's head against boundary markers ensured he would remember their location; annual evocations of Exodus transform the Israelites' escape from Egypt into a personal experience for each celebrant. In Passover and Seder ceremonies 'both the language and the gesture are geared to spur, not so much a leap of memory as a fusion of past and present', writes Yerushalmi. 'Memory here is no longer recollection, which still preserves a sense of distance, but reactualization', as articulated in the dirge:

> A fire kindles within me as I recall – *when I left Egypt*
> But I raise laments as I remember – *when I left Jerusalem.*[382]

Some societies need no re-enactment to reactivate history; the process seems to be ingrained, habitual. Unassuaged injuries and injustices often lead men to conflate remote with recent times and even with the present. Many Irish continue to experience the Danish invasions, the devastations of Laud, the Famine of 1847, as almost contemporaneous events. Irish memory has been likened to historical paintings in which Virgil and Dante converse side by side.[383] But the Irish do not 'live in the past; rather, Ireland's history "lives in the present". All previous traitors and all previous heroes remain alive in it', as in the 'bottomless memory' of an O'Faolain character in which 'one might see, though entangled beyond all hope of unravelling', the entire saga of Ireland's decay.[384]

The enduring import of family bonds often conflates past generations. 'Yes, 1852, that was the year ... I fought King Ta'ufa'ahau', reports a Tongan; but in fact it was his great-great-great-grandfather who had done so.[385] West Indian small-islanders have spoken to me of eighteenth-century progenitors as if they were still living or had only recently died, 'remembering' them in no less intimate detail than grandparents.[386] At dinner parties in Toulouse 'you may hear families solemnly comparing the role of their ancestors in the mediaeval woad trade or the revolt against Richelieu', John Ardagh reports.

'Did your family fight in the First or the Second?' I heard one scion ask another. He was not referring to this century's World Wars, but to the Crusades. Another Toulousain said to me, 'We are all deeply marked here by the Roman Conquest, ...' and then added, 'We're marked by the Nazi Occupation too' – as if the two events were roughly contemporary.[387]

To reactivate vivid memory, as we have seen, requires a renewed sensation in the present. Through the sound of a spoon against a glass, the feel of a damask napkin, the uneven paving stones trod in the Guermantes' courtyard, Proust fully recaptured the past, as

---

[381] Vansina, *Oral Tradition*, pp. 36–8. See Baier, 'Mixing memory and desire', p. 200.

[382] *Zakhor: Jewish History and Jewish Memory*, pp. 43–4. 'In each and every generation let each person regard himself as though *he* had emerged from Egypt' is the Talmudic dictum central to the Passover Haggadah (p. 45). On the revelatory significance of Passover and Seder, see R. M. Brown, 'Uses of the past'; Kern, *Culture of Time and Space*, p. 51.

[383] Lippmann, *Public Opinion*, p. 144.

[384] Edwin Ardener, 'Cosmological Irishman', *New Society*, 14 Aug. 1975, p. 362; O'Faolain, *Nest of Simple Folk*, p. 39. See McHugh, 'Famine in Irish oral tradition', pp. 391, 395–6, 436; Rodgers, *Ulstermen and Their Country*, p. 14; Cahalan, *Great Hatred, Little Room*, pp. 37, 120.

[385] Sahlins, 'Other times, other customs: the anthropology of history', pp. 522–3.

[386] Lowenthal, *West Indian Societies*, p. 106.

[387] *Tale of Five Cities*, p. 290. Claud Cockburn records a similar conversation shortly after the Second World War with Ladino-speaking Jews in Sofia, one of whom said, 'Our family used to live in Spain before they

with the unforgettable *madeleine* which his aunt Leonie used to give him on Sunday mornings.

And as soon as I had recognised the taste of the piece of madeleine soaked in her decoction of lime-blossom ... immediately the old grey house upon the street, where her room was, rose up like a stage set ... and the whole of Combray and of its surroundings, taking shape and solidity, sprang into being ... from my cup of tea.[388]

Regaining the past through sights, sounds, and smells re-experienced was a stock theme of nineteenth-century literature; renewing old sensations recalled both the original experiences and the feelings that went with them. The scent of violets recalled for Tennyson 'The times when I remember to have been / Joyful and free from blame'; the scent of a geranium leaf brought back for David Copperfield Dora's straw hat, blue ribbons, and curls; cold water on his bared arm 'Fetched back from its thickening shroud / ... a sense of that time / And the glass we used, and the cascade's rhyme' for Hardy's reminiscent lover.[389]

Piling history on memory redoubled the sense of the past. The medieval figures in William Morris's early poems dream of earlier experiences and look back on what is to *them* the past. The tales in *Earthly Paradise* are ancient even to their narrators; Guinevere relates her 'Defence' as a recollection; the dreams within dreams in 'The Land East of the Sun and West of the Moon' distance more from less remote pasts.[390] Guinevere's 'memory from old habit of the mind / Went slipping back upon the golden days ... / moving through the past unconsciously', and historical memories bring Tennyson's past into the present as well as distancing it.[391] Friends and lovers portrayed in Pre-Raphaelite paintings lend their ancient themes a certain contemporaneity, while deliberate modernisms of dress and gesture emphasize the pastness of their archaistic scenes.[392]

Artifacts as metaphors in history and memory

Memory, history, and relics have long served as mutual metaphors. The writer fitting together jigsaw puzzles from the past becomes 'the archaeologist of memory'; psychologists and philosophers habitually refer to recollections as artifacts. 'Memory is a repository or reservoir of records, traces, and engrams of past events analogous to records preserved in geological strata', in Hans Meyerhoff's words; 'like the earth (geological records) or the tools and instruments of man (archaeological records) ... the human mind is also a "recording instrument"'.[393]

moved to Turkey. I asked how long it had been since their family lived there. He said, it was approximately five hundred years, but spoke of those events as though they had occurred a couple of years ago' (*Crossing the Line*, p. 155). See Finley, 'Myth, memory and history', pp. 293–4.

[388] *Remembrance of Things Past*, 1:51. See Shattuck, *Proust's Binoculars*, pp. 70–4. Mink notes that 'Proust's memory was a little *madeleine* and a lot of imagination' ('Everyman his or her own annalist', p. 235).

[389] Tennyson, 'A dream of fair women' (1832), lines 79–80, p. 445; Dickens, *David Copperfield*, Ch. 26, p. 396; Hardy, 'Under the waterfall' (1911–12), pp. 315–16. See Gent, '"To flinch from modern varnish": the appeal of the past to the Victorian imagination', p. 15; Quinn, 'Personal past in the poetry of Thomas Hardy and Edward Thomas', p. 20.

[390] Ellison, '"The undying glory of dreams": William Morris and the Northland of old', pp. 148–50.

[391] 'Guinevere' (1859), lines 376–7, pp. 1734–5. See J. D. Hunt, 'Poetry of distance: Tennyson's "Idylls of the king"', p. 99.

[392] Gent, 'Appeal of the past to the Victorian imagination', p. 30; Buckley, 'Pre-Raphaelite past and present', p. 136.

[393] *Time in Literature*, p. 20. See Allen Tate, *Memories and Essays*, p. 12.

The notion of retrieving memories like checked baggage from storage long antedates the camera and the phonograph. Plato and Aristotle thought that sensory images impressed the mind as a signet ring does a block of wax; to this day similes of wax tablets, record grooves, and tapes dominate descriptions of memory.[394] To be sure, memory traces are only representations of things recalled, whereas relics *are* things, but writers on memory often overlook the distinction. Among the nerve cells of the temporal lobe, according to Penfield, 'runs the thread of time, the thread that has run through each succeeding wakeful hour of the individual's past life', and when 'the neurosurgeon's electrode activates some portion of that thread, there is a response as though that thread were a wire recorder, or a strip of cinematographic film, on which are registered all those things of which the individual was once aware . . . Time's strip of film . . . seems to proceed again at time's own unchanged pace.'[395]

Archaeological analogies have obsessed explorers of history and memory from Petrarch to Freud. Metaphors of disinterment and resuscitation pervaded humanist thought, as we saw in Chapter 3. Retrieval of antiquity meant resurrecting both buried artifacts and buried texts, and the unearthing of relics was equated with the restoration of classical learning. 'Sub-reading' texts and pictures to make out the vestigial forms beneath, deciphering historical knowledge hidden under the visual or verbal surfaces, 'the reader divines a buried stratum', in Greene's phrase, 'as a visitor to Rome divines the subterranean foundations of a temple'.[396]

Four centuries later these Renaissance metaphors became central to psychoanalytic insights. Like archaeologists and humanists, analysts sought to reconstruct the past from submerged artifacts – their patients' repressed memories – 'which had somehow preserved their form and even their life despite their seemingly final disappearance'.[397] Freud repeatedly invoked the resemblance between psychoanalysis and prehistoric excavation. Likening himself to an archaeologist who had made the dumb stones speak and reveal their forgotten past, he claimed in 1896 to have 'unearthed' unconscious memory traces of infantile sexual traumas, and when he later came to think that these memories reflected fantasies rather than actual seductions, he none the less retained the archaeological metaphor, aiming now to '"excavate" the inner subjective history of desire'.[398] 'This fragment might possibly belong to the period about which we are curious but it is not precise enough and not complete' was a characteristic Freudian reaction to one such memory; 'We have to go on digging and wait until we find something more representa-

[394] Marshall and Fryer, 'Speak, memory! an introduction to some historic studies of remembering and forgetting', pp. 304; Sorabji, *Aristotle on Memory*, p. 5; Heil, 'Traces of things past'. A typical instance: 'Dread and anticipation first soften the tablets of memory, so that the impressions which they bring are clearly and deeply cut, and when time cools them off the impressions are fixed like the grooves of a gramophone record' (Lyttelton, *From Peace to War*, p. 152).

[395] Penfield, 'Permanent record of the stream of consciousness', p. 68.

[396] *Light in Troy*, p. 99. For humanists this was no mere analogy but an actual identity, Foucault suggests, reflecting Renaissance views that accorded written texts and physical relics the same status. The world itself was a tissue of words and signs, the discourse of the Ancients a faithful mirror of what they described. Visible marks and legible words called for the same kind of interpretation; what was seen and what was read yielded knowledge of the same order (*Order of Things*, pp. 33–4, 38–40, 56).

[397] Ernest Jones, *Life and Work of Sigmund Freud*, 3:318.

[398] Freud, 'Aetiology of hysteria' (1896), 3:192; Toews, 'Inner and outer reality: Freud's abandonment of the seduction theory and the crisis of liberal culture in Western Europe', pp. 1, 6.

tive.'[399] In restoring what was missing Freud claimed to 'follow the example of those discoverers whose good fortune it is to bring to the light of day after their long burial the priceless though mutilated relics of antiquity'.[400] Himself a passionate collector who kept his latest finds within constant view, Freud wrote in the same vein of one analytic discovery that 'It is as if Schliemann had dug up another Troy which had hitherto been believed to be mythical.'[401]

Freud treated the retention as well as the unearthing of memory traces archaeologically. Just as the burial of ancient artifacts often preserved them, and Pompeii's relics only began to decay when they were dug up and made visible, so did conscious memory wear away, leaving only what was buried and unconscious unchanged; memory fragments were 'often most powerful and most enduring when the process which left them behind was one which never entered consciousness'. The difference was that 'every effort was made to preserve Pompeii, whereas people were anxious to be rid of tormenting ideas' like those his patients manifested.[402] And psychoanalysis 'works under more favourable conditions than' archaeology, whose significant evidence may well have been destroyed; for the analyst 'all of the essentials are preserved; even things that seem completely forgotten are present somehow and somewhere'.[403]

Critics contend that Freud's archaeological analogies unjustifiably reify his patients' memories, as if they were actual objects open to verification by others or to comparison with actual past events. The archaeologist formed his picture of the past from existing material artifacts, Freud from verbalized memories and images continually being deformed by analytic interaction. The patients' verbal utterances were creations of the present, and the analyst was not only discovering a past but also helping to create it.[404] 'Like a conscientious archaeologist', Freud claimed, 'I have not omitted to mention . . . where the authentic parts end and my constructions begin.'[405] But this too implied a material authenticity, Donald Spence notes, suggesting that Freud was privy to what had actually happened to his patients.[406] Terms like 'uncovering', 'fragment', and 'reconstruction' do seem to presuppose access to the 'true' past, which Freud could not have had. But such a return is no more possible for archaeologists, in fact, than for psychoanalysts.

[399] Bernfeld, 'Freud and archeology', p. 111. See Gay, 'Freud for the marble tablet', pp. 17–22.
[400] 'Fragment of an analysis of a case of hysteria' (1905), 7:12.
[401] To Wilhelm Fliess, 21 Dec. 1899, in his *Origins of Psycho-Analysis*, p. 305. Contrary to Bernfeld's assertion that Freud refers here to his own self-analysis, the letter clearly relates to 'Herr E.'.
[402] *Beyond the Pleasure Principle* (1920), 18:25; 'Notes upon a case of obsessional neurosis' (1909), 10:177. 'Everything conscious was subject to a process of wearing away while what was unconscious was relatively unchangeable; and I illustrated my remark by pointing to the antiques standing about my room . . . Their burial had been their preservation; the destruction of Pompeii was only beginning now that it had been dug up' (p. 176). See also Freud, *Leonardo da Vinci and a Memory of His Childhood* (1910), 11:83–4. Repression is hence a process of preserving as well as of suppressing data; a repressed memory persists as it was: 'Ideas which have become pathological have persisted in such freshness and affective strength because they have been denied the normal wearing-away processes (Freud, 'On the psychical mechanism of hysterical phenomena' (1893), p. 11; see Klein, *Psychoanalytic Theory*, p. 248).
[403] Freud, 'Constructions in analysis' (1937), 23:259–60: Unlike the analyst, the archaeologist could not check his constructs with some surviving Trojan or Babylonian (Lewin, *Selected Writings*, pp. 291–2).
[404] Jacobson and Steele, 'From present to past: Freudian archaeology', pp. 349, 359–61; Spence, *Narrative Truth and Historical Truth*, p. 267.
[405] Freud, 'Fragment of an analysis of a case of hysteria', 7:12.
[406] *Narrative Truth and Historical Truth*, pp.160–1, 165, 176.

36 Freud's *Gradiva*: archaeology, psychoanalysis, commemoration (Chris Cromarty)

As with his distinction between 'narrative truth' and 'historical truth', Spence exaggerates the difference between verbalized memories and physical relics.

A childhood memory restored by bringing the Pompeiian past to life is the theme of the novel *Gradiva*, which Freud analyzed in detail.[407] For Wilhelm Jensen's protagonist, a reclusive German archaeologist, old 'marble and bronze were not dead, but rather the only really vital thing'. Rejecting the present, 'he sat in the midst of his walls, books, and pictures, with no need of other intercourse'. He shuns living women but is entranced by the classical bas-relief of a girl from buried Pompeii; envisaging his 'Gradiva' striding along the ancient streets, her 'enviroment rose before his imagination like an actuality. It created for him, with the aid of his knowledge of antiquity, the vista of a long street, ... lively colors, gaily painted wall surfaces, pillars with red and white capitals.'[408]

Impelled to wander among the ruins at Pompeii, he comes to see that his science 'merely gnawed at the dry rind of the fruit of knowledge without revealing anything of its content' and taught 'a lifeless, archaeological view'. Truly to comprehend the past he 'had to stand here alone, among the remains of the past ... Then the sun dissolved the tomb-like rigidity of the old stones, a glowing thrill passed through them, the dead awoke, and Pompeii began to live again.' His beloved Gradiva reappears in the guise of a forgotten childhood friend. 'Can't you remember?' she tries to reawaken his early memories. 'It seems to me as if we had eaten our bread together like this once, two thousand years ago ... To think that a person must first die to become alive; but for archaeologists that is necessary, I suppose.'[409] By the end, Freud shows, the archaeologist's repressed childhood has been excavated intact from the Vesuvian ashes.[410]

Freud later found in the Vatican Museum the Greek prototype of the *Gradiva* relief that had inspired Jensen's story, and hung a plaster cast of it in his consulting room to symbolize the interplay between memory and artifact. As tokens of their veneration of Freud, other analysts subsequently had the *Gradiva* photographed for their own offices.[411] Thus an ancient work of art, reflected as memory and history in Jensen's novel, became for Freud an archaeological emblem of repression and rediscovery, and at length a commemorative image for his followers.

Changing routes to the past

The roles of history, memory, and relics in understanding the past vary with stages both in life and in civilization. Most things that surround the young, like most of the history they learn, were there before them; as we grow older, more and more of our own past

---

[407] Jensen, *Gradiva: A Pompeiian Fancy* (1903); Freud, *Delusion and Dream* (1906).

[408] *Gradiva*, pp. 159, 150. The story was not original with Jensen; it had been a stock theme of the Romantic imagination. Gautier's 'Arria Marcella' (1852) revives the age of Titus among Pompeii's ruins, and his hero enjoys a love affair with a maiden of the period. See also Gautier, 'Pied de momie'; A. B. Smith, *Théophile Gautier and the Fantastic*, pp. 64–5, 97; Daemmrich, 'Ruins motif', p. 37.

[409] *Gradiva*, pp. 179, 216, 230.

[410] *Delusion and Dream*. Slochower suggests that Freud's fascination with the Gradiva–Pompeiian theme stemmed from a need to have his own love-object 'dug out of the ruins again' ('Freud's *Gradiva*', p. 646).

[411] *Delusion and Dream*, 'Appendix to the second edition', p. 121; Jones, *Freud*, 2:342; *Berggasse 19*, pp. 58–9 and plate 12. When I saw the *Gradiva* in Freud's London consulting room in 1973, Anna Freud confirmed its significance as a psychoanalytic symbol.

becomes history. And our lengthened memories come to encompass more and more of what is historically known, including some history that antedates our birth.

Today's lengthened life spans extend both the remembered and the historical past and promote their convergence: more of us can now look back over longer stretches of time. And just as the old show particular interest in the past, so do societies with high proportions of elderly people. Two centuries ago, when the median age in the United States was 18 and the average length of life about 35, few could remember much of the past or had time to spare for it. With a median age of 35 and an average life span of 70, Americans today can recall a period twice as long, and being older are more disposed to do so. And more of what they remember is the subject of historical research. But the elderly also tend to focus on their own private, more manipulable past, substituting relics and recollections for history.[412]

As time distances events beyond personal recall, memory within any society gives way to history, and relics gain renewed significance. Once great events pass beyond the realm of memory and oral verification, they take on a different look. Thus a half century after the Revolution, notes Michael Kammen, Americans began to mythologize its history and to preserve its relics, cherishing the physical traces and reanimating the historical spirit of an epoch slipping beyond remembrance.[413]

The course of history itself has tipped the balance toward historical knowing; written history has by and large gained at the expense of memory and artifacts.[414] In cultures that lack writing or cannot store records of past events, memory plays the major role in transmitting heritage. Mnemonic devices common to oral and scribal cultures facilitate the recall of vast quantities of data; medieval 'memory theatres' held keys to tens of thousands of recollectable buildings, landscapes, and artifacts.[415] The modern book-trained mind may be no less capable of mnemonic feats, but information storage and retrieval makes such imagery unnecessary. 'If I distrust my memory, . . . I am able to supplement and guarantee its workings by making a note in writing', as Freud put it; 'I have only to bear in mind the place where this "memory" has been deposited and I can then "reproduce" it any time I like, with the certainty that it will have remained unaltered.'[416] Freud's recipe for recall makes it obvious why history has dethroned memory: physiology ultimately limits memory capacity, but the potential for historical knowledge is boundless. To be sure, lengthening life spans enlarge the variety of images we can recall, but that increase is trivial compared with the expansion of historical materials since the invention of printing.

Land-survey techniques illustrate the shift from relics and recollections to historical records. Traditionally, natural features and artifacts – trees and rocks, mountains and

---

[412] Kastenbaum, 'Time, death and ritual in old age', pp. 26–8; Rowles, 'Place and personal identity in old age'; Rowles, 'Reflections on experiential field work', p. 183.

[413] *Season of Youth: The American Revolution and the Historical Imagination*, pp. 21, 163.

[414] Writing was feared as a threat to memory. 'This invention will produce forgetfulness in the minds of those who learn to use it, because they will not practise their memory. Their trust in writing . . . will discourage the use of their own memory' (Plato, *Phaedrus*, p. 563). 'Abundance of books makes men less studious', destroying memory and enfeebling the mind (Hieronimo Squarciafico (1477), in Ong, *Orality and Literacy*, p. 80). See also Gerhardsson, *Memory and Manuscript*, pp. 123, 157. But as we have seen, literacy did not impair ability to remember, and verbatim memory is rare in non-literate societies.

[415] Rawles, 'Past and present of mnemotechny'; Yates, *Art of Memory*.

[416] 'Note upon the "mystic writing-pad"' (*c.* 1924), 19:227. See Cool, 'Petrarchian landscape as palimpsest', p. 92.

rivers, meadows and pastures, buildings and roads – demarcated both private and civil boundaries. King Edmund's charter granting Bishop Aelfric land in Berkshire in A.D. 944 illustrates the physical specificity of old-time boundaries: 'Up to the great tumulus beneath the wild garlic wood, then . . . up along the stone way to the tall crucifix at Hawk Thorn, . . . to the third thorn tree at bog-myrtle hangar . . . up to the Hill of Trouble, then west to rough lynchet . . . to the heathen burial places.'[417] Landowners and local officials committed these landmarks to memory by regularly perambulating the bounds, and preserved such landmarks as irreplaceable evidence of possession. Printing, aerial photography, and mathematical cartography have changed all this: we now trace boundaries on an abstract grid and reproduce them mechanically, obviating the need either to recall or to retain old physical features.[418]

Pictures along with print enhance knowledge of the past and diminish needs for recall. While relics yield to print's superior powers to preserve and convey information, *images* of artifacts have become more and more consequential. The very notion of 'seeing' the past gained currency from the late eighteenth-century proliferation of book illustrations that began to accustom people to the past as a visual experience.[419] Photography made such images accurate and ubiquitous, replacing not only the tangibly antique but history and memory as well. To have a daguerreotype was 'very nearly the same thing as carrying off the palace itself', wrote Ruskin from Venice; 'every chip of stone & stain is here – and, of course, there is no mistake about *proportions*'. By contrast with recollections and reports of the past, moments captured on film are verisimilar, precisely replicable, and indefinitely durable. Once people grew used to absorbing visual information from them, photographs became the norm of faithful representation, obviating needs for detailed recollection.[420]

The impact of photographs on our sense of the past involves more than this, however. To some they depict only frozen, static moments severed from lived experience, conveying no sense of diachronic connection.[421] Others regard photos as instant antiques, adjuncts to the generalized pathos of looking back. From the start, photographers fancied themselves historians recording a vanishing world, and were employed to do precisely that: Viollet-le-Duc commissioned daguerreotypes of Notre-Dame in Paris in 1842 before beginning its restoration.[422] Profound historical empathy led the photographer Walker Evans to see things around him as destined for extinction and to portray them as prospective relics.[423] Family photographs serve both as goads to memory and as aids to its verification, making our recollections more faithful to the actual past. Our first home was not really so big as we remembered it, our favourite uncle not really so handsome.[424] In poring over an old family

417 Quoted in Drabble, *A Writer's Britain*, p. 17.
418 Stilgoe, 'Jack-o'-lanterns to surveyors: the secularization of landscape boundaries'. The injunction 'Remove not the ancient landmark, which thy fathers have set' (Proverbs 22.28) has become obsolete.
419 Boase, 'Macklin and Bowyer', pp. 170–4; Strong, *And When Did You Last See Your Father?* p. 20.
420 Ruskin to his father, 7 Oct. 1845, *Ruskin in Italy*, p. 220; Kern, *Culture of Time and Space*, pp. 38–9; Ivins, *Prints and Visual Communication*, pp. 94–5.
421 John Berger, 'Uses of photography', pp. 50–2; Bann, *Clothing of Clio*, pp. 88–9, 134–6.
422 Sontag, *On Photography*, pp. 70–1, 79–80.
423 Arbus, 'Allusions to a presence' (review of Walker Evans, *First and Last*), *The Nation*, 11 Nov. 1978, pp. 497–8.
424 Hirsch, *Family Photographs*, p. 45. The effect of memory may so overwhelm such visual evidence, however, that we continue to recall the past as grander and greater than it was (Olney, 'Wole Soyinka as autobiographer', p. 85).

album, Michael Lesy suggests, children become aware of how their own private past converges with that of the family, the country, and bygone times in general.[425]

While reducing reliance on written history, audio-visual devices expand other consciousness of the past: television, museum displays, and historic sites promote visual rather than verbal images. Thousands nowadays visit Stoke Poges and Selborne who never read Gray's *Elegy* or Gilbert White's *Natural History*; millions watched *The Barchester Chronicles* and *The Forsyte Saga* on television who never turned a page of Trollope or Galsworthy. And Kenneth Clark's *Civilisation* remains far better known as a television series than as a book.

Films make history both intense and plausible; figures seen moving and speaking in locales redolent of the past seem more alive than ever. 'Thanks to the cinema, the twentieth century and its inhabitants stand in a different relation to time from any previous age', writes a film critic. 'We can conjure up the past, moving – and for the past 50 years – talking just like life.'[426] Sights and sounds stored on film and tape give increasing access to bygone events, and every passing year adds both to the bulk of such records and to their temporal remoteness. And they not only secure but enormously amplify personal memory. A few hundred people may today know your face at 40, but only a few score of these knew it when you were 20, perhaps a handful of them when you were 6; by extending potential access to the ways we used to look, snapshots enhance our own connections with our former selves.[427]

Yet every advance in our knowledge of the past paradoxically makes it more remote, less knowable. Few until this century fully realized that the past cannot be directly confronted, that it is largely inaccessible notwithstanding confirmed evidence, and that we unavoidably transform what we learn about it to suit our own needs.

The sense of loss attending increased knowledge is an old story, however. Exuberant Renaissance response to classical art later succumbed to a surfeit of information; by the seventeenth century people no longer asked of an ancient statue 'Why is it so sublime?', in Gombrich's phrase, but 'What lost work does it reflect?'[428] Every new discovery brought antiquity closer in accurate detail while distancing it in feeling. Growing awareness of anachronism especially has detached us from the past. Through the eighteenth century, anachronism referred only to errors that distorted or misdated something of the past; in the nineteenth century the term came to refer to past survivals or revivals in the *present*, in the pejorative sense of being outdated, of having outlived their time.[429] The better we know the past, the more we find we have outgrown it. Indeed, we begin to feel we have similarly outgrown our own life histories; the pace of external change and of internal re-evaluation make it hard to sustain coherent images of ourselves and our purposes. Looking back with anachronistic misgivings, we replace old memories not merely unwittingly, as people have always done, but with abashed deliberation; we can now recall the past all too well for present comfort.[430]

[425] *Time Frames: The Meaning of Family Pictures*, pp. xv–xvi.
[426] David Robinson, 'The film immutable against life's changes', *The Times*, 7 Dec. 1983, p. 11.
[427] Lesy, *Time Frames*, p. xiii. Lesy posits fewer recognitions at each age.   [428] 'Perfection's progress', p. 5.
[429] Blaas, *Continuity and Anachronism*, pp. 29–30.   [430] Peter Berger, *Invitation to Sociology*, pp. 71–6.

Such awareness also makes our view of the present increasingly unlike the past it self-consciously absorbs. 'In earlier ages when there was not enough historical background to project the present against, the present appeared largely inevitable', writes Walter Ong. 'Because we have access to so much history ... the present can be examined for Renaissance, medieval, classical, preclassical, Christian, Hebrew, and countless other elements ... Our knowledge of the histories of a great many other cultures and how they accord with and differ from our own' further sets the present apart.[431]

As the past seems to recede from us, we seek to re-evoke it by multiplying paraphernalia *about* it – souvenirs, mementoes, historical romances, old photos – and by preserving and rehabilitating its relics. These surrogates resemble those of the later Victorians,[432] but whereas they felt confident they had captured the real past, we suspect we have not. Conscious of contriving substitutes, we alter the inherited past more radically than did our precursors who felt closer to it. These transformations of the past – the modes of effecting them, and the reasons they are made – are the subject of the next chapter.

---

[431] *Rhetoric, Romance, and Technology*, p. 326.   [432] Buckley, *Triumph of Time*, p. 105.

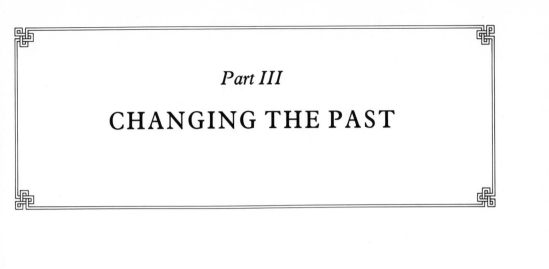

Part III

CHANGING THE PAST

6

CHANGING THE PAST

If you do not like the past, change it.

William L. Burton, 'The use and abuse of history'[1]

Every act of recognition alters survivals from the past. Simply to appreciate or protect a relic, let alone to embellish or imitate it, affects its form or our impressions. Just as selective recall skews memory and subjectivity shapes historical insight, so manipulating antiquities refashions their appearance and meaning. Interaction with a heritage continually alters its nature and context, whether by choice or by chance.

Such changes can be profoundly disturbing, for they cast doubt on all historical knowledge. As Chapter 2 showed, we need a stable past to validate tradition, to confirm our own identity, and to make sense of the present. How can we rely on a past that is fluid and alterable? One solution is to remain unaware that the past has been changed, like many who depend wholly on oral tradition. Another is to suppose such alterations inconsequential, leaving the past essentially what it was. A third is to believe that we can rectify previous changes, like science-fiction time wardens restoring traces and relics to their original state. A fourth is to accept alterations as necessary evils, conserving past remains against still worse erosion and despoliation.

None of these stances wholly allays suspicions that, like memory and history, the reliquary past is a will-o'-the-wisp. Time corrupts its surviving traces whether we wish it to or no, making relics ever more outdated, less recognizable, and subject to graver misinterpretation. Philip Larkin suggests how the centuries eroded the original meaning of the medieval hand-linked figures in 'An Arundel Tomb'.

> Side by side, their faces blurred,
> The earl and countess lie in stone
>   *   *   *
> They would not think to lie so long.
> Such faithfulness in effigy
> Was just a detail friends would see:
> A sculptor's sweet commissioned grace

[1] *American Historical Association Newsletter*, 20:2 (1982), p. 14.

Thrown off in helping to prolong
The Latin names around the base.
    ★ ★ ★

Now, helpless in the hollow of
An unarmorial age . . .
    ★ ★ ★

Only an attitude remains:
Time has transfigured them into
Untruth . . .[2]

Ensuing consequences likewise alter how we view relics. Surviving Georgian structures look different in 1985 than they did in 1885 not simply because they are now older and scarcer but because a further century has added to the scene a host of neo-Georgian structures. New insights and needs, new memories and forgettings force each generation to revise what relics it notices and how to interpret them.

For many of these alterations we are not responsible; nothing can prevent them. Others involve interactions with history and antiquities that are to some extent matters of choice. In either case, any treatment of the past, however circumspect, invariably alters it. What kinds of change are thereby induced, and what occasions them, is the subject of this chapter. The first two parts focus primarily on how changes affect material relics, notably artifacts; Chapter 5 surveyed similar alterations of history and memory. The motives and reasons that underlie all these alterations are reviewed in the third part of this chapter.

Relics undergo two types of transformation. One affects them directly: protection, iconoclasm, enhancement, reuse alter their substance, form, or relation to locale. Action of these kinds wasted British abbeys into ruins, concentrated classical antiquities at the British Museum, transplanted London Bridge to Arizona. The second type of transformation is indirect, impinging less on the physical condition of survivals than on how they are seen, explained, illustrated, and appreciated. Relics inspire copies, replicas, models, emulations, depictions; monuments and re-enactments commemorate people and events. Action of these kinds converted Edinburgh into 'the Athens of the North', made simulated half-timbering an inter-war suburban hallmark, littered Victorian England with innumerable medieval reminders, and embellished the bicentennial American scene with Revolutionary pageantry.

No sharp boundary separates these activities, and the results are often analogous. Copying, imitating, and emulating antiquities may stem from or arouse a desire to protect or enhance the originals; safeguarding relics often determines how they are displayed. Yet each form of impact has particular effects, some more drastic than others. From identifying, displaying, and protecting relics to removing, embellishing, and readapting them tends to involve increasingly radical alterations.[3]

---

[2] *Whitsun Weddings*, pp. 45–6. See John Bayley, 'The last romantic', *London Review of Books*, 5–18 May 1983, pp. 11–12; Clausen, 'Tintern Abbey to Little Gidding', pp. 422–4. In fact, the hand-in-hand pose was not original but the work of a Victorian restorer.

[3] For degrees of intervention, ranging from preservation to restoration, conservation, consolidation, adaptive use, reconstruction, and replication, see Fitch, *Historic Preservation*, pp. 44–7, and Feilden, *Conservation of Historic Buildings*, pp. 8–12.

ALTERING RELICS

All patterns and moulds we can skilfully make
You won't tell the difference between ours and a fake!
So if you want your building to look like the real thing
Just pick up the phone and give J. R. a ring.

'Ode to GRP', advertisement for glass-reinforced plastic[4]

One always rebuilds the monuments in his own way. But it is already something gained to have used only the original stones.

Marguerite Yourcenar, 'Reflections on the composition of *Memoirs of Hadrian*'[5]

Identifying

Valuing antiquity leads us to proclaim its existence: here it is, we want to say, an early, original, or ancient feature. And so we mark the site or the relic. Designation locates the antiquity on our mental map and lends it status; the signpost heralding its age also distinguishes it from present-day surroundings. Like a painting in a gallery, the marked antiquity becomes an exhibit contrived for our attention.

Markers may echo the past even if the things they identify are not themselves old, like European place-names given to American settlements. Knowingly anachronistic street and pub signs in British suburbia – Sylvan Walks, Dells, Hop Poles, Woodmans, Wheatsheafs, Ploughs – celebrate a generalized rural past. More English house-names are chosen as reminders of previous homes or past holidays than for any other purpose – hence the proliferation of Windermeres and Braemars in the 1930s, of San Remos, Tossas, and Riminis today.[6] A family or functional name on a building is more likely to identify a previous owner or use than the present one. 'The Schoolhouse' is a building that *used* to be a school; on a present-day school such a sign would be redundant.

The past thus identified may long antedate present memory. Thousands of American towns attest their founders' hunger for the sanction of antiquity; even hybrid innovations like Thermopolis, Minneapolis, Itasca, Spotsylvania, embody some lustre of age. Innumerable Euclid Drives, Appian Ways, and Phaeton Roads suggest ancient felicities, and Greek initials bedeck fraternity houses as though the Eleusinian mysteries were modern rites.[7]

Some traces of antiquity are so faint that only contrivance secures their recognition. In the absence of signposts, how many visitors to an old battlefield could tell that it was an historical site? But for markers, people would generally pass by most ancient monuments unaware of their antiquity. One risk of deleting archaeological sites from the British Ordnance Survey, as has been proposed, is that landowners and local governments are apt to scant the value if not to doubt the very existence of antiquities no longer pinpointed on maps, thus hastening their actual extinction.[8] Historic plaques similarly rescue from

[4] John Rogers (London) Ltd., in *Building Conservation*, 3:5 (1981), 22.   [5] *Memoirs of Hadrian*, p. 341.
[6] Survey by Joyce Miles, cited in 'Favourite house names', *Sunday Times*, 3 Feb. 1980, p. 49.
[7] H. M. Jones, *O Strange New World*, p. 228. See also Zelinsky, 'Classical town names in the United States'.
[8] There is 'a firm impression that unless a site of antiquity is shown on an OS map it has no reliable authority for its existence' (Graham Webster, 'Mapping buried history', letter, *The Times*, 31 Oct. 1977, p. 13).

37 Restoring and signposting: old iron mine, Roxbury, Connecticut, before renovation

38 After renovation

39 Marking the invisible past: Revolutionary conflict, Castine, Maine

40 Marking the inconsequential past: accident, Harrow on the Hill, Middlesex

obscurity homes of the famous. Except for the rare Monticello or Kelmscott, displaying Jefferson's own genius and Morris's own memorabilia, few houses are visibly distinctive simply for having sheltered great men; they become evocative only through subsequent markers.

An imposing marker may overshadow the relic it designates; if some signposts save history, others drown it in trivia. Local interest lends notoriety to places that 'marked some event almost too meager to comprehend', along such lines as 'Near this site . . . was believed to be . . . the original shed where Josiah Dexter, an early settler of Dexterville, hid from four Hessians'.[9] Many designations are avowedly speculative. At Top Withens, a farm associated with Emily Brontë's *Wuthering Heights*, a sign cautions pilgrims that 'The buildings, even when complete, bore no resemblance to the house she described. But the situation may have been in her mind when she wrote of the moorland setting.'[10] Other markers are frankly counter-factual, like the claim in an American Civil War park that 'Had General Lee been less troubled by the approach of battle he would have enjoyed the view of this fine pinewood forest'; the sign on a watering-trough that 'This is where Paul Revere would have watered his horse had he come this way'; the advertisement for a neo-Tudor time-share property that 'Queen Elizabeth would like to have slept here'; and the 'Seed from a lotus plant, that might have been picked by Christopher Columbus, had the American continent not got in the way.'[11]

Written signs obtrude both as objects and as linguistic symbols whose meaning and perhaps veracity must be pondered. After the parish council complained about the misleading word 'Castle' on a National Trust signpost at Bramber, a Norman relic in Sussex, the word 'ruin' was appended. Familiarity renders some notices invisible, others increasingly obtrusive: a sign identifying the churchyard through which Wordsworth's daughter ran to him as 'Dora's Field' at first lends emphasis to but subsequently encumbers the scene. If we do not need to be shown the way to or told the name of an historic site, why should our view be cluttered for the sake of others less knowledgeable or venturesome? To be temporarily 'lost' is often better than to be over-informed.[12]

Yet markers can also enhance the past. To American visitors European village names conjure up a thousand years of history. Places need not conform to the historical images their names imply; to provide a distinct impression of *some* past is enough. We do not feel cheated to find Bath more Georgian than Roman, Finchingfield substantially a nineteenth-century rather than a medieval village, or London's 'Roman' Barbican with only scanty pre-medieval traces. Markers magnify our sense of the past simply by echoing the condition of being *historical*; the echo alone may suffice. More commonly they help, like patina, to validate antiquity. 'That 1537 over the way is TRUE', exulted Frederick Law Olmsted on his visit to Chester, for 'I can see the sun shine into the figures.'[13]

---

[9] William Zinsser, 'Letter from home', *N.Y. Times*, 18 Aug. 1977, p. C16.

[10] Brontë Society plaque, 1964, in John Allwood and Ray Taylor, 'Signs of the times', *Parks*, 5:1 (1980), 20.

[11] Marcella Sherfy told me of the Lee sign; Arthur A. Newkirk, 'Artifact or artefact?' *Science*, 180 (1973), 1232; Elmers Court Timeshare, Lymington, advertisement, *Sunday Times*, 3 Oct. 1982, p. 8; *New Scientist*, 28 Oct. 1982, p. 272.

[12] Beazley, 'Popularity: its benefits and risks', p. 201.

[13] *Walks and Talks of an American Farmer in England* (1852), p. 88.

41 'Yes, I remember Adlestrop': this author beneath the sign that inspired Edward Thomas

Adlestrop (1915)

Yes, I remember Adlestrop –
The name, because one afternoon
Of heat the express-train drew up there
Unwontedly. It was late June

The steam hissed. Someone cleared his throat.
No one left and no one came
On the bare platform. What I saw
Was Adlestrop – only the name

Collected Poems, p. 71

Awareness of the tangible past is shaped as well as sharpened by signs telling where it is and what it was. Markers celebrating this relic or forbidding access to that one profoundly influence what we make of them. Even the least conspicuous sign on the most dramatic site affects how history is experienced. For example, signs identifying the keeps, donjons, and garderobes of ancient castles, the refectories, chapels, and libraries of ruined monasteries, induce an academic frame of mind by encouraging viewers to *compare* one ruin with another, these relics with those. They sort antiquities into history-book order, endowing the reliquary past with the flavour of the written record. And just as 'treasure-hunt' questionnaires at museums lead children to concentrate not on the exhibits but on the labels and notices, so some visitors to history-laden places attend more to the markers than to what they celebrate.[14]

---

[14] Rainey, 'Reflections on battlefield preservation', p. 75; Joel Stratte-McClure, 'In Paris, plaquetice makes perfect strolling', *IHT*, 12–13 Apr. 1980, p. 8; MacCannell, *Tourist*, p. 127.

42 Marking an intended past: restoring the aboriginal Kansas prairie

43 Marking a sentiment: honouring the reformer Shaftesbury, Harrow School

Mere recognition thus transforms the visible past. Identifying and classifying may tell us much about relics but often occludes our view of them, sacrificing communion with the past to facts about it.

Displaying

Showing off the past is the common result of identifying it. Labelling a relic affirms its historical significance; displaying it enhances its appeal. Antiquities in museums are enshrined in glass cases, mounted on cushions, flattered by spotlighting. Relics *in situ* are freed of surrounding encumbrances. *Son-et-lumière* programmes dramatize the past and set it off from nearby excrescences and modern obtrusions.

Cultural norms about how relics should be displayed determine the type and extent of alteration. For a picturesquely overgrown sixteenth-century ruined Italian nymphaeum, architects from several countries recently proposed highly diverse treatments. An English idea was to provide an entry to the site through a rough grassy walk, with unobtrusively weather-proofed ruined arches framing the distant city; an American scheme replaced the grass with paving and covered the ruin with metal and plastic corrugated roofing; a Jordanian rebuilt the building, adding vaulting and three supported domes; a West African replaced the grass with plastic turf, left the ruin as it was, and fenced out the public.[15]

Each of these solutions treated display along with protection, appearance, and function; indeed, these aims are often impossible to isolate. Original intent and use, historical authenticity, and contemporary aesthetics may buttress one or another treatment of antiquities. Preservationists seek to save views of St Paul's from tower-block obstruction; developers counter that the Cathedral was meant to be glimpsed intermittently from built-up streets. Against criticism that proposed council houses would destroy a superb open view of Beverley Minster, local planners retort that the Minster is no isolated art object and should be reincorporated into the community that built and sustained it.[16] Defenders of the ivy on Harvard College buildings wished to retain the familiar 'Ivy League' look that lends the Yard a picturesque unity; ivy detractors noted that look was of recent origin, cited the recurring cost of clearing the roots, and felt the buildings should be seen as their builders intended.[17]

Demands for intelligibility often justify altering ruins; the picturesque but shapeless Roman sites, medieval castles, and monastic ruins in British state care have been made more comprehensible by lowering ground surfaces, heightening walls, revealing buried details. Subsequent additions that 'confuse' the scene are removed (wartime Nissen huts and nineteenth-century pigsties but not eighteenth-century dovecotes or seventeenth-century gateways). The surrounding sward, cropped with military tidiness, enhances the

[15] Linstrum, 'Education for conservation', pp. 680–1.
[16] Ken Powell, *Beverley*; letters in *The Times*, 23 and 26 Mar., 2 Apr. 1981; *Sunday Times*, 29 Mar. 1981.
[17] David Harris Sacks, in 'The College pump', *Harvard Mag.*, 84:6 (1982), 96; 'Plan to cut hallowed ivy threatens Harvard image', *IHT*, 22 Apr. 1982. The ivy dates only from the 1880s.

44 Ruins made tidy: medieval remains, Yorkshire

45 Ruins left incomprehensible: medieval rubble, Bury St Edmunds, Suffolk

bleak, austere, and majestic mood the public has come to expect from ruins.[18] 'It's worth erring towards order and control', notes a heritage-guide reviewer, 'to offer something to people who are not specialists in medieval history.'[19]

The paraphernalia of display orchestrate and at times dominate the view. It is already 'difficult to appreciate the glories of Gothic architecture filtered through a mesh of ladders, exhibition stands, moulded plastic chairs and badly-placed, cluttered notice boards', and some fear that every historic building open to the public may soon require a new structure nearby to house the interpretive apparatus.[20] Some visitor centres are designed to clash with the ancient features they display; an ultra-modern geodesic dome was built for Connecticut's Dinosaur State Park, the State Commissioner explained, 'for the contrast between the very new and the 200 million year old tracks'.[21]

Whether blatantly modern or unobtrusively in keeping, ancillary attractions can eclipse the actual relics. The most conspicuous landmark at Gettysburg Battlefield is the tower that yields a bird's-eye perspective no Civil War participant ever had. To see the 'living' farm, the cyclorama, and the electric map at the Gettysburg Visitor Center takes longer than most visitors can spare for the entire battlefield.[22] Few who visit the Minute Man National Historical Park between Concord and Lexington get beyond the display centre into the remnants of the Revolutionary landscape. Some structures literally overwhelm the antiquities they are meant to display: the Lincoln 'birthplace' log cabin and Lenin's tomb seem puny and insignificant inside the great marble temples that house them. Other traces of past events remain invisible even when well advertised – like the tree in the Bois de Boulogne purportedly hit by Czar Alexander II's would-be assassin. Neither bullet nor bullet-hole could be seen, but 'the guides will point it out to visitors for the next eight hundred years', wrote Mark Twain, 'and when it decays and falls down they will put up another there and go on with the same old story'.[23]

Promotional efforts leave their own imprint, deplored by some and hailed by others. Floodlighting is held to free York Minster from visual pollution, but to turn Canterbury Cathedral into Dracula's castle.[24] Those who deprecate interpretive 'noise' think advance knowledge and unobtrusive guidebooks ample; others look for ways to make antiquities accessible to the widest possible public.[25] It is clear that the more interpretation becomes available, the more people rely on it; they prefer to imbibe history in comfort in heritage centres and are seldom conscious of, or worried about, the alterations of the past that interpretation implies.

[18] M. W. Thompson, *Ruins*, pp. 22–31; John Harvey, *Conservation of Buildings*, pp. 188–9.
[19] Ena Kendall, 'The sightseers' almanac', *Observer Mag.*, 24 May 1981, p. 56. See Lowenthal, 'Age and artifact', pp. 109–12.
[20] Johnstone and Weston, *Which? Heritage Guide*, p. 8. 'To be faced, on one's final arrival, by a notice board, an iron railing and a turnstile is more than can be borne' (Piper, 'Pleasing decay', p. 96). See Rainey, 'Battlefield preservation', p. 82.
[21] Stanley J. Pac, quoted in 'Dinosaur Park dedication', *Connecticut Woodlands*, 43:1 (1978), p. 14.
[22] Robert M. Utley, National Park Service, interview 2 Aug. 1978.
[23] *Innocents Abroad* (1869), p. 101. On involvement with markers, see MacCannell, *Tourist*, pp. 109–33.
[24] John Shannon, York Civic Trust, and Lois Lang-Sims, Canterbury, interviews 20 Sept. and 26 Aug. 1978.
[25] Beazley, 'Popularity', pp. 194–6.

46 Display overwhelms: the Lincoln 'birthplace cabin' in its marble memorial carapace,
Hodgensville, Kentucky, 1911 (Walter H. Miller)

47 Display denatures: Plymouth Rock, Massachusetts

Protecting

Display arouses the impulse to conserve, but also increases the need for it. Protective measures may detract from the appearance or intelligibility of relics, yet without them they vanish or decay all the sooner. The erosion of Niagara Falls poses a dilemma common to many 'natural' relics that survive only by dint of much artifice. The celebrated view of the Falls supports a multi-million-dollar tourist industry. But man, not nature, sustains that view, threatened by build-up of talus at the base and by demands for power that episodically vary the flow of water. To keep the Falls as immortalized in painting and literature – and in tourist brochures – would require arresting the river's headward erosion, an immensely costly engineering task. Erosion will in the long run – a few million years, perhaps – utterly destroy Niagara no matter what is done. But preservation is not concerned with so long a run. What are the short-run alternatives? Should the Falls remain moulded to our image of them? Or should nature take its course, and visitors be made to get used to seeing the Falls change?[26]

The granite nose of the Old Man of the Mountain at Franconia Notch, New Hampshire, would crumble away were it not bolted to the face. Only periodic scouring keeps visible the Neolithic white horses outlined on Britain's chalk scarps; regular recarving prevents erosion from disfiguring Gutzon Borglum's four sculpted presidential heads on Mt Rushmore.

Architectural antiquities require similar intervention. The Leaning Tower of Pisa must be kept leaning; left to fall or set upright, it would lose most of its historical identity. Protection often entails disfiguring artifice: many Gothic churches and cathedrals were saved from collapse only by nineteenth-century restorations later condemned as meretricious.

Protective action may engender or augment erosive processes. Ancient earthworks fenced off against mechanized agriculture attract burrowing rabbits displaced from ploughed fields. The iron clamps with which earlier conservators kept Acropolis columns and caryatids from crumbling are now, owing to expansive corrosion, themselves a major agency of destruction. Exposure to mass admiration magnifies existing menaces and spawns new ones. Fragile antiquities do not survive much handling. Tapestries soon get dirty and deteriorate with frequent washing; old furniture is roped off so it will not be sat on, books pinioned against removal from shelves. Furnishings and fabrics must be shielded against the effects of light – curtains installed, blinds kept down, slipcovers added. Such precautions are bound to alter the feel of the past.[27]

Public viewing can threaten the very survival of ancient sites, as instanced in the fading, cracking, and destructive mould on the cave paintings at Lascaux and Altamira. English cathedral steps, paving stones, and floor memorials are sorely vulnerable to tourism.

---

[26] Krieger, 'What's wrong with plastic trees?' pp. 447–8; Harwell, 'Recovering the "lost" Niagara'; Reyner Banham, 'Goat Island story', *New Society*, 13 Jan. 1977, pp. 72–3; Keith Tinkler, 'The downfall of Niagara', *New Scientist*, 15 Nov. 1979, pp. 506–9. Patrick McGreevy notes that writers' and artists' exaggerations helped form images of what the Falls *ought* to be ('Niagara as Jerusalem', *Landscape*, 28:2 (1985), 26–32).

[27] J. E. Harris and Crossland, 'Mechanical effects of corrosion', pp. 21–2; Greece, Ministry of Culture and Sciences, *Work on the Acropolis, 1975–1983*; John Cornforth, 'Housekeeping and house keeping', *National Trust*, No. 29 (Spring 1978), 13.

48 Protection trivializes: Casa Grande Ruins National Monument, Arizona (Richard Frear)

Canterbury Cathedral has suffered manifold woes: paving in the south aisle worn down more than an inch, a stone lost from a mosaic in the Trinity Chapel, inscriptions on the floor of the southwest transept rendered unreadable, the edges of brass fittings in the Martyrdom worn smooth, the bell tower unvisitable owing to wear on the roof leading, graffiti-marked piers, walls, and columns. To minimize wear and tear, cathedrals more and more ration access, rope off or cover up fragile areas, make visitors don felt overshoes, and replace relics with replicas.[28]

Preservative action often involves prolonged disturbance subversive of display. Like modern airports, medieval cathedrals seem forever wrapped in scaffolding and builders' rubble, detracting from their flavour of antiquity. Protection can debase the ambience of antiquities even when their fabric remains intact; Casa Grande, an ancient American Indian adobe structure in Arizona, is overwhelmed by its glass and steel protective roof. As with Lincoln's and Lenin's marble carapaces, the canopy reduces Casa Grande to triviality, and 'it now takes powers of imaginative reconstruction far beyond anything that can be inculcated by current "visitor-orientation" techniques to see the abode as the great monument of the plain'.[29]

Popularity threatens the fabric and the feeling of history; to prevent or mitigate such

[28] Hanna, 'Cathedrals at saturation point?'; English Tourist Board, *English Cathedrals and Tourism*, pp. 32–6, 60–3.
[29] Banham, 'Preservation adobe'. The protective canopy in fact accelerates erosion by drying out the adobe beneath (Douglas H. Scovill, National Park Service, interview, 26 Apr. 1984).

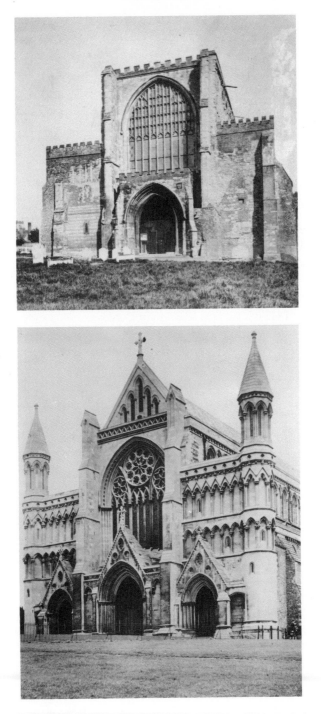

49–50 Antiquity reconstituted: St Albans Cathedral west front, before and after restoration by Lord Grimthorpe in 1879

damage further affects surviving relics. Thus preservation sets in train the extensive remodelling of the very past it aims to protect.

Reconstituting

We also remould the past to our expectations by embellishing its relics. Although revision is seldom the ostensible motive, removing dirt or rust, reconstructing a ruin, restoring an old building to what it might or should have been, and adding to extant remains all in fact aim at improving on what has survived.

That improving the past meant changing it long went unrecognized. Nineteenth-century restorers who purged medieval churches of later additions fancied they were reconstituting the true past. The purpose of many such alterations was ideological; in excising 'harmful' accretions and restoring 'pure' Gothic, ecclesiological reformers sought to retrieve the atmosphere and thereby rekindle the spirit of early Christian faith. To that end more than seven thousand medieval English churches – over half those surviving – were profoundly transformed.[30]

Restored structures were not only dead but anachronistic. Not even the most pains-taking renovation conformed with original work. 'Restoration is impossible', wrote Francis Palgrave in 1847 of attempts to do so in Bordeaux. 'You cannot grind old bones new. You may repeat the outward form (though rarely with minute accuracy), but you cannot the material, the bedding and laying, and above all the tooling...There is an anachronism in every stone.' In any renovation of antiquity 'the sensation of sham is invincible', he commented later. 'In the most perfect resuscitation of Henry the Third "Early English", the tooling and well-tempered town-made chisel inscribes "Victoria and Albert" upon every stone.'[31] Similarly, the men who had built St Mark's Venice 'drew everything by hand, set out everything by eye, and seem to have had an instinctive delight in curved and rounded and irregular surfaces and outlines everywhere', noted G. E. Street. By contrast, those engaged in restoring the cathedral in the 1880s had 'to have every angle perfectly square, every dimension exact, and every line straight . . . [Since] no single axiom of the perfect nineteenth century workman was ever regarded by the old builders and decorators with an atom of respect', it was grotesque to patch up a medieval building with modern work.[32]

Appalled by the destructive renovation of English churches and cathedrals, Ruskin and then Morris and the Society for the Protection of Ancient Buildings denounced all reconstitution of the past:

In the course of this double process of destruction and addition the whole surface of the building is necessarily tampered with; so that the appearance of antiquity is taken away from such old parts of

[30] Tschudi-Madsen, *Restoration and Anti-Restoration*, p. 25.
[31] Palgrave to Dawson Turner, 19 July 1847, in 'Biographical memoir', *Collected Historical Works*, 1:[xlv]; idem, *History of Normandy and England*, 1:xxix. Palgrave, deputy keeper of public records from 1838 to 1861, antedated Ruskin in expressing concern over ecclesiological renovation. 'To bring back the days of Edward III and of Catholicism appears to me to be an affectation', he wrote of the intended removal of Merton College's seventeenth-century woodcarvings; ' – *repair* when and where is needed, but never *restore* (to Dawson Turner, Oct. 1836, 1:[xxv]). Obituaries of both men noted certain similarities (Richard Garnett, 'Sir Francis Palgrave as a precursor of Ruskin' (1901), cited in Ruskin, *Complete Works*, 38:180), and Ruskin befriended two of Palgrave's sons, but there is no evidence of direct influence.
[32] Street, 'Report to S.P.A.B.' (1880–6).

51 Antiquity sustained: Arch of Titus, before restoration by Giuseppe Valadier, 1820s:
Piranesi, *Vedute dell'Arco di Tito*, *c.* 1760

52 Arch of Titus, after restoration: Herschel Levit photo, *c.* 1960

the fabric as are left, and there is no laying to rest in the spectator the suspicion of what may have been lost; and in short, a feeble and lifeless forgery is the final result.

The proper way to treat a relic was to leave it alone: 'Resist all tampering with either the fabric or ornament of the building as it stands; if it has become inconvenient for its present use, . . . raise another building rather than alter or enlarge the old one', Morris concluded. Ancient buildings were 'monuments of a bygone art, created by bygone manners, that modern art cannot meddle with without destroying'.[33]

Morris's 'anti-scrape' tenets came to guide the care of architectural and other relics throughout Europe. Restorers were constrained to respect the attritions and additions of time alone with the original structures. And where renovation was essential it was made obvious; historical honesty required that modern replacements be clearly distinguishable from surviving relics. To ensure that no one mistook them for the old, textures and colours of replacement materials were chosen to contrast with the original fabric. But while such flagrant disparities between old and new alerted viewers to the fact of restoration, they detracted from the aura of antiquity. Plugging holes in the Arch of Constantine with material of much lighter tone and harder outline than the surrounding stonework, for example, destroyed its unity of character.[34]

Other aesthetic considerations nowadays temper anti-scrape purism. Replacements are meant to harmonize with original surviving elements, and to be detectable only by expert inspection of the tooling on new stonework, of dates on new stained glass and wood, or of their slightly differing tints. Replacements 'should seem to recede visually behind the original material, yet be so harmonious as not to detract but rather to add to the whole'. Filling lacunae with marginally less textured materials coloured nearly like the original stonework has kept the Arch of Titus's sense of unity. At Herculaneum, faint lines on dull-toned plaster carry the eye over and beyond gaps in the frescoes.[35] New heads of fourteenth-century figures from the west front of York Minster harmonize with the bodies, yet differ enough not to deceive spectators into thinking them original.

But the propriety of restoration still generates passionate dispute. Oxford dons and graduates, fond of the old Sheldonian busts of Roman household guardians eroded beyond recognition, criticized proposed replacements as modern anachronisms. At Wells Cathedral those who saw charm and authenticity in the erosive veneer of age termed sculptural replacements 'a disaster, negating the rhythm and vitiating the deeply personal nature of the original carvings'; even inspired new carvings were 'at best a crude substitute for the medieval sculpture, however battered and fragmented'.[36]

The wider public, however, unabashedly enjoys reconstructions. Few have the taste or the training to appreciate the past simply from fragmentary remains. Heaps of fallen stones convey nothing to the ordinary spectator; only reconstitution makes them coherent

---

[33] Morris, 'Restoration' (1877), in SPAB, *Manifesto* and *Repair not Restoration*, which also reprint selections from Ruskin's *Seven Lamps of Architecture* (1848). See Chapter 4, above, p.151.

[34] Frycz, 'Reconstruction des monuments d'architecture', p. 21; Feilden, *Conservation of Historic Buildings*, pp. 246–55.

[35] Ibid., p. 247. See Linstrum, 'Giuseppe Valadier et l'arc de Titus'; for the treatment of lacunae generally, Mora, Mora, and Philippot, *Conservation of Wall Paintings*, pp. 301–24.

[36] W. F. Oakeshott, *Oxford Stone Restored*, pp. 46–7; John Schofield and Alban Caroe, letters, *The Times*, 8 and 21 Feb. 1973, pp. 17 and 15; Philip Vening, SPAB, ibid., 8 Dec.1984, p. 13; 'Making sense of Wells', SPAB *News*, 5 (1984), 42–3.

53 Renewing antiquity: the ragged Roman regiment around the Sheldonian Theatre, Oxford, 1868 restorations of seventeenth-century originals (photo 1965)

54 The heads replaced, Michael Black, sculptor, 1972

and evocative. Having excavated Knossos, Sir Arthur Evans restored the palace to make it comprehensible; his reconstruction 'was wrong, but boatloads of cultural tourists to Crete have been grateful to him', for it 'helps them interpret and understand the site'.[37] Many popular sites in Greece – the Erechtheum, the Temple of Nike, the Treasury of Delphi – are largely restorations. The taste for fragments discussed in Chapter 4 may lend cachet to the incomplete, but ruinous vestiges usually require some restoration to be appreciated. Reconstructing a henge monument, a stretch of Hadrian's Wall, an Iron Age fort to their original wholeness, a British observer suggests, might restore 'some of our great sites to something of their ancient glory'.[38]

Some reconstituted relics displace the present along with the past. In Old Jerome, an early twentieth-century Arizona mining town, tourist promoters envisage restoration as total replacement. 'I can see the old awnings going back on the shops, like in the 1900s', predicts a developer; 'I can see the old streetlights coming back. I can see where when you step into Jerome you'll be stepping into the true past.'[39] Old Jerome turns Finney's *Time and Again* from science fiction into reality.

The true past eludes recapture, however. Consider Rouen Cathedral, whose sixteenth-century timber spire gave way in 1822 to a cast-iron replacement unable to bear its own weight. A new spire is now needed. Should it honour the original or the historical continuity embodied in the fraud of a non-weightbearing load? Faithfulness to the original structure would deprive the cathedral of history's additions; faithfulness to continuity would deprive it of functional and legible unity.[40] Or consider the church of Saint-Sernin, Toulouse, whose neo-Romanesque restoration by Viollet-le-Duc is now adjudged 'technically bad and aesthetically mediocre'. Should the church be left as it is, with all its inferior additions? Or should it be re-restored to a conjectural original state, as Viollet himself might have done?[41] And where does obeisance to continuity end? If nineteenth-century alterations are sacrosanct, why not late twentieth-century embellishments? If everything that has happened to a relic is sanctified as part of its history, no criteria remain to identify, let alone to celebrate, its past.

Moving

Relics are profoundly altered by being moved away from – or back to – their place of origin. Removal subsumes a wide range of actions: antiquities as small as a nail or as large as a temple may be shifted a few inches or halfway round the world, transported entire or reassembled, broken up into segments or reunited from separate fragments. Some artifacts – books, paintings, bronzes, medals – were made to be portable; others, whose

---

[37] Feilden, *Conservation of Historic Buildings*, p. 252. For assessments of Evans's reconstructions, see Macaulay, *Pleasure of Ruins*, pp. 111–12; Cadogan, *Palaces of Minoan Crete*, p. 51; Horwitz, *Find of a Lifetime*, pp. 200–1.
[38] Ronald Dew, 'Restoring the past', *Popular Archaeology*, 1:9 (1980), 23.
[39] Bob Koble, quoted in Haas, 'Secret life of the American tourist', p. 27.
[40] Parent, 'Doctrine for the conservation and restoration of monuments and sites', pp. 63–4.
[41] 'The world of conservation: Yves Boiret', pp. 19–25; Durliat, Boiret, and Costa, 'Saint-Sernin de Toulouse'. See Dupont, 'Viollet-le-Duc and restoration in France'; Pevsner, 'Ruskin and Viollet-le-Duc', p. 52.

meaning and value derive from and enliven their surroundings, are displaced with grave loss. Some artifacts are moved because everything cognate around them has changed; others, previously uprooted by war, theft, or accident, may be returned to former locales. Some relics are dispersed from centres of origin or collection, others brought together from scattered sites.

The practice of concentrating antiquities is prefigured in late Renaissance paintings that depict far-flung classical monuments in close proximity, often embellished with imaginary mutilations or restorations. One artist set the *Laocoön* in front of a broken wall to suggest the moment it was unearthed; another grouped relics amid antique temples by the shores of Troy.[42] The idealized ancient city in Jean Lemaire's *Roman Senators Going to the Forum* is a patchwork of well-known ruins – the Triumphal Arch at Orange, Verona's Town Gate, the Pantheon portico, the Septizoneum, the Colosseum. A real sixteenth-century vestige and a fictitiously ruined Mannerist statue stand alongside the authentic Constantinian Arco di Gione in Jan Baptist Weenix's *Roman Campagna*.[43]

The taste for ruins encouraged eighteenth-century painters to group ancient monuments as decorative accessories; rearranged classical sculptures and Roman ruins fill the backgrounds of Pompeo Batoni's portraits of British worthies on the Grand Tour, and the French ambassador in Rome commissioned from Giovanni Panini an imaginary picture gallery stocked with the scenic treasures of ancient Rome.[44] Like a family portrait or a mantel full of snapshots that gather one's dear ones together, such pictures let the lover of antiquity gaze on all his favourite monuments at once. National pride likewise concentrated historical images. To enhance the effect of 'several of the monuments characteristic of the past history of our country, and which will soon cease to exist', the Irish painter George Petrie's *Pilgrims at Clanmacnoise* depicted a round tower, a Celtic cross, and a half-ruined Hibernian Romanesque church in contrived juxtaposition.[45] Modern collages display historic houses of many epochs cheek by jowl, as though they existed door-to-door on the same street.

The Victoria and Albert Museum's Cast Court juxtaposes full-scale copies of architectural relics, including Trajan's Column cut into two lengths for easier viewing, and a Romanesque medley of the San Zemo doors inserted into the Portico della Gloria from Santiago de Compostela.[46] And at Austria's 'Minimundus' the models of the Tower of London and the Arc de Triomphe lie on opposite sides of Berlin's Brandenburg Gate.[47]

---

[42] Haskell and Penny, *Taste and the Antique*, p. 21.

[43] *Gods & Heroes*, Catalogue nos. 21, 57, and plates pp. 28, 51. The statue in the Weenix painting is Gianbologna's famous *Rape of the Sabines* (1583).

[44] E. P. Bowron, 'Introduction', *Pompeo Batoni*, pp. 15–17; Haskell and Penny, *Taste and the Antique*, p. 84 and fig. 45.

[45] Starobinski, *Invention of Liberty*, p. 179; Petrie, letter to Committee of the Royal Irish Art Union, in William Stokes, *Life and Labours . . . of George Petrie*, p. 15. See Sheehy, *Rediscovery of Ireland's Past*, p. 22 and plate 11.

[46] Malcolm Baker, *Cast Courts*. William Feaver terms the assemblage of classical and Gothic casts 'a stupendous High Victorian experience' ('Splendid illusions', *Observer*, 2 May 1982, p. 34).

[47] *Minimundus: Die Kleine Welt am Wörthersee*, Klagenfurt: Kärtner Universitäts-Druckerei, 1983. My thanks to Minimundus manager Dr Josef Kleindienst.

56 Antiquity dismembered: bisected copy of Trajan's Column, Cast Court, Victoria and Albert Museum, London

55 Antiquity rearranged: Pompeo Batoni, *Thomas Dundas*, on the Grand Tour, 1764

Actual antiquities are likewise brought into closer proximity. Most 'historic' American villages include imported structures: Portsmouth's Strawbery Banke incorporates many buildings brought in from remote or imperilled locales; Mystic Seaport's buildings come from all over New England; Old Sturbridge Village as an entity dates only from 1929, when several dozen old structures were brought together.[48] Singleton Village in Sussex comprises fourteenth- to nineteenth-century buildings from the whole of southeast England. On their new sites some of these old buildings acquire a past bizarrely at odds with historical reality. For example, Henry Ford grouped Greenfield Village's log structures, a slave-overseer's cabin next to Abraham Lincoln's Logan County Courthouse next to the George Washington Carver Memorial Cabin, to illustrate the march from slavery to freedom to black genius.[49]

Removal has become a major mode of historical salvage. The same technology that nowadays menaces relics of the past can move the most massive antiquities out of danger. Modern engineering made it possible to cut and lift the Abu Simbel temples from Philae to Agilka, and some find the temples more impressive on the bare rock than in their former palm-tree setting.[50] Less congruous is London Bridge, re-erected in the Arizona desert along with lamps cast from Napoleon's cannon and an imitation City of London pub. Arizona's most popular site after the Grand Canyon, the salvaged bridge attracts two million visitors a year, but the sense of context and even of age are gone, London's sooty patina having peeled off in the dry desert air.[51]

For many relics export is the only alternative to terminal decay or demolition. From a warehouse in Texas, the stained-glass ceiling of the Fulham Free Library, the copper-leaded portals of the former Bank of India, and the brass doors of the Café Royal are auctioned to restaurants whose New World patrons crave an Olde English ambience. Liverpool Stock Exchange fittings decorate a Beverly Hills restaurant; bits of the Morecambe pier adorn a Las Vegas casino; a Middlesbrough convent has become a Kansas City eatery.[52] Britain also exports the oak beams of rural structures dating back to the fifteenth century – historically documented, pest-free, and guaranteed to last another five centuries. 'We are preserving these buildings for *mankind* . . . rather than letting them deteriorate and vanish', maintains the agent, 'salvaging those buildings which are just not being cared for'. American appetites are such that one architect predicts 'you would have to tear down all of Tudor and Stuart England to meet the demand'.[53] Neo-Gothic and neo-Renaissance French chateaux otherwise scheduled for destruction are likewise dis-

---

[48] Candee, 'Second thoughts on museum villages as preservation', p. 16, and 'From model village to village model: ... Old Sturbridge Village (unpublished typescripts); Hosmer, *Preservation Comes of Age*, pp. 108–21, 332–40.

[49] Charles Phillips, 'Greenfield's changing past', p. 11. See Roger Butterfield, 'Henry Ford, the Wayside Inn, and the problem of "History is bunk"'; Hosmer, *Preservation Comes of Age*, pp. 75–97, 987–92.

[50] Berg, 'Salvage of the Abu Simbel temples'.

[51] Chamberlin, *Preserving the Past*, pp. 127–31; Muriel Bowen, 'Vanishing soot upsets London Bridge buyers', *Sunday Times*, 22 Oct. 1972, p. 2.

[52] 'Where our heritage goes', *Sunday Times*, 20 Oct. 1980, p. 32; Ronald Faux, 'Transatlantic Steptoe turns to home market', *The Times*, 21 Feb. 1983, p. 3.

[53] John Durtnell, quoted in Ian Ball, 'Barns take U.S. by storm', *Sunday Telegraph Mag.*, 17 May 1980, pp. 51, 48; American architect, quoted in Ian Ball, 'U.S. imports old British farmhouses', *Daily Telegraph*, 2 Aug. 1979, p. 19.

mantled and shipped abroad; some buyers faithfully restore these castles, others reshuffle their stones like Lego bricks.[54]

Several benefits accrue from moving remnants of the past. First, relics are saved which would otherwise be lost. Second, concentrating antiquities often makes them more accessible and meaningful, especially if only small fragments remained on the original sites. Third, the removal of relics may benefit the locales they come from: moving Martha's Vineyard's oldest house out of its rural setting leaves an almost primeval solitude in a landscape now devoid of artifacts, 'a greater presence than before'.[55] Fourth, transplanted relics confer talismanic virtues on their new homes. Fragments from ancient structures the world over give the Chicago Tribune building a composite historical aura. The Washington Monument gains vicarious antiquity from memorial stones that include a 2,000-year-old bust from the Temple of Augustus in Egypt, a stone from a Swiss chapel honouring William Tell, and a piece from the 'Temple of Aesculapius' in Paros.[56] People not only expect but like much of the tangible past to be manipulated in this way, so long as personal or local attachments are not jeopardized. Four out of every five Toronto residents recently questioned preferred to see historical and archaeological relics in museums or in other public arenas (such as shopping centres) rather than *in situ*.[57]

Yet such removals also exact a toll. Transport hazards seriously inhibit sending precious relics on tour, and if disassembled, lack of space or money or planning permission may prevent or delay their reconstitution. Financial or site constraints may impoverish antiquities during the process of rebuilding, as Illinois' early eighteenth-century Cahokia Courthouse well illustrates. After a varied career as a private home and a saloon, the much-deteriorated courthouse was reconstructed for the St Louis World's Fair of 1904 with its four original rooms reduced to one (the left-over walnut timbers were turned into souvenir cigar boxes). Again dismantled and reassembled at Jackson Park, Chicago, the courthouse was now bereft of its fireplace, its roof-lines and windows altered, the logs mispositioned. A generation later Cahokians agitated for the courthouse's return, and the surviving remnants, fleshed out to the original size with replica materials, were re-erected in southern Illinois in 1940.[58]

Aesthetic integrity is another victim of fragmentation and dispersal. Antiquities are dismembered for ease of transport or, like the huge Tiepolo *Madonna* taken to France by Napoleon, sawn in two to suit a later taste. Prudery pruned a Poussin *Venus*, her immodest legs cut off by a French nobleman; avarice led to the dismemberment of two Toulouse-Lautrec canvases. Once disjoined, each piece embarks on its own career; the fragments of a once-harmonious Sienese altarpiece are now scattered in Berlin, Dublin,

[54] Robin Smyth, 'Now there's a take-away chateau shop', *Observer*, 2 Sept. 1979, p. 7; Diane Shah with Elaine Scilino, 'Chateaux under siege', *Newsweek*, 10 Sept. 1979, p. 59.

[55] Hough, *Soundings at Sea Level*, pp. 123–4.

[56] F. L. Harvey, *History of the Washington National Monument*, p. 48; Olszewski, *History of the Washington Monument*, pp. 12–13. So symbolically significant were these stones that anti-papists stole the Vatican's memorial gift – actually a pagan relic from the ruins of Rome's Temple of Concord – and dumped it in the Potomac in 1854.

[57] Konrad, 'Orientations toward the Past in the Environment of the Present', p. 225; 'Presenting our native heritage in public parks'.

[58] E. R. Moore, 'Cahokia Courthouse'. For another removal keenly resented but never returned, see Robinson, 'Henry Ford and the Postville Courthouse'.

Paris, Glasgow, Toledo, Ohio, and Williamstown, Massachusetts.[59] A 1968 exhibition temporarily reunited a Veneziano polyptych in the Louvre with fragments in Ajaccio and Toulouse, and the halves of a Persian carpet originally commissioned but found too large for the altar steps at Cracow Cathedral.[60]

Not every dispersal is to be condemned, nor do all dismembered relics deserve reconstitution. Transplantation may infuse a work with new life, lending it decorative or iconographic value. Putting icon screens back in Russian churches would sacrifice their aesthetic impact for the sake of trivial historical authenticity: replaced in its original location in the Kremlin Cathedral of the Annunciation, an exquisite painting of Theophanes the Greek became discernable only through binoculars.[61] A niche showing books and other objects in *trompe l'œil* cut out of a panel of the *Aix Annunciation* in the eighteenth century subsequently passed for the first French still life; 'the very fact that it had been mutilated was responsible for its reputation amongst scholars and art-lovers'.[62] Along with disputes over ownership, the varying environmental fortunes of dismembered fragments may preclude amalgamation; damaged by clumsy restoration, the fragment of Poussin's *Venus and the Liberal Arts* at Dulwich would mar rather than enhance the main canvas in the Louvre, which in any case would still lack important missing pieces.[63]

Fragmentation also affects collections meant to be integral; the dispersal of an artist's *œuvre* may dismember the past no less than the division of a single work. Inherited by two different families, half of the Flemish painter Justus of Ghent's twenty-eight portraits of *Famous Men* are now in Urbino, the rest in the Louvre.[64] So with the dispersal of furnishings specifically designed for particular houses. 'Separated from each other, out of context, they lose two-thirds of their meaning', one critic termed the selling off of baroque furniture commissioned in the eighteenth century for St Giles' House, Dorset. Family portraits handsome and meaningful on their own walls likewise lose value when dispersed: 'considered on its own merits, each piece becomes at best a pleasing if slightly boring conventional portrait'. Smaller antiquities long gathered together also accrue value as an ensemble. The recent breakup of the great collection of Greek vases assembled at Castle Ashby in the 1820s was held to blot out 'part of the collective memory of a nation':[65] the nation referred to was not Greece but Britain, the memory not of the vases themselves but of the early nineteenth-century passion for collecting them.

Perhaps the most grievous effect of dispersing antiquities is the loss of environmental context. The removal of relics whose lineaments are indissolubly of their place annuls their testamentary worth and forfeits their myriad ties with place. The whole value of many antiquities inheres in their locale; the landmark must stay put if it is to mark the land. 'It's a dreadful thing to do', says Lucy Boston's *Green Knowe* child when the local Standing

[59] On Tiepolo, Robert Adams, *Lost Museum*, pp. 12, 142–5, and Pesenti, 'Dismembered works of art – Italian painting', pp. 25, 48–51; on Poussin, Louis Henri de Loménie, Comte de Brienne, Discours sur les Ouvrages des plus Excellents Peintres, Mss, cited in Thuillier, 'Dismembered works of art – French painting', pp. 90–1; see also pp. 92, 108–9.

[60] Hak, 'Introduction: UNESCO's action to promote the reconstitution of dismembered works of art', pp. 15–16.

[61] Danilova, 'Dismembered works of art – Russian painting', p. 178.

[62] Thuillier, 'Dismembered French painting', pp. 90, 98–101.

[63] Ibid., pp. 93, 102–3; see also Lavalleye, 'Dismembered works of art – Flemish painting', p. 55.

[64] Lavalleye, 'Dismembered Flemish painting', pp. 52, 62–3.

[65] Souren Melikian, 'A collection lost forever', *IHT*, 5–6 July 1980, p. 8.

Stones are carted off to a museum. 'They were in their own place. Out of it they will be dead.'[66] Some movers of antiquities go to heroic lengths to retain the context of locale, as Henry Ford did with Edison's famous laboratory at Greenfield Village:

Before he moved the [Menlo Park] laboratory here, he went out to New Jersey – the land where the building was originally – and dug up tons of dirt, just tons of it. Then he had it all carted out here and dumped it all over this site before they stuck the building down on top of it. That was his idea of complete restoration. This place had been built on New Jersey soil, so it should be restored on New Jersey soil. Stuff like that drove the experts crazy.[67]

Moving reminders of the past has vital consequences, above all, for national and cultural identity. Removal becomes desecration if a national symbol is at stake. When P. T. Barnum bid for Shakespeare's birthplace, *The Times* envisaged his 'taking it from its foundations and trundling it about on wheels like a caravan of wild beasts, giants, or dwarfs'.[68] Removing the Assurian statues of winged beasts from Nimrod's palace seemed to A. H. Layard himself almost an act of sacrilege: 'They were better suited to the desolation around them for they had guarded the palace in its glory, and it was for them to watch over it in its ruin.'[69] Lord Elgin's dismemberment of the Parthenon may have spared the marbles some further mishaps but impoverishes the temple and deprives the Greek nation of its supreme symbol of identity. But the crusade for the restitution of lost heritage is a topic that warrants a book in itself.

Readapting

We refashion antiquities most radically, sometimes altering them beyond recognition, in adapting them to present-day purposes. But without adaptive reuse most old artifacts would soon perish. Had the Parthenon not served variously as a mosque, a harem, even as a powder magazine, it would have succumbed to plunder and decay. Prolonged survival usually requires subsequent uses utterly unlike the original one, for things normally become less and less suited to initial uses themselves often extinguished by time. Later technology made obsolete the defence of the realm at the Tower of London; Christian worship cannot now alone sustain the fabric of Canterbury Cathedral; most eighteenth-century jails no longer serve as prisons nor workhouses as indigent abodes, not merely because they have decayed but because convicts and the poor are now differently defined and treated. Few old dwellings are habitable without alteration; current standards of comfort, social life, safety, and decor are bound to violate inherited integrity. While adaptation may protect and even highlight some relic features, modern appliances and furnishings conceal or replace many others.

Adaptive reuse arouses conflicting reactions. New uses for old structures may seem a sacrilege; rather than reconvert redundant Anglican churches, one prominent spokesman prefers them left vacant as reminders of eternal spiritual values.[70] At the other extreme,

---

[66] *Stones of Green Knowe*, p. 120.   [67] Interpreter quoted in Phillips, 'Greenfield's changing past', p. 10.

[68] Kozintsev, *Shakespeare: Time and Conscience*, pp. 10–11. See also Roger Pringle, 'The history of Shakespeare as a tourist attraction', *Interpretation*, No. 21 (1982), 17–18.

[69] Quoted in Chamberlin, *Preserving the Past*, p. 124. See E. A. Freeman, *Preservation and Restoration*, pp. 36–7.

[70] Lord Anglesey, presidential address, Friends of Friendless Churches, cited in 'New uses for redundant churches opposed', *The Times*, 8 Sept. 1977, p. 14.

American preservationists take special pride in the wide range of functions well-known places have served: Washington's Lafayette Square, for example, for having been successively a cherry orchard, the site of Andrew Jackson's raucous inaugural party, a sheep pasture during the First World War, and now an urban visual amenity.[71] Reuse through alteration was the credo of the recent French exhibition '*Hier pour Demain*', showing how old things are adjusted to later needs: 'A heritage is something to be preserved and understood', explained the show's curator, 'but also to be modified to meet the needs of a changing world.'[72]

The extreme in adaptive reuse involves treasuring relics as museum pieces. Like a 'discarded hubcap ... launched on a second life as a planter for a nice cactus assortment', in Haas's phrase,[73] their workaday function gives way to decorative, pedagogic, or nostalgic uses. A cartoonist envisions the Statue of Liberty redeveloped into luxury flats whose residents can 'sleep in the splendor of a national monument', with doormen 'dressed in the native costumes of their grandparents'.[74]

Recycled relics often end in the museum. A sword begins as a warrior's weapon; after his death it may be transformed into a sacred object for ceremonial use; taken as loot it becomes a token of wealth and a souvenir of conquest; ultimately it is found by archaeologists and put on display. But only its previous retention for military, sacred, and treasure purposes enabled the sword to survive to the museum stage, while less valued objects have rusted, rotted, and vanished from view.[75]

Display need not be antiquities' final use, however, as Rome's rebirth from ancient ruins attests. An unending sequence of reuse characterizes Italo Calvino's 'Clarice', a city whose inhabitants recycle relics at every stage of extinction and of rebirth. When Clarice dies, its survivors

grabbed everything that could be taken from where it was and put it in another place to serve a different use: brocade curtains ended up as sheets; in marble funerary urns they planted basil; wrought-iron gratings torn from the harem windows were used for roasting cat meat on fires of inlaid wood.

When Clarice prospers again the reused artifacts are remembered as survivors from an earlier past, and 'the shards of the original splendor that had been saved, by adapting them to more obscure needs, were again shifted. They were now preserved under glass bells, locked in display cases, set on velvet cushions' so that people could reconstruct the previous Clarice in their minds' eye.[76] Thus each successive stage reshuffles the fragments of what remains from former uses, sacred or profane, functional or decorative. Heritage appreciation, complains a Canadian geographer, 'has done little more than to turn museums into communities and, what is worse, communities into museums'.[77] But as we have seen, these transitions occur all the time, with or without deliberate intent.

---

[71] Architour, *Architectural Tour of Lafayette Square* brochure, *c.* 1979.
[72] Jean Cuisenier, quoted in Michael Gibson, 'Preserving France's heritage from before the (Industrial) Revolution', *IHT*, 5–6 July 1980, p. 8.
[73] 'Secret life of the American tourist', pp. 14, 21.   [74] Bill Day, *Preservation News*, 20:8 (1980), 4.
[75] Fisher, 'The future's past', pp. 587–90.
[76] *Invisible Cities*, pp. 106–7.   [77] Norris, 'Preserving Main Street', p. 128.

ADDING TO RELICS

If we need another past so badly, is it inconceivable that we might discover one, that we might even invent one?

Van Wyck Brooks, 'On creating a usable past'[78]

We alter the surviving past not only by changing its lineaments but also by adding to them, creating or decorating with bygone themes and images. Some additions replace antiquities too fragile to withstand erosion or attention; others are surrogates for what has been or is likely to be lost; still others transmute past forms or motifs. Whether or not antecedents of new artifacts are recognized and their derivation acknowledged, 'everything made now is either a replica or a variant of something made a little while ago', as George Kubler writes, 'and so on back without break to the first morning of human time'.[79]

Copying or celebrating relics makes the originals better known and alters our view of them. The visitor to Philadelphia sees Independence Hall through the lens of familiarity with dozens of replicas, the Eiffel Tower through the perspective of innumerable travel posters. Along with original relics, our inheritance includes a congeries of later imitations and commemorations. Thus impressions of the past reflect all subsequent acts of appreciation and derogation, our own included.

The impact of these additions depends on how far they resemble or how close their affinity with the actual relics. Each act that supplements the past – imitation, emulation, reproduction, commemoration – is in some measure distinctive. Imitations and re-enactments aim to replicate admired originals fairly faithfully; models and images often deliberately depart from their exemplars; emulations use the past to inspire new creations; monuments and memorials frequently commemorate the past in present-day forms or motifs.

Duplicates

Facsimiles, which aim simply to duplicate admired relics, embrace three distinct types: copies imitate existing or lost originals; forgeries pretend to *be* the originals; replicas reproduce well-known prototypes in other locales. Few facsimiles correspond with their originals in every detail, but imitation in the narrow modern sense of the word is their principal if not sole aim.

Viewers often fail to realize, even after repeatedly being told, that vanished or threatened relics have been replaced by modern contrivances. Facsimile restorations in the Suffolk town of Sudbury depart significantly from the originals, yet passers-by – including natives long familiar with the original structures and witnesses to their demolition – suppose they are seeing the old façades.[80] The restored medieval cores of war-torn Polish cities were so verisimilar that ten years later, according to Warsaw's restoration chief, 'even the elders do not realize in their everyday life that this town, which appears old, is to a great extent new. And they do not feel it to be an artificial creation.'[81] But some who are

---

[78] 1918, p. 339.   [79] *Shape of Time*, p. 2.
[80] John Popham, Suffolk Preservation Society, interview 15 June 1978.
[81] Lorentz, 'Reconstruction of the old town centers of Poland', p. 52.

aware of it find the replacement uncanny. 'The house I was born in was destroyed violently thirty-six years ago – but I can go into the bedroom I had as a boy, look out of the exact same window at the exact same house across the courtyard', says an architect. 'There's even a lamp bracket with a curious twist in it hanging in the same place. It's unnerving, when you come to think of it. Is it "real" or isn't it?'[82]

Replacements of antiquities endangered by erosion, pollution, or theft engender similar doubts, especially if the originals are close by. A facsimile of Michelangelo's *David* has stood outside Florence's Palazzo Vecchio for the past century, with the actual statue in the Accademia; replicas have replaced original elements from French Gothic monasteries installed only fifty years ago at the Cloisters in New York; Venice's ancient bronze horses are kept free from corrosion in a museum, glass-fibre copies taking their place in St Mark's Square. Some predict that protection may soon require all original works to 'be embalmed in some inaccessible stronghold while the public is fed on replicas'.[83]

Replicas that masquerade as originals pretend to be previously lost or undiscovered relics. The appetite for antiquities has long made forgery a major enterprise. Salvaging ancient beams, the French craftsman André Mailfert's workshop produced 50,000 'rare old pieces' of 'antique' furniture during the 1910s and 1920s, together with thousands of fake old master paintings.[84] Huge demand spurs the manufacture of 'Valamasters' – photographs of old paintings with brushstrokes hand-applied in a transparent covering glaze, said to resemble the originals so closely that even experts need a second look.[85] Sophisticated detection techniques inspire ever more clever forgeries. A fabricator of 'Etruscan' terra-cottas and 'Greek' vases visually indistinguishable from true antiques claims he can even circumvent thermoluminescence tests.[86]

Fakes of lost originals alter our image of the past by seeming to bring what once existed back to life. Other forgeries add to an artist's supposed *œuvre* or augment the output of a past epoch, enlarging the stock of relics within some well-known tradition. In line with the adage that 'a forgery can be distinguished from an original because it looks more genuine',[87] forgers aim at verisimilitude; their additions to the past must not appear novel. Yet forgeries reflect as much credit on their exemplars as honest replicas; even when exposed, they are often valued as excellent copies of ancient masterpieces.[88]

No intent to deceive taints such reproductions as Britain's Palladian villas or copies of America's Independence Hall. And no matter how faithful in form, such replicas inevitably depart from their prototypes in ambience. Nashville's reinforced-concrete Parthenon of the 1920s is a case in point. Like many replicas, it is more complete than the original: plaster casts of the Elgin Marbles, supplemented by sculptures of live models posing as described in Pausanias's *Periegesis*, supply the east pediment's missing figures. So 'authentic' is their replica, Tennesseeans brag, that the Greeks would have to study the correct details in Nashville in order to rebuild the original. But authenticity ends outside

---

[82] Pietor Tsiolkowski, quoted in Chamberlin, *Preserving the Past*, pp. 8–9.
[83] Thomson, 'Conservation of antiquities', p. 42.
[84] Mailfert, *Au Pays des antiquaires*, pp. 23, 145.
[85] Reg Bell, ' . . . copies', *Observer Suppl.*, 7 Sept. 1980; Leo Vala, telephone interview, 13 Jan. 1984.
[86] Karl Meyer, *Plundered Past*, p. 113.
[87] Ernest Bloch, quoted in Rieth, *Archaeological Fakes*, p. 7. See also Greenhalgh, *Classical Tradition in Art*, p. 59.
[88] Sagoff, 'Aesthetic status of forgeries'.

57 Replication: the Nashville Parthenon, 1922–32

58 Replication: Anne Hathaway's Cottage, Victoria, British Columbia

the portico. Nashville's Parthenon builders dispensed with the steep rise up to the actual Acropolis because 'it was feared that the effort needed to climb the hill might discourage visitors'; a mere ten-foot mound is meant to give it a 'commanding place'. Yet the replica has made Nashville 'the Athens of the South'.[89]

Replicas like replacements may be preferred to their prototypes. The nineteenth-century English view that 'a happy imitation is of much more value than a defective original' has its twentieth-century counterpart in Walt Disney's boast that Disneyland's 'Vieux Carré' was just like the 1850s original, but 'a lot cleaner'.[90] Whether or not they improve on the originals, however, replicas lack their history of felt relationships. 'A child dies, leaving behind a worn, dirty, and much-hugged teddy bear. Would a molecular reproduction, known to be such, have the same value to the parents?' asks a philosopher. Even a replica similarly marked by wear and tear could not replace the original, for it would not be the bear that child had hugged. A replica Grand Canyon in, say, New Jersey, would be still more deficient. 'What we respond to in hiking down the Bright Angel Trail is the way in which the canyon has been whittled, particle by particle, by water and wind: we do not have this experience in the Bayonne Grand Canyon, however, because it was fabricated quite mechanically, all at once'.[91] *Pace* Henry James, ascending worn steps to an ancient cathedral or touching smooth banisters in an old house links visitors with the long history that wore and smoothed them – a history no replica, known as such, could ever convey.

On the other hand, some newly minted reproductions convey historical immediacy better than originals do. 'Although the boy or girl of today may be denied the undoubted thrill of putting on the actual garment of a former age, by means of the substitute it may be possible to recreate the feeling which the first wearer may have felt', writes an educator. 'Who is to say that wearing the copy affords any less of a true historical experience than putting on the original?'[92] Some *have* said so, as we saw in Chapter 5, but the point deserves consideration. The sheer ingenuity of replication can help bring history to life – as with Knott's Berry Farm's 'Liberty Bell' that was frozen in dry ice and then 'authentically cracked' with a heli-arch torch applied to a built-in fracture line.[93] Authenticity in manufacture matters no less than in the product. Nowell's 'Victorian' fixtures can't be told from the originals because 'we make them one at a time by hand, exactly the way the originals were made, and ... of exactly the same materials. And we make them well enough to hang right next to period originals without looking out of place.'[94] Indeed, the original may seem out of place, for habituation to replicas tends to persuade us that antiquities should look complete and 'new'. The copy may afford an historical experience as 'true' as the original, but it is a *different* experience.

[89] Creighton, *Parthenon in Nashville*, quotations on pp. 22, 48.
[90] James Dallaway, *Anecdotes of the Arts in England* (1800), quoted in Kenneth Clark, *Gothic Revival*, p.113; 'New scene at Disneyland simulates New Orleans', *N.Y. Times*, 26 July 1966, p. 25. See also R. W. Freeman, 'Integrity in the Vieux Carré'.
[91] Battin, 'Exact replication in the visual arts', pp. 154–5. Even if accurately made of marble from the original quarry the Tennessee Parthenon would not be considered genuine, whereas the actual Parthenon if transported to Nashville would keep its identity even in that diminished setting (Margolis, 'Art, forgery, and authenticity', p. 167).
[92] Fairley, *History Teaching through Museums*, pp. 127–8.
[93] Maass, 'Architecture and Americanism or pastiches of Independence Hall', pp. 24–5. The replica bell was dedicated 4 July 1966.
[94] *Preservation News*, 20:4 (1980), 9.

59 Precious authenticity: 70-year-old 'Harry White', deaf in one ear

Reproductions seem inferior to the *cognoscenti* simply because they are not originals. 'Genuineness' is said to be preferable to 'authenticity' because 'genuineness is the real thing ... It is solid wood, not plastic veneer ... It has meaning because it puts us in the presence of what was – the experience of history – not a later impression of what something looked like.' Without genuine bits of the past, 'our sense of values and ability to judge the real from the fake is damaged – or worse, never developed'.[95] But much as most of us know the *Iliad* and the Bible only through translation, so our awareness of the tangible past is based mainly on copies, reflections, and subsequent impressions; most people not only cannot tell originals from replicas, they are just as pleased with the latter. The copy reflects 'the past' no less than the original.

Re-enactments

Imitations reproduce past artifacts; re-enactments reproduce past events. Some re-enactors simply seek to entertain, some to convince themselves or others of the reality of the past, some to heighten history's revelatory significance, some for a sense of purpose or excitement lacking in the present. Live actors repeat what was supposedly done in the past, and restored or replica houses are staffed with 'replica people' or 'human artifacts'.[96] Like restorers, re-enactors start with known elements and fill in the gaps with the typical, the probable, or the invented.

Some re-enactments portray particular episodes and personages, others activities characteristic of the past. Theatrical restaging ranges in scale from school Nativity plays to once-in-a-lifetime spectaculars, like the late Shah of Iran's £3 million, 3,500-man pageant in reconstructed Persepolis to celebrate Cyrus's founding of the Persian Empire 2,500 years before.[97]

In the United States, re-enactments are a *sine qua non* of popular participation in history. Scarcely a skirmish of the Revolution went unrepeated during the 1976 bicentennial celebrations. Many battle participants spend large sums on equipment and uniforms, wax fanatical over details of dress down to the contents of their pockets, and designate 'historians' to research battles and troop movements.[98] A growing cult of authenticity is said to have driven 'a wedge between the once-a-year "paraders" ... and the fanatical "button-counters" who make their pants from patterns preserved in the Smithsonian, and who may think nothing of a trip to England to determine the exact shade of blue worn by the Royal Artillery'. These conflicting perspectives may determine who play British or American roles. In 'American' eyes, 'the British units go too far in pursuit of authenticity and chase away the spontaneous fun of it all ... The British, on the other hand, are often openly contemptuous of the "ragtag colonials"' with makeshift uniforms and harum-scarum deployment; in their view, the Americans haven't improved in two centuries. 'They started as a rabble in 1775', sneered a 'British' officer as a 'colonist' sauntered past, 'and now they are authentically portraying a rabble.'[99]

Re-enactments often slant the past for nationalist aims. But re-enactment also differs from history as it happened simply because unembellished replay would soon pall on participants and spectators alike. Yorktown won't be re-enacted because 'it can't be',

---

[95] An architectural journal, quoted in Bishop, 'Perception and the Importance of Time in Architecture', pp. 272–3.
[96] Robert Marten, Plimoth Plantation, letter to the author, Aug. 1981.
[97] Chamberlin, *Preserving the Past*, pp. 18–24.
[98] Elder, 'War games', p. 8; Forester, 'Weekend warriors', pp. 417–18. 'Willfully ignoring authenticity is a crime', a Second World War re-enactment buff told Jay Anderson (*Time Machines*, p. 73; also pp. 145–7).
[99] Tim Clark, 'When the paraders meet the button-counters at Penobscot Bay', pp. 49, 134–5.

explained a National Park spokesman. 'You can't reenact a siege. Everybody would get bored and go home.'[100] Impatient with the unadorned past, a drama leader in Lively's *Judgement Day* wants to enliven a Levellers' Masque by having a militia colonel's wife tearfully recognize a prisoner as her lover. But 'it didn't happen', she is told. 'All right. So it didn't. But it might have done ... How's anyone to know what happened and what didn't? ... No way do I rehearse that scene again like it was. It's dull dull dull.'[101]

Some bicentennial celebrants unabashedly manufactured Revolutionary episodes. Not every eighteenth-century village hosted one of Washington's 'tactical withdrawals', but this was no bar to celebrating; 'You give us the Bicentennial, we'll provide the battle', they said in Queens, New York.[102] Baltimore improved on the past by staging a mythical battle of the War of 1812 in a pageant depicting British soldiers arresting city fathers. 'So what?' retorted Baltimore officials when reminded the event had no historical basis. 'Just because it never happened doesn't detract from it.'[103]

Patent inaccuracies and unavoidable reductions in scale and scope lead some historians to denounce battle replays as 'a sham put over on the American public', a demeaning mockery of the past. Appalled that people would 'seek enjoyment out of what was literally a human tragedy', the National Park Service finally called a halt to all battle re-enactments.[104]

The replay of prototypical events – the hourly shooting of a desperado at Old Fort Dodge, the ritual confrontation of militiaman and Redcoat at Old North Bridge, Confederate infantrymen at Stones River Battlefield talking about their wartime experiences – add drama to the everyday past and play a major role at outdoor museums. Visitors at Olde Illinois see a cooper making a barrel for salt pork, watch a woman hanging out a pumpkin rind to dry, smell the odour of boiling sorghum – all activities 'typical of the nineteenth century, yet you are experiencing them today!' exclaims an interpreter.[105] So real seems this dramatic past that visitors hesitate to enter 'Lincoln's log cabin' while a 'period meal' is being eaten.[106] But re-enactment often ends there. Period-garbed coopers and black-smiths explain what they are doing and why, but their speech and know-how are mostly modern; in conveying up-to-date facts about the past, they preclude intimacy with it.

By contrast, 'character imposters' at Plimoth Plantation dress and act their parts, answering questions in the dialect and with the perspectives of 'Elder' Brewster and other specified folk of 1627. 'Every effort is made to portray an accurate picture of seventeenth-century life – from outward appearances to innermost beliefs and attitudes', expounds the brochure. 'Busy as they are, the villagers are always eager for conversation ... You are invited to explore their community, to ask about their lives, ... to examine their possessions, habits and values.' Unlike a modern community, the past is a world into which time travellers may pry without embarrassment or fear of rebuff.

---

[100] Roy Graybill, quoted in Elder, 'War games', p.12.   [101] P. 138. I have conflated the dialogue.
[102] Murray Schumach, 'Queens gets battle of '76 at last', *N.Y. Times*, 28 May 1976, pp. C1–2.
[103] Walter Orlinsky and William Schafer, quoted in 'Undeterred', *IHT*, 24 June 1975, p. 14. See my 'Bicentennial landscape', pp. 259–60.
[104] Edwin C. Bearss and Ben Levy, quoted in Elder, 'War games', pp. 9, 11.
[105] James Allen, 'Living the past in Illinois', p. 3.
[106] Vance, 'History lives at Lincoln's log cabin', p. 10.

60 Re-enacting the past: Plimoth Plantation as of 1627

61 Re-enacting the past: Youth Theatre children in period costume
at the National Portrait Gallery, London

Animated re-enactment of the Plimoth type expanded in the late 1970s, after marketing surveys showed that activities attract more people than do artifacts.[107] Yet tourists often seem reluctant to 'share a riddle, a joke, a bit of gossip' with these 'warm, friendly folk'; beyond technical questions about household skills, crops, and beverages, most moderns seem at a loss.[108] The press of numbers also inhibits a sense of the past: it is hard to suspend disbelief about the seventeenth century with hundreds of other twentieth-century folk milling about.

As with battle replays, verisimilitude can be overdone. True-to-eighteenth-century militiamen at Canada's restored Louisbourg Fortress offended tourists with their rumpled uniforms and rude ways; even when told that the 'militiamen' were slovenly and demoralized because that was how they *had* been, back then, visitors were ill at ease, as they were with ticket collectors posing as 'syphilitic whores'. In the end Louisbourg abandoned realistic animation altogether.[109]

Participation enhances the re-enacted everyday past: while horse-shoeing, grain-grinding, glass-blowing are usually confined to experts, visitors sometimes till the soil and do cooking, dairy work, spinning and weaving. A Maine farm re-creating 1870s' life conveys the sense of the past through its privations; in the icy mid-winter visiting children 'go to the outhouse, and *it's* icy. Those kids were feeling history right in the seat of their pants.'[110] To feel 'what it was like to wear medieval dress and serve at a medieval table', costumed children at Derby Museum prepare a 'typical' medieval green stew (eggs and cheese stained green with parsley) for dinner at a trestle table furnished with trenchers, replica medieval pottery, and horn beakers.[111]

The re-enactment of bygone daily life is especially popular in America, where the common man's past excites keen interest and yesteryear is traditionally seen in theatrical guise; some eight hundred outdoor museums regularly present living history programmes.[112] The British have more doubts about all this. Guides in period dress seem superfluous where *real* history is so plentiful, and National Trust members are said even to feel 'above' guided tours.[113] The Duke of Bedford, whose Woburn Abbey is one of England's most popular historical sites, derided the idea of historic-house owners having to 'sit around all day creaking in armour with swords dripping in blood or in wigs and crinolines armed with smoking warming pans; ... Sir Francis Dashwood would draw vast

---

[107] *Old Sturbridge Village: An Exploration of the Motivations and Experiences of Visitors and Potential Visitors* (1979); 'History stumbles', *Landscape*, 25:1 (1981), 35; Kelsey, 'Reflections on the character and management of historical and tourist parks in the 1980s'; Anderson, *Time Machines*, pp. 43–52.

[108] Plimoth Plantation brochure, *Have the Time of Their Life*; I visited in 1981.

[109] Fortier, 'Louisbourg: managing a moment in time'; *idem*, 'Thoughts on the re-creation and interpretation of historical environments'; *idem*, *Fortress of Louisbourg*; Fortier to the author, 1 Dec. 1980; Proudfoot, 'How Louisbourg restored looks today', p. 30; Louisbourg Fortress Staff Notice No. 1979–10, 24 May 1979. French–English conflict long afflicted modern Louisbourg: in the late 1960s French Canadians vandalized several displays at the site; in retaliation for his victory, a statue of General Wolfe lost its nose to a hammer blow (Schuyler, 'Images of America', p. 32). At Plimoth Plantation, the 'Pilgrims'' long hair and dirty feet likewise upset visitors at first (Anderson, *Time Machines*, pp. 60–1).

[110] Billie Gammon, quoted in Craig, 'Retreat into history', p. 15.

[111] Fairley, *History Teaching through Museums*, pp. 128–9.

[112] Jay Anderson, 'Living history', p. 295.

[113] Dolly Pile, lecture at Why Interpret Historic Landscapes? conference, Hebden Bridge, Yorkshire, 19 Mar. 1983.

crowds' by re-enacting his eighteenth-century forebear's orgies at Hell Fire Caves, but Bedford doubted that modern High Wycombe could supply enough virgins to meet the demand.[114] Avoidance of historical simulation is carried to such a length that interpreters at British farm museums don white laboratory coats to harrow their fields. Compared with the spirited presentations that make the American past come alive, much of the British historical experience is felt to be locked up in glass cases, and 'history on the Continent is dead; beautifully embalmed, but dead'.[115]

An American study of interpretation at Tatton Park, Cheshire, one of the British National Trust's most popular historic houses, underscores these differences. The U.S. National Park Service felt that Tatton Park's attendants behaved more like guards than interpreters; instead, costumed butlers and ladies' maids should demonstrate and talk about their duties. The kitchen needed a 'worked-in' look; the meat model should be 'a more realistic replica, or, on occasion, the real thing'. Guides should eschew dates and facts to focus on 'the humaness of the participants in Tatton's evolutionary story', the 'common humanity shared by today's visitor and Tatton's medieval residents'. An 'authentic medieval house' in the village should be peopled by a hypothetical peasant family (mother, father, children, livestock). These suggestions and a self-guided medieval village trail have proved highly popular.[116]

American-style animation has increased elsewhere in Britain too. Re-enactments at Blickling Hall, Norfolk, feature the Earl of Buckinghamshire in eighteenth-century costume; other National Trust houses theatrically transport schoolchildren back to Tudor days; Kentwell Hall, Suffolk, re-creates a particular seventeenth-century year each summer. The Civil War Society advertises historical re-enactments; the Jousting Association runs a Knights Training School and supplies historic houses with medieval entertainment; the Practical History Society involves entire communities in re-creating the past.[117]

In fact, Britain has a long tradition of fanciful re-enactment. In Elizabethan times allegories of the *Faerie Queene* were acted in mock-fortified castles like Bolsover, and mock-medieval battles were waged alongside the real war against Spain. The mid nineteenth-century saw the spectacular medieval tournament at Eglinton, the Buckingham Palace masked ball to which Victorians came as their Elizabethan counterparts, and

[114] Bedford, 'Historic homes', letter, *The Times*, 9 Sept. 1976, p. 15.

[115] Burcaw, 'Can history be too lively?' p. 5. See also Anderson, 'Living history', p. 292; Peter Addyman, York Archaeological Trust, in Barri Jones, 'A new look for our museums', *Popular Archaeology*, 4:10 (1983), 2. Said to 'blend the techniques of Schliemann and Disney' (*N.Y. Times*, 2 Aug. 1984, p. 2), York's Jorvik Viking Centre may allay complaints that British heritage interpretation lacks innovation ('Understanding our surroundings', 1981). But R. T. Schadla-Hall ('Slightly looted – a review of the Jorvik Viking Centre', *Museums Journal*, 84 (1984), 62–4) finds Jorvik's techniques flawed. On European reluctance to animate the past see Iorwerth C. Peate, 'Reconstructing the past', *Folk Life*, 6 (1968), 113–14; and Anderson, *Time Machines*, pp. 22–3.

[116] U.S. National Park Service, *Tatton Park Interpretive Study*, pp. 31, 33–4, App. II, pp. ii, x; Pile, 'Interpreting Old Hall, Tatton Park'; *idem*, at Why Interpret Historic Landscapes? conference. Tatton had 100,000 visitors in both 1982 and 1983 (National Trust (Britain), *Annual Report*, 1983, App. 2, p. 28).

[117] Philip Howard, 'Blickling's ghosts dramatise our heritage', *The Times*, 27 Apr. 1978, p. 6; Rich, 'Ten thousand children in need of a sponsor'; Robert Low, 'Saving the hay – in 1569 style', *Observer*, 3 July 1983, p. 5; Charles Kightly, '17th century fun', *Interpretation*, No. 15 (1980), 10–12.

the expansion of the knighthood from 350 at the start of Victoria's reign to nearly 2,000 at the end.[118]

Besides recalling the past, re-enactments may help confirm or deny hypotheses about it. In the Butser Iron Age Farm reconstruction, at Lejre in Denmark, and elsewhere, as with Thor Heyerdahl's *Kon-Tiki*, work with replicated tools and bred-back livestock test archaeologists' surmises about the past.[119] But a recent year-long attempt, by a dozen volunteers chosen from several hundred applicants, to 'relive' the Iron Age in southwest England, showed modern circumstances and expectations incompatible with Iron Age life to be insurmountable obstacles. Unlike today's counterparts, Iron Age farmers did not have to contend with rats, nor did they suffer cloistered isolation; on the other hand, re-enactors insisted on certain modern comforts – pen and paper, tampax, contraceptives, antibiotics – and argued endlessly whether it was authentic or anachronistic to use an old ploughshare as a pot holder, or a piece of glass as a mirror.[120] Visitors who 'go back' to 1870s' Maine are warned that 'you won't take a shower for three days, you'll sleep on a cornhusk mattress in the dead of winter ... This is *real*' – but historical reality yields to such concessions as 'window screens in summer and toilet paper year round'.[121]

Re-enactment differs from enactment above all in that actors and audiences, like historians, know the *future* of the past portrayed. In English Civil War replays Cromwell looks smug and Charles I glum because they know the outcome all too well.[122] To eliminate hindsight some re-enactors aim to convert the past into a present with outcomes still unresolved; American Revolutionary fanatics 'are already planning and engaging in the next logical step – 18th-century war games, where British and American units can test their mettle in combat situations without foreordained conclusions'.[123]

Re-enactments are patent anachronisms. But they do not always seem anachronistic; some actors become so involved in bygone events that they feel as though they are really living them. In making a film about the Napoleonic Wars those who portrayed officers and soldiers were paid at the same rate, but after a few days 'the officers of this celluloid army began to eat at a separate table from the mere privates and NCOs', Le Roy Ladurie reports; 'later on, an actual partition was put up to divide the "officers' mess" from the *vulgum pecus*'. As a World War II Re-enactment Society 'paratrooper' put it, 'You've got to

---

[118] Girouard, *Return to Camelot*, pp. 17, 26, 92–115, 228. Twain's *Connecticut Yankee* assailed not only medieval England but the Victorian medievalist cult reflected in and encouraged by 'chivalric' re-enactments (Salomon, *Twain and the Image of History*; Strout, *Veracious Imagination*, pp. 98–103, 282–3); significantly, Twain's illustrator gives Merlin the features of Tennyson, whose poetry 'had worked a kind of spell, inducing people to regard the Dark Ages and chivalry as noble and admirable' (Tuveson, *Redeemer Nation*, p. 226; also pp. 215–31). On earlier (Carolingean) re-enactments, see Anne Barton, 'Harking back to Elizabeth: Ben Jonson and Caroline nostalgia', *ELH*, 48 (1981), 706–31.

[119] Coles, *Experimental Archaeology*; idem, *Archaeology by Experiment*; Reynolds, *Iron-Age Farm: The Butser Experiment*; Anderson, *Time Machines*, pp. 85–131.

[120] Percival, *Living in the Past*, pp. 16, 25–6, 37, 111, 115, 127. Similar problems bedevilled a briefly relived Great Plains' pioneer experience (Welsch, 'Very didactic simulation'). 'To pretend that modern people, wrenched from their environment and placed in a totally alien situation, can thereupon fall into a way of life extinct for centuries and millennia, is a fallacy' (Coles, *Experimental Archaeology*, p. 249).

[121] Billie Gammon, quoted in Craig, 'Retreat into history', p. 15.   [122] Westall, *Devil on the Road*, p. 7.

[123] Clark, 'When the paraders meet the button-counters', p. 143.

be pretty stable not to get re-enacting and real life confused.'[124] In battle re-enactments, such 'time warps' can be really dangerous. 'Participants sometimes lose sight of the fact that it is all in play, and feel the same emotions their ancestors felt on the spot', writes Tim Clark; 1961 re-enactors of the Civil War Battle of Manassas (Bull Run) ended up clubbing each other with rifle butts.[125]

The time warp is not confined to participants; spectators too get carried away by simulated history, viciously assaulting 'British' soldiers at American Revolutionary replays. 'We went down to Faneuil Hall in Boston', said one 'British' soldier, 'and we could have been wearing Nazi uniforms, for the reaction – there was the same feeling of hatred as 200 years ago.' During a 1979 'tarring-and-feathering' at Penobscot Bay, 'militiamen' had to protect a 'British sympathizer' from onlookers who 'wanted to get in there and tear and grab and hurt people'.[126] Watching his children re-enact a hanging, a father lost some of his enthusiasm for the seventeenth century. 'Sometimes I'm afraid', he said, 'they take authenticity too far.'[127]

Re-enactments enliven history for millions who turn a blind or bored eye on ancient monuments, not to mention history books. But they risk turning venerable places into jokey or self-conscious replicas of themselves, or worse, persuading participants and even spectators that one can escape to the past. The pageantry of re-enactment transports today's locales into a fictitious yesterday purged of historical guilt, where people act out fantasies denied them in the contemporary world.[128]

Copies

Relics of the past are profoundly affected by being copied and depicted. Like duplicates, copies celebrate or call to mind aspects of the past; unlike duplicates, they aim at no strict fidelity to their models, and often intentionally depart from them in scale, materials, dimension, or form. Unlike emulations, however, copies mainly follow and reflect the past. Both their resemblances to and their differences from their models affect our perception of the originals.

The present pejorative meaning of 'copy' is of relatively recent origin. During antiquity, copying was not distinguished from creative innovation; all works of art and architecture

---

[124] Emmanuel Le Roy Ladurie, 'Democracy and modernity', *London Review of Books*, 17 Feb.–2 Mar. 1983, p. 10; Tom Sullivan, 1982, quoted in Anderson, *Time Machines*, p. 155. Not only amateurs and actors are trapped by such time warps; archaeologists too are tempted to think that 'the feelings engendered by carrying out prehistoric experiments with prehistoric implements in prehistoric surroundings, somehow had objective validity and could be treated as experimental data' (Bibby, 'Experiment with time', pp. 100–1). At Lejre, Iron Age experimental staff deliberately wear modern clothing lest they begin believing themselves Vikings (Anderson, *Time Machines*, pp. 86, 95), and archaeologists in Errett Callahan's Pamunkey Project in eastern Virginia took similar precautions so as not to persuade themselves they were really living in or actually resurrecting the American Indian past (Coles, *Experimental Archaeology*, p. 214). Total simulation makes careful documentation impossible.

[125] 'When the paraders meet the button-counters', pp. 138–41; Elder, 'War games', p. 10.

[126] Don Daley and John Skillin, quoted in Clark, 'When the paraders meet the button-counters', pp. 135, 141.

[127] Forester, 'Weekend warriors', p. 418.

[128] Anderson, 'Living history', p. 291; J. B. Jackson, *Necessity for Ruins*, p. 102.

62 Classical replicas, Syon House, Middlesex

63 *Venus*, after Clodion, in parian ware, *c.* 1862   64 St Basil's Cathedral, Thorpe Park, Surrey

62–4 Antiquity multiplied and miniaturized

were viewed as copies taken from nature or from the human form. In late-Roman and Hellenistic times, collectors valued works of art for their beauty, rarity, and antiquity, and identified as 'masterpieces' works then reproduced by copyists. Throughout the Middle Ages, artists and craftsmen copied their own masters and other prototypes with no notion that originality was desirable.[129]

Self-conscious reproduction became a hallmark of humanist historical awareness. Architects and sculptors copied great works of antiquity (or more often their Hellenistic copies) and artists copied each other. Although the Romantic stress on original creativity gave the word a bad name, painters continued to learn from and reinterpret their predecessors by assiduously copying them. In sculpture, plaster casts of antique works established a canonical set of much-copied masterpieces – the *Laocoön*, *Farnese Hercules*, *Apollo Belvedere*, Vatican *Cleopatra*, *Venus de' Medici*, the *Nile*, the bronze equestrian *Marcus Aurelius*, *Alexander and Bucephalus*, and reliefs on the triumphal arches and on the Trajan and Antonine columns.[130] In architecture, copying extended beyond classical structures to Palladian and other derivatives and eventually to Gothic prototypes in revivals that long dominated the built environment of the Western world.

Most connoisseurs became familiar with great works of the past only through copies, for private sequestration and difficulty of travel curtailed access to the originals. Up to the late nineteenth century, most antiquities were beyond the ken of all but a few, and acquaintance with admired relics was confined to reproductions and written descriptions. Only in our day has familiarity with originals become at all common, and thanks to advances in printing, metallurgy, paper-making, and photography, copies scarcely distinguishable from the originals are widely available.[131]

Full-scale plaster casts of antique sculptures in Italian papal and ducal collections were first made in the sixteenth century, and seventeenth-century French monarchs, notably Louis XIV, were their earliest assiduous collectors. Visiting Paris in 1665, Bernini stressed the importance of antique casts for the study of art and spurred the taking of moulds in Rome. In eighteenth-century England, antique casts and copies dominated the Adam rooms at Syon House, and Holkham, Kedleston, and Croome displayed substantial collections. Even American contempt for slavish devotion to the past did not preclude their acquisition of cast copies.[132]

Plaster was not the only material in which marble relics were copied. Bronze reproductions, ceramic statuettes, and lead copies of sculptures vied in popularity with plaster casts. Such was the mania for reproductions of canonical antiques that Woburn Abbey once housed sixteen marble copies of the *Medici Vase*, also copied in cast iron at Alton Towers; the *Dying Gladiator* appeared in stone at Rousham, in marble at Wilton, in bronze at Syon; the *Apollo Belvedere* in parian ware reached thousands of English homes in the 1860s.[133] Nowadays vernacular relics, too, are copied in exotic materials.

Many such copies are miniatures. Porcelain replicas and Staffordshire earthenware figurines date from the mid eighteenth century; Italian firms churned out small bronze

[129] Kidson, 'Figural arts', pp. 425–7.
[130] Haskell and Penny, *Taste and the Antique*, pp. 16, 136–40, 148–51, 184–7, 252–5.
[131] Haskell, *Rediscoveries in Art*, pp. 166–8; Ivins, *Prints and Visual Communication*, pp. 90–1, 97.
[132] Haskell and Penny, *Taste and the Antique*, pp. 16, 35–9, 87–91.
[133] Ibid., pp. 93, 252, 316, 225; *idem, Most Beautiful Statues*, p. xii.

copies of antique sculpture, and statues and temples in Tuscan alabaster.[134] Wedgwood's mass-produced antique cameos and intaglios derived from the 'mechanic skill' praised by Samuel Rogers:

> Be mine to bless the more mechanic skill,
> That stamps, renews, and multiplies at will;
> And cheaply circulates, thro' distant climes,
> The fairest relics of the purest times.[135]

But nineteenth-century plaster-cast makers, marble workshops, and bronze foundries relied more and more on machine reductions, and as their replicas multiplied the quality of their work declined.[136]

Copies also miniaturize architectural relics. Many historical models are three-fifths the original size, large enough to seem like real buildings yet small enough to feel quaint. Some locales that echo the past give the impression of being miniatures even when they are not: at Norman Shaw's 'seventeenth-century' Bedford Park village, Yeats felt 'we were living among toys', much as today's visitor feels large and gawky amid the cosy neatness of the reconstructed past.[137] Other replicas are little larger than dolls' houses: at Thorpe Park near London, the Uffington White Horse in concrete is one-fifth size, and the Taj Mahal, the Temple of Artemis, the Great Pyramid, Bodiam Castle only 5 to 10 feet high, surrounded by life-size flowers that accentuate the reduction.

Many historic miniatures make their impact as souvenirs. Anne Hathaway's cottage adorns millions of mantels and appends innumerable key rings. 'Limited-edition' replicas vaunt their authenticity: Bruce McCall's 'miniature pewterine reproductions, authenticated by the World Court at The Hague, of the front-door letter slots of Hollywood's 36 most beloved character actors and actresses' catches their bizarre mixture of precision and triviality, as do his 'Ornamental Handles of Walking Canes of the Hohenzollern Princelings' made during 'the equivalent of three centuries of painstaking historical research', and his 'Great Cookie Jars of the Restoration, just as Congreve the boy must have pilfered from . . . so authentic that you can actually smell them with your nose'.[138]

Pictorial likenesses transform perceptions of relics still more radically, especially since printing made images on paper ubiquitous. Prints of famous classical sculpture were disseminated soon after 1500; an illustrated inventory of Roman antique statues was published in 1556; Bernard de Montfaucon's catalogue of 1719 contained over thirty thousand images of ancient art; from 1762 on, the sketches of Stuart and Revett made Greek antiquities increasingly familiar.[139] Ease and fidelity of pictorial reproduction increasingly favours the visual apprehension of history; even when we read about the past we now envisage it pictorially.

Moreover, surrogates like miniatures are less burdensome than full-scale vestiges. The

---

[134] Haskell and Penny, *Taste and the Antique*, pp. 94–6.
[135] 'Epistle to a friend' (1799), lines 65–8, p. 12. See Mankowitz, *Wedgwood*, pp. 104–7, 214–15, 221–3.
[136] Haskell and Penny, *Taste and the Antique*, pp. 122–3; J. M. Crook, 'Canon of the classical'.
[137] Yeats, quoted in Nicholas Taylor, *Village in the City*, p. 60; Frederika Randall, 'Unreconstructed past', *The Nation*, 7–14 Aug. 1982, p. 122.
[138] 'Rolled in rare Bohemian onyx, then vulcanized by hand', *New Yorker*, 21 Dec. 1981, p. 39.
[139] Haskell and Penny, *Taste and the Antique*, pp. 17–21, 43.

65 Mission models, San Gabriel Mission courtyard, California

66 *The Last Supper*, Bibleland, Santa Cruz, California

Somerset town of Taunton gladly shed many of its older buildings in the 1950s and 1960s; postcards and tea towels portraying these banished landmarks soon afterwards became locally popular.[140] When still extant these structures were sad reminders of a scruffy and impoverished past; only when the actual relics were gone could their images be appreciated.

Many prefer Disneyland's 'historic' facsimiles precisely because they *are* copies, not demanding the solemn awe felt to be due to the originals.[141] Affection for images of the past may reflect our distance from their prototypes. Old photos substitute for ancestors estranged by the erosion of family coherence, suggests Hirsch; the pictures of these tanned peasants or careworn peddlers bespeak our remoteness from them, not our intimacy with them.[142]

Changing skills and tastes can make copies more valuable than originals. Renaissance sculpture surpasses its debased Hellenistic exemplars, which now come alive only through copies of them that clear away inferior accretions. 'Looking at a terra cotta by Maderno, a bronze by Susini, or a drawing by Batoni', write Haskell and Penny, 'we may sense the compelling power ... the sculptures which these artists were reproducing ... once held.'[143]

Whether or not copies improve on relics, familiarity with copies shapes how the originals are subsequently seen: reactions to antiquities are mainly predetermined by reproductions. Until recently, their effect was thought beneficial; multiplying copies of ancient masterpieces would 'most effectually prevent the Return of Ignorant and barbarous Ages', wrote Josiah Wedgwood – though he was, to be sure, addressing potential customers. Copies diffused good taste, instructed the public eye, and improved the arts while enhancing the prototype, Wedgwood went on, 'for the more Copies there are of any Works, as of the Venus Medicis for instance, the more celebrated the Original will be ... Everybody wishes to see the Original of a beautiful Copy.'[144]

In fact, the *Venus de' Medici*'s reputation began seriously to decline just as she was most multiplied. The prestige of ancient masterpieces rested partly on their scarcity and inaccessibility; over-exposure dimmed their canonical excellence and turned the touchstones into clichés.[145] Mass replication tarnishes a relic's reputation; the image of Shakespeare is simply demeaned, a visitor to Stratford complained, when one is made to eat an omelette off a likeness of the Bard's face or to stub out a cigarette on it.[146]

While reproduction has stimulated public interest in original relics, it has also debased them. Viewers throng to the *Mona Lisa*, as they goggle at movie stars, largely because they

[140] Somerset County planning officers, Taunton, interviews 3 Mar. 1978; Robin Bush, *The Book of Taunton* (Chesham: Barracuda, 1977). L. S. Lowry's paintings likewise became popular after the industrial scenes they portrayed had become defunct (Randolph Langenbach, 'The challenge facing Oldham', in *Satanic Mills: Industrial Architecture in the Pennines*, p. 11; John Berger, 'Lowry and the industrial North', pp. 90–3).

[141] Goldberger, 'Dangers in preservation success', p. 161.   [142] *Family Photographs*, p. 119.

[143] *Most Beautiful Statues*, p. xiii.

[144] Wedgwood & Bentley 1779 catalogue, transcription in Mankowitz, *Wedgwood*, pp. 253, 229. Nelson Rockefeller similarly claimed that replicas of his collection helped make art 'for the first time the common heritage of all mankind'; art dealers complained that they were 'sold as substitutes for, rather than reminders of, "the real thing"' (Grace Glueck, 'Dealers take on Rockefeller', *IHT*, 8 Dec. 1978).

[145] Bolgar, 'Introduction', *Classical Influences*, p. 28; Haskell and Penny, *Taste and the Antique*, p. 122; Crook, 'Canon of the classical'.

[146] Kozintsev, *Shakespeare*, p. 7. On the effects of mass-produced copies, see Walter Benjamin, 'Work of art in the age of mechanical reproduction', pp. 220–3; Dorfles, *Kitsch*, pp. 31–2, 94–7.

have so often seen its likeness; they admire it because they recognize its fame. 'Oh my, it was beautiful', exclaimed a recent viewer at the Louvre. 'It was just like all those copies I've seen.'[147] As famous originals become pop symbols they shed historical significance. Antique costumes remind viewers not of historical figures but of the entertainers who portrayed them. A guide book identifies the sixteenth-century Duke of Norfolk entombed in Framlingham church, Suffolk, as having 'figured prominently in the TV series, *The Six Wives of Henry VIII*'.[148] Relics become simulacra of their modern representations, like Harold Bloom's anxious poets reversing the direction of influence between forerunner and successor.

Depictions of ancient artifacts often detract from subsequent impressions of the originals; the anticipatory viewer may be thrilled to recognize a relic but is deprived of a fresh unmediated experience. And because photographs screen out the banal or the irrelevant and show ancient monuments at awe-inspiring angles, they arouse expectations that reality often disappoints. They so accustom us to the solemn majesty of the Parthenon's west front, the splendid columns of Persepolis, that the visitor finds it 'a shock to see that these are isolated survivors arising out of something like a builder's yard'. The antiquities seen by a sampling of British tourists elicited such responses as 'It was much smaller than I expected', 'It was all broken up – I couldn't make head or tail of it', 'It was sort of scruffy.'[149] Just as live performances sound thin to ears jaded by souped-up recordings, so have ultra-glossy reproductions in art books corrupted the public eye; as faces cloud over with disappointment on seeing the original paintings, viewers wonder 'Where were those gorgeous coach-work colors?'[150]

The liberties taken in modern duplication and revision further diminish old masterpieces. Originally seen as a prototype of naturalistic realism, the *Mona Lisa* came in the nineteenth century to stand for enigmatic seduction; twentieth-century copies have made it such common coin that, in Harold Rosenberg's phrase, it seems more like Aunt Jemima than a great painting.[151] The beard and moustache added to the original in Marcel Duchamp's *L.H.O.O.Q.* (1919) have themselves become prototypes of satirical and commercial manipulation.[152]

Artists and photographers alter perspectives on the past by adorning historical events with anachronistic symbols. Emmanuel Leutze's *Washington Crossing the Delaware* (1851) elevated a minor episode of the American Revolution to a mythic event, and new additions and legends continually alter the historical message of Custer's Last Stand, the most

---

147 Robert Goldberg, 'Jostling over Mona Lisa', *IHT*, 5–6 July 1980, p. 8. See W. H. Cohn, 'History for the masses', p. 282. Reproductions also tempt restorers to emulate the stark colours, flat plane, and homogenized texture of art book photographs, turning paintings into 'two-dimensional shadows of their former selves' (Walden, *Ravished Image*, p. 6).

148 The Victoria and Albert's exhibition of costumes used in a television series about Henry VIII far outdrew its permanent display of real Tudor costumes (Thomson, 'Conservation of antiquities', p. 42); Castle Howard is touted – and largely visited – as the locale of the television series *Brideshead Revisited*.

149 Chamberlin, *Preserving the Past*, p. 66. Everyday reality often spoils the picture in the mind's eye. Thus at Balbec Proust's Marcel is appalled to find the statue of the Virgin, long adored in his imagination, 'reduced now to its own stone semblance, ... coated with the same soot as defiled the neighbouring houses, ... transformed, as was the church itself, into a little old woman whose height I could measure and whose wrinkles I could count' (*Remembrance of Things Past*, 1:709–10).

150 Richardson, 'Crimes against the Cubists', p. 34.

151 Boas, 'Mona Lisa in the history of taste'; Rosenberg, 'Mona Lisa without a mustache', p. 48.

152 McMullen, *Mona Lisa*; Storey, *Mona Lisas*; Roy Fuller, 'The Venus pin-up', *New Society*, 23 Oct. 1975, p. 222; Ducousset, 'Epidémie des parodies'.

67 Updating the patriotic past: Archibald M. Willard, *Spirit of '76*, 1876

68 Updating the patriotic past: Sheraton Hotels advertisement, 1976

reproduced event in American history.[153] Archibald Willard's *Spirit of '76* (originally *Yankee Doodle*), first made familiar by chromolithographs in every photographer's studio, changes meaning with every national crisis. Deliberately staged parallels with Willard's figures made the Iwo Jima flag scene an icon of American fortitude in the Second World War, and during the bicentennial the *Spirit of '76* shed lustre on Budget-Rent-a-Car, Sesame Street, the American Chiropractic Association, Kentucky Fried Chicken and, not least, Disneyland.[154] Down Main Street, U.S.A., in the heart of Disney World, came 'America on Parade', and there, 'at the head of the parade, bearing drum and fife ... and patched with bandages, stand the three symbols of the American Revolution: Mickey Mouse, Donald Duck, and Goofy'.[155]

Copies of the past thus take on careers of their own, often submerging their prototypes in the service of subsequent demands.

Emulations

Many additions to surviving relics are free, even fanciful, readaptations. But it is in self-conscious period revivals – respectful yet creative reworkings of earlier forms and styles – that the past manifests its most pervasive influence.

Such revivals transcend mere copying. Even structures inspired solely by obeisance to an exemplar are bound to reflect their own time; the most faithful followers exhibit modern departures. 'Artists should never be afraid of their work appearing derivative and unoriginal, for whatever they produce inevitably retains the flavour of their [own] epoch.'[156] Fidelity to history did not prevent Victorians from gilding Greek or Gothic with nineteenth-century gold, and cultural nostalgia and liturgical reaction yielded 'medieval' architecture that was manifestly mid nineteenth-century. 'Under the guise of "revival"', remarks Nicholas Taylor of the nostalgic utopias of Pugin, Ruskin, and Morris, 'their authors were in fact being highly original and inventive.'[157]

Yet revivals expand perspectives of the emulated epoch too. Indeed, artifacts later inspired by past exemplars loom larger in the present landscape than do its original relics. Not only are emulations more numerous than surviving originals, but many a past now survives only or mainly in subsequent refractions of it: awareness of all but the most recent past derives less from its own remains than from subsequent copies and emulations. Our image of 'classical', for example, depends far less on actual Greek and Roman survivals than on Hellenistic and later evocations. And present-day notions of Gothic owe less to scanty medieval remains than to subsequent additions that reflect and rework Gothic style or spirit. Elizabethan and Jacobean nostalgia led to neo-medieval chivalry and the battlements and keeps, vaulted halls and ogee-arched fireplaces of

[153] Kammen, *Season of Youth*, pp. 81–3; Anne Hawkes Hutton, *Portrait of Patriotism: 'Washington Crossing the Delaware'* (Philadelphia: Chilton, 1959); Don Russell, 'Whatever happened at Custer's Last Stand?'.

[154] Pauly, 'In search of "The Spirit of '76"'.

[155] Dick Schaap, 'Culture shock: Williamsburg & Disney World, back to back', *N.Y. Times*, 28 Sept. 1975, Travel sect. p. 1.

[156] Lees-Milne, *Ancestral Voices*, diary entry 24 Mar. 1942, p. 40. Carew's toga-clad statue of Huskisson in Chichester Cathedral inspired this reflection.

[157] *Village in the City*, p. 32.

69 George Washington and the cherry tree: the original myth. Grant Wood, *Parson Weems'*
Fable, 1939 (Amon Carter Museum, Fort Worth, Texas)

70 A modern explanation: 'Give a kid a hatchet, he's going to chop things', Kraus, *New Yorker*,
1969

71 Technology tarnishes the fable: 'Father, I cannot tell a lie', Fredon, *New Yorker*, 1954

72 The classical: the Pantheon, Rome, 27 B.C., rebuilt A.D. 117–125

73 Classical derivatives: John Soane, Dairy, Hamels Park, Hertfordshire, 1783 (demolished);
sketch by G. Richardson

74 National Monument, Calton Hill, Edinburgh, by C. R. Cockerell and W. H. Playfair,
1822–9

75 Forest Lawn Memorial Park mortuary, Glendale, California, 1920s

76 G. P. W. Custis residence, Arlington, Virginia, by George Hadfield, 1820
(Wayne Andrews)

77 Bank façade, Madison, Wisconsin, 1972

78 The Gothic: Bodiam Castle, Sussex, 1386

79 Gothic derivatives: James Malton, design for a hunting-lodge, *c*. 1802

80 Capitol, Baton Rouge, Louisiana, by J. H. Dakin, 1847 (Wayne Andrews)

81 'Lyndhurst', Tarrytown, New York, by Alexander Jackson Davis, 1838–65
(Wayne Andrews)

82 Strawberry Hill, Twickenham, by Horace Walpole, *c.* 1760

83 William Burges, design for Church of St Mary, Alford-cum-Studley, Yorkshire, *c.* 1872

84 Oxfordshire County Hall, by John Plowman, 1840–1

85 Salvation Army, Poole, Dorset

86 Mortuary, Encinitas, California

houses only symbolically Gothic; the decorative fortifications of eighteenth-century Gothick suited the gunpowder age, not the days of pikes; the prototype fairy-tale castle that today denotes 'Gothic' – central keep and rectangular ramparts with four corner turrets – is a picturesque amalgam of Palladian planning with a 'medieval' silhouette.[158] But 'Gothic may lose *all* those features by which we know it', as a Victorian architect remarked, 'and yet for our purposes be Gothic in the truest sense after all';[159] indeed, neo-Gothic changed the letter so as to keep the spirit. Unlike medieval Gothic as such revivals were, they are now more Gothic than anything else. Medieval ruins, Tudor castles, Romantic Gothick follies, ecclesiological and municipal Gothic, and the battlements of the Salvation Army comprise a composite Gothic landscape that most viewers would find hard to disaggregate. Few admirers of the classical can tell Roman from Grecian, let alone Hellenistic; revivals are commonly mistaken for survivals. The passage of time dissolves distinctions between originals and emulations, and augments their confluence.

Purists often censure this commingling of derivates with originals. Harrow's Conservation Area planners caution potential developers against designing in an 'historical' style, as such buildings would 'devalue the merits of the existing genuine buildings'.[160] Neo-Georgian is disowned by The Georgian Group, lest the offspring's excesses diminish the parent's prestige.[161] But for most people such adaptations merge quite companionably with original prototypes and with other derivatives. Only a quarter of those surveyed

---

[158] J. M. Crook, 'Origins of the Gothic Revival', pp. 50–3.
[159] T. G. Jackson, *Modern Gothic Architecture* (1873), p. 113.
[160] London Borough of Harrow, *Conservation Areas*, 'Advice on new buildings' (1983).
[161] Eleanor Murray, Georgian Group, interview 15 May 1978.

87 The eclectic past: Osbert Lancaster, 'Bypass Variegated'

in Guildford made any distinction between original and derivative architecture.[162] Preservationists in Metroland fight as hard to save Edwardian half-timbering and thatched roofs as they do any surviving originals, and 1930s mock-Tudor has begun to take on the sacred aura of the long-ago look it sought to copy.[163]

Copies and revivals often have commemorative intents or consequences. Reminders of ancient Greece so enveloped Americans that to 'separate ourselves entirely from the influence of all those memorials', remarked Daniel Webster in the Senate in 1824, we would have to 'withdraw ourselves from this place, and the scenes and objects which here surround us'; urging American recognition of Greek independence, he noted that 'even the edifice in which we assemble, these proportioned columns, this ornamented architecture, all remind us that Greece has existed, and that we, like the rest of mankind, are greatly her debtors'.[164]

The eclectic or haphazard commingling of revival styles also reshapes our sense of the broader past, like the 'infernal amalgam [of] quaint gables culled from Art Nouveau; . . . twisted beams and leaded panes of Stockbrokers Tudor', Pont Street Dutch terra-cotta plaques, 'Wimbledon Transitional porch', and vaguely Romanesque red brick garage of Osbert Lancaster's immortal Bypass Variegated,[165] the aggregate of these disparate components redefining the whole architectural heritage.

---

[162] Bishop, 'Perception and Importance of Time in Architecture', p. 263.
[163] Saunders, 'Metroland: half-timbering and other souvenirs in the Outer London suburbs', pp. 168, 172–3; Clive Aslet, 'Let's stop mocking the neo-Tudor', *The Times*, 11 June 1983, p. 8.
[164] 'Revolution in Greece', 5:61.   [165] *Here, Of All Places*, p. 152.

88 Commemorative motifs from Egypt: Grove Street Cemetery, New Haven, Connecticut, by Henry Austin, 1845–6 (Wayne Andrews)

89 Commemorative and contemporary: Milford, Connecticut

90 Unique and apposite commemoration: concrete and stone tent, mausoleum of Richard F. Burton of *The Arabian Nights*, Mortlake, Surrey, 1890

91 Collective and generic commemoration: monument to soldiers of successive wars, Hartland, Vermont

Commemorations

Monuments and memorials embellish the past by evoking some epoch's splendour, some person's power or genius, some unique event. What most such evocations have in common is being made after the event; they celebrate the past in later guise. And their form and features may in no way resemble what they are expressly built to recall.

Although commemorative emblems often derive from or symbolize antiquity, many memorials simply reflect the iconographic fashions of their own days. Thus effigies loll on their elbows among cherubs, skulls, scythes, twisted columns and similar seventeenth-century icons of death and immortality; while the rediscovery of Egypt made pyramids, obelisks, sphinxes, and sarcophagi popular memorial features in the late eighteenth century.[166]

Heroes are often memorialized in garb reflecting a retrospective ideal. The Roman toga draped around George Washington in pictures and statues symbolized republican virtues; Pakistan's founding father Jinnah, a fastidious Westerner in dress, is now everywhere depicted in the close-fitting, high-buttoned national *sherwani*.[167] Like an earlier plea that a

---

[166] Curl, *Celebration of Death*, pp. 40, 363–5. Funerary adornments in late sixteenth-century England were purged of traditional Catholic symbolism (John Phillips, *Reformation of Images*, pp. 118–19).
[167] 'Redressing history', *The Times*, 29 Mar. 1982, p. 6.

monument to Washington should bear witness 'to the good taste and judgment of those who erect it', Edward Everett sought a Bunker Hill Monument which would both call to mind the Revolutionary struggle and teach posterity 'that the people of Massachusetts of *this* generation' had thought of it.[168]

Monuments are more numerous and imposing in the Old World than the New, and memorial purposes remain more hortatory. 'Every tacky little fourth-rate déclassé European country has monuments all over the place and one cannot turn a corner without banging into an eighteen-foot bronze of Lebrouche Tickling the Chambermaids at Vache while Planning the Battle of Bledsoe, or some such', observes Donald Barthelme. 'Whereas Americans tend to pile up a few green cannon balls next to a broken-down mortar and forget about it.'[169]

Until recently, most monuments were exhortations to imitate the virtues they commemorated; they reminded people what to believe and how to behave. Commemoration likewise came to evince a recollective rather than a hortatory purpose in post-Civil War America. The contrast between Lincoln's 'Gettysburg Address' and the subsequent designation of the battlefield exemplifies the change, J. B. Jackson suggests. Lincoln dedicated 'us the living . . . to the unfinished work which they who fought here have thus far so nobly advanced', implying that 'on a specific occasion a contract was entered into, a covenant was made, and the monument is to remind us of that contract; just as it confers a kind of immortality on the dead, it determines our actions in years to come'. After the Civil War, Gettysburg Battlefield became its own monument, the mere designation a sufficient memorial. 'It was no longer a reminder; it no longer told us what to do; it simply explained the battle.'[170]

Paralleling this change, Americans commemorated the Civil War in terms less of individual leaders than of all its participants, often erecting statues to a literally unknown soldier. Other memorials increasingly honoured ordinary people and ways of life. Following Daniel Chester French's *Minute Man* at Concord in 1876 came monuments to prototypical Americans – the anonymous cowboy, newsboy, Gloucester fishermen, even boll weevil.[171] Across the Atlantic, the national or collective past had already become worthy of recall, with late eighteenth-century monuments to fallen soldiers prefiguring mass-produced French 'Mariannes' and British 'Tommys'.[172] And we increasingly commemorate, just as we restore and re-enact, not to follow a past example but simply to recall how life used to be.

Monuments may be remote from their subjects in space as well as in decor. As commemorative purposes increasingly prevailed over judgemental aims, funerary statues were detached from tombs to become significant elements of the urban landscape. 'A thickening forest of monuments', in Marvin Trachtenberg's phrase, epitomized late nineteenth-century nationalist glorification of the past, 'almost threaten[ing] to choke the city

---

[168] William Tudor (1816), and Everett (pre-1865), quoted in Neil Harris, *Artist in American Society*, p. 197; my italics.
[169] Barthelme and Sorel, 'Monumental folly', p. 33.
[170] *Necessity for Ruins*, p. 93; 'Gettysburg Address' (1863).
[171] Jackson, *Necessity for Ruins*, pp. 94–5; Schwartz, 'Social context of commemoration', pp. 390–5.
[172] Ariès, *Hour of Our Death*, pp. 547–9; Hobsbawm, 'Mass-producing traditions', pp. 271–2.

squares and picturesque sites of Europe'.[173] Many memorials adorn locations that had no connection with the celebrated person or event, like Poets' Corner in Westminster Abbey or Nelson's Column at Trafalgar Square. Statues of former rulers grace localities half a world away from their own scenes of action. Caesar is commemorated far beyond the former Roman Empire; Washington bestrides a horse in countless city squares; Victoria oversees traffic as far from home as Benares and Berbice.

Famous figures are most suitably commemorated in locales they have vitally affected or been influenced by. 'An author is expected to have been associated with a building over a considerable time and to have written some important work', rules Britain's Department of the Environment, 'before we consider listing for historic reasons.'[174] But it is beginnings and endings, all the same, that arouse the keenest memorial interest. Where a famous man was born or died may have little bearing on his historical role, yet the public expects monuments to mark them.[175]

The reason is clear: the memorial act implies termination. We seldom erect monuments to ongoing events or to people still alive. Hence our queasiness when *we* are commemorated. On visits home Updike's protagonist in *Of the Farm* finds himself increasingly enshrined in old pictures, schoolboy medals, certificates 'permanized' in plastic; 'I was so abundantly memorialized it seemed I must be dead'. The author later fell victim to his own fictional memorial: a 1982 BBC programme showed Updike reading *Of the Farm* in the very room the book commemorates, the camera picking out the mementoes the text describes.[176]

Tombstones make up the great bulk of all memorials. But cemeteries now matter more as fields of remembrance for the living than as repositories of the dead, whose place of burial becomes still less consequential once they moulder into dust or are removed to make way for others. Distinctively personal monuments dominate some graveyards; in others the memorial feeling is collective. Massed identical crosses and anonymous graves in military cemeteries recall not the individual soldiers but the general carnage of the Great War.[177] But all old graveyards become increasingly collective: as the interred lose personal significance for the living, their monuments no longer recall particular forebears but bespeak the common ancestral past.[178]

Long-enduring monuments acquire an antiquity that deserves its own recognition; in Crabbe's words, 'Monuments themselves Memorials need.'[179] Their patinaed forms, the archaic content and calligraphy of their engraved messages, add layers of remembrance to those their makers intended.[180] This flavour of antiquity ultimately joins the landscape of

[173] Ariès, *Hour of Our Death*, pp. 215, 230, 235; Trachtenberg, *Statue of Liberty*, p. 100.
[174] Quoted in Saunders, 'Protection of property', p. 30.
[175] Ashley Barker, Greater London Council, Historic Buildings Division, interview 4 May 1978.
[176] *Of the Farm*, p. 17; Valentine Cunningham, 'Authenticating the poet', *TLS*, 5 Feb. 1982, p. 134.
[177] Zelinsky, 'Unearthly delights: . . . the changing American afterworld'; Stamp, *Silent Cities*; Ariès, *Hour of Our Death*, p. 550.
[178] Warner, *The Living and the Dead*, p. 319.
[179] *The Borough*, Letter 2, p. 18. Crabbe's line is a gloss on Juvenal's 'seeing that sepulchres, too, have their allotted fate' (*Satire* 10, line 146, p. 210).
[180] People 'saw their chronicles upon the marble', wrote an early Victorian of ancient inscriptions. 'The lines were read by the fathers, the children, and grandchildren, and after the lapse of age, the moss-grown characters add the most powerful charms to the majestic ruin' (*Civil Engineer and Architects' Journal*, 1839, quoted in Ellen Frank, *Literary Architecture*, p. 248).

commemoration with other additions to the past. Indeed, memorials are often put among other relics. Monuments dating from the 1876 centennial adorn Concord's reconstructed Old North Bridge, overlooked by Hawthorne's 'Old Manse'; one memorial stone commemorates the British dead in Lowell's lines against the tyranny of tradition:

> They came three thousand miles, and died,
> To keep the Past upon its throne.[181]

When other relics have perished, commemorative creations survive as our only physical reminders of the past. They are deliberately made durable to recall treasured lineaments for as long as possible. Semblances of Ireland's early architecture – a chapel, a high cross, a round tower – festooned George Petrie's proposed tomb for Daniel O'Connell, so that even when 'the wreck of time and the devastations of ignorance' had wasted other extant vestiges, the memorial would keep alive those forms and features.[182]

Yet memorials are far more than mere reflections of what they celebrate, for they add to the landscape a new medley of funerary and hortatory symbols. They not only remind us about the past but impress us with its significance and our loss, reinforcing our reluctant recognition that it is forever gone.

We change the past, then, not only by altering antiquities but by using them as stimuli for subsequent creations. Innumerable acts of imitation and emulation, of re-enactment and commemoration, of imagery and reproduction, add to the stock of what passes for the past and transforms the impact of its surviving relics. The resultant past is a cluster of original fragments, much altered by erosion and appreciation, embedded among myriad later additions. New technologies and increased historical awareness encourage more such insertions. Among the proliferation of new and altered pasts it becomes ever harder to distinguish those relics that are original.

WHY WE CHANGE THE PAST

> I'm going to fix up everything just the way it was before.
>
> F. Scott Fitzgerald, *The Great Gatsby*[183]

> The mythic instinct erelong begins to shape things as they ought to have been, rather than as they were.
>
> James Russell Lowell, 'The Rebellion: its causes
> and consequences'[184]

The present looks back at some great figure of an earlier century and wonders, Was he on our side? Was he a goodie? What a lack of self-confidence this implies: the present wants both to patronise the past by adjudicating on its political acceptability,

---

[181] 'Lines suggested by the graves of the English soldiers on Concord battle-ground', 9:272.
[182] Petrie, 'Report to the Committee of the O'Connell Monument' (1851), in Stokes, *George Petrie*, p. 434.
[183] 1925, p. 102. See Steinbrink, '"Boats against the current"'; Stallman, 'Gatsby and the hole in time', p. 4.
[184] 1864, 6:145.

and also to be flattered by it, to be patted on the back and told to keep up the good work.

Julian Barnes, *Flaubert's Parrot*[185]

Why do we change the past? What moves us to alter and elaborate our heritage in all these ways? And in other ways too, for we transform not only tangible relics but also historical records and personal memories as shown in Chapter 5. To be sure, we cannot avoid altering our inheritance; modern perspectives are bound to reinterpret all relics and recollections. Seeing the past in our own terms, we necessarily revise what previous interpreters have seen in their terms, and reshape artifacts and memories accordingly. But beyond involuntary alterations, explicit aims prompt us to replace or add to an inadequate past.

We all want more or other than what we have been left. The bare remains of antiquity on the ground, in texts, and in our recollections seldom suffice the needs elaborated in Chapter 2, let alone the dreams of Chapter 1. 'The people of Crete', says a Saki character, 'unfortunately make more history than they can consume locally.'[186] That is a rare circumstance; in most countries the demand exceeds the supply. If William James was appalled at Stratford by 'the absolute extermination and obliteration of every record of Shakespeare save a few sordid material details',[187] his brother Henry mocked at their manufacture for history-hungry pilgrims. 'Don't they want also to see where He had His dinner and where He had His tea?' 'They want everything . . . They want to see where He hung up His hat and where He kept His boots and where His mother boiled her pot.'[188]

Among the history hungry today, antiquing is a widespread avocation. Copies outnumber and often obscure actual survivals; newly minted places replicate nostalgically imagined scenes. Seeing a quaint Mediterranean town, a visitor who asks about its past is told 'the town *has* no history, Signore. It was built from scratch three years ago, entirely for the tourist trade.'[189]

As with memory, we reinterpret relics and records to make them more comprehensible, to justify present attitudes and actions, to underscore changes of faith. The unadulterated past is seldom sufficiently ancient or glorious; most heritages need ageing and augmenting. Individually and collectively we revise the inherited past to enhance self-esteem, to aggrandize property, to validate power. Hence genealogies are fabricated to bolster titles of nobility, decrees forged to justify papal dominion, relics planted to demonstrate pre-Columbian discoveries.

To specify such motives, however, is not to say that all these alterations are deliberate. We are often innocent of conscious intent to change what we mean simply to conserve or celebrate. What impelled our predecessors to change the past – the biases of bygone historians, restorers, curators – is clear enough in hindsight. We can now see how pedagogic and patriotic commitments shaped Henry Ford's Greenfield and John D.

---

[185] 1984, p. 130.
[186] 'Jesting of Arlington Stringham' (1910), p. 135. See Langguth, *Saki*, p. 110. Minus the word 'unfortunately', Saki's remark served to promote tourism in Crete in an advertisement which added that 'Today, their descendants loyally preserve and present the evidence' (*Sunday Times*, 23 Apr. 1978, p. 67).
[187] To Charles Eliot Norton, 4 May 1902, in William James, *Letters*, 2:166.
[188] 'Birthplace', 11:437. See Conn, *Divided Mind*, p. 25; Edel, *Henry James*, 2:464, 473, 475–6, 478–9.
[189] Stevenson cartoon, *New Yorker*, 8 May 1965, p. 120.

Rockefeller's Williamsburg.[190] But we cannot detect our own preconceptions, which warp the past no less than Ford's or Rockefeller's. To be aware of our own biases is beyond a point impossible: we fail to recognize not only *why* we alter history, but often *that* we do. Thus we tend to misconceive the past as a fixed verity from which others have strayed, but to which we can and should remain unswervingly faithful.

Though the past is malleable, its alteration is not always easy: the stubborn weight of its remains can baulk intended revision. When relics and records obstinately resist a desired interpretation, we may have to change our minds rather than alter the evidence. In fact we commonly do both at once: the consensual past is in continual flux between long-held views reluctantly abandoned and a heritage perennially transformed.

In this section I first examine how far changing the past is conscious or deliberate, and the consequences of such awareness for history and its remains. Next I discuss the qualities and features we like to put into the past and the goals to which they conduce. Finally I survey the impact of such changes on our surroundings and on ourselves, as participants in a continuing dialogue between ever-modernizing pasts and ever-passing presents.

Awareness of alteration

We may be fully conscious, partially and hazily aware, or wholly unconscious of what prompts us to alter the past. Many such changes are unintended; others are undertaken to make a supposed legacy credible; relatively few are expressly sought. The more strenuously we build a desired past, the more we convince ourselves that things really were that way; what ought to have happened becomes what did happen. If we profess only to rectify our predecessors' prejudices and errors and to restore pre-existing conditions, we fail to see that today's past is as much a thing of today as it is of that past; to bolster faith that the past originally existed in the form we now devise, we minimize or forget our own alterations.

In this belief George Gilbert Scott, who substituted his own 'Gothic' for surviving Norman and other styles, discounted the wholesale changes he introduced, claiming he always regarded 'an original detail ... though partly decayed and mutilated [to be] infinitely more valuable than the most skilful attempt at its restoration'; he had sought 'the least possible displacement of old stone', replacing only those 'features which have actually been destroyed by modern mutilation'. Persuaded to 'restore' the dilapidated fifteenth-century chapel on the bridge at Wakefield, Scott was later 'filled with wonder how I ever was induced to consent to it at all, as it was contrary to the principles of my own report ... I think of this with the utmost shame and chagrin.'[191]

---

[190] Rockefeller expressly stated his aim to free Williamsburg 'entirely from alien or inharmonious surroundings' and 'preserve the beauty and charm of the old', and felt proud that the restoration 'teaches of the patriotism, high purpose, and unselfish devotion of our forefathers to the common good' (John D. Rockefeller, Jr, 'The genesis of the Williamsburg restoration', *National Geographic*, 71:4 (1937), 401). John Candee maintains that Old Sturbridge Village was begun as a tax shelter, and that Rockefeller selected Williamsburg for restoration to link his name with Washington, Jefferson, and Patrick Henry; no lesser place would have done ('American preservation movement: a reassessment', lecture at Historic Preservation symposium, Boston University, 2 Dec. 1978).

[191] *Plea for the Faithful Restoration of Our Ancient Churches* (1850), quoted in Pevsner, *Some Architectural Writers*, p. 172; *Recollections*, quoted in Briggs, *Goths and Vandals*, pp. 176, 173.

The architect George Edmund Street exhibited a similar disparity between conscious precept and unconscious practice: he criticized the reconstructions of Burgos Cathedral and St Mark's, Venice, for the same historical insensitivity that led Street himself to replace the fourteenth-century eastern arm of the choir of Dublin's Christ Church Cathedral with a pastiche of the 'original' choir; yet Street was neither a vandal nor a hypocrite.[192] Like Orwell's Ministry of Truth, which continually revised the past to show that the Party had always been right, we brainwash ourselves into believing that we simply reveal the true past – a past which is unavoidably, however, partly of our own manufacture.

In oral societies, the absence of permanent records inhibits awareness of alteration, and reluctance to recognize change characterizes scribal cultures as well. Only the fixity of print, Eisenstein shows, finally forced scholars to realize how seriously copyists had corrupted such embodiments of tradition as the Old Testament.[193] Even peoples who lack writing, however, may knowingly alter the past that has come down to them. To preserve social institutions, certain African chroniclers must transmute received history into new forms. Social function, Vansina shows, determines how far oral accounts consciously falsify the past: historical narrators alter testimony intentionally for their own purposes, unintentionally for the sake of collective tradition; hence communal aims incite erroneous accounts of the past, whereas private aims encourage deliberate falsifications. Tradition generally omits, or prohibits the recounting of, facts about the past that might undermine ruling institutions: the Bushongo proclaim that their ruling dynasty was the first in the country, although they know this is not true, and official Akan history holds that the ruling class was indigenous, though members of the royal clan know well that they were immigrants.[194]

Failure to realize how deeply we ourselves affect the received version of our past derives partly from feeling that the past is sacred and ought not to be tampered with. Those who deliberately falsify the historical record rarely confess except under compulsion; those who revise it unconsciously or to set the record straight are reluctant to face up to their own biases. And because their perpetrators remain unaware or unrepentant, many alterations of the past never come to light.

Faith in the ultimate stability of the past's lineaments also explains unwillingness to admit one has tampered with it; people prefer to believe that exposing lies and expunging fabrications, securing historical fidelity against villainous manipulators, will regain the 'true' past. Faith in the fixed reality of the past buttresses the belief that by sloughing off previous alterations we can celebrate antiquity exactly as it was.

Even those conscious of their own actions often fail to see that they put the surviving past at risk. Latter-day Romans who quarried marble from imperial temples and statuary, contractors who demolish archaeological remains, farmers who plough up traces of medieval villages seldom realize that they subvert the historical legacy.

---

[192] *Some Account of Gothic Architecture in Spain*, 1:29n: 'In dealing with old buildings it is absolutely impossible to be too conservative . . . when we find old work we cannot be wrong in letting well alone.' See John Harvey, *Conservation in Buildings*, pp. 92–3.

[193] *Printing Press*, pp. 114–16, 289–90, 319–26. See Peel, 'Making history', pp. 128–9.

[194] Vansina, *Oral Tradition*, pp. 76–85. Peel ('Making history', pp. 124–7) shows how Yoruba villagers manipulate written records to alter or escape the consequences of a fixed tradition.

Admirers of antiquity also unwittingly erode its relics. Visitors who wear down the floor of Canterbury Cathedral do not stop to consider the cumulative impact of thousands of pairs of shoes; those whose breath and body heat threatened Lascaux's paintings had no notion of the corrosive effect of their mere presence in the cave. The imperfect knowledge of experts too can have dire consequences: conservators who secured the Parthenon pillars with iron bolts early in this century little dreamt that rust and metal expansion would make them agents of destruction. Few who signpost historical sites, copy old master paintings, or emulate period styles imagine that such acts of appreciation may also affect how the original relics are seen. Perhaps motives unconsciously held explain their perpetrators' blindness to impacts that are patent to others.

Just because it seems so laudable, 'setting the record straight' involves more self-deception than any other motive for changing the past. Convinced that they at last see the past in its true light, revisionists stripping away previous accretions remain unaware that they are adding new accretions of their own. Some reshape relics to conform with the documentary record; others rewrite history to accommodate artifactual evidence; still others restore tangible and written remains to what they might have been but for attrition and interference. Yet faith in a vital document, a rare relic, a unique memory, an *idée fixe* often entails the neglect or revision of other evidence that tells discordant tales of the past.

We feel impelled to right previous wrongs and repair previous errors whatever motivated them. Wanton extirpation like the Nazi destruction of Poland's medieval town centres; revision animated by aesthetic morality like Victorian Gothic church fittings; well-meant but ill-informed or ineptly executed previous restorations – all are zealously rectified. Some restore to expiate their own guilt; Henry Ford's Greenfield Village re-created an earlier America his automobiles had done much to destroy.[195]

The rectified past aims to be seen as the true original. 'Historic' villages that have corrected pedagogic and patriotic invention now claim to portray an archaeologically authentic past. But because the up-to-date truth they profess is a point of pride, doubts about the authenticity of their own revisions are apt to be brushed aside, conflicting evidence ignored.

Those who remake the past as it *ought* to have been, as distinct from what it presumably was, are more keenly aware of tampering with its residues. They deliberately improve on history, memory, and relics to give the past's true nature better or fuller expression than it could attain in its own time. The transition from oral to written records in twelfth- and thirteenth-century England often required such interventions to make the written record conform both with common sense and with concepts of authenticity. 'A charter was inaccurate and should be corrected if it failed to give the beneficiary a privilege which the author had obviously intended it to have, had he still been alive to express his wishes', notes M. T. Clanchy. (Most donors' words could not have been exactly recorded in any case, for charters had to be written in Latin.) Unfamiliarity with actual past forms made other changes necessary: 'A good oral tradition or an authentic charter of an early Anglo-Saxon king might be rejected by a court of law because it seemed strange, whereas a

---

[195] John Wright, director of the Henry Ford Museum and Greenfield Village, believes that 'Ford built this place out of guilt' (quoted in Phillips, 'Greenfield's changing past', p. 11); Greenfield is 'preservation by expiation' (Brian Horrigan, 'Car hopping', *Historic Preservation*, 32:3 (1980), 55).

forged charter would be acceptable because it suited contemporary notions of what an ancient charter should be like.'[196]

In aiming to bring out what was nascent in their forebears' views, those who thus fix up the record impose their own standards on the past. Thus Benjamin Jowett insisted that the homosexual relationships celebrated in *Phaedrus* should be seen as heterosexual; Plato had written of love between men only because women in ancient Athens could not be men's intellectual helpmates, and 'had he lived in our times he would have made the transposition himself'.[197] In restored Colonial Williamsburg, paints and fabrics brighter than colonists ever had were justified on the ground that eighteenth-century folk would surely have used such colours if they could have found and afforded them.[198] Commissioning a painting of the banquet commemorating the invention of the electric light, Henry Ford deliberately revised history to include his grandchildren, who 'couldn't be at the party because they were ill', he told the painter; but 'this is our picture, and they should, by all means, be in there'.[199]

Many refashion antiquity to realize past intentions originally constrained by lack of resources or skills. In his use of sixteenth-century English Gothic the American architect Ralph Adams Cram sought 'not to turn back the clock so much as to set a much finer clock ticking again without readjusting the hands'.[200] In copying old pictures darkened by time and neglect and profaned by retouching, Hawthorne's Hilda not only restores them to pristine glory but does 'what the great Master had conceived in his imagination, but had not so perfectly succeeded in putting upon canvas'; Hilda is 'a finer instrument . . . by the help of which the spirit of some great departed Painter now first achieved his ideal'.[201] Evelyn Waugh's fictional Forest Lawn reconstruction of Oxford's 'St Peter-without-the-walls' gains acclaim as not merely a replica, but what 'the first builders dreamed of', an inspired realization of 'what those old craftsmen sought to do, with their rude implements of bygone ages'.[202] The 'Tudor' cottages in Potton's 1982 'Heritage' range mirror Waugh's fiction in modern English fact. 'We *have* turned the clock back', boast the builders, and 'if Oliver Cromwell or even Inigo Jones walked into the house they wouldn't find a brick or an oak beam out of place', a critic observed, ' – except, of course, that the beams aren't actual oak'; they are preservative-impregnated Canadian Douglas fir. Thwarted in their pre-scientific day by wormwood, mould, and rot, the sixteenth-century builders' aims are at last fulfilled in ours.[203]

Architecture in Renaissance Italy exhibits a transition from unawareness of change to deliberate alteration in conformity with supposed past intentions. Initially, architects supposed their copies identical to ancient buildings. Later they professed to imitate what ruins had been when whole. Then they sought to 'improve' antique practice in the light of antique precepts: strict followers of Vitruvius 'corrected' deviations thought due to early imperfect knowledge or subsequent corruption. Thus in seeking to reconstruct the

[196] *From Memory to Written Record*, pp. 253, 249.
[197] Jowett, 'Introduction to the *Phaedrus*' (1875), p. 120. See Turner, *Greek Heritage in Victorian Britain*, pp. 424–7.
[198] Boorstin, *America and the Image of Europe*, p. 94.
[199] Irving Bacon, quoted in Wallace, 'Visiting the past', pp. 74–5.
[200] Kidney, *Architecture of Choice*, p. 39.   [201] *Marble Faun*, p. 59.   [202] *The Loved One*, pp. 64–5.
[203] Potton Timber Engineering Co. catalogue, 1982, p. 3; Robert Troop, 'Buy yourself a date in history', *Sunday Times*, 28 Mar. 1982, p. 19.

Pantheon, Carlo Fontana reverted to what he considered correct, austere principles, excising Agrippa's ornate additions in favour of a humble structure in line with supposed early republican principles.[204]

All these motives involve some self-deception, some lingering faith that the past thus preserved or restored is not being altered. By contrast, those who deliberately invent evidence usually aim to sow error. Some falsify the past because what actually happened embarrasses or impoverishes or frightens them; others forge paintings or salt sites with fake antiquities to gain wealth or to perpetrate a hoax; still others invent history to inflame pride or patriotism. The Donation of Constantine was fabricated to sustain papal claims to temporal powers; James Macpherson's 'Ossian' served to purify the Homeric epic tradition and to provide the Gaels with a heroic antiquity. So common were forgeries that, as we have seen, many scholars came to dismiss chronicles as mendacious accounts fabricated by self-serving historians and their patrons.[205]

Pure mischief inspires other forgeries, exemplified in the Cardiff Giant. Irked by a fundamentalist minister's loudly reiterated belief that 'There were giants in the earth in those days' (Genesis 6.4), a nineteenth-century American sceptic carved a block of gypsum in his own likeness and buried it near Cardiff, New York, to be 'discovered' by well-diggers the following year. Some who thronged to see the 'Cardiff Giant' thought it a petrified body, others a great work of ancient art. A Yale academic found 'Phoenician inscriptions' on its right arm; Oliver Wendell Holmes saw 'anatomical details' through a hole he bored behind its left ear. Several 'Giant Saloons' and 'Goliath Houses' refreshed the curious, who kept coming even after the hoax was revealed. Barnum had it copied, and the imitation humbug outdrew the real one.[206] Now in the Farmers' Museum at Cooperstown, the giant has much deteriorated, its legs broken by being shunted about to county fairs, its toes and genitals eroded by half a century of freezing and thawing.[207]

Like the Cardiff Giant, many hoaxes are meant to be unmasked – few so indisputably as the runic inscription found at Mullsjö, Sweden, which read (in modern English): 'Joe Doakes went East 1953. He discovered Europe. Holy smoke!'[208] But although hoaxers may intend the truth eventually to come out, professional reputations sometimes make it difficult to reveal them. Thus the Piltdown forgery 'was merely a delicious joke – . . . at first', contends Stephen Jay Gould, 'to see how far a gullible professional could be taken', but the experts 'tumbled too fast and too far' for the hoaxer to find a moment when the truth could be told.[209]

All these reasons for fabricating the past may become inextricably tangled. The novel *Krasnoye Derevo* depicts 'holy charlatans' refashioning ancient Russian relics and conning customers into buying reproduction furniture as real antiques. These fakes symbolize the Party's revision of history – selling a false view of the Russian past, replacing real with distorted memories, and substituting a shoddy modern simulacra for genuine past ideals.

---

[204] Buddensieg, 'Criticism of ancient architecture in the sixteenth and seventeenth centuries', pp. 338–46, citing Fontana, *Templum Vaticanum et ipsius origo* (1694); a retrograde step from Raphael, who had accepted ancient architecture as it was and refused to 'improve' it by 'correcting' supposed mistakes.

[205] J. H. Franklin, *Jean Bodin and the Sixteenth-Century Revolution in the Methodology of Law and History*, pp. 89–101, 121–2; Chapter 5, p. 244, above.

[206] Dunn, 'Cardiff Giant hoax'; and *Antiquity*, 47 (1973), 89–91.   [207] Edmund Wilson, *Upstate*, p. 33.

[208] Daniel, 'Minnesota petroglyph', p. 267n.

[209] *Hen's Teeth and Horse's Toes*, pp. 201–40, quotation on p. 225.

But whereas history and memories are unconsciously subverted, the artifacts are knowingly antiqued.[210]

The reactions of those who are fooled depends partly on the fabricators' supposed motives. Unlike fakes designed to deceive, good intentions extenuate the crimes of those who distort or destroy original relics under the illusion of restoring them. And faith that the actual past is too closely interwoven to be permanently subverted also mitigates the offence of tampering with history, for few expect the alterations to endure.

Motives for changing the past

What impels us to tamper with history? And what do we add to or substitute for what we inherit? We feel more at home with our past, whether manufactured or inherited, when we have put our own stamp on it. Some occupants of old houses seek to exorcise the imprint of previous occupants, to replace their predecessors' pasts with their own. To connect with a valued tradition, we must, like the humanists, replicate, transform, and fragment it; in order to link their own lives intimately with events of wider significance, as shown in Chapter 5, people 'remember' having been present at historic events they were nowhere near. Pasts made famous by interpretation or depiction, like Haley's Juffure, often become present actuality. The East Anglian scenes celebrated by Constable have become a synthetic Constable-scape juxtaposing carports, pylons, and motorways with cottages, livestock, and vegetation out of *The Haywain*, like Julian Fane's picturesque village which 'looked as if it had been not only painted hundreds of times but designed by Abel Duncan'.[211]

Other relics are fragmented to yield time-honoured souvenirs. Chips from the piers of Remagen Bridge became $20 paperweight mementoes a generation after the U.S. Army crossed the Rhine, and a thousand crosses, authenticated by four bishops, were cut for sale from the carpet on which Pope John Paul held mass in Cardiff in 1982.

We alter the past to become part of it as well as to make it our own. Graffitists bent on nominal immortality have defaced ancient monuments at least since Renaissance visitors scribbled on the walls of the Catacombs. The temptation seems irresistible; the eighteenth-century painter Robert Ker Porter inscribed his own name alongside those of other celebrities he had scolded for doing the same thing.[212] Those who clean and repair historic stonework add their own carved initials: 'The architects get furious and call us vandals', said a Westminster Abbey cleaner. 'They do it, of course – but that's called signing their work.'[213] The phrase 'Tolfink carved these runes in this stone', inscribed in Carlisle Cathedral, bears 'witness at least to the existence of Tolfink, a human being unwilling to dissolve entirely into his surroundings'.[214]

---

[210] Falchikov, 'Rerouting the train of time: Boris Pil'nyak's *Krasnoye Derevo*', pp. 146–7.

[211] Fane, 'Abel Duncan and success', p. 61. On Constable, see Blythe, Commentary, p. 159. Comparing Constable paintings with present-day views, Peglitsis' *Sketches of Dedham Vale as John Constable Saw It* (1982) omits modern intrusions to emphasize the resemblances and show how little the countryside has changed.

[212] Panofsky, *Renaissance and Renascences in Western Art*, p. 173; Porter (1823), cited in Rose Macaulay, *Pleasure of Ruins*, pp. 145–6.

[213] Quoted in Chamberlin, *Preserving the Past*, p. 190.

[214] Le Guin, 'It was a dark and stormy night', p. 194.

Even the crudest disfigurements may in time embellish history. James Lees-Milne censured Canadian troops for cutting their names and addresses inches deep in the James Paine bridge at Brocket Park, Hertfordshire, yet 'what an interesting memorial this will be thought in years to come', he reflected, 'and quite traditional, like the German mercenaries' names scratched in 1530 on the Palazzo Ducale in Urbino'.[215] Whatever the carver's name, it adds a timeworn aura to historical ambience. Heavily inscribed desks from Harrow and Eton fetch high prices, and hand- and footprints of Hollywood film stars set in concrete gave Grauman's Chinese Theater historic fame.

The desire to leave his own mark prompted the painter Robert Rauschenberg to mutilate a Willem de Kooning drawing; deliberate obliteration would also lend salutary emphasis to the inexorable erosion of time. Persuaded by this argument, de Kooning handed over one of his finer drawings, which Rauschenberg then painstakingly effaced. 'It wasn't easy', he recalled. 'The drawing was done with a hard line, and it was greasy, too, so I had to work very hard on it, using every sort of eraser. But in the end ... I felt it was a legitimate work of art.' Below the barely detectable original lines an inscription reads:

ERASED DE KOONING DRAWING
ROBERT RAUSCHENBERG
1953

Cited as 'the first work with an exclusively art-historical content and produced expressly for art historians',[216] *Erased de Kooning* also exemplifies the wish for involvement that motivates many to alter their heritage.

Most of all we alter the past to 'improve' it – exaggerating aspects we find successful, virtuous, or beautiful, celebrating what we take pride in, playing down the ignoble, the ugly, the shameful. The memories of most individuals, the annals and monuments of all peoples highlight supposed glories; relics of failure are seldom saved and rarely memorialized.

What changes achieve these emphases? What qualities do we instil into our inheritance? The preferences surveyed in Chapters 1 and 2 herald the answers: a past that is long, honourable, distinguished, manifesting continuity of tradition or a return to earliest principles; a past rich in meaning and virtue that respects ancestral precept and harmonizes with the present's best impulses. If missing or scanty in actual remains, these desired traits abound in subsequent additions to the written record, to relics, and to works of emulation and commemoration.

Magnified traditions especially bolster peoples embittered by subjugation or newly come to nationhood. Hence Muslim panegyrists made Spanish Islam the fountainhead of European art and science, Turkish schoolchildren learn that civilization originated on the Anatolian plateau, and government murals in Accra show Ghanaians inventing the alphabet and the steam engine.[217] The European image of classical Greece led nineteenth-

---

[215] *Ancestral Voices*, diary entry 7 Jan. 1942, p. 5.
[216] Rauschenberg, quoted in Tomkins, 'Moving out', p. 59; Rosenberg, 'American drawing and the Academy of the Erased de Kooning', p. 108.
[217] Bernard Lewis, *History Remembered, Recovered, Invented*, pp. 74–7, 38–9; Kedourie, 'Introduction', *Nationalism in Asia and Africa*, pp. 48–52; David Gordon, *Self-Determination and History in the Third World*, pp. 88–97; Plumb, *Death of the Past*, p. 73n.

century Greek nationalists to adopt the guise of ancient Athenians and pen their 1822 national charter (the Constitution of Epidaurus) in language so archaic few Greeks could understand it; to reaffirm continuity with antiquity, Greek folklorists later cleaned up and reclassified tales which failed to exhibit such links in line with appropriately Greek precepts.[218]

Britain's Celtic fringe furnishes innumerable instances of such revisions. In subjugated eighteenth-century Wales, Prys Morgan shows, loss of national heritage impelled patriots to glorify its ancient remnants and to create new traditions, including the eisteddfod, choral singing, and a homogeneous national costume. The Druids were remoulded from arcane obscurantists tainted by human sacrifice into Welsh intellectuals and sages, celebrated in miniature Stonehenges erected for that purpose; William Owen re-created modern Welsh as a language of purity, patriarchal tradition, and 'infinite copiousness'; landscape legends like the 'grave of Gelert' cairn ascribed by a Caernarfonshire hotelier to Prince Llewellyn were fabricated for tourist consumption. And purported Welsh remnants among American Indian tribes bolstered an identity shattered by English conquest, spurring Welsh emigration to the United States.[219]

The Scottish Highland tradition embodies other retrospective inventions. After 1745, the Highlanders were stereotypically transformed from idle predatory barbarians into romantic primitives with the added charm, in Trevor-Roper's phrase, of being an endangered species. A pedigree showing the kilt to be a relic of once universal medieval dress formed part of the 'Sobieski' Stuarts' romantic scheme, similar to Pugin's revival of Gothic architecture, to restore Catholic Celtic culture; but the kilt was in fact invented by an English Quaker industrialist in the eighteenth century, not to preserve the traditional Highland way of life but to replace the old belted plaid with a garment better suited to factory work.[220]

The nineteenth-century Irish antiquarian revival exalted the past to comfort the present. To help forge a respectable national identity in the face of English suzerainty, the episodes, symbols, and styles of a distinctively Irish past were rediscovered and deployed in every aspect of life. The Book of Kells, the newly found Tara Brooch, and Celtic crosses became sources of inspiration for art and architecture; furniture and ornaments carved out of ancient bog oak exhumed from peat served as emblems of Irish history similarly disentombed; shamrocks, harps, wolfhounds, and round towers proliferated on tea services, glassware, jewellery, bookcovers, workboxes, banners, and tombstones.[221] Although the Irish Revival largely failed in its aims, most of these emblems of the past endure in the present-day national landscape. And similar motives have recently turned Irish antiquities into ambassadors. 'Sending the treasures abroad was a political decision', Ireland's education minister wrote in 1974 of the 'Treasures of Early Irish Art' displayed in New York. 'The image of Ireland, which has become associated with violence and strife,

---

[218] Herzfeld, *Ours Once More: Folklore, Ideology, and the Making of Modern Greece*, pp. 6, 20, 85–6. See Koraes, 'Report on the present state of civilization in Greece' (1803); Clogg, 'Waving the standard of Hellenism', *TLS*, 12 Aug. 1983, p. 861.

[219] Morgan, 'From a death to a view: the hunt for the Welsh past in the Romantic period', pp. 72–4 (on William Owen), 86–7 (on the grave of Gelert); Gwyn Williams, *Madoc*.

[220] Trevor-Roper, 'Invention of tradition: the Highland tradition of Scotland; pp. 25, 34–7, 20–2.

[221] Sheehy, *Rediscovery of Ireland's Past.*

92 National symbols of the Irish Celtic Revival: Pat McAuliffe, Central Hotel façade, Listowel, County Kerry, Eire (George Mott)

will benefit from this demonstration that we are a nation with a rich and deep cultural past.'[222]

Many remade histories are narrowly chauvinist, excluding the alien so as to emphasize native or ethnic achievements. Poles have favoured Slavonic antiquities while neglecting some of Teutonic provenance; and the Irish have pulled down or left unprotected fine Georgian buildings, viewed askance as symbols of English oppression to be swept away and replaced by the 'peasant–Gaelic' architecture of an independent Eire.[223] 'I was glad to see them go', said Ireland's Minister of Culture in 1961; 'they stand for everything I hate.'[224]

---

[222] Richard Burke, quoted in David H. Wright, 'Shortchanged at the Met', *N.Y. Review of Books*, 4 May 1978, p. 32.

[223] Gruszecki, 'Cultural and national identity and the protection of foreign fortifications in Poland', p. 47 (older Teutonic castles like Malbork, popularized by Sienkiewicz, are cherished, but Poles shun more recent foreign fortresses, such as Dęblin and Zamość; John Harvey, *Dublin: A Study in Environment*, p. 17).

[224] Desmond Guinness, quoted in Kearns, 'Preservation and transformation of Georgian Dublin', p. 273. Irish hostility to Ascendancy structures – 'no one wanted these walls of memories around. The sooner they go, the

Preservation in America can be equally selective: Southerners involved in a Washington, D.C., conservation programme asked the planner in charge, 'Why save those damn Yankee buildings?'[225]

To denigrate a rival heritage its antiquities may be hidden or demolished. The Mexican Emperor Itzcoatl destroyed an earlier Náhuatl codice to leave the official Aztec version of history uncontested; the Spanish concealed the impressive Inca masonry at Cuzco lest observers conclude the Indians were not a 'depraved' and 'idle' race; under white Rhodesian rule, the Great Zimbabwe ruins were displayed as the creation of Europeans.[226] Nineteenth-century British Ecclesiastical Commissioners razed the remains of Irish churches, Irish nationalists charged, 'to destroy evidences of past civilisation in order to reconcile men to the notion that they are "a people without a history" who ought ... to occupy an inferior position'; and the British government was said to have scuttled the Irish Ordnance Survey because the local interest it generated in antiquities aroused Irish nationalist sentiment.[227]

Men displaced from power or made insecure by a sorry present can derive solace from a romantically magnified past. Faced with upstart entrepreneurs, the older gentry in seventeenth- and eighteenth-century England harked back nostalgically to a time when their forebears' status was supposedly unquestioned. Fearful of uncouth immigrants and of industrial populism, as we saw in Chapter 3, New England Brahmins of the late nineteenth century repeopled the colonial past with upright, thrifty, frugal forebears, exaggerating old-time virtues the better to censure modern evils.[228]

By contrast, others so devalue their own national past that they ignore indigenous in favour of foreign features or persuade themselves that native antiquities are exotic: antiquarians long tried to prove English monumental remains Greek or Egyptian or Phoenician or almost anything, so long as they were not British.[229] Dismissing all history as an encumbrance, others strive to diminish or tarnish the entire past; Chapter 3 showed how characteristic this was of early national Americans. Some find it easier to expunge or slight a shameful inheritance than to contrive a worthy one: those whom the past has mocked with its false hopes and promises are less likely to revere than to sell off its remains. 'Bad debt that it is, the optimistic past must be brought into line and chopped up

---

better' (McLaren, *Ruins: The Once Great Houses of Ireland*, p. ii); 'these "symbols of oppression" should be swept away to be replaced by the bright new architecture of an independent Ireland' (Nowlan, 'Conservation and development', p. 8) is giving way to recognition that much Georgian work was created by Irish craftsmen (Kearns, 'Preservation', p. 274). In 1962 architectural students marched about with banners proclaiming 'Dublin must not be a museum'; by 1969 they were occupying threatened historic buildings to prevent their destruction (Kearns, *Georgian Dublin*, pp. 76–7).

[225] Kevin Lynch, 'Conservation of two historic districts in Washington: when is whose history?' lecture at Historic Preservation symposium, Boston University, 2 Dec. 1978.

[226] Léon-Portilla, *Pre-Columbian Literature of Mexico*, p. 119; Adams, *Lost Museum*, p. 139; Garlake, *Great Zimbabwe*, pp. 12–13, 71–5; idem, 'Prehistory and ideology in Zimbabwe', pp. 1, 11, 14–16.

[227] Samuel Ferguson, 'Architecture in Ireland' (1846), quoted, and Patrick McSweeney, *A Group of Nation Builders, O'Donovan, O'Curry, Petrie* (1913), cited in Sheehy, *Rediscovery of Ireland's Past*, pp. 58, 20. For the impact of the Ordnance Survey on Irish sensibilities, see Brian Friel's play, *Translations* (1981), set in County Donegal in 1833.

[228] Plumb, 'Historian's dilemma', p. 40.

[229] Daniel, *Idea of Prehistory*, pp. 20–4. Stukeley eventually saw Stonehenge and everything ancient in Britain as Druidic (Piggott, *Druids*, pp. 112–31).

into souvenirs', concludes Haas; 'it must be made to amuse us now, as punishment for misleading us all that time.'[230]

Those bent on contriving a prideful past may have to mediate between traditionalist and modernist goals. The desire to affirm continuity with a pre-colonial heritage and to 'restore' non-Western traditions often conflicts with an equally urgent need to demonstrate that the new country and its people have long been 'modern'.[231] But whichever kind of past triumphs, it must be one of ancient vintage.

History is customarily made more venerable. Those who magnify their past are especially prone to amplify its age. Relics and records count for more if they antedate rival claims to power, prestige, or property; envy of antecedence plays a prime role in lengthening the past.

Most peoples exaggerate their cultural antiquity or conceal its recency. The English used to date Oxford from Alfred the Great, Parliament from the Romans, and native Christianity from Joseph of Arimathea.[232] Olof Rudbeck's *Atlantica* established ancient Sweden as the fount of modern culture; Germans and then the English and Americans ascribed the roots of democracy to early Goths; African arts are said to antedate the Assyrians.[233] With threadbare traditions and an ignoble recent past, the Welsh, as we have seen, fell back on ancient Druidic and Celtic sources for a remote and romantic cultural heritage. English songs translated into Welsh only in the late eighteenth century, for example, soon became ancient native melodies, and by the mid nineteenth century the whole recently developed musical tradition was attributed to hoary antiquity.[234]

The backwardness of Germanic prehistory revealed by excavation dismayed Adolf Hitler. 'Why do we call the whole world's attention to the fact that we have no past? Isn't it enough that the Romans were erecting great buildings when our forefathers were still living in mud huts?' While Himmler enthused over every potsherd and stone axe the archaeologists found, Hitler grumbled that 'all we prove by this is that we were still throwing stone hatchets and crouching over open fires when Greece and Rome had already reached the highest point of culture. We really should do our best to keep quiet about this past.'[235]

Illusory antiquity has bolstered countless causes. From the edicts of Diocletian to a fifteenth-century carving that metamorphosed a contest between Athene and Poseidon into a portrayal of the Fall, a halo of forged and borrowed antiquity has enshrined

---

[230] 'Secret life of the American tourist', p. 20. See also Walden, *Ravished Image*, pp. 10–11.
[231] Gordon, *Self-Determination and History*, pp. 134, 181–9. The people of Qatar, given to dismissing the past as unprogressive – 'before oil, not interesting' – are now urged to admire their heritage ('A museum to preserve the force of national roots', *IHT*, 28 Dec. 1978, p. 38).
[232] Joan Evans, *History of the Society of Antiquaries*, p. 11.
[233] Michell, *Megalithomania*, pp. 42–3; Kliger, *Goths in England*; G. P. Marsh, *Goths in New-England*; Lowenthal, *George Perkins Marsh*, pp. 56, 58–63; David Levin, *History as Romantic Art*, pp. 74–92; Dorothy Ross, 'Historical consciousness in nineteenth-century America', pp. 918–21; Kedourie, 'Introduction', *Nationalism in Asia and Africa*, pp. 54–6. Terming ancient Egyptians Negro, and Ethiopia 'the first country to appear on earth', a Jamaican black nationalist ascribed the origin of writing, astronomy, history, architecture, the plastic arts, navigation, agriculture, and the textile industry to Black Africa (Blyden, 'Negro in ancient history' (1871); see Hollis Lynch, *Edward Wilmot Blyden*, pp. 54–7).
[234] Morgan, 'Hunt for the Welsh past', pp. 76–9.
[235] Quoted in Speer, *Inside the Third Reich*, p. 141.

Christian claims. The Turks were 'the first cultured peoples of the world', insisted Ataturk's historians; theirs was 'not the history of a tribe of four hundred tents, but that of a great nation' founded 12,000 years before Christ – a retrospective renaissance that enhanced the prestige of the Turkish Revolution.[236] Many British eagerly embraced Piltdown Man as proof of Britain's humanoid primacy; indeed, Piltdown's spurious antiquity held even broader implications, for if this 'earliest Englishman was the progenitor of white races', in Gould's words, 'then whites crossed the threshold to full humanity long before other people'.[237]

The monarchy provides Britain with a more successful fabulation of antiquity. By George VI's coronation in 1937, royal pomp and ceremony introduced as recently as 1901 had already become 'immemorial'; in Richard Dimbleby's phrase, envious Americans knew 'that they must wait a thousand years before they can show the world anything so significant or so lovely'. Ceremonial that had been rudimentary and poorly performed in Victoria's reign was now so well staged that the British believed they always had been good at ritual.[238]

British faith in hoary tradition extended to British Africa, where twentieth-century admirers of age-old custom sought to 'return' Africans to their tribal identities; but what administrators considered customary law, customary land-rights, customary political structure and so on were in the main invented by colonial codification – often to the dismay of their intended beneficiaries. In India the British Raj from the 1860s on zealously preserved 'Indian' tradition and 'reinstated' 'traditional' Mughal and Indian turbans, sashes, and tunics.[239]

Pre-Columbian misattributions lent New World civilization a respectable antiquity. To compensate for 'an empty land peopled only by naked wandering savages', Americans longed to find traces of grand precursors.[240] Hebrews, Greeks, Persians, Romans, Vikings, Hindus were variously fancied as builders of the huge Indian mounds in the Ohio and Mississippi valleys; meteoric fragments mistaken for cast iron 'proved' that 'ancient millions of mankind had their seats of empire in America'.[241] It suited Americans busy dispossessing Indians to think of them as savage interlopers whose forebears had brutally shattered an earlier high civilization.[242] A reviewer of E. G. Squier and E. H. Davis's lavish *Ancient Monuments of the Mississippi Valley* (1848) rejoiced that Americans could now refute

the reproach [of] the excessive modernness and newness of our country ... as being bare of old associations as though it had been made by a journeyman potterer day before yesterday ... We have

[236] Arnau, *Three Thousand Years of Deception*, p. 27; Alp, 'Restoration of Turkish history', p. 210.
[237] 'Smith Woodward's folly', p. 44.
[238] Cannadine, 'British monarchy and the "invention of tradition"', pp. 145–50, 160; Dimbleby, 'My coronation commentary', p. 85: 'I might be watching something that happened a thousand years before. In all that time there has been no major change in our Coronations' (p. 84). Many 'age-old' countryside traditions likewise turn out to be nineteenth- or twentieth-century revivals (Jennings, *Living Village*, pp. 76–7).
[239] Ranger, 'Invention of tradition in colonial Africa', pp. 247–51; B. S. Cohn, 'Representing authority in Victorian India', p. 183.
[240] Silverberg, *Mound Builders*, pp. 1, 5, 34–5.
[241] Josiah Priest, *American Antiquities and Discoveries in the West* (1833), quoted in Silverberg, *Mound Builders*, p. 42.
[242] Silverberg, *Mound Builders*, p. 30.

93 'Earlying up' the past: G. E. Moody cartoon, *Punch*, 28 Sept. 1938

94 Cashing in on a fraudulent past: Viking logo in Alexandria, Minnesota

here, what no other nation on the known globe can claim: a perfect union of the past and present; the vigor of a nation just born walking over the hallowed ashes of a race whose history is too early for a record.[243]

A cult of antique origins likewise inspired the Church of the Latter-day Saints. According to the fabulous gold tablets unearthed by Joseph Smith in 1823, Nephites (the supposed mound builders) and Jaredites had come from the Old World in remote antiquity, flourishing in America until the fourth century, when God destroyed them for their corruption. Mormons still believe that America was long ago settled from the Near East and that the great mounds are relics of this earlier civilization.[244]

A magnified or invented antiquity also aggrandizes localities and individuals. Tracing Elizabethan lineages back to Roman and Trojan origins legitimated family claims, and royal contenders cited Noah or Adam as direct forebears.[245] Retroactive conversion of their ancestors enhances modern Mormon solidarity. Though long since exposed as a fabrication, the Kensington Runestone in Alexandria, Minnesota, remains a fixture of the local scene; a replica runestone twelve times the size of the original and 'the world's largest Viking' embellish the town.[246]

Lust for the ancient may entail the sacrifice of more recent relics. Some restorers virtually raze buildings in order to return them to their supposed original state. Style and

---

[243] 'The Western mound builders', *Literary World* (1848), quoted in Stanton, *Leopard's Spots*, p. 85; see my *George Perkins Marsh*, pp. 89–91.

[244] Silverberg, *Mound Builders*, pp. 44–7.

[245] Fussner, *English Historical Writing and Thought, 1580–1640*, pp. 15–16, 42–4; Wagner, *English Genealogy*, p. 305.

[246] Wahlgren, *Kensington Stone*; Daniel, 'Minnesota petroglyph'. Barry Fell, *America B.C.: Ancient Settlers in the New World* (1976) typifies the unquenchable yearning for pre-Columbian origins.

decor attributed to earlier times replace what is disparaged as later: nineteenth- and early twentieth-century English terraced houses accrete simulated details of seventeenth- and eighteenth-century façades, and American towns 'early up' their Victorian main streets to look Colonial.

Besides antiquating the past, we make it sumptuous or seemly, like Renaissance painters who depicted the Nativity in the ambience of magnificent palaces. Great victories and glorious deeds still dominate our histories, aristocratic forebears our ancestries, castles and cathedrals our reliquary landscapes. Leaving out the commonplace dross of which the present shows us quite enough, historical romance still fits the purpose Archibald Alison defined in 1845: it 'discards from human annals their years of tedium, and brings prominently forward their eras of interest, giving us the truth of history without its monotony'.[247] The preferred past is mostly seen from the purview of the rich, the well born, the powerful. Like the time travellers and reincarnated souls of Chapter 1, so often figures of consequence or eminence, Harvard staff and students named a fourteenth-century Tunica chief, Queen Elizabeth, a high-born lady in sixteenth-century Dubrovnik, a late eighteenth-century Viennese aristocrat, the nineteenth-century master of Sissinghurst as the people they would want to be in the past of their choice.[248] Historic preservation even behind the Iron Curtain has concentrated on the grandiose remains of feudalism and imperialism. These 'class-hostile' structures appeal not only to foreign tourists; the indigenous masses reject folk architecture and 'relics of the workers' movements' in favour of legacies of capitalism.[249]

The past is habitually reshaped by the criteria of Henry James's duchess, anxious to make sure that 'Stories from English History' is suitable for her little niece:

'Is it all right?'
'I don't know . . . There have been some horrid things in English history.'
'Well, darling, Mr. Longden will recommend to you some nice historical work – for we love history, don't we? – that leaves the horrors out. We like to know . . . the cheerful, happy, *right* things. There are so many, after all.'[250]

The right things are those that make the past seem virtuous, successful, or beautiful. Like Rameses II, who despite having to acknowledge Hittite equality with Egypt continued to represent himself in monumental inscriptions as their conquerer, we augment relics and records that evince desired deeds and traits and ignore or erase contrary evidence. History becomes a chronicle of progress interrupted by only minor setbacks, and a quaint serenity softens the stress of past reality.[251]

Modern parents still follow Henry James's duchess. 'We take the children to

[247] 'Historical romance', p. 346.
[248] 'Century game' (1973). Most living-history re-enactors 'assume a persona that is based on the upper socioeconomic class', but serious buffs often opt for a craft: 'Being a poor person "ain't much fun" but most were – so try it' (R. H. Griffiths, 1983, quoted in Anderson, *Time Machines*, p. 187).
[249] Stankiewicz, 'Conflits de la doctrine de conservation et de la conscience de l'identité culturelle et sociale', p. 30; 'Czech relics criticized as "class-hostile"', *Times Higher Education Suppl.*, 12 Oct. 1984, p. 10.
[250] *Awkward Age* (1899), p. 180.
[251] Van Seters, *In Search of History*, p. 177; Bommes and Wright, 'The public and the past', pp. 300–1. 'We want to know the beautiful or useful things that were built and the originality that was shown, . . . the grace-notes to life that were sounded' (Hyman, 'Empire for liberty', p. 1).

Stonehenge', writes Penelope Lively, 'but we'd probably shrink from exposing them to a candid account of Bronze Age beliefs and practices. We like the past gutted and nicely cleaned up.'[252] The filth and stench of early town life, the foraging of pigs in city streets, the din of horse-drawn vehicles on cobblestones, the terror of pain before modern anaesthesia are never reproduced.[253] It was exceptional to hear a period-costumed guide in the nineteenth-century apothecary shop at Mystic Seaport detail the harsh consequences of tight corsets, arsenic, and leeches, concluding: 'Aren't you really glad you're living *today?*'

The past appears to best advantage in renovated relics of everyday activities: grist mills at historic reconstructions always function, printshops unfailingly turn out facsimile broadsides, medieval herb gardens seem invariably fruitful; 'nothing needs to be fixed, raked, painted: there is no dung, no puddles, no weeds'. Nature's normal vicissitudes and mankind's customary tribulations seldom afflict life in the past as we portray it. Views of early Bruges, for example, typically gloss over the seamy side of things, bathing the city in sunshine. 'Paintings were commissioned by rich men for their drawing rooms', explains a local art teacher. 'They didn't want to look at sniveling wretches in the rain.'[254]

In the sanitized American past not even slaves are wretched: porch columns and chimneys raise the restored slave quarters to the standard of overseers' dwellings.[255] Restored Port Arthur, Tasmania's notorious prison, almost persuades us that nineteenth-century convicts were lucky to live in so idyllic a setting.[256] The touristic past jettisons seedy reality for spurious romance. Like Scott's Jonathan Oldbuck, historical entrepreneurs in Old Jerome look askance at the past's messier human vestiges. 'The only thing that's holding us back', complains a promoter, 'is some of those old relics who live in town.'[257]

Faced with the reality of early New England – 'Stark. Bleak. No trees, only stumps. Cowpats. Horse dung. Pig manure. Smoke-blackened rooms. Unwashed illiterate people huddled against the cold. Trampled dirt around the house' – Jane Langton's preservationist ladies are

shocked by this perversion of their common vision of the past, with its butter-churning, candle-making, musket-seizing forefathers – those large comfortable families beaming around their jolly hearthsides where great black pots were bubbling over blazing logs; the women bustling around the kitchen in aprons and ruffled mobcaps; ... and then at bedtime everyone picking up those little pewter candlesticks – that nice gift shop in Concord had some just like them – and climbing the stairs to their plump featherbeds.[258]

[252] 'Children and the art of memory', p. 201.
[253] Whitehill, '"Promoted to Glory": the origin of preservation in the United States', p. 43.
[254] Leone, 'Relationship between artifacts and the public in outdoor history museums', p. 301; Bruno Van Dycke, quoted in Rona Dobson, 'Through new/old Bruges', *IHT*, 12–13 July 1980, p. 9.
[255] Tina Laver, 'In the name of preservation', p. 21; Ralph Christian, American Association for State and Local History, Nashville, interview Dec. 1978.
[256] Derek Linstrum, '"Whatever is good of its kinde": some thoughts on architectural conservation', lecture at Art Historians' conference, London, 26 Mar. 1983; Robertson, *Early Buildings of Southern Tasmania*, 2:368–76. The bullpen in Colonial Williamsburg 'looked so freshly cleaned and sterilized that it seemed impossible to imagine a drunk had ever committed a nuisance in its virgin space' (Parr, 'History and the historical museum', p. 58).
[257] George Latka, quoted in Haas, 'Secret life of the American tourist', p. 24. Oldbuck's passion for relics similarly alienated him from genuine living traditions and folk survivals (*The Antiquary*; see also David Brown, *Walter Scott and the Historical Imagination*, pp. 53–4).
[258] Langton, *Natural Enemy*, pp. 61–2.

To sustain a featherbed image of the past, evidence is often ignored or misinterpreted. As 'reconstructed' in Los Angeles, Hugo Reid's original crude adobe pioneer home is tricked out with a tile floor and roof, elaborate furnishings, and a Spanish patio; it has become the rancho house of a wealthy Don.[259] Historical annals are upgraded to comport with similar desires. Mid Victorians exaggerated ancient chivalry and elevated Arthurian legend into fact so as to re-enact the medieval past in their own self-image; nineteenth-century Americans rewrote Revolutionary history to imbue it with a salutary domestic and guerilla colour.[260] Disregarding the fact that Christianity had become the Roman Empire's official religion, nineteenth-century novelists persuaded readers that pagan immorality had caused Rome to fall; to make the classical past more reputable, scholars conflated Greek myth with biblical tradition and rejected archaeological evidence from Troy and Mycenae that threatened Homer's suitability for Victorian readers.[261] Late nineteenth-century Americans made Dante's *Divine Comedy* a tract exemplifying character formation through self-control, transforming medieval Catholics into proto-Protestant apostles of duty and will-power.[262]

Relics and memories of ill repute are likewise obliterated, infamous events omitted from re-runs of the past. Celebrants of Newburyport's tercentenary 'ignored this or that difficult period of time or unpleasant occurrence or embarrassing group of men and women; they left out awkward political passions; they selected small items out of large ... contexts, seizing them to express today's values'.[263] Tarrytown long withheld historical recognition from A. J. Davis's Tudoresque 'Lyndhurst' (see Illus. 81) the former home of the reprehensible robber-baron Jay Gould.[264] Benedict Arnold was totally ignored in bicentennial festivities at Norwich, Connecticut, Arnold's birthplace. 'What can you do when what you've got is Benedict Arnold?' sighed the president of the local bicentennial commission. 'If only he'd gotten killed before going bad. Then we'd have a hero and it would all be so much easier.'[265] A tableau depicting Arnold's expedition to Canada, which the Jewish community had been asked to sponsor, had to be withdrawn from Newburyport's tercentenary celebration owing to Arnold's unsavoury reminder of Judas.[266] Disaffected minorities reject unsavoury roles impersonating their forefathers: descendants of slaves on the island of St John, U.S. Virgin Islands, refused to don slave costumes for a 'living history' programme.[267]

Evil associations jeopardize relics. The ancient bust of a Greek Venus unearthed in fourteenth-century Siena was destroyed out of fear of pagan malevolence. English

[259] Schuyler, 'Images of America', p. 30.
[260] Girouard, *Return to Camelot*; Dellheim, *Face of the Past*; Forgie, *Patricide in the House Divided*, pp. 210–13; Kammen, *Season of Youth*, Ch. 6, 'The American Revolution as a national *rite de passage*', pp. 186–220.
[261] Highet, *Classical Tradition*, pp. 462–3; Turner, *Greek Heritage in Victorian Britain*, pp. 169–72. The best known of these novels were E. G. E. L. Bulwer Lytton, *The Last Days of Pompeii* (1834), Charles Kingsley, *Hypatia* (1853), Lew Wallace, *Ben Hur* (1880), Henryk Sienkiewicz, *Quo Vadis?* (1896).
[262] Lears, *No Place of Grace*, pp. 158–9.   [263] Warner, *Living and the Dead*, p. 110.
[264] 'Tarrytown urging U.S. to cancel law for a Gould shrine'; 'Jay Gould mansion wins status as a museum'; Thomas W. Ennis, 'Jay Gould mansion: Hudson's Gothic castle', *N.Y. Times*, 16 Sept. p. 33, 30 Oct. p. 31, 19 Nov. p. 41, 1964.
[265] Marian O'Keefe, quoted in Michael Knight, 'Benedict Arnold – a bicentennial nonperson', *IHT*, 8 Mar. 1976, p. 3.
[266] Warner, *Living and the Dead*, pp. 119, 200–3.
[267] Olwig, 'National parks, tourism and the culture of imperialism', p. 255 n. 5. See Schlebecker, 'Social functions of living historical farms in the United States', p. 147.

churchmen fulminated against Avebury's stone circle as a sinister relic of black magic.[268] A memorial to the 'world's oldest profession' – the prostitutes who had served California gold-rush miners – was demolished by officials embarrassed to flaunt so sordid a past. Banished memorials may later be reinstated, like the famous statue of Frederick the Great that Communists removed from Unter den Linden to signal their break with Germany's past, but replaced thirty years later to cap the restoration of Berlin's old centre.[269]

A past negatively portrayed can be stood on its head. The figures in *Uncle Tom's Cabin*, written to expose the oppressive cruelty of Southern slavery, were inverted in the late nineteenth-century novels of Joel Chandler Harris and Thomas Nelson Page to limn a paternalistic society of kindly slaveholders and contented slaves.[270] Abraham Lincoln's frontier Illinois environment, previously seen as a handicap the young man had struggled to overcome, became more estimable from the 1890s thanks to Frederick Jackson Turner's portrayal of the frontier as the seed-bed of democracy; once termed a 'stagnant putrid pool' and a 'dung-hill', New Salem became the 'sacred spot' that had shaped Lincoln's character.[271]

Retrospective needs for success shaped bicentennial re-enactments of the American Revolution. In reality, while winning independence Americans had lost many of the battles along the way. But in the 1976 replays they emerged with glory almost every time. Defeats became draws, routs were termed tactical withdrawals. Re-enacting Lafayette's flight, Conshohocken dignitaries boasted that 'we didn't run like Lafayette's men did'. And 'to hear them talk about it now in Conshohocken', commented a state official, 'Lafayette's decision to cross the river to escape from superior forces was the greatest victory in American history'.[272] Nothing less than victory will do for some spectators. Turning her back on the re-enactment of the Battle of Penobscot Bay, a woman grumbled, 'Why couldn't they at least do one that we win?'[273] To propitiate French visitors, organizers of a mock Battle of Waterloo at Brighton in 1983 allowed France to 'win' on one day of the battle.

The virtues of bygone heroes are likewise inflated. Admired forebears acquire qualities esteemed today, however anachronistic, and their faults are concealed or palliated. Popular modern depictions of Washington and Jefferson, for example, are utterly at variance with their lives as eighteenth-century slave-holding planters, just as Luther is now lauded in East Germany as a champion of the proletariat.[274]

Americans for whom history has to be a chronicle of national greatness shun reminders of what seems shameful or demeaning. The only villains compatible with historical virtue

268 Burl, *Prehistoric Avebury*, pp. 36–40.
269 'East Germany to restore statue of Frederick', *IHT*, 30–31 Aug. 1980; Henry Tanner, 'East Germany rehabilitates Prussia to bolster its historical legitimacy', *IHT*, 23 Mar. 1984, p. 6.
270 Riggio, '*Uncle Tom* reconstructed'.
271 R. S. Taylor, 'How New Salem became an outdoor museum', p. 2.
272 William Collins and Oran Henderson, quoted in Israel Shenker, 'U.S. bicentennial cures history's warts', *IHT*, 5–6 July 1975, p. 5.
273 Quoted in Clark, 'When the paraders meet the button-counters', p. 44. So popular were American Civil War centennial re-enactments, however, that Southerners commemorated their defeats as well as their victories (Karl Betts, testimony at House Appropriations Committee, 1961, quoted in Anderson, *Time Machines*, p. 141).
274 Peterson, *Jeffersonian Image in the American Mind*, discusses the needs that shaped reverence for Jefferson but bypasses the gulf between facts and images; 'Luther lauded', in 'Times diary', *The Times*, 24 Sept. 1982.

are Western bad men, whose anti-heroic stance reflects post-war Hollywood's self-deprecatory style.[275] But American 'history is still so full of heroes that it is a mighty relief to see a few treated, however clumsily, with the disrespect they deserve', suggests an English reviewer of Doctorow's *Ragtime*. By contrast, the British 'method of historical inculcation, which results in half our national figures being better known for their foibles than for . . . their achievements, has disrespect built into it'.[276] On the other hand, British devotees of antiquity, who see ley lines and stone circles as evidence of advanced science at the dawn of history and hold prehistoric folk in exaggerated awe, seem 'obsessed with romanticizing ancient societies and making them as capable as ourselves'.[277]

Other improvers revise the past's aesthetic standards to accord with their own. Those who equated classical beauty with the 'purity' of whiteness were appalled when Canova tinted statues according to actual antique practice.[278] Triptyches shorn of religious significance lose their side panels and tops to confirm with the gallery image of a 'picture'. Modern love of contrast subverts medieval and Renaissance decorative aims in renovations of church interiors, emphasizing distinctions between flat surfaces, sculptural features, and architectural elements that were intended to flow harmoniously together.[279] Australian restorers added white exteriors, green shutters and doors, and polished cedar joinery to conform English 'Late Georgian' 'to what they wished it to be or what they thought it should have been'.[280] Modern taste often overrides historical truth in furnishing period interiors; thus formally aligned chairs customary in eighteenth-century salons are rejected as stilted in favour of more casual layouts with a 'lived-in' look.[281] In old houses that are actually lived in the past is also compromised: curators of historic (1920s) Cedar Crest, now the Kansas governor's residence, are 'bringing back as much of Kansas history as possible while staying within the parameters of good decorating'.[282]

Tenets of taste and comfort also shape the past in restorations and re-enactments. To 'offer visitors the least common denominator between what we believe to be accurate and what we presume they want to see', curators cast aside the unpleasant or the ordinary for

---

[275] The National Association and Center for Outlaw and Lawman History, founded in 1974 at Utah State University and now affiliated with the University of Wyoming, reflects this interest.

[276] Russell Davies, 'Mingle with the mighty', *TLS*, 23 Jan. 1976, p. 77.

[277] John Patrick, quoted in Douglas Aiton, 'Stonehenge theory challenged in Australia', *The Times*, 22 Mar. 1980, p. 5. See Heggie, *Megalithic Science*; Williamson and Bellamy, *Ley Lines in Question*; Burl, 'Science or symbolism: problems of archaeo-astronomy'; Burl and Michell, 'Living leys or laying the lies?'. The cult of prehistoric science owes much to Stukeley's *Stonehenge* (1740): 'our predecessors, the Druids of Britain . . . advanc'd their inquiries, under all disadvantages, to such heights, as should make our moderns asham'd, to wink in the sunshine of learning and religion' (p. vii).

[278] Greenhalgh, *Classical Tradition in Art*, pp. 217–18. As recently as the 1950s, the copy of the Attalus Stoa erected by the American School of Classical Studies in Athens eschewed red and blue paint as untrue, not to the original, but to the modern stereotype (Horne, *Great Museum*, p. 29). The late nineteenth-century Colonial Revival similarly whitened greyish blue and green colonial American woodwork (Flaherty, 'Colonial Revival house', p. 9).

[279] Paul Philippot, 'Conservation and the art historian', lecture at the Architectural Association, London, 29 Feb. 1984; Walden, *Ravished Image*, pp. 6, 13, 92, 144.

[280] Clive Lucas, quoted in 'World of Conservation: an interview with Clive Lucas', p. 237.

[281] J. T. Butler, 'Historic rooms at Sleepy Hollow restorations', p. 69. 'The impulse to decorate in conformity with 20th-century taste is commonly allowed to prevail . . . Often, after professional research reveals the actual paper that was used in a room, the results are ignored by members of an influential committee who consider the paper ugly and therefore "inappropriate"' (Frangiamore, *Wallpapers in Historic Preservation*, p. 2). See Parr, 'History and the historical museum', pp. 58–9.

[282] Nel Richmond, quoted in Craig, 'Champions of history', p. 10.

the museum-worthy *crème de la crème* and an imaginary serenity.[283] How to celebrate Christmas in 1836 at Conner Prairie Pioneer Settlement illustrates other pressures on historical truth. Up to 1978, visitors to this Indiana frontier replica community enjoyed a round of 'traditional' Christmas activities. But research showed that Christmas had been scarcely recognized back then, let alone celebrated, and so the staff decided to treat it like any other winter day of 1836, with 'pioneers' realistically butchering a hog. The new accuracy outraged visitors who 'could not believe that we actually had dropped the "true", early-American Christmas' they had come for. The drop in attendance forced a compromise: in 1979 every December day became 'Christmas Eve' 1836, and settlers' biographies were 'adjusted' to permit Christmas talk and activity: the upstate New York origins of a Methodist family were shifted toward the Hudson River 'to acquire sufficient Dutch influence to have come across ... St. Nicholas'; a few strokes of a pen converting the doctor's wife from Presbyterian to Episcopalian 'left just enough room for some more Christmas greens to slip into their house'.[284] Like Hexter's prototypical historian, Conner Prairie's curators changed the facts in order to convey the past to audiences which would otherwise have stayed away. At most historic sites it is nostalgia that pays the bills. Hence 'even the less appalling unpleasantnesses that we know were part of daily life – the lack of fuel for heat, the smells of spoiling food, then common diseases – seem to be unacceptable for presentation in a homelike setting'.[285]

Past discord is likewise simplified or played down, making times of violent strife seem remarkably benign and orderly. Mount Vernon was saved as a symbol of early American concord then quite lacking, and re-enactments counterfeit friendliness between Union and Confederate troops, minimizing the Civil War's agony and squalor.[286] The film *The Birth of a Nation* (1914) depicted the North and the South as virtually identical peoples, the Civil War itself as without any cause.[287] Pallid history texts in which both sides figure 'as perfectly reasonable people without strong prejudices' similarly denature that conflict; no one could 'infer from any text written since the thirties the passions that animated the war', concludes Frances Fitzgerald.[288]

The past is not always benignly exhibited; on occasion its infamies too are exaggerated. Partisan historians invent or magnify enemy depravities. The public gloats over gory tales of Jack the Ripper, scenes of execution at the Tower of London, the chamber of horrors at Madame Tussaud's, indulging tastes for the macabre safely displaced to bygone times. The London Dungeon advertises 'History written in blood! – the full horror of medieval Britain' as a family day-outing, and advocates Black Plaques to mark sites of executions, torture, squalor, and the plague pits and prisons of the past; 'it seems ridiculous to let this aspect of British history go unrecorded when it could help boost ... London's second

[283] Mary Stevens, 'Wistful thinking: the effect of nostalgia on interpretation', p. 11.
[284] Ronsheim, 'Christmas at Conner Prairie', quotations on p. 16.
[285] Stevens, 'Wistful thinking', p. 10. Aero Park and Flambard Village in Culdrose, Cornwall, likewise display pasts said to conform more to public expectations than to historical facts (Kavanagh, 'History and the museum: the nostalgia business').
[286] David Hall, 'Preserving what is best from the past', *Bostonia*, Dec. 1971, pp. 13–16; Hill, Mahan, and Johns, 'The changing view from Mt. Vernon'; Hosmer, *Presence of the Past*, pp. 41–62; Forgie, *Patricide*, pp. 168–72; Rainey, 'Battlefield preservation', p. 85.
[287] Sorlin, *Film in History*, pp. 91–5.   [288] *America Revised*, p. 156.

95 Cashing in on an evil past: witch postcard, Salem, Massachusetts

largest money-earner'.[289] Salem, Massachusetts, where nineteen people were hanged as witches, today exploits its ancient infamy as 'The Witch City' – 'You would not have liked being here in 1692', but 'you really ought to experience it now . . . Stop by for a spell.'[290] The Lizzie Borden murder case, once a memory shunned, has become a mystery whose grisly artifacts Fall River itches to capitalize on. 'I see her as the best marketing tool we have', says the city's tourism director. 'We want to make sure everybody associates Lizzie Borden with Fall River.'[291]

A penitential stance encourages 'realistic' displays of the seamy side of the past – slave quarters, prisons, early factories – and of episodes which excite shame rather than pride. At Andersonville, the infamous Civil War prison, visitors see wells that were desperately dug with bare hands, tunnels to abortive escape routes, and Sweetwater Creek, which once ran red with death.[292] Americans have a new penchant for historical self-flagellation,[293] but other nations have also begun to display the gore along with the glory of their pasts. The awful din of the spinning and weaving machines, the stench of the dyeing vats, dominate the nineteenth-century past shown at Bradford's textile mills, and a 'smell of

[289] Annabel Geddes, quoted in 'Plague and plaque', 'Times diary', *The Times*, 20 Oct. 1981, p. 14. See Helen Chappell, 'Horror, degradation, etc', *New Society*, 3 Sept. 1981, pp. 381–2.
[290] Salem Witch Museum brochure, 1984. See Michael Carlton, 'New England's witch town', *N.Y. Post*, 12 Aug. 1980; Kay, 'Salem: fly beyond the witch image'; Wallace, 'Visiting the past', p. 71.
[291] Kenneth Raymond, quoted in 'Lizzie Borden: new tourist lure?' *Sacramento Bee*, 5 Aug. 1982, p. A8.
[292] Watkins, 'A heritage preserved. Listening: Andersonville'. The site was designated in 1970.
[293] Kenneth L. Adelman, 'Stronger voice for U.S.', *N.Y. Times*, 1 Aug. 1980, p. A23. U.S. National Park Service battlefield interpretations today focus so much on the horrors of war that some suspect pacifist leanings (Rainey, 'Battlefield preservation', p. 77).

poverty' was fabricated for Lord Montagu's reconstructed peasant's cottage at Buckler's Hard.[294]

The past's worst horrors are beyond the power of replication, but the cult of violence and the callousness engendered by television permit the portrayal of infamies unthinkable even fifteen years ago, including the tortures of the Inquisition, the branding of slaves, and the gas ovens of Auschwitz. Now a World Heritage site, Auschwitz serves as a monument to the suffering of martyrs; Washington's National Holocaust Museum is 'a testament to man's moral imperfections'.[295] Nothing seems too horrendous to commemorate: death-camp mementoes were displayed at a reunion of Holocaust survivors in Jerusalem in 1981. But such grim reminders often fail to convey the real horror. The film *Holocaust* was enormously successful 'because it was deliberately made bearable', Gitta Sereny suggests. 'Its manipulated history and prettified characters offered an easy way out to millions who had felt vaguely guilty for their own resistance to the subject.'[296]

Changing needs again remould the past as time outmodes previous alterations. Historians and biographers of the 1920s tended to debunk early American achievements, those of the 1930s to exalt them; formerly magnified by historical fiction, the past today is more often deflated.[297] The novelist Siegfried Lenz shows attitudes toward museum relics on display in the Masurian borderland shifting with the fortunes of war; in the light of successive Russian or German conquests things which local people 'had previously thought poignant they now saw as tasteless or even incriminating'.[298] Prejudices are overcome to accommodate newly fashionable relics: now praised for its architecture, a once-repudiated Arkansas brothel acquired a revised social pedigree to match. 'It wasn't just the transients who came here', says the founder of the Fort Smith Heritage Foundation; 'Some very prominent people frequented Miss Laura's House.'[299] The current tendency to proletarianize the past has converted General Sam Houston's Greek Revival clapboard home in Texas into a rough-hewn log cabin which Houston himself would have disdained.[300]

Rivalry between a homely and a handsome past embroiled historians at the Lyndon Baines Johnson National Historic Site in Texas. While still President, Johnson in 1964 had built on the site of his birthplace a small house similar to the one he was born in, furnishing

[294] Ian Bradley, 'Bradford, gateway to the past', *The Times*, 13 Mar. 1982, p. 6; 'Historic smells waft into AIM museums', *Quarterly Bulletin of the Association of Independent Museums*, 23:3 (1983). Poverty's odour was not specified, but Beaulieu's technical services head suggested to me a possible blend of cooked cabbage, excreta, and unwashed human bodies (John Willrich, 25 Jan. 1985).

[295] World Heritage List, Nomination Form for Auschwitz Concentration Camp, 1978; Georges Fradier, 'Wonders of the world', *UNESCO Courier*, 33:8 (1980), 34; Vice-President George Bush, quoted in 'Ground broken for Holocaust museum', *N.Y. Times*, 1 May 1984. See Horne, *Great Museum*, pp. 244–7.

[296] 'BBC condones distorted history', *New Statesman*, 29 Aug. 1980, p. 9.

[297] A. H. Jones, 'Search for a usable past in the New Deal era', pp. 712–14, 720; Strout, *Veracious Image*, p. 171.

[298] *Heritage*, p. 452.

[299] Julia Yadon, quoted in P. L. Brown, 'The problem with Miss Laura's house', p. 19. Today's permissive mores enable Westerners to cherish aspects of the past once shunned as shameful (Grace Lichtenstein, 'Cities in West are starting to protect architectural relics of a gaudy past', *N.Y. Times*, 19 Aug. 1975, p. 67).

[300] Michael Leccese, 'Sow's ear from silk purse? Texas landmark endangered', and 'Epilogue: cabin conversion complete', *Preservation News*, 20:12 (1980), 1, 10, and 22:6 (1982), 12. On the tendency to invent rustic simplicity, see Gowans, *Rural Myth and Urban Fact in the American Heritage*, pp. 14–16. Cary Carson, 'Living museums of everyman's history' (1981), explains – and praises – the new populism at Colonial Williamsburg and elsewhere.

it with memorabilia from his own and Lady Bird's later years. After his death, some National Park Service officials sought to replace Johnson's version with a facsimile of the unadorned original. But others, backed by Lady Bird, argued successfully that the sentimental reality of what the President thought his birthplace *ought* to have been mattered more than a lifeless and largely conjectural facsimile of the actual birthplace. The Birthplace Cottage was eventually restored back to the way it looked between 1964 and 1972, as 'the nation's only presidential birth place to be reconstructed, refurnished, and interpreted by an incumbent chief executive'.[301]

Relics and records of ethnic groups likewise emerge, disappear, and resurface in response to changing stereotypes. Formerly implacable adversaries, American Indians degenerated into cigar-store-and-movie buffoons in the 1920s and 1930s, vanished from public awareness in the 1940s and 1950s, and re-emerged in the 1960s as native victims of racist imperialism.[302] At Dartmouth College, founded in the eighteenth century to convert the Indians, an Indian Studies Symbols Committee banned racially offensive caricatures – the 1930s' dining-room mural of unfrocked squaws is boarded over, the giant Indian head emblazoned on the basketball court sanded down, traditional Indian cheers of 'Scalp 'em' and 'Wah-hoo-wah' silenced, Indian-head sweatshirts and decals outlawed.[303]

The past is always altered for motives that reflect present needs. We reshape our heritage to make it attractive in modern terms; we seek to make it part of ourselves, and ourselves part of it; we conform it to our self-images and aspirations. Rendered grand or homely, magnified or tarnished, history is continually altered in our private interests or on behalf of our community or country.

Consequences of changing the past

All these changes affect both our historical environment and ourselves. Above and beyond achieving a past more splendid, virtuous, ancient, or even horrific than the way things actually were, alteration reflects unintended changes that reorganize the past's spatial and temporal character. It is to these unintended changes that I now turn.

Exaggeration is one evident effect. We make the past more vivid by focusing on its greatest or basest residues and amalgamating them in a contrived unity.[304] 'Even the most faithful histories', wrote Descartes, 'if they neither change nor augment the significance of things to make them more readable, almost always omit the most commonplace and least striking of the attendant circumstances, thereby distorting the remainder.'[305] More than three centuries later Descartes's observation still holds true. A cult of the everyday now competes with the bias toward the magnificent and the unique, as noted above. But

---

[301] Bearss, *Furnishing Study: Lyndon B. Johnson National Historic Site*, p. 3. According to Lady Bird Johnson, the President had 'never for a moment considered it as an authentic reconstruction' (3 Mar. 1978, quoted on p. 4). I am grateful to Robert M. Utley and Edwin C. Bearss, National Park Service, for interviews, 2 Aug. 1978 and 25 Apr. 1984 respectively.

[302] Fitzgerald, *America Revised*, pp. 90–3; Bataille and Silet (eds.), *Pretend Indians*, especially Donald L. Kaufmann, 'Indian as media hand-me-down' (1975), pp. 22–34, and John A. Price, 'The stereotyping of North American Indians in motion pictures' (1973), pp. 75–91.

[303] Dena Kleiman, 'Dartmouth alumni trying to "Bring back the Indian"', *N.Y. Times*, 3 Aug. 1980, p. 16.

[304] Bate, *Burden of the Past*, p. 67.   [305] *Discours de la méthode* (1637), p. 7.

selective preservation and attention continue to make the past seem more vivid than it usually was or than the present usually is.[306]

A past thus made vivid conforms to our expectations, for modern perceptions require stimuli which an unadorned past could seldom supply. Habituated to a far wider range of artifacts and locales than our forebears, we would scarcely notice, let alone admire, the drabber and less diversified products of most previous epochs.

What we know of the past, however, more and more conflicts with how we feel it should be experienced. History tells us that everyday medieval life was hard and poor – quite unlike the colourful, high-spirited world of castles, cathedrals, and chivalry familiar from romance. The modern lass in *Doctor Who and the Time Warrior* chides her medieval captors for their overly authentic reek of savagery: 'I know things were pretty scruffy in the middle ages, but really! You might leave the tourists a bit of glamour and illusion.'[307] In defiance of known facts we continue to envisage a rose-coloured past. For example, pre-Gutenberg books conjure up a world of splendid illuminated manuscripts, although we know that such work was scarce and seen by far fewer than are nowadays bedazzled by the lurid paperbacks in any bookshop. But we admire the medieval manuscript as an emblem of ancient learning, whereas the tawdry thriller symbolizes the debasement of modern culture.

Altering the past also conflates it, making all its variegated segments seem somehow alike. We reduce the diversity of previous experience either to a few themes within a narrow time span or to generalized uniformity. Such conflation sounds paradoxical; after all, both speech and writing elaborate the history they transmit, scholarship elucidates ever more remote and numerous pasts, waves of nostalgia now lap at the very shores of the present, and historical evidence – textual analysis, radiocarbon dating – permits ever finer discriminations of age and style. Yet we minimize the distinctiveness of these proliferating pasts, unite former 'greats' by viewing them all as 'old', and impart the same vintage aroma to most of our relics and memories.[308] Revived and surviving pasts collapse into a single realm, temporal specificity yields to a blurred continuum. We increasingly seek an indeterminate past 'without the trivial and reachable individuality of a year attached to it', in Robert Harbison's phrase.[309] For modern worshippers of antiquity the times of Stonehenge's construction and ruination have not the slightest consequence; to them it just grandly conveys 'the past', and calendric specificity would only detract from their awed appreciation of its pervasive antiquity.[310]

The past's apparent homogeneity stems from several causes. For one, things of the same

[306] A selective haze likewise promotes the remote and demotes the recent past. 'The thirteenth century is celebrated as if it were summed up by St. Thomas Aquinas, Dante, and the Virgin of Chartres, while the twentieth century is reduced to Hitler, Hearst, and the sex queens of Hollywood' (H. J. Muller, *Uses of the Past* (1952), p. 23).

[307] Dicks, *Doctor Who and the Time Warrior*, p. 64.

[308] Malraux, *Voices of Silence*, p. 591; Bate, *Burden of the Past*, p. 70. To Robert Lowell during bouts of insanity 'all history became a simultaneous event where it was possible for everyone to meet everyone ... the distinctions of time vanished altogether, and the world was peopled by a series of tyrants and geniuses all jostling with one another' (Jonathan Miller, interview 1980, in Ian Hamilton, *Robert Lowell*, p. 314). Helen Vendler thinks 'that this vast theater of competing events *is* the European past as Americans must see it' ('American poet', *N.Y. Review of Books*, 2 Dec. 1982, pp. 4–6).

[309] *Deliberate Regression*, p. 161.

[310] James Mitchell, 'Druids at Stonehenge', *The Times*, 30 June 1978, p. 19. See 'Solstice invasion of Stonehenge', letters, *The Times*, 28 June 1978, p. 17.

96 The past as *mélange:* Disneyland, Anaheim, California

material weather in roughly similar ways whatever their age; decay affects an Attic temple and the Albert Memorial in the same general fashion. Obsolescence also has a homogenizing effect; all relics now functionally useless fall into one temporal category, equally anachronistic ten years out of date as ten centuries.

Alterations and additions to the past strengthen the feeling that it is all essentially one. Popular historical icons – half-timbering, cut-glass pub windows, signposted castles, cloche hats, steam engines – come to stand not simply for a particular period or episode but for the past as a whole, triggering a generalized sense of bygone days. W. I. Thompson dismisses Southern California's composite ambience of the 'past' – plastic paddlewheel steamers, medieval castles, rocket ships – as a landscape of 'shattered ... discontinuities',[311] but these nostalgic images, spanning so much of history, in fact coalesce to carry the imagination back to a time universally seen as 'olden'.

[311] *At the Edge of History*, p. 12.

The conformation of relics and records likewise makes the past all more homogeneous. The reworked heritage acquires a studied air of coherent uniformity foreign to the ramshackle and discrepant nature of the inviolate past, let alone to the detritus that time unaided has bequeathed us. When restorers aim for 'charming and rich effects suitable to . . . today's decorator taste', observes Ada Louise Huxtable, 'the result is that most restored houses look as if they'd had the same decorator. They are all . . . Williamsburged.'[312]

Even reconstructions that leave accretions alone to emphasize ever-changing continuities often end up seeming homogeneous. In a house exhibiting a sequence of building styles each room is apt to be restored back to its own peak period, which creates the impression that these epochs coexisted rather than succeeded one another. The peaks of perfection all bear a family likeness; despite evident differences from room to room, the visitor senses their similarity as capstones of achievement.

Adaptations such as Ghirardelli Square, Quincy Market, and Covent Garden exhibit particularly marked resemblances. 'The idea, after all, is not that the places remain distinctive for their histories', says Haas, 'but that they use their histories as an excuse to become more and more like each other, to the reassurance of their tourist audience.' Even restorations that try to escape the influence succumb to the Ghirardelli–Quincy mould, like the Schoolhouse complex in Old Jerome, which 'in its small way, precisely duplicates the appearance and merchandise' of its precursors.[313]

Refitted historical structures tend to look alike, finally, because present-day demands and techniques impose a uniform gloss on whatever individuality they once had. Whether an old-time precinct is purportedly neolithic, medieval, or Edwardian, the visitor is apt – and hence apt to expect – to see it tricked out in the same way and surrounded by the same paraphernalia. Standard display and restoration practices apply today's veneer to relics of all epochs.[314]

For familiar reasons, Georges Duby suggests, remote ancestors described in medieval French genealogies strikingly resemble one another down through the generations. Lacking even memorial evidence much beyond a century back, the genealogist 'projects his own dream into the dark night beyond memory', portraying

imagined beings whose attitudes and dress reproduce those of the masters for whom he writes, those masters who wish their mores to be the model, from the virtues they profess to the failings of which they are proud . . . These supple unfurlings then stretch back toward the present life, binding it to a reflection of what the living would wish to be.

Thus family members depicted over several centuries 'all wear the same costume, parade in the same figures, [exhibit] the behaviour judged fitting, at the moment when this narration was written, by those who ordered its composition'.[315] The normative features of the present are imprinted on the whole length of the past.

[312] 'The old lady of 29 East Fourth St.', *N.Y. Times*, 28 June 1972, sect. 2, p. 22.
[313] Haas, 'Secret life of the American tourist', pp. 22, 24. 'Blindfold a tourist and drop him in Canal Square in Washington or Ghirardelli Square in San Francisco or Quincy Market in Boston – and it would be impossible to say whose history he is re-enacting or remembering . . . Restoration developments are interchangeable in design as well as content' (Andrew Kopkind, 'Kitsch for the rich', *The Real Paper* (Cambridge, Mass.), 19 Feb. 1977, p. 22). See Thorne, *Covent Garden Market*, pp. 87–90.
[314] Trillin, 'Thoughts brought on by prolonged exposure to exposed brick', pp. 100, 104; Liebs, 'Remember our not-so-distant past?' p. 33.
[315] Duby, 'Memories with no historian', pp. 12, 14.

97 Domesticating classical antiquity: Lawrence Alma-Tadema, *A Favourite Custom*, 1909

BRITAIN · NEEDS

YOU · AT · ONCE

98 Manipulating the medieval: British recruiting poster, First World War

Remaking the past to embody their own wished-for virtues was a major Victorian enter-prise, as we saw in Chapter 3. By modernizing the Greeks and archaizing themselves, the Victorians could view the ancients as living contemporaries.[316] The unblemished classical characters in Lytton's *The Last Days of Pompeii*, W. H. Mallock's *The New Republic*, the paintings of Alma-Tadema idealized nineteenth-century upper-class life as it might have appeared, in Jenkyns's words, 'with the traffic and the hoardings excluded'.[317] Kenelm Digby's refined version of chivalry bowdlerized the brutal medieval actuality; English radicals infected by medieval taste viewed the Great Hall as a symbol of class togetherness; *fin-de-siècle* Americans idealized the Middle Ages as a straightforward, unquestioning epoch blessed with imaginative and emotional responses denied to their introspective present.[318] Traditionalists dreamed of replacing the present with the past; but today was usually brought in line with yesteryear by conforming yesteryear with today's desires.[319]

[316] Turner, *Greek Heritage in Victorian Thought*, pp. xii, 8, 229, 263, 383.
[317] *Victorians and Ancient Greece*, pp. 316–17.
[318] Girouard, *Return to Camelot*, pp. 60, 146, 179, 70, 76; Lears, *No Place of Grace*, pp. 149, 163.
[319] Blaas, *Continuity and Anachronism*, p. 141; Burrow, *Liberal Descent*, pp. 224–8. 'The fervour of the Whig historian very often comes from ... the transference into the past of an enthusiasm for something in the

Presentist bias still strews such anachronisms across the American past. Revolutionary heroes are depicted as tolerant, egalitarian, concerned for the common weal – traits that we, their inheritors, ought to live up to. Could Franklin and Washington and Jefferson see how things had turned out, one scholar imagines, our standing army and our swollen aristocracy of wealth would appal and mystify them; 'indeed, their very Declaration of Independence indicts us as surely as it ever indicted King George, since the crimes of which it accused him characterize our own existence'.[320] Another exhorts history teachers to forestall the decline of the republic by rekindling 'willingness to return to the Spartan and self-sacrificing values that led Englishmen to build new lives and a new nation in America'.[321] But, both the crimes and the spirit of self-sacrifice are modern conceptions, not those of the earlier times. Beneath their period veneer, faces and behaviour in historical fiction, too, are emphatically of our time. 'In Louis L'Amour's West', boasts the publisher of America's best-selling frontier romances, 'women walk beside men, not behind them';[322] L'Amour shows the past the way his readers think the present ought to be.

Similar illusionist criteria affect tangible relics. To be credible historical witnesses, antiquities must to some extent conform with modern stereotypes; unless medieval structures are castellated, New England Colonial farmhouses furnished with candlesticks and spinning-wheels, Gothic churches fitted with encaustic tiles and canopied sedilia, they fall short of current expectations as relics; yet all these features are in fact anachronistic additions.[323] Moreover, the very process of conforming to current expectations tempts renovaters to feel that the past they reconstruct is not only faithful, but *more* faithful than what once existed, just as they themselves are more knowledgeable about times past than those who lived in them.[324]

The ubiquity of such anachronisms helps to explain why revivals often seem more 'correct' than originals, for revivals are faithful less to the relics of the past than to modern views of supposed past intentions only partly manifest in surviving structures. The revivalist gives final form to the genius of the past, but in the spirit of his own time; his work accords better with his own epoch's perception of that past than does the unadulterated past.[325] It was because certain seventeenth-century stained glass seemed *too* correctly Gothic that Pevsner suspected it had undergone Victorian alteration.[326]

Even a knowingly manipulated or adulterated past can coexist easily with unaltered relics. In historic-village compounds, old houses *in situ* nestle side by side with others brought in from far and wide, with replicas of extinct local buildings, and with generic antiquities. Signs and guidebooks usually specify which of these is which, but visitors soon

present, an enthusiasm for democracy or freedom of thought or the liberal tradition' (Butterfield, *Whig Interpretation of History*, p. 96).

[320] Zuckerman, 'Irrelevant Revolution', p. 238.

[321] Ivor Noël Hume, quoted in Cary Carson, 'Living museums of everyman's history', p. 32.

[322] Bantam Books advertisement, 1982.

[323] Kenneth Clark, *Gothic Revival*. 'The Tudor we now look upon is not sixteenth century Tudor but Tudor made in the image of what twentieth century builders think Tudor ought to look like' (Prince, 'Reality stranger than fiction', p. 14); Arthur Evans's art-nouveau style frescoes at Knossos have formed the modern image of what Minoan must have been like (Sparshott, 'Disappointed art lover', p. 249).

[324] 'As the recent Getty Museum demonstrates, the fragments of Pompeian villas may be recreated with an accuracy that is . . . greater than the original' (Jencks, 'Introduction', *Post-Modern Classicism*, p. 10).

[325] Hitchcock and Seale, *Temples of Democracy*, p. 205.   [326] Cited in Adams, *Lost Museum*, p. 88.

99 Original and 'authentic': Harrow School building, by Mr Sly, 1608–15 (left), modified by Samuel and C. R. Cockerell to conform with their matching right wing, 1820

forget, if they ever note, differences between authentic and imitated, untouched and restored, specific and generic.[327] 'Most visitors do not distinguish between reconstructed and original buildings though they are very concerned about authenticity'; 'there seems to be no real feeling that the structures must be original in order to be interesting'; 'while the public shows some surprise at the fact that these are not the original edifices, they are ... only very rarely disappointed to find that the buildings have been reconstructed' – these are typical curatorial judgements.[328] In any case, the buildings all get much the same custodial and interpretive treatment as a matter of cost, convenience, or taste for coherence. The commingling of originals and fabrications seems to distress the proprietors no more than the public.

The confusion is actually a source of pride for some who parade their contrivance as equal to (if not better than) the real old thing. 'It is always flattering', concludes an advertisement for do-it-yourself reproduction furniture, 'to have your own creations mistaken for originals.'[329] Another urges owners 'tired' of their modern furniture to 'Let us antique it for you. Send for our illustrated booklet showing pieces we have Chippen-

---

[327] Utley, 'Preservation ideal', p. 44. 'I don't know how many times a day', says an interpreter at Greenfield, 'I hear somebody say, "Why, I never realized Henry Ford, Thomas Edison, Noah Webster and the Wright Brothers all lived in the same town"' (quoted in Phillips, 'Greenfield's changing past', p. 44).

[328] Letters to the author from David A. Armour, Mackinac Island State Park Commission, Michigan, 1 Dec. 1980; Jean C. Smith, Liberty Village Foundation, Flemington, N.J., 25 Nov. 1980; Ronald G. Wilson, Appomattox Courthouse National Historical Park, Virginia, 25 Nov. 1980. Visitors to homes of the famous do, however, crave artifacts actually used by them (Irwin, 'Visitor response to Interpretation at Selected Historic Sites', pp. 153–5).

[329] *Cohasset Colonials*, Hagerty catalog, 1967.

daled, Sheratoned, etc.'[330] The deception is inconsequential – any expert could spot the difference. What matters is the delight taken in authentically replicating the past. Indeed, in this sense only a replica can be authentic.

Many enjoy the actual knowledge of contrivance. Renovated relics seem superior to untouched antiquities because they *are* remade for *us*; we feel comfortable with a contrived past because it is partly a product of the present, of people like us – not wholly the work of strange folk of long ago, with their weird and outlandish ways.

History thus transformed becomes larger than life, merging intention with performance, ideal with actuality. Acting out a fantasy our own time denies us, we remake the past into an epoch much like the present – except that we have no responsibility for it. The present cannot be moulded to such desires, for we share it with others; the past is malleable because its inhabitants are no longer here to contest our manipulations.

Imbuing the past with present-day intention and artifice also distances it, however, segregating it in its own world – quintessentially the world of the museum. Relics absolved from functional contexts can be moulded solely for display, and appreciative veneration underscores the distinction between the now useless but attractive past and the workaday present. 'On one side plastic, formica, gadgets, nothingness; on the other beauty and culture, mummified in a museum.'[331] With 'lustre cream pitchers that held no cream, the Dutch oven that held no bread, chairs with tapes across where no one could sit, pineapple-post beds where no one slept, and the rooms that no one lived in', museums necessarily deprive the past of life. And like museum reconstructions, the 'determinedly instructive air' of many historic house interiors 'lose the sense of life and warmth' of centuries 'of continuous use and development'.[332] The very process of classification distances and diminishes the past, as with Chamberlin's vignette of old papers being sorted for archival use: 'The piles of paper dwindled slowly into their classes, losing personality as they gained the pale immortality of a Special Collection.'[333]

Many antiquities are more accessible in a museum showcase than in such original locations as a cathedral ceiling or a Central American jungle, as noted above. But if bringing relics within walls makes them easier to see it also abridges the viewer's temporal awareness. In an antique building or landscape one moves in time among survivals; in a museum they are shorn of duration. The most artful placement, the most breathtaking proximity, cannot compensate for that detachment. The sculptures Lord Elgin removed from the Parthenon may be seen in absorbing close-up detail in the British Museum, but remain divorced there from diachronic context; at the Acropolis they were an integral part of an enduring local landscape and could be experienced as a past connected with the present.[334]

[330] Peterborough, 'Applied art?' *Daily Telegraph*, 24 July 1979, p. 14.
[331] Marrey, *Grands magasins*, p. 246.
[332] Benson, 'Spirit of '76', p. 24; Watkin, *Rise of Architectural History*, p. 187. 'What a long walk it is from one end of the Museum to the other, and how singularly lifeless the loveliest things appear' (Betjeman, 'Antiquarian prejudice' (1937), p. 69). Many museums are now much more lively, but no animation can bring their relics into the present.
[333] *Preserving the Past*, p. 107.
[334] This is not to assert that all antiquities should remain *in situ*; as noted above, most people prefer them in more accessible places. Great works of art may gain value if freed from contexts of time and place, as their creators often intended them to be. 'Our age is infected with a mania for showing things only in the environment that properly belongs to them, thereby suppressing the essential thing, the act of mind which isolated them from

The adjuncts of appreciation similarly distance relics left in place. Signposts, fences, admission booths, shaven greensward detach the surviving past from its present-day environment; the clutter of visitation divorces a recognized antiquity from local context. Marooned as it is among commercial huts and visitors' vehicles, Stonehenge might almost as well be in Trafalgar Square as on Salisbury Plain.[335] Even without the clutter of appreciation, change around them tends to make relics look less and less at home in their surroundings. While the lives of cherished structures are being extended, everything else of their vintage is being replaced. The preserved antiquity is ultimately left adrift in a modern sea, an isolated feature that stands out because it *alone* is old.

Special protection for antiquities may thus result in startling incongruities. Until New York City's air-rights ordinance of 1971, many landmarks seemed doomed by high-rise development. The new ordinance enabled rights to unused space above old buildings to be transferred to adjacent sites, where new structures could exceed statutory height and setback requirements to compensate for space 'wasted' above the historical landmarks. This helped to save some old structures but left them dwarfed by ever-higher buildings.[336] Manhattan's Trinity Church and the Old Stock Exchange and Customs House, already miniscule among neighbouring giants, may be further diminished by this well-meant tactic, while the midtown Italianate Villard Houses have been 'preserved' by the disharmonious juxtaposition of a massive hotel tower.

Crowds attracted to historic sites and structures themselves demean the experience. According to a 1970 survey, Westminster Abbey fell below the 'minimum comfort level' (35 square feet per person) more than half the time, with tourists often subject to intolerable congestion, noise, heat, and delay.[337] In many museums world-famous relics can scarcely be seen for the hordes of visitors. 'I've heard the Mona Lisa is quite a painting', writes a critic, 'but in all the times I've been to the Louvre, I've never seen it. I have seen the glass box it's housed in, and once I almost caught a glimpse, but I was pushed back to the benches.'[338]

Over-popularity has long detracted from historic ambience. At Kenilworth in 1877 Henry James resented 'a row of ancient pedlars outside the castle wall, hawking twopenny pamphlets and photographs', and 'half a dozen beery vagrants sprawling on the grass'. As at other historic places 'there are always people on the field before you, and there is usually something being drunk on the premises'. It was not just the numbers but the vulgarity James minded: at 'most romantic sites in England, there is a constant cockneyfication with which you must make your account ... The very echoes of the beautiful ruin seemed to have dropped all their *h*'s.'[339] Mass enjoyment today

---

that environment' in the first place. The tendency is as common today as it was in Proust's era. But a masterpiece contemplated 'in the midst of furniture, ornaments, hangings of the same period, stale settings ... does not give us the exhilarating delight that we can expect from it only in a public gallery', whose neutral and uncluttered background accords far better with 'those innermost spaces into which the artist withdrew to create it' (*Remembrance of Things Past*, 1:693–4).

[335] Chippindale, 'What future for Stonehenge?'; *idem, Stonehenge Complete*; Royal Commission on Ancient Monuments, *Stonehenge and Its Environs*.

[336] Costonis, *Space Adrift*, pp. 54–61; Goldstone and Dalrymple, *History Preserved: Guide to New York City Landmarks*, p. 25; Huxtable, *Kicked a Building Lately?* pp. 269–72.

[337] Hanna, 'Cathedrals at saturation point?' pp. 179–81; English Tourist Board, *English Cathedrals and Tourism*, pp. 56–9.

[338] Goldberg, 'Jostling over Mona Lisa', *IHT*, 5–6 July 1980, p. 8.   [339] *English Hours*, pp. 124–5.

100 The present dwarfs the past: McKim, Mead, and White,
Villard Houses, New York City, 1886

101 The present dwarfs the past:
Memory Lane Lounge beneath Detroit's Renaissance Center

greatly exacerbates these problems, diminishing the ambience of most noteworthy relics.

Much as eighteenth-century landscaped parks excluded signs of the workaday world, managers of many historic sites segregate their patch of the past; the invisibility of the present enhances visitors' sense of being in bygone times. With cement plants, housing developments, even modern farming equipment screened out, everything seen from within Stones River Battlefield seems to belong to the 1860s, including fields growing only old-fashioned varieties of cotton.

Favouring the early at the expense of the recent also distances past from present. 'Earlying up' reinforces notions of the past as a realm apart, only remotely and peripherally connected with life today. The conversion of Sacramento's early twentieth-century warehouses into early nineteenth-century boutiques and candle shops thus obliterated one observer's remembered landmarks; his childhood scene, his personal links with history, were replaced by a quaint, irrelevant antiquity.[340] Preservation focused on the distant past 'moves people only momentarily, at a point remote from their vital concerns', writes Kevin Lynch. 'It is impersonal as well as ancient. Near continuity is emotionally more important than remote time, though the distant past may seem nobler, more mysterious, or intriguing to us.' Our real ties are with 'the near and middle past'.[341]

Preservation from a single period, as at Williamsburg, also makes the past seem decidedly unlike the present. When everything in the preserved precinct dates from one selected time and nothing from any other, the effect is peculiarly static, unlike present-day landscapes, in which new and old everywhere commingle. 'No generation starts from scratch' anywhere but a pioneer settlement; 'the artifacts of previous generations do not vanish but clutter up the place'.[342]

Even where past and present physically intermingle, interpretation betokens segregation. The use of two names on Boston street signs, the 'Olde Name' beneath the modern one, divides attention *between* past and present, urging visitors to look now at the historical elements of the scene, now at the contemporary – never at both together. The deliberate highlighting of antique features in a room – furniture, *objets d'art*, souvenirs, all framed or otherwise set apart – similarly proclaims their separate historicity. Indeed, any management of relics sets the safeguarded past apart from the surrounding present.

Relics are more likely to be self-consciously segregated where they are rare. Compared with the awesome respect Americans accord their antiquities, the English seem almost casual about their more substantial heritage.[343] Yet a century ago Ruskin thought his fellow countrymen far less well-endowed and hence more prone to meddle with relics than the French or Italians:

---

[340] Thomas Frye, 'My history is missing', *Preservation News*, 17:12 (1977), 16.

[341] *What Time Is This Place?* p. 61. 'Anything before the eighteenth century is just too foreign for me', confessed a colleague of Anderson's at Plimoth Plantation (*Time Machines*, p. 81).

[342] Steinberg, 'Has anyone seen the Zeitgeist?' p. 24. See Lowenthal, 'American way of history'. Economic and technical constraints also engender static, uniform temporal concentration; American living historical farms cluster around 1850 in the North, 1870 in the South, because tools from earlier periods are hard to obtain and tractors and reapers of more recent times require costly maintenance (Schlebecker, 'Social functions of living historical farms', pp. 147–8).

[343] 'We corrupted Old-Worlders are much more sloppy and imprecise with our ancient monuments; we have lived with them for centuries and treat them like old pieces of family furniture, to be patched and repaired at need. And we made most of them ourselves, so – what the hell – they are ours to deal with as we think fit' (Banham, 'Preservation adobe', p. 24).

Abroad, a building of the eighth or tenth century stands ruinous in the open street; the children play round it, peasants heap their corn in it, the buildings of yesterday nestle about it, and fit their new stones into its rents, and tremble in sympathy as it trembles. No one wonders at it, or thinks of it as separate, and of another time; we feel the ancient world to be a real thing, and one with the new.

By contrast with this intermingled past and present, 'We, in England, have our new street, our new inn, our green shaven lawn, and our piece of ruin emergent from it – a mere *specimen* of the middle ages put on a bit of velvet carpet', whereas 'on the Continent, the links are unbroken between the past and present'.[344]

But those links remain unbroken only so long as the tangible past goes unrecognized. Imagine the effects of a visit to that French ruin of even a small fraction of Ruskin's readers. *They* would wonder at it, think it of another time, sketch and photograph it. Villagers would provide lodgings, sell souvenirs, and become picturesque likenesses on film. Publicity would swell the press of visitors and require the ruin to be fenced off, guards stationed, and admission charged to defray these costs. Conscious appreciation of antiquity inevitably sets it apart.[345]

We think, talk, and act toward the past as our ancestors rarely did – as a realm of particular concern to the present yet one essentially apart from it.[346] Self-consciousness distances past from present, emphasizing that then is not now. Nations strive to defend or regain relics as tangible emblems of great present consequence, but the effort of retrieval also enshrines those relics in a special past. The child who asks her grandmother about olden times may identify with her when she was young, but in so doing makes her now seem a quaint denizen of a remote time, less contemporaneous than before those questions were put.[347] Labelling and exhibiting family photos may refresh our memories but also segregates them from the present by emphasizing their subjects' irretrievable pastness – a pastness reinforced by the antiquarian flavour of the clothing and hair styles, the frames and the sepia prints. Rescuing ancient buildings from the bulldozer removes them from the limbo of the unremarked present into an ostentatious past. Once an artifact, an idea, or a memory is recognized and valued as historic, it is severed from the surrounding present. It becomes 'a work of art, free from irrelevancies and loose ends', in Beerbohm's words. 'The dullards have all disappeared . . . Everything is settled. There is nothing to be done about it.'[348]

The managed past may end up not merely segregated but unwittingly destroyed. In Massachusetts, for example, the Concord–Lexington 1775 combat route was set aside for the Minute Man National Historical Park in the 1960s. To display the story of that day, residents were evicted, post-Revolutionary houses demolished, and traditional farming brought to an end. The remaining houses were boarded up, fields and pastures reverted to brush, and within a few years the whole countryside ceased to bear any resemblance to the Revolutionary epoch's usage. Instead of a living landscape with past and present visibly

---

[344] *Modern Painters*, IV, Pt 5, Ch. 1, sects. 3 and 4, pp. 3–4. On the distinction between living relic and dead specimen, see Bann, *Clothing of Clio*, pp. 17, 82, 91, 131.

[345] Lynch, *What Time Is This Place?* p. 237; Lowenthal, 'Age and artifact', pp. 124–5.

[346] Ong, *Rhetoric, Romance, and Technology*, pp. 325–6.

[347] Thorndike, 'Renaissance or prenaissance?' p. 66; Panofsky, *Renaissance and Renascences*, pp. 36–7; Lowenthal, 'Past time, present place', pp. 13–14.

[348] *Lytton Strachey*, p. 345.

and functionally linked, a sumptuous visitor centre now shows surrogate relics and events of 1775 in audiovision; outdoors, where the skirmishes actually happened, elaborate notices along a measured wood-chipped trail interpret the historical views that could have been seen before the National Park Service obliterated them.[349]

Even examining the past can be fatal to it. Archaeological excavation unhappily demonstrates that 'We murder to dissect.'[350] 'The antiquarians had felled the tree that they might learn its age by counting the rings in the trunk', commented a nineteenth-century traveller on the excavation of the Roman Forum: 'They had destroyed, that they might interrogate.'[351] The mummified head of Otokar II of Bohemia rapidly disintegrated when his thirteenth-century tomb was reopened, in Prague's St Vitus's Cathedral in 1977, to see what could be learned from it.[352] Most poignant is Herbert Winlock's account of penetrating beneath the robber-rifled Meket-Rē' tomb at Thebes in 1920. Turning his flashlight on the hitherto untouched chamber of miniatures, the explorer fancied that he momentarily glimpsed the little green men coming and going in uncanny silence – who then instantly froze, motionless, forever; 'Winlock had looked into a cavity and seen the past in motion, and stilled it with his torch.'[353] The risk is more than fanciful: 'Shine a light bright enough to see an object', a conservator warns, 'and it will fall apart before your very eyes.'[354] Only its deliberate destruction secures Lenz's beleaguered Masurian past against misuse: to prevent their misappropriation for propaganda purposes, the curator of Masurian relics sets fire to his own museum, so that when 'the treasured finds have crumbled away, the traces have been obliterated', he will have brought 'the collected witnesses to our past into safety, a final, irrevocable safety, ... where they could never again be exploited for this cause or that'.[355] The collector of antiquities may fancy himself a preserver, but his passion destroys the context in which his cherished relics were once part of a living tradition.[356] 'There was somebody', remarks the custodian of Shakespeare's birthplace in Henry James's tale. 'But They've [the visitors] killed Him. And dead as He is, They keep it up, They do it over again, They kill Him every day.'[357]

To murder the past may portend a like fate for the murderer. The rifling of Bronze Age artifacts led Thai villagers to fabricate their own 'antique' pottery and thus better their material lot – at the cost of their traditional network of community relations. 'People destroy the archaeological finds', an observer commented, 'and the finds destroy the people.'[358] In Loren Eiseley's words, 'to tamper with the past, even one's own, is to bring

---

[349] Historical continuity has been sacrificed in the interest of future reversion to the original scene; the Park Service's aim, through massive archival research, 'is the eventual recreation of the landscape which once existed on that momentous day' (Malcolm, *Scene of the Battle, 1775*, p. 6).

[350] Wordsworth, 'Tables turned' (1798), line 28.   [351] Hillard, *Six Months in Italy* (1853), 1:299.

[352] Malcolm W. Browne, 'Prague protects its medieval architecture', *IHT*, 25 Jan. 1977, p. 3.

[353] Winlock, 'Diggers luck' (1921), p. 3; quotation from Eiseley, *All the Strange Hours*, p. 104.

[354] Jonathan Ashley-Smith, Keeper of Conservation, Victoria and Albert Museum, 'Conservation and information', lecture at Art Historians' conference, London, 26 Mar. 1983.

[355] Lenz, *Heritage*, p. 458.   [356] Arendt, 'Introduction: Walter Benjamin', pp. 39–45.

[357] 'Birthplace', 11:440. 'How one might love it', muses a James protagonist on the past around him in a sleepy English village, 'but how one might spoil it! To look at it too hard was positively to make it conscious, and to make it conscious was positively to wake it up. Its only safety ... was to be left still to sleep' ('Flickerbridge', 11:337).

[358] Debra Weiner, 'Treasures from the Thai earth', *IHT*, 26–7 June 1982, p. 6. See Alicia Levin, 'Thai town's specialty: making "antiques"', *IHT*, 23 Sept. 1981, p. 5.

at times that slipping, sliding, tenuous horror which . . . may draw disaster from the air, or make us lonely beyond belief'.[359]

Enlarged or diminished, embellished or purified, lengthened or abbreviated, the past becomes more and more a foreign country, yet also increasingly tinged with present colours. But in spite of its modern overlay the altered past retreats from the present more rapidly than the untouched past, and suffers earlier extinction. Only the continual addition of more recent history prevents the past we revise from becoming marooned in ever remoter antiquity.

Such alterations segregate and homogenize us along with our relics: as we reshape the past to fit present-day images, our perceptions of it become more like those of our contemporaries. Whereas an unrevised past elicits diverse explanations, a past formed to fit received views reduces the variety of historical perspectives and limits the range of historical experience. Less idiosyncratically encountered, the remade past is more mono-lithically interpreted: the restorers and guides through whose eyes we see it fit us all with the same distorting lenses.

History continually tailored to our conceptions is more and more a joint enterprise; your past resembles mine not only because we share a common heritage but also because we have changed it in concert. But this fabricated consensus is highly evanescent. We outdate history with increasing speed, so that even quite recent views of the past, available in voluminous detail on tape and film, now seem unbelievably strange. Textbooks bring the 'truth' about American history quickly and thoroughly up to date, notes Fitzgerald, but because each generation of schoolchildren reads only one such version of the past, 'that transient history is those children's history forever'.[360] A past remoulded in the image of the ever-changing present may enable a whole age group to share perspectives, but cuts them off from those historical perspectives that preceded and will follow them.

Incessant historical revision makes our predecessors' sense of the past more remote and less accessible. We have lost our parents' and our grandparents' view of history, not to mention that of earlier times, not merely because time has interpolated new pasts and altered what we know of older ones, but also because each new consensus transforms the very structure and syntax of historical understanding.

[359] *All the Strange Hours*, p. 97.   [360] *America Revised*, p. 17; see also p. 47.

CREATIVE ANACHRONISM

> Forward into the past!
>
> Motto of The Eldon League

The Eldon League would restore feudalism and abolish the present and future tense; an American counterpart pretends to rejoice in the return of sod shanties, quinsy, and the croup; the Society for Creative Anachronism glories in a mock-medieval 'tradition which has outlived its original purpose, but which survived just because it's a lot of fun'.[1] Such caprices conceal a serious issue: what use can be made of a past increasingly seen as flawed or irrelevant? What can be done with relics and attitudes now irrevocably obsolete? Beyond display in a musuem, has the past any value at all?

A 'creative anachronism' is a contradiction in terms. Yet nothing that survives is wholly anachronistic. Every generation disposes its own legacy, choosing what to discard, ignore, tolerate, or treasure, and how to treat what is kept. Such choices are not unconstrained: decisions to remember or forget, to preserve or destroy, largely depend on forces beyond our control, often beyond conscious awareness. But current feelings about the past largely determine what becomes of its residues.

This chapter explores perspectives on the past prevalent since the turn of this century. Some contend that the past is dead, that industrial and democratic society, enlightened by a rational and dispassionate study of history, has dispelled antiquity's hold on men's minds and deeds. Yet passionate concern with roots and widespread nostalgic attachments evince the past's durability rather than its demise.

New information and insights have expanded historical perspectives and multiplied specialized knowledge. But they have also deprived us of many modes of communion with the past that once were common. I explain why these modes of historical apprehension are

---

[1] Russell Baker, 'The 1833 bandwagon', *IHT*, 17 Apr. 1981, p. 12; SCA *Pleasure Book* (1979), quoted in Jay Anderson, *Time Machines*, p. 170. The SCA in fact aims 'to re-create the Middle Ages not as it was but as it should have been, doing away with the strife and pestilence' (p. 167). The Eldon League takes its name from John Scott, 1st Earl of Eldon, England's most backward-thinking Lord High Chancellor (1802–6, 1807–27), whose sole aim was 'to maintain things as he found them' and 'for nearly forty years . . . fought against every improvement' (*Encyclopedia Britannica*, 11th edn, 9:167d).

no longer available, review modernist antagonism to tradition, and discuss the resulting breach with the past, which maroons us amidst a valued but ever less familiar legacy.

One consequence of that breach is the popularity of preservation. Bereft of creative connection with the past, we zealously save its relics. I explore the scope of preservation and the impulses that animate it – the felt pace of change and loss, the role of national and neighbourhood landmarks, the linking of personal with public histories. These impulses, noteworthy at the end of the eighteenth and nineteenth centuries, are again prominent in our day. I go on to discuss the benefits and costs of preservation in economic and social terms, and finally in the context of alternative ways of using the past, a persisting yet malleable realm shaped by us as well as shaping us.

DEATH AND ENDURANCE OF THE PAST

> We've inherited all sorts of old ideas and old dead beliefs . . . They're not actually alive in us but they're rooted there all the same, and we can't rid ourselves of them.
>
> Henrik Ibsen, *Ghosts*[2]

> The 'past' has given way to 'history'.
>
> Michael Neve, 'Up market in Manhattan'[3]

The past long exerted a powerful and in many ways malign influence; it 'seeped through the interstices of society, staining all thought, creating veneration for customs, traditions and inherited wisdom', acting as a 'bulwark against innovation and change', according to J. H. Plumb. But better understanding of history is at last emancipating mankind from those shackles; objective inquiry has dispelled antiquity's mythical powers, fateful portents, and claims to authority. 'The old past is dying . . . and so it should. Indeed, the historian should speed it on its way, for it was compounded of bigotry, of national vanity, of class domination.' The history that is replacing that evil old past will 'help to sustain man's confidence in his destiny, and create for us a new past as true, as exact, as we can make it.'[4]

Historical insight has indeed progressed. Awareness of the past as a web of contingent events subject to unceasing re-evaluation supplant notions of a predestined unfolding or moral chronicle. Antiquity no longer automatically confers power or prestige, nor do primordial origins seem the sole key to destiny's secrets. The old exemplary use of the past has 'been undermined, battered and exploded by the growth of history itself'.[5]

Technological advance likewise weakens the everyday role of the past, in Plumb's view. 'Industrial society, unlike the commercial, craft and agrarian societies which it replaces, does not need the past . . . The new methods, new processes, new forms of living of scientific and industrial society have no sanction in the past and no roots in it'; we now look back only as 'a matter of curiosity, of nostalgia, a sentimentality . . . The strength of the past in all aspects of life is far, far weaker than it was a generation ago; indeed, few societies

---

[2] 1882, Act II, p. 61.   [3] *TLS*, 4 Mar. 1983, p. 208.

[4] Plumb, *Death of the Past*, pp. 66, 115. Plumb distinguishes 'the past' and 'history' partly in terms of class: 'The past has only served the few; perhaps history may serve the multitude' (p. 16).

[5] Ibid., p. 44.

have ever had a past in such galloping dissolution as this.'[6] Psychoanalysis is similarly credited with freeing individuals from the tyranny of their childhoods; guided recollection relieves patients of obsessive regression and enables them to live in the present rather than the past. Freed from the dead weight of history, modern man no longer stands on the shoulders of past generations 'like acrobats in the circus', in Ortega y Gasset's phrase,[7] but 'leaps from their shoulders and swings to the top of the circus tent alone and free'.[8]

Avowed emancipation from the past has not wholly superseded previous dependence, however. Michael Oakeshott, for one, terms Plumb's 'belief that an "historical" attitude towards the past is now more common than it used to be' an illusion; most people continue to use – and abuse – history for their own immediate purposes.[9] Former perspectives on the past may be academically discredited, but they are not vanquished; the old views linger alongside the new, just as relics mingle with novelties, and historical romance with futurist science fiction. As recently as 1969 Plumb thought 'the need for personal roots in time' much weaker than 'a mere hundred or even fifty years ago'[10] – an assertion that I doubt anyone would repeat today.

Far from being of less consequence, the past seems to matter more and more; innumerable facets of modern life reflect its heightened import. Physical relics are treasured national talismans – a global concern manifest in World Heritage Convention designations. Third World demands for the restitution of antiquities from Western collections, not to mention the Greek crusade for the return of the Elgin Marbles, highlight the critical role of relics and records as symbols of collective identity; nothing so inflames national sentiment as threats to the artifactual and archival heritage. Indeed, Paul Valéry's indictment of historical passion strikingly resembled Plumb's diatribe against the sinister *non*-historical past:

History is the most dangerous product the chemistry of the intellect has concocted . . . It produces dreams and drunkenness. It fills people with false memories, exaggerates their reactions, exacerbates old grievances, and encourages either a delirium of grandeur or a delusion of persecution. It makes whole nations bitter, arrogant, insufferable, and vainglorious.[11]

And 'history' is still as revered, as risky – and as manipulated – as 'the past' has always been. A century on, Nietzsche's conclusions seem an apt rebuttal to the death of Plumb's past: 'There are no more living mythologies, you say? Religions are at their last gasp? Look at the religion of the power of history, and the priests of the mythology of Ideas, with their scarred knees!'[12]

For individuals as for nations, things salvaged from the past have come to embody greater value – and are preserved in greater quantity and variety – than ever before. Ancient Egypt entombed artifacts only for the benefit of the dead; early Christendom treasured no tangible survivals other than religious relics. Renaissance cabinets of curiosities held few objects valued for antiquity *per se*, and copies of a handful of works sufficed antiquarian appetites. Eighteenth-century *cognoscenti* admired new archaeological finds but took few actual trophies. Devotees of Walter Scott's historical novels and Gilbert

---

[6] Ibid., p. 14.   [7] *Man and Crisis*, p. 53.
[8] A. N. Gilbert, 'Introduction', *In Search of a Meaningful Past*, p. vi.
[9] 'Activity of being an historian', p. 165.   [10] *Death of the Past*, p. 49.   [11] 'On history' (1931), 10:114.
[12] *Use and Abuse of History* (1874), p. 52.

102 The past all-pervasive: 'Well, Emmeline, what's new?' B. Tobey, *New Yorker*, 1976

Scott's historical architecture enjoyed tangible mementoes of heritage, to be sure, but 'how many rooms, in Europe or in America', speculates an historian, 'were filled in 1880 with the furniture of 1780?' Our great-grandparents would find far more that was familiar in the current vogue for Victoriana than *their* great-grandparents would have found in homes of a century ago.[13] More than any previous generation, we cram our houses with furnishings that deliberately evoke the past, adorn walls with family photos and mantels with memorabilia, and convert public streets into 'Memory Lanes'.

Present-day absorption with the past reflects needs that transcend partisan purposes or personal nostalgia. A view of man as conceived and created by history, suggests Eliade, impels Western culture to seek out and reconstitute the entire past.[14] Dreams of re-experiencing dominate much of what we read, see, and hear: beyond mere curiosity lies a deep fascination with how things used to be, an eagerness for lifelike insights into the past, near or remote, familiar or arcane. Popular history, biography, autobiography, and historical fiction deluge bookshops and television screens; classroom re-enactments emphasize the immediacy and malleability of past events; 'family history' has transformed genealogy from an elite pursuit into a popular preoccupation; oral archives celebrate the annals of hitherto unsung masses and local histories their most humdrum details, the narrator becoming 'a kind of beachcomber among the casually washed-up detritus of the past', in Simon Schama's phrase, 'ministering to a culture terrified by the fragility of the contemporary, and seeking in chronicle an inverted form of augury'.[15] Older forms of augury also persist in cults of megalithic magic and reincarnated spirits.

New means of access make modern concern with the past supremely self-conscious and self-confident. Every age thinks it best understands its predecessors, but our epoch has extra reason to believe it can depict the past more fully and truly than ever. Archival and archaeological progress enables historians to date and elaborate things previously only vaguely known, opening to minute scrutiny the everyday life as well as the outstanding events of distant times. Other resources tap times nearer the present. Recordings and films put an ever-lengthening past literally before our eyes and ears, and make the physical look of the recent past common property.

The new media also make the past more compelling. Films engross sustained attention; viewers feel they participate in the past. The books and pictures, relics and ruins, that supplemented the memory of previous generations were both more taxing and less convincing; they required interpretation and reconstruction. Movies and snapshots plunge us into a vivid past – or bring that past directly into the present – seemingly without mediation. And they inspire faith as records of reality surpassing books and artifacts – for books have been contrived by later minds, and artifacts have suffered subsequent erosion. 'Unlike the monastic scribe or the newspaper reporter', we suppose the camera 'cannot lie, because it cannot think'; as noted in Chapter 5, historical films seem to show us the actual

---

[13] John Lukacs, 'Obsolete historians', p. 82. 'The Albert Memorial Issue', *Observer Mag.*, 9 Oct. 1983, amply illustrates this vogue.

[14] *Myth and Reality*, p. 136.

[15] 'Monte Lupo story', *London Review of Books*, 18 Sept.–1 Oct. 1980, p. 23. See Ronald G. Witt, 'Teaching history through reenactment', paper at American Historical Association meeting, Dec. 1982, pp. 6–7. An eminent figure now in his eighties told me that as a boy at Harrow School he had striven to suppress the knowledge that his grandfather was a common labourer; today he would want to shout it from the roof-tops.

past.[16] Forgetting that camera angles are selected, tapes and films edited and distorted, we attend to them as raw glimpses of what actually happened. The feeling that the past is open to perusal as never before creates an illusion that *we*, at last, can know what it was *really* like.[17]

The value now ascribed to historical truth buttresses this naïve confidence. Fidelity to the facts is ever the claim of chroniclers, but only recently have historians been *exclusively* preoccupied with the disinterested study of the past.[18] Historical site curators are likewise newly bent on portraying the naked truth, though often frustrated, as we saw in Chapter 6, by patrons' tastes and visitors' preferences. Previously, historical fidelity mattered less than inspiring awe and veneration: readers were told and viewers shown a celebrated, glamorous, elegant, quaint, or sometimes horrific past, never what passed for the unvarnished whole. But audiences already persuaded that the past is important can perhaps be shown history straight, suggests Elizabeth Stillinger: now that the worth of American antiques is firmly established, we are 'free to engage in serious inquiry into just how our ancestors *did* live, rather than creating the charming imaginary settings in which we *wish* they had lived'.[19] Although best-selling nostalgia continues to purvey a wishful 'living past' to a credulous public, serious historians and curators disdain such 'obscene necromancy', in Oakeshott's epithet;[20] rather, they painstakingly document every detail so as to present the past entire, warts and all. In fact, the past modern historians and curators select for display is no less biased or presentist than that of their predecessors, as shown in Chapter 5. Awareness of the pitfalls of subjectivity and efforts to preclude such bias as they can recognize make their view of the past more self-conscious than their precursors', but no less subjective.

Greater familiarity alters our experience of the past. When less definitively known, its lineaments were commonly vague and shadowy. The exhaustive detail in which previous epochs are now limned makes them more plausible, notwithstanding the *longueurs* and horrors often disclosed; indeed, yesteryear seems authentic *because* it is shown in such presumably faithful detail. Factual fidelity may dispel some of the past's enchantment, but for most people today (as for nineteenth-century audiences) realism heightens its appeal. Temporal distance increases needs for verisimilitude; bone china 'King Arthur Plates' 'chosen by three of the most eminent experts on Arthurian history' are advertised as 'an authentic expression of the world of the Knights of the Round Table'.[21] Yet details of the recaptured past also sharpen the contrast between then and now. Television gives a similar kaleidoscopic shape to today and to yesterday but exaggerates their felt differences: watching an old movie, we are at once struck by even minor shifts in fashion, speech, transport. The cinematic detail that makes the recent past so real also makes it alien; seen through today's eyes, Herbert Hoover's ways seem hardly less weird than those of Hammurabi.

Yet despite their apparent veracity, relics and records are increasingly known to have

---

[16] Paul Smith, 'Fiction film as historical source', p. 204.
[17] Gane, 'History and film', pp. 184–7; Kent, 'Film and history teaching in the secondary school'; Duckworth, '"Filmic" vs. "real" reality in the historical film'.
[18] Munz, *Shapes of Time*, p. 169.   [19] *The Antiquers*, p. 282.   [20] 'Activity of being an historian', p. 166.
[21] Plates by James Marsh for the International Arthurian Society, L'Atelier Art Editions brochure, 26 Feb. 1979.

been altered. The survivals that form our views of the past are now seen as continually reshaped. And widespread awareness of manipulation makes the past seem in some ways more like the present. The same forces that affect new creations impinge on what is left of the old; growing demands to supplement a missing or deficient tangible heritage, growing capacities to transport and to copy vestiges lead us to expect our past to be one remade for us, rather than part of the past as it originally was. Later in this chapter I show that while this expected past stems from the quest to preserve the heritage, it also casts doubts on the validity of that quest. But first let us review what previous uses of the past modern insights have made obsolete.

PASTS WE HAVE LOST

Just once, you should walk down the same street your great-grandfather walked.

Pan American Airways advertisement, 1983

Modern historical insights include awareness of how our precursors felt about their own pasts. Holding different beliefs and values, people in other epochs looked to the past for other sustenances than we do. The benefits categorized in Chapter 2 embrace both our ways of using the past and theirs, but growing knowledge and differing assumptions make some of these benefits more valid or important, others less. Many once customary ways of recognizing and engaging with the heritage have become increasingly outgrown, discredited, and inaccessible. What were these previous uses of the past? How far have we lost them, and why? And how does the loss affect our awareness and treatment of the heritage?

Tradition

The earliest common use of the past was to validate the present. This perspective is still habitual in 'traditional' societies lacking a written language and wholly reliant on folk memory. In such societies empirical inquiry seldom revises received views, and tradition is the pre-eminent guide for behaviour, especially if the precedent is believed ancient and constant. The past is an infallible source of truth and merit; things are deemed correct simply because they have happened; to paraphrase Pope, 'Whatever *was*, is right.'

Societies that have written and printed records remain attached to tradition, but not in the same way or to the same degree. They continue to validate many attitudes and actions by reference to former practices, as detailed in Chapter 2. But to believe tradition perpetuated unbroken from remotest antiquity they would have to deny historical changes implicit in their annals. Those who know they have a history and habitually distinguish past from present must curtail appeals to tradition.

In most history-conscious societies, 'tradition' denotes not total or unswerving stability but the value of *particular* precedents, the unfolding of practice from immemorial specific instances. English common law reflects such a use of tradition. From Coke to Blackstone, lawyers have rooted the laws and liberties of England in Magna Carta, and that charter itself in a body of law still more ancient. 'The minds of all our lawyers and legislators, and of all the people whom they wish to influence, have always been filled', wrote Edmund

Burke, with a 'powerful prepossession towards antiquity.'[22] Tradition itself was a traditional virtue: Burke maintains that the English had *always* appealed to the past. 'There really did exist a habit of conducting political discussion in England "upon the principle of reference to antiquity"', concludes J. G. A. Pocock. Burke was 'not calling upon his contemporaries to return to a seventeenth-century habit of mind, but assuming that it was still alive and meaningful among them'.[23] Regularly shorn of what ceased to be useful, common law was thus continuous since time immemorial yet also always up to date. But for common-law tradition to be authoritative, P. B. M. Blaas points out, the past had to remain unknown, lest knowledge of actual historical detail subvert the assurance of its authority. The true past would at once be seen as anachronistic; 'neglecting the concrete facts made it easier to . . . commandeer authority in the present by means of that very past'.[24] Customary law 'quietly passes over obsolete laws, which sink into oblivion, and die peacefully, but the law itself remains young, always in the belief that it is old'.[25]

The supposed continuity of tradition shaped English historical perspectives throughout the nineteenth century, and remnants of this faith still suffuse popular thought – for example, in the imagined antiquity of royal ceremony revived or invented in the twentieth century. Many continue to cherish 'the belief that English institutions, like no other in the Western world, were the result of slow growth from Saxon days; that, like a coral reef, precedent had fallen on precedent, erecting a bulwark of liberty, creating institutions such as Parliament or constitutional monarchy', as Plumb himself agrees. 'Many centuries and much tribulation had been required to bring these to perfection; their antiquity, their slow growth, endowed them with a special virtue.'[26]

The appeal to tradition embodied in common-law precepts and in the Whig view of history is, however, fatally at odds with modern awareness of change. Only an immemorial and unknowable past can conform tradition to current usage and thus deny the newness of the present. By contrast, in any historically understood past things are bound to change; new departures continually occur, and what is old becomes *passé*. By the turn of this century, as Blaas shows, awareness of historicity could no longer be repressed, and 'tradition' in the old sense came to be equated with useless antiquarianism or paralyzing anachronism.[27]

The age-old appeal to tradition is generally obsolete because past and present now seem too dissimilar to make it a safe or valid guide. The word's very meaning has changed: 'tradition' now refers less to how things have always been done (and therefore should be done) than to allegedly ancient traits that endow a people with corporate identity. And the 'tradition' nowadays invoked on behalf of earlier ways is seldom alive; more often it signals

---

[22] *Reflections on the Revolution in France* (1790), p. 118. 'The very idea of the fabrication of a new government, is enough to fill us with disgust and horror. We . . . wish to derive all we possess as an inheritance from our forefathers' (p. 117).

[23] *Language, Politics and Time*, p. 208; also pp. 252–4.

[24] *Continuity and Anachronism*, pp. 252–3. See also Pocock, 'Origins of the study of the past', pp. 232–3; Ong, *Orality and Literacy*, p. 98; Clanchy, *From Memory to Written Record*, p. 233.

[25] Fritz Kern, *Kingship and Law in the Middle Ages*, p. 179.   [26] *Death of the Past*, p. 70.

[27] *Continuity and Anachronism*, pp. xi–xiv, 28, 141, 202, 238–9. 'In us the word "tradition" excites no reverence, for the expert knows that those who appeal to it do so in default of any proof for the origin they seek to claim' (J. H. Round, 'Historical genealogy', quoted in Blaas, p. 57). See Hughes, *Consciousness and Society*, pp. 33–7, 189.

a sterile reluctance to change. 'What was good enough for my father is good enough for me' no longer affirms the virtues of the past; it simply spurns what is new and untried – like old Skullion, Tom Sharpe's head porter who 'was prepared to give his qualified approval to improvements provided there was no suggestion that it was the past that had been improved upon'.[28] Governing bodies and committees that fall back on precedent do not celebrate a living past but seek refuge in one safely dead. In any case, self-consciousness precludes tradition in its original sense; one cannot restore a former tradition to gratify nostalgic fancy. 'There is no hope in returning to a traditional faith after it has once been abandoned', writes Kedourie, 'since the essential condition in the holder of a traditional faith is that he should not know he is a traditionalist'.[29]

The past as example

The pedagogic past has been as vital as the traditional, with which it is often confused. But they are quite disparate. Tradition flowed unchanged into the present, explaining nothing; pedagogy gave insight into today's affairs by comparison with yesterday's. People learned from both similarities and differences to profit by some historical examples and take warning from others.

Nineteenth-century insights progressively abandoned belief in universal human nature, thereby devaluing historical analogy, as discussed in Chapters 2 and 5. Historical explanation was increasingly vested in traits and events unique to each people. When every culture and epoch had to be understood in its own terms, the lessons of history became invalid, and the past ceased to be the great teacher of life.

What invalidated the pedagogic past was not animus against it, but growing awareness that past and present were too unlike for comparative lessons to apply. Although exemplary history endures in popular thought and folk belief, it is no longer taken seriously by historians. We recognize in 'patronizing' fashion 'that simpler cultures benefited from values that we have lost', charges John Coolidge, but 'we act as if those vanished values could have little relevance to the sophisticated problems of our day'.[30] In fact, we are no more patronizing about the past than eighteenth-century *philosophes* who believed in the efficacy of its lessons; they thought themselves superior to the ancients precisely because, living after them, they could profit by their experience.[31] That faith we no longer share. 'It is a normal human desire', thinks an interpreter of living history, 'to believe that those in other times and places, especially our ancestors, felt and acted as we do today.'[32] But however pervasive this desire, historical perspectives no longer sustain the belief.

The ideal past

Investing some particular epoch with every virtue is another once-favoured use of the past now out of vogue. According to earlier common belief, there was once a time when all

---

[28] *Porterhouse Blue*, p. 46.   [29] 'Introduction', *Nationalism in Asia and Africa*, p. 66.
[30] 'Foreword', *Gods & Heroes*, p. 9.
[31] Becker, *Heavenly City of the Eighteenth-Century Philosophers*, p. 96.
[32] Ronsheim, 'Christmas at Conner Prairie', p. 17.

things were perfect. But the perfection was mythic, not historical; 'the people of the golden age have left us no monuments of genius, no splendid columns, no paintings, no poetry';[33] specificities were wholly lacking. Yet the supposed felicities of particular times and places supplied compelling images of a golden age. The pastoral poems of Ovid and Virgil, conflating Sicily and Arcadia, and the paintings of Claude and Poussin giving them scenic form, held up to view prototypical idealized pasts.

The golden age for Renaissance humanists was classicial antiquity, whose ideals they sought to realize in their own creations. In the eighteenth century artists aimed anew to distil the essence – truth, purity, simplicity, primitive virility – of antiquity. But historical knowledge already made it hard to idealize any particular past. Renaissance attainments themselves showed that classical antiquity had no monopoly on achievement; to the Enlightenment, in Felix Gilbert's phrase, the Romans thus 'became different people rather than patterns for all times'.[34] Historical relativism today makes any golden age an evident fiction. Even those most besotted with the past know too much to invest a particular period with perfection. Great bygone epochs still compel admiration, but their virtues are neither archetypal nor transmissible. Today we hanker less for a golden age – always a land of fantasy, even when derived from some fancied past – than for the past in general or for more recent if less inspiring Good Old Days.[35]

Imitation

Incorporating past exemplars into contemporary life is another mode of appropriation now out of favour. The Renaissance use of classical models ranged, as shown in Chapter 3, from slavish copying to eclectic variation and cumulative transformation. Humanists imitated Greek and Roman works to bring classical glories into their own life and thought. Petrarch urged students 'to catch the sound of classical Latin; . . . to make the tone of their writing appropriate to the natural level of the subject as it was in the best classical authors, . . . to collect their stocks of phrases on every subject'.[36] Lexicons, grammars, and collections like Erasmus's *Adages* enabled humanists to draw turns of speech, imagery, situations, and characters from ancient sources, and thereby make classical categories and theories their own.[37] When the classics permeated vernacular literature and everyday speech, the classical heritage came more and more into the general stock of thought; transmitted through English versions of Plutarch and Italian *novelle*, Horace's *Ars poetica* made Shakespeare, though all but ignorant of Latin, no less a beneficiary of classical models than Racine or Schiller.[38] Almost every schoolboy in England, it was said (or at least hoped), learned to write and even to think like Cicero.[39]

Imitation of antiquity remained common practice, but by the nineteenth century its pattern had changed and its purpose had narrowed. Now amplified and corrected by

---

[33] Sampson Reed, Harvard M.A. oration, 29 Aug. 1821, quoted in Emerson, *Journals and Miscellaneous Notebooks*, 1:293–4.

[34] 'Italy', p. 41.   [35] Lerner, *Uses of Nostalgia*, pp. 243–6.

[36] Bolgar, *Classical Heritage and Its Beneficiaries*, p. 266.

[37] Bolgar, 'Greek legacy', pp. 455–8; *Classical Heritage*, pp. 273–5, 297–300.

[38] Rosenmeyer, 'Drama', p. 121. See *Transmission of Ideas of Early Modern Europe*.

[39] 'Greek legacy', p. 458.

archaeological discoveries, classical texts ceased to be infallible guides. Greater knowledge and new techniques made those who transmitted ancient images better able to authenticate them and more concerned to do so; fidelity to classical or medieval models became a *sine qua non* of revivalist art and architecture. Imitation undertaken in this spirit, however, aimed not to rival antiquity but to confirm or relive it. And as the classics became common knowledge they came to be taken for granted; for many antiquity ceased to be a living force. Bereft of their former pioneering function, classical languages served increasingly to preserve traditional values and perpetuate existing elites.[40]

Creative imitation had given humanists 'an extraordinary understanding of their models, an understanding which far surpasses the normal knowledge of [today's] historian', concludes R. R. Bolgar. We cannot equal their achievements because 'we lack that final purpose which breathed life into their work. We do not read the classics in order to learn to write or in order to solve our daily problems of conduct.'[41] We have not ceased to imitate antiquity, nor could we if we wished; classical exemplars profoundly influence even those who ignore or condemn them. But conscious imitation became antithetical to Romantic and then to modernist ways of thought and feeling. As technology perfected modes of imitation, the notion of imitation became profoundly distasteful; many assume that the creative process should depend wholly on self-discovery and self-expression and owe nothing to the past. We are no longer allowed to borrow or appropriate from others; to be creative we must be wholly original. 'No dogma of the Classical creed is more alien to 20th-century views of art than [its] acceptance of authority', in Gombrich's words, and abhorrence of past models permeates most aspects of modern life.[42]

Communion

Empathetic identification with great precursors, like idealization and imitation, derived from the urge to reanimate the past in the present. 'Alexander walked in the footsteps of Miltiades', and Caesar 'took Alexander as his prototype. Such "imitation" meant far more than we mean by the word today. It was a mythical identification.'[43] Renaissance and Enlightenment worthies fancied themselves in intimate converse with classical poets and philosphers and cited them as contemporaries. Petrarch felt himself among Roman authors as he read them: 'It is with these men that I live at such times and not with the thievish company of today', he 'told' Livy.[44] Machiavelli recounts entering into the presence and converse of the ancients through their books; a Vatican curator talked to his classical statues 'as if they were living', reported John Evelyn, 'sometimes kissing & embracing them'.[45]

This love was at best symbolically requited, as noted in Chapter 3. 'The idea of a "direct conversation" with ancient Romans seems to point to an intimacy that is incompatible

---

[40] Bolgar, *Classical Heritage*, pp. 300–3; Jenkyns, *Victorians and Ancient Greece*, pp. 63, 67, 70.
[41] *Classical Heritage*, p. 389.
[42] 'Perfection's progress', p. 3. [43] Thomas Mann, 'Freud and the future', p. 424.
[44] 22 Feb. 1349 (?) in *Petrarch's Letters to Classical Authors*, pp. 101–2. See Peter Burke, *Renaissance Sense of the Past*, p. 22.
[45] Machiavelli to Francesco Vittori, cited in Pocock, *Machiavellian Moment*, p. 62; Evelyn, *Diary and Correspondence*, 27 Feb. 1644, p. 150, referring to Hippolito Vitellesco. See Houghton, 'English virtuoso in the seventeenth century', p. 191.

with' holding them at an historicized distance, in Eisenstein's view;[46] but the ancients' failure to respond kept humanists poignantly aware of that distance. Their felt closeness to the great classical authors was not reciprocated, their deep yearning for transaction almost by definition unquenchable. Ancient mentors who have deserved 'friendship or love or thanks at my hands, never lost in the same by being no longer there', claimed Montaigne; 'I have better paid and more carefully rewarded them' in their absence.[47] But his was a rare generosity. To most, the beloved ancients 'maintained a marble or a bronze repose that could break hearts', in Greene's phrase, and 'the pathos of this incomplete embrace' was the price humanists paid for the pride of their intimacy.[48]

Eighteenth-century *philosophes* likewise wrapped themselves in the togas of Cicero and Lucretius to re-enact ancient stances. 'Continuously preoccupied with Rome and Athens', wrote Rousseau while reading Plutarch, 'living ... with their great men, ... I pictured myself as a Greek or a Roman.'[49] The philosopher d'Holbach hunted and walked days on end enthralled by 'the ever-charming conversation of Horace, Virgil, Homer and all our noble friends of the Elysian fields'.[50] Ancient heroes permeated Enlightenment consciousness. 'He has all the eloquence of Cicero, the benevolence of Pliny, and the wisdom of Agrippa', wrote Frederick the Great in 1740 after meeting Voltaire, who retorted after another meeting that Frederick 'talked in as friendly a manner to me as Scipio to Terence'.[51] Napoleon identified himself first with Alexander, then with Charlemagne, saying '"I am Charlemagne"' – not that he was *like* Charlemagne or that '"My situation is like Charlemagne's"', but quite simply: '"I am he."'[52]

Longings to feel at one with the past outlasted such fantasized communion. Niebuhr meant his history of Rome to shed such a light for his readers that the Romans would stand before their eyes, 'distinct, intelligible, familiar as contemporaries, with their institutions and the vicissitudes of their destiny, living and moving'.[53] Nineteenth-century enthusiasms took the form of colloquies between classical heroes, such as Walter Savage Landor's *Imaginary Conversations*: 'To-day there came to visit us a writer who is not yet an author: his name is Thucydides ... Sophocles left me about an hour ago ... Euripedes was with us at the time.'[54] Unfettered by chronology, many 'conversations' involved figures who could never have met, conflating centuries in the fashion Gibbon had mocked.[55] The mode was itself Greek-inspired; 'how much instruction has been conveyed to us in the form of conversations at banquets, by Plato and Xenophon and Plutarch', exclaims Peacock's Dr. Opimiam. 'I read nothing with more pleasure than their Symposia.'[56] Such communion led Victorians to attribute to the Greeks a strange obsession with the future, notes Jenkyns; fancying himself an ancient, the Victorian had an insistent 'urge to buttonhole

---

[46] *Printing Press*, p. 190.
[47] 'Of vanitie', 3:246. See also Schiffman, 'Montaigne's perception of ancient Rome', p. 351.
[48] *Light in Troy*, p. 43.   [49] *Confessions*, Bk I (1781), p. 20.
[50] To John Wilkes, 3 Dec. 1746, British Library, Addison Mss 30.867 f.18.
[51] Andrews, *Voltaire*, pp. 42, 47.   [52] Mann, 'Freud and the future', p. 424.
[53] *History of Rome* (1811), 1:5.
[54] Landor, *Pericles and Aspasia* (1836); letters 141, 145, 154, 2:28, 36, 53. Shaftesbury likewise communed with Plato, Aristotle, Plotinus, Seneca, Marcus Aurelius, and Epictetus (Cassirer, *Philosophy of the Enlightenment*, p. 313).
[55] *Index Expurgatorius* (c. 1768–9), No. 30, 5:566.
[56] *Gryll Grange* (1861), p. 197. See Buxton, *Grecian Taste*, pp. 121–5.

one of those old Greeks and Romans and tell him what the future had in store'.[57] But retrospective prophecy did not spare them humanist pathos; as Hazlitt wistfully put it, 'We are always talking of the Greeks and Romans; – *they* never said any thing of us.'[58]

Communing with great figures from the past still holds appeal. 'Newton, Cromwell, Byron, Milton, Tennyson, Pepys, Darwin: You ought to try living with them some time', an American university tempts students to its summer programme in Cambridge. 'Sit under the same apple tree that gave Sir Isaac Newton a headache – and the world the theory of gravitation. Stroll through the courts, quads, and pathways that inspired Milton, Pepys and Tennyson.'[59] Perhaps the habit endures longest in the New World; an English historian marvels that Virginians still talk about Jefferson as though he might at this moment be training his telescope on them from Monticello.[60] But at least one evocative variant is English: tracing back chains of forebears and mentors, correspondents to *The Times* revel in calculating their own hand-to-hand contact with antiquity.[61]

A few moderns still claim actual contact with precursors. Wilmarth Lewis, who spent most of his life immortalizing Horace Walpole, at times felt literally in touch with him. But such empathy is much rarer nowadays; few are steeped enough in the classics to claim Horace or Livy or Homer as intimates. And historical relativism distances even the most admired exemplars; only the naïve or the unschooled can now engage in whole-hearted communion with folk from any past.

Rumination

Musing over the vestiges of the past was a customary Romantic trait now more extinct than the ruins themselves. Relics of every kind once moved sensitive souls to the sublime and melancholy reflections discussed in Chapter 4. Ruins and tombstones, lichen and moss, decayed and eroded artifacts evoked associations between the observer's own impending demise and the transience of all life, the failure of memory, the futility of fame, the irretrievability of the past; and by the eighteenth century such vestiges acquired value as fragments in their own right. Diderot's reaction to Hubert Robert's paintings exemplifies the musings of his age – and underscores their remoteness from our own:

The ideas aroused in me by ruins are lofty . . . How old this world is! . . . Wherever I turn my eyes, the objects that surround me foretell an end and help me resign myself to the one that awaits me. What is my ephemeral existence compared to that of this stone collapsing with antiquity, of this deepening valley, of this forest tottering with age![62]

Ruins long remained evocative, and traces of that taste survive in modern fondness for the fragmentary, the indistinct, the suggestively incomplete.[63] But physical decay today spurs no contemplations like Diderot's, and the sentimentality that once accompanied such reflections is even more outdated. We view the greatest scenes of antiquity with a

---

[57] *Victorians and Ancient Greece*, p. 52.   [58] 'Schlegel on the drama' (1816), 16:66.
[59] UCLA Extension advertisement, *N.Y. Review of Books*, 22 Jan. 1981, p. 20.
[60] Pole, 'American past: is it still usable?' p. 63.
[61] Bernard Levin, 'How to shake hands with a legend', *The Times*, 5 Mar. 1980, p. 16, and letters of 8, 11, 14, 20, 26 Mar., and 'Times diary', 1 Apr. 1980.
[62] *Salons* (1767), 3:228–9. See Carlson, *Hubert Robert*, p. 21.
[63] M. W. Thompson, *Ruins*, p. 95; Jencks, 'Introduction', *Post-Modern Classicism*, pp. 10–12.

drier eye than, for example, Burne-Jones, who returned from an 1854 pilgrimage to the Godstow Abbey ruins, the burial place of the 'Fair Rosamund', 'in a delirium of joy' induced by 'pictures of the old days, the abbey, and long processions of the faithful, banners of the cross, copes and crosiers, gay knights and ladies by the river bank, hawking parties and all the pageantry of the golden age' in his mind's eye; 'it made me feel so wild and mad . . . I never remember having such an unutterable ecstasy'.[64] But the desperate search for a land of lost content that engaged the attention of poets ever since Words-worth's 'Tintern Abbey' has since given way to a merely antiquarian interest, the mild curiosity of 'some ruin-bibber, randy for antique', of Philip Larkin's 'Church Going'. Unlike Arnold, Hardy, or Eliot, Larkin finds the ancient church 'not in the least haunted, . . . merely old'; he observes it not as a participant but as an 'anthropologist who has accidentally happened upon a minor shrine of a dead civilization'.[65] Our attachment to reminders of the past is now less personal, less emotional, altogether less involved.[66]

CONSEQUENCES OF THE LOST PAST

Modern culture is . . . a titanic and deliberate effort to undo by technology, rationality, and governmental policy the givenness of what came down from the past.

Edward Shils, *Tradition*[67]

What do all these losses signify? The extinction of some modes of connection with the past – self-justifying traditionalism, for example – is no cause for regret. But the lapse of other modes grievously reduces our capacity to engage with what we have inherited. Some erosion of feeling was evident even before the end of the Renaissance: by the late sixteenth century 'the image of antiquity had been recovered but at the same time it ceased to speak directly to the modern world', writes Myron Gilmore. 'History was becoming academic. What it discovered might be archeologically true but it was irrelevant to the concerns of a later age.'[68] It was not only history's irrelevance that dismayed later generations. As historical knowledge undermined medieval certitudes, 'the past ceased to be a repository of true doctrines and became an incoherent heap of errors and inhumanities', in Richard Southern's words. The Renaissance and Enlightenment kept this realization at bay, as I have shown; not until late in the nineteenth century did the inadequacies of the whole framework of inherited ideas become widely apparent. Threatened with alienation from their past, Victorians found a remedy in the 'vigorous and sensitive cultivation of historical understanding', replacing 'intellectual certainty by an emotional cohesion within which all the experiences of the past could coexist'. Thus they could jettison the intellectual structure for an 'imaginative appropriation' of past experiences.[69]

Our own more comprehensive losses are less easily requited, nor have their implications for our treatment of the past been assessed. Much enlarged by scholarship, the past exerts

---

[64] Burne-Jones, *Memorials*, 1:97.

[65] Larkin, *Less Deceived*, pp. 28–9; Clausen, 'Tintern Abbey to Little Gidding', pp. 422–3.

[66] 'We have many accounts of people at mid-[nineteenth] century being moved to tears by a Thomas Cole landscape, so great were its religious and philosophical associations. The same painting today is viewed with a dryer eye' (Reiff, 'Memorial Hall', p. 40).

[67] 1981, p. 197.   [68] *Humanists and Jurists*, p. 37.

[69] Southern, 'Aspects of the European tradition of historical writing: 4. the sense of the past', p. 244.

as strong a fascination as ever; but current knowledge of its legacy is as restricted as our ways of using it are curtailed. In the United States, the public evinces an insatiable appetite for history while the numbers of trained historians dwindle; majors in history declined during the 1960s and 1970s from 10 to barely 2 per cent of university graduates. Historical thinking may have entered the American blood but has little place in the American mind, John Lukacs concludes.[70] In France, the popularity of a few historians rivals that of film stars but historical ignorance is rife. Throughout Western Europe from the fifteenth up to the twentieth century, an art historian judges, 'the understanding of the past was . . . more subtle and varied than is our own'.[71]

Above all, we have lost the wellnigh universal tradition of the educated: intimate acquaintance with the classical and Scriptural past. Access to much of history requires an informed appreciation of the classics, observes Jenkyns, if we are 'to understand how the minds of those who governed, thought, created or invented were furnished'.[72] But this once living tradition has become a sterile academic preserve. 'In 1921 ancient Greece was a sounding-board which teachers and preachers used to echo and magnify their live preoccupations; in the 1980s we behave as though it were a mausoleum to which only certified experts are allowed access, a necropolis to be cautiously and correctly described.'[73]

More than the Greek and Latin languages, more than a host of ancient texts and allusions, we have lost the whole richly peopled classical world that was for over four centuries the lingua franca of a large and influential elite. What that elite made and inspired – architecture, art, and literature – is the major part of our cultural landscape; but since classical emblems and associations suffuse all these creations, it is a landscape we now wander through like bewildered strangers from another planet. The churches and cathedrals, palaces and gardens, paintings and sculpture that have exalted a dozen generations still grace us with their evident glories; but few who see them are more than vaguely aware of their historical contexts and connotations.[74]

The classical and mythological allusions in Monteverdi's *Orfeo*, notes a recent explication of that opera, enhanced the appreciation of its original auditors in 1607; on the modern audience the same allusions are almost wholly lost. Most educated people of the seventeenth century knew, often by heart, the accounts of Orpheus in Ovid and Virgil. The classical legend that Orpheus's music could attract mountains and animals; Apollo's warning of the jealous Maenids who endangered Orpheus's life; the implications of Hades summoned up by Charon's mention of naked souls in torment – these were familiar

---

[70] 'Obsolete historians', p. 82. History graduates declined from 44,663 in 1971 to 18,301 in 1980–1 (*American Historical Association Perspectives*, 22:8 (1984), 3).

[71] Coolidge, 'Foreword', *Gods & Heroes*, p. 9.   [72] 'Keeping up Greek'.

[73] Taplin, 'Guide to the necropolis'. In the United States the necropolis has been sealed off for some time; of a Harvard comparative literature class in 1912, not one student in a hundred knew when Aristotle lived (though half a dozen guessed it was before 1840); the *Saturday Evening Post* lauded their ignorance, because 'knowing when Aristotle lived, or anything else about him, is one of the least profitable uses to which lay human brains can be put' (quoted in John Lukacs, *Outgrowing Democracy*, p. 297). Attractively packaged classical texts in translation now abound, but for most readers they are almost wholly sundered from their context (Arendt, 'Introduction: Walter Benjamin', p. 46).

[74] 'The educated public which shared knowledge of the ancient classics and the main works of world literature . . . has become so attenuated that the general culture of a university teacher is frequently little different from that of the ordinary intellectually uninterested graduate' (Shils, *Tradition*, p. 248). See Kubler, *Shape of Time*, pp. 29–30.

references then, and for three centuries thereafter. Today they are virtually meaningless to all but a few.[75] Like the libretti of Monteverdi's operas, the stones of Venice and the marbles of Michelangelo have become dimly apprehended wonders, mere fragments of a densely textured past now gone almost as irretrievably as its creators.

Many Freudian allusions likewise now fall on deaf ears because 'most readers have only a nodding acquaintance with classical European literature'. Key words that once 'carried deep meaning and were vibrant with specific humanistic resonances' have lost most of those connotations. In choosing the term 'Oedipus complex', for example, Freud 'assumed that his readers would be cultivated people who had been schooled in the classics, as he had been', writes Bruno Bettelheim; most no longer are and thus trivialize or simply misconceive the Oedipal metaphor.[76] What would Freud have made of today's students who cannot identify Socrates?

Scriptural tradition has become similarly attenuated. Well into the nineteenth century, Bible stories throughout Western Europe were invested with special mythic significance and were intimately interrelated with other forms of knowledge; the smallest details of the geography of Israel, as of Greece, 'imposed themselves on our consciousness until they [became] part of the map of our imaginative world'. That intimacy is now rare, Northrop Frye judges; and because 'a student of English literature who does not know the Bible does not understand a good deal of what is going on in what he reads', he continually misconstrues its meaning and implications.[77]

Merely to know *about* the past is not enough; what is needed is the sense of intimacy, the intensely familiar interaction with antiquity that was a distinguishing and self-defining mark of European thought. To know the past in this fashion demands T. S. Eliot's perception 'not only of the pastness of the past, but of its presence'.[78] Assiduous archaeologists, epigraphers, philologists, numismatists have vastly extended knowledge of the ancient world, but no generation since the Middle Ages ever held it in smaller regard; some advanced modernists are 'even prepared to dismiss the Parthenon as the sacred cow of a discredited past'.[79] No public leader today would exhort his constituents as did a Western Australia mayor at the turn of the century: 'Citizens of Perth, follow me and I will make this city a fairer Athens and a freer Rome.'[80]

Many explicitly rejected the classical tradition for its felt antithesis with modern technology, politics, and aesthetics. Industrial society was said to demand the training not of humanists but of technicians; egalitarianism ran counter to the aristocratic genius of Greek and Roman culture; the modernist cult of originality scorned anything bound by established rules or requiring long apprenticeship.[81] Beyond these antipathies, the Nietzschean view that history was futile and the past a destructive incubus suited the

---

[75] David Freeman, 'Some thoughts on *Orfeo*', programme notes for Monteverdi/Striggio, *Orfeo*, London: English National Opera, *c*.1981.

[76] *Freud and Man's Soul*, pp. 7–10. For Freud's own transformations of the Oedipus legend, see Schorske, *'Fin-de-Siècle' Vienna*, pp. 199–200; it was Freud's Oedipus, not that of the Greeks, who aimed to escape his fate and to acquire self-knowledge.

[77] *Great Code*, pp. 33, 229, 218, x.   [78] 'Tradition and the individual talent', p. 14.

[79] Kidson, 'Architecture and city planning', p. 376.

[80] W. G. Brookman (1900–1), quoted in Richards, 'Historic public gardens in Perth', p. 69 n.1.

[81] Marrou, 'Education and rhetoric', pp. 199–200. Deriving from Tullius's gradation of Roman society and use of the word for the first class only, 'classical' originally meant 'excellent' or 'choice'; hence it rightly suggests 'authority, discrimination, even snobbery' (Rykwert, *First Moderns*, p. 1).

weary decadence of late nineteenth-century Europe. *Fin-de-siècle* anti-traditionalism posited the worthlessness of the entire past. Rebellion against inherited forms reached anti-rational or even irrational levels early in the new century.[82] The very concept of history was resented for binding men to antiquated institutions, ideas, and values; now reduced to studying the past for its own sake, the historian became in modernist eyes an antiquarian fleeing from the present or a 'cultural necrophile'. Hostility to 'feverish rummaging among the ruins' expressed unconscious fear, in an atmosphere of impending doom, of a future too dreadful to contemplate.[83] Literature mirrored these suspicions: a surfeit of her husband's historical research stultified Ibsen's Hedda Gabler; obsessive concern with dead cultures made Gide's archaeologist acutely ill; history was the 'nightmare' from which Joyce's Stephen Dedalus sought to awake.[84]

Architects too found the past a crippling burden. Otto Wagner urged modern architects to liberate themselves from history, and the Viennese 'Secession' association aimed to break the manacles of tradition by creating a new, untrammelled style. In Wagner's view, the deadening eclecticism of Vienna's Ringstrasse exemplified failure to keep pace with social change; architects unable to respond to today's needs and circumstances had instead dredged up and reused all past styles.[85]

These modernist indictments made *fin-de-siècle* Europeans curiously like Strehlow's Australian aborigines:

Since every feature of the landscape . . . in central Australia is already associated with one or another of these [ancestral] myths, . . . the thoroughness of their forefathers had left them not a single unoccupied scene which they could fill with creatures of their own imagination. The present-day natives are on the whole merely the painstaking, uninspired preservers of a great and interesting tradition. They live almost entirely on the traditions of their forefathers.[86]

Spokesmen for the new gloried in trying to scuttle the whole corpus of inherited European culture. Tired of obeisance to an encumbering past, early twentieth-century leaders in the arts defiantly broke with it – discarding exemplars, denying forerunners, denouncing reverence for tradition. Abstraction in painting, atonal music, stream-of-consciousness in fiction, *vers libre* in poetry all reflected convictions that the old repertory of forms no longer spoke to the meaning of modern life.[87] And the cult of originality

---

[82] Harbison, *Deliberate Regression*, p. 176; Shils, *Tradition*, pp. 231–7; Lears, *No Place of Grace*, p. 5; Conn, *Divided Mind*, p. 13; Hughes, *Consciousness and Society*, p. 338. As noted in Chapter 5, there is a correlation between the ends of centuries and the peculiarity of our imagination, that it always chooses to be at the end of an era. The death of Nietzsche and the publication of Freud's *Interpretation of Dreams*, of Husserl's *Logic*, of Russell's critical exposition of Leibniz, and of Planck's quantum theory, combined to give '1900, like 1400 and 1600 and 1000, . . . the look of a year that ends a *saeculum*' (Kermode, *Sense of an Ending*, pp. 96–8).

[83] Hayden White, 'Burden of history', pp. 125, 119. See Harpham, 'Time running out: the Edwardian sense of cultural degeneration'; Rasch, 'Literary decadence', pp. 213–15.

[84] *Hedda Gabler* (1890) (see Saari, 'Hedda Gabler; the past recaptured'); *Immoralist* (1902), pp. 52–3, 137–8, 145; *Ulysses* (1922), p. 42. For the pessimistic fatalism that commenced with the 1880s, see Stephen Kern, *Culture of Time and Space*, p. 327 n.45.

[85] Inaugural address, Vienna Academy of Fine Arts, 1894, and *Moderne Architektur* (1895), in Schorske, '*Fin-de-Siècle*' Vienna, pp. 82–4.

[86] *Aranda Traditions*, p. 6.

[87] Malcolm Bradbury and McFarlane, 'Name and nature of Modernism', p. 26; Cahm, 'Revolt, conservatism and reaction in Paris, 1905–25'; Kubler, *Shape of Time*, p. 70; Toliver, *Past That Poets Make*, p. 162. 'We are now concerned . . . with an abrupt end with all tradition . . . The aim of five centuries of European effort is openly abandoned' (Herbert Read, *Art Now* (1933), pp. 57–9).

continues to narrow experience to what we regard as new. Readers of poetry today 'listen to hear a distinctive voice', writes Harold Bloom, and unless it is 'differentiated from its precursors ... we tend to stop listening'.[88]

Modernists literally swept away models of past excellence. During the 1920s and 1930s American museums and art schools consigned historical cast collections to the scrap-heap; Gombrich recalls a Midwestern university where casts 'were thrown out of the window and smashed in a belated ritual of liberation'.[89] Nothing should be treasured so long that it became old: 'Written poetry is worth reading once and then should be destroyed', prescribed the surrealist Antonin Artaud. 'Let the dead poets give way to the living.'[90]

The Futurist ideology embodying these views first arose in northern Italian cities – Turin, Genoa, Milan – transformed by industrialization over a few short years. The bizarre survival of antique and Renaissance forms in a landscape of radical technological change may help to explain Futurist manifestoes against the past.[91] Why 'waste all your best powers in this eternal and futile worship of the past?' asked the poet Marinetti. He boasted of having 'provoked a growing nausea for the antique, for the worm-eaten and moss-grown' in seeking 'to free this land from its smelly gangrene of professors, archeologists, ciceroni and antiquarians. For too long has Italy been a dealer in second-hand clothes. We mean to free her from the numberless museums that cover her like so many graveyards'.[92] In place of the outmoded past Marinetti worshipped mechanical transience and speed, terming a roaring motor car more beautiful than the Hellenistic *Winged Victory of Samothrace* in the Louvre.[93]

Futurist tastes soon gained architectural expression. Sant'Elia proscribed preserving, restoring, or copying ancient monuments, for modern technology had banished 'the monumental, the massive, the static' in favour of light, elastic, expendable architecture. 'Our houses will last less time than we do, and every generation will have to make its own.'[94] Similar echoes of Hawthorne's imprecations against old buildings came from other modernist architects. 'We throw the out-of-date tool on the scrap-heap', wrote Le Corbusier; architects must likewise get rid of the 'old and hostile environment [with its] stifling accumulation of age-long detritus'.[95] In futurist and modernist eyes, twentieth-century life rendered all past architecture obsolete; only styles newly created could express the uniquely new perspectives. 'Modern life and art are removing the oppression of the

---

[88] *Anxiety of Influence*, p. 148.
[89] 'Perfection's progress', p. 3. For similar episodes, see H. H. Reed, 'Classical tradition in modern times', p. 25.
[90] *Théâtre et son double* (c. 1933), 4:94. See de Man, *Blindness and Insight*, p. 147.
[91] Banham, *Theory and Design in the First Machine Age*, pp. 100–1; Carrà, 'Idea of art and the idea of life'.
[92] 'Founding and manifesto of Futurism' (1909); 'Birth of a Futurist aesthetic' (1911–15); 'Founding and manifesto', in his *Selected Writings*, pp. 43, 81, 42. Enlightenment visitors had indignantly contrasted Italy's ignoble present with her glorious past (Venturi, 'History and reform in the middle of the eighteenth century', p. 223).
[93] 'Founding and manifesto', p. 41. See also Lynton, 'Futurism'; Rawson, 'Italian Futurism'. Frank Lloyd Wright echoed Marinetti's admiration for the ocean liner, the plane, and the car (Conn, *Divided Mind*, pp. 221–4).
[94] *Messaggio* (1914) and *Città nuova* (1914), quoted in Banham, *First Machine Age*, pp. 129, 135. See Frampton, *Critical History of Modern Architecture*, pp. 84–9.
[95] *Towards a New Architecture* (1923), pp. 17, 268.

past', believed Mondrian, enabling people to escape from the tyrannical influence of old buildings.[96]

Bias against the past dominated architectural theory and practice well beyond the Second World War. 'The post-war era is the first to abandon confidence not just in the styles of previous ages, but in almost its entire building legacy', states Marcus Binney. 'No previous age has ever indulged in such wholesale condemnation of the architecture of the past.' Modernists banned references to existing and past buildings and put classical and Gothic tradition alike beyond the pale of current practice, denying students the experience of working with and imitating precedents.[97]

Two generations of modernism left a body of artists and architects, not to mention their clients, largely unfamiliar with classical and other legacies of Western culture. Many now deplore that hiatus. 'To cut ourselves off from this tradition in the mindless pursuit of novelty and orginality is to alienate ourselves from culture', judges Allen Greenberg. 'One might as well jettison the English language, with its unrivalled heritage and power of expression, in order to communicate in ... Esperanto.'[98] Recalling Lewis Mumford's embarrassment in the 1950s that so praiseworthy a monument as New York's Pennsylvania Station 'should be sheathed in classical garb', an architectural historian suggests that perhaps it 'was so good not in spite of its being classical ... but because it was classical'; Penn Station 'made sense on Seventh Avenue' because it had 'made sense in Rome'.[99] The languages of historical architecture 'carry very few overtones that are commonly understood', concludes Robin Middleton; 'the inferences, the subtle inflexions, of past usage have not been recorded and have been lost. We have become, quite simply, illiterate.'[100]

But newly felt nostalgia for time-honoured traditions seldom envisions creative exemplars for the present and future; instead it aims mostly to preserve past lineaments, whether glorious or familiar. And even that aim is jeopardized by ignorance. 'Forty years of the modern movement have left us with virtually no architects less than 60 years old who have been brought up with a knowledge of classical architecture – a knowledge necessary to cope with the current pressure of conservation of buildings'.[101] At Yale in the late 1940s, Vincent Scully remembers 'a whole bunch of old gentlemen who had been trained in the Beaux Arts – the great academic classical tradition – who had tenure so they couldn't be fired, but they didn't have any students. Nobody paid any attention to them. Now everybody wishes they were around again.'[102]

The breathtaking new world the modernists substituted for the old now strikes many as

---

[96] *Liberation from Oppression of Art and Life* (1941), quoted in Tafuri, *Theories and History of Architecture*, p. 38. Classicism deeply absorbed such modernists as Le Corbusier and Mies van der Rohe, to be sure; but classical models interested them mainly as exemplifications of beginnings and of timelessness, and their use of them was rhetorical, not contextual (Curtis, 'Modern transformation of classicism'; Searing, 'Speaking a new classicism', pp. 11–13).

[97] Binney, 'Oppression to obsession', p. 210; Machado, 'Old buildings as palimpsest', p. 48.

[98] 'A sense of the past: an architectural perspective', p. 48.

[99] Goldberger, *On the Rise: Architecture and Design in the Postmodern Age*, p. 30. Ever since the 1893 Chicago World's Fair, in Mumford's view, 'the white cloud of classicism hung poisonously over the whole country' ('A backward glance', in his *Roots of Contemporary American Architecture*, p. 14).

[100] 'Use and abuse of tradition in architecture', p. 732.

[101] Cecil Elsom, quoted in David White, 'Don't shoot the architect', *New Society*, 21 June 1978, pp. 707–8.

[102] James Lardner, 'Vincent Scully', *IHT*, 5 Apr. 1983, p. 16.

103 Post-modern classical: Charles Moore, Piazza d'Italia, New Orleans, 1978 (Alan Karchmer)

inhuman, sterile, unliveable. The past two decades have witnessed growing reaction against avant-garde amnesia: historical eclecticism in the arts, traditionalism in literature, post-modern classicism in architecture. The last vogue illustrates both the enduring pull of antiquity and the difficulty of resuming intimacy with it after the modernist breach. Architects employ classical motifs in a witty or ironic way, as if embarrassed to be caught admiring them.[103] They 'may be rediscovering the past, but their knowledge of it is still so spotty, their enthusiasm so arbitrary and episodic, that a lot of what we are getting is do-it-yourself history'.[104] Philip Johnson's 'Chippendale' skyscraper in New York uses classical elements for new decorative effects, and Charles Moore's stainless steel and neon Piazza d'Italia in New Orleans provides a stunning classical collage; but neither displays the assured synthesis of pre-modernist forerunners at ease with an established tradition, who sought to capture the spirit of the past, not to revive its

---

[103] Jencks, 'Introduction', *Post-Modern Classicism*. One architect thinks 'irony is indispensable to any attempt to use classical vocabulary today . . . If the object is not clearly *intended* as ironic, it can only become the *object* of irony itself' (Edward S. Levin, in *Speaking a New Classicism*, p. 36).

[104] Huxtable, 'Troubled state of modern architecture', p. 26.

details.[105] Despite a dazzling spectrum of techniques – direct quotation and indirect allusion, faithful reproduction and tantalizing inversion – post-modernists rarely seem at home with antique exemplars. Condemning rival classic revivalism as 'a fad pretending to relate to the past' by means of 'stylistic caprice' or 'ornamental provocation', a spokesman for Ricardo Bofill's Taller de Arquitectura unconsciously parodies his firm's Marne-la-Vallée complex as 'the Cape Canaveral of the Classical space age'.[106]

Unfamiliarity with the past is a marked deficiency of the space age. A civilization sure of its values would not need to stress references to canonical texts and monuments, Gombrich argues; because 'our own past is moving away from us at such frightening speed, ... to keep open the lines of communication which permit us to understand the greatest creations of mankind we must study and teach the history of culture more deeply and more intensely than was necessary a generation ago, when many more of such resonances were still to be expected as a matter of course'.[107] Post-modern classicists continually refer to ancient monuments and reproduce their characteristics, but often fail to convey their essential meaning. Treating the past as a spare-parts warehouse, in Moshe Safdie's phrase, they select historical motifs out of context and in ignorance or defiance of their origins and relationships.[108] But history is a gathering body of experience, not a 'stylistic warehouse'; arbitrary reference or quotation is a poor substitute for the temporal associations inherent in traditional buildings. 'The leaders of the profession today seem to be trivializing the past', concludes an architectural historian, 'they are composing with fragmentary rubbish; historical study has not served to enlarge their perceptions or strengthen their powers. They are merely proliferating the motifs and elements of the past.'[109]

Post-modern classicism has scarcely begun to reconnect with history. 'Turning in despair towards a past without any idea of how to use it', writes Manfredo Tafuri, modern Italian architects salvage not history but their own emotions, nostalgia, autobiographical incidents, their 'rescue' of history merely 'a gutless and indecisive attempt to get free from the *tradition of the new*'.[110] Indeed, post-modern classicism is so eclectic that it seems to embrace *any* historically derivative style 'that contemporary architects evoke or mis-quote'.[111]

Another symptom of the loss of the past is the unstructured eclecticism of our historical interest. Our tradition is no longer an organized historical corpus but a pot-pourri of everything that ever happened, in which a 1930s cinema attracts the same degree and type of interest as the Parthenon. 'We appear to be living', in Loren Eiseley's words, 'amidst a

---

[105] Longstreth, 'Academic eclecticism in American architecture', pp. 78–80; Huxtable, 'Is modern architecture dead?' On the Piazza d'Italia, see 'Place debate' (1984), including a local Italian–American reaction: 'We just wish he would have done something more Sicilian, and not quite so Roman' (p. 17).

[106] Searing, 'Speaking a new classicism', pp. 9–10; Peter Hodgkinson, in 'TA talk to AR', *Architectural Review*, 121:6 (1982), 32. See Annabelle d'Huart, 'Los espacios de Abraxas', in *Ricardo Bofill: Taller de Arquitectura*, Barcelona: Gustavo Gili, 1984, pp. 32–43.

[107] 'Research in the humanities: ideals and idols', p. 2; *In Search of Cultural History*, quotation on p. 45.

[108] Rossi, 'The Greek Order', p. 19; Safdie, 'Private jokes in public places', p. 68. Few observers questioned in a recent study caught the intended historical associations of modern historicist buildings (Groat and Canter, 'Does Post-Modernism communicate?' p. 87).

[109] Middleton, 'Use and abuse of tradition in architecture', p. 736.

[110] *Theories and History of Architecture*, pp. 54, 52, 59.

[111] Nicholas Penny, 'Cross purposes', *TLS*, 3 Apr. 1981, p. 383. 'Buildings which would have been called variations on the modern a decade ago are now hailed as classical' (Reed, 'Classical tradition in modern times' (1981), p. 25).

meaningless mosaic of fragments. From ape skull to Mayan temple we contemplate the miscellaneous debris of time like sightseers to whom these mighty fragments, fallen gateways, and sunken galleys convey no present instruction.'[112]

Unwilling or unable to incorporate the legacy of the past into our own creative acts, we concentrate instead on saving its remaining vestiges. The less integral the role of the past in our lives, the more imperative the urge to preserve its relics. Because we seldom understand what those relics meant, what part they played, what aspirations they reflected, what values they embodied in the active life of the past, we do little more than simply save them. They no longer belong to our actual world; they no longer stimulate artists and architects to create anew; they no longer form part of a living past, however much we respect their survival or yearn to adapt them to modern uses. Because earlier modes of response to the past are now closed to us, because much of what survives is now foreign to us, preservation has become the principal, often the exclusive, way of deriving sustenance from our heritage.

PRESERVATION

In a world of concrete, Concorde and computers, it is vital that we preserve what remains of individuality. If everything were modern, everywhere would look pretty much the same.

Timothy Cantell, 'Why care about old buildings?'[113]

It was natural to be nineteenth century in the nineteenth century, and anyone could do it, but in the twentieth it takes quite a lot of toil.

Malcolm Bradbury and Michael Orsler,
'Department of amplification'[114]

A civilization which tends to conserve is a civilization in decline.

Pierre Boulez, *Conversations with Célestin Deliège*[115]

The crusade for cultural amnesia coincided with the rise of nostalgic time travel (Chapter 1) and the manipulation of history as a commodity (Chapter 6); all three trends converge in the impulse to preserve. But the modern passion for preservation reflects a half millennium of changing attitudes and artifacts. This section surveys the current state of preservation, explains why it became prominent, summarizes its supposed benefits and alleged risks, and reviews its broader implications.

Preserving material objects is not the only way to conserve a heritage. The great Ise Shinto temple in Japan is dismantled every twenty years and replaced by a faithful replica built of similar materials exactly as before. Physical continuity signifies less to the Japanese than perpetuating the techniques and rituals of re-creation; craftsmen trained in the old

---

[112] *Unexpected Universe*, p. 6. 'The vast increase in our knowledge of the past [has made] all pasts essentially comparable in both completeness and complexity' (L. B. Meyer, *Music the Arts and Ideas*. p. 192). See Ong, *Rhetoric, Romance, and Technology*, pp. 325–6.
[113] 1980, p. 7.   [114] 1960, p. 59.   [115] 1975, p. 33.

skills are themselves designated 'Living National Treasures' – prized exemplars of cultural heritage.[116]

The Japanese thus avoid the dilemma inherent in conserving objects – its ultimate impossibility. Everything we think of as 'preserved' is more or less altered; it is really the form that endures, not the substance. And most things are identified on that basis. A barrel whose original hoops and staves have all been replaced remains for us the same old barrel. Chemistry ceaselessly transforms the constituents of all artifacts, yet we go on seeing them as originals until their final dissolution: a building or a pair of shoes remains that building and those shoes from the moment of their making until the building falls into rubble, the shoes into rubbish.

Living things likewise keep their identity despite obvious physical replacement. Trees annually lose and grow new leaves, are reshaped by growth and decay, and may be transplanted elsewhere; yet they remain recognizeable entities. We too retain identities over a lifetime, experiencing remembered and present selves, however altered, as the same individual.[117] The concept of conservation thus goes far beyond the acts of material preservation on which Western societies concentrate their efforts.

Scope

Only in this generation has saving the tangible past become a major global enterprise. Vestiges of the past, whole, dismembered, or discernable only in traces, lie everywhere around us, yet throughout history men have mainly overlooked most of these remnants. Taking their collective material inheritance much for granted, they have allowed antiquity to survive, to decay, or to disappear as the laws of nature and the whims of their fellow men dictated.

Instances of preservation can be documented from time immemorial, to be sure, and certain remnants – interred mortal remains, relics of religious faith, tangible icons of power – are habitually treasured. But to retain a substantial portion of the past is signally a latter-day goal. Only with the nineteenth century did European nations closely identify themselves with their material heritage, and only in the twentieth have they launched major programmes to protect it. And concerted efforts to secure relics against destruction and decay have come mainly in the past few decades.

Preservation is now a ubiquitous crusade; virtually every state strives to safeguard its

---

[116] Kobayashi, 'Case of the Ise Grand Shinto temple in Japan'. Sixty-six Living National Treasures on government stipends include potters, lacquer-makers, wood-workers, weavers, paper-makers, swordsmiths, silk-dyers, temple-bell makers, and performers in Kabuki, Noh, and Bunraki (puppet) theatres and on ancient string instruments (Christine Chapman, 'Living national treasures: cultural anachronisms who keep a rich heritage alive for the future', *IHT*, 21 Mar. 1983, p. 12). See Arnheim, 'On duplication', p. 237; Margolis, 'Art, forgery, and authenticity', p. 166.

[117] 'An oak, that grows from a small plant to a large tree, is still the same oak; tho' there be not one particle of matter, or figure of its parts the same' (David Hume, *Treatise of Human Nature*, Bk I, Pt 4, sect. 6, 1:538). See Fain, *Between Philosophy and History*, pp. 74–80; E. A. Freeman, *Preservation and Restoration*, pp. 38–9; Wiggins, *Identity and Spatio-Temporal Continuity*, pp. 8–18; Chisholm, *Person and Object*, pp. 89–113. Yet to learn the identity of someone we used to know, after having first failed to recognize him, is an admission that the person one remembers no longer exists, and 'that what is now here is a person whom one did not know to exist'; Proust is dumbfounded that a name 'could be used to describe both the fair-haired girl, the marvellous waltzer, whom I had known in the past, and the massive white-haired lady making her way through the room with elephantine tread' (*Remembrance of Things Past*, 3:982).

104 The humble past reclaimed: Sawyers' Hall, Erdigg, Clwyd, Wales (John Bethell)

historic monuments. Attachments are manifest where antiquities are ancient and abundant as well as where they are rare and largely recent, under communist or capitalist regimes, by former imperial powers along with newly liberated colonies. A proliferation of agencies – the International Council of Museums (ICOM), the International Council on Monuments and Sites (ICOMOS), the International Centre for the Study of the Preservation and the Restoration of Cultural Property (ICCROM), the International Institute for Conservation of Historic and Architectural Works (IIC), the World Heritage Convention – attest the global character of concern for tangible heritage.

The growth of preservation has been most spectacular in the realm of old buildings. Groups devoted to the architectural legacy multiplied many times over during the 1960s and 1970s. In the United States, preservation in 1960 was still the hobby of a small well-to-do elite; by 1980 more than half of American construction work involved rehabilitation, and in fiscal year 1983 more than two billion dollars' worth of such projects received preservation tax credits.[118] Almost two-thirds of a recent Harvard College alumni class were engaged in restoring old houses – an avocation that the previous generation of graduates had deemed highly eccentric.[119] In Britain the demand for old houses is intense: half the population seems to be seeking converted old barns, watermills, or oast houses. The number of historic structures potentially protected by listing exceeded 300,000 in 1984 and is scheduled to reach half a million by 1987, 4 per cent of Britain's building stock.[120] Eastern Europe exhibits similar trends: Prague spent over six times as much on historic preservation in 1980 as in 1964.[121]

Buildings deemed worth saving have become more various as well as more numerous. The conserved past now includes structures as recent as the 1960s, representative together with archetypal features, homes of the humble along with mansions of the mighty, landmarks cherished for local familiarity in addition to monuments of universal renown. And preservation reaches beyond individual structures to embrace neighbourhoods and entire towns. Landscapes too rank as precious relics: Egdon Heath in Dorset, its unique flora and its association with Thomas Hardy both threatened by nuclear power, is termed 'as irreplaceable as a Gothic cathedral'.[122]

What warrants preservation expands with what is thought historically significant. Unsung figures and events gain fresh stature; entire aspects of the past become newly worth saving. The homes of presidents and patriots, battle sites and frontier forts used to be America's major shrines; preservation priorities now focus on industry, the arts, and hitherto neglected minorities. Tourists at antebellum plantation houses throng restored slave huts once shunted aside as historically embarrassing; servants' quarters at National

---

[118] *Preservation News*, 27:1 (1983), p. 3. See my 'Conserving the heritage: Anglo-American comparisons', pp. 228–33; Lee, 'Profiteers vs. antiquarians'.

[119] Lukacs, 'Obsolete historians', p. 80. Harvard's Class of '68 were surveyed in 1980.

[120] SPAB *Annual Report*, 1981–2, p. 5. There may be as many as 750,000 protected buildings by 1987, for one listing often includes several structures (Richard Griffith, Greater London Council, Historic Building Division, lecture at University College London, 30 Jan. 1984).

[121] Carter, *Conservation Problems of Historic Cities in Eastern Europe*, p. 32. See *idem*, 'Balkan historic cities'; Tarnoczi, 'Conservation et reintegration des monuments historiques . . . en Hongrie', pp. 19–30; Lorentz, 'Protection of monuments'.

[122] Christopher Booker, 'The nuclear threat to Hardy's heath', *The Times*, 20 Feb. 1982, p. 6. The heaths of Hardy's childhood in fact became collectively 'Egdon' in his writings (Hawkins, *Hardy's Wessex*, pp. 24–5, 46–8).

Trust houses attract British visitors whose parents, a generation ago, had eyes only for the sumptuous and the aristocratic.[123]

Preservation efforts formerly reserved for features of renown and widely venerated monuments are now extended to everyday neighbourhoods of purely local import. 'The locality where we belong . . . is a centre of reassurance [identifiable] more by the tenacity of its users than by its architecture', writes Lionel Brett. 'It may even be ugly, will generally be shabby, will invariably be overcrowded . . . Civic societies passionately defend its every cobblestone', but they defend 'more than bricks and mortar; it is the need for what Simone Weil called *l'Enracinement*, rootedness.'[124] Many communities wish to save structures and scenes that would never qualify as 'aesthetic' or 'historic', perhaps not even as pleasant or comfortable. Preservation in this spirit extends to the industrial landscape, embracing not just factories but entire working-class towns. 'Our identity lies in this urban industrial past', says the originator of America's first urban historic park, Lowell, Massachusetts; Lowell's revival secures the collective heritage of the city's inhabitants as a 'confirmation of their past'.[125]

Yet congeniality remains a prime motive for preserving; most survivals are treasured for their beauty or harmony. Attractiveness, variety, and historical assocations were the main reasons people in Guildford wanted old buildings conserved.[126] Historic buildings offer 'a richer source of environmental well-being than contemporary architecture', concludes a large-scale study of English preferences.[127] Three out of four first-time British buyers wanted older houses than they had, a recent building society survey shows; fewer than one in four who sought Victorian houses could get them.[128]

Surviving older buildings are found gracious and liveable for good reasons: because the materials used in their construction usually exceed closely calculated modern minimum requirements, they are often stronger, roomier, warmer in winter, cooler in summer, and better insulated against noise and vibration than new buildings. 'The average minimum standard mid-20th-century house', concludes the American National Trust, 'is certainly no match in general soundness to the average 19th-century house', and shoddy post-war housing in Britain likewise deteriorates much faster than what remains from Victorian times.[129]

Not every relic is seemly or desirable, to be sure. Like the past in general, inherited property is a mixed blessing; along with 'the Old Master over the carved surround of the saloon fireplace, each perhaps with a high intrinsic merit', the old family mansion contains 'the peeling wallpaper in the servant's bedroom'.[130] Survivals may be simultaneously adored and detested. Picking his way through cabbages, diesel six-wheelers, and theatre

[123] Martin Drury, National Trust, interview 12 Sept. 1978. See Waterson, *Servants' Hall*, pp. 9–18.
[124] Brett, *Parameters and Images*, p. 143. For the distinction between 'public images' and 'fields of care', see Tuan, 'Space and place', pp. 237–45.
[125] Patrick Mogan, paraphrased in Jane Holtz Kay, 'Lowell, Mass. – new birth for us all', *The Nation*, 17 Sept. 1977, p. 246. See Lowell, Mass., *Lowell Historic Canal District Commission*, 1977, App. 2, pp. 70–84.
[126] Bishop, 'Perception and Importance of Time in Architecture', Table 28, p. 218.
[127] Colin Morris, 'Townscape Images', p. 268. See *idem*, 'Townscape images: a study in meaning', pp. 267, 269, 274, 283–4.
[128] Alliance Building Survey, 1978, cited in Jenny Freeman, 'Mortgage myopia', p. 293.
[129] Stephen, *Rehabilitating Old Houses* (1976), p. 2; Jon Nordheimer, 'London 1983: everything is falling down', *IHT*, 29 July 1983, pp. 1–2.
[130] Faulkner, 'Philosophy for the preservation of our historic heritage', p. 455.

props in old Covent Garden, Tom Baistow conceived 'a preservationist's passion for this tight-packed, smelly, rakishly scruffy and vital corner of London that was only equalled by a deep conviction ... that the whole bloody lot ought to be bulldozed'.[131] A writer who termed Lancashire quixotic in 'clinging to its vast, old industrial monuments' none the less urged their retention, for 'in fighting to remove the greyness of its economy, it would be a pity to tamper with its soul'. Even the soul may perish in north-of-England weather, however; Mancunian rain so depressed one lover of the past that she sympathized with 'the perverse mentality of the dyed-in-the-wood Labour councillor who advocated removing all evidence of Victorian and Edwardian times from the town'.[132]

Buildings are the chief catalyst of collective historical identity because they seem intrinsic to their surroundings and outlast most other relics.[133] But preservation interest also embraces manuscripts and motor cars, silent films and steam engines; many if not most household objects are cherished for the sense of heritage, of antiquity, of continuity their presence confers. The valued past ranges from the greatest monuments to the most trifling memorabilia, and from the most enduring remains to the merest shadows of what things once were. Virtually any old thing which twenty years ago would have been junked today finds a place both in popular history and in collectors' hearts. We are well on the way to salvaging every kind of survival either for functional reuse or as souvenirs.

Different motives, to be sure, animate lovers of architectural relics, archaeological sites, ancient landscapes, antiques and collectables of various kinds. But whatever the specific focus, their aims have much in common.[134] Relics saved enhance our sense of history, link us with our own and other people's pasts, and shed glory on nations, neighbourhoods, and individuals. Amidst bewildering novelty, historic sites and antique objects spell security, ancient bricks and mortar offer tangible assurances of stability. From photo-enshrined mantels and antiques-laden parlours to conserved Pompeii and restored Williamsburg, preservation provides havens imbued with the peace or the thrill, the majesty or the intimacy, of *some* past. To halt demolition and stave off erosion approaches a precious permanence, a virtual immortality that defies the tooth of time.

Origins and motives

The urge to preserve derives from several interrelated presumptions: that the past was unlike the present; that its relics are necessary to our identity and desirable in themselves; and that tangible remains are a finite and dwindling commodity. So swift is the pace of change, so conspicuously does the present differ from even the recent past, so precious and fragile seems much of our material legacy, that we forget how recent are these facets of awareness. For many millennia most people lived under much the same circumstances as their forebears, were little aware of historical change, and scarcely differentiated past from present. Men were hard put to distinguish other times from

---

[131] 'The Covent Garden to come', *New Statesman*, 19 Apr. 1968, p. 511.
[132] Dennis Johnson, 'Masochism in Lancashire', ibid., 1 Mar. 1968, p. 262; Anne Angus, 'What's wrong with the North?' *New Society*, 13 July 1967, p. 55.
[133] Parent, 'Doctrine for the conservation and preservation of monuments and sites', p. 47.
[134] Csikszentmihalyi and Rochberg-Halton, *Meaning of Things*, pp. 62–96, give various reasons for attachments to old furniture, art works, photographs, books, plates, and silver.

their own.[135] Few sought to preserve, if only because the sense of the past as a state of things no longer existing had not yet emerged; to medieval man the great Gothic architectural works 'did not represent a past state of things, but a present', as E. A. Freeman observed.[136] Indeed, until the twentieth century, in C. P. Snow's view, social change had been 'so slow, that it would pass unnoticed in one person's lifetime'.[137]

The disjunction of past from present became significantly apparent only during the Renaissance, when rapport with antiquity made humanists exaggerate the unlikeness of more recent medieval times, as we saw in Chapter 3, and feel poignantly their remoteness from ancient Rome. But for all their attachment to the classical past, humanists took little interest in preserving its surviving remnants. Antiquarians strove to safeguard classical manuscripts and inscriptions, but that concern seldom extended to other material remains; the rescue of saintly relics consoled Flavio Biondo for the loss of classical architecture.[138] Admirers of antiquity were less apt to save ancient temples and sculptures than to mine them for their own creations: to extract marble from an old ruin was cheaper than to import it from Carrara. Rome's marble cutters and lime burners were virtually licensed destroyers of ancient monuments, even taxed for the purpose by the Holy See.[139]

But it was the passion for rebuilding along classical lines, Roberto Weiss concludes, that destroyed most of what was left of ancient Rome. Works begun under Pope Nicholas V (1447–55) eliminated any vestiges of antiquity that stood in the way of a straightened road or a new church. Pius II deplored the neglected state of Rome's ruins and issued a bull to protect them in 1462, but tore down the eastern colonnade of the Portico of Octavia and other ancient monuments to use their stones in new Vatican buildings. Sixtus IV (1471–84) curtailed the export of ancient statues and building stones and founded the Vatican antiquities collection, but did nothing to stop the demolition of the Temple of Hercules in the 'Forum Boarium' and the conversion into cannon-balls of other antique remains. The famed 'Meta Romuli' pyramid made way in 1499 for the new Via Alessandrina, and Leo X (1513–21) sacrificed other ancient buildings to straighten the road to the Capitol. Distressed to see 'the corpse of this noble city ... so grievously torn and disfigured', Raphael persuaded Leo X to stop quarrying antiquities for St Peter's, and was formally authorized in 1515 to halt the destruction, but his powers were nugatory, and the conservation programme was abandoned after his death in 1520.[140] And even Raphael had sought to preserve antiquities not for their own sake but as inspirations for future efforts, to 'keep alive the examples of the ancients so as to equal and surpass them'.[141]

To be sure, ancient buildings still in use – the Pantheon, Castel Sant' Angelo, the Capitol – were frequently repaired and restored, but aside from Raphael almost no one

---

[135] 'Words and phrases by which we express our sense that the past was not the same, but something different from the present, ... are all of them modern, and most of them, indeed, of very recent introduction' (Logan Pearsall Smith, *English Language*, p. 227).

[136] *Preservation and Restoration* (1852), p. 15. See Michael Hunter, 'Germanic and Roman antiquity and the sense of the past in Anglo-Saxon England', pp. 46–7; Hay, *Annalists and Historians*, p. 91.

[137] Snow, *Two Cultures and the Scientific Revolution*, p. 40. See John Berger, 'Painting and time'.

[138] *Roma instaurata* (1447), cited in Burckhardt, *Civilization of the Renaissance in Italy*, 1:186; Weiss, *Renaissance Discovery of Classical Antiquity*, pp. 65–70.

[139] Weiss, *Renaissance Discovery*, p. 98; J. B. Ross, 'A study of twelfth-century interest in the antiquities of Rome', p. 309; Greene, *Light in Troy*, p. 236.

[140] Weiss, *Renaissance Discovery*, pp. 98–101.

[141] Raphael and Castiglione to Leo X, cited in Portoghesi, *Rome of the Renaissance*, p. 36.

bothered to save antiquities that lacked utilitarian value. A few special relics – the Arch of Titus, the Temple of Vesta – were partly protected under Paul II and Sixtus IV, but after 1484 even these were abandoned to decay. In sum, the ruins, arches, baths, theatres, and forums of ancient Rome were abandoned to the ravages of weather, the greed of building contractors and stonemasons, and the ambitions of city planners.[142] The lamentations of a handful of humanists fell on deaf ears. Not until the late eighteenth century did Romans begin to conserve their antiquities in earnest, and then were animated 'not from taste, not from respect for antiquity, but only from avarice', a French visitor recorded; ancient monuments were valued mainly as tourist attractions.[143]

Parsimony, greed, and emulative ambition do not wholly account for Renaissance disinclination to save antiquity's material vestiges. Humanists believed the past's glories were better preserved in language than in physical remains. Achilles was still remembered through Homer, noted Du Bellay, whereas those commemorated by colossi and pyramids had long been forgotten. Relics were not only ephemeral but widely scattered and deeply buried; much was now lost or had crumbled to dust; although old Rome's extant remains were 'fully adequate to carry away the present age with admiration', Montaigne saw them as mere ruins of ruins, 'the least worthy [of] disfigured limbs'.[144]

It was not to salvage ancient fragments that antiquities were disinterred, as we saw in Chapter 3, but to bring dead monuments back to life, to reconstruct the dismembered classics. Very few humanists sought, so did the sixteenth-century architect Sebastiano Serlio, to incorporate the broken, the ruined, the anachronistic into new buildings, broadening their expressive range and adding a past tense to the architectural grammar of the present. Instead, most viewed such fragments as pathetic, if not hideously senile or dead. They aimed not to embalm but to revitalize relics by refashioning them whole and new.[145]

Concern for preserving past remains, as distinct from reshaping or imitating them, sprang from several late eighteenth- and nineteenth-century developments. One was the dawning awareness that history was not structured by destiny or by any constants of human nature, but was an organic, multifaceted, varied process subject to manifold contingencies. As every people came to seem unique and each epoch unrepeatable, tangible monuments and physical relics became crucial to historical understanding, and the premium placed on original and authentic physical sources lent impetus to their conservation. Yet even as awareness of historicity infused more and more of life with an historical dimension, topics that had previously been seen and studied as part of the grand human story – nature, language, wealth, to cite Foucault's examples – now took on separate careers of their own, dispossessing general history of much of its former manifest

---

[142] Weiss, *Renaissance Discovery*, pp. 103–4. 'Ironic as it may seem, the Renaissance brought more destruction on the Roman ruins than any other age: the new Rome of the Renaissance meant the annihilation of the old' (p. 205).

[143] L. E. F. Ch. Mercier Dupaty, *Lettres sur l'Italie, en 1785*, quoted in Mortier, *Poétique des ruines*, p. 149. The historian Charles Duclos felt that the names of the popes who had allowed ancient Roman monuments to be destroyed should be proscribed (*Considérations sur l'Italie* (1767), in Mortier, p. 146).

[144] Du Bellay, *Deffence et illustration de la langue francoyse* (1549), Bk II, Ch. 5; Montaigne, *Travel Journal*, 26 Jan. 1581, p. 79.

[145] Greene, *Light in Troy*, p. 235, and Ch. 8, 'Poliziano: the past dismembered', p. 147–70. See Ackerman, 'Planning of Renaissance Rome', p. 13; M. W. Thompson, *Ruins*, p. 15.

105 Removal excites protective legislation: Rood-loft, Cathedral of St John, Hertogenbosch, Netherlands, *c.* 1610, purchased by Victoria and Albert Museum, London, 1871

content and shattering the old unity of cosmic chronology and macro–micro analogy. A growing mystique of historical consciousness and an avid attachment to documents and physical traces of the past helped to compensate for these mental erosions; men seized on material tokens of the roles that still remained to history proper, things whose historicity reflected a self-image no longer timeless and universal, but now organic, heterogeneous, and specific to period and place.[146]

A related impulse toward preservation was nationalism: vernacular languages, folk-lore, material arts, and antiquities became foci of group consciousness and folk identity for Europe's emergent – and often beleaguered – nation-states. As Munz observes, relics lent continuity to tradition and served as visible guarantors of national identity:

Since the doctrine of nationalism required people to believe that every nation had existed for many centuries even when its existence was not socially and politically noticeable, the proof for its existence depended on the continuity of its linguistic and cultural coherence. Since not even that coherence was obvious to the naked eye, historians had . . . to demonstrate that the ruins and documents of the past . . . were part of the cultural heritage of each nation, monuments to the existence of cultural continuity.[147]

Cologne Cathedral, restored and completed in old Gothic style by Karl Friedrich Schinkel and his successors, was celebrated as 'the greatest of Germany's bulwarks, which she will either guard or perish, and which will only fall when the blood of the last Teuton has mingled with the waves of Father Rhine'.[148] Hesse's pioneering protective decree of 1818, also inspired by Schinkel, was expressly patriotic and pedagogic in intent: 'The surviving monuments of architecture are among the most important and interesting evidence of history, in that from them may be inferred the former customs, culture, and civil conditions of the nation, and therefore their preservation is greatly to be wished.'[149] Crusading against the notorious Bande Noire, brigands who demolished old monuments to sell their stones, Victor Hugo defended France's ancient buildings as sacred national shrines and sources of poetic inspiration, and Montalembert urged France to safeguard her antiquities, for 'long memories make great peoples'.[150]

Removal or threatened loss lent impetus to the preservation of antiquities as tokens of national heritage. Early nineteenth-century English antiquarians like John Sell Cotman and Dawson Turner were appalled by the derelict state of many of Normandy's ancient abbeys, churches, and castles, damaged before or during the French Revolution, vandal-ized and neglected since. 'It is the English alone who labour to preserve the memory of the structures of Normandy, which are doomed to destruction by the disgraceful sloth and ignorance of the French', concluded Francis Palgrave in 1821. The French hated 'all memorials of ancient times; the task of illustrating the ancient monuments of France has

[146] Michael Hunter, 'Preconditions of preservation', pp. 25–8; Foucault, *Order of Things*, pp. xxiii, 367–70.

[147] *Shapes of Time*, p. 154. See Harbison, *Deliberate Regression*, Ch. 5, 'Romantic localism'.

[148] *Der Kölner Dom und Deutschland's Einheit* (1842), quoted in Robson-Scott, *Literary Background of the Gothic Revival in Germany*, p. 288, and pp. 287–301; Wolff, 'Completion of Cologne Cathedral in the nineteenth century', pp. 26–9.

[149] Ludwig I of Hesse, 22 Jan. 1818, reprinted in John Harvey, *Conservation of Buildings*, p. 27. For the anti-Jacobin background to Hesse's medievalism, see Honour, *Romanticism*. p. 177.

[150] Hugo, 'Bande noire' (1824; see also his 'Sur la destruction des monuments en France', 1825); Montalembert, in G. B. Brown, *Care of Ancient Monuments*, p. 74. See also Mortier, *Poétique des ruines*, pp. 213–14; Daemmrich, 'Ruins motif as artistic device in French literature', pp. 35–6; Lagarde, *Mémoire des pierres*, pp. 54–78.

thus devolved upon us ... Whilst the owners of these noble structures are dull to their beauties and incapable of appreciating their value, we have made them English property ... Abandoned by their possessors, the fields have become our own, by the tillage which we have bestowed upon them.' Shamed by this accusation, and perhaps alarmed lest the metaphors of possession become actualities, the pioneer archaeologist Arcisse de Caumont founded the Société des Antiquaires de Normandie in 1823, forerunner of Guizot's French national monuments conservation agency.[151]

The Victoria and Albert Museum's 1869 purchase of the early seventeenth-century rood-loft of St John Hertogenbosch, after that Dutch cathedral had dismantled and sold it to a dealer, became a scandalous *cause célèbre* that inspired the creation of the Rijksmonumentenzorg, the Netherlands' official preservation body. And it was an American syndicate's dismantling of Tattershall Castle's fifteenth-century fireplaces, along with a threat of the castle's imminent demolition – only the fact that much of it was brick was said to prevent the Americans from taking it all away – that led the Marquis of Curzon to buy and restore it. Curzon then went on to champion the Ancient Monuments Act of 1913, which gave the British government its first real powers to protect buildings deemed of national importance in the event their owners could not resist the blandishment of American millionaires. Seventy-five years later, alarms re-echo over similar threats posed by Getty billions. As an art historian remarks, in discussing the Mellon Collection of British paintings at Yale, 'our so-called heritage never means more to us than when we see it inherited by someone else'.[152]

A third preservationist impulse was the acute sense of loss resulting from unexampled change. After the French Revolution and the Napoleonic Wars all that had gone before seemed to belong to a world forever lost. Traditional patterns of life disrupted, monuments vandalized, art treasures pillaged – all this aroused conservation-minded reaction, not least in France; Napoleon himself decreed in 1809 that Rome's classical buildings be preserved, and helped to defray the cost.[153] The care of ancient monuments came to symbolize conservation in the broadest sense, as in Cuvier's comment on fossil bones that he 'had to learn ... to restore those monuments of past revolutions'.[154] The very word 'revolution', which had meant 'revolvement' or 'restoration' but now came to refer to the overthrow of the established order and to radical innovation in general,[155] underscored the irretrievability of even the recent past.

Hard on the heels of these convulsions came those of the Industrial Revolution, most notably in Britain, where the miseries attendant on rapid urbanization heightened

[151] Palgrave, 'Normandy – architecture of the Middle Ages', p. 147; 'Organisation de functionnaires chargés de veiller à la Conservation des Monuments nationaux', *Revue Normande*, 1 (1831), 275–83. British antiquarians were especially devoted to Normandy's churches and abbeys as prototypes of their own Romanesque. But the records of the Society of Antiquaries in London do not substantiate the reiterated French charge that the British intended to buy up Normandy's medieval structures and re-erect them in England (Monnet, 'Care of ancient monuments in France', p. 35; Lagarde, *Mémoire des pierres*, pp. 31–3).

[152] Avery, *Rood-Loft from Hertogenbosch*, pp. 1–2; Dale, *Historic Preservation in Foreign Countries: I: ... The Netherlands*, p. 105; Curzon and Tipping, *Tattershall Castle*, pp. 143–4; Kennet, *Preservation*, pp. 35–6; Nicholas Penny, 'Constable: an English heritage abroad', *Sunday Times*, 11 Nov. 1984, p. 43.

[153] Linstrum, 'Giuseppe Valadier et l'Arc de Titus', p. 52.

[154] 'Recherches sur les ossemens fossiles' (1825), quoted in Rudwick, 'Transposed concepts from the human sciences', p. 69.

[155] Felix Gilbert, 'Revolution', 4:152–6.

nostalgia for olden times. The monastic dissolution had stunned many observers in the sixteenth century, but awareness of – and regret for – material change first became widespread in the early nineteenth, when more people than ever were sundered from familiar scenes.[156]

A fourth new perspective was the growing awareness of individual identity discussed in Chapter 5. Looking back at their earlier selves and viewing life as a career in which past actions had continuing consequences, people also found meaning in recalling and revisiting childhood scenes. And attachment to the locales of one's own past aroused the impulse not only to see them again but to have them kept in their remembered state – and to grieve when they were not.[157]

Fifthly, the rediscovery of ancient sites and monuments excited sentiment for preserving them. The excavation of cradles of civilization in the Nile and the Mediterranean and the growth of antiquarian activity at home kindled interest in material remains, and the expansion of education and leisure made 'more people ... susceptible to the intrinsic interest of the past than ever before'.[158] For many, that interest involved not just viewing and collecting but also seeking to preserve relics.

These developments did not all culminate at one given moment. Like the preservation ethos, their inception varied with place and circumstance, previous perspectives enduring alongside later ones. Yet the early nineteenth century marked a watershed when these impulses became especially intense, arousing unprecedented initiatives for preserving relics of the past.

The end of the nineteenth century marked another such divide. Rising doubts about the continuance of progress, disquietude over social and political instability, growing awareness that the present was utterly unlike any past all engendered acute anxiety over the direction and pace of change – an anxiety exemplified in Brooks Adams's prognosis of imminent dissolution.[159] 'The series of events comes swifter and swifter', thought Carlyle, 'velocity increasing ... as the square of time'; the future was unimaginable.[160] 'Material, physical, mechanical change in human life' in the century since Watt and Arkwright seemed to an English historian 'greater than occurred in the thousand years that preceded, perhaps even in two thousand years or twenty thousand', and to be constantly accelerating; Charles Péguy felt in 1913 that 'the world has changed less since Jesus Christ than it has done in the last thirty years'.[161]

Whether or not these ominous judgements were valid, they were widely held. One consequence was nostalgia, manifest in idealizations of rural life, in vernacular-revival

---

[156] Aston, 'Dissolution and the sense of the past'; Burrow, 'Sense of the past'.

[157] Salvesen, *Landscape of Memory*, pp. 1–45, 137–66. The theme is prefigured in Goldsmith's "Deserted Village"; see Goldstein, 'Auburn syndrome: change and loss in "The Deserted Village" and Wordsworth's Grasmere'.

[158] Hudson, *Social History of Archaeology*, pp. 20, 53, 73–83.

[159] *Law of Civilization and Decay* (1896), pp. 292–5, 307–8. See also Henry Adams, *Education of Henry Adams* (1918), pp. 486–98.

[160] 'Shooting Niagara: and after?' (1867), 3:590.

[161] Frederic Harrison, 'A few words about the nineteenth century' (1882), p. 424; Péguy, *L'Argent* (1913), p. 10. See Shattuck, *Banquet Years*, p. 1. Of the 1890s, Talcott Parsons wrote that 'A revolution of such magnitude in the prevailing empirical interpretations of human society is hardly to be found occurring within the short space of a generation, unless one goes back to the sixteenth century' (*Structure of Social Action*, p. 5).

architecture, in arts-and-crafts movements, and in a surge of preservation activity. Country after country enacted laws to protect ancient monuments, founded agencies to cherish one or another aspect of the past, and set aside historic houses as treasured memorials. 'I don't like pulling down anything . . . Keep everything', E. A. Freeman exclaimed.[162] To give the wayfarer 'not only something authentic, but everything veritable to dwell upon', the Society for the Protection of Ancient Buildings sought 'to preserve what is left of the past in the most indiscriminate way; whether good or bad, old or new, preserve it all'.[163]

Similar trends again intensify the impulse to preserve in our own time. Resurgent national and ethnic allegiances require symbolic links with the past. Developmental psychology and psychoanalysis explore the childhood roots of adult behaviour, emphasizing needs to reassess the personal past. Prevailing disaffection with the present and pessimism about the future fuel nostalgia. And the increasingly accessible splendours of antiquity give hundreds of millions a greater stake in their survival.

Above all, destructive and disruptive change has accelerated. Technological innovation, rapid obsolescence, the radical modernization of the built environment, massive migration, and increased longevity combine to leave us in ever less familiar surroundings, remote even from our own recent pasts. 'Every man is a traveller from another time', said William Jovanovich, 'and if the journey is long he ends up as a stranger.'[164] In today's kaleidoscopic world, even a brief journey from the past can estrange us.

Outright annihilation threatens most aspects of the tangible heritage not already in a museum. Historic buildings and traditional scenes are helpless against developmental pressures augmented by new technology: the lost country houses, urban dwellings, churches and chapels, public, commercial, and industrial architecture documented by SAVE Britain's Heritage make appalling reading,[165] and losses elsewhere, if less well documented, are equally extensive.

This generation has also destroyed more of prehistory than was previously known to exist. 'The tempo of destruction is presently so great', warns Karl Meyer, 'that by the end of the century most remaining important archaeological sites may well be plundered or paved over.'[166] In Britain, recent ploughing has denuded or eradicated many barrows and mounds, erasing settlement traces that had endured two millennia of grazing and traditional cultivation; afforestation poses grave threats to other sites. The fast-growing hobby of treasure-hunting is another threat to the archaeological heritage: licenses for metal detectors, used largely to unearth relics for profit, doubled in Britain between 1974 and 1981.[167]

---

[162] To Ugo Balzani, 3 Jan. 1886, in W. R. W. Stephens, *Life and Letters of Edward A. Freeman*, 2:341. See Chapter 3, pp. 102–4 above.

[163] Kerr, 'English architecture thirty years hence' (1884), p. 309. Kerr was criticizing the SPAB for excessive historicity (Wiener, *English Culture*, pp. 68–9).

[164] Quoted in Hough, *Soundings at Sea Level*, p. 206.

[165] Roy Strong, Marcus Binney, and John Harris, *Destruction of the Country House 1875–1975* (1974); Binney and Burman, *Future of Our Churches*; Ken Powell, *New Iconoclasts*; idem, *Fall of Zion*; Binney, Harris, and Emma Winnington, *Lost Houses of Scotland* (1980); Binney and Hanna, *Preservation Pays*, pp. x–xiv; Binney and Emma Milne, *Vanishing Houses of England* (1982); idem, *Time Gentlemen Please!* (1983).

[166] *Plundered Past*, p. xv. See Brinkley-Rogers, 'Big business of artifacts theft'; Bator, *International Trade in Art*.

[167] Cunliffe, *The Past Tomorrow*, pp. 7–10; Lambrick, *Archaeology and Agriculture*; Barker, 'Scale of the problem'; Shoard, *Theft of the Countryside*, pp. 175–6; 'Should metal detectors be banned as archaeological

Widespread destruction is not a uniquely modern phenomenon, to be sure. In 1861, Thomas Bateman noted the 'rapid disappearance and exhaustion' of Celtic crania and vases 'arising from agricultural improvements, and the ill-conducted pillage of idle curiosity'.[168] Public curiosity a century ago seemed to imperil ancient monuments throughout Britain. 'The very fact that attention is drawn to them', feared an archaeological observer, 'makes them increasingly the prey of the ignorant sightseer on the one hand or the needy owner of the soil on the other.'[169]

Yet the pace of destruction has unquestionably accelerated. Modern machinery can now metamorphose a city or a landscape virtually at a stroke; urban skylines are transformed unrecognizeably every few years, street scenes altered almost in the blink of an eye. Where demolition might once have been stayed, today trees are felled, hedgerows uprooted, buildings obliterated before a protest can be lodged; in 1980 a bulldozer took only 45 minutes to demolish Monkspath Hall by 'mistake' and in 1982 local authorities vandalized Kensington Town Hall overnight to forestall an impending order to preserve it. Pollution erases masterpieces that have withstood centuries of travail; to safeguard the Acropolis and *The Last Supper* against atmospheric sulphur would require ridding Athens and Milan of automobiles and industry; industrial pollution causes Cracow's ancient buildings to decay at a thousand times the pre-war rate.[170]

Redevelopment is the past's main rival, but other impulses aggravate the technological toll. Bombs enable iconoclasts to eradicate a detested legacy and put every tangible relic at risk. Popularity also speeds the past's destruction. As shown in Chapter 6, mass tourism aggravates theft and erosion at historic sites. Visitors no longer carry away slivers of Shakespeare's supposed chair at Stratford nor hire hammers to chip keepsakes from Stonehenge,[171] but these gains in decorum are small compared with modern losses. Tourist footsteps have worn out the turf around the Stonehenge sarsens; cathedral sightseers rub inscriptions to illegibility; antiquities' collectors promote illicit traffic that devastates ancient sites: entire Mayan temples are hacked to pieces for clandestine export. Growing appreciation saves many old decorative features from demolition but creates a demand that threatens their survival *in situ*; thieves posing as preservation officers make off with old chimneypieces, balustrades, and Adam fireplaces. 'We have educated the public so well', an expert in Victoriana ruefully comments, 'that they now know what is worth stealing.'[172]

aids?' *Everything Has a Value*, No. 13 (Oct. 1981), 36–9; 'Treasure hunters and archaeologists', *Treasure Hunting*, 3:7 (1980), 4–8; Henry Cleere, Council for British Archaeology, 'Treasure hunt through British heritage', letter, *The Times*, 16 July 1983, p. 9. The urban archaeological heritage is perhaps most imperilled: 'The most important towns of all historical periods will be lost to archaeology within twenty years, if not before' (Martin Biddle, 'Preface', in Heighway, *Archaeology and Planning in Towns*, p. vi; see also Biddle, 'Future of the urban past', p. 101). Many archaeologists today would halt virtually all excavation, partly because the backlog of unreported digs is so great, partly because non-destructive topographic analysis now yields incomparable evidence, partly so as not 'to deprive all future archaeologists . . . of their chance to make new and dramatic discoveries' (Thomas, 'Ethics in archaeology', pp. 270, 272; Fowler, *Approaches to Archaeology*, pp. 35–67, 189–90).

[168] *Ten Years' Diggings in Celtic and Saxon Grave Hills*, pp. v–vi.   [169] '*Archæologia*' (1881), pp. 120–1.

[170] Lloyd Timberlake, 'Poland – the most polluted country in the world?' *New Scientist*, 22 Oct. 1981, pp. 348–50.

[171] 'We cutt off a Chip according to the Custom' (John Adams, 'Notes on a tour of English country seats, &c., with Thomas Jefferson', 4–10 (?) Apr. 1786, in his *Diary and Autobiography*, 3:185; see also Howland, 'Travelers to Olympus', p. 150); Chippindale, 'What future for Stonehenge?' p. 180.

[172] Rory O'Donnell, quoted in Judith Judd, 'Thieves with a taste for Adam fireplaces', *Observer*, 20 June 1983, p. 3. See W. G. Blair, 'Half of architectural art objects lost in demolition', *N.Y. Times*, 20 July 1980, pp. R1, 8; Deyan Sudjic, 'The elegant rip-off', *Sunday Times*, 6 June 1982.

The high cost of protecting historic sites and relics also serves to doom them. Effective safeguards are often too expensive or onerous to install and maintain: the stringent enforcement of modern fire regulations requires insulation and escape routes that few historic-house owners can afford, and connoisseurs fear that this 'could spell the end of Georgian and Victorian domestic architecture'. By rigidly applying height, lighting, and staircase rules meant for new structures, British public health officers are said to 'habitually destroy the character of 17th-century buildings'.[173]

The transience of artifacts of all kinds – houses, clothes, books, furniture, crockery – transforms our surroundings no less than outright destruction. More plentiful than ever, objects also perish at an unprecedented pace. When materials were expensive and labour cheap, many things were made to last, often handed down from generation to generation. Today we replace rather than repair. Who now protects fabrics with dust covers? How many turn cuffs and collars or darn socks? Manufacturing makes it cheaper to buy whole new aggregates than to furnish old structures with new parts. Because profits depend on high turnover, old goods become obsolete even when still serviceable. 'It is an increasing commonplace that a machine less than ten years old can no longer be repaired because the design has been abandoned', writes Chamberlin. '"They're not making them any more", and the machine becomes, literally, a museum piece.'[174]

Built-in obsolescence further speeds dissolution. Rapidly fading colours, rotting paper, jerry-built houses distressed Ruskin back in 1857, when most things lasted a lot longer than now; ephemeral materials, he warned, invited careless craftmanship, for no 'workman worthy the name will put his brains into a cup, or an urn, which he knows is to go to the melting-pot in half a score years'. A Dürer engraving could still be handled two hundred years later, but contemporary paintings deteriorated markedly within twenty years, and a century would reduce them to rag fragments.[175] Nowadays paper decays much faster: impregnated with sulphuric acid to prevent the feathering of ink, modern hardcover books last only fifty years, paperbacks thirty; one-third of the Library of Congress's six million volumes are badly deteriorated. The fugacity of books is a measure of our culture's acceptance of obsolescence.[176]

Entire categories of objects rapidly become useless and die out. 'Hitherto, the active life of almost any given class of artefact could be measured in centuries, if not millennia', adds Chamberlin; 'there was little difference ... between a plough used by a Roman and one used by a nineteenth-century Dorset farmer. Now the cycle of invention, use and obsolescence can be completed not merely in a generation but within a decade or less.'[177] We live in circumstances that are uniquely ephemeral: as Marinetti envisioned, most things we wear, use, and see around us are shorter-lived than we

---

[173] Patricia Brown, 'Safety in older buildings', *The Times*, 8 Apr. 1978, p. 15; SPAB *Annual Report*, 1981–2, p. 4. See Dobby, *Conservation and Planning*, pp. 152–3; Lord James of Rusholme, Royal Fine Art Commission, 'Fire regulations in historic buildings', letter, *The Times*, 8 Sept. 1978, p. 15; Lewis Sturge, 'The price of preservation', *Daily Telegraph*, 2 Apr. 1979, p. 14.

[174] *Preserving the Past*, p. 79.   [175] Ruskin, 'Education in art' (1858), in his *Lamp of Beauty*, p. 302.

[176] Arthur Magida, 'Our printed legacy is turning to dust'. Deacidification in a vacuum chamber now promises to multiply the lifetime of books ten-fold (J. C. Williams, 'Chemistry of the deacidification of paper', pp. 16–18; Adrian C. Sclawy and John C. Williams, 'Alkalinity – the key to paper "permanence"', *Tappi*, 64:5 (1981), 49–50; *Paper and Its Preservation: Environmental Controls*).

[177] *Preserving the Past*, p. 79.

are.[178] At the same time, increased longevity and propensity to move leave ever fewer of us in the same localities, let alone the same houses, we were born in. Hence what surrounds us in later life is seldom what we grew up with, and the disposable things we make and build are also more apt to be left behind.

The impulse to preserve is partly a reaction against the increasing evanescence of things and the speed with which we pass them by. In the face of massive change we cling to the remaining familiar vestiges. And we compensate for what is gone with an interest in its history. Like a newcomer to an old village who acquires roots by joining the local historical society, the buyer of new goods becomes nostalgically attached to the articles they replace. When things cease to be useful they are admired because they are old. Preserving them gives the objects we once used a genealogy, places them in a temporal context, makes up for the longevity we deprived them of by having cast them off so soon. Interest in each remnant of the past mounts as it threatens to disappear – steam engines, thatched roofs, canals, pottery ovens now evoke an affection they seldom elicited when still plentiful. Nothing so quickens preservation sympathies as the fear of imminent extinction, whether of a building, a bird, or a folkway.

Attachment to scenes recalled and to things that were here before us mitigates the alien quality of unfamiliar environments, and affection for old buildings reflects 'a rational hunger for some degree of permanence' when the pace of change exceeds people's capacity to absorb it.[179] 'The more rapidly society changes, the less readily should we abandon anything familiar which can still be made to serve a purpose', advises Peter Marris. 'The townscape ought to reflect our needs for continuity.' However efficient or handsome the new, abrupt discontinuity with the old can inflict intolerable stress.[180]

The more the past is destroyed or left behind, the stronger the urge to preserve and restore. Threatened by technology, pollution, and popularity, surviving vestiges command attention as never before, and painstaking expertise is devoted to their care. The machines that demolish also help locate and salvage history hitherto hidden under the ground, beneath the sea, behind the varnish of a painting. And new conservation techniques mend old materials that would once have decayed beyond hope of repair.

Losses and gains

All this salvaging however requires money, time, and effort; against the benefits of preservation must be set its costs. Both advocates and detractors tend to exaggerate: preservationists decry every demolition as vandalism; critics charge them with hanging on to the entire past. 'Of course I'm all in favour of conservation – I'm a member of the National Trust', an official told SAVE Britain's Heritage; 'but some of these people, they want to preserve everything.'[181] Indeed, even Britain's Minister for the Arts recently stated that 'If I had the power I would almost prohibit the tearing down of any building at all.'[182]

---

[178] Kendig and Hutton, *Life-Spans*, pp. xiii–xiv, 163. To be sure, most houses in the past were far more ephemeral than many built today.

[179] Glyn England (1981), quoted in Binney, 'Oppression to obsession', p. 208.

[180] *Loss and Change*, p. 150.

[181] U.K. Property Services Agency officer, quoted in Binney, 'Oppression to obsession', p. 205.

[182] Paul Channon, address at SPAB annual general meeting, London, 11 Nov. 1982.

Nostalgic and Futurist hyperbole apart, no one wants to save or to destroy everything. But the proper balance between preservation and replacement, like that explored in Chapters 2 and 3 between past and present generally, is hard to assess; it varies with the durability or evanescence of everything around us; with changing needs for permanence and for novelty, and with economic, cultural, and aesthetic costs and benefits.[183]

Preservation is often viewed as a luxury expendable when times are hard. Old buildings in particular 'like divorced wives ... cost money to maintain', in John Summerson's phrase. 'They are often dreadfully in the way. And the protection of one may exact as much sacrifice from the community as the preservation of a thousand pictures, books or musical scores.'[184] In Britain, which may have half a million old buildings with some claim to maintenance, the cost of preservation may come to seem overwhelming. Even Americans sometimes find it disproportionate. When preservationists met in New York in 1981 to lobby against impending federal budget cuts, one official confessed that she was embarrassed to seek aid for historic preservation in view of severe reductions in school-lunch, food-stamp, and welfare programmes.[185] Weighed against such necessities, preservation funding seems clearly expendable; no one will be homeless, suffer malnutrition, or go without medical care for lack of it. 'At a time like this you spend too long pitying that dead plumage', argues a British Labourite, 'and forget the dying public services.'[186]

These are valid distinctions. But the comparison overlooks the fact that preservation is never *just* an expense; it means keeping a capital asset. A relic's worth depends on its state of repair, on who owns and looks after it, and on what use it serves; but everything surviving from the past has some value which is forfeited unless it is preserved.

Far from wasting resources, saving and reusing historic buildings often makes economic and social sense. Preservation can conserve energy and materials, create jobs, and save money. Many older buildings provide lower-cost space and yield higher profits than new ones. 'Re-using older buildings usually requires less capital ... and take[s] less time to complete than new buildings [so] that money is tied up for shorter periods before rents begin to repay loans', an architectural journal concludes. 'Preservation and remodeling efforts require more workers and craftsmen than do new buildings ... The revitalization of sound structures and viable neighborhoods is both less expensive and less socially disorganizing than ... new construction.'[187]

These arguments commonly buttress preservation in the United States. Preservationists publicize how many thermal units are saved by refurbishing old buildings and how little heat and air-conditioning they consume compared with modern structures. As the building industry uses one-third of U.S. energy, such savings are substantial: urban rehabilitation often needs only half as much energy, materials, and capital as building anew.[188] Preservation thus promises ecological thrift along with heritage and environmental felicity.

---

[183] Hägerstrand, 'On the survival of the cultural heritage'.   [184] 'The past in the future', p. 221.

[185] 'The future of historic preservation: new directions and forecasts', panel discussion at 4th Annual Convocation of Preservation Alumni, Columbia University, 11 Apr. 1981.

[186] Phillip Whitehead, 'Preserving the past, failing the future', *The Times*, 17 Mar. 1984. p. 8.

[187] David Morton, 'Looking forward to the past', *Progressive Architecture*, 35:11 (1976), 45. On economic issues, see my 'Conserving the heritage', pp. 239–44.

[188] U.S. Advisory Council on Historic Preservation, *Annual Reports*, 1979 and 1980; National Trust, *New Energy from Old Buildings*, pp. 16, 23, 27, 119.

Such savings are less often cited as rationales for preservation in Britain, partly because taxes (notably value added tax) actually penalize repair and rehabilitation.[189] Yet reusing old buildings saves capital costs, and historic milieux benefit firms whose personnel enjoy the ambience of the past; 'historic environment was an influential or deciding factor' in many office relocations, and 'places and areas that have adopted positive conservation policies have enjoyed economic benefits as a result'.[190] The touristic values of preservation are manifold; Britain's historic buildings contribute significantly 'through tourism to earnings of foreign exchange, to local employment and prosperity, and to central government taxation'. Visits to historic houses, ancient monuments, and old churches rank first in popularity with foreign tourists; visitors contribute half the income of several cathedrals and over two-thirds the running costs of Westminster Abbey; building preservation in small towns and villages 'is clearly the most vital factor underpinning their income from tourism'.[191]

On the other hand, critics contend that rehabilitating old housing often 'represents poor value today and a large-scale maintenance problem for the next generation'.[192] Old buildings destroyed, like Monkspath and Kensington Town Hall, or neglected until they have to be pulled down for safety's sake, show how burdensome historic structures seem to local authorities and developers.[193] Few tempted by period homes realize the unremitting expense their upkeep entails, or that 'Many features of period charm' is a vendor's euphemism for 'doorways low enough to stun anyone taller than four-feet six, and window frames which feed in constant cold air.'[194] Preservation is alleged to take an excessive share of public resources; a British conservation minister recently warned that supporting old buildings might come to cost as much as the National Health Service. But the miniscule sums actually allocated belie the spectre of preservation as a crippling burden.[195] In fact, the allocation of neither costs nor benefits is well understood. Shopkeepers seem not to know that much of their trade comes from visitors to nearby historic attractions; governments scant the contribution made by tourist taxes and foreign exchange. Yet displaying the past for profit also multiplies maintenance costs and imperils its fabric and ambience, as discussed in Chapter 6. These burdens do not negate the profitability of the heritage. But there is ultimate truth in a preservationist's comment that 'You can't keep the 19th century without paying for it in the 20th.'[196]

The drawbacks go beyond repair and maintenance costs. Saving old things runs counter

189 Binney and Grenfell, *Drowning in V.A.T.* See also Historic Buildings Council, *Annual Report*, 1979–80, p. 2, 1980–81, p. 12; Suddards, *Listed Buildings*, pp. 203–28.

190 Hanna and Binney, *Preserve and Prosper*, p. 33 and Introduction, n.p.

191 Binney and Hanna, *Preservation Pays: Tourism and the Economic Benefits of Conserving Historic Buildings*, pp. ix, 135; Hanna, 'Cathedrals at saturation point?' p. 189. See also English Tourist Board, *Putting On the Style* (1981), 'a guide to stately English settings for those special business occasions'.

192 Owen Luder, 'Luder on conservation: shouting rude words at the vicar', *Building*, 15 Dec. 1978, p. 35.

193 George Allan, 'When an "alteration" is "demolition"', *Period Home*, 2:3 (1981), 26. 'The Department of the Environment's commendable zeal in adding historic buildings to the list of those protected by law is not matched by its enthusiasm for ensuring that listed buildings stay upright', Allan later noted. 'On the contrary, the laws protecting listed buildings from decay, demolition and damage are so inadequate as to bring the whole listing process into disrepute' ('Legal notes', ibid., 6:1 (1985), 16).

194 John Ridley-Walker, '"Period delights"', ibid., 3:3 (1982), 18.

195 'Lady Birk spells out Government conservation policy', *Architects' Journal*, 167 (1978), 1142; Binney, 'Oppression to obsession', p. 206.

196 Margot Wellington, New York Municipal Art Society, quoted in P. L. Brown, 'Is South Street Seaport on the right track?' p. 19.

to the very spirit of modern enterprise. Over a century ago, preserving old buildings was held inimical to improving British living standards and needs for development.[197] In Britain today, no profitable use can be found for many large older buildings, and preservation is felt to impede recovery in the building trades, re-employment prospects, and business generally.[198] Some fear that conserving relics of the Industrial Revolution will discourage new industry; anxious to jettison its old mill-town image, Burnley met preservation proposals with 'active hostility'.[199] Emphasizing preservation implies entrepreneurial lassitude; 'the image of history and Beefeaters', attests a government official, 'was making it difficult for British exporters to sell our goods abroad'.[200] Critics charge that the cult of preservation may at length make England valuable only as a relic. Half a century ago, Clough Williams-Ellis termed England a museum and accused archaeologists and antiquaries of preserving dead things to the detriment of the living.[201] Since then the appetite for relics of earlier life-styles has reduced 'the stately homes of England, and even whole nations, like the prototypically picturesque Spain', observes Cesar Graña, 'to the conditions of *objets d'art*'.[202]

Such a condition may have its compensations. 'Shudder as we may, perhaps the creation of a living history book in this clutch of islands is not so bad a prospect', Labour politician Andrews Faulds suggests. He envisions Britain as 'a sort of Switzerland with monuments in place of mountains ... to provide the haven, heavy with history, for those millions ... who will come seeking peace in a place away from the pulsating pressures and the grit and grievances of their own industrial societies'. Already 'millions of visitors flood in ... to gape and marvel at our heritage. Should we not be doing our utmost to enhance it?'[203] But most Britons draw the line at becoming full-time purveyors of their past, quaint old codgers – or cultural prostitutes – in a fairy-tale historyland. Fears are voiced lest industrial archaeology turn Wales into 'a nation of museum attendants' minding the world's 'biggest mausoleum'.[204] 'Tourism reduces all nations to Ruritania', warns another critic. 'It encourages their citizens to become hucksters and grovellers after tips.'[205] And the more profitable the past as show-place, the graver the risks. Tourist receipts may help to check physical erosion, but even the strictest surveillance can merely mitigate the vulgarity and loss of ambience that popularity entails.

Preservation is accused not only of deterring progress but of being inimical to moral or social well-being – complaints sometimes conjoined. 'Does the Church really want to go on keeping alive, as if they had a terminal disease, buildings which have no hope of

[197] *The Antiquarian* (1871), cited in Hudson, *Social History of Archaeology*, p. 55.
[198] *Britain's Historic Buildings: A Policy for Their Future Use*, pp. 18–19; Charles McKean, 'Fears over conserving buildings', *The Times*, 13 Apr. 1982, p. 8.
[199] Ken Powell, *Burnley: Mill-Town Image: Burden or Asset?* p. 1.
[200] Quoted in Binney, 'Oppression to obsession', p. 205.
[201] *England and the Octopus* (1928), pp. 108, 131–2. As early as 1890 Havelock Ellis thought 'we may already trace the development of England as a museum of antiquities' (*New Spirit*, p. 24); but unlike Williams-Ellis, Ellis thought this highly desirable.
[202] *Fact and Symbol*, p. 98.
[203] 'Ancient assets that may be our salvation', *The Times*, 19 Jan. 1976, p. 12.
[204] Hywel Francis, quoted in Robert Merrill, 'Cefn Coed coal & steam centre: the interpretation of a mining community', *Interpretation*, No. 17 (1981), 13.
[205] Frank Johnson, 'Ruritania here we come', *The Times*, 23 June 1981. A Prussian historian and diplomat voiced the same view in 1845: 'It is better to build, to found, and to act', he wrote in praise of the United

self-support?' asks an authority on preservation law, conjuring up an image of clergy too busy reglazing windows to spread the Word; Anglicans oppressed by redundant churches – 'the weight of masonry which hangs around our necks' – agree that their mission is to save souls, not buildings.[206] Gentrified villages conserve old houses at the expense of the old community, which can no longer afford to buy – or to resist selling – ancient cottages. When rehabilitation fever sweeps a quaint old American neighbourhood, low-income residents are typically displaced by 'restoration block-busting'.[207] Billingsgate traders resented the concern lavished on the doomed old fish market while they themselves were neglected; as one of them said, 'I hope the whole bloody lot falls down.'[208] Dismissing the Colosseum as 'one big urinal', many Romans condemn archaeological plans for the ancient centre as a scheme to turn still more of the living city over to the dead.[209]

As such complaints suggest, preservation remains tainted by elitism despite its claims to popular support. It is by and large the rich who wish to save old buildings – and who receive grants or tax benefits for doing so. Many of the poor associate historic buildings 'with an archaic degrading phase of history during which . . . the leisured classes indulged in conspicuous waste'.[210] Preservation holds little appeal for those whose sense of the past is sullied by insalubrious memories. 'There wasn't even a whimper of complaint' when a new highway sliced through historic cotton mills in Fall River, Massachusetts, in the early 1970s, 'there was more like a cheer', reported an industrial archaeologist. 'The dirt, noise, bad smells, hard labor and other forms of exploitation associated with these kinds of places' make preservation ludicrous. '"Preserve a steel mill?" people say, '"It killed my father. Who wants to preserve that?"'[211]

But the fearsome industrial past is by no means universally rejected, as the Lowell and Bradford responses indicate. Reactions to the 'Satanic Mills' exhibition of nineteenth-century Pennine cloth manufactories showed how much their survival meant to those who had worked in them, even when they found life hard and thought the buildings ugly. By no means nostalgic for her childhood days of toil, one visitor was none the less glad to know that her mill was still there: its survival validated her memories.[212] In northern England, as in old New England mill towns,

States, 'than to have ruins pointed out by tourist guides' (von Raumer, *America and the American People*, p. 300).

206 R. W. Suddards, 'Do the empty churches a service – knock them down', *The Times*, 29 May 1982, p. 10; Archbishop Coggan, address at Church of England General Synod, 1975, quoted in Powell, *New Iconoclasts*, p. 1.

207 Roddewig and Young, *Neighborhood Revitalization and the Historic Preservation Incentives of the Tax Reform Act of 1976* (1979), quoted in McGee, 'Historic preservation and displacement', p. 12. See Singer, 'When worlds collide'.

208 Interviewed by Jacquelin Burgess, 1982. See George Hill, 'The city smell will never be the same again', *The Times*, 10 Nov. 1981, p. 10.

209 Federico Zeri, quoted in Sari Gilbert, 'City of living, city of dead', *IHT*, 1 June 1981, pp. 7–8S. For the background, see Spiro Kostof, *The Third Rome 1870–1950: Traffic and Glory*, Berkeley, Calif.: University Art Museum, 1973.

210 Dobby, *Conservation and Planning*, pp. 28–9. On veneration of archaic, obsolete, and clumsy hand-made book production, typified by the Kelmscott Press, see Veblen, *Theory of the Leisure Class* (1899), pp. 116–17.

211 Robert Vogel, quoted in Theo Richmond, 'Sites and soundings', *Guardian*, 28 Aug. 1973, p. 12. Manchester, N.H., would go on demolishing its Amoskeag mills 'as long as anybody's alive who ever had to work in them', said an inhabitant (quoted in Greiff, *Lost America* (1974), pp. 11–12); within a few years Amoskeag's stunning preservation programme proved him wrong (Hareven and Langenbach, *Amoskeag*, 1978).

212 *Satanic Mills: Industrial Architecture in the Pennines*; Hareven and Langenbach, 'Living places, work places and historical identity', pp. 112–14.

the assumptions of social reformers and planners that the working-class past in these industrial settings must be eradicated because it symbolizes poverty, grimness, and exploitation, misses what the workers themselves feel about their world . . . They were willing, and at times eager, to recall the bitter times along with the good. Both were part of their entire life story and were deeply enmeshed with their sense of place.[213]

Others slate preservation for crippling initiative. This defect of the past was often expressed by American visitors in the Old World long before preservation became practice, as noted in Chapter 3. Rome's wellnigh indestructible houses seemed as sinister to Hawthorne's Americans as Apollo's boon of immortality to the Sibyl of Cumae. 'All towns should be made capable of purification by fire, or of decay within each half-century. Otherwise, they become the hereditary haunts of vermin and noisomeness, besides standing apart from the possibility of such improvements as are constantly introduced into the rest of man's contrivances.'[214]

This view was soon explicitly extended to preservation. 'We cannot allow our lives to be overburdened and crushed down by the mere accumulation of the dead things of the past', said a member of Parliament in 1878. *'Let dead things go, let living things be kept.'*[215] A century on, the director of the Victoria and Albert Museum echoes that charge: 'Worship of the past and what it has created has been taken to an extreme unknown to any previous century . . . Nothing is deader than dead heritage and there is too much dead heritage around. The past has swallowed us up.'[216]

Devotion to the architectural heritage is particularly felt to inhibit creativity and to foreclose the future. Old buildings pre-empt space and talent; regard for antiquity stifles innovation. 'If we let the paranoid preservers manoeuvre us into keeping everything', charges Reyner Banham, 'we shall bring the normal life-processes of decay and replacement to a half, we shall straitjacket ourselves in embalmed cities of the past.'[217] Had conservation been as pervasive in the past as it is today, opponents are fond of stressing, structures now thought splendid or sacrosanct would never have been built.[218] 'Conservationists rob us of our cultural self-confidence', runs a typical indictment. 'We can no longer create, construct, imagine something new. We have to conserve, preserve, restore.'[219] Even an historian devoted to traditional architecture considers the present vogue for preservation excessive, reflecting a failure of nerve.[220] 'With planners scared or unwilling to plan, builders ashamed or unwilling to build', Hunter Davies fears 'we will then be left with preservation as our only growth industry.'[221]

Such complaints caricature the preservation movement and exaggerate its influence, but the misgivings they reflect about attachment to relics of the past are genuine and pervasive.

Preservation can fairly be charged with segregating the past. Consciousness of the past as a separate realm arouses the urge to save it; doing so then further sunders it from the

[213] Ibid., p. 16.   [214] *Marble Faun*, pp. 301–2.
[215] Leonard Courtney, in SPAB *Report*, 1878, quoted in Dellheim, *Face of the Past*, p. 91.
[216] Roy Strong, 'Taking the age out of heritage', *The Times*, 24 Sept. 1983, p. 8.
[217] 'Preserve us from paranoid preservers', *Observer Mag.*, 21 Oct. 1973, p. 15.
[218] Dobby, *Conservation and Planning*, p. 29; RIBA president Michael Manser, 'Down with mediocrity . . . up with originality!' *Observer Mag.*, 3 May 1981, p. 31; 'Luder on conservation' (see note 192 above).
[219] Douglas Johnson, 'Not what it used to be', *Vole*, 5 (1978), 43.
[220] Middleton, 'Use and abuse of tradition', p. 736.
[221] 'Preserve us from the preservers', *Sunday Times*, 19 Jan. 1975, p. 21.

present. The very effort of salvage is self-conscious and crisis-starred. And it encumbers the landscape with artifacts which no longer attest a living antiquity but celebrate what is dead. Emphasis on preservation typically substitutes a separable and saleable past for 'traditional' stream-of-time continuity.[222] Like collectors generally, as Walter Benjamin realized, preservers destroy as they salvage;[223] what is deliberately withheld from the natural course of decay and evanescence, as we saw in Chapter 6, ceases to be part of a living entity and ends up as a fragment sundered from context.

Preservation thus confirms the temporal distinction which helped engender it to begin with. It is museums' express function to sequester relics so as to save and display them. But survivals adapted to new uses are equally set apart from present-day things, their anachronisms highlighted, their antiqueness emphasized, the obsolescence of their original use underscored. Whether museumized or readapted, the preserved past is strongly differentiated from the everyday milieu.

Segregation is the usual fate of surviving relics no matter how they are treated. Stripping buildings of later accretions and replacing missing parts, for example, both nineteenth-century ecclesiastical restorers and twentieth-century historic-house curators sought to return them to an idealized original state. In reaction, 'anti-scrape' conservers sought to quarantine the past against modern meddling and let it speak for itself. Although these practices reflect opposing views of what relics are and why they matter, each treats the past as a realm quite unlike the present – in the restorers' case, uncontaminated by subsequent change; in the anti-scrape, untouched by ourselves. 'By granting ancient buildings the quasireligious status of virtually untouchable places', Dellheim concludes, the Society for the Protection of Ancient Buildings 'deprived them of their mundane functions' and turned them into museums – even though this was the opposite of their intention.[224]

Museum perspectives suffuse preservation work, for we tend 'to see our historic towns as "pictures" somehow divorced from the reality of everyday life', in Roy Worskett's words. But whereas Worskett decries such segregation for trivializing 'the intensely valuable and irreplaceable',[225] champions of modern architecture half a century ago expressly aimed to mummify the past, fencing off ancient structures in special preserves where they would not interfere with the contemporary scene. Architectural relics should be enshrined like carefully tended cemeteries, advised Le Corbusier, for 'in this way the past becomes no longer dangerous to life'.[226] Frank Lloyd Wright likewise deplored Britain's preservation of old buildings *in situ*. 'London is senile', he warned. 'Had you a grandmother hopelessly senile, you probably would not embalm her and preserve her in a glass case if she died.' Old London should be honoured, 'preserving the best of it as a memorial in a great green park', but not allowed to stand in the way of the new.[227]

Seen in this perspective, preservation actually underscores our freedom from antiquity.

---

[222] Spender, *Love–Hate Relations*, pp. 35, 219–20, 239–40.
[223] Arendt, 'Introduction: Walter Benjamin', p. 39–45.
[224] *Face of the Past*, p. 129.
[225] 'New buildings in historic areas', p. 150; also *idem*, 'I'm worried about Walt'.
[226] *City of To-morrow* (1925), pp. 287–8.
[227] *Organic Architecture* (1939), p. 41; also pp. 16, 34–5. Wright would preserve only 'the better houses and palaces, historic old streets and lanes and public buildings and churches' (p. 35).

Our very eagerness to save its vestiges shows how much we have overcome it. 'Every nicely motivated effort to preserve nature, primitives and the past, and to represent them authentically', argues Dean MacCannell, makes the present 'more unified against its past, more in control of nature, less a product of history.' The vogue for preservation reflects the victory of the modern. So complete is this victory that we can afford to save, reproduce, and redistribute innumerable relics of our now distanced heritage. 'Restored remnants of dead traditions are essential components of the modern community and consciousness. They are reminders of our break with the past and with tradition, even our own tradition.'[228]

Relics are enjoyed all the more because they matter so little; it is their felt remoteness, their lack of consequence for the present, that lends preserved things their charm. 'Men have restored what they cease to resent.'[229] Like Calvino's mythical Maurilia, the old city seems beautiful now that a new one has superseded it.[230] What would once have been banished as reminders of too potent or encumbering a past is now cherished. Remains are most admired when new ideas or technology make them obsolete; it is the traces of Plumb's dead past whose permanence we strive to secure.

Crusading zeal further sunders then from now; the tangible past contrasts more acutely with the present because its advocates and detractors are so embattled. Is the past essential to the present or an encumbrance to it? The debate polarizes along a single spectrum of concern; preservation becomes the sole criterion for appreciating (or neglecting) the heritage, hence the *only* way to use it.

Setting apart things specially preserved from the commonplace present forecloses other uses of them. Such relics seldom become sources of creative inspiration; they are valued for their own sake, not for how we might reshape them. Appreciation today means protecting ancient structures, not making new ones after their example. We save old buildings but rarely or ineffectually use them as models. Indeed, it would be difficult to select creative exemplars from a legacy so widely and indiscriminately preserved. Unable to use the past creatively, we further isolate what we preserve; what we make may conform with treasured relics but seldom extends their living virtues; what we save is property and artifacts rather than ideas or culture.[231]

By contrast, many artists and architects from the Renaissance to the nineteenth century were excited more by the *spirit* of ancient times than by their remains. As we have seen, they cared less to preserve the past than to have it inspire their own work. Historical visions drawn from books, pictures, artifacts, and landscapes moved them not simply to revere but to rival antiquity: their cities, gardens, houses, furnishings, paintings, sculpture recalled classical or Gothic forms and patterns. Most of what the past five centuries made and built expresses this use of tradition. Men did sometimes fear lest admiration of the past preclude originality. But only in this century has originality become creativity's sole criterion.

[228] MacCannell, *Tourist*, p. 83. On cutting the past down to size, see Walden, *Ravished Image*, p. 10.
[229] 'They cease to resent what seems safely lodged in history' (Levenson, *Confucian China and Its Modern Fate*, 3:v).
[230] *Invisible Cities*, pp. 30–1.
[231] Bommes and Wright, '"Charms of residence": the public and the past', p. 269.

PASTS WE HAVE GAINED

I do not propose a return to Renaissance or any other mode of dealing with the past; to do so would be futile and anachronistic. It is useless to prescribe or proscribe how to treat the past, for our view of it is embedded in everything that we are and do. Yet few scholars seem to resist giving such advice. If 'we were to study the classical masterpieces with the same attention to detail' as Renaissance humanists 'and with the impulse to create works as good as the ones we read', Bolgar suggests, 'we too would [possibly] discover solutions to the new problems that vex us ... A line of enquiry which proved eminently successful in the past is unlikely to have lost all its original value.'[232] But we cannot study the classics in this way, for we have replaced Renaissance perspectives with our own, which allow imitation no role in creativity. If we gave up 'our easy contemporary way of acculturating the remote, appropriating the shards of all eras', surmises Greene, we could perhaps regain 'that shock of confrontation which might assist us to situate ourselves more knowingly in time'. But we are now too self-conscious to stop domesticating the past; the diffusion of historical knowledge no longer allows its 'fragments to withdraw into their proper strangeness' or lets us scan its alien embers 'in their tragic, spectral dimness';[233] *our* past is irreversibly lucid, comfortable, and artificial.

To enter vicariously into our predecessors' modes of experiencing *their* pasts, however, and to compare our own feelings with those of other times, may itself prove illuminating. We cannot emulate Dante in walking with Virgil, Petrarch in corresponding with Livy, or d'Holbach in enjoying conversations with Horace, or gaze on ruins with the sentiments of Diderot or Shelley; but in assessing the strength of these empathetic bonds we become aware that the past can pull in directions other than our own. We may doubt the reciprocity of humanist and *philosophe* rapport with their beloved Ancients, but we cannot deny that antiquity truly inspired them. We may be thankful to escape the enduring Irish sense of past grievances, but we should admire the imaginative force with which story-tellers have brought the Irish past to life. We view Victorian obsessions with Anglo-Saxon origins as more *outré* than the anachronisms of Alex Haley's *Roots*, but we may envy the Victorians for their capacity to draw communal sustenance from historical paintings, architecture, and literature. And 'we begin to see these creations in a different light', as Roy Strong says, 'only when we try to relive their excitement as they recaptured the past, as they relived it, as they used it to point a moral and give hope to a mass audience'.[234] Noting how 'Virgil, Dante, Shakespeare, Milton placed themselves in remote lands and in remote ages', the modern poet, comments Wallace Stevens, 'will wonder at those huge imaginations, in which what is remote becomes near, and what is dead lives with an intensity beyond any experience of life.'[235]

Alert to other routes to the past, we may see our own relations with it as less binding and destined at length to give way to other modes of appreciation. Our grandchildren may wonder at our passion for authentically restored old buildings much as we smile at

---

[232] *Classical Heritage*, p. 385.   [233] Greene, *Light in Troy*, p. 293.
[234] *And When Did You Last See Your Father?* p. 43.
[235] 'The noble rider and the sound of words' (1942), p. 23.

the naïvety of our grandparents, who thought that viewing a shrine where a hero fought would elevate the visitor's character and excite his patriotism.

Awareness of the myriad ways others have appreciated their heritage could enlarge our tolerance for manipulations of the past often decried as false or bizarre. A sanitized, Disneyfied heritage has some virtues; Ye Olde Englishe, mock-Tudor, and instant mansards are popular partly because they convey more lively or up-to-date impressions of things past than do many scrupulously kept survivals or laboriously self-conscious post-modern creations. Better a misinformed enjoyment of history than none, a lighthearted dalliance with the past than a wholesale rejection of it. Our heritage is amusing as well as serious, incongruous as well as harmonious. We can afford to smile at the anachronisms that make bygone times seem like old *Punch* cartoons fitted with new captions. The past is often funny because it *is* old hat. The very notion of preservation invites mockery at its extravagances – the several heads of John the Baptist[236] and the fourteen foreskins of Christ preserved in various churches;[237] the viscera of Henry V, which released an authentically unpleasant smell on being unearthed from a pot buried in France, and were then deep-frozen before being rejoined with that king's other remains in Westminster Abbey;[238] the cabin built of wood from forty-eight states that Henry Ford had reconstructed from George Washington Carver's memory of the one he lived in as a boy.[239] The pleasures of archaistic celebration outlive the veneration that inspires it, as with William Theed's wistful statue emphasizing Victoria and Albert's Anglo-Saxon affinities. Restorations and reconstructions need not always strive to be wholly authentic; even a patently altered or brazenly contrived past can have its uses.

Other perspectives help to compensate for modes of response to the past now lost. Our awareness of antiquity in many respect transcends our predecessors'. The elaboration of historical inquiry to lengthened reaches of chronology and culture sharpens our sense of

---

[236] Reputed heads were at Amiens, Nemours, St-Jean d'Angeli (France), San Silvestro in Capite (Rome), Emesa (Phoenicia) (Tillemont, *Ecclesiastical Memoirs* (1693), 1:85–6, 407–17; Charles L. Souvay, 'John the Baptist, Saint', *Catholic Encyclopedia* (New York: 1907–12), 8:490).

[237] Among the places with holy prepuces were Poitiers, Coulombs, Charraux, Hildesheim, Puy-en-Velay, Antwerp, and the Church of St John Lateran, Rome. See Steinberg, *Sexuality of Christ*, pp. 159, 202, citing Bernardino Carvajal, *Oratio in die circumcisionis* (1484). The Poitiers prepuce was long famed, but that at St John Lateran was declared authentic in the sixteenth century, only to be stolen and taken to Calcata, near Viterbo, ending up in the local Church of SS Cornelius and Cyprian. Following German Protestant ridicule, a papal decree of 1900 confined public showing of the prepuce to the annual Feast of the Circumcision, and prohibited all publicity, even excising its mention from Italian Touring Club guides (Peyrefitte, *Keys of St Peter*, pp. 263–83, 321–5). The Calcata prepuce was again recently stolen from the home of the parish priest, its disappearance this time relieving the Church of embarrassment (Tana de Zulueta, 'Mystery over theft of tiny "divine" relic', *Sunday Times*, 15 Jan. 1984, p. 12).

[238] Ian Murray, 'French soil yields trace of England's royal past', *The Times*, 8 June 1978, p. 1. As of October 1984, they had not yet reached the Abbey. Hearts and entrails often served as relics in lieu of skeletal remains (Hallam, 'Burial places of English kings', p. 45). During the late Middle Ages the felt connection between saving the soul and preserving moral remains made it desirable to multiply the number of one's burial places. The body of William the Conquerer was buried in Caen, his heart in Rouen, his bowels in Chalus; Bernard de Guesclin, constable to Charles V, had four separate tombs (heart, bowels, flesh, bones). Subsequently hearts instead of being buried were carried around as family souvenirs, later being replaced by less cumbersome and corruptible locks of hair (Ariès, *Hour of Our Death*, pp. 261–2, 387–8).

[239] Charles Phillips, 'Greenfield's changing past', p. 11. The vogue for preserving 1930s buildings, John Summerson surmises, lies in 'the very grimness of their Thirtyish humour; ... they bring out, as it were in caricature, the contradictions and neurosis of the time', but if we decide to preserve 'funny old things just for the hell of it, and for the entertainment of all and sundry ... the test is: "Are they funny enough?"' ('Demolishing the Thirties myth', *The Times*, 17 Dec. 1983, p. 8).

both continuities and discontinuities. Gone are the days when the standard text in architectural history could dismiss all buildings outside greater Europe as 'non-historical' because 'they exercise little direct influence on . . . Western Art'.[240] Less myopic moderns experience a past enriched by a broader substantive range, appreciating not only the traces of antiquity but the succession of events that connect them with countless echoes of the past.[241]

Mere touches of the past can give restored or modern structures some sense of history. Boston's Quincy Market preserves the past mainly in emblem and insignia, the fresh-minted classicism of the renovated Bulfinch dome juxtaposed against the worn lettering of nineteenth-century shopkeepers' signs lending the twentieth-century mercantile setting an aura of composite antiquity. At South Salem, New York, a new church has replaced the nineteenth-century meeting-house; at first glance a replica, it is in fact only reminiscent of it, streamlining the old church's steeple setbacks and jettisoning the Colonial shutters. Inside all is transformed, the nave itself turned at right angles; but behind the new altar a picture window gives onto the old burial ground, affording a picturesque glimpse of the past.

Consciousness of how time has linked us with locale also enhances modern perceptions. We celebrate the landscape as a living tapestry woven and tenanted by our forebears and ourselves. It is to disclose continuities, rather than to flaunt fame or antecedence, that many today explore family pasts. Such explorations fructify the middle ground of personal history and collective memory. No previous age matches the affectionate insight of Ronald Blythe's collage of a Suffolk village seen through octogenarian natives' eyes; or Dorothy Gallagher's compassionate exploration of six coexisting generations of American mothers and daughters; or Rowland Parker's absorbing chronicle of a Cambridgeshire hamlet; or John Baskin's evocations of two centuries of life and death in a doomed Ohio village.[242]

Crucial to such perspectives is appreciation of change – change not only from past to present, but as successive generations have seen the past. It may be unnerving to know that later impressions reshape previous assessments of the past; but it is also liberating. And it can be inspiring to know that the past we now recognize is an inheritance enlarged by our own acts and anticipations.

Our impact on surviving vestiges can reinforce awareness that the past is ever changing. Self-evidently both of earlier times and of today, such vestiges come to us visibly affected by the vicissitudes of nature and history. The impact of time is apparent in their structure, appearance, and function. Traces of the alterations that remould antiquities enrich our perception and enhance our experience. 'What the majority of us celebrate as natives is native improvements', Blythe writes of the Suffolk landscapes continuously transformed by his farming forebears. 'The shapes, colours and scents have an ancestral significance, and what moves us is that the vista . . . is a series of constructions made by our labouring fathers.'[243] And made by ourselves, as well.

[240] Fletcher, *History of Architecture on the Comparative Method* (1950), p. 888.
[241] 'Not for Caravaggio or Claude our awed awareness of the three millennia and the few feet of earth which at Sardis separate prehistoric skeletons from Byzantine bronzes!' (Coolidge, 'Foreword', *Gods & Heroes*, p. 10).
[242] Blythe, *Akenfield* (1969); Parker, *Common Stream* (1975); Gallagher, *Hannah's Daughters* (1976); Baskin, *New Burlington* (1976).
[243] 'Inherited perspective', p. 12.

A portrait of any past also reflects the painter's own time. Until recently, most historians sought to eliminate traces of the present. But rather than try to get rid of modern intrusions, those who paint the past today often deliberately insert them. The fictional excavations of Günter Grass, Thomas Pynchon, and Gabriel García Márquez throw extraordinary light on the present. Present awareness vividly informs past circumstances in the novels of J. G. Farrell, where motives and events are faithful to their historical periods but also prefigure modern perceptions. Such revelatory anachronisms may seem bizarre but are consistent with reality as experienced; any modern reader is similarly bound to invest historical scenes with his own knowledge and perspectives.

CONCLUSION

Recognizing the impact of the present on the past, we confront anew the paradox implicit in preservation. Vestiges are saved to stave off decay, destruction, and replacement and to keep an unspoiled heritage. Yet preservation itself reveals that permanence is an illusion. The more we save, the more aware we become that such remains are continually altered and reinterpreted. We suspend their erosion only to transform them in other ways. And saviours of the past change it no less than iconoclasts bent on its destruction.

What reassurance can be gained from vestiges of a past so prone to vicissitude? What virtue has a heritage whose permanence is chimerical? The answer is that a fixed past is not what we really need, or at any rate not all we need. We require a heritage with which we continually interact, one which fuses past with present. This heritage is not only necessary but inescapable; we cannot now avoid feeling that the past *is* to some extent our own creation. If today's insights can be seen as integral to the meaning of the past, rather than subversive of its truth, we may breathe new life into it.

Memory displays comparable fusions and transformations, as Chapter 5 showed. Recollections of what we have done, where we have been, how things looked and felt, alter with changing notions of how things *ought* to have been. Original recall is filtered through memories of our own earlier memories and by what others have told us; new experience and revised expectations continually reshape them. And we expect memories to alter as they recede into the past and our own self-image changes.

Preservation, by contrast with memory, segregates a tangible past required to be unlike the present. But such segregation conflicts with our awareness of reality. The things that surround us all have a past, and are recognizable because we share that past. With the relics we preserve, as with the memories we cherish, we live simultaneously in present and past. And while preservation formally espouses a fixed and segregated past, it cannot help revealing a past all along being altered to conform with present expectations. What is preserved, like what is remembered, is neither a true nor a stable likeness of past reality.

Humanity's continuous impact on the relics of the past may seem self-evident, but awareness of it is only recent. Historic preservation has helped us to see how much the past is altered to suit the present. Old buildings and artifacts have long been adapted to new uses, but the impulse to preserve has made such adaptation much more self-conscious. Adaptive alterations violate anti-scrape scruples but also reinforce them. Do not strip old buildings of later accretions or foist on them later images of the past, say the followers of

Ruskin and Morris; leave them alone, except for daily care, to show the marks of time and use. But this dictum can never be realized. Even minimal protection of ancient buildings from erosion – or from appreciation – has manifold and often unforeseeable consequences.

Such consequences are in themselves neither desirable nor deplorable; they are simply inevitable. We should not deceive ourselves that we can keep the past stable and segregated. Ruskin and Morris condemned restoration as a fraudulent modern contrivance, but modern contrivance is inescapable. Whether we restore or refrain from restoring we cannot avoid reshaping the past; no recognized vestige is devoid of present intentions. When we realize that past and present are not exclusive but inseparable realms, we cast off preservation's self-defeating insistence on a fixed and stable past. Only by altering and adding to what we save does our heritage remain real, alive, and comprehensible.

Preservation narrowly construed cannot improvise or adapt to the implacable pressures of change. Seen as part of the process of change, however, preservation takes its place among other fruitful ways of treasuring a heritage. Without a past that is malleable as well as generously preserved, the present will lack models to inspire it and the future be deprived of a lifeline to its past.

By changing relics and records of former times, we change ourselves as well; the revised past in turn alters our own identity. The nature of that impact depends on the purpose and power of those who instigate the changes. The transformation of history in totalitarian regimes can persuade people that free will and chance play no part in their lives, that everything is predetermined. New historical perspectives can, on the other hand, free people from archaic conventions, outworn rules, age-old tyrannies. And other revisions of the past deeply influence beliefs and affect personality.

To recognize that the past has been altered understandably arouses anxiety. A past seen as open to manipulation not only undermines supposed historical verities but implies a fragile present and portends a shaky future. When we know that hoary documents are regularly forged, old paintings imitated, relics contrived, ancient buildings modernized and new ones antiquated, the identity of everything around us becomes dubious. When a past we depend on for heritage and continuity turns out to be a complex of original and altered remains enlarged by subsequent thoughts and deeds, if not an outright sham, we lose faith in our own perceptions.

Yet to see why and how we ourselves change the past helps to free us from myths that constrained previous perceptions. To achieve such demystification, psychoanalysis encourages us to re-examine – and hence reconstruct – our personal past. Obsessive behaviour is often based on earlier perceptions mired in an outgrown past. Bringing to consciousness long-concealed feelings and events helps shake off dependence on the past and conduces toward a freely chosen future. No longer captive to a misconstrued life history, we refashion one that is coherent and believable in present terms. But knowing that today's circumstances determine what and how we reconstruct, we remain aware that each new life history is bound to be further revised; our new past is no more final than the previous one.

Plumb contended that 'objective' history based on firm canons of evidence has largely dispelled dependence on a fixed and fearsome past. As I have shown, this conclusion is dubious: the cult of nostalgia, the yearning for roots, the demand for heritage, the passion for preservation show that the spell of the past remains potent. Indeed, history can never bring about the death of the past, for every act we take, every plan we make, entail the past's more or less conscious re-evaluation, revision, and re-creation.[244] But a past known to be altered and alterable sheds at least some of its enchantment, sacred or malign. Once aware that relics, history, and memory are continually refashioned, we are less inhibited by the past, less frustrated by a fruitless quest for sacrosanct originals.

We must reckon with the artifice no less than the truth of our heritage. Nothing ever made has been left untouched, nothing ever known remains immutable; yet these facts should not distress but emancipate us. It is far better to realize the past has always been altered than to pretend it has always been the same. Advocates of preservation who adjure us to save things unchanged fight a losing battle, since even to appreciate the past is to transform it. Every relic is a testament not only to its initiators but to its inheritors, not only to the spirit of the past but to the perspectives of the present.

Some preservers believe they save the real past by preventing it from being made over. But we cannot avoid remaking our heritage, for every act of recognition alters what survives. We can use the past fruitfully only when we realize that to inherit is also to transform. What our predecessors have left us deserves respect, but a patrimony simply preserved becomes an intolerable burden; the past is best used by being domesticated – and by our accepting and rejoicing that we do so.

The past remains integral to us all, individually and collectively. We must concede the ancients their place, as I have argued. But their place is not simply back there, in a separate and foreign country; it is assimilated in ourselves, and resurrected into an ever-changing present.

---

[244] Peel, 'Making history', p. 129.

BIBLIOGRAPHY AND CITATION INDEX

Titles listed all refer to works cited in the text or footnotes; page numbers are in bold face at the end of each item. Excluded from the bibliography are items from newspapers, most brief or peripheral articles from weekly and monthly periodicals, and fugitive matter such as advertisements and brochures; all these are fully cited in the relevant footnotes. When such items are cited several times or seem to me of topical significance, however, they are included here. Brackets around dates refer to first publication; square brackets refer to dates of composition.

ABBREVIATIONS

ICOMOS   International Council on Monuments and Sites
IHT   *International Herald Tribune*
SPAB   Society for the Protection of Ancient Buildings (U.K.)
TLS   *Times Literary Supplement*

Abraham, Gerald. *The Tradition of Western Music*, Oxford University Press, 1974. **242**

Ackerman, James. 'The planning of Renaissance Rome', in Ramsey, *Rome in the Renaissance*, q.v., pp. 3–17. **391**

Acton, John E. E. Dalberg, Lord. 'Inaugural lecture on the study of history' (1895), in his *Lectures on Modern History*, ed. J. V. Figgis and R. N. Laurence, London: Macmillan, 1921, pp. 1–28. **68**

Adams, Brooks. *The Law of Civilization and Decay*, 2nd edn. (1896), New York: Vintage, 1955. **395**

Adams, Charles Francis. 'Hutchinson's third volume', *North American Review*, 38 (1834), 134–58. **118**

Adams, Henry. *The Education of Henry Adams: An Autobiography* (1906), Boston: Houghton Mifflin, 1918. **395**

  Mont-Saint-Michel and Chartres (1912), London: Constable, 1950. **9**

Adams, John. *Diary and Autobiography*, ed. L. H. Butterfield, 3 vols., Harvard University Press, 1961. **397**

  Novanglus, or, a History of the Dispute with America, from Its Origin, in 1754, to the Present Time (1774), *Works*, 10 vols., Boston, 1857, 4:1–177. **107**

Adams, Robert. *The Lost Museum: Glimpses of Vanished Originals*, New York: Viking, 1980. **161, 172, 287, 354**

Addison, Joseph. *Critical Essays from the 'Spectator'*, ed. Donald F. Bond, 5 vols., Oxford: Clarendon, 1965. **94, 160**

Adler, Thomas P. 'Pinter's *Night*: a stroll down Memory Lane', *Modern Drama*, 17 (1974), 461–5. **193**

Æ (George William Russell). *The Candle of Vision*, London: Macmillan, 1918. **18**

Agard, Walter R. 'Classics on the Midwest frontier', in Walker D. Wyman and Clifton B. Kroeber (eds.), *The Frontier in Perspective*, University of Wisconsin Press, 1965, pp. 165–83. **110, 113**

Agee, James, and Evans, Walker. *Let Us Now Praise Famous Men* (1941), Boston: Houghton Mifflin, 1969. **151**

Aldiss, Brian W. *An Age*, London: Faber and Faber, 1967. **22, 23, 31**
Frankenstein Unbound, London: Cape, 1973. **4**

Alexander, Edward P. *Museums in Motion: An Introduction to the History and Functions of Museums*, Nashville, Tenn.: American Association of State and Local History, 1979. **244**

Algarotti, Francesco. *Essay on Painting*, London, 1764. **149, 160**

Alison, Archibald. 'The historical romance', *Blackwood's Magazine*, 58 (1845), 341–56. **340**

Allardyce, Gilbert. 'The rise and fall of the Western Civilization course', *American Historical Review*, 87 (1982), 695–725. **222**

Allen, James. 'Living the past in Illinois', *Historic Illinois*, 1:4 (1978), 3, 11. **296**

Alp, Tekin. 'The restoration of Turkish history' (from his *Le Kemalisme*, 1937), in Kedourie, *Nationalism in Asia and Africa*, q.v., pp. 207–24. **46, 337**

Althöfer, Heinz. 'Fragmente und Ruine', *Kunstforum International*, 19 (1977), 57–169. **172, 173**

Alverson, Charles. *Time Bandits*, London: Sparrow, 1981. **68**

Amis, Kingsley. *New Maps of Hell: A Survey of Science Fiction*, London: Gollancz, 1961. **24**

Anderson, Jay. 'Living history: simulating everyday life in living museums', *American Quarterly*, 34 (1982), 290–306. **299, 301**
Time Machines: The World of Living History, Nashville, Tenn.: American Association for State and Local History, 1984. **24, 28, 31, 49, 246, 295, 298, 299, 301, 340, 343, 359, 363**

Anderson, Jervis. 'Sources' (review of Haley, *Roots*, q.v.), *New Yorker*, 14 Feb. 1977, pp. 112–23. **51, 197**

Anderson, Poul. *Guardians of Time*, London: Pan, 1977. **24, 26, 27, 31, 32**
'The man who came early', in his *The Horn of Time*, Boston: Gregg, 1968, pp. 68–90. **29**
There Will Be Time, London: Sphere, 1979. **30**

Anderson, Quentin. *The Imperial Self: An Essay in American Literary and Cultural History*, New York: Knopf, 1971. **110**

Andrews, Wayne. *Voltaire*, New York: New Directions, 1981. **374**

Anscombe, G. E. M. 'Experience and causation', in H. D. Lewis, *Contemporary British Philosophy*, q.v., pp. 15–29. **196**
'The reality of the past', in Max Black, *Philosophical Analysis: A Collection of Essays*, Englewood Cliffs, N. J.: Prentice-Hall, 1963, pp. 36–56. **28**

Appian's Roman History, 4 vols., London: Heinemann, 1912. **46**

'Archaeologia; or, miscellaneous tracts relating to antiquity', *Edinburgh Review*, 154 (1881), 101–21. **397**

Ardagh, John. *A Tale of Five Cities: Life in Provincial Europe Today*, London: Secker & Warburg, 1979. **250**

Arendt, Hannah. *The Human Condition*, University of Chicago Press, 1958. **39**
'Introduction: Walter Benjamin: 1892–1940', in Benjamin, *Illuminations*, q.v., pp. 1–55. **361, 377, 405**

Ariès, Philip. *The Hour of Our Death*, London: Penguin, 1983. **61, 131, 177, 322, 323, 408**

Aristides. 'Disremembrance of things present', *American Scholar*, 49 (1980), 157–63. **205**

Arkell, W. J. *Oxford Stone*, London: Faber and Faber, 1947. **164**

Armstrong, William A. 'Introduction' to Bacon, *Advancement of Learning*, q.v., pp. 1–47. **90**

Arnau, Frank (H. Schmitt). *Three Thousand Years of Deception in Art and Antiques*, London: Cape, 1961. **14, 64, 152, 153, 170, 171, 337**

Arnheim, Rudolf. 'On duplication', in Dutton, *Forger's Art*, q.v., pp. 232–45. **385**

Arnold, Matthew. *Culture & Anarchy: An Essay in Political and Social Criticism* (1869), London: Macmillan, 1938. **96**

Arragon, R. F. 'History's changing image: "with such permanence as time has"', *American Scholar*, 33 (1964), 222–33. **218, 231**

Artaud, Antonin. *Le Théâtre et son double* (c. 1933), *Œuvres complètes*, Paris: Gallimard, 1964, Vol. 4. **380**

Ashton, Francis. *The Breaking of the Seals*, London: Andrew Dakers, 1946. **20**

Asimov, Isaac. 'The dead past', in his *Earth Is Room Enough*, London: Granada/Panther, 1957, pp. 9–50. **23**

Aston, Margaret. 'English ruins and history: the Dissolution and the sense of the past', *Journal of the Warburg and Courtauld Institutes*, 36 (1973), 231–55. **144, 173, 175, 395**

Ausonius. 'Epitaphs', *Works*, 2 vols., London: Heinemann, 1919, 1:141–61. **126**

Austen, Jane. *Love and Freindship, and Other Early Works*, London: Chatto & Windus, 1922, pp. 85–97. **157**

Austin, Alfred. *Haunts of Ancient Peace*, London: Macmillan, 1902. **9**

Avery, Charles. *The Rood-Loft from Hertogenbosch*, reprint from *Victoria and Albert Museum Yearbook*, 1 (1969), 110–36. **394**

d'Azevedo, Warren L. 'Tribal history in Liberia', in Neisser, *Memory Observed*, q.v., pp. 258–68 (first published as 'Uses of the past in Gola discourse', *Journal of African History*, 3 (1962), 11–34). **235**

Babbage, Charles. *The Ninth Bridgewater Treatise: A Fragment*, London, 1837. **19**

Bacon, Francis. *The Advancement of Learning, Book I* (1605), ed. William A. Armstrong, London: Athlone, 1975. **89, 91**

   Novum Organum (1620), in his *Works*, ed. James Spedding, R. L. Ellis, and D. D. Heath, 7 vols., London, vol. 4, 1858. **89, 90**

Baier, Annette. 'Mixing memory and desire', *American Philosophical Quarterly*, 13 (1967), 213–20. **250**

Bailyn, Bernard. *The Ideological Origins of the American Revolution*, Harvard University Press, 1967. **112, 142**

Baker, Ernest. *A Guide to Historical Fiction*, New York: Argosy-Antiquarian, 1968. **224**

Baker, Malcolm. *The Cast Courts, Victoria and Albert Museum*, London: H.M.S.O., 1982. **283**

Balderston, John L., with Squire, J. C. *Berkeley Square: A Play in Three Acts*, London: Longmans, Green, 1929. **24, 33**

Ball, Adrian. *Cleopatra's Needle: The Story of 100 Years in London*, Havant, Hants.: Kenneth Mason, 1978. **151**

Ballard, J. G. 'The sound-sweep', in his *The Four-Dimensional Nightmare*, Penguin, 1977. **20**

Baltrušaitis, Jurgis. *Le Moyen Age fantastique: antiquités et exotismes dans l'art gothique*, Paris: Armand Colin, 1955. **176**

Banham, Reyner. 'The last boom-town', *New Society*, 13 May 1982, pp. 264–5. **6**

   'Preservation adobe', ibid., 2 Apr. 1981, pp. 23–4. **276, 359**

   Theory and Design in the First Machine Age, London: Architectural Press, 1960. **380**

Bann, Stephen. *The Clothing of Clio: A Study of the Representation of History in Nineteenth-Century Britain and France*, Cambridge University Press, 1984. **221, 227, 257, 360**

Barante, Prosper de. 'Sur l'acquisition du Musée du Sommerard', rapport fait à la Chambre des Pairs, 15 July 1843, in his *Etudes littéraires et historiques*, 2 vols., Paris, 1858, 2:417–26. **245**

Barkan, Leonard. *Nature's Work of Art: The Human Body as Image of the World*, Yale University Press, 1975. **136, 141**

Barker, Philip. 'The scale of the problem', in Rahtz, *Rescue Archaeology*, q.v., pp. 28–34. **396**

Barnes, Julian. *Flaubert's Parrot*, London: Cape, 1984. **325**

Baron, Hans. *The Crisis of the Early Italian Renaissance: Civic Humanism and Republican Liberty in an Age of Classicism and Tyranny*, rev. edn., Princeton University Press, 1966. **76, 77, 79**

   'The *Querelle* of the Ancients and the Moderns as a problem for Renaissance scholarship', *Journal of the History of Ideas*, 20 (1959), 3–22 (reprinted in P. O. Kristeller and P. P. Wiener (eds.), *Renaissance Essays*, New York: Harper & Row, 1968, pp. 95–114). **76, 77, 79, 86**

Barry, Dave. 'Why I like old things', *Historic Preservation*, 35:1 (1983), 49–50. **13, 44**

Barthelme, Donald, and Sorel, Edward. 'Monumental folly', *Atlantic Monthly*, 237:2 (1976), 33–40. **322**

Bartlett, Frederic C. *Remembering: A Study in Experimental and Social Psychology* (1932), Cambridge University Press, 1967. **202**

Baskin, John. *New Burlington: The Life and Death of an American Village*, New York: Norton, 1976. **409**

Bataille, Gretchen M., and Silet, Charles L. P. (eds.). *The Pretend Indians: Images of Native Americans in the Movies*, Iowa State University Press, 1980. **348**

Bate, Walter Jackson. *The Burden of the Past and the English Poet*, London: Chatto & Windus, 1971. **73, 94, 137, 348, 349**

Bateman, Thomas. *Ten Years' Diggings in Celtic and Saxon Grave Hills, in the Counties of Derby, Stafford, and York, from 1848 to 1858 ...*, London, 1861. **397**

Bator, Paul M. *The International Trade in Art*, University of Chicago Press, 1983. **396**

Battin, M. Pabst. 'Exact replication in the visual arts', *Journal of Aesthetics and Art Criticism*, 38 (1979), 153–8. **293**

Beams, David W. 'Consciousness in James's "The Sense of the Past"', *Criticism*, 5 (1963), 148–72. **33**

Bearss, Edwin C. *Furnishing Study: Lyndon B. Johnson Birthplace-Cottage, Stonewall, Gillespie County, Texas*, Denver: U.S. Dept. of the Interior, National Park Service, 1979. **348**

Beauvoir, Simone de. *Old Age*, Penguin, 1977. **131, 133, 192, 210**

Beazley, Elisabeth. 'Popularity: its benefits and risks', in Lowenthal and Binney, *Our Past Before Us*, q.v., pp. 193–202. **268, 273**

Becker, Carl L. 'Everyman his own historian' (reprinted from *American Historical Review*, 37 (1932), 221–36), in Winks, *Historian as Detective*, q.v., pp. 3–23. **39, 211, 212, 216, 240**
  The Heavenly City of the Eighteenth-Century Philosophers, Yale University Press, 1932. **95, 371**

Beecher, Henry Ward. *Star Papers; or, Experiences of Art and Nature* (1855), rev. edn., New York, 1873. **114**

Beerbohm, Max. *Lytton Strachey* (Rede Lecture, 1943), in his *The Incomparable Max: A Selection*, London: Heinemann, 1962, pp. 339–57. **360**
  Seven Men and Two Others (1919), Oxford University Press, 1966. **3**

Bellow, Saul. *Mr. Sammler's Planet*, New York: Viking, 1970. **198**

Bellringer, Alan W. 'Henry James's *The Sense of the Past*: the backward vision', *Forum for Modern Language Studies*, 17 (1981), 201–16. **32**

Belmont, John M. 'Individual differences in memory: the cases of normal and retarded development', in Gruneberg and Morris, *Aspects of Memory*, q.v., pp. 153–85. **193**

Benjamin, B. S. 'Remembering' (reprinted from *Mind*, 65 (1956), 312–31), in Donald F. Gustafson (ed.), *Essays in Philosophical Psychology*, London: Macmillan, 1967, pp. 171–94. **195**

Benjamin, Walter. *Illuminations*, New York: Schocken, 1969:
  'The storyteller: reflections on the works of Nicolai Leskov', pp. 83–109. **209**
  'The work of art in the age of mechanical reproduction', pp. 217–51. **306**
  Arendt, 'Introduction', q.v.

Benson, Sally. 'Spirit of '76', *New Yorker*, 25 Dec. 1954, pp. 20–5. **356**

Bentham, Jeremy. *Auto-Icon; or, Farther Uses of the Dead to the Living. A Fragment from the Mss*, ed. John Hill Burton, n.p., 1842. **61**

Berg, Lennart. 'The salvage of the Abu Simbel temples', *Monumentum*, 17 (1978), 25–54. **285**

Berger, John. *About Looking*, London: Writers and Readers, 1980:
  'Lowry and the industrial North', pp. 87–95. **306**
  'Uses of photography', pp. 48–63. **257**
  'Painting and time', *New Society*, 27 Sept. 1979, pp. 684–5. **390**

Berger, Peter L. *Invitation to Sociology: A Humanistic Perspective*, Penguin, 1966. **199, 201, 258, 306**

Berggasse 19: Sigmund Freud's Home and Offices, Vienna 1938: The Photographs of Edmund Engelman, New York: Basic Books, 1976. **255**

Bergson, Henri. *Creative Evolution* (1922), London: Macmillan, 1954. **185**

Matter and Memory (1896), New York: Macmillan, 1911. **17**

La Pensée et le mouvant (1934), in his *Œuvres*, ed. André Robinet, 3rd edn., Paris: Presses Universitaires de France, 1970, pp. 1251–1482. **17**

Berington, Joseph. *The History of the Lives of Abeillard and Eloisa*, 2nd edn., 2 vols., Basel, 1793. **236**

Berkeley, George. *The Works of George Berkeley, Bishop of Cloyne*, 9 vols., London, 1848–57. **108**

Berlin, Isaiah. *Vico and Herder: Two Studies in the History of Ideas*, London: Hogarth, 1976. **141, 211, 233, 245**

Bernfeld, Suzanne Cassirer. 'Freud and archeology', *American Imago*, 8 (1951), 107–28. **35, 239, 253**

Bertaux, Daniel (ed.). *Biography and Society: The Life History Approach in the Social Sciences* (Sage Studies in International Sociology 23), Beverly Hills, Calif.: Sage, 1981. Includes essays by Gagnon; Hankiss; Kohli.

Bester, Alfred. 'Hobson's choice', in his *Starburst*, New York: New American Library/Signet, 1958, pp. 133–48. **24, 29, 31, 33**

'The men who murdered Mohammed' (1958), in *The Light Fantastic: The Great Short Stories of Alfred Bester*, London: Gollancz, 1977, pp. 113–29. **32**

Betjeman, John. 'Antiquarian prejudice' (1937), in his *First and Last Loves*, London: Arrow, 1960, pp. 54–72. **356**

Bettelheim, Bruno. *Freud and Man's Soul*, New York: Knopf, 1983. **378**

'The problem of generations', *Daedalus*, 91 (1962), 68–96. **72**

Bibby, Geoffrey. 'An experiment with time', *Horizon*, 12:2 (1970), 97–101. **301**

Bibikov, Sergei N. 'A Stone Age orchestra', *UNESCO Courier*, 28:6 (1975), 28–31. **242**

Biddle, Martin. 'The future of the urban past', in Rahtz, *Rescue Archaeology*, q.v., pp. 94–112. **397**

'Preface' to Carolyn M. Heighway (ed.), *The Erosion of History: Archaeology and Planning in Towns*, London: Council for British Archaeology, 1972, pp. vi–vii. **397**

Binney, Marcus. 'Oppression to obsession', in Lowenthal and Binney, *Our Past Before Us*, q.v., pp. 203–12. **153, 381, 399, 401, 402**

Binney, Marcus, and Burman, Peter (eds.). *Change and Decay: The Future of Our Churches*, London: Studio Vista, 1977. Includes essay by Schofield. **396**

Binney, Marcus, and Grenfell, Laura. *Drowning in V.A.T.*, London: SAVE Britain's Heritage, 1980. **401**

Binney, Marcus, and Hanna, Max. *Preservation Pays: Tourism and the Economic Benefits of Conserving Historic Buildings*, ibid., 1978. **396, 401**

Binns, C. K. 'The importance of patina on old English furniture', *Antiques Collector*, 42 (1971), 58–64. **145, 156**

'Restored and unrestored pieces of early oak furniture', ibid., 41 (1970), 184–90. **152**

Binyon, Michael. *Life in Russia*, London: Hamish Hamilton, 1983. **6, 35, 62**

Biro, J. I. 'Hume on self-identity and memory', *Review of Metaphysics*, 30 (1976–7), 19–38. **197**

Bishop, Reid. 'The Perception and Importance of Time in Architecture', Ph.D. thesis, University of Surrey, 1982. **222, 295, 319, 388**

Blaas, P. B. M. *Continuity and Anachronism: Parliamentary and Constitutional Development in Whig Historiography and in the Anti-Whig Reaction between 1890 and 1930*, The Hague: Nijhoff, 1978. **41, 102, 217, 233, 258, 353, 370**

Black, Robert. 'Ancients and Moderns in the Renaissance: rhetoric and history in Accolti's *Dialogue on the Preeminence of Men of His Own Time*', *Journal of the History of Ideas*, 43 (1982), 3–32. **76**

Blavatsky, Helena Petrovna. *Isis Unveiled: A Master-Key to the Mysteries of Ancient and Modern Science and Technology*, 2 vols., New York, 1877. **19**

Blegen, Theodore. 'Singing immigrants and pioneers', in Joseph J. Kwiat and Mary C. Turpie (eds.), *Studies in American Culture: Dominant Ideas and Images*, University of Minnesota Press, 1960, pp. 171–88. **42**

Bloch, Marc. *The Historian's Craft* [1941–4], Manchester University Press, 1954. **55, 245**

Bloch, Maurice. 'The past and the present in the present', *Man*, 12 (1977), 278–92. **220, 231**

Blomfield, Reginald. *Modernismus*, London: Macmillan, 1934. **163**

Bloom, Harold. *The Anxiety of Influence: A Theory of Poetry*, Oxford University Press, 1975. **70, 71, 73, 380**

   Poetry and Repression: Revisionism from Blake to Stevens, Yale University Press, 1976. **93, 113**

Blyden, Edward Wilmot. 'The Negro in ancient history' (1871), in Kedourie, *Nationalism in Asia and Africa*, q.v., pp. 250–74. **336**

Blythe, Ronald. *Akenfield: Portrait of an English Village*, London: Allen Lane/Penguin, 1969. **409**

   Commentary, in Paul Hallberg (ed.), *The Feeling for Nature and the Landscape of Man* (Proceedings of the 4th Nobel Symposium (1978), Royal Society of Arts and Sciences of Göteberg, 1980), p. 159. **331**

   'An inherited perspective', in his *From the Headlands*, London: Chatto & Windus, 1982, pp. 1–13. **409**

   The View in Winter: Reflections on Old Age, London: Allen Lane, 1979. **130, 131, 133, 134**

Boas, George. 'The Mona Lisa in the history of taste', *Journal of the History of Ideas*, 1 (1940), 207–24. **307**

Boase, T. S. R. *Death in the Middle Ages: Mortality, Judgment and Remembrance*, London: Thames and Hudson, 1972. **176**

   'Macklin and Bowyer', *Journal of the Warburg and Courtauld Institutes*, 26 (1963), 148–77. **257**

Boiret, Yves. *See* 'World of conservation: Yves Boiret'.

Bolgar, R. R. *The Classical Heritage and Its Beneficiaries*, Cambridge University Press, 1954. **372, 373**

   'The Greek legacy', in Finley, *Legacy of Greece*, q.v., pp. 429–72. **225, 372, 407**

   (ed.). *Classical Influences on European Culture, A.D. 1500–1700*, Cambridge University Press, 1976. Includes his 'Introduction', pp. 1–30; Buddensieg, q.v. **306**

Bolingbroke, Viscount Henry St John. *The Idea of a Patriot King, with Respect to the Constitution of Great Britain*, London, *c.* 1740. **141**

   Letters on the Study and Use of History, 2 vols., London, 1752. **234**

Bommes, Michael and Wright, Patrick. '"Charms of residence": the public and the past', in *Making Histories: Studies in History-Writing and Politics* (Centre for Contemporary Cultural Studies, University of Birmingham), London: Hutchinson, 1982, pp. 253–301. **37, 340, 406**

Boorstin, Daniel. *America and the Image of Europe: Reflections on American Thought*, New York: Meridian, 1960. **145, 329**

   The Americans: The National Experience, New York: Random House/Vintage, 1967. **108**

   'The enlarged contemporary' (Reith Lectures, 1975), *The Listener*, 11 Dec. 1975, pp. 786–9. **xvii, 66**

   The Lost World of Thomas Jefferson, Boston: Beacon, 1960. **108**

Borges, Jorge Luis. 'The creation and P. H. Gosse' (1941), in his *Other Inquisitions 1937–1952*, New York: Washington Square Press, 1966, pp. 22–5. **189**

   'Doctor Brodie's report', in book of same title, New York: Bantam, 1973, pp. 133–46. **3**

   A Personal Anthology, London: Cape, 1967:

      'Funes, the memorious', pp. 35–43. **205**

      'A new refutation of time' (1946), pp. 44–64. **204**

      'The witness', p. 178. **195**

   'Tlön, Uqbar, Orbis Tertius' (1961), in his *Labyrinths*, Penguin, 1970, pp. 27–43. **187, 195**

Bosanquet, Bernard. *A History of Aesthetic* (1932), rev. edn., New York: Meridian, 1957. **135**

Boston, Lucy M. *The Stones of Green Knowe*, Penguin/Puffin, 1979. **288**

Boulez, Pierre. *Conversations with Célestin Deliège (Par volonté et par hazard)*, London: Eulenberg, 1976. **124, 384**

Bousquet, J., and Devambez, P. 'New methods in restoring ancient vases in the Louvre', *Museum*, 3 (1950), 177–80. **171**

Bovey, John. 'Boats against the current: notes of a returning exile', *Virginia Quarterly Review*, 54 (1978), 577–600. **164**

Bowron, E. P. 'Introduction', *Pompeo Batoni (1708–87) and his British Patrons*, Greater London Council, 1982, pp. 7–20. **283**

Bradbury, Malcolm, and McFarlane, James (eds.). *Modernism 1890–1930*, Penguin, 1976. Includes essays by Cahm; Rawson; the editors.

    'The name and nature of modernism', in their *Modernism*, q.v., pp. 19–55. **379**

Bradbury, Malcolm, and Orsler, Michael. 'Department of amplification', *New Yorker*, 2 July 1960, pp. 58–62. **384**

Bradbury, Malcolm, and Palmer, David (eds.). *Victorian Poetry* (Stratford-upon-Avon Studies 15), London: Edward Arnold, 1972. Includes essays by Buckley; Ellison; Gent; Hunt, J. D.; Miller, J. H.; Peckham.

Bradbury, Ray. 'The machine-tooled happyland – Disneyland', *Holiday*, 38:4 (1965), 100–4. **190, 248**

    'A scent of sarsaparilla', in his *The Day It Rained Forever*, Penguin, 1963, pp. 192–8. **7, 248**

    'A sound of thunder', in his *R Is for Rocket*, London: Pan, 1972, pp. 73–86. **31**

Bradstreet, Anne. 'Of the four ages of man' (1678), in *The Works of Anne Bradstreet*, ed. Jeannine Hensley, Harvard University Press, 1967, pp. 51–64. **130**

Brandi, Cesare. 'The cleaning of pictures, in relation to patina, varnish and glaze', *Burlington Magazine*, 91 (1949), 183–8. **160**

Brandt, Anthony. 'A short natural history of nostalgia', *Atlantic Monthly*, 242:6 (1978), 58–63. **66**

Bray, J. W. *A History of English Critical Terms*, Boston, 1898. **101**

Breitling, Peter. 'The origins and development of a conservation philosophy in Austria', in Kain, *Planning for Conservation*, q.v., pp. 49–61. **44**

Brennan, Penny L., and Steinberg, Laurence P. 'Is reminiscence adaptive? Relations among social activity level, reminiscence, and morale', *International Journal of Aging and Human Development*, 18 (1984), 99–110. **43**

Brett, Lionel. *Parameters and Images: Architecture in a Crowded World*, London: Weidenfeld and Nicolson, 1970. **42, 388**

Briggs, Asa. *Victorian Cities*, London: Odhams, 1963. **97**

Briggs, Martin S. *Goths and Vandals: A Study of the Destruction, Neglect and Preservation of Historical Buildings in England*, London: Constable, 1952. **67, 326**

Brinkley-Rogers, Paul. 'The big business of artifacts theft', *Historic Preservation*, 33:1 (1981), 17–21. **396**

Britain's Historic Buildings: A Policy for Their Future Use, London: British Tourist Authority, 1980. **402**

British Steel Corporation, *Cor-Ten Steel* brochure, Publication GSD/MS/OL/3–73. **164**

Brockelman, Paul. 'Of memory and things past', *International Philosophical Quarterly*, 15 (1975), 309–25. **196, 201, 203**

Brommelle, Norman. 'Material for a history of conservation: the 1850 and 1853 reports on the National Gallery', *Studies in Conservation*, 2 (1956), 176–87. **160**

Bronner, Simon J. '"Visible proofs": material culture study in America', *American Quarterly*, 35 (1983), 316–38. **245**

Brooks, Van Wyck. 'On creating a usable past', *The Dial*, 64 (1918), 337–41. **290**

    The World of Washington Irving, Philadelphia: Blakiston, 1945. **115**

Brown, B. Floyd, *et al.* (eds.). *Corrosion and Metal Artifacts – A Dialogue between Conservators and Archaeologists and Corrosion Scientists* (National Bureau of Standards Special Publication 479), Washington: U.S. Dept. of Commerce, 1977. Includes essays by Foley, R. T.; Nielson; Organ; Smith, C. S.; Weil, P. D.

Burne-Jones, Georgiana. *Memorials of Edward Burne-Jones*, 2 vols., London: Macmillan, 1904. **98, 376**

Burnet, Thomas. *The Sacred Theory of the Earth* (1684), 1691 edn., London: Centaur, 1965. **88, 137, 138, 140**

Burns, E. Bradford. 'Teaching history: a changing clientele and an affirmation of goals', *American Historical Association Perspectives*, 21:1 (1983), 19–21. **237**

Burrow, J. W. *A Liberal Descent: Victorian Historians and the English Past*, Cambridge University Press, 1981. **41, 102, 233, 353**
  'The sense of the past', in Laurence Lerner (ed.), *The Victorians*, London: Methuen, 1978, pp. 120–38. **96, 97, 98, 102, 245, 395**

Burrows, Edwin G., and Wallace, Michael. 'The American Revolution: the ideology of nationalism and the psychology of national liberation', *Perspectives in American History*, 6 (1972), 165–206. **106, 107**

Burton, Robert G. 'The human awareness of time: an analysis', *Philosophy and Phenomenological Research*, 36 (1975–6), 303–18. **195, 200**

Bury, J. B. *The Idea of Progress: An Enquiry into Its Origin and Growth* (1932), New York: Dover, 1955. **95**

Butler, Joseph T. 'Historic rooms at Sleepy Hollow restorations', *Historic Preservation*, 20:2 (1968), 69–73. **344**

Butler, Ronald J. 'Other dates', *Mind*, 68 (1959), 16–33. **188, 190**

Butterfield, Herbert. *The Historical Novel: An Essay*, Cambridge University Press, 1924. **186, 215, 226, 227**
  Man on His Past: The Study of Historical Scholarship, Cambridge University Press, 1969. **221**
  The Whig Interpretation of History, London: G. Bell, 1931. **41, 55, 354**

Butterfield, Roger. 'Henry Ford, the Wayside Inn, and the problem of "History is bunk"', *Massachusetts Historical Society Proceedings*, 77 (1965), 53–66. **244, 285**

Buxton, John. *The Grecian Taste: Literature in the Age of Neo-Classicism 1740–1820*, London: Macmillan, 1978. **374**

Byron, George Gordon, Lord. *Childe Harold's Pilgrimage*, in *Poetical Works*, ed. Frederick Page, Oxford University Press, 1970, pp. 179–252. **181**

Cadogan, Gerald. *Palaces of Minoan Crete*, London: Barrie and Jenkins, 1975. **282**

Cahalan, James. *Great Hatred, Little Room: The Irish Historical Novel*, Syracuse University Press, 1983. **250**

Cahm, Eric. 'Revolt, conservatism and reaction in Paris, 1905–25', in Bradbury and McFarlane, *Modernism*, q.v., pp. 162–71. **379**

Calvino, Italo. *Invisible Cities*, New York: Harcourt Brace Jovanovich, 1972. **289, 406**

Campbell, Donald. 'Blunden Shadbolt 1879–1949: architect of the House Desirable', *Thirties Society Journal*, No. 3, 1982 (1983), 17–24. **62, 153**

Cannadine, David. 'The context, performance and meaning of ritual: the British monarchy and the "invention of tradition", c. 1820–1977', in Hobsbawm and Ranger, *Invention of Tradition*, q.v., pp. 101–64. **57, 97, 337**

Cantell, Timothy. 'Why care about old buildings?' *Period Home*, 1:3 (1980), pp. 5–8. **384**

Carlson, Victor. *Hubert Robert: Drawings & Watercolors*, Washington, D.C.: National Gallery of Art, 1978. **168, 375**

Carlyle, Thomas. *Critical and Miscellaneous Essays*, 3 vols., London, 1887–8:
  'Biography' (1832), 2:245–60. **62**
  'Shooting Niagara: and after?' (1867), 3:586–627. **395**
  'Sir Walter Scott', 3:165–223. **225**

Carne-Ross, D. S. 'Scenario for the new year: 3. the sense of the past', *Arion* (University of Texas), 8 (1969), 230–60. **64, 192, 249**

Carr, John Dickson. *The Devil in Velvet*, Penguin, 1957. **21, 27, 32**

Carrà, Massimo. 'The idea of art and the idea of life', in Caroline Tisdall and Angelo Bozzolla (compilers), *Futurismo 1909–1919: Exhibition of Italian Futurism*, Newcastle upon Tyne: Northern Arts, 1972, n.p. **380**

Carson, Cary. 'Living museums of everyman's history', *Harvard Magazine*, 83:7 (1981), 22–32. **347, 354**

Carson, Robin. *Pawn of Time: An Extravaganza*. New York: Henry Holt, 1957. **24, 29, 31**

Carter, Francis W. 'Balkan historic cities: pollution vs. conservation', in *Proceedings of the Anglo-Bulgarian Modern Humanities Symposium*, London: School of Slavonic and East European Studies, 1985, 2:1–25. **387**

    Conservation Problems of Historic Cities in Eastern Europe, Dept. of Geography, University College London, Occasional Paper No. 39, 1981. **387**

Casey, Edward S. 'Imagining and remembering', *Review of Metaphysics*, 31 (1977), 187–209. **3, 206**

Cassirer, Ernst. *The Philosophy of the Enlightenment*, Princeton University Press, 1951. **374**

Cather, Willa. *O Pioneers!* (1913), Boston: Houghton Mifflin, 1941. **42**

Cave, Terence. *The Cornucopian Text: Problems of Writing in the French Renaissance*, Oxford: Clarendon, 1979. **80, 85**

'The century game', *Harvard Bulletin*, 75:6 (1973), 3, 21–9. **340**

Cervantes, Miguel de. *The History of Don Quixote de la Mancha* (1615), 2 vols., London: Navarre Society, 1923. **225**

Chamberlin, E. R. *Preserving the Past*, London: Dent, 1979. **285, 288, 291, 295, 307, 331, 356, 398**

Charlton, D. G. *New Images of the Natural in France: A Study in European Cultural History 1750–1800*, Cambridge University Press, 1984. **178, 179**

Charteris of Amisfield, Lord. 'The work of the National Heritage Memorial Fund', *Journal of the Royal Society of Arts*, 132 (1984), 325–38. **37**

Chastellux, Francois Jean de. *An Essay on Public Happiness*, London: 2 vols., 1774. **95**

Chateaubriand, Francois-René de. *The Genius of Christianity or the Spirit and Beauty of the Christian Religion* (1802), 2nd rev. edn., Baltimore, 1856. **53, 141, 189**

Cheever, John. *The Stories of John Cheever*, New York: Knopf, 1978: **51**
    'The Duchess', pp. 347–58. **249**
    'The Lowboy', pp. 404–12. **43, 64, 67**

Chernela, Janet. 'In praise of the scratch: the importance of aboriginal abrasion on museum ceramic ware', *Curator*, 12 (1969), 174–9. **153**

Chesterfield, Lord (Philip Dormer Stanhope). *Letters Written . . . to His Son, Philip Stanhope, Esq.*, 2 vols., London, 1774. **74**

Chinard, Gilbert. 'Polybius and the American Constitution', *Journal of the History of Ideas*, 1 (1940), 38–58. **112**

Chippindale, Christopher. *Stonehenge Complete*, London: Thames and Hudson, 1983. **357**
    'What future for Stonehenge?' *Antiquity*, 57 (1983), 172–80. **357, 397**

Chisholm, Roderick M. *Person and Object: A Metaphysical Study*, London: Allen & Unwin, 1976. **385**

Chorley, Richard J., Dunn, Antony J., and Beckinsale, Robert P. *The History of the Study of Landforms, or the Development of Geomorphology*, 2 vols., London: Methuen, vol. 1, 1964; vol. 2 (Chorley, Beckinsale, and Dunn), 1973. **139, 140**

Christie, Agatha. *By the Pricking of my Thumbs*, London: Fontana/Collins, 1971. **208**

'Church architecture in New-York', *United States Magazine and Democratic Review*, 20 (1847), 139–44. **111**

Cicero, Marcus Tullius. *De Inventione*, London: Heinemann, 1909. **81**

Clanchy, M. T. *From Memory to Written Record: England, 1066–1307*, Harvard University Press, 1979. **221, 231, 235, 329, 370**

Clarendon, 1st Earl of (Edward Hyde). *Of the Reverence Due to Antiquity* (1670), in *A Collection of Several Tracts of the . . . Earl of Clarendon*, London, 1727, pp. 218–40. **91, 92**

Clark, Kenneth. *The Gothic Revival: An Essay in the History of Taste* (1928), 4th edn., London: Murray, 1974. **168, 293, 354**

Clark, Tim. 'When the paraders meet the button-counters at Penobscot Bay', *Yankee* (July 1980), 44–9, 129–43. **295, 300, 301, 343**

Clarke, Arthur C. 'Time's arrow' (1950), in his *Reach for Tomorrow*, London: Corgi, 1976, pp. 132–48. **22**

Clarke, Edward Daniel. *Greek Marbles Brought from the Shores of the Euxine, Archipelago, and Mediterranean . . .*, Cambridge University Press, 1809. **171**

Clausen, Christopher. 'Tintern Abbey to Little Gidding: the past recaptured', *Sewanee Review*, 84 (1976), 405–24. **8, 264, 376**

Clegg, Jeanne. *Ruskin and Venice*, London: Junction Books, 1981. **159, 179**

Cobb, Richard. 'Becoming a historian', in his *A Sense of Place*, London: Duckworth, 1975, pp. 7–48. **221**

Cochrane, Eric. *Historians and Historiography in the Italian Renaissance*, University of Chicago Press, 1981. **36, 77, 225, 244**

Cockburn, Claud. *Crossing the Line: Being the Second Volume of Autobiography*, London: MacGibbon & Kee, 1958. **250**

Cohen, Kathleen. *Metamorphosis of a Death Symbol: The Transi Tomb in the Late Middle Ages and the Renaissance*, University of California Press, 1973. **175, 176**

Cohn, Bernard S. 'Representing authority in Victorian India', in Hobsbawm and Ranger, *Invention of Tradition*, q.v., pp. 165–209. **37**

Cohn, William H. 'History for the masses: television portrays the past', *Journal of Popular Culture*, 10 (1976), 280–9. **307**

Coker, Francis W. *Organismic Theories of the State: Nineteenth Century Interpretations of the State as Organism or as a Person* (Columbia University Studies in History, Economics, and Public Law No. 101), New York, 1910. **128**

Colbourn, H. Trevor. *The Lamp of Experience: Whig History and the Intellectual Origins of the American Revolution*, University of North Carolina Press, 1965. **108, 119**

Colden, Cadwallader D. *Memoir, at the Celebration of the Completion of the New York Canals*, New York, 1825. **109**

Cole, Thomas. 'Essay on American scenery' (1835), in John Conron (ed.), *The American Landscape: A Critical Anthology of Prose and Poetry*, New York: Oxford University Press, 1973, pp. 568–78. **115**

See also Noble, L. L.

Cole, Thomas R. 'Aging, meaning, and well-being: musings of a cultural historian', *International Journal of Aging and Human Development*, 19 (1984), 329–36. **129**

Colegrove, F. W. 'The day they heard about Lincoln', in Neisser, *Memory Observed*, q.v., pp. 41–8 (abridged from 'Individual memories', *American Journal of Psychology*, 10 (1899), 228–55). **197**

Coles, John. *Archaeology by Experiment*, London: Hutchinson, 1973. **300**
Experimental Archaeology, London: Academic Press, 1979. **300, 301**

Collingwood, R. G. *The Idea of History*, New York: Oxford University Press/Galaxy, 1956. **46, 213, 218**
'The limits of historical knowledge', *Journal of Philosophical Studies*, 3 (1928), 213–22 (reprinted in Winks, *Historian as Detective*, q.v., pp. 513–22). **188**
'Some perplexities about time, with an attempted solution', *Proceedings of the Aristotelean Society*, n.s. 26 (1926), 135–50 (reprinted in Charles M. Sherover (ed.), *The Human Experience of Time*, New York University Press, 1975, pp. 558–71). **186**

Collins, William. 'An epistle addressed to Sir Thomas Hanmer, on his edition of Shakespeare's Works' (1744), in *The Poems of Thomas Gray, William Collins, Oliver Goldsmith*, ed. Roger Lonsdale, London: Longmans, Green, 1969, pp. 389–400. **93**

Commager, H. S. *The Empire of Reason: How Europe Imagined and America Realized the Enlightenment*, New York: Doubleday/Anchor, 1976. **108**

Compton-Burnett, Ivy. *A Father and His Fate*, London: Gollancz, 1957. **14**

Conklin, Groff (ed.). *Science Fiction Adventures in Dimension*, London: Grayson and Grayson, 1955. Includes stories by Gross; Long.

Conn, Peter. *The Divided Self: Ideology and Imagination in America, 1898–1917*, Cambridge University Press, 1983. **104, 123, 325, 379**

Constable, John. *John Constable's Discourses*, ed. R. B. Beckett, Ipswich: Suffolk Records Society, vol. 14 (1970):
  'Lecture on landscape' (1834–5), pp. 69–74. **100**
  'Various subjects of landscape characteristic of English scenery' (1833), pp. 7–27. **100**

Constable, W. G. 'Curators and conservation', *Studies in Conservation*, 1 (1954), 97–102. **160**

Constant, Benjamin. *Adolphe* (1816), London: Philpot, 1924. **48**

Cool, Kenneth E. 'The Petrarchian landscape as palimpsest', *Journal of Medieval and Renaissance Studies*, 11 (1981), 83–100. **256**

Coolidge, John. See *Gods & Heroes*.

Cooper, James Fenimore. *The Headsman; or, The Abbaye des Vignerons*, 3 vols., London, 1833. **64**
  Home as Found (1849), Mohawk edn., New York, 1896–7. **110**

Corkery, Daniel. *The Hidden Ireland: A Study of Gaelic Munster in the Eighteenth Century* (1924), Dublin: Gill and Macmillan, 1970. **48**

Cormack, Patrick. *Heritage in Danger*, London: Quartet, 1978. **37**

Cory, William Johnson. *Ionica* (1858), London: George Allen, 1905. **179**

Costonis, John. *Space Adrift: Landmark Preservation and the Marketplace*, University of Illinois Press for the National Trust for Historic Preservation, 1974. **357**

Cottle, Thomas J. *Perceiving Time: A Psychological Investigation with Men and Women*, New York: Wiley, 1976. **14, 21, 36**
  Time's Children: Impressions of Youth, Boston: Little, Brown, 1971. **197**

Cottle, Thomas J., and Klineberg, Stephen L. *The Present of Things Future: Explorations of Time in Human Experience*, London: Macmillan/Free Press, 1974. **193**

Coulton, G. G. *Friar's Lantern* (1906), London: Watts, 1948. **33**

Cowper, Richard. 'The Hertford Manuscript', *Fantasy and Science Fiction*, 51:4 (1976), 6–37. **29**

Cowper, William. *Correspondence* . . . , ed. Thomas Wright, 4 vols., London: Hodder and Stoughton, 1904. **157**
  The Task, in his *Poetical Works*, ed. H. S. Milford, Oxford University Press, 1934, pp. 129–241. **203**

Cox, Harvey. 'The restoration of a sense of place: a theological reflection on the visual environment', *Ekistics*, 25 (1968), 422–4. **247**

Crabbe, George. *The Borough, a Poem, in Twenty-Four Letters* (1810), London: Hatchard, 1916. **159, 323**

Craig, Tracey Linton. 'Retreat into history', *History News*, 38:6 (1983), 10–19. **298, 300**
  'Champions of history', ibid., 38:5 (1983), 6–16. **344**

Craven, Wayne. 'Thomas Cole and Italy', *Antiques*, 114 (1978), 1016–27. **178**

Creighton, Wilbur F. *The Parthenon in Nashville*, Nashville: privately printed, 1968. **293**

Crèvecœur, Michel-Guillaume Jean de (J. Hector St John). *Journey into Northern Pennsylvania and the State of New York* (1801), University of Michigan Press, 1964. **112**

Crick, Bernard. 'Orwell and biography', *London Review of Books*, 7–20 Oct. 1982, pp. 22–4. **207**

Croce, Benedetto. *History as the Story of Liberty*, London: Allen & Unwin, 1941. **233**

Croly, Herbert. *Progressive Democracy*, New York: Macmillan, 1914. **123**

Crook, J. A. *Law and Life of Rome*, London: Thames and Hudson, 1967. **72, 304**

Crook, J. Mordaunt. 'The canon of the classical' (review of Haskell and Penny, *Taste and the Antique*, q.v.), *TLS*, 3 Apr. 1981, p. 373. **306**
  'Introduction: the origins of the Gothic Revival', in Charles L. Eastlake, *A History of the Gothic Revival* (1872), Leicester University Press, 1978, pp. 13–57. **318**
  William Burges and the High Victorian Dream, London: Murray, 1981. **97, 98, 101**

Cross, Amanda (Carolyn Heilbrun). *Poetic Justice*, New York: Avon, 1979. **8**

Csikszentmihalyi, Mihaly, and Rochberg-Halton, Eugene. *The Meaning of Things: Domestic Symbols and the Self*, Cambridge University Press, 1981. **52, 54, 61, 389**

Cunliffe, Barry S. *The Past Tomorrow: An Inaugural Lecture*, University of Southampton, 1970. **396**

Curl, James Stevens. *A Celebration of Death*, London: Constable, 1980. **178, 179, 321**

Curti, Merle. *The Roots of American Loyalty*, Columbia University Press, 1946. **109, 121**

Curtis, William. 'Modern transformation of classicism', *Architectural Review*, 176:7 (1984), 39–47. **381**

Curzon, George Nathaniel, Marquis Curzon of Kedleston, and Tipping, H. Avray. *Tattershall Castle: A Historical & Descriptive Survey*, London: Cape, 1929. **394**

Daemmrich, Ingrid G. 'The ruins motif as artistic device in French literature', *Journal of Aesthetics and Art Criticism*, 30 (1972), 449–57; 31 (1972), 30–41. **156, 173, 255, 393**

Daiches, David. 'Sir Walter Scott and history', *Études Anglaises*, 24 (1971), 458–77. **99**

Dale, Antony. *Historic Preservation in Foreign Countries: Vol. I: France, Great Britain, Ireland, The Netherlands, Denmark*, ed. Robert E. Stipe, Washington, D.C.: US/ICOMOS, 1982. **394**

Dangerfield, George. *The Awakening of American Nationalism, 1815–1828*, New York: Harper Torchbook, 1965. **118**

Daniel, Glyn. *The Idea of Prehistory*, Penguin, 1964. **238, 245, 335**
'The Minnesota petroglyph', *Antiquity*, 32 (1958), 264–7. **330, 339**

'Daniel Webster: his political philosophy in 1820', *United States Magazine and Democratic Review*, 22 (1848), 129–38. **113**

Danilova, Irina. 'Dismembered works of art–Russian painting', in UNESCO, *Illustrated Inventory*, q.v., pp. 175–87. **287**

Danto, Arthur C. *Analytical Philosophy of History*, Cambridge University Press, 1965. **189, 190**
'Narrative sentences', *History and Theory*, 2 (1962–3), 146–79. **32, 218**

David, Percival. *Chinese Connoisseurship* (translation of Ko Ku Yao Lun, *The Essential Criteria of Antiquities*, 1388), London: Faber and Faber, 1971. **49, 156**

Davidson, Marshall. 'Whither the course of Empire?' *American Heritage*, 8:6 (1957), 52–61, 104. **175**

Davies, Gordon L. *The Earth in Decay: A History of British Geomorphology 1578–1878*, London: Macdonald, 1969. **88, 128, 136, 139, 188**

Davies, Robertson. *The Rebel Angels*, Penguin, 1983. **69, 185**

Davis, Fred. 'Nostalgia, identity and the current nostalgia wave', *Journal of Popular Culture*, 11 (1977), 414–24. **10, 13**
Yearning for Yesterday: A Sociology of Nostalgia, New York: Free Press, 1979. **12, 194, 195**

Davis, William Morris. 'Physical geography as a university study' (1894), in his *Geographical Essays*, Boston: Ginn, 1909, pp. 165–92. **140**

Delacroix, Eugène. *Journal*, ed. André Joubin, 3 vols., rev. edn., Paris: Plon, 1950. **151**

Dellheim, Charles. *The Face of the Past: The Preservation of the Medieval Inheritance in Victorian England*, Cambridge University Press, 1982. **104, 342, 404, 405**

de Man, Paul. *Blindness and Insight: Essays in the Rhetoric of Contemporary Criticism*, 2nd edn., London: Methuen, 1983. **70, 93, 380**

Demos, John. 'Old age in early New England', in David D. Van Tassell (ed.), *Aging, Death and Completion of Being*, University of Pennsylvania Press, 1979, pp. 115–64. **129**
'Oedipus in America: historical perspectives on the reception of psychoanalysis in the United States', *Annual of Psychoanalysis*, 6 (1978), 23–39. **72, 107**

Denney, Alan, and O'Brien, Turlogh. 'An introduction to weathering steels', *Architects' Journal*, 156 (1972), 959–79. **164**

Dennis, Nigel. *Cards of Identity* (1955), London: Weidenfeld and Nicolson, 1974. **xv, 12**

De Quincey, Thomas. *Confessions of an English Opium-Eater* (1822) (pp. 1–145) . . . and *Suspira de Profundis* (1845–54) (pp. 229–79), London: Constable, 1927. **16, 203, 204**

Descartes, René. *Discours de la méthode pour bien conduire la raison et cherchez la vérité dans les sciences* (1637), ed. Etienne Gilson, Paris: Vrin, 1947. **348**

Durliat, Georges, Boiret, Yves, and Costa, Georges. 'Saint-Sernin de Toulouse', *Monuments Historiques*, No. 112 (1980), 49–64. **282**

Dutton, Denis (ed.). *The Forger's Art: Forgery and the Philosophy of Art*, University of California Press, 1983. Includes essays by Arnheim; Margolis; Sagoff; Sparshott.

Dyer, John. *Grongar Hill* (1761), ed. Richard C. Boys, Johns Hopkins Press, 1941. **157, 178**

Dymond, D. P. *Archaeology and History: A Plea for Reconciliation*, London: Thames and Hudson, 1974. **114**

Dywan, Jane, and Bowers, Kenneth. 'The use of hypnosis to enhance recall', *Science*, 222 (1983), 184–5. **19**

Earle, William. 'Memory', *Review of Metaphysics*, 10 (1956), 3–27. **190, 194**

'The East and the West', *United States Magazine and Democratic Review*, 22 (1848), 401–9. **113**

Edel, Leon. *The Life of Henry James*, 2 vols., Penguin, 1977. **325**

Edwards, Amelia. *A Thousand Miles Up the Nile* (1877), reprint of 1888 edn., London: Century, 1982. **43, 246, 247**

Ehman, Robert R. 'Temporal self-identity', *Southern Journal of Philosophy*, 12 (1974), 333–41. **198**

Ehrenzweig, Anton. *The Hidden Order of Art: A Study in the Psychology of the Artistic Imagination*, University of California Press, 1971. **55**

Eiseley, Loren. *All the Strange Hours: The Excavation of a Life*, New York: Scribner's, 1975. **361, 362**

    The Invisible Pyramid, London: Rupert Hart-Davis, 1971. **67**

    The Unexpected Universe, New York: Harcourt, Brace & World, 1969. **384**

Eisenstein, Elizabeth L. 'Clio and Chronos: an essay on the making and breaking of history-book time', *History and Theory*, Beiheft 6 (1966), 36–64. **220, 221, 222**

    The Printing Press as an Agent of Change: Communications and Cultural Transformations in Early-Modern Europe, Cambridge University Press, 1979. **84, 88, 89, 90, 214, 238, 327, 374**

Elder, Betty Doak. 'War games: recruits and their critics draw battle lines over authenticity', *History News*, 36:8 (1981), 8–12. **295, 296, 301**

Eliade, Mircea. *Myth and Reality*, London: Allen & Unwin, 1964. **67, 85, 367**

Eliot, George. *Letters*, ed. Gordon S. Haight, 9 vols., Yale University Press, 1964–6. **99**

    Impressions of Theophrastus Such, Edinburgh, 1879. **98**

Eliot, T. S. 'Tradition and the individual talent' (1917), in his *Selected Essays*, 2nd rev. edn., London: Faber and Faber, 1934, pp. 13–22. **191, 235, 378**

Ellis, Havelock. *The New Spirit*, London, 1890. **402**

Ellis, P. G. 'The development of T. S. Eliot's historical sense', *Review of English Studies*, 23 (1971), 291–301. **198**

Ellison, R. C. '"The undying glory of dreams": William Morris and the "Northland of Old"', in Bradbury and Palmer, *Victorian Poetry*, q.v., pp. 139–75. **251**

Elson, Ruth Miller. *Guardians of Tradition: American Schoolbooks of the Nineteenth Century*, University of Nebraska Press, 1964. **112, 115, 116, 121**

Ely, David. 'Time out', in his *Time Out*, London: Secker & Warburg, 1968, pp. 80–132. **190, 191**

Emerson, Ralph Waldo. *The Complete Works*, Century edn., 12 vols., Boston: Houghton Mifflin, 1904–12:

    'Nature' (1836) 1:1–77. **113**

    'Self-reliance', 2:43–90. **113**

    'Works and days' (*Society and Solitude*, 1870), 7:155–85. **105**

    Journals and Miscellaneous Notebooks, ed. W. H. Gilman, *et al.*, 16 vols., Harvard University Press, 1960–82. **113, 372**

    Letters, ed. Ralph L. Rusk, 6 vols., Columbia University Press, 1939. **118**

    The Portable Emerson, New York: Viking, 1946:

        'Historic notes of life and letters in New England' (1883), pp. 513–43. **114**

        'Quotation and originality', pp. 284–303. **70**

English Tourist Board. *English Cathedrals and Tourism: Problems and Opportunities*, London, 1979. **276, 357**

Erasmus, Desiderius. *Complete Works*, 24 vols., University of Toronto Press, 1976–78:
'Copia': *Foundations of the Abundant Style*, transl. Betty I. Knott, 24: 279–659. **197, 225**
Correspondence, transl. R. A. P. Mynors and D. F. S. Thomson, vol. 3. **84**

Erikson, Erik H. *Life History and the Historical Moment*, New York: Norton, 1975. **73**

Evans, Joan. *A History of the Society of Antiquaries*, Oxford University Press, 1956. **336**

Evelyn, John. *The Diary of John Evelyn*, ed. E. S. de Beer, Oxford University Press, 1959. **245, 373**

Everett, Edward. 'Circular' of the Bunker Hill Monument Association, in George Washington Warren, *The History of the Bunker Hill Monument Association*, Boston, 1877, pp. 109–16. **119**

Fagan, Brian M. *The Rape of the Nile: Tomb Robbers, Tourists, and Archaeologists in Egypt*, London: Macdonald and Jane's, 1977. **44, 49**

Fain, Haskell. *Between Philosophy and History: The Resurrection of the Speculative Philosophy of History within the Analytic Tradition*, Princeton University Press, 1970. **188, 385**

Fairley, John A. *History Teaching through Museums*, London: Longman, 1977. **246, 293, 298**

Falchikov, Michael. 'Rerouting the train of time: Boris Pil'nyak's *Krasnoye Derevo*' [1929], *Modern Language Review*, 75 (1980), 138–47. **331**

Fane, Julian. 'Abel Duncan and success', in his *Happy Endings*, London: Hamish Hamilton, 1979, pp. 58–85. **331**

Farmer, Philip José. *Time's Last Gift*, London: Granada/Panther, 1975. **24, 32**
To Your Scattered Bodies Go (1971), Boston: Gregg, 1980. **22**

Faulkner, Patrick A. 'A philosophy for the preservation of our historic heritage: three Bossom lectures', *Journal of the Royal Society of Arts*, 126 (1978), 452–80. **388**

Febvre, Lucien. *A New Kind of History*, New York: Harper & Row, 1973. **65**

Fedden, Robin. 'Introduction: an anatomy of exile', in Fedden, *et al.*, *Personal Landscape: An Anthology of Exile*, London: Editions Poetry, 1945, pp. 7–15. **59**
'Problems of conservation: the Trust and its buildings', *Apollo*, 81 (1965), 376–9. **60**

Feilden, Bernard M. *Conservation of Historic Buildings*, London: Butterworth, 1982. **264, 280, 282**

Felstiner, Mary Lowenthal. 'Family metaphors and the language of an independence revolution', *Comparative Studies in Society and History*, 25 (1983), 154–80. **107**

Ferguson, Adam. *Essay on the History of Civil Society* (1767), ed. Duncan Forbes, Edinburgh University Press, 1968. **90**

Ferguson, Margaret. 'The exile's defense: Du Bellay's *La Deffence et illustration de la langue francoyse*', *Publications of the Modern Language Association*, 93 (1978), 275–89. **79, 83, 84**

Ferguson, Wallace K. *The Renaissance in Historical Thought: Five Centuries of Interpretation*, Boston: Houghton Mifflin, 1948. **53**

Fielding, Henry. *Amelia* (1751), ed. Martin B. Battestin, Oxford: Clarendon, 1983. **141**

Fields, James T. *Yesterdays with Authors* (1872), London, 1881. **115**

Filmer, Robert. *Patriarcha, or the Natural Powers of Kings Asserted*, London, 1680. **106**

Finley, M. I. 'Myth, memory, and history', *History and Theory*, 4 (1964–5), 297–302. **250**
(ed.). *The Legacy of Greece: A New Appraisal*, Oxford: Clarendon, 1981. Includes essays by Bolgar; Kidson; Marrou; Rosenmeyer.

Finney, Jack. *The Clock of Time*, London: Panther, 1961:
'I'm scared', pp. 24–37. **11**
'Such interesting neighbours', pp. 5–20. **31**
Time and Again, New York: Simon and Schuster, 1970. **20, 21, 24, 25, 31, 32, 145, 239**

Fischer, David Hackett. *Growing Old in America*, expanded edn., Oxford University Press, 1978. **129, 130**
Historians' Fallacies: Toward a Logic of Historical Thought, New York: Harper Colophon, 1970. **221**

Fisher, Philip. 'The future's past', *New Literary History*, 6 (1975), 587–606. **172, 289**

Fitch, James Marston. *Historic Preservation: Curatorial Management of the Built World*, New York: McGraw-Hill, 1982. **264**

Fitzgerald, Frances. *America Revised: History Schoolbooks in the Twentieth Century*, New York: Random House/Vintage, 1980. **121, 168, 195, 222, 345, 348, 362**

Fitzgerald, F. Scott. *The Beautiful and the Damned* (1921), Penguin, 1966. **180**

The Great Gatsby (1925), in *The Portable F. Scott Fitzgerald*, New York: Viking, 1945, pp. 1–168. **324**

Flaherty, Carolyn. 'The Colonial Revival house', *The Old-House Journal*, 6:1 (1978), 1, 8–10. **344**

Flavell, John H. *Cognitive Development*, Englewood Cliffs, N.J.: Prentice-Hall, 1977. **201**

Fledelius, Karsten, *et al.* (eds.). *History and the Audio-Visual Media* (Studies in History, Film and Society 1), Copenhagen: Eventus, 1979. Includes essays by Duckworth; Gane; Kent; Smith, Paul. **230**

Fleming, Ronald Lee. 'Lovable objects challenge the Modern Movement', *Landscape Architecture*, 71:1 (1981), 89–92. **175**

Fletcher, Banister. *A History of Architecture on the Comparative Method*, 15th edn., New York: Scribner's 1950. **409**

Flicker, David J., and Weiss, Paul. 'Nostalgia and its military implications', *War Medicine*, 4 (1943), 380–7. **11**

Fliegelman, Jay. *Prodigals and Pilgrims: The American Revolution against Patriarchal Authority, 1750–1800*, Cambridge University Press, 1982. **106, 107**

Fodor, Nandor. 'Varieties of nostalgia', *Psychoanalytic Review*, 37 (1950), 25–38. **11**

Foley, Barbara. 'From *U.S.A.* to *Ragtime*: notes on the forms of historical consciousness in modern fiction', *American Literature*, 50 (1978), 85–105. **227**

Foley, R. T. 'Measures for preventing corrosion in metals', in B. F. Brown, *Corrosion and Metal Artifacts*, q.v., pp. 67–76. **155**

Fontenelle, Bernard. *Digression sur les anciens et les modernes* (1688), in his *Entretiens sur la pluralité des mondes* and *Digression . . .* , ed. Robert Shackleton, Oxford: Clarendon, 1955, pp. 161–76. **89**

Forester, Tom. 'Weekend warriors', *New Society*, 10 Sept. 1981, pp. 417–18. **295, 301**

Forgie, George B. *Patricide in the House Divided: A Psychological Interpretation of Lincoln and His Age*, New York: Norton, 1979. **117, 118, 119, 120, 342, 345**

Fornara, Charles William. *The Nature of History in Ancient Greece and Rome*, University of California Press, 1983. **46, 225, 227**

Fortier, John. *Fortress of Louisbourg*, Toronto: Oxford University Press, 1979. **xv, 298**

'Louisbourg: managing a moment in time', in Peter E. Rider (ed.), *The History of Atlantic Canada: Museum Interpretations*, Ottawa: National Museum of Man (Mercury Series, History Division Paper No. 32), 1981, pp. 91–123. **298**

'Thoughts on the re-creation and interpretation of historical environments', *International Congress of Maritime Museums*, 3rd Conference Proceedings, Mystic, Conn., 1978, pp. 251–62. **298**

Foucault, Michel. *The Archaeology of Knowledge*, London: Tavistock, 1972. **55, 393**

The Order of Things: An Archaeology of the Human Sciences, New York: Pantheon, 1970. **200, 252, 393**

Fowler, Peter J. *Approaches to Archaeology*, London: Black, 1977. **397**

'Archaeology, the public and the sense of the past', in Lowenthal and Binney, *Our Past Before Us*, q.v., pp. 56–68. **224**

Fraisse, Paul. *The Psychology of Time*, rev. edn., London: Eyre & Spottiswoode, 1964. **36, 39, 48, 196, 208**

Frampton, Kenneth. *A Critical History of Modern Architecture*, London: Thames and Hudson, 1980. **380**

Frangiamore, Catherine Lynn. *Wallpapers in Historic Preservation*, Washington, D.C.: U.S. Dept. of the Interior, National Park Service, Office of Archeology and Historic Preservation, 1977. **344**

Frank, Ellen Eve. *Literary Architecture: Essays toward a Tradition*, University of California Press, 1979. **323**

Frank, Joseph. 'Spatial form in modern literature', *Sewanee Review*, 37 (1945), 221–40. **205**

Franklin, Benjamin. 'Old mistresses apologue', 25 June 1745, *The Papers*, ed. L. W. Larabee and W. J. Bell, Yale University Press, 1961, 3:30–1. **134**

Franklin, Julian H. *Jean Bodin and the Sixteenth-Century Revolution in the Methodology of Law and History*, Columbia University Press, 1963. **330**

Fraser, Julius T., and Lawrence, N. *The Study of Time II*, Berlin: Springer, 1975. Includes essays by Green, H. B.; Kastenbaum.

Freeman, Edward A. *The Growth of the English Constitution from the Earliest Times* (1872), 3rd edn., London, 1890. **233**

    The History of the Norman Conquest of England, Its Causes and Its Results, 6 vols., Oxford, 1867–79. **57**

    The Preservation and Restoration of Ancient Monuments, Oxford, 1852. **232, 385, 390**

  See also Stephens, W. R. W.

Freeman, Jenny. 'Mortgage myopia', *Chartered Surveyor*, 112 (1980), 291–8. **388**

Freeman, Richard W., Jr. 'Integrity in the Vieux Carré', in National Trust for Historic Preservation, *Economic Benefits of Preserving Old Buildings*, q.v., pp. 110–15. **293**

Freud, Sigmund. *The Complete Psychological Works*, London: Hogarth Press and the Institute of Psycho-Analysis, 1966–74:

    'The aetiology of hysteria' (1896) 3:191–222. **252**

    Beyond the Pleasure Principle (1920), 18:1–64. **71, 253**

    Civilization and Its Discontents (1930), 21:64–145; pagination from 3rd edn., London: Hogarth Press, 1946. **239**

    'Constructions in analysis' (1937), 23:257–69. **253**

    Delusion and Dream (1906) and 'Appendix' to the 2nd edn. (1911), 9:7–95; pagination from *Delusion and Dream and Other Essays*, Boston: Beacon, 1956, pp. 25–118 and 119–21. **255**

    'Fragment of an analysis of a case of hysteria' (1905), 7:1–122. **253**

    Leonardo da Vinci and a Memory of His Childhood (1910), 11:57–137. **253**

    'A note upon the "mystic writing-pad"' (c. 1924), 19:227–32. **256**

    'Notes upon a case of obsessional neurosis' (1909), 10:153–318. **253**

    'On the psychical mechanism of hysterical phenomena: preliminary communication' (1893) (*Studies in Hysteria*, with Josef Breuer), 2:3–17. **253**

    The Psychopathology of Everyday Life (1901), vol. 6; pagination from London: Benn, 1966. **17, 200, 239**

    'Remembering, repeating and working-through' (1914), 12:147–66. **17**

    'Screen memories' (1899), 3:299–322. **209**

    Totem and Taboo: Some Points of Agreement between the Mental Lives of Savages and Neurotics (1913), 13:1–161; pagination from London: Routledge & Kegan Paul, 1950. **18**

    The Origins of Psycho-Analysis: Letters to Wilhelm Fliess. Drafts and Notes: 1887–1902, ed. Marie Bonaparte, Anna Freud, and Ernst Kris, London: Imago, 1954. **253**

Froude, James Anthony. *History of England from the Fall of Wolsey to the Defeat of the Spanish Armada* (1856), rev. edn., 12 vols., London, 1893. **233**

    The Nemesis of Faith (1849), Farnborough, Hants: Gregg, 1969. **8**

Frycz, Jerzy. 'Reconstruction des monuments d'architecture', in *Problems of Heritage and Cultural Identity in Poland*, q.v., pp. 20–4. **280**

Frye, Northrop. *The Great Code: The Bible and Literature*, London: Routledge & Kegan Paul/Ark, 1983. **85, 212, 219, 378**

Fuentes, Carlos. *Terra Nostra*, Penguin, 1978. **134**

Fuller, Peter. *Art and Psychoanalysis*, London: Writers and Readers, 1980. **172**

Fussner, F. Smith. *The Historical Revolution: English Historical Writing and Thought 1580–1640*, London: Routledge & Kegan Paul, 1962. **47, 339**

Gagnon, Nicole. 'On the analysis of life accounts', in Bertaux, *Biography and Society*, q.v., pp. 47–60. **207**

Gaius. *Elements of Roman Law*, Oxford: Clarendon, 1881. **72**

Galbraith, V. H. 'Historical research and the preservation of the past', *History*, n.s. 22 (1938), 303–14. **66, 233, 246**

Gallagher, Dorothy. *Hannah's Daughters: Six Generations of an American Family, 1876–1976*, New York: Crowell, *c.* 1976. **409**

Gane, Judith H. 'History and film – some reflections on the authenticity question', in Fledelius, *History and the Audio-Visual Media*, q.v., pp. 181–97. **368**

García Márquez, Gabriel. *One Hundred Years of Solitude*, Penguin, 1972. **198, 236**

Garlake, Peter S. *Great Zimbabwe*, London: Thames and Hudson, 1973. **335**

  'Prehistory and ideology in Zimbabwe', in J. D. Y. Peel and Terence Ranger (eds.), *Past and Present in Zimbabwe*, Manchester University Press, 1983, pp. 1–19. **335**

Gaskell, Elizabeth. *Sylvia's Lovers* (1863), London: Dent, 1964. **234**

Gauld, Alan, and Stephenson, Geoffrey M. 'Some experiments relating to Bartlett's theory of remembering', *British Journal of Psychology*, 58 (1967), 39–49. **202**

Gaunt, William. *Bandits in a Landscape: A Study of Romantic Painting from Caravaggio to Delacroix*, London: Studio, 1937. **49, 168, 178**

Gautier, Théophile. *Contes fantastiques*, Paris: José Corti, 1962:
  'Arria Marcella: souvenir de Pompeii' (1852), pp. 213–51. **255**
  'Pied de momie' (1840), pp. 147–63. **255**
  L'Art' (1857) (*Émeaux et camées*), *Poésies complètes*, ed. René Jasinski, 3 vols., rev. edn., Paris: A. G. Nizet (1870), 3:128–30. **126**

Gay, John, Pope, Alexander, and Arbuthnot, John. *Three Hours after Marriage* (1717), Augustan Reprint Society of Dublin, Nos. 91–2 (1758 Dublin ed.), ed. John Harrington Smith, Los Angeles: William Andrews Clark Library, UCLA, 1962, pp. 139–222. **138**

Gay, Peter. *The Enlightenment: An Interpretation*, 2 vols., New York: Knopf, 1966. **65, 220**
  'Introduction: Freud for the marble tablet', in *Berggasse 19*, q.v., pp. 13–54. **253**
  A Loss of Mastery: Puritan Historians in Colonial America, New York: Random House/Vintage, 1968. **105**

Gent, Margaret. '"To flinch from modern varnish": the appeal of the past to the Victorian imagination', in Bradbury and Palmer, *Victorian Poetry*, q.v., pp. 11–35. **65**

George, J. Mishell. 'James Kirke Paulding, a Literary Nationalist', M.A. thesis, Columbia University, 1941. **109**

George, M. Dorothy. *Hogarth to Cruikshank, Social Change in Graphic Satire*. London: Allen Lane/Penguin, 1967. **153**

Gerhardsson, Birger. *Memory and Manuscript: Oral Tradition and Written Transmission in Rabbinic Judaism and Early Christianity* (Acta Seminarii Neotestamentici Upsaliensis 22), Lund: Gleerup, 1961. **194, 200, 256**

Gerrold, David. *The Man Who Folded Himself*, New York: Random House, 1973. **24**

Gettens, Rutherford J. 'Patina: noble and vile', in Suzannah Doeringer, D. G. Mitten, and Arthur Steinberg (eds.), *Art and Technology: A Symposium on Classical Bronzes*, Cambridge, Mass.: M.I.T. Press, 1970, pp. 57–72. **163**

Ghost Towns and Mining Camps: Selected Papers. Washington, D.C.: Preservation Press for the National Trust for Historic Preservation, 1977. Includes essays by Hart; Nelson. **169**

Giamatti, A. Bartlett. 'Hippolytus among the exiles: the romance of early humanism', in his *Exile and Change in Renaissance Literature*, Yale University Press, 1984, pp. 12–32. **84, 85**

Gibbon, Edward. *Autobiography* (1796), ed. M. M. Reese, London: Routledge & Kegan Paul, 1970. **245**
  The Decline and Fall of the Roman Empire (1776–88), 3 vols., New York: Modern Library, n.d. **66, 178, 212**
  Index Expurgatorius (*c.* 1786–9), in *The Miscellaneous Works*, ed. John Lord Sheffield, 5 vols., London, 1814, 5:548–79. **374**

Gide, André. *The Immoralist* (1902), London: Cassell, 1953. **379**
  So Be It, or The Chips Are Down, London: Chatto & Windus, 1960. **133**
Gilbert, Arthur N. (ed.). *In Search of a Meaningful Past*, Boston: Houghton Mifflin, 1972. **365**
Gilbert, Felix. 'Italy', in Orest Ranum (ed.), *National Consciousness, History, and Political Culture in Early-Modern Europe*, Johns Hopkins University Press, 1975, pp. 21–42. **372**
  'Revolution', in *Dictionary of the History of Ideas*, ed. Philip P. Wiener, 4 vols., New York: Scribner's, 1973, 4:152–67. **394**
Gilmore, Myron P. *Humanists and Jurists: Six Studies in the Renaissance*, Harvard University Press, 1963. **46, 225, 232, 376**
Gilpin, William. *A Dialogue upon the Gardens of the Right Honourable the Lord Viscount Cobham, at Stow in Buckinghamshire*, London, 1748. **175**
  Observations on the River Wye, and Several Parts of South Wales, &c, relative chiefly to Picturesque Beauty; made in the Summer of the Year 1770, 3rd edn., London, 1792. **156, 157**
  Observations, relative chiefly to Picturesque Beauty, Made in the Year 1772, on . . . the Mountains, and Lakes of Cumberland, and Westmoreland, 2 vols., London, 1796. **157, 159**
  Remarks on Forest Scenery and Other Woodland Views . . . , 3 vols., London, 1794. **168, 175**
Gilson, Etienne. *Painting and Reality*, London: Routledge & Kegan Paul, 1957. **126, 163**
Girouard, Mark. *The Return to Camelot: Chivalry and the English Gentleman*, Yale University Press, 1981. **4, 9, 38, 97, 233, 300, 342, 353**
  Sweetness and Light: The 'Queen Anne' Movement 1860–1900, Oxford: Clarendon, 1977. **9, 104**
Gissing, George. *By the Ionian Sea* (1901), London: Richards, 1956. **16**
Godkin, E. L. 'The Constitution, and its defects', *North American Review*, 99 (1864), 117–45. **118**
Gods & Heroes: Baroque Images of Antiquity, New York: Wildenstein Gallery, 1968. **283, 371, 377, 409**
Goethe, Johann Wolfgang von. *Goethe: Conversational Encounters*, ed. David Lake and Robert Pick, London: Oswald Wolff, 1966. **70, 93**
  Gedenkausgabe der Werke, Briefe, und Gespräche, 24 vols., Zurich: Artemis, 1949–52:
  'Teilnahme Goethes aus Manzoni' (1827), 14:812–44. **228**
  'Die Vereinigten Staaten' (1812), 2:405–6. **110**
Goldberger, Paul J. 'The dangers in preservation success', in National Trust for Historic Preservation, *Economic Benefits of Preserving Old Buildings*, q.v., pp. 159–61. **306**
  On the Rise: Architecture and Design in the Postmodern Age, New York: Times Books, 1983. **381**
Golding, William. 'Envoy extraordinary' (1956), in his *The Scorpion God*, London: Faber and Faber, 1971, pp. 115–78. **26**
Goldsmith, Oliver. *An Enquiry into the Present State of Polite Learning in Europe* (1759), *Collected Works*, ed. Arthur Friedman, 5 vols., Oxford: Clarendon, 1966, 1:243–341. **94**
Goldstein, Laurence. 'The Auburn syndrome: change and loss in "The Deserted Village" and Wordsworth's Grasmere', *ELH*, 40 (1973), 352–71. **395**
Goldstone, Harmon H., and Dalrymple, Martha. *History Preserved: A Guide to New York City Landmarks and Historic Districts*, New York: Schocken, 1976. **357**
Gombrich, E. H. 'Controversial methods and methods of controversy', *Burlington Magazine*, 105 (1963), 90–3. **161, 163**
  'Dark varnishes, variations on a theme from Pliny', ibid., 104 (1962), 51–5. **163**
  'The dread of corruption', *The Listener*, 15 Feb. 1979, pp. 242–5. **55**
  In Search of Cultural History, Oxford: Clarendon, 1967. **383**
  Norm and Form: Studies in the Art of the Renaissance, London: Phaidon, 1966:
  'The Renaissance conception of artistic progress and its consequences' (1952), pp. 1–10. **36, 77, 86**
  'The style *all'antica*: imitation and assimilation' (1961), pp. 122–8. **80**
  'Perfection's progress' (review of Haskell and Penny, *Taste and the Antique*, q.v.), *London Review of Books*, 5–18 Nov. 1981, pp. 3–5. **77, 258, 373, 380**
  'Research in the humanities: ideals and idols', *Daedalus*, 102:2 (1973), 1–10. **383**

'Style', *International Encyclopedia of the Social Sciences* (New York: Macmillan, 1968), 15:352–61. **126**

Goodman, Nelson. 'Twisted tales; or, story, study, and symphony', in Mitchell, *On Narrative*, q.v., pp. 99–115. **223**

Goodrich, S. G. *Recollections of a Lifetime, or Men and Things I Have Seen*, 2 vols., New York, 1857. **119**

Goody, Jack. *The Domestication of the Savage Mind*, Cambridge University Press, 1977. **220**

Goody, Jack, and Watt, Ian. 'The consequences of literacy' (reprinted from *Comparative Studies in Society and History*, 3 (1963), 304–45), in Goody (ed.), *Literacy in Traditional Societies*, Cambridge University Press, 1968, pp. 27–68. **214, 231, 237**

Gordon, David C. *Self-Determination and History in the Third World*, Princeton University Press, 1971. **332, 336**

Gordon, Jan B. 'Origins, history, and the reconstitution of family: Tess' journey', *ELH*, 43 (1976), 366–88. **64**

Gosse, Edmund. *Father and Son: A Study of Two Temperaments* (1907), London: Heinemann, 1964. **189**

Gosse, Philip Henry. *Omphalos: An Attempt to Untie the Geological Knot*, London, 1857. **188, 189**

Gossman, Lionel. *Medievalism and the Ideologies of the Enlightenment: The World and Work of La Curne de Sainte-Palaye*, Johns Hopkins Press, 1968. **232, 236**

Goubert, Pierre. *Louis XIV and Twenty Million Frenchmen*, London: Allen Lane/Penguin, 1970. **130**

Gould, Stephen Jay. *Hen's Teeth and Horse's Toes*, New York: Norton, 1983. **330**
    'Smith Woodward's folly', *New Scientist*, 5 Apr. 1979, pp. 42–4. **337**

Gowans, Alan. *Images of American Living*, Philadelphia: Lippincott, 1964. **112, 121, 181**
    Rural Myth and Urban Fact in the American Heritage, Wilmington, Del.: Wemyss Foundation, 1965. **347**

Grafton, Anthony T. 'Joseph Scaliger and historical chronology', *History and Theory*, 14 (1975), 156–85. **221**

Grahame, Elspeth. *First Whisper of 'The Wind in the Willows' by Kenneth Grahame*, Philadelphia: Lippincott, 1945. **9**

Graña, César. *Fact and Symbol: Essays in the Sociology of Art*, Oxford University Press, 1971. **402**

Gravelle, Sarah Stever. 'Humanist attitudes to convention and innovation in the fifteenth century', *Journal of Medieval and Renaissance Studies*, 11 (1981), 193–209. **79**

Graves, Robert. *Seven Days in New Crete*, London: Cassell, 1949. **50**

Greece, Ministry of Culture and Sciences, Committee for the Preservation of the Acropolis Monuments. *Research, Studies, Work on the Acropolis 1975–1983*, Athens, 1983. **275**

Greek Lyric Poetry, transl. Willis Barnstone, New York: Schocken, 1972. **131**

Green, Anne. *Flaubert and the Historical Novel: Salammbô Reassessed*, Cambridge University Press, 1982. **227**

Green, H. B. 'Temporal stages in the development of self', in Fraser and Lawrence, *Study of Time II*, q.v., pp. 1–19. **42**

Green, John Richard. *Stray Studies from England and Italy*, London, 1876. **245**

Greenberg, Allen. 'A sense of the past: an architectural perspective', *Chicago Architectural Journal*, 1 (1981), 42–8. **381**

Greene, Thomas M. *The Light in Troy: Imitation and Discovery in Renaissance Poetry*, Yale University Press, 1982. **70, 72, 77, 80, 82, 85, 86, 252, 374, 390, 391, 407**

Greenhalgh, Michael. *The Classical Tradition in Art*, London: Duckworth, 1978. **55, 291, 344**

Greenwood, George. *Rain and Rivers, or Hutton and Playfair against Lyell and All Comers*, London, 1857. **139**

Greif, Lucien R. 'Cleaning up the treasures of history', *Curator*, 13 (1970), 290–9. **149**

Greiff, Constance M. *Lost America: From the Atlantic to the Mississippi*, Princeton, N.J.: Pyne Press, 1974. **403**

Groat, Linda, and Canter, David. 'Does Post-Modernism communicate?' *Progressive Architecture*, 60:12 (1979), 84–7. **383**

Gross, Marion. 'The good provider', in Conklin, *Science Fiction Adventures in Dimension*, q.v., pp. 167–71. **28**

'Growing old: an exchange', *New York Review of Books*, 15 Sept. 1977, pp. 47–9. **129**

Gruman, Gerald J. 'A history of ideas about the prolongation of life: the evolution of prolongevity hypotheses to 1800', *Transactions of the American Philosophical Society*, 56:9 (1966), 1–102. **129**

Gruneberg, Michael M., and Morris, Peter (eds.). *Aspects of Memory*, London: Methuen, 1978. Includes essays by Belmont; Marshall and Fryer.

Gruneberg, M. M., Morris, P. E., and Sykes, R. N. (eds.). *Practical Aspects of Memory*, London: Academic Press, 1978. Includes essays by Linton; Rawles. **193**

Gruszecki, Andrzef. 'Cultural and national identity and the protection of foreign fortifications in Poland', in *Problems of Heritage and Cultural Identity in Poland*, q.v., pp. 45–9. **334**

Gummere, Richard M. *The American Colonial Mind and the Classical Tradition: Essays in Comparative Culture*, Harvard University Press, 1963. **112**

Gutman, Herbert G. 'Whatever happened to history?' *The Nation*, 21 Nov. 1981, pp. 521, 553–4. **44, 237**

Haas, Charlie. 'The secret life of the American tourist', *New West*, 5:16 (1980), 13–29. **282, 289, 336, 341, 351**

Haber, Carole. 'From senescence to senility: the transformation of senile old age in the nineteenth century', *International Journal of Aging and Human Development*, 19 (1984), 41–5. **129**

Hägerstrand, Torsten. 'On the survival of the cultural heritage', *Ethnologia Scandinavia* (1977), 7–12. **400**

Haggard, H. Rider. *Allan and the Ice-Gods: A Tale of Beginnings*, London: Andrew Melrose, 1927. **26**

   She: A History of Adventure (1887), London: Macdonald, 1948. **16, 134**

Hak, Selim Abdul. 'Introduction: Unesco's action to promote the reconstitution of dismembered works of art', in UNESCO, *Illustrated Inventory*, q.v., pp. 13–17. **287**

Hakewill, George. *An Apologie or Declaration of the Power and Providence of God in the Government of the World Consisting in an Examination and Censure of the Common Errour Touching Nature's Perpetuall and Universal Decay*, 3rd edn., 2 vols., Oxford, 1635. **88, 136, 137, 143**

Halbwachs, Maurice. *The Collective Memory*, New York: Harper Colophon, 1980. **50, 196, 198, 209**

Haldane, J. B. S. *The Man with Two Memories*, London: Merlin, 1976. **17**

Hale, David George. *The Body Politic: A Political Metaphor in Renaissance English Literature*, The Hague: Mouton, 1971. **128**

Hale, John. 'Museums and the teaching of history', *Museum*, 21 (1968), 67–72. **243**

Haley, Alex. *Roots*, London: Hutchinson, 1977. **55, 228**

Hallam, Elizabeth M. 'The burial places of English kings', *History Today*, 31:7 (1981), 44–7. **408**

Hamilton, Ian. *Robert Lowell: A Biography*, New York: Random House/Vintage, 1983. **349**

Hamlin, Talbot. *Greek Revival Architecture in America* (1944), New York: Dover, 1964. **111, 112**

Handlin, Oscar and Mary F. *Facing Life: Youth and the Family in American History*, Boston: Little Brown, 1971. **107**

Hanff, Helene. *The Duchess of Bloomsbury Street*. London: Deutsch, 1974. **246**

Hankiss, Agnes. 'Ontologies of the self: on the mythological rearranging of one's life-history', in Bertaux, *Biography and Society*, q.v., pp. 203–9. **207**

Hanna, Max. 'Cathedrals at saturation point?' in Lowenthal and Binney, *Our Past Before Us*, q.v., pp. 178–92. **276, 357, 401**

Hanna, Max, and Binney, Marcus. *Preserve and Prosper: The Wider Economic Benefits of Conserving Historic Buildings*, London: SAVE Britain's Heritage, 1983. **401**

Harbison, Robert. *Deliberate Regression*, New York: Knopf, 1980. **233, 349, 379, 393**

Hardy, Thomas. *A Laodician: or, The Castle of the De Stancys*, 3 vols., London, 1881. **49**

   Tess of the d'Urbervilles: A Pure Woman (1891), Penguin, 1978. **64**

'Under the waterfall' (1911–12), *Collected Poems*, 4th edn., London: Macmillan, 1930. **251**

Hareven, Tamara K., and Langenbach, Randolph. *Amoskeag: Life and Work in an American Factory-City*, New York: Pantheon, 1978. **403**

    'Living places, work places and historical identity', in Lowenthal and Binney, *Our Past Before Us*, q.v., pp. 109–23. **403, 404**

Harpham, Geoffrey. 'Time running out: the Edwardian sense of cultural degeneration', *Clio*, 5 (1976), 283–301. **379**

Harris, J. E., and Crossland, I. G. 'Mechanical effects of corrosion: an old problem in a new setting', *Endeavour*, 3:1 (1979), 15–26. **275**

Harris, Neil. *The Artist in American Society: The Formative Years 1790–1860*, New York: Braziller, 1966. **323**

Harris, Victor. *All Coherence Gone*, University of Chicago Press, 1949. **87, 88, 136, 137, 138, 139**

Harrison, Frederic. 'A few words about the nineteenth century' (1882), in his *The Choice of Books and Other Literary Pieces*, London, 1886, pp. 417–47. **395**

    The Meaning of History, and Other Historical Pieces, London: Macmillan, 1894. **55**

Harrison, Henry. *A Rebel in Time*, New York: Tor, 1983. **27**

Harrisson, Tom. *Living through the Blitz*, London: Collins, 1976. **7, 206, 207**

Hart, A. A. 'Interpretive case study: Custer, Idaho', in *Ghost Towns and Mining Camps*, q.v., pp. 25–8. **169**

Hartley, L. P. *The Go-Between*, London: Hamish Hamilton, 1953. **xvi**

Hartmann, Günter. *Die Ruine im Landschaftsgarten: Ihre Bedeutung fur den frühen Historismus und die Landschaftsmalerei der Romantik*, Worms: Werner'sche, 1981. **156**

Harvey, Frederick L. *A History of the Washington National Monument and the Washington National Monument Society*, 57 Cong. 2 Sess., Sen. Doc. 224, Washington, D.C., 1903. **286**

Harvey, John. *Conservation of Buildings*, London: John Baker, 1972. **60, 273, 327, 393**

    Dublin: A Study of Environment, London: Batsford, 1949. **334**

Harvey, Peter. *Reminiscences and Anecdotes of Daniel Webster*, Boston, 1877. **60, 113, 392**

Harwell, Faye B. 'Recovering the "lost" Niagara', *Landscape Architecture*, 71 (1981), 450–5, 510. **275**

Hasbany, Richard. '*Irene*: considering the nostalgic sentiment', *Journal of Popular Culture*, 9 (1976), 816–26. **13**

Haskell, Francis. 'The manufacture of the past in nineteenth-century painting', *Past and Present*, No. 53 (1971), 109–20. **62**

    Rediscoveries in Art: Some Aspects of Taste, Fashion and Collecting in England and France, 2nd edn., Oxford: Phaidon, 1976. **97, 141**

Haskell, Francis, and Penny, Nicholas. *The Most Beautiful Statues: The Taste for Antique Sculpture 1500–1900*, Oxford: Ashmolean Museum, 1981. **303, 306**

    Taste and the Antique: The Lure of Classical Sculpture 1500–1900, Yale University Press, 1981. **170, 283, 303, 304, 306**

Hatch, Nathan O. *The Sacred Cause of Liberty: Republican Thought and the Millennium in Revolutionary New England*, Yale University Press, 1977. **119**

Hawkins, Desmond. *Hardy's Wessex*, London: Macmillan, 1983. **387**

Hawthorne, Nathaniel. *Doctor Grimshawe's Secret*, Boston: Houghton Mifflin, 1883 ('Etherege', in *Works*, q.v., 12:90–342). **48, 59, 64, 116**

    The English Notebooks, ed. Randall Stewart, New York: Modern Language Association of America, 1941. **66, 115, 159**

    Works, Centennial edn., 14 vols., Ohio State University Press, 1962–80:

        'About Warwick' (1862) (*Our Old Home*), 5:65–89. **96**

        The American Notebooks, ed. Claude M. Simpson, vol. 8. **118**

        'Consular experiences' (1863) (*Our Old Home*), 5:6–40. **115**

        'Earth's holocaust' (1844) (*Mosses from an Old Manse*), 10:381–404. **111**

        'The gray champion' (1835) (*Twice-Told Tales*), 9:9–18. **130**

The House of the Seven Gables (1852), vol. 2. **111, 113, 119**

'Leamington Spa' (1862) (*Our Old Home*), 5:41–64. **116**

'Main-street' (1849) (*Aesthetic Papers*), 11:49–82. **113**

The Marble Faun; or, The Romance of Monte Beni (1859), vol. 4. **48, 60, 115, 116, 166, 239, 329, 404**

'The old manse' (1846) (*Mosses from an Old Manse*), 10:3–35. **246**

'Septimius Felton' (1872), 13:3–194. **119**

Hawthorne, Sophia. *Notes on England and Italy*, New York: Putnam, 1870. **114**

Hay, Denys. *Annalists and Historians: Western Historiography from the Eighth to the Eighteenth Centuries*, London: Methuen, 1977. **220, 221, 390**

Haydon, Benjamin Robert. *Diary*, ed. William Bissell Pope, 5 vols., Cambridge University Press, vol. 2, 1960. **172**

Hays, Samuel P. *The Response to Industrialism, 1885–1914*, University of Chicago Press, 1957. **121**

Hazard, Paul. *The European Mind (1680–1715)* (1935), New York: World/Meridian, 1963. **89, 95**

Hazlitt, William. *Complete Works*, ed. P. P. Howe, 21 vols., London: Dent, 1930–4:

'Fine arts, whether they are promoted by academies and public institutions' (1814), 18:37–51. **100**

'[W. A.] Schlegel on the drama' (1816), 16:57–99. **99, 375**

'Why distant objects please' (*Table-Talk*, 1821–2), 8:255–64. **16**

Head, Joseph, and Cranston, S. L. (eds.). *Reincarnation: An East–West Anthology*, Wheaton, Ill.: Theosophical/Quest Book, 1968. **18**

Heggie, Douglas. *Megalithic Science: Ancient Mathematics and Astronomy in North-west Europe*, London, Thames and Hudson, 1981. **344**

Heil, John. 'Traces of things past', *Philosophy of Science*, 45 (1978), 60–72. **252**

Heine, Heinrich. 'Ueber die französische Bühne: Vertraute Briefe an August Lewald' (1837), *Sämtliche Werke*, Hamburg: Hoffman und Campe, vol. 12/1, 1980, pp. 229–90. **100**

Heller, Agnes. *Renaissance Man*, London: Routledge & Kegan Paul, 1978. **75**

A Theory of History, ibid., 1982. **186, 234**

Hemans, Felicia Dorothea. *Poems*, Edinburgh, 1872. **135**

Henderson, Harry B. III. *Versions of the Past: The Historical Imagination in American Fiction*, Oxford University Press, 1974. **64**

Hendricks, Jon, and Davis, C. 'The age old question of old age: was it really so much better back when?' *International Journal of Aging and Human Development*, 8 (1977), 139–54. **130**

Henige, David P. 'The disease of writing: Ganda and Nyoro kinglists in a newly literate world', in Miller, *African Past Speaks*, q.v., pp. 240–61. **231**

The Chronology of Oral Tradition: Quest for a Chimera, Oxford: Clarendon, 1974. **220**

Henretta, James A. 'Social history as lived and written', *American Historical Review*, 84 (1979), 1293–1322. **223**

Herder, Johann Gottfried von. *Reflections on the Philosophy of the History of Mankind* (1784–91), ed. Frank E. Manuel, University of Chicago Press, 1968. **69, 142**

Herzfeld, Michael. *Ours Once More: Folklore, Ideology, and the Making of Modern Greece*, University of Texas Press, 1982. **131, 333**

Hesse, Hermann. *The Glass Bead Game*, Penguin, 1972. **20**

Heusden, Willem van. *Ancient Chinese Bronzes of the Shang and Chou Dynasties*, Tokyo: privately published, 1952. **156**

Hewison, Robert. *John Ruskin: The Argument of the Eye*, London: Thames and Hudson, 1976. **166**

Hexter, J. H. *The History Primer*, London: Allen Lane/Penguin, 1972. **216, 229**

'The rhetoric of history', *International Encyclopedia of the Social Sciences* (New York: Macmillan, 1968), 6:368–94. **218, 219, 224, 236**

Higham, John. *Strangers on the Land: Patterns of American Nativism, 1860–1925*, Rutgers University Press, 1955. **121**

Highet, Gilbert. *The Classical Tradition: Greek and Roman Influences on Western Literature*, Oxford: Clarendon, 1949. **91, 93, 186, 342**

Hijia, James A. 'Roots: family and ethnicity in the 1970s', *American Quarterly*, 30 (1978), 548–56. **233**

Hill, John W., Mahan, Catherine, and Johns, Ferdinand S. 'The changing view from Mt. Vernon: Geo. Washington watched here', *Landscape Architecture*, 71:1 (1981), 73–6. **345**

Hillard, George Stillman. *Six Months in Italy*, 2 vols., Boston, 1853. **361**

Hillier, Bevis. *Austerity Binge: The Decorative Arts of the Forties and Fifties*, London: Studio Vista, 1975. **6**

  The Style of the Century: 1900–1980, London: Herbert, 1983. **6**

Hindle, Brook. 'How much is a piece of the True Cross worth?' in Quimby, *Material Culture and the Study of American Life*, q.v., pp. 5–20. **246**

Hirsch, Julia. *Family Photographs: Content, Meaning, and Effect*, Oxford University Press, 1981. **257, 306**

Historic Preservation Today, Charlottesville, Va.: National Trust for Historic Preservation and Colonial Williamsburg, 1966. Includes essays by Dupont; Lancaster; Lorentz.

Hitchcock, Henry-Russell. *The Architecture of H. H. Richardson and His Times*, rev. edn., Cambridge, Mass.: M.I.T. Press, 1966. **181**

Hitchcock, Henry-Russell, and Seale, William. *Temples of Democracy: The State Capitols of the USA*, New York: Harcourt Brace Jovanovich, 1976. **354**

Hobbes, Thomas. 'The answer of Mr. Hobbes to Sir William Davenant's preface before Gondibert' (1650), *The English Works of Thomas Hobbes*, ed. William Molesworth, 11 vols., London, 1839–45, 4:441–58. **89**

Hobsbawm, Eric. 'Mass-producing traditions: Europe, 1870–1914', in Hobsbawm and Ranger, *Invention of Tradition*, q.v., pp. 263–307. **322**

Hobsbawm, Eric, and Ranger, Terence (eds.). *The Invention of Tradition*, Cambridge University Press, 1983. Includes essays by Cannadine; Cohn, B. S.; Hobsbawm; Morgan, Prys; Ranger; Trevor-Roper.

Hofer, Johannes. 'Medical dissertation on nostalgia, … 1688', transl. Carolyn Kiser Anspach, *Bulletin of the History of Medicine*, 2 (1934), 376–91. **10, 11**

Hoffman, Charles Fenno. *A Winter in the West*, 2 vols., New York, 1835. **54**

Hogg, Thomas Jefferson. *The Life of Percy Bysshe Shelley*, 4 vols., London, 1858. **16**

Holdsworth, Deryck. 'Natives vs. newcomers: different views of the past', in David Lowenthal and Victor Konrad (eds.), *The Uses and Misuses of the Past: Essays on Historic Preservation*, Duxbury, Mass.: Guilford, forthcoming. **42**

Holmes, Oliver Wendell. *Our Hundred Days in Europe*, Boston, 1887. **48**

Honour, Hugh. *Neo-classicism*, Penguin, 1968. **94, 156**

  Romanticism, Penguin, 1981. **99, 225, 233, 393**

Hopkins, W. Thurston. *Rudyard Kipling's World*, London: Robert Holden, 1925. **9**

Horne, Donald. *The Great Museum: The Re-Presentation of History*, London: Pluto, 1984. **55, 344, 347**

Horwich, Paul. 'On some alleged paradoxes of time travel', *Journal of Philosophy*, 72 (1975), 432–44. **32**

Horwitz, Sylvia L. *The Find of a Lifetime: Sir Arthur Evans and the Discovery of Knossos*, London: Weidenfeld and Nicolson, 1981. **282**

Hoskins, W. G. *Provincial England: Essays in Social and Economic History*, London: Macmillan, 1963. **57**

Hosmer, Charles B., Jr. *Presence of the Past: A History of the Preservation Movement in the United States before Williamsburg*, New York: Putnam's, 1965. **120, 247, 249, 345**

  Preservation Comes of Age: From Williamsburg to the National Trust, 1926–1949, 2 vols., University Press of Virginia, 1981. **244, 285**

Hough, Henry Beetle. *Soundings at Sea Level*, Boston: Houghton Mifflin, 1980. **181, 286, 396**

Houghton, Walter E., Jr. 'The English virtuoso in the seventeenth century (II)', *Journal of the History of Ideas*, 3 (1942), 190–219. **373**

  The Victorian Frame of Mind, 1830–1870, Yale University Press, 1957. **96, 98**

Hussey, Christopher. *The Picturesque: Studies in a Point of View* (1927), London: Cass, 1967. **160,**
166, 168

Huxtable, Ada Louise. 'Is modern architecture dead?' *N.Y. Review of Books*, 16 July 1981,
pp. 17–22. **383**

Kicked a Building Lately? New York Times/Quadrangle, 1978. **357**

'The troubled state of modern architecture', *N.Y. Review of Books*, 1 May 1980, pp. 22–9. **382**

Huyghe, René. 'The Louvre Museum and the problem of the cleaning of old pictures', *Museum*, 3
(1950), 191–206. **161, 163**

Hyman, Sidney. 'Empire for liberty', in *With Heritage So Rich*, q.v., pp. 1–27. **340**

Ibsen, Henrik. *Ghosts* (1882), Penguin, 1964. **364**

Hedda Gabler (1890), London: Methuen, 1967. **379**

ICOMOS (International Council on Monuments and Sites). *Nessun futuro senza passato*, Acts of the
6th General Assembly, Rome, 1981. Includes essays by Kobayashi; Linstrum; Parent.

Irenaeus. *Adversus Haereses* (c. 180), excerpted in *The Early Christian Fathers: A Selection*, ed. Henry
Bettenson, Oxford University Press, 1956, pp. 29–50. **131**

Irving, Washington. *Abbotsford and Newstead Abbey*, Paris, 1835. **43**

Irwin, Lucinda Lou. 'Visitor Response to Interpretation at Selected Historic Sites', M.Sc. thesis,
Texas A & M University, 1978. **355**

Isaac, Glynn Ll. 'Whither archaeology?' *Antiquity*, 25 (1971), 123–9. **238**

Ivins, William M., Jr. *Prints and Visual Communication*, London: Routledge & Kegan Paul, 1953.
171, 257, 303

Jackson, John Brinckerhoff. *American Space: The Centennial Years, 1865–1876*, New York: Norton,
1972. **121**

The Necessity for Ruins, and Other Topics, University of Massachusetts Press, 1980. **301, 322**

Jackson, T. G. *Modern Gothic Architecture*, London, 1873. **318**

Jacobson, Paul B., and Steele, Robert S. 'From present to past: Freudian archaeology', *International
Review of Psycho-Analysis*, 6 (1979), 349–62. **18, 253**

James, Henry. *The American Scene* (1907), Indiana University Press, 1968. **54, 151**

The Awkward Age (1899), Penguin, 1966. **62, 340**

The Complete Tales, ed. Leon Edel, 12 vols., London: Rupert Hart-Davis, 1964:

'The Birthplace' (1903), 11:403–65. **325, 361**

'Flickerbridge' (1903), 11:327–50. **361**

English Hours, New York: Orion, 1960. **48, 357**

Hawthorne, London: Macmillan, 1879. **38, 115, 116**

Novels and Tales, New York edn., New York: Scribner's, 24 vols., 1908–9:

A Passionate Pilgrim (1871), 13:333–434. **125**

'The private life' (1893), 17:215–66. **98**

The Reverberator (1888), 13:1–211. **117**

Selected Letters of Henry James, ed. Leon Edel, London: Rupert Hart-Davis, 1956. **230**

The Sense of the Past, New York: Scribner's, 1917; includes 'Notes', pp. 289–358. **24, 29, 30, 33,**
60, 117, 204

A Small Boy and Others (1913), in *Autobiography*, ed. Frederick W. Dupee, London: W. H.
Allen, 1956, pp. 3–236. **205**

The Spoils of Poynton (1897), Penguin, 1963. **48**

James, William. *The Letters*, ed. Henry James, 2 vols., London: Longmans, Green, 1920. **325**

Jantz, R. K., Seefeldt, A., Galper, A., and Serock, K. *Children's Attitudes toward the Elderly: Final
Report*, Dept. of Educational Development, College of Education, University of Maryland,
1976. **133**

Jefferies, Richard. *The Life of the Fields* (1884), London: Lutterworth, 1948. **36**

Jefferson, Thomas. *The Writings*, ed. Albert Ellery Bergh, 20 vols., Washington, D.C.: Thomas
Jefferson Memorial Association, 1907. **108**

Jencks, Charles (ed.). *Post-Modern Classicism: The New Synthesis*, special issue, *Architectural Design*,
50 (1980, 5/6). **354, 375, 382**

Jenkyns, Richard. 'Keeping up Greek' (review of A. E. Hillard and C. G. Botting, *Elementary Greek Exercises*), *TLS*, 7 Aug. 1981, p. 917. **377**

   The Victorians and Ancient Greece, Oxford: Blackwell, 1980. **16, 52, 98, 99, 102, 142, 159, 230, 353, 373, 375**

Jennings, Paul. *The Living Village: A Report on Rural Life in England and Wales*, London: Hodder and Stoughton, 1968. **337**

Jensen, Gordon D., and Oakley, Fredericka B. 'Aged appearance and behavior: an evolutionary and ethological perspective', *Gerontologist*, 20 (1980), 595–7. **131**

Jensen, Oliver. *America's Yesterdays: Images of Our Lost Past Discovered in the Photographic Archives of the Library of Congress*, New York: American Heritage, 1978. **51**

Jensen, Wilhelm. *Gradiva: A Pompeiian Fancy* (1903), in Freud, *Delusion and Dream*, q.v., pp. 145–235. **255**

Johnson, James William. 'Chronological writing: its concepts and development', *History and Theory*, 2 (1962), 124–45. **221**

Johnson, Samuel. *Works*, ed. W. J. Bate and Albrecht B. Strauss, 3 vols., Yale University Press, 1969. **93**

Johnstone, Clive, and Weston, Winifred. *The Which? Heritage Guide*, London: Consumers' Association and Hodder & Stoughton, 1981. **273**

Jones, Alfred Haworth. 'The search for a usable past in the New Deal era', *American Quarterly*, 23 (1971), 710–24. **41, 347**

Jones, Ernest. *The Life and Work of Sigmund Freud*, 3 vols., New York: Basic Books, 1953–7. **252, 255**

Jones, Howard Mumford. *O Strange New World; American Culture: The Formative Years*, New York: Viking, 1964. **114, 265**

Jones, Richard Foster. *Ancients and Moderns: A Study of the Rise of the Scientific Movement in Seventeenth-Century England*, 2nd edn., University of California Press, 1965. **76, 90, 91, 92, 144**

Joppien, Rüdiger. 'The iconography of the Burke and Wills expedition in Australian art', in Quartermaine, *Readings in Australian Arts*, q.v., pp. 49–61. **54**

Josephy, Alvin M. 'Awesome space: a historian speculates on interpretations of the Old West', *History News*, 37:6 (1982), 26–30. **192**

Jowett, Benjamin. 'Introduction to the *Phaedrus*', in his (ed.) *Dialogues of Plato*, 4th edn., 4 vols., Oxford: Clarendon, 1953, 3:117–32. **329**

Joyce, James. *Ulysses* (1922), London: Bodley Head, 1960. **379**

Juvenal. *The Satires*, transl. Rolfe Humphries, Indiana University Press, 1958. **131, 323**

Kain, Roger (ed.). *Planning for Conservation*, London: Mansell, 1981. Includes essays by Breitling; Morris, Colin.

Kames, Henry Home, Lord. *Elements of Criticism*, 3 vols., Edinburgh, 1762. **178**

   Sketches of the History of Man, rev. edn., 4 vols., Edinburgh, 1788. **94**

Kammen, Michael. 'Introduction: the historian's vocation', in his (ed.) *The Past Before Us: Contemporary Historical Writing in the United States*, Cornell University Press for the American Historical Association, 1980, pp. 19–46. **236**

   A Season of Youth: The American Revolution and the Historical Imagination, New York: Knopf, 1973. **256, 309, 342**

   'Vanitas and the historian's vocation', *Reviews in American History*, 10:4 (1982), 1–27. **237**

Kander, Lotte. *Die Deutsche Ruinenpoesie des 18. Jahrhunderts bis in die Anfänge des 19. Jahrhunderts*, Wertheim am Main: Bechstein, 1933. **173**

Kant, Immanuel. 'An answer to the question: "What is enlightenment?"' (1784), in *Kant's Political Writings*, ed. Hans Reiss, Cambridge University Press, 1971, pp. 54–60. **107**

Kastenbaum, Robert. 'Memories of tomorrow', in Bernard S. Gorman and Alden E. Wessman (eds.), *The Personal Experience of Time*, New York: Plenum, 1977, pp. 193–214. **196**

   'Time, death and ritual in old age', in Fraser and Lawrence, *Study of Time II*, q.v., pp. 20–38. **43, 209, 256**

Kastenbaum, Robert, and Ross, Barbara. 'Historical perspectives on care', in John C. Howells (ed.), *Modern Perspectives in the Psychiatry of Old Age*, Edinburgh: Churchill-Livingstone, 1975, pp. 421–49. **130, 131**

Kaufmann, Walter. *Time Is an Artist*, New York: Reader's Digest Press, 1978. **133, 171, 173, 199**

Kavanagh, Gaynor. 'History and the museum: the nostalgia business', *Museums Journal*, 83 (1983), 139–41. **345**

Kay, Jane Holtz. 'Salem: fly beyond the witch image for an unforgettable experience in architectural history', *American Preservation*, 1:2 (1977–8), 9–20. **346**

Kearns, Kevin Corrigan. *Georgian Dublin: Ireland's Imperilled Architectural Heritage*, Newton Abbot: David & Charles, 1983. **335**

'Preservation and transformation of Georgian Dublin', *Geographical Review*, 72 (1982), 270–90. **334, 335**

Keats, John. *Poetical Works*, ed. H. W. Garrod, 2nd edn., Oxford: Clarendon, 1958. **159**

Kedourie, Elie (ed.). *Nationalism in Asia and Africa*, London: Weidenfeld and Nicolson, 1971. Includes essays by Alp; Blyden; Koraes; his own introduction. **332, 336, 371**

Keller, Hans D. 'Time out: the discontinuity of historical consciousness', *History and Theory*, 14 (1975), 275–96. **211**

Kelley, Donald R. *Foundations of Modern Historical Scholarship: Language, Law, and History in the French Renaissance*, Columbia University Press, 1970. **86, 88, 186, 214**

Kelly, Francis. *Art Restoration*, Newton Abbot: David & Charles, 1971. **126, 152, 161**

Kelsey, Darwin P., Jr. 'Reflections on the character and management of historical and tourist parks in the 1980s', paper from Australian Historical and Tourist Parks Association Conference, 1980. **298**

Kemble, Frances Anne (Butler). *Journal of a Residence in America*, Paris, 1835. **126**

Kendig, Frank, and Hutton, Richard. *Life-Spans or How Long Things Last*, New York: Holt, Rinehart and Winston, 1979. **126, 399**

Kennet, Wayland. *Preservation*, London: Temple Smith, 1972. **394**

Kent, David A. 'Film and history teaching in the secondary school', in Fledelius, *History and the Audio-Visual Media*, q.v., pp. 87–102. **368**

Kermode, Frank. *The Sense of an Ending: Studies in the Theory of Fiction*, Oxford University Press, 1968. **221, 379**

Kern, Fritz. *Kingship and Law in the Middle Ages* (1914), Oxford: Blackwell, 1948. **370**

Kern, Stephen. *The Culture of Time and Space 1880–1918*, London: Weidenfeld and Nicolson, 1983. **17, 250, 257, 379**

Kerner, Karen. 'The malevolent ancestors: ancestral influence in a Japanese religious sect', in Newell, *Ancestors*, q.v., pp. 205–17. **67**

Kerr, Robert. 'English architecture thirty years hence' (1884), reprinted in Pevsner, *Some Architectural Writers of the Nineteenth Century*, q.v., App. I, pp. 291–314. **396**

His Excellency the Ambassador Extraordinary, 3 vols., London, 1879. **98**

Kidney, Walter C. *The Architecture of Choice: Eclecticism in America 1880–1930*, New York: Braziller, 1974. **153, 329**

Kidson, Peter. 'Architecture and city planning' and 'The figural arts', in Finley, *Legacy of Greece*, q.v., pp. 376–400 and 401–28. **81, 142, 303, 378**

Kierkegaard, Søren. *Either/Or* (1843), 2 vols., Oxford University Press, 1944. **12**

Kindler, Roger A. 'Periodical criticism 1815–40: originality in architecture', *Architectural History*, 17 (1974), 22–37. **99, 101**

Kinser, Samuel. 'Ideas of temporal change and cultural process in France, 1470–1535', in Anthony Molho and John A. Tedeschi (eds.), *Renaissance Studies in Honor of Hans Baron*, Northern Illinois University Press, 1971, pp. 713–55. **80, 84**

Kissane, James. 'Tennyson: the passion of the past and the curse of time', *ELH*, 32 (1965), 85–109. **210**

Klein, George S. *Psychoanalytic Theory: An Exploration of Essentials*, New York: International Universities Press, 1976. **253**

Kliger, Samuel T. *The Goths in England: A Study in Seventeenth and Eighteenth Century Thought*, Harvard University Press, 1952. **336**

Knight, Richard Payne. *An Analytical Inquiry into the Principles of Taste*, 3rd edn., London, 1806. **100**

Ko Ku Yao Lun, *see* David, Percival.

Kobayashi, Bunji. 'The case of the Ise Grand Shinto Temple in Japan', in ICOMOS, *Nessun futuro senza passato*, q.v., pp. 185–91. **385**

Kohli, Martin. 'Biography: account, text, method', in Bertaux, *Biography and Society*, q.v., pp. 61–75. **213**

Konrad, Victor Alexander. 'Orientations toward the Past in the Environment of the Present: Retrospect in Metropolitan Toronto', Ph.D. thesis, McMaster University, 1978. **37, 286**

'Presenting our native heritage in public parks', *Recreation Canada*, 35:3 (1977), 18–25. **286**

Konrad, Victor A., and Taylor, S. Martin. 'Retrospective orientations in metropolitan Toronto and their implications for preservation and presentation of the historical environment', *Urban History Review*, 11:2 (1980), 65–86. **37**

Koraes, Adamantios. 'Report on the present state of civilization in Greece' (1803) (reprinted from his *Mémoire de l'état actuel de la civilisation dans la Grèce*, in Kedourie, *Nationalism in Asia and Africa*, q.v., pp. 153–88. **333**

Kozintsev, Grigori. *Shakespeare: Time and Conscience*, London: Dobson, 1967. **288, 306**

Kracauer, Siegfried. 'Time and history', *History and Theory*, Beiheft 6 (1966), 65–78. **208, 220**

Kramer, Leonie. 'The sense of the past in modern Australian poetry', in Quartermaine, *Readings in Australian Arts*, q.v., pp. 23–34. **54**

Kramnick, Isaac. *Bolingbroke and His Circle: The Politics of Nostalgia in the Age of Walpole*, Harvard University Press, 1968. **141**

Krieger, Martin H. 'What's wrong with plastic trees?' *Science*, 179 (1973), 446–55. **275**

Krieger, Murray. *Arts on the Level: The Fall of the Elite Object*, University of Tennessee Press, 1981. **70**

Kris, Ernst. 'The recovery of childhood memories', *Psychoanalytic Study of the Child*, 11 (1956), 54–88. **209, 210**

Kristeller, Paul Oskar. 'The modern system of the arts: a study in the history of aesthetics', *Journal of the History of Ideas*, 12 (1951), 496–527; 13 (1952), 17–46. **92**

Kroeber, Karl. *Romantic Landscape Vision: Constable and Wordsworth*, University of Wisconsin Press, 1975. **178**

Kubler, George. *The Shape of Time: Remarks on the History of Things*, Yale University Press, 1962. **67, 126, 187, 191, 290, 377, 379**

Kurz, Otto. 'Time the painter', *Burlington Magazine*, 105 (1963), 94–7. **160, 161**

'Varnishes, tinted varnishes, and patina', ibid., 104 (1962), 56–9. **159, 160, 163**

Lafferty, R. A. *Nine Hundred Grandmothers*, New York: Ace Books, 1970:

'Nine hundred grandmothers', pp. 7–19. **23**

'Through other eyes', pp. 282–96. **29**

'Thus we frustrate Charlemagne' pp. 171–84. **26**

Lagarde, Pierre de. *La Mémoire des pierres*, Paris: Albin Michel, 1979. **393, 394**

Lambrick, George. *Archaeology and Agriculture: A Survey of Modern Cultivation Methods and Problems of Assessing Plough Damage to Archaeological Sites*, Oxford: Council for British Archaeology and the Oxfordshire Archaeological Unit, 1977. **396**

Lancaster, Osbert. 'The future of the past: some thoughts on preservation', *Cornhill Magazine*, 174 (Summer 1964), 122–32 (reprinted as 'Some thoughts on preservation', in *Historic Preservation Today*, q.v., pp. 187–98). **240**

Here, of All Places, Boston: Houghton Mifflin, 1958. **319**

Landor, Walter Savage. *Pericles and Aspasia* (1836), 2 vols., London, 1890. **374**

Lang, S. 'Richard Payne Knight and the idea of modernity', in John Summerson (ed.), *Concerning Architecture: Essays on Architectural Writers and Writing Presented to Nikolaus Pevsner*, London: Allen Lane/Penguin, 1968, pp. 85–97. **100**

Langenbach, Randolph. *See* Hareven, Tamara; and *Satanic Mills*.

Langer, Alfred. *Wilhelm Leibl*, Leipzig: Seemann, 1961. **172**

Langer, Susanne K. *Feeling and Form: A Theory of Art*, London: Routledge & Kegan Paul, 1953. **39, 206**

Langguth, A. J. *Saki: A Life of Hector Hugh Munro*, London: Hamish Hamilton, 1981. **325**

Langton, Jane. *Natural Enemy*, New Haven: Ticknor & Fields, 1982. **341**

Larkin, Philip. *A Girl in Winter*, London: Faber and Faber, 1975. **133, 242**

    The Less Deceived, London: Marvell Press, 1955. **376**

    The Whitsun Weddings, London: Faber and Faber, 1964. **264**

Laski, Marghanita. *The Victorian Chaise Longue*, New York: Ballantine, 1953. **30**

Lassels, Richard. *An Italian-Voyage, or, A Compleat Journey through Italy* (1670), 2nd edn., 2 parts, London, 1698. **134**

Laumer, Keith. *Dinosaur Beach*, New York: Daw, 1971. **22, 30, 31**

    The Great Time Machine Hoax, New York: Grosset and Dunlap, 1963. **27, 29**

Lavalleye, Jacques. 'Dismembered works of art – Flemish painting', in UNESCO, *Illustrated Inventory*, q.v., pp. 52–87. **287**

Laver, James. *Taste and Fashion from the French Revolution to the Present Day*, rev. edn., London: Harrap, 1945. **51**

Laver, Tina. 'In the name of preservation', *Historic Preservation*, 33:5 (1981), 16–23. **341**

Lawrence, D. H. *Letters*, ed. Aldous Huxley, London: Heinemann, 1932. **9**

Leacock, Stephen. 'Old junk and new money' (1928), *The Bodley Head Leacock*, ed. J. B. Priestley, London, 1957, pp. 272–6. **153**

Lears, T. J. Jackson. *No Place of Grace: Antimodernism and the Transformation of American Culture 1880–1920*, New York: Pantheon, 1981. **104, 200, 342, 353, 379**

    See also 'Writing history: an exchange'.

Lebra, Takie Sugiyama. 'Ancestral influence on the suffering of descendants in a Japanese cult', in Newell, *Ancestors*, q.v., pp. 219–30. **67**

Le Corbusier (C. E. Jeanneret). *The City of Tomorrow and Its Planning* (1925), London: John Rodker, 1929. **142, 405**

    Towards a New Architecture (1923), rev. edn., London: Architectural Press, 1946. **380**

    When the Cathedrals Were White: A Journey to the Country of Timid People (1937), New York: McGraw-Hill, 1964. **144**

Lee, Antoinette J. 'Profiteers vs. antiquarians', in David Lowenthal and Victor Konrad (eds.), *The Uses and Misuses of the Past* (see Holdsworth), forthcoming. **387**

Lees-Milne, James. *Ancestral Voices*, London: Chatto & Windus, 1975. **309, 332**

    Caves of Ice, ibid., 1983. **105**

Leff, Gordon. *History and Social Theory*, New York: Doubleday/Anchor, 1971. **213, 216, 234**

Le Goff, Jacques, *et al. La Nouvelle Histoire*, Paris: Retz-CEPL, 1978. **211**

Le Guin, Ursula K. 'It was a dark and stormy night; or, Why are we huddling about the campfire?' in Mitchell, *On Narrative*, q.v., pp. 187–95. **331**

Leiber, Fritz. *The Big Time*, London: Four Square/New English Library, 1965. **31**

    'Try and change the past' (1958), in Robert Silverberg, ed., *Trips in Time*, Nashville, Tenn.: Nelson, 1977, pp. 93–101. **32**

Lenz, Siegfried. *The Heritage*, New York: Hill and Wang, 1981. **347, 361**

Leonardo da Vinci. *On Painting. A Lost Book ('Libro A')* [1508–15], ed. Carlo Pedretti, London: Peter Owen, 1965. **83**

Leone, Mark P. 'The relationship between artifacts and the public in outdoor history', *Annals of the New York Academy of Sciences*, 376 (1981), 301–13. **xxiv, 341**

Léon-Portilla, Miguel. *Pre-Columbian Literature of Mexico*, University of Oklahoma Press, 1969. **335**

Lerner, Laurence. *The Uses of Nostalgia: Studies in Pastoral Poetry*, London: Chatto & Windus, 1972. **372**

Le Roy, Louis. *De la vicissitude ou variété des choses en l'univers* (1575), excerpted as 'The excellence of this age', *The Portable Renaissance Reader*, ed. James Bruce Ross and Mary Martin McLaughlin, New York: Viking, 1953, pp. 91–108. **88**

Le Roy Ladurie, Emmanuel. *Montaillou: Cathars and Catholics in a French Village 1294–1324*, London: Scolar, 1978. **223, 232**

Lesy, Michael. *Time Frames: The Meaning of Family Pictures*, New York: Pantheon, 1980. **258**

Levenson, Joseph R. *Confucian China and Its Modern Fate*, 3 vols., London: Routledge & Kegan Paul, vol. 3, *The Problems of Historical Significance*, 1965. **406**

Levin, Betty. *A Griffon's Nest*, New York: Macmillan, 1975. **20**

    'Peppers' progress: one hundred years of the Five Little Peppers', *Horn Book Magazine*, 57 (1981), 161–73. **41**

    The Sword of Culann, New York: Macmillan, 1973. **20**

Levin, David. *History as Romantic Art: Bancroft, Prescott, Motley, and Parkman*, Stanford University Press, 1959. **115, 246, 336**

Levin, Edward S. See *Speaking a New Classicism*.

LeVine, Robert A. 'Adulthood and aging in cross-cultural perspective', Social Science Research Council *Items* (New York), 31/32:4/1 (1978), 1–5. **199**

Lévi-Strauss, Claude. *The Savage Mind*, London: Weidenfeld and Nicolson, 1966. **61**

Levstik, Linda S. 'Living history – isn't', *History News*, 37:5 (1982), 28–9. **244**

Lewin, Bertram D. *Selected Writings*, ed. Jacob A. Arlow, New York: Psychoanalytic Quarterly, 1973. **17, 253**

Lewis, Bernard. *History Remembered, Recovered, Invented*, Princeton University Press, 1975. **332**

Lewis, Clarence Irving. *An Analysis of Knowledge and Valuation*, La Salle, Ill.: Open Court, 1946. **187, 188, 190, 200, 215**

Lewis, C. S. *Out of the Silent Planet*, New York: Collier, 1962. **39**

Lewis, David. 'The paradoxes of time travel', *American Philosophical Quarterly*, 13 (1976), 145–52. **32**

Lewis, H. D. (ed.). *Contemporary British Philosophy: Personal Statements. Fourth Series*, London: Allen & Unwin, 1976. Includes essays by Anscombe; Walsh, W. H.

Lewis, Philippa. 'Peasant nostalgia in contemporary Russian literature', *Soviet Studies*, 28 (1976), 548–69. **6, 35**

Lewis, R. W. B. *The American Adam: Innocence, Tragedy, and Tradition in the Nineteenth Century*, University of Chicago Press/Phoenix, 1955. **110**

Leyden, Wolfgang von. 'Antiquity and authority: a paradox in the Renaissance theory of history', *Journal of the History of Ideas*, 19 (1958), 473–92. **89**

    'Categories of historical understanding', *History and Theory*, 23 (1984), 53–77. **215, 218**

Liebs, Chester H. 'Remember our not-so-distant past?' *Historic Preservation*, 30:1 (1978), 30–5. **351**

Lifton, Robert Jay. 'Individual patterns in historical change: imagery of Japanese youth', *Comparative Studies in Society and History*, 6 (1964), 369–83. **71**

Lincoln, Abraham. *The Collected Works*, ed. Roy P. Basler, 8 vols., Rutgers University Press, 1953:

    'Address before the Young Men's Lyceum of Springfield, Illinois' (1838), 1:108–15. **119, 120**

    'Annual message to Congress', 1 Dec. 1862, 5:518–37. **120**

    'Gettysburg Address', 19 Nov. 1863, 7:20. **322**

    'Speech at Edwardsville, Illinois', 11 Sept. 1858, 3:91–6. **120**

Linstrum, Derek. 'Education for conservation', in ICOMOS, *Nessun futuro senza passato*, q.v., pp. 679–89. **271**

    'Giuseppe Valadier et l'Arc de Titus', *Monumentum*, 25 (1982), 43–71. **280, 394**

Linton, Marigold. 'Memory for real-world events', in D. A. Norman and D. E. Rumelhart (eds.), *Explorations in Cognition*, San Francisco: Freeman, 1975, pp. 376–404. **197**

    'Real-world memory after six years: an *in vivo* study of very long term memory', in Gruneberg, Morris, and Sykes, *Practical Aspects of Memory*, q.v., pp. 69–76. **206**

'Transformations of memory in everyday life', in Neisser, *Memory Observed*, q.v., pp. 77–91. **206, 207**

Lippard, Lucy C. *Overlay: Contemporary Art and the Art of Prehistory*, New York: Pantheon, 1983. **55**

Lippmann, Walter. *Public Opinion* (1922), New York: Macmillan, 1960. **250**

Litman, Vicki Halper. 'The cottage and the temple: Melville's symbolic use of architecture', *American Quarterly*, 21 (1969), 630–8. **166**

Lively, Penelope. *According to Mark*, London: Heinemann, 1984. **14, 197**

'Children and the art of memory', *Horn Book Magazine*, 54 (1978), 17–23, 197–203. **222, 341**

'Children and memory', ibid., 49 (1973), 400–7. **61**

Going Back, London: Heinemann, 1975. **206**

The House in Norham Gardens, London: Pan, 1977. **20, 61, 243, 247**

Judgement Day, London: Heinemann, 1980. **296**

The Road to Lichfield, London: Heinemann, 1977. **67, 222**

A Stitch in Time, London: Pan, 1978. **21**

Treasures of Time, London: Heinemann, 1979. **144**

Locke, John. *The Conduct of the Understanding* (1706), London, 1825. **95**

Some Thoughts Concerning Education (1693), Menston: Scolar, 1970. **106**

Two Treatises of Government (1690), ed. Thomas I. Cook, New York: Hafner, 1947. **106**

Loewald, Hans W. *Psychoanalysis and the History of the Individual*, Yale University Press, 1978. **48, 72**

Loftus, Elizabeth F. and Geoffrey R. 'On the permanence of stored information in the human brain', *American Psychologist*, 35 (1980), 409–20. **17**

Long, Amelia R. 'Reverse phylogeny' (1937), in Conklin, *Science Fiction Adventures in Dimension*, q.v., pp. 31–43. **17**

Longfellow, Henry Wadsworth. *The Writings*, Riverside edn., 11 vols., London: Routledge, 1886–93:

Hyperion (1839), 2:13–285. **116**

Outre-Mer (1835), 1:9–278. **114**

Longstreth, Richard W. 'Academic eclecticism in American architecture', *Winterthur Portfolio*, 17 (1982), 55–82. **383**

Lorentz, Stanisław. 'Protection of monuments', in *Poland: A Handbook*, Warsaw: Interpress, 1974, pp. 418–22. **46, 387**

'Reconstruction of the old town centers of Poland', in *Historic Preservation Today*, q.v., pp. 43–72. **46, 290**

Lovejoy, Arthur O. 'Herder and the Enlightenment philosophy of history', in his *Essays in the History of Ideas*, Johns Hopkins University Press, 1948, pp. 166–84. **64, 234**

Lowell, James Russell. *The Complete Writings*, Elmwood edn., 16 vols., Boston: Houghton Mifflin, 1904:

'Lines suggested by the graves of the soldiers on Concord battle-ground', 9:271–2. **324**

'The Rebellion: its causes and consequences' (1864), 6:145–85. **324**

'Self-possession *vs.* prepossession', *Atlantic Monthly*, 8 (1861), 761–9. **118**

Lowell, Massachusetts. *Report on the Lowell Historic Canal District Commission*, Washington, D.C.: U.S.G.P.O., 1977. **388**

Lowenthal, David. 'Age and artifact: dilemmas of interpretation', in Donald W. Meinig (ed.), *The Interpretation of Ordinary Landscapes: Geographical Essays*, New York: Oxford University Press, 1979, pp. 103–28. **273, 360**

'The American way of history', *Columbia University Forum*, 9:3 (1966), 27–32. **51, 359**

'Australian images: the unique present, the mythical past', in Quartermaine, *Readings in Australian Arts*, q.v., pp. 84–93. **54**

'The bicentennial landscape: a mirror held up to the past', *Geographical Review*, 67 (1977), 253–67. **296**

'The Caribbean region', in Marvin W. Mikesell (ed.), *Geographers Abroad: Essays on the Problems and Prospects of Research in Foreign Areas*, University of Chicago, Dept of Geography Research Paper No. 152, 1973, pp. 47–69. **54**

'Conserving the heritage: Anglo-American comparisons', in John Patten (ed.), *The Expanding City: Essays in Honour of Jean Gottmann*, London: Academic Press, 1983, pp. 225–76. **387, 400**

George Perkins Marsh: Versatile Vermonter, Columbia University Press, 1958. **108, 244, 336, 339**

'Past time, present place: landscape and memory', *Geographical Review*, 65 (1975), 1–36. **360**

'The pioneer landscape: an American dream', *Great Plains Quarterly*, 2 (1982), 5–19. **42**

'The place of the past in the American landscape', in Lowenthal and Bowden, *Geographies of the Mind*, q.v., pp. 99–117. **105, 122**

West Indian Societies, Oxford University Press, 1972. **250**

Lowenthal, David, and Binney, Marcus. *Our Past Before Us: Why Do We Save It?* London: Temple Smith, 1981. Includes essays by Beazley; Binney, Fowler; Hanna; Hareven and Langenbach; Hunter, M.; Saunders.

Lowenthal, David, and Bowden, Martyn (eds.). *Geographies of the Mind: Essays in Historical Geosophy in Honor of John Kirtland Wright*, New York: Oxford University Press, 1975. Includes essays by Lowenthal; Zelinsky.

Lowenthal, David, and Prince, Hugh C. 'English landscape tastes', *Geographical Review*, 55 (1965), 186–222. **151**

Lowenthal, David, and Riel, Marquita. *Structures of Environmental Associations* (Publications in Environmental Perception No. 6), New York: American Geographical Society, 1972. **127**

Milieu and Observer Differences in Environmental Associations, ibid., No. 7. **127**

Environmental Structures: Semantic and Experiential Components, ibid., No. 8. **127**

Lucas, Clive. *See* 'World of conservation: an interview with Clive Lucas'.

Luck, Georg. 'Scriptor classicus', *Comparative Literature*, 10 (1958), 150–8. **245**

Lukacher, Brian. 'Gandy's dream revisited', in *Joseph Michael Gandy*, London: Architectural Association, 1982, pp. 4–25. **168**

Lukács, Georg. *The Historical Novel*, Penguin, 1969. **226, 229**

Lukacs, John. 'Obsolete historians', *Harpers*, 261 (Nov. 1980), 80–4. **237, 367, 377, 387**

Outgrowing Democracy: A History of the United States in the Twentieth Century, Garden City, N.Y.: Doubleday, 1984. **377**

Luria, A. R. *The Man with a Shattered World: The History of a Brain Injury*, London: Cape, 1973. **197**

Lynch, Hollis R. *Edward Wilmot Blyden: Pan-Negro Patriot 1832–1912*, Oxford University Press, 1967. **336**

Lynch, Kevin. *What Time Is This Place?* Cambridge, Mass.: M.I.T. Press, 1972. **xviii, 42, 50, 179, 244, 359, 360**

Lynes, Russell. *The Tastemakers*, New York: Grosset & Dunlap, 1954. **121**

Lynn, Kenneth S. *A Divided People* (Contributions in American Studies No. 30). Westport, Conn.: Greenwood, 1977. **107**

Lynton, Norbert. 'Futurism', in Nikos Stangos (ed.), *Concepts of Modern Art*, rev. edn., London: Thames and Hudson, 1981, pp. 97–105. **380**

Lyons, John O. *The Invention of Self: The Hinge of Consciousness in the Eighteenth Century*, Southern Illinois University Press, 1978. **232**

Lyttelton, Oliver, Viscount Chandos. *From Peace to War: A Study in Contrast, 1857–1918*, London: Bodley Head, 1968. **252**

Maass, John. 'Architecture and Americanism or pastiches of Independence Hall', *Historic Preservation*, 22:2 (1970), 17–25. **293**

Macaulay, Rose. *Pleasure of Ruins*, New York: Walker, 1953. **57, 168, 173, 238, 282, 331**

Macaulay, Thomas Babington. 'Hallam' (1828), *Critical and Historical Essays*, ed. F. C. Montague, 3 vols., London: Methuen, 1903, 1:115–202. **225**

The History of England, from the Accession of James II, 5th edn., 10 vols., London, vol. 1, 1848. **239**

The Letters of Thomas Babington Macaulay, ed. Thomas Pinney, Cambridge University Press, 1974. **233**

McCann, Willis H. 'Nostalgia: a descriptive and comparative study', *Journal of Genetic Psychology*, 62 (1943), 97–104. **11**

'Nostalgia – a review of the literature', *Psychological Bulletin*, 38 (1941), 165–82. **11**

MacCannell, Dean. *The Tourist: A New Theory of the Leisure Class*, New York: Schocken, 1976. **269, 273, 406**

McCarthy, Mary. *The Oasis*, New York: Random House, 1949. **24**

McCullagh, C. Behan. *Justifying Historical Descriptions*, Cambridge University Press, 1984. **215, 216**

McFarland, Thomas. *Romanticism and the Forms of Ruin: Wordsworth, Coleridge, and Modalities of Fragmentation*, Princeton University Press, 1981. **171**

McGarry, Daniel D., and White, Sarah H. *World Historical Fiction Guide*, 2nd edn., Metuchen, N.J.: Swallow Press, 1973. **227**

McGee, Henry W., Jr. 'Historic preservation and displacement: regeneration or resegregation? *UCLA Center for Afro-American Studies Newsletter*, 6:1 (1981), 11–16. **403**

Machado, Rodolfo. 'Old buildings as palimpsest: toward a theory of remodeling', *Progressive Architecture*, 57 (1976), 47–9. **381**

McHugh, Roger J. 'The Famine in Irish oral tradition', in A. Dudley Edwards and T. Desmond Williams (eds.), *The Great Famine, Studies in Irish History 1845–52*, Dublin: Browne and Nolan, 1956, pp. 391–436. **250**

McIntyre, James Lewis. *Giordano Bruno*, London: Macmillan, 1903. **137**

McKechnie, George. 'The Environmental Response Inventory in application', *Environment and Behavior*, 9 (1977), 255–75. **36**

McKenna, John M. 'Original historical manuscripts and the undergraduate', *American Historical Association Newsletter*, 16:3 (1978), 6–7. **153**

McLaren, Duncan. *Ruins: The Once Great Houses of Ireland*, New York: Knopf, 1980. **335**

McMullen, Roy. *Mona Lisa: The Picture and the Myth*, Boston: Houghton Mifflin, 1975. **307**

Maddock, Ieuan. 'Why industry must learn to forget', *New Scientist*, 11 Feb. 1982, pp. 368–70. **69**

Magida, Arthur. 'Our printed legacy is turning to dust', *Historic Preservation*, 33:4 (1981), 50–5. **398**

Mahon, Denis. 'Miscellanea for the cleaning controversy', *Burlington Magazine*, 104 (1962), 460–70. **149, 153, 160**

Mailfert, André. *Au Pays des antiquaires: confidences d'un 'maquilleur' professionel*, Paris: Flammarion, 1935. **291**

Maitland, Frederic William. 'A survey of the century' (1901), *The Collected Papers*, ed. H. A. L. Fisher, 3 vols., Cambridge University Press, 1911, 3:432–9. **233**

Township and Borough, Cambridge, 1898. **216**

Maiuri, Amadeo. 'Recent excavations at Pompeii', *Museum*, 3 (1950), 102–4. **164**

Malcolm, Joyce Lee. *The Scene of the Battle, 1775: Historic Grounds Report, Minute Man National Historical Park: Cultural Resource Management Study*, Boston, Mass.: U.S. Dept. of the Interior, National Park Service, 1983. **361**

Mallet, David. *The Excursion: a Poem in Two Books*, London, 1728. **157**

Malraux, André. *The Voices of Silence*, London: Secker & Warburg, 1954. **172, 349**

Mankowitz, Wolf. *Wedgwood*, London: Batsford, 1953. **304, 306**

Mann, J. G. 'Instances of antiquarian feeling in medieval and Renaissance art', *Archaeological Journal*, 99 (1939), 254–74. **241**

Mann, Thomas. 'Freud and the future' (1936), in his *Essays of Three Decades*, London: Secker & Warburg, n.d., pp. 411–28. **373, 374**

Manuel, Frank E. *Shapes of Philosophical History*, Stanford University Press, 1965. **94, 141, 142**

Margolis, Joseph. 'Art, forgery, and authenticity', in Dutton, *Forger's Art*, q.v., pp. 153–71. **293, 385**

Marinetti, Filippo Tommaso. *Marinetti: Selected Writings*, ed. R. W. Flint, London: Secker & Warburg, 1972. **142, 380**

Marmoy, C. F. A. 'The "Auto-Icon" of Jeremy Bentham at University College London', *Medical History*, 2:2 (1958), 1–10. **61**

Marrey, Bernard. *Les Grands Magasins des origines à 1939*, Paris: Picard, 1979. **356**

Marris, Peter. *Loss and Change*, London: Routledge & Kegan Paul, 1974. **399**

Marrou, H.-I. 'Education and rhetoric', in Finley, *Legacy of Greece*, q.v., pp. 185–201. **378**

Marryat, Frederick. *Diary in America* (1839), ed. Jules Zanger, Indiana University Press, 1960. **109**

Marsh, George P. *The American Historical School*, Troy, N.Y., 1847. **244**

  The Goths in New-England, Middlebury, Vt., 1843. **108, 336**

  Man and Nature (1864), ed. David Lowenthal, Harvard University Press, 1965. **xvii, 19**

  'The study of nature', *Christian Examiner*, 68 (1860), 33–62. **19**

Marsh, Jan. *Back to the Land: The Pastoral Impulse in Victorian England, from 1880 to 1914*, London: Quartet, 1982. **104**

Marshall, John C., and Fryer, David M. 'Speak, memory! an introduction to some historic studies of remembering and forgetting', in Gruneberg and Morris, *Aspects of Memory*, q.v., pp. 1–25. **252**

Martin, C. B., and Deutscher, Max. 'Remembering', *Philosophical Review*, 75 (1966), 161–96. **196**

Marx, Karl. *The Eighteenth Brumaire of Louis Napoleon* (1852), New York, 1898. **65**

Matheson, Richard. *Somewhere in Time*, London: Sphere, 1980 (published in 1977 as *Bid Time Return*). **14**

Matthews, Albert. 'Some sobriquets applied to Washington', *Publications of the Colonial Society of Massachusetts, Transactions*, 8 (1903), 275–87. **112**

Maxwell, William. *Ancestors*, New York: Knopf, 1971. **60**

  So Long, See You Tomorrow, New York: Ballantine, 1980. **185**

Mazzeo, Joseph Anthony. *Varieties of Interpretation*, University of Notre Dame Press, 1978. **69, 73**

Mazzocco, Angelo. 'The antiquarianism of Francesco Petrarch', *Journal of Medieval and Renaissance Studies*, 7 (1977), 203–24. **78, 148**

  'The case of Biondo Flavio', in Ramsey, *Rome in the Renaissance*, q.v., pp. 185–95. **78**

Mbiti, John S. *African Religions & Philosophy*, London: Heinemann, 1969. **195**

Meacham, John A., and Leiman, Burt. 'Remembering to perform future actions', in Neisser, *Memory Observed*, q.v., pp. 327–36. **193**

Meerloo, Joost A. M. *The Two Faces of Man: Two Studies on the Sense of Time and on Ambivalence*, New York: International Universities, 1954. **42**

Meiss, Millard. 'Discussion' of 'The aesthetic and historical aspects of the presentation of damaged pictures', *Studies in Western Art* (Acts of the 20th International Congress of the History of Art), 4 vols., Princeton University Press, 1963, 4:163–6. **172**

Melville, Herman. *Writings*, Northwestern University Press and Newberry Library, 8 vols., 1968–82:

  Mardi (1849), vol. 3. **148**

  Pierre: or the Ambiguities (1852), vol. 7. **166**

Mendilow, A. A. *Time and the Novel*, London: Peter Nevill, 1952. **185, 196, 205**

Merriman, James D. 'The other Arthurians in Victorian England', *Philosophical Quarterly*, 56 (1977), 249–53. **38**

Merton, Robert K. *On the Shoulders of Giants: A Shandean Postscript*, New York: Harcourt Brace Jovanovich, 1965. **89**

Merwin, Sam, Jr. *Three Faces of Time*, London: John Spencer/Badger, 1960. **25, 27, 29**

Métraux, Guy S. *Le Ranz des vaches: du chant de bergers à l'hymne patriotique*, Lausanne: Editions 24 Heures, 1984. **10**

Metzger, Gustav. *Auto-Destructive Art*, London: Architectural Association, 1965. **172**

Meyer, Karl E. *The Plundered Past*, London: Hamish Hamilton, 1974. **50, 152, 291, 396**

Meyer, Leonard B. *Music the Arts and Ideas: Patterns and Predictions in Twentieth-Century Culture*, University of Chicago Press, 1967. **192, 384**

Meyerhoff, Hans. *Time in Literature*, University of California Press, 1955. **251**

Michelet, Jules. *Ma jeunesse* (1884), Paris: Flammarion, n.d. **245**

Michell, John. *Megalithomania: Artists, Antiquarians and Archaeologists at the Old Stone Monuments*, London: Thames and Hudson, 1982. **336**

Middlekauff, Robert. *Ancients and Axioms: Secondary Education in Eighteenth-Century New England*, Yale University Press, 1963. **112**

Middleton, Arthur Pierce, and Adair, Douglass. 'The case of the men who weren't there: problems of local pride' (abridged from 'The mystery of the Horn papers', *William and Mary Quarterly*, 3rd ser., 4 (1947), 409–43), in Winks, *Historian as Detective*, q.v., pp. 142–77. **246**

Middleton, Robin. 'The use and abuse of tradition in architecture', *Journal of the Royal Society of Arts*, 131 (1983), 927–39. **381, 383, 404**

Miles, Edwin A. 'The young American nation and the classical world', *Journal of the History of Ideas*, 35 (1974), 259–74. **112, 113**

Mill, John Stuart. 'The spirit of the age' (1831), in his *Essays on Literature and Society*, ed. J. B. Schneewind, New York: Collier, 1965, pp. 27–78. **93, 97, 100, 130**

Miller, Joseph C. 'Introduction: listening for the African past', in his *African Past Speaks*, q.v., pp. 1–59. **214, 220, 238**

 (ed). *The African Past Speaks: Essays on Oral Tradition and History*, Folkestone, Kent: Dawson, 1980. Includes essays by Henige; Miller, J. C; Vansina.

Miller, J. Hillis. 'History as repetition in Thomas Hardy's poetry: the example of "Wessex Heights"', in Bradbury and Palmer, *Victorian Poetry*, q.v., pp. 223–53. **16, 234, 248**

Miller, Perry. 'The romantic dilemma of American nationalism and the concept of nature', *Harvard Theological Review*, 48 (1955), 239–43. **109**

 The Life of the Mind in America from the Revolution to the Civil War, New York: Harcourt, Brace and World, 1965. **111**

Miller, Shirley M., Blalock, Jan, and Ginsburg, Harvey J. 'Children and the aged: attitudes, content, and discriminative ability', *International Journal of Aging and Human Development*, 19 (1984), 47–53. **133**

Milosz, Czeslaw. 'The Nobel lecture, 1980', *N.Y. Review of Books*, 5 Mar. 1981, pp. 11–14. **224**

Milton, John. '*Naturam non pati senium*' (c. 1627), *The Poems*, ed. John Carey and Alistair Fowler, London: Longmans, 1968, pp. 61–5. **138**

Mink, Louis O. 'Everyman his or her own annalist', in Mitchell, *On Narrative*, q.v., pp. 233–9. **212, 221, 229, 251**

 'History and fiction as modes of comprehension', *New Literary History*, 1 (1970), 541–58. **220**

 'Narrative form as a cognitive instrument', in Robert H. Canary and Henry Kozicki (eds.), *The Writing of History: Literary Form and Historical Understanding*, University of Wisconsin Press, 1978. **218**

Minkowski, Eugène. *Lived Time: Phenomenological and Psychopathological Studies* (1933), Northwestern University Press, 1970. **192, 202, 203, 204**

Mitchell, W. J. T. (ed.). *On Narrative*, University of Chicago Press, 1981 (from *Critical Inquiry*, 7, 1980–1). Includes essays by Goodman; Le Guin; Mink; Schafer, Roy.

Momigliano, Arnaldo D. 'Ancient history and the antiquarian' (1950), in his *Studies in Historiography*, London: Weidenfeld and Nicolson, 1969. pp. 1–39. **89, 244**

 'Time in ancient historiography' (1966), in his *Essays in Ancient and Modern Historiography*, Oxford: Blackwell, 1977, pp. 179–204. **141**

Monk, Samuel H. *The Sublime: A Study of Critical Theories in XVIIIth-Century England* (1935), University of Michigan Paperback, 1960. **144, 173**

Monnet, Bertrand. 'The care of ancient monuments in France', *Architectural Association Quarterly*, 2:2 (1970), 27–36. **394**

Montaigne, Michel de. 'Of vanitie', *Essays*, transl. John Florio, London: Dent, 1910, 3:183–253. **128, 374**

 Travel Journal, transl. Donald M. Frame, San Francisco: North Point, 1983. **391**

Montesquieu, Charles de Secondat de. *Persian Letters* (1721), transl. John Davidson, London: Routledge, n.d. **137**

Moorcock, Michael. *Behold the Man*, London: Fontana/Collins, 1980. **27**
  The English Assassin: A Romance of Entropy, London: Alison & Busby, 1972. **7**
Moore, Brian. *The Great Victorian Collection*, London: Cape, 1975. **147**
Moore, Evelyn R. 'The Cahokia Courthouse', *Historic Illinois*, 3:2 (1980), 1–3. **286**
Moore, Ward. *Bring the Jubilee* (1955), London: New English Library, 1976. **23, 30, 32**
Mora, Paolo and Laura, and Philippot, Paul. *The Conservation of Wall Paintings*, London: Butterworth, 1984. **280**
More, Paul Elmer. 'Criticism', *Shelburne Essays, Seventh Series*, New York: Putnam's, 1910, 213–44. **198**
Morgan, Prys. 'From a death to a view: the hunt for the Welsh past in the Romantic period', in Hobsbawm and Ranger, *Invention of Tradition*, q.v., pp. 43–100. **46, 333, 336**
Moriarty, Sandra Ernst, and McGann, Anthony F. 'Nostalgia and consumer sentiment', *Journalism Quarterly*, 60 (1983), 81–8. **13**
Morison, Samuel Eliot. *Admiral of the Ocean Sea: A Life of Christopher Columbus*, 2 vols., Boston: Little Brown, 1942. **246**
Morris, Colin John. 'Townscape Images: A Study in Meaning and Classification', Ph.D. thesis, University of Exeter, 1978. **388**
  'Townscape images: a study in meaning', in Kain, *Planning for Conservation*, q.v., pp. 259–87. **388**
Morris, George Pope. *The Deserted Bride and Other Poems*, New York, 1838. **135**
Morris, William. *Collected Works*, ed. May Morris, 24 vols., London: Longmans, Green, 1910–15:
  'The beauty of life' (1880) 22:51–80. **164**
  'The hopes of civilisation' (1885), 23:59–80. **24–5**
  'The revival of architecture' (1888), 22:318–20 (reprinted in Pevsner, *Some Architectural Writers*, q.v., pp. 315–24). **101**
  'Restoration' (1877), reprinted as SPAB, *Manifesto*; in SPAB, *Repair not Restoration*; and in Tschudi-Madsen, *Restoration and Anti-Restoration*, q.v., Annex VI. **151, 280**
Morris, Wright. *Cause for Wonder*, University of Nebraska Press, 1978. **35**
Mortier, Roland. *Le poétique des ruines en France: ses origines, ses variations de la Renaissance à Victor Hugo*, Geneva: Droz, 1974. **134, 148, 168, 171, 173, 179, 391, 393**
Motley, John Lothrop. 'The polity of the Puritans', *North American Review*, 69 (1849), 470–98. **115**
Muller, Herbert J. *The Uses of the Past: Profiles of Former Societies*, Oxford University Press, 1952. **346**
Muller, Jeffrey M. 'Rubens's theory and practice of the imitation of art', *Art Bulletin*, 64 (1982), 229–47. **81, 82, 83, 84, 88**
Mullett, Charles F. 'Classical influences on the American Revolution', *Classical Journal*, 35 (1939), 92–104. **112**
Mulvey, Christopher. *Anglo-American Landscapes: A Study of Nineteenth-Century Anglo-American Travel Literature*, Cambridge University Press, 1981. **231, 247**
Mumford, Lewis. 'A backward glance', in his (ed.), *Roots of Contemporary American Architecture* (1952), New York: Dover, 1972, pp. 1–30. **381**
  The Culture of Cities, New York: Harcourt, Brace & World, 1938. **245, 248**
Munchhausen, K. F. H. von. *Travels and Adventures of Baron Munchausen* (1785), London: Nelson, 1941. **20**
Munz, Peter. *The Shapes of Time: A New Look at the Philosophy of History*, Wesleyan University Press, 1977. **215, 218, 223, 229, 232, 235, 236, 243, 368, 393**
Murphey, Michael G. *Our Knowledge of the Historical Past*, Indianapolis: Bobbs-Merrill, 1973. **189, 190, 213, 235**
Musset, Alfred de. *La Confession d'un enfant du siècle* (1836), *Œuvres complètes: Prose*, Paris: Gallimard, 1960, pp. 65–288. **101**
Muto, LaVerne. 'A feminist art – the American memorial picture', *Art Journal*, 35 (1976), 352–8. **178**

Nowlan, Kevin B. 'Conservation and development', in Nowlan, *et al.* (eds.), *Dublin's Future: The European Challenge. A Conservation Report*, London: Country Life for An Taisce, 1980, pp. 8–13. **335**

Oakeshott, Michael. 'The activity of being an historian' (1955), in his *Rationalism in Politics and Other Essays*, London: Methuen, 1967. **237, 365, 368**
    On History and Other Essays, Oxford: Blackwell, 1983. **237**

Oakeshott, W. F. *Oxford Stone Restored: The Work of the Oxford Buildings Trust 1957–1974*, Oxford University Press, 1975. **280**

O'Brien, Justin. 'Proust confirmed by neuro-surgery', *PMLA*, 85 (1970), 295–7. **17**

O'Connell, Donald N., Shor, Ronald E., and Orne, Martin T. 'Hypnotic age regression', *Journal of Abnormal Psychology*, 76/2 (Monograph Suppl. No. 3, 1970), 1–32. **19**

O'Faolain, Sean. *A Nest of Simple Folk*, London: Cape, 1933. **250**

Old Sturbridge Village: An Exploration of the Motivations and Experiences of Visitors and Potential Visitors, New York: Fine, Travis, and Levine, 1979. **298**

Oliphant, Laurence. *Minnesota and the Far West*, Edinburgh, 1855. **112**

Olmsted, Frederick Law. *Walks and Talks of an American Farmer in England* (1852), University of Michigan Press, 1967. **247, 268**

Olney, James. 'Wole Soyinka as autobiographer', *Yale Review*, 73 (1983), 72–93. **257**

Olszewski, George J. *A History of the Washington Monument 1844–1968*, Washington, D.C.: U.S. Dept. of the Interior, National Park Service, 1971. **286**

Olwig, Karen Fog. 'National parks, tourism and the culture of imperialism', *Transactions of the Finnish Anthropological Society*, No. 2 (1977), 243–56. **54, 342**
    'National parks, tourism, and local development: a West Indian case', *Human Organization*, 39 (1980), 22–31. **54**

Ong, Walter J. *Orality and Literacy: The Technologizing of the Word*, London: Methuen, 1982. **256, 370**
    Rhetoric, Romance, and Technology: Studies in the Interaction of Expression and Culture, Cornell University Press, 1971. **232, 259, 360, 384**

Organ, R. M. 'The current status of the treatment of corroded metal artifacts', in B. F. Brown, *Corrosion and Metal Artifacts*, q.v., pp. 107–42. **163**

Orne, Martin T., Soskis, David A., Dinges, David F., and Orne, Emily Carota. 'Hypnotically induced testimony', in Gary F. Wells and Elizabeth F. Loftus (eds.), *Eyewitness Testimony: Psychological Perspectives*, Cambridge University Press, 1984, pp. 171–213. **19**

Ortega y Gasset, José. *Man and Crisis*, London: Allen & Unwin, 1959. **365**

Orwell, George. *Coming Up for Air* (1939), Penguin, 1962. **134**
    Nineteen Eighty-Four (1948), Penguin, 1954. **190**

O'Sullivan, John Louis. 'The great nations of futurity', *United States Magazine and Democratic Review*, 6 (1839), 426–30. **110**

Otto, Bishop of Freising. *The Two Cities: A Chronicle of Universal History in the Year 1146 A.D.*, ed. Austin P. Evans and Charles Knapp, Columbia University Press, 1928. **136**

'Our new homes', *United States Magazine and Democratic Review*, 21 (1847), 392–5. **111**

Ovid. *Tristia*, transl. Arthur Leslie Wheeler, London: Heinemann, 1924. **131**

Paine, Thomas. 'The American crisis', III (1777), *Writings*, ed. Moncure D. Conway, New York, 1894, 1:196–229. **107**
    The Complete Writings of Thomas Paine, ed. Philip S. Foner, 2 vols., New York: Citadel, 1945: 'Dissertation on the first principles of government', 2:570–88. **108**
    The Rights of Man (1791–2), 1:243–458. **110**

Palgrave, Francis. *The Collected Historical Works*, ed. R. H. Inglis Palgrave, 10 vols., Cambridge University Press, 1919–22: **278**
    The History of Normandy and England (1851), 4 vols. **278**
    'Normandy – architecture of the Middle Ages', 10:363–402 (from *Quarterly Review*, 25 (1821), 112–47). **394**

Palmer, A. H. *The Life and Letters of Samuel Palmer, Painter & Etcher*, London, 1892. **36**

Pane, Roberto. 'Some considerations on the meeting of experts held at UNESCO House 17–21 October 1949', *Museum*, 3 (1950), 49–89. **164**

Panikkar, Raimundo. 'Time and history in the tradition of India: Kāla and Karma', in *Cultures and Time*, Paris: UNESCO, 1976, pp. 63–88. **212**

Panofsky, Erwin. 'The first page of Giorgio Vasari's "Libro": a study on the Gothic style in the judgment of the Italian Renaissance' (1930), in his *Meaning in the Visual Arts: Papers in and on Art History*, Garden City, N.Y.: Doubleday Anchor, 1955, pp. 169–225. **78, 128**

'Father Time', in his *Studies in Iconology: Humanistic Themes in the Art of the Renaissance* (1939), New York: Harper & Row, Icon edn., 1972, pp. 69–93. **131**

Renaissance and Renascences in Western Art (1960), London: Paladin, 1970. **78, 331, 360**

Tomb Sculpture: Its Changing Aspects from Ancient Egypt to Bernini, London: Thames and Hudson, 1964. **176**

Paper and Its Preservation: Environmental Controls, Washington, D.C.: Library of Congress, Preservation Leaflet No. 2, 1983. **398**

Parent, Michel. 'Doctrine for the conservation and restoration of monuments and sites', in ICOMOS, *Nessun futuro senza passato*, q.v., pp. 37–70. **282, 389**

Parker, Rowland. *The Common Stream*, London: Collins, 1975. **409**

Parker, Samuel. *Journal of an Exploring Tour beyond the Rocky Mountains . . . 1835, '36, and '37*, Ithaca, N.Y., 1838. **114**

Parr, Albert Eide. 'History and the historical museum', *Curator*, 15 (1972), 53–61. **341**

Parsons, Talcott. *The Structure of Social Action: A Study in Social Theory with Special Reference to a Group of Recent European Writers*, 2nd edn., Glencoe, Ill.: Free Press, 1949. **395**

Pascal, Blaise. 'Fragment d'un traité du vide' (*c.* 1651), in *Pensées de Pascal*, ed. Ernest Havet, 2 vols., Paris, 1881, 2:266–77. **89**

Pascal, Roy. *Design and Truth in Autobiography*, London: Routledge & Kegan Paul, 1960. **42**

Pater, Walter. *Marius the Epicurean: His Sensations and Ideas*, 2nd edn., 2 vols., London, 1885. **49, 102**

Pauly, Thomas H. 'In search of "The Spirit of '76"', *American Quarterly*, 28 (1976), 444–64; reprinted in Zenderland, *Recycling the Past*, q.v., pp. 29–49. **309**

Pavese, Cesare. *This Business of Living: A Diary 1935–1950 (Il Mestiere di vivere*, 1952), London: World Distributors/Consul, 1961. **65**

Peabody, Andrew Preston. 'Arnold *and* Merivale: the History of Rome', *North American Review*, 72 (1851), pp. 442–65. **120**

Peacham, Henry. *The Complete Gentleman* (1622), ed. Virgil B. Heltzel, Cornell University Press for the Folger Shakespeare Library, 1962. **245**

Peacock, Thomas Love. *Four Ages of Poetry* (1820), in *Percy Reprints No. 3*, ed. H. F. B. Brett-Smith, Oxford: Blackwell, 1921, pp. 1–19. **12, 13, 141**

Gryll Grange (1861), London: Constable, 1924. **374**

Peardon, Thomas Preston. *The Transition in English Historical Writing 1760–1830*, Columbia University Press, 1933 (Studies in History, Economics, and Public Law No. 390). **49, 225**

Peckham, Morse. 'Afterword: reflections on historical modes in the nineteenth century', in Bradbury and Palmer, *Victorian Poetry*, q.v., pp. 277–300. **199**

The Triumph of Romanticism, University of South Carolina Press, 1970. **199, 226**

Peel, J. Y. D. 'Making history: the past in the Ijesha present', *Man*, 19 (1984), 111–32. **67, 214, 220, 232, 327, 412**

Peglitsis, Nicolas. *Sketches of Dedham Vale as John Constable Saw It*, Dedham, Essex: CPRE Countryside Centre, 1982. **331**

Péguy, Charles. *L'Argent* (1913), Paris: Gallimard, 1932. **395**

Penfield, Wilder. 'The permanent record of the stream of consciousness', *Acta Psychologica*, 11 (1955), 47–69. **17, 252**

Percival, John. *Living in the Past*, London: BBC, 1980. **300**

Perham, Margery. *Lugard: The Life of Frederick Dealtry Lugard*, 2 vols., London: Collins, 1956. **246**

Perkins, Howard Cecil (ed.). *Northern Editorials on Secession*, 2 vols., New York: Appleton, for the American Historical Association, 1942. **117**

Perry, John. 'Personal identity, memory, and the problem of circularity', in his (ed.), *Personal Identity*, University of California Press, 1975, pp. 135–55. **201**

Persons, Stow. *American Minds: A History of Ideas*, New York: Holt, Rinehart & Winston, 1958. **109**
  'Progress and the organic cycle in eighteenth-century America', *American Quarterly*, 6 (1954), 147–63. **109, 142**

Pesenti, Franco Renzo. 'Dismembered works of art – Italian painting', in UNESCO, *Illustrated Inventory*, q.v., pp. 18–51. **287**

Pesetsky, Bette. 'The hobbyist', in her *Stories Up to a Point*, London: Bodley Head, 1982, pp. 35–43. **12**

Peterson, Merrill D. *The Jeffersonian Image in the American Mind*, Oxford University Press/Galaxy, 1962. **343**

Petrarch, Francesco. *Letters from Petrarch*, ed. Morris Bishop, Indiana University Press, 1966. **76, 81, 83, 373**
  Petrarch's Letters to Classical Authors, transl. Mario Emilio Cosenza, University of Chicago Press, 1910. **8, 85**

Petrie, George. *See* Stokes, William.

Pevsner, Nikolaus. *Some Architectural Writers of the Nineteenth Century*, Oxford: Clarendon, 1972. Includes essays by Kerr; Morris, William. **100, 101, 326**
  'Ruskin and Viollet-le-Duc: Englishness and Frenchness in the appreciation of Gothic architecture', in *Eugène Emmanuel Viollet-le-Duc 1814–1879* (*Architectural Design* Profile), London: Academy Editions, 1980, pp. 48–53. **282**

Peyrefitte, Roger. *The Keys of St. Peter*, New York: Criterion, 1957. **408**

Phillips, Charles. 'Greenfield's changing past', *History News*, 37:11 (1982), 9–14. **288, 328, 355, 408**

Phillips, John. *The Reformation of Images: Destruction of Art in England, 1535–1660*, University of California Press, 1973. **321**

Philp, Peter. 'Restoring furniture and clocks', *Antique Dealers and Collectors Guide*, Aug. 1978, pp. 57–61. **149, 169**

Piaget, Jean, and Inhelder, Bärbel. *Memory and Intelligence*, London: Routledge & Kegan Paul, 1973. **191, 194, 202, 209**

Piggott, Stuart. *The Druids*, Penguin, 1974. **335**
  Ruins in a Landscape: Essays in Antiquarianism, Edinburgh University Press, 1976. **175**

Pigman, G. W. III. 'Imitation and the Renaissance sense of the past: the reception of Erasmus' *Ciceronianus*', *Journal of Medieval and Renaissance Studies*, 9 (1979), 155–77. **78, 79, 83**
  'Versions of imitation in the Renaissance', *Renaissance Quarterly*, 33 (1980), 1–32. **75, 81, 82**

Pile, Dolly. 'Interpreting Old Hall, Tatton Park', *Interpretation*, No. 17 (1981), 3–5. **299**

Piper, John. 'Pleasing decay' (1947), in his *Buildings and Prospects*, London: Architectural Press, 1948, pp. 89–116. **145, 164, 165, 169, 273**

'Place debate' [on the Piazza d'Italia], *Places*, 1:2 (1984), 7–31. **383**

Plato. *Phaedrus*, in *Works*, Loeb edn., 12 vols., Harvard University Press, 1914, 1:405–579. **256, 329**

Plenderleith, H. J., and Organ, R. M. 'The decay and conservation of museum objects of tin', *Studies in Conservation*, 1 (1953), 63–72. **163**

Plumb, J. H. 'The historian's dilemma', in his (ed.), *The Crisis in the Humanities*, Penguin, 1964, pp. 24–44. **335**
  The Death of the Past (1969), Penguin, 1973. **xxv, 64, 69, 233, 332, 364, 365, 370**

Pocock, J. G. A. *The Machiavellian Moment: Florentine Political Thought and the Atlantic Republican Tradition*, Princeton University Press, 1975. **109, 373**
  'The origins of the study of the past: a comparative approach', *Comparative Studies in Society and History*, 4 (1962), 209–46. **211, 213, 214, 370**

Politics, Language and Time: Essays on Political Thought and History, London: Methuen, 1972. **41, 370**

Pole, J. R. 'The American past: is it still usable?' *Journal of American Studies*, 1 (1967), 63–78. **375**

Pollard, Albert Frederick. 'Historical criticism', *History*, 5 (1920), 21–9. **217**

Pope, Alexander. *An Essay on Criticism* (1711), in *The Poems*, ed. E. Aubra and Aubrey Williams, 11 vols., London: Methuen, 1961, 1:237–326. **87**

Porter, Dale H. *The Emergence of the Past: A Theory of Historical Explanation*, University of Chicago Press, 1981. **223**

Portoghesi, Paolo. *Rome of the Renaissance*, London: Phaidon, 1972. **390**

Posner, Donald. *Annibale Carracci: A Study in the Reform of Italian Painting around 1590*, 2 vols., London: Phaidon, 1971. **81**

Post, Robert C. (ed.). *1876: A Centennial Exhibition*, Washington D.C.: National Museum of History and Technology, Smithsonian Institution, 1976. **145**

Poulet, Georges. *Studies in Human Time*, Johns Hopkins University Press, 1956. **16, 48, 198, 203**
   'Timelessness and Romanticism', *Journal of the History of Ideas*, 15 (1954), 3–22. **16, 204**

Pound, Roscoe. *The Formative Period of American Law*, Boston: Little Brown, 1938. **108**

Powell, Ken. *Beverley: Will Housing Sprawl Engulf Minster?* London: SAVE Britain's Heritage, 1981. **271**
   Burnley: Mill-Town Image: Burden or Asset? ibid., 1980. **402**
   The Fall of Zion: Northern Chapel Architecture and Its Future, ibid., 1980. **396**
   The New Iconoclasts, ibid., 1981. **396, 403**

Powell, Mary. 'Variations on a theme of dying trees', *Landscape Research*, 6:1 (1981), 26–7. **135**

Praz, Mario. *On Neoclassicism*, Northwestern University Press, 1969. **247**

Preston, Joseph H. 'Was there an historical revolution?' *Journal of the History of Ideas*, 38 (1977), 353–64. **232**

Price, H. H. *Thinking and Experience*, 2nd edn., London: Hutchinson, 1969. **190**

Price, Uvedale. *Essays on the Picturesque, as Compared with the Sublime and the Beautiful . . .* , 3 vols., London, 1810:
   A Dialogue on the Distinct Characters of the Picturesque and of the Beautiful, in Answer to the Objections of Mr. Knight (1801), 3:181–400. **156, 166, 168**
   Essay on Architecture and Buildings (1794), 2:171–370. **175**
   An Essay on Artificial Water, and on the Method in which Picturesque Banks may be Practically Formed (1794), 2:1–167. **157**
   On the Picturesque, &c, vol. 1. **156**

Priestley, J. B. *I Have Been Here Before: A Play in Three Acts*, London: Samuel French, 1939. **64**

Priestley, Joseph. *Lectures on History and General Policy*, Birmingham, 1788. **93**

Prince, Hugh C. 'Reality stranger than fiction', *Bloomsbury Geographer*, 6 (1973), 2–22. **40, 354**

Problems of Heritage and Cultural Identity in Poland, Warsaw: Polish National Committee of International Council on Monuments and Sites, 1984. Includes essays by Frycz; Gruszecki; Stankiewicz.

Proudfoot, Dan. 'How Louisbourg restored looks today', *Canadian Geographical Journal*, 93:1 (1976), 28–33. **298**

Proust, Marcel. *Remembrance of Things Past* (1913–27), transl. C. K. Scott-Moncrieff and Terence Kilmartin, 3 vols., Penguin, 1983. **xxv, 16, 49, 203, 205, 206, 209, 241, 251, 307, 357, 385**

'Public buildings of Edinburgh', *Blackwood's Edinburgh Magazine*, 6 (1820), 370–5. **99**

Quartermaine, Peter (ed.). *Readings in Australian Arts*, University of Exeter, 1978. Includes essays by Joppien; Kramer; Lowenthal.

Quimby, Ian M. G. (ed.). *Material Culture and the Study of American Life*, New York: Norton for the Winterthur Museum, 1978. Includes essays by Hindle; Hume, I. N.

Quinn, Maire A. 'The personal past in the poetry of Thomas Hardy and Edward Thomas', *Critical Quarterly*, 16 suppl. (1974), 7–28. **251**

Quinones, Ricardo J. *The Renaissance Discovery of Time*, Harvard University Press, 1972. **84, 198**

Rabelais, François. *The Five Books of Gargantua and Pantagruel* (1535), New York: Modern Library, 1944. **20**

Radcliffe, Ann. *The Romance of the Forest* (1791), London: Routledge, 1904. **177**

Rahtz, Philip A. (ed.). *Rescue Archaeology*, Penguin, 1974. Includes essays by Barker; Biddle.

Rainey, Reuben M. 'The memory of war: reflections on battlefield preservation', in *The Yearbook of Landscape Architecture: Historic Preservation*, ed. Richard L. Austin *et al.*, New York: Van Nostrand Reinhold, 1983, pp. 68–89. **269, 273, 345, 346**

Raleigh Walter. *The History of the World*, London, 1614. **128, 137**

Ralling, Christopher. 'What is television doing to history?' *The Listener*, 10 Jan. 1980, pp. 41–3. **230**

Ramsey, P. A. (ed.). *Rome in the Renaissance: The City and the Myth*, Binghamton, N.Y.: Center for Medieval and Early Renaissance Studies (Texts and Studies, Vol. 18), 1982. Includes essays by Ackerman; Mazzocco; Schiffman.

Ranger, Terence. 'The invention of tradition in colonial Africa', in Hobsbawm and Ranger, *Invention of Tradition*, q.v., pp. 211–62. **337**

Rasch, Wolfdietrich. 'Literary decadence: artistic representation of decay', *Journal for Contemporary History*, 17 (1982), 201–18. **179, 379**

Rattansi, P. M. Review of Jones, *Ancients and Moderns*, q.v., *British Journal for the Philosophy of Science*, 18 (1967), 250–5. **91**

Raumer, Frederick von. *America and the American People*, New York, 1846. **119, 403**

Rawles, R. E. 'The past and present of mnemotechny', in Gruneberg, Morris, and Sykes, *Practical Aspects of Memory*, q.v., pp. 164–71. **256**

Rawson, Judy. 'Italian Futurism', in Bradbury and McFarlane, *Modernism*, q.v., pp. 243–58. **380**

Ray, John. *Miscellaneous Discourses Concerning the Dissolution and Changes of the World*, London, 1692. **137**

Read, Herbert. *Art Now: An Introduction to the Theory of Modern Painting and Sculpture*, 3rd edn., London: Faber and Faber, 1945. **379**

Reed, Henry Hope. 'The classical tradition in modern times: a personal assessment', in *Speaking a New Classicism*, q.v., pp. 23–5. **380, 383**

Reiff, Daniel D. 'Memorial Hall: the splendor beneath the dust', *Harvard Bulletin*, 74:3 (1972), 29–42. **376**

'Reminiscences of a walker round Boston', *United States Magazine and Democratic Review*, 3 (1838), 79–87. **117**

Renfrew, Colin. *Towards an Archaeology of the Mind*, Cambridge University Press, 1982. **243**

Repplier, Agnes. 'Old wine and new', *Atlantic Monthly*, 77 (1896), 688–96. **9**

Repton, Humphry. *Sketches and Hints on Landscape Gardening* (1795), in his *The Art of Landscape Gardening*, ed. John Nolan, London: Constable, 1907. **168**

'Restoration of the Parthenon in the National Monument', *Blackwood's Edinburgh Magazine*, 6 (1819), 137–48. **101**

Rethinking History: Time, Myth, and Writing, ed. Marie-Rose Logan and John Frederick Logan, *Yale French Studies*, No. 59, 1980. Includes essays by Duby; Robin.

Reynolds, Mack. 'Compounded interest' (1956), in Judith Merril (ed.), *SF: The Best of the Best*, New York: Dell, 1967, pp. 199–213. **27**

Reynolds, Peter J. *Iron-Age Farm: The Butser Experiment*, London: British Museum/Colonnade, 1979. **300**

Rhodes, John G., Smith, David A., and Shishtawi, Ahmed S. 'Manor Farm, Cogges: a museum of farming and the countryside in Oxfordshire', *Museums Journal*, 79 (1979), 13–16. **151**

Rich, Lawrence. 'Ten thousand children in need of a sponsor', *National Trust*, No. 35 (1981), 8–9. **15, 299**

Richards, Oline. 'A fairer Athens and a freer Rome: historic public gardens in Perth, W.A.', *Heritage Australia*, 1:1 (1982), 66–9. **378**

Richardson, John. 'Crimes against the Cubists', *N.Y. Review of Books*, 16 June 1983, pp. 32–4. **172, 307**

Riegl, Alois. *Der moderne Denkmalkultus: Seine Wesen und seine Entstehung*, Vienna: W. Brau-müller, 1903. **179**

Rieth, Adolf. *Archaeological Fakes*, London: Barrie and Jenkins, 1970. **152, 291**

Riggio, Thomas P. 'Uncle Tom reconstructed: a neglected chapter in the history of a book', in Zenderland, *Recycling the Past*, q.v., pp. 66–80. **343**

Riley, Robert B. 'Speculations on the new American landscapes', *Landscape*, 24:3 (1980), 1–9. **13**

Robertson, E. Graeme. *Early Buildings of Southern Tasmania*, 2 vols., London: Routledge & Kegan Paul, 1970. **341**

Robin, Régine. *Le Cheval blanc de Lénine ou l'histoire autre*, Brussels: Roment, 1979. **239**
'Toward fiction as oblique discourse', in *Rethinking History*, q.v., pp. 230–42. **239**

Robinson, Erik. 'Henry Ford and the Postville Courthouse', *Historic Illinois*, 3:3 (1980), 1–3, 13–15. **286**

Robson-Scott, W. D. *The Literary Background of the Gothic Revival in Germany*, Oxford: Claren-don, 1965. **393**

Rodgers, W. R. *Ulstermen and Their Country*, London: Longmans, Green, for the British Council, 1947. **250**

Rogers, Samuel. *An Epistle to a Friend, with Other Poems*, London, 1799. **304**
The Pleasures of Memory and Other Poems (1792), London, 1802. **10**

Rogin, Michael Paul. *Fathers and Children: Andrew Jackson and the Subjugation of the American Indian*, New York: Knopf, 1975. **106, 117**

Ronsheim, Robert. 'Christmas at Conner Prairie: reinterpreting a pioneer holiday', *History News*, 36:12 (1981), 14–17. **345, 371**

Rooke, Hayman. 'Some accounts of the Brimham Rocks in Yorkshire', *Archaeologia*, 8 (1787), 209–17. **114**

Rose, Mark. *Alien Encounters: An Anatomy of Science Fiction*, Harvard University Press, 1981. **14**

Rosenberg, Harold. 'American drawing and the Academy of the Erased de Kooning', *New Yorker*, 22 Mar. 1976, pp. 106–10. **332**
'The Mona Lisa without a mustache: art in the media age', *Art News*, 75:5 (1976), 47–50. **307**

Rosenblum, Robert. 'The origin of painting: a problem in the iconography of romantic classicism', *Art Bulletin*, 39 (1957), 279–90. **55**
Transformations in Late Eighteenth Century Art, Princeton University Press, 1967. **55, 157, 178, 182**

Rosenmeyer, Thomas G. 'Drama', in Finley, *Legacy of Greece*, q.v., pp. 120–54. **372**

Ross, Dorothy. 'Historical consciousness in nineteenth-century America', *American Historical Review*, 89 (1984), 909–28. **109, 233, 336**

Ross, James Bruce, 'A study of twelfth-century interest in the antiquities of Rome', in James Lea Cate and Eugene N. Anderson (eds.), *Medieval and Historiographical Essays in Honor of James Westfall Thompson*, University of Chicago Press, 1938, pp. 302–21. **390**

Rossabi, Morris. 'Comment' on Allardyce, q.v., *American Historical Review*, 87 (1982), 729–32. **222**

Rossi, Aldo. 'The Greek Order' (excerpt from his *Scritti scelti sull'architettura e la città, 1956–1972*), in Demetri Porphyrios (ed.), *Classicism Is Not a Style*, special issue; *Architectural Design*, 52 (1982, 5/6), 19–21. **383**

Rousseau, Jean-Jacques. *Confessions* (1781), Penguin, 1953. **374**
The Social Contract or Principles of Political Right (1762), in his *Political Writings*, ed. Frederick Watkins, Edinburgh: Nelson, 1953, pp. 1–155. **106**

Rowles, Graham D. 'Place and personal identity in old age: observations from Appalachia', *Journal of Environmental Psychology*, 3 (1983), 299–313. **43, 152, 256**
'Reflections on experiential field work', in David Ley and Marwyn Samuels (eds.), *Humanistic Geography*, London: Croom Helm, 1978, pp. 173–93. **256**

Rowntree, Lester B., and Conkey, Margaret W. 'Symbolism and the cultural landscape', *Annals of the Association of American Geographers*, 70 (1980), 459–74. **44**

Royal Commission on Ancient Monuments (England). *Stonehenge and Its Environs: Monuments and Land Use*, Edinburgh University Press, 1979. **357**

Rubin, William. 'Modernist primitivism', in his *'Primitivism' in Twentieth Century Art*, pp. 1–79. **55** (ed.). *'Primitivism' in Twentieth Century Art: Affinity of the Tribal and the Modern*, 2 vols., New York: Museum of Modern Art, 1984. Includes essays by Rubin; Varnedoe.

Rudwick, Martin J. S. 'Transposed concepts from the human sciences in the early work of Charles Lyell', in L. J. Jordanova and Roy S. Porter (eds.), *Images of the Earth: Essays in the History of the Environmental Sciences*, Chalfont St Giles: British Society for the History of Science, 1979, pp. 67–83. **394**

Ruhemann, Helmut. *The Cleaning of Paintings*, London: Faber and Faber, 1968. **160, 169**

Ruml, Beardsley. 'Some notes on nostalgia', *Saturday Review of Literature*, 29 (22 June 1946), 7–9. **11, 13**

Rupke, Nicolaas A. *The Great Chain of History: William Buckland and the English School of Geology (1814–1859)*, Oxford, Clarendon, 1983. **188**

Ruskin, John. *Complete Works*, ed. E. T. Cook and Alexander Wedderburn, 39 vols., London: George Allen, 1903–12: **278**

'Education in art' (1858), 16:143–51; reprinted in *The Lamp of Beauty: Writings on Art by John Ruskin*, ed. Joan Evans, London: Phaidon Press, 1959, pp. 292–318. **398**

Letters, vol. 37. **97**

'The three aeras' (1875) (*Deucalion*), 26:115–23. **139**

Modern Painters, 4 vols., New York: John Wiley & Sons, 1886. **99, 164, 165, 166, 168, 247, 360**

Ruskin in Italy: Letters to His Parents, ed. Harold I. Shapiro, Oxford: Clarendon Press, 1972. **50, 257**

The Seven Lamps of Architecture (1849), New York: Noonday Press, 1961. **157, 164, 280**

Russell, Bertrand. *The Analysis of Mind*, London: Allen & Unwin, 1921. **188, 201**

Russell, Don. 'Whatever happened at Custer's Last Stand?' *Art News*, 77:10 (1978), 63–70. **309**

Ryan, Susan. 'The architecture of James Gamble Rogers at Yale University', *Perspecta* (Yale Architectural Journal), 18 (1982), 25–42. **153**

Rycroft, Charles. 'Viewpoint: analysis and the autobiographer', *TLS*, 27 May 1983, p. 541. **205, 207**

Rykwert, Joseph. *The First Moderns: The Architects of the Eighteenth Century*, Cambridge, Mass.: M.I.T. Press, 1980. **378**

Saari, Sandra A. 'Hedda Gabler: the past recaptured, *Modern Drama*, 20 (1977), 299–316. **379**

Sadleir, Michael. '"All horrid?": Jane Austen and the Gothic romance', in his *Things Past*, London: Constable, 1944, pp. 167–200. **178**

Safdie, Moshe. 'Private jokes in public places', *Atlantic Monthly*, 248 (Dec. 1981), 62–8. **383**

Sagoff, Mark. 'The aesthetic status of forgeries', *Journal of Aesthetics and Art Criticism*, 35 (1976), 169–80 (reprinted in Dutton, *Forger's Art*, q.v., pp. 131–52). **291**

Sahlins, Marshall. 'Other times, other customs: the anthropology of history', *American Anthropologist*, 85 (1983), 517–44. **250**

St. Clair, William. *Lord Elgin and the Marbles*, Oxford University Press, 1967. **171**

'St Paul's: black or white?' *Architectural Review*, 135 (1964), 243–5. **151**

Saki (H. H. Munro). 'The jesting of Arlington Stringham' (1910), *The Complete Works of Saki*, London: Bodley Head, 1980, 133–6. **325**

Salomon, Roger B. *Twain and the Image of History*, Yale University Press, 1961. **300**

Salvesen, Christopher. *The Landscape of Memory: A Study of Wordsworth's Poetry*, London: Edward Arnold, 1965. **199, 395**

Samuel, Raphael. 'History Workshop I: truth is partisan', *New Statesman*, 15 Feb. 1980, pp. 247–50. **233**

Sanders, Andrew. *The Victorian Historical Novel 1840–1880*, London: Macmillan, 1978. **98, 225, 226**

Sanderson, William. *Graphice, or, The Use of Pen and Pensill*, London, 1658. **152**

Santayana, George. *The Life of Reason or the Phases of Human Progress*, 5 vols., London: Constable, 1905. **47**

Santmyer, Helen Hooven. *Ohio Town*, Ohio State University Press, 1962. **42, 60**

Satanic Mills: Industrial Architecture in the Pennines, London: SAVE Britain's Heritage, 1978. **306, 403**

Saunders, Matthew. 'Metroland: half-timbering and other souvenirs in the Outer London suburbs', in Lowenthal and Binney, *Our Past Before Us*, q.v., pp. 165–74. **319**

'The protection of property: do we "demolish" the people who made history?' *Period Home*, 1:2 (1980), 28–30. **322**

Schachtel, Ernest G. *Metamorphosis: On the Development of Affect, Perception, Attention, and Memory*, New York: Basic Books, 1959. **195, 202**

Schafer, Roy. 'Narrative in the psychoanalytic dialogue', in Mitchell, *On Narrative*, q.v., pp. 25–49. **209**

A New Language for Psychoanalysis, Yale University Press, 1976. **200**

The Psychoanalytic Life History, London: H. K. Lewis for University College London, 1976. **200**

Schafer, R. Murray. 'The music of the environment', *Cultures*, 1 (1973), 15–52. **37**

The Tuning of the World, Toronto: McClelland and Stewart, 1977. **37**

Scheffer, John D. 'The idea of decline in literature and the fine arts in eighteenth-century England', *Modern Philology*, 34 (1936–7), 156–78. **92, 93, 94, 95**

Schiffman, Zachary S. 'Montaigne's perception of ancient Rome: biography as a form of history', in Ramsey, *Rome in the Renaissance*, q.v., pp. 345–53. **374**

Schlanger, Judith E. *Les Métaphores de l'organisme*, Paris: Vrin, 1971. **128, 135, 142**

Schlebecker, John T. 'Social functions of historical living farms in the United States', *Museum*, No. 143 (1984), 146–9. **342, 359**

Schlereth, Thomas J. *Artifacts and the American Past*, Nashville, Tenn.: American Association for State and Local History, 1980. **145**

'Pioneers of material culture: using American things to teach American history', *History News*, 37:9 (1982), 28–32. **244**

(ed.). *Material Culture Studies in America*, Nashville, Tenn.: American Association for State and Local History, 1982. **244**

Schochet, Gordon J. *Patriarchalism in Political Thought: The Authoritarian Family and Political Speculation and Attitudes Especially in Seventeenth-Century England*, Oxford: Blackwell, 1975. **106, 255**

Schofield, John. 'Repair not restoration', in Binney and Burman, *Change and Decay*, q.v., pp. 153–4. **145**

Scholes, Robert, and Kellogg, Robert. *The Nature of Narrative*, Oxford University Press/Galaxy, 1968. **194, 199, 217, 225**

Schorske, Carl. *'Fin-de-Siècle' Vienna: Politics and Culture*, New York: Random House/Vintage, 1981. **101, 378, 379**

Schramm, Percy Ernest. *A History of the English Coronation*, Oxford: Clarendon, 1937. **57**

Schug, Albert. 'Dismembered works of art – German painting', in UNESCO, *Illustrated Inventory*, q.v., pp. 140–74. **172**

Schuyler, Robert. 'Images of America: the contribution of historical archaeology to national identity', *Southwestern Lore*, 42 (1976), 27–39. **298, 342**

Schwartz, Barry. 'The social context of commemoration: a study in collective memory', *Social Forces*, 61 (1982), 374–402. **118, 322**

Schwartzbach, Bertram Eugene. 'Antidocumentalist apologetics: Hardouin and Yeshayahu Leibowitz, *Revue de Théologie et de Philosophie*, 115 (1983), 373–390. **232**

Scott, Walter. *The Antiquary* (1816), London: Dent/Everyman, 1907. **198, 341**

Ivanhoe (1820), Edinburgh: Black, 1981. **229**

The Lady of the Lake (1810), *Poetical Works*, ed. J. Logie Robinson, Oxford University Press, 1904, pp. 207–312. **139**

The Prefaces to the Waverley Novels, ed. Mark A. Weinstein, University of Nebraska Press, 1978. **229**

Seabury, Paul. 'The histronaut', *Columbia University Forum*, 4:3 (1961), 4–8. **27**

Searing, Helen. 'Speaking a new classicism: American architecture now', in book of same title, q.v., pp. 9–22. **381, 383**

Seefeldt, Carol. 'Children's attitudes toward the elderly: a cross-cultural comparison', *International Journal of Aging and Human Development*, 19 (1984), 319–28. **133**

Senden, M. von. *Space and Sight: The Perception of Space and Shape in the Congenitally Blind before and after Operation*, London: Methuen, 1960. **39**

Seneca the Younger. *Ad Lucilium epistulae morales*, transl. Richard M. Gummere, 3 vols., London: Heinemann, 1920. **72**

Shaftesbury, Anthony Ashley Cooper, 3rd Earl. *The Moralists; a Philosophical Rhapsody*, London, 1709. **139**

Sharpe, Tom. *Porterhouse Blue*, London: Pan, 1976. **371**

Shattuck, Roger. *The Banquet Years: The Arts in France*, London: Faber and Faber, 1959. **395**
    Proust's Binoculars: A Study of Memory, Time, and Recognition in 'A la recherche du temps perdu', London: Chatto & Windus, 1964. **203, 205, 210, 251**

Shaw, Bob. *Other Eyes, Other Days*, London: Gollancz, 1972. **20**

Sheehy, Jeanne. *The Rediscovery of Ireland's Past: The Celtic Revival 1830–1930*, London: Thames and Hudson, 1980. **46, 283, 333, 335**

Shelley, Percy Bysshe. *Alastor, or The Spirit of Solitude* (1815), *Complete Poetical Works*, ed. Neville Rogers, 4 vols., Oxford: Clarendon, 1972–5, 2:43–64. **53**
    Hellas, a Lyrical Drama (1822), ed. Thomas J. Wise, 2nd edn., London, 1886. **99**

Shepard, Paul. *Man in the Landscape: A Historic View of the Esthetics of Nature*, New York: Knopf, 1967. **114**

Sherfy, Marcella. 'The craft of history', *In Touch* (Interpreters Information Exchange, National Park Service, U.S. Dept. of the Interior), No. 13 (1976), 4–7. **217**

Sherred, T. L. 'E for effort', *Astounding Science Fiction*, 39:3 (1947), 119–62. **21, 27**

Shils, Edward. *Tradition*, London: Faber and Faber, 1981. **41, 69, 185, 214, 376, 377, 379**

Shipler, David K. *Russia: Broken Idols, Solemn Dreams*, New York Times Books, 1983. **6, 62**

Shippey, Tom. 'History in SF', in Nicholls, *Encyclopedia of Science Fiction*, q.v., pp. 283–4. **26**

Shoard, Marion. *The Theft of the Countryside*, London: Temple Smith, 1980. **198, 396**

Shore, Elizabeth M. 'Virginia Woolf, Proust, and *Orlando*', *Comparative Literature*, 31 (1979), 232–45. **203**

Sidney, Algernon. *Discourses Concerning Government* (1698), London, 1751. **92**

Sidney, Margaret (Harriet Lothrop). *Five Little Peppers Midway*, London, 1890. **41**

Siegel, Jerrold E. '"Civic humanism" or Ciceronian rhetoric? the culture of Petrarch and Bruni', *Past and Present*, No. 34 (1966), 3–48. **76**

Silverberg, Robert (historian). *The Mound Builders*, New York: Ballantine, 1974. **14, 337, 339**

Silverberg, Robert (science fiction). 'In entropy's jaws', in his *Unfamiliar Territory*, London: Hodder and Stoughton/Coronet, 1977, pp. 158–94. **32**

Simak, Clifford D. *Catface*, London: Methuen/Magnum, 1980. (U.S. title: *Mastodonia*.) **23, 24, 27, 31**

Singer, Amy. 'When worlds collide', *Historic Preservation*, 36:4 (1984), 32–9. **403**

Sivesind, Ray S. 'Historic interiors in Wisconsin', ibid., 20:2 (1968), 74–7. **51**

Skinner, Quentin. 'Meaning and understanding in the history of ideas', *History and Theory*, 8 (1969), 3–53. **216**

Slive, Seymour, and Hoetink, H. R. *Jacob van Ruisdael*, New York: Abbeville, 1981. **173**

Slochower, Harry. 'Freud's Gradiva: *Mater nuda redidiva*: a wish-fulfilment of the "memory" on the Acropolis', *Psychoanalytic Quarterly*, 40 (1971), 646–62. **255**

Smith, Albert B. *Théophile Gautier and the Fantastic*, University of Missouri, Romance Monographs No. 23, 1977. **255**

Smith, Arthur Hamilton. 'Lord Elgin and his collection', *Journal of Hellenic Studies*, 36 (1916), 163–372. **171**

Smith, Cyril Stanley. 'Some constructive corrodings', in B. F. Brown, *Corrosion and Metal Artifacts*, q.v., pp. 143–53. **155**

Smith, Hedrick. *The Russians*, rev. edn., New York Times Books, 1983. **6**

Smith, John Thomas. *Remarks on Rural Scenery with Twenty Etchings of Cottages . . . Relative to the Picturesque*, London, 1797. **157**

Smith, K. C. P., and Apter, M. J. 'Collecting antiques: a psychological interpretation', *Antiques Collector*, 48:7 (1977), 64–6. **246**

Smith, Logan Pearsall. *The English Language*, London: Williams and Norgate, 1912. **390**

Smith, Paul. 'The fiction film as historical source: problems and approaches', in Fledelius, *History and the Audio-Visual Media*, q.v., pp. 201–11. **368**

Snow, C. P. *The Two Cultures and the Scientific Revolution* (Rede Lecture), Cambridge University Press, 1959. **390**

Solnit, Albert J. *Memory as Preparation: Development and Psychoanalytic Perspectives* (Freud Memorial Inaugural Lecture), University College London, 1984. **xxiv**

Somkin, Fred. *Unquiet Eagle: Memory and Desire in the Idea of American Freedom, 1815–1860*, Cornell University Press, 1967. **108, 109**

Sontag, Susan. *On Photography*, Penguin, 1979. **43, 257**

Sophocles. *Oedipus at Colonus*, transl. Robert Fitzgerald, New York: Harcourt, Brace, 1941. **126**

Sorabji, Richard. *Aristotle on Memory*, London: Duckworth, 1972. **252**

Sorlin, Pierre. *The Film in History: Restaging the Past*, Oxford: Blackwell, 1980. **230, 345**

Southern, Richard W. 'Aspects of the European tradition in historical writing: 4. the sense of the past', *Transactions of the Royal Historical Society*, 5th ser. (1973), 243–63. **376**

'The historical experience' (Rede Lecture), *TLS*, 24 June 1977, pp. 771–3. **212**

Southworth, Emma D. E. N. *Self-raised; or, From the Depths* (1864), New York, 1884. **110**

Spacks, Patricia Meyer. *Imagining a Self: Autobiography and Novel in Eighteenth-Century England*, Harvard University Press, 1976. **141, 198, 201**

Sparshott, Francis. 'The disappointed art lover', in Dutton, *Forger's Art*, q.v., pp. 246–63. **354**

Speaking a New Classicism: American Architecture Now, Northampton Mass.: Smith College Museum of Art, 1981. Includes essays by Reed; Searing. **382**

Speer, Albert. *Inside the Third Reich*, New York: Avon, 1970. **336**

Spence, Donald P. *Narrative Truth and Historical Truth: Meaning and Interpretation in Psychoanalysis*, New York: Norton, 1982. **209, 210, 218, 253**

Spender, Stephen. *Love–Hate Relations: A Study of Anglo-American Sensibilities*, London: Hamish Hamilton, 1974. **50, 64, 65, 181, 405**

Spengler, Oswald. *The Decline of the West* (1918), London: Allen & Unwin, 1932. **142**

Spenser, Edmund. *The Faerie Queene* (1590), ed. J. C. Smith, 3 vols., Oxford: Clarendon, vol. 2, 1909. **138**

Spiegel, Gabrielle M. 'Forging the past: the language of historical truth in the Middle Ages', *The History Teacher*, 17 (1984), 267–83. **225**

Sprague de Camp, L. 'A gun for dinosaur' (1956), in *The Best of L. Sprague de Camp*, New York: Ballantine/Del Rey, 1978, pp. 272–302. **22, 31**

Lest Darkness Fall (1941), London: Sphere, 1979. **26, 29**

Sprat, Thomas. *History of the Royal Society* (1667), facs. reproduction, St. Louis: Washington University Studies, 1959. **91**

Staël, Germaine Necker de. *Corinne, ou l'Italie* (1807), 2 vols., Paris, 1836. **114**

Stallman, R. W. 'Gatsby and the hole in time', *Modern Fiction Studies*, 1:4 (1955), 2–16. **324**

Stamp, Gavin. *Silent Cities: An Exhibition of the Memorial and Cemetery Architecture of the Great War*, London: Royal Institute of British Architects, 1977. **323**

Stankiewicz, Jerzy. 'Conflits de la doctrine de conservation et de la conscience de l'identité culturelle et sociale', in *Problems of Heritage and Cultural Identity in Poland*, q.v., pp. 25–31. **340**

Stanton, William. *The Leopard's Spots: Scientific Attitudes toward Race in America, 1815–59*, University of Chicago Press, 1960. **339**

Starobinski, Jean. *1789: The Emblems of Reason*, University Press of Virginia, 1982. **55, 232**

'The idea of nostalgia', *Diogenes*, 54 (1966), 81–103. **10, 11**

'The inside and the outside', *Hudson Review*, 28 (1975), 333–51. **55**

The Invention of Liberty 1700–1789, Geneva: Skira, 1964. **198, 283**

Stegner, Wallace. *Wolf Willow*, University of Nebraska Press, 1980. **42, 196, 203, 240**

Steinbeck, John. *Grapes of Wrath*, London: Heinemann, 1939. **43**

Steinberg, Jonathan. 'Has anyone seen the Zeitgeist?' *New Society*, 3 Apr. 1980, pp. 23–4. **359**

'"Real authentick history" or what philosophers of history can teach us', *Historical Journal*, 24 (1981), 453–74. **235, 236**

Steinberg, Leo. *The Sexuality of Christ in Renaissance Art and in Modern Oblivion*, New York: Pantheon, 1983. **408**

Steinbrink, Jeffry. '"Boats against the current": mortality and the myth of renewal in *The Great Gatsby*', *Twentieth Century Literature*, 26 (1980), 157–70. **324**

Stendhal (Henri Beyle). *A Roman Journal* (1827), ed. Haakon Chevalier, London: Orion, 1959. **168**

Stephen, George. *Rehabilitating Old Houses* (National Trust for Historic Preservation, Information Series), Washington, D.C.: Preservation Press, 1976. **388**

Stephens, W. R. W. *The Life and Letters of Edward A. Freeman*, 2 vols., London, 1895. **345, 396**

Sterne, Laurence. *The Life and Opinions of Tristram Shandy* (1760–7), 4 vols., London: Navarre Society, n.d. **205**

Stevens, Mary Lynn. 'Wistful thinking: the effect of nostalgia on interpretation', *History News*, 36:12 (1981), 10–13. **345**

Stevens, Wallace. 'The noble rider and the sound of words' (1942), in his *The Necessary Angel: Essays on Reality and Imagination*, London: Faber and Faber, 1960, pp. 1–36. **407**

Stilgoe, John R. 'Jack-o'-lanterns to surveyors: the secularization of landscape boundaries', *Environmental Review*, 1 (1976), 14–31. **257**

Stillinger, Elizabeth. *The Antiquers . . . , 1850–1930*, New York: Knopf, 1980. **122, 368**

Stokes, Adrian. *The Invitation in Art*, London: Tavistock, 1965. **60**

Stokes, William. *The Life and Labours in Art and Archaeology of George Petrie*, London, 1868. **283, 324**

Stone, Lawrence. 'The revival of narrative: reflections on a new old history', *Past and Present*, No. 85 (1979), 3–24; reprinted in his *The Past and the Present*, London: Routledge & Kegan Paul, 1981, pp. 74–96. **224**

'Walking over grandma' (review of Fischer, *Growing Old in America*, q.v.), *N.Y. Review of Books*, 12 May 1977, pp. 10–16. **129**

Storey, Mary Rose. *Mona Lisas*, London: Constable, 1980. **307**

Stothard, Charles Alfred. *The Monumental Effigies of Great Britain . . .* (1832), London, 1876. **248**

Stratton, George M. 'The mnemonic feat of the "Shass Pollak"', *Psychological Review*, 24 (1917), 244–7; reprinted in Neisser, *Memory Observed*, q.v., pp. 311–14. **200**

Street, George Edmund. 'Report to S.P.A.B.' in 'St. Mark's, Venice, Part II 1880–1886', *SPAB News*, 3 (1982), 31. **278**

Some Account of Gothic Architecture in Spain, 2 vols., London: Dent, 1914. **327**

Strehlow, T. G. H. *Aranda Traditions*, Melbourne University Press, 1947. **61, 379**

Strömberg, Gustaf. *The Soul of the Universe*, 2nd edn., Philadelphia: McKay, 1948. **17**

Strong, Roy. *And When Did You Last See Your Father? The Victorian Painter and British History*, London: Thames and Hudson, 1978. **257, 407**

Strout, Cushing. *The American Image of the Old World*, New York: Harper and Row, 1963. **115, 121**

The Veracious Image: Essays on American History, Literature, and Biography, Wesleyan University Press, 1981. **223, 227, 300**

Stukeley, William. *Stonehenge: A Temple Restored to the British Druids*, London, 1740. **344**

Styron, William. *The Confessions of Nat Turner*, London: Cape, 1978. **227**

Suddards, Roger W. *Listed Buildings: Law and Practice*, London: Sweet and Maxwell, 1982. **401**

Summerson, John. 'The evaluation of Victorian architecture', *Victorian Society Annual*, 1968–9, pp. 36–47. **101**

'The past in the future' (1947), in his *Heavenly Mansions and Other Essays on Architecture*, New York: Norton, 1963, pp. 219–42. **168, 400**

Swift, Jonathan. 'The battle of the books' (1698), in *A Tale of the Tub and Other Satires*, London: Dent, 1975, pp. 37–65. **92**

Gulliver's Travels (1726), Penguin, 1967. **129**

'Thoughts on various subjects' (1706?), *Works*, ed. Herbert Davis, 13 vols., Oxford: Blackwell, 1957–9, 4:243–54. **129**

Szacka, Barbara. 'Historical consciousness: conclusions drawn from empirical studies', *Polish Sociological Bulletin*, 1976, No. 3, pp. 19–30. **36**

'Two kinds of past-time orientation', ibid., 1972, Nos. 1–2, pp. 63–75. **14, 36**

Tafuri, Manfredo. *Theories and History of Architecture*, London: Granada, 1980. **381, 383**

Takeda, Chosu. 'Recent trends in studies of ancestor worship in Japan', in Newell, *Ancestors*, q.v., pp. 129–37. **53**

Tanner, Tony. *City of Words: American Fiction 1950–1970*, London: Cape, 1971. **72, 228**

Taplin, Oliver. 'A guide to the necropolis' (review of Finley, *Legacy of Greece*, q.v.), *TLS*, 30 Apr. 1982, p. 491. **377**

Tarnoczi, Laurent. 'Conservation et reintegration des monuments historiques et des sites dans l'organisation de l'éspace en Hongrie', *Acta Geografica*, 26 (1976), 19–38. **387**

Tate, Allen. *Memories and Essays: Old and New 1926–1974*, Manchester: Carcanet, 1976. **251**

Tate, Peter. *The New Forest: 900 Years After*, London: Macdonald and Jane's, 1979. **53**

Taylor, Laurie. 'Living with things', *New Society*, 5 Aug. 1976, pp. 297–8. **147**

Taylor, Nicholas. *The Village in the City*, London: Temple Smith, 1973. **304, 309**

Taylor, Richard S. 'How New Salem became an outdoor museum', *Historic Illinois*, 2:1 (1979), 1–3. **343**

Taylor, S. Martin, and Konrad, Victor A. 'Scaling dispositions toward the past', *Environment and Behavior*, 12 (1980), 283–307. **36**

Temple, William. *An Essay upon the Ancient and Modern Learning*, in his *Essays*, ed. J. E. Spingarn, Oxford: Clarendon, 1909, pp. 1–42. **92**

Tennyson, Alfred, Lord. *The Poems*, ed. Christopher Ricks, London: Longmans, Green, 1969:

'A dream of fair women' (1832), pp. 440–53. **251**

'Guinevere' (1859), pp. 1724–42. **251**

'Ode to memory' (1830), pp. 211–14. **210**

Thackeray, William Makepeace. *The English Humourists of the Eighteenth Century* (1853), London: Grey Walls, 1949. **225**

The History of Henry Esmond (1852), Penguin, 1970. **225**

Thomas, Charles. 'Ethics in archaeology', *Antiquity*, 45 (1971), 268–74. **397**

Thomas, Edward. *The Collected Poems*, ed. R. George Thomas, Oxford: Clarendon, 1978. **269**

Thomas, Keith. *Religion and the Decline of Magic: Studies in Popular Beliefs in Sixteenth- and Seventeenth-Century England*, Penguin, 1973. **84**

Thompson, Michael. *Rubbish Theory: The Creation and Destruction of Value*, Oxford University Press, 1979. **49, 52, 240**

Thompson, M. W. *Ruins: Their Preservation and Display*, London: British Museum/Colonnade, 1981. **273, 375, 391**

Thompson, William Irwin. *At the Edge of History: Speculations on the Transformation of Culture*, New York: Harper Torchbooks, 1979. **129, 350**

Thomson, Garry. 'The conservation of antiquities: developments in planning', *Journal of World History*, 14 (1972), 24–47. **291, 307**

Thoreau, Henry David. *The Journal*, ed. Bradford Torrey and Francis H. Allen, 14 vols., Boston: Houghton Mifflin, 1949. **115**

Walden (1854), New York: Modern Library, 1937, pp. 1–297. **111**

A Week on the Concord and Merrimack Rivers (1849), New York: New American Library, 1961. **54**

Thorndike, Lynn. 'Renaissance or prenaissance?' *Journal of the History of Ideas*, 4 (1943), 65–74. **360**

Thorne, Robert. *Covent Garden Market: Its History and Restoration*, London: Architectural Press, 1980. **351**

Thuillier, Jacques. 'Dismembered works of art – French painting', in UNESCO, *Illustrated Inventory*, q.v., pp. 88–115. **287**

Tilden, Freeman. *Interpreting Our Heritage: Principles and Practices for Visitor Services in Parks, Museums, and Historic Places*, University of North Carolina Press, 1957. **248**

Tillemont, Sébastien Le Nain de. *Ecclesiastical Memoirs of the First Six Centuries . . .* (1693), 2 vols., London, 1733. **408**

Tillinghast, Pardon E. *The Specious Past*, Reading, Mass.: Addison-Wesley, 1972. **22**

Tindall, Gillian. *The Fields Beneath: The History of One London Village*, London: Granada/Paladin, 1980. **9, 42, 243, 249**

Tocqueville, Alexis de. *Democracy in Ameria* (1834–40), 2 vols., New York: Knopf/Vintage, 1945. **107, 111**

Toews, John. 'Inner and outer reality: Freud's abandonment of the seduction theory and the crisis of liberal culture in Central Europe', paper at American Historical Association meeting, Dec. 1982. **252**

Toffler, Alvin. *Future Shock*, London: Pan, 1971. **50**

Toliver, Harold. *The Past That Poets Make*, Harvard University Press, 1981. **379**

Tomkins, Calvin. 'Moving out', *New Yorker*, 29 Feb. 1964, pp. 39–85. **332**

Trachtenberg, Marvin. *The Statue of Liberty*, Penguin, 1977. **323**

Traherne, Thomas. 'Fourth Century', in his *Centuries, Poems, and Thanksgivings*, 2 vols., ed. H. M. Margoliouth, Oxford: Clarendon, 1958, 1:169–225. **170**

The Transmission of Ideas in Early Modern Europe c. 1350–1700, Oxford: Past and Present Society, 1979. **372**

Trevelyan, George Macaulay. 'Autobiography of an historian', in his *Autobiography and Other Essays*, London: Longmans, Green, 1949. **185**

Trevor-Roper, Hugh. 'The invention of tradition: the Highland tradition of Scotland', in Hobsbawm and Ranger, *Invention of Tradition*, q.v., pp. 15–41. **333**

Trillin, Calvin. 'U.S. journal: thoughts brought on by prolonged exposure to exposed brick', *New Yorker*, 16 May 1977, pp. 101–7. **351**

Trollope, Anthony. *Barchester Towers* (1857), Oxford University Press, 1925. **159**

Trompf, Garry W. *The Idea of Historical Recurrence in Western Thought: From Antiquity to the Reformation*, University of California Press, 1979. **128, 136, 140, 141**

Trowbridge, John T. 'We are a nation', *Atlantic Monthly*, 14 (1864), 769–75. **121**

Trumbach, Randolph. *The Rise of the Egalitarian Family: Aristocratic Kinship and Domestic Relations in Eighteenth-Century England*, New York: Academic Press, 1978. **106**

Tschudi-Madsen, Stephan. *Restoration and Anti-Restoration: A Study in English Restoration Philosophy*, 2nd edn., Oslo: Universitetsforlaget, 1976. **144, 151, 278**

Tuan, Yi-Fu. *Dominance and Affection: The Making of Pets*, Yale University Press, 1984. **129**
    'The significance of the artifact', *Geographical Review*, 70 (1980), 462–72. **59, 238**
    'Space and place: humanistic perspective', in *Progress in Geography: International Review of Current Research*, Vol. 6, London: Edward Arnold, 1974, pp. 211–52. **388**

Tucker, Paul Hayes. *Monet at Argenteuil*, Yale University Press, 1982. **40**

Tucker, Wilson. *The Lincoln Hunters*, London: Hodder and Stoughton/Coronet, 1979. **23, 24**
    The Year of the Quiet Sun (1970), reprint edn., Boston: Gregg, 1979. **22**

Tuckerman, Henry T. 'American society', *North American Review*, 81 (1855), 26–50. **120**

Tulving, Endel. *Elements of Episodic Memory*, Oxford University Press, 1983. **201**

Turner, Frank M. *The Greek Heritage in Victorian Britain*, Yale University Press, 1981. **233, 329, 342, 353**

Turner, Frederick Jackson. 'The significance of the frontier in American history' (1893), in his *The Frontier in American History*, New York: Holt, 1920, pp. 1–38. **119**

Tuveson, Ernest Lee. *Millennium and Utopia: A Study in the Background of the Idea of Progress* (1949), Gloucester, Mass.: Peter Smith, 1972. **88, 97**

　Redeemer Nation: The Idea of America's Millennial Role, University of Chicago Press, 1968. **109, 300**

Twain, Mark (Samuel L. Clemens). *A Connecticut Yankee in King Arthur's Court* (1889), New York, 1899. **25, 26, 29, 300**

　The Innocents Abroad, or the New Pilgrim's Progress (1869), New York: New American Library/ Signet, 1966. **116, 273**

　'The legend of the Capitoline Venus', in *Sketches New and Old* (1875), London: Chatto & Windus, 1922, pp. 285–92. **153**

Tyler, Anne. *The Clockwinder*, New York: Popular Library, 1977. **197**

Uchendu, Victor C. 'Ancestorcide! are African ancestors dead?' in Newell, *Ancestors*, q.v., pp. 283–96. **195**

'Understanding our surroundings' [interview with Geoffrey Lord, Carnegie UK Trust], *Heritage Outlook*, 1 (1981), 96–8. **299**

UNESCO. *An Illustrated Inventory of Famous Dismembered Works of Art: European Painting*, Paris, 1974. Includes essays by Danilova; Hak; Lavalleye; Pesenti; Schug; Thuillier.

Updike, John. *Buchanan Dying: A Play*, New York: Knopf, 1974, 'Afterword', pp. 181–262. **229, 248**

　Of the Farm, Greenwich, Conn.: Fawcett, 1965. **323**

U.S. National Park Service. *Tatton Park Interpretive Study*, Cheltenham, Gloucs.: Countryside Commission, 1975. **299**

Utley, Robert M. 'A preservation ideal', *Historic Preservation*, 28:2 (1976), 40–4. **355**

Uttley, Alison. *A Traveller in Time* (1939), Puffin, 1978. **19, 26, 248**

Valéry, Paul. *The Collected Works*, 15 vols., London: Routledge & Kegan Paul, 1971–5:

　'Letter about Mallarmé' (1927), 8:240–53. **70**

　'On history' (1931), 10:114–17. **365**

Vanbrugh, John. *Complete Works*, ed. Bonamy Dobrée and Geoffrey Webb, 4 vols., London: Nonesuch, 1925–8:

　Aesop (1697), 2:1–65. **46**

　Letters, vol. 4. **36**

Vance, Tom. 'History lives at Lincoln's log cabin', *Historic Illinois*, 1:4 (1978), 1–3, 10. **296**

Vansina, Jan. 'Memory and oral tradition', in J. C. Miller, *African Past Speaks*, q.v., pp. 262–79. **200, 205, 210**

　Oral Tradition: A Study in Historical Methodology, Routledge & Kegan Paul, 1965. **194, 214, 217, 224, 235, 250, 327**

Van Seters, John. *In Search of History: Historiography in the Ancient World and the Origins of Biblical History*, Yale University Press, 1983. **46, 340**

Van Tassell, David D. *Recording America's Past: An Interpretation of the Development of Historical Studies in America 1607–1884*, University of Chicago Press, 1960. **109, 121, 142**

Varnedoe, Kirk. 'Contemporary explorations', in Rubin (ed.), *'Primitivism' in Twentieth Century Art*, q.v., pp. 661–85. **55**

Vasari, Giorgio. *Lives of the Painters, Sculptors & Architects* (1551), 4 vols., London: Dent, 1927. **54, 78, 131, 141, 149, 152**

　Le Vite de' pui eccelenti pittori scultori ed architettori, in *Le Opere*, ed. Gaetano Milanese, 9 vols., Florence: Sansoni, 1878–85. **171**

Vaughan, Henry. *Works*, Oxford: Clarendon, 1957:

　'Corruption', in *Silex Scintillans* (1655), pp. 387–545. **136**

　'Daphnis. An elegaic eclogue' (1666), pp. 676–80. **136**

Veblen, Thorstein. *The Theory of the Leisure Class* (1899), London: Allen & Unwin, 1970. **403**

Vendler, Helen. 'All too real', *N.Y. Review of Books*, 17 Dec. 1981, pp. 32–6. **234**

Venturi, Franco. 'History and reform in the middle of the eighteenth century', in J. H. Elliott and H. G. Koenigsberger (eds.), *The Diversity of History: Essays in Honour of Sir Herbert Butterfield*, London: Routledge & Kegan Paul, 1970, pp. 223–44. **380**

Vernant, J.-P. 'Death with two faces', in Humphries and King, *Mortality and Immortality*, q.v., pp. 285–91. **198**

Vico, Giambattista. *The New Science* (1744), 3rd edn., transl. Thomas Goddard Bergin and Max Harold Frisch, Cornell University Press, 1948. **141, 245**

 On the Study Methods of Our Time (1709), transl. Elio Gianturco, Indianapolis: Bobbs-Merrill, 1965. **93**

Vida, Marco Girolamo. *De arte poetica*, transl. Ralph G. Williams, Columbia University Press, 1976. **82**

Vidal, Gore. *1876: A Novel*, London: Heinemann, 1976. **228**

Vines, Gail, and Barnes, Michael. 'Hypnosis on trial', *New Scientist*, 6 Jan. 1983, pp. 12–16. **19**

Volney, Constantin Francois, Comte de. *The Ruins: or, A Survey of the Revolutions of Empire* (1789), 5th edn., London, 1807. **95, 175**

Wagenknecht, Edward. *Henry Wadsworth Longfellow: A Full-Length Portrait*, New York: Longmans, Green, 1955. **116**

Wagner, Anthony Richard. *English Ancestry*, Oxford University Press, 1961. **38**

 English Genealogy, Oxford: Clarendon, 1960. **38, 339**

Wahlgren, Erik. *The Kensington Stone: a Mystery Solved*, University of Wisconsin Press, 1958. **339**

Walcott, Derek. 'The muse of history: an essay', in Orde Coombs (ed.), *Is Massa Day Dead? Black Moods in the Caribbean*, New York: Doubleday/Anchor, 1974, pp. 1–27. **227**

Walden, Sarah. *The Ravished Image*, London: Weidenfeld and Nicolson, 1985. **160, 163, 170, 307, 336, 344, 406**

Wallace, Michael. 'Visiting the past: history museums in the United States', *Radical History Review*, 25 (1981), 63–96. **121, 329, 346**

Walsh, James P. 'Holy time and sacred space in Puritan New England', *American Quarterly*, 32 (1980), 79–95. **105**

Walsh, W. H. 'The constancy of human nature', in H. D. Lewis, *Contemporary British Philosophy*, q.v., pp. 275–91. **232**

Wardman, Alan. *Rome's Debt to Greece*, New York: St. Martin's 1976. **75**

Warner, W. Lloyd. *The Living and the Dead: A Study of the Symbolic Life of Americans* (Yankee City Series, 5), Yale University Press, 1959. **216, 323, 342**

Waters, Bruce. 'The past and the historical past', *Journal of Philosophy*, 52 (1955), 253–69. **201**

Waterson, Merlin. *The Servants' Hall: A Domestic History of Erdigg*, London: Routledge & Kegan Paul, 1980. **388**

Watkin, David. *The Rise of Architectural History*, London: Architectural Press, 1980. **356**

Watkins, T. H. 'A heritage preserved. Listening: Andersonville', *American Heritage*, 31:3 (1980), 100–1. **346**

Waugh, Evelyn. *The Loved One: An Anglo-American Tragedy* (1948), London: Chapman & Hall, 1965. **329**

Webster, Daniel. *The Writings and Speeches*, 18 vols., Boston: Little, Brown, 1903:
 'The Bunker Hill monument' (1825), 1:235–54. **118**
 'The completion of the Bunker Hill monument' (1843), 1:259–83. **118**
 'The revolution in Greece' (1824), 5:60–93. **319**
 See also 'Daniel Webster'.

Webster, John. *The Duchess of Malfi* (1614), ed. F. L. Lucas, London: Chatto & Windus, 1958. **143**

Webster, Noah. 'On the education of youth in America' (1787–8), in Frederick Rudolph (ed.), *Essays on Education in the Early Republic*, Harvard University Press, 1965, pp. 41–77. **107, 117**

Wedgwood, C. Veronica. *Truth and Opinion: Historical Essays*, London: Collins, 1960:
 'Literature and the historian', pp. 62–81. **227**
 'Sense of the past', pp. 19–41. **30, 227, 246**

Weil, Phoebe Dent. 'Contributions toward a history of sculpture techniques: I. Orfeo Boselli on the restoration of antique sculpture', *Studies in Conservation*, 12 (1967), 81–101. **170**

'A review of the history and practice of patination', in B. F. Brown, *Corrosion and Metal Artifacts*, q.v., pp. 77–92. **155, 159**

Weil, Simone. *The Need for Roots*, New York: Harper Colophon, 1971. **44**

Weinshenker, Anne Betty. 'Diderot's use of the ruin-image', *Diderot Studies*, 16 (1973), 309–29. **175**

Weintraub, Karl J. 'Autobiography and historical consciousness', *Critical Inquiry*, 1 (1975), 821–48. **199**

The Value of the Individual: Self and Circumstance in Autobiography, University of Chicago Press, 1978. **199**

Weiss, Roberto. *The Renaissance Discovery of Classical Antiquity*, Oxford; Blackwell, 1959. **148, 390, 391**

Wellman, Manly Wade. *Twice in Time* (1940), New York: Galaxy, 1958. **26**

Wells, H. G. *The Dream*, London: Collins, 1929. **16**

The Time Machine (1895), London: Pan, 1979. **22, 27, 30**

Welsch, Roger L. 'Very didactic simulation: workshops in the Plains pioneer experience at the Stuhr Museum', *History Teacher*, 3 (1974), 356–64. **300**

Werrell, Kenneth P. 'History and fiction: challenge and opportunity', *American Historical Association Newsletter*, 17:3 (1979), 4–6. **228**

Westall, Robert. *The Devil on the Road*, London: Macmillan, 1978. **29, 300**

Whistler, Laurence. *The Initials in the Heart*, London: Hart-Davis, 1964. **131**

White, Hayden V. 'The burden of history', *History and Theory*, 5 (1966), 111–34. **227, 228, 236, 379**

'Foucault decoded: notes from the underground', *History and Theory*, 12 (1973), 23–54. **212**

White, Jerry. 'History Workshop 3: beyond autobiography', *New Statesman*, 29 Feb. 1980, pp. 325–7. **224**

Whitehill, Walter Muir. '"Promoted to Glory . . .": the origin of preservation in the United States', in *With Heritage So Rich*, q.v., pp. 35–44. **341**

Whitrow, G. J. *The Natural Philosophy of Time*, 2nd edn., Oxford: Clarendon, 1980. **205**

The Nature of Time, Penguin, 1975. **15**

Wiener, Martin J. *English Culture and the Decline of the Industrial Spirit, 1850–1980*, Cambridge University Press, 1981. **9, 104, 151, 396**

Wiggins, David I. *Identity and Spatio-Temporal Continuity*, Oxford: Blackwell, 1971. **385**

Wilde, Oscar. *The Picture of Dorian Gray* (1891), London: Dent, 1930. **36, 134**

Williams, Eunice. 'Introduction' to *Gods & Heroes*, q.v., pp. 13–24. **239**

Williams, Gordon. *Change and Decline: Roman Literature in the Early Empire*, University of California Press, 1978. **75**

Williams, Gwyn A. *Madoc: The Making of a Myth*, London: Eyre Methuen, 1979. **333**

Williams, John C. 'Chemistry of the deacidification of paper', *Bulletin of the American Group-IIC*, 12 (1971), 16–32. **398**

Williams, Raymond. *The Country and the City*, London: Chatto & Windus, 1973. **13**

Williams-Ellis, Clough. *England and the Octopus*, London: Geoffrey Bles, 1928. **402**

Williamson, George. 'Mutability, decay, and seventeenth-century melancholy', *ELH*, 2 (1935), 121–50. **87**

Williamson, Tom, and Bellamy, Liz. *Ley Lines in Question*, London: World's Work, 1983. **344**

Wills, Garry. *Cincinnatus: George Washington and the Enlightenment*, New York: Doubleday, 1984. **112**

Wilson, Arthur M. *Diderot*, Oxford University Press, 1972. **91**

Wilson, Edmund. *Upstate: Records and Recollections of Northern New York*, New York: Farrar, Straus and Giroux, 1971. **330**

Wilson, Ian. *Reincarnation: The Claims Investigated*, Penguin, 1983 (rev. edn. of *Mind Out of Time?* 1981). **18**

Winks, Robin W. (ed.). *The Historian as Detective: Essays on Evidence*, New York: Harper & Row, 1969. Includes essays by Becker; Collingwood; Middleton and Adair.

Winlock, Herbert E. 'Diggers luck' (1921), in his *Models of Daily Life in Ancient Egypt* (Metropolitan Museum of Art Egyptian Expedition, vol. 18), Harvard University Press, 1955. **361**

With Heritage So Rich. New York: Random House, 1966. Includes essays by Howland; Hyman; Whitehill.

Wolff, Arnold. 'In retrospect: the completion of Cologne Cathedral in the nineteenth century', *Monumentum*, 26 (1983), 23–42. **393**

Wollheim, Richard. 'Preface' to Adrian Stokes, *Invitation in Art*, q.v., pp. ix-xxxi. **55**

Wood, Gordon S. 'Star-spangled history', *N.Y. Review of Books*, 12 Aug. 1982, pp. 4–9. **237**
    See also 'Writing history: an exchange'.

Wood, Michael. 'Nostalgia or never: you can't go home again', *New Society*, 7 Nov. 1974, pp. 343–6. **7, 12, 13**

Wood, Robert. *The Ruins of Palmyra, Otherwise Tedmore, in the Desart*, London, 1773. **43, 247**

Woodward, C. Vann. 'The future of the past', *American Historical Review*, 75 (1970), 711–26. **108, 111**

Woolf, Virginia. *Moments of Being: Unpublished Autobiographical Writings*, ed. Jeanne Schulkind, London: Chatto & Windus for Sussex University Press, 1976. **13, 48, 196**
    Orlando (1928), New York: New American Library, 1960. **59, 198**

Wordsworth, William. *The Poetical Works*, ed. Ernest de Selincourt and Helen Darbyshire, 5 vols., Oxford: Clarendon, 1940–59:
    'Lines composed a few miles above Tintern Abbey' (1798), 2:259–63. **210**
    'Memorials, of a tour in Scotland, 1803', 3:64–96. **135**
    'The tables turned' (1798), 4:57. **361**
    'To enterprise' (1832), 2:280–6. **53**
    The Prelude, or Growth of a Poet's Mind, Bk III (1805–6), 2nd edn., Oxford: Clarendon, 1959. **196, 199**

'World Heritage List established', *Parks*, 3:3 (1978), 12–14. **54, 55**

'The world of conservation: an interview with Clive Lucas', *Monumentum*, 25 (1982), 235–49. **344**

'The world of conservation: Yves Boiret', ibid., 9–27. **282**

Worskett, Roy. 'I'm worried about Walt', *Heritage Outlook*, 2:2 (1982), 34–5. **405**
    'New buildings in historic areas: I. conservation: the missing ethic', *Monumentum*, 25 (1982), 129–54. **405**

Wotton, William. *Reflections upon Ancient and Modern Learning*, London, 1694. **92, 160**

Wright, Austin. *The Morley Mythology*, New York: Harper & Row, 1977. **195**

Wright, Frank Lloyd. *An Organic Architecture, the Architecture of Democracy*, London: Lund Humphries, 1939. **405**

'Writing history: an exchange', *N.Y. Review of Books*, 16 Dec. 1982, pp. 58–9. **236**

Wyatt, Frederick. 'In quest of change: comments on R. J. Lifton's "Individual patterns in historical change"', *Comparative Studies in Society and History*, 6 (1964), 384–92. **4, 71**
    'The reconstruction of the individual and of the collective past', in Robert W. White (ed.), *The Study of Lives: Essays on Personality in Honor of Henry A. Murray*, New York: Atherton, 1964, pp. 304–20. **41**

Wyndham, John. 'Pillar to post', in his *The Seeds of Time*, Penguin, 1975, pp. 140–69. **39**

Yardley, Jonathan. 'The narrowing world of the historian', *American Historical Association Perspectives*, 20:6 (1982), 21–2. **237**

Yates, Frances A. *The Art of Memory*, Penguin, 1969. **208, 256**

Yerushalmi, Yosef Hayim. *Zakhor: Jewish History and Jewish Memory*, University of Washington Press, 1982. **66, 210, 250**

Young, Edward. *Conjectures on Original Composition*, 2nd edn. (1759), ed. Edith J. Morley, Manchester University Press, 1918. **89, 94**

Yourcenar, Marguerite. *Memoirs of Hadrian*, New York: Farrar, Straus & Giroux, 1963, 'Reflections on the composition', pp. 317–47. **265**

Zelinsky, Wilbur. 'Classical town names in the United States', *Geographical Review*, 57 (1967), 463–95. **112, 265**

    'Unearthly delights: cemetery names and the map of the changing American afterworld', in Lowenthal and Bowden, *Geographies of the Mind*, q.v., pp. 171–95. **323**

Zenderland, Leila (ed.). *Recycling the Past: Popular Uses of American History*, University of Pennsylvania Press, 1978. Includes essays by Pauly; Riggio.

Ziegler, Arthur P., Jr. *Historic Preservation in Inner City Areas*, Pittsburgh, Pa.: Ober Park Associates, 1974. **51**

Zilsel, Edgar. 'The origins of William Gilbert's scientific method', *Journal of the History of Ideas*, 2 (1941), 1–32. **90**

Zuckerman, Michael. 'The irrelevant Revolution: 1776 and since', *American Quarterly*, 30 (1978), 224–42. **354**

Zwart, P. J. *About Time: A Philosophical Inquiry into the Origin and Nature of Time*, Amsterdam: North-Holland, 1976. **143**

Zweig, Paul. 'Paris and Brighton Beach', *American Scholar*, 47 (1977–8), 501–13. **247**

ADDENDUM

Works listed below reached me after this book was in page proof; their topical relevance is paginated as above.

Buckley, Jerome Hamilton. *The Turning Key: Autobiography and the Subjective Impulse since 1800*, Harvard University Press, 1984. The role of creative recollection in 'calculated self-portraiture and unintentional self-betrayal' (p. 42) since Wordsworth's *The Prelude*. **196, 199**

Davis, Lennard J. *Factual Fictions: The Origins of the English Novel*, Columbia University Press, 1983. Changing categories of 'fact' and 'fiction' in seventeenth- and eighteenth-century English literature. **198, 207**

Haber, Carole. *Beyond Sixty-Five: The Dilemma of Old Age in America's Past*, Cambridge University Press, 1983. How colonial fathers kept authority over grown sons through economic control (pp. 10–15); how changing social and medical conceptions increasingly derogated and segregated the elderly in the nineteenth century (pp. 28–81). **106, 129**

Kotre, John. *Outliving the Self: Generativity and the Interpretation of Lives*, Johns Hopkins University Press, 1984. How current needs shape childhood memories (pp. 30, 142–6), enabling parents to master a painful or deficient past and leave a better heritage to offspring (pp. 168–9, 274). **199, 207, 209–10**

Levine, Joseph M. 'Ancients, Moderns, and history: the continuity of English historical writing in the later seventeenth century', in Paul J. Korshin (ed.), *Studies in Change and Revolution: Aspects of English Intellectual History 1640–1800*, Menston: Scolar Press, 1972, pp. 43–75; *idem*, 'Ancients and Moderns reconsidered', *Eighteenth Century Studies*, 15 (1981–2), 72–89. Shared as well as conflicting views about the virtues of the classics and the proper uses of the past gave rise to substantial agreement, notwithstanding polemical invective, between antagonists in the *querelle* from Temple and Wotton on. **92, 95**

Morris, Kevin L. *The Image of the Middle Ages in Romantic Victorian Literature*, London, Croom Helm, 1984. Medievalism in all its guises, as an anti-classical, quasi-religious, and nostalgic genre. **24–5, 49, 97–8, 353, 376**

Nora, Pierre. 'Entre mémoire et histoire: la problématique des lieux', in his (ed.), *Les Lieux de mémoire: I. La République*, Paris: Gallimard, 1984, pp. xv–xlii. How history and memory differ as routes to personal and collective pasts; how history has increasingly displaced memory since the French Revolution, heightening impulses toward genealogical, monumental, and commemorative heritage. **38, 212–14, 256, 259, 384**

Reinhold, Meyer. *Classica Americana: The Greek and Roman Heritage in the United States*, Wayne State University Press, 1984. The colonial cult of antiquity; opposition to classicism during and after the Revolution; post-Revolutionary philhellenism. **112, 113**

Williams, Huntington. *Rousseau and Romantic Autobiography*, Oxford University Press, 1983. How memory and reverie, prolonging the present through awareness of the past, gave rise to a new sense of personal identity (pp. 78–81), and the mystique of subjectivity elevated fictional life histories to reality. **198, 207**

Zonabend, Françoise. *The Enduring Memory: Time and History in a French Village*, Manchester University Press, 1984. Memory, the dating of events, and distinctions and linkages between the awareness of historical time (objective, linear, developmental) and that of communal and family time (stable, cyclical, reversible) in a rural community. **208, 213–14, 220, 250**

GENERAL INDEX

The asterisk before some names indicates that the author also appears in the Bibliography and Citation Index on other pages from those indicated in the General Index, or that there is more than one item listed.